BEN AND HIS MATES

The War diaries, letters
and photographs of
Lieutenant Ben Champion 1st AIF, 1915–1920

Edited by
Penny Ferguson

ECHO BOOKS

First published in 2018 by Barrallier Books Pty Ltd,
trading as Echo Books

Registered Office: 35-37 Gordon Avenue, West Geelong, Victoria 3220,
Australia.

www.echobooks.com.au

National Library of Australia Cataloguing-in-Publication entry: (paperback)

Author: Ferguson, Penny. Editor

Title: Ben and his Mates : The War diaries, letters and photographs of
Lieutenant Ben Champion 1st AIF, 1915-1920

ISBN: 9780648308270 (Hardback)

Front cover image: *Ben and his mates, Tel el Kebir, Egypt, February 1916. Back, l-r
Ben, Billy Hunt, Harry Newing. Front Rupe Neil.*

Book and cover design by Peter Gamble Graphic Design, Canberra.

Set in Garamond Premier Pro 12/17, MinervaSculptura and MinervaModern.

www.echobooks.com.au

Contents

Preface

This book aims to educate, commemorate and inspire. It is a unique insight into the mind and heart of a young man, Ben Champion, aged 18 years, eager to participate in the First World War as a member of the Australian Imperial Force (AIF). He set out in 1915 with his best mate, Arthur 'Art' Felton, as members of the 7th Reinforcements to the 1st Battalion for the Gallipoli Peninsula via the training camps of Egypt to join his compatriots, many of them friends and acquaintances from his home town and district, to fight in a doomed campaign that would be engraved forever into Australia's national identity. He joined the 1st Battalion that became a brotherhood home that would take him to the bloody battlefields of France and comfort him after he returned wounded from the front in April 1918.

During this momentous time for 19-year-old Ben in Gallipoli and France, he wrote and received letters. His primary correspondent was his beloved Frances Julia Niland, whom he mainly called 'Frank' but also many other names such as Gug, Franco, Old Pal. He also wrote less frequently to Frank's mother, whom he addressed formally as 'Mrs Niland' and other family members. Letters to Frank were not only communications of love and friendship, but were also personal descriptions of Ben's wartime experiences, softened and abbreviated in places so that Frank would not be too concerned for his welfare and safety. These letters constitute a warm testimony to the way young middle-class Australians wooed each other and shared their personal worlds in challenging times.

His letters to Frank sat undisturbed for decades in a box Ben made for Frank. They were discovered recently still tightly packed in their envelopes in Ben's daughter Ruth's home. When asked about the letters Ruth said she had long forgotten about them and had not wanted to read her parents love letters anyway.

It must be remembered how young both he, 18 and Frank, aged 16 were at the start of Ben's war and it is obvious when these letters are read just how innocent in terms of love letters they are. The letters were censored not only by the military but also by Frank's mother.

Side-by-side with these letters are Ben's journal entries that also describe in more detail the life and times of a young soldier and his mates at war. Ben's journal is a treasure trove of anecdotes and observations. Entries change as his experiences change, mature and harden Ben and his mates. Ben takes readers to the frontline as well as the life of the AIF between battles.

The book is enriched and its aperture literally and figuratively widened by Ben's photographs of people and places in Liverpool Camp, Sydney, Egypt, Gallipoli and France. Images in the book include items, such as post

cards and menus, and other documents that have special meaning and tell their own stories vividly. They are pictures of the people, times and places, and contribute to the feelings of mateship that these young Australians held for each other.

Ben's photos taken with his baby Kodak, although not of an excellent quality, have been included to document a very real moment in Ben's life. When reading the diary entries and letters one can easily forget that Ben was actually right there in the trenches, waist deep in mud and a long way from home. The photos add a reminder: he was there.

The publication of Ben's diaries, letters and photographs give a wide readership access to those who served in 'The Great War', especially those who died single and childless and have no direct descendants to remember and commemorate them. Many of the men who returned home were damaged to varying degrees, either physically or emotionally, or both, with consequent effects on their families as well as themselves. It is not often acknowledged how many men died within a few years of returning to Australia.

The chapters Home 1918-1920 mention many who lived in the Wahroonga area and it is hoped that this will be of interest to those who have connections to the area. Some of Ben's adventures and reminisces may also bring back memories from bygone years. Ben writes of returned soldiers seeking new employment; the painstakingly slow rehabilitation process; the arrival of new brides who they had married while in England; and importantly, the process of learning to live without the constant camaraderie of their fellow soldiers. For many, the return home meant readjusting to life without the structure of military service and learning to fit back into the family structure. This was easier for some than others.

The book has an appendix of the names and summaries of the service of the individuals named in Ben's letters and diaries. This is another layer of information that should be remembered and cherished. Most of the men listed were wounded or ill more than once during their service and were patched up and sent back to the war several times.

Thanks to Ben, extended family members may now know more of their boy's Cook's Tour as 6 shilling- a- day tourists and remember them as fun-loving young men on their big adventure, rather than just memorialising heroes who made great sacrifices. Ben gives those who read his letters and journals, as well as viewing his photographs, insight into facing adversity and inspires readers to put their own life challenges into perspective.

This is not a military book but should appeal to those who are interested in military events. It is also a family history and hopefully the customs and social standards of the early 20th century may also be of interest to those who are not related to Ben. Families of those men who passed through Ben's life hopefully will find it interesting to know more about their often-forgotten family member.

Ben's letters are written from his perspective, and we do not have Frank's replies, however, one can read between the lines and guess what she is writing to Ben based on his news and replies to her questions.

The letters add an important social layer to the factual military events written in the diaries. Ben writes of his emotions, what he is seeing, events, customs and social history. He writes to Frank that these letters were to be a part of his diary in the event he was unable to write at any time, so it is apparent that he intended to do something with both the letters and diaries in the future.

There was no punctuation in his diaries as he wrote as his thoughts came to him. We have attempted to correct this in order to make it easier to read without removing the honesty and charm in which the letters and diaries are written. He was not careful in the spelling of surnames, but he may not have been aware of this. Names such as Mackenzie/McKenzie, Macdonald/McDonald, Reid/Read, Smith and Jones were common throughout the diaries and to know which Smith or Jones Ben was writing about was only made possible by the Nominal roll of the Diary of the First Battalion, the lists 1-10 reinforcements to 1st Battalion at the AWM made by Ben's friend Billy Hunt and checking against military records for relevant dates online at The Australian National Archives.

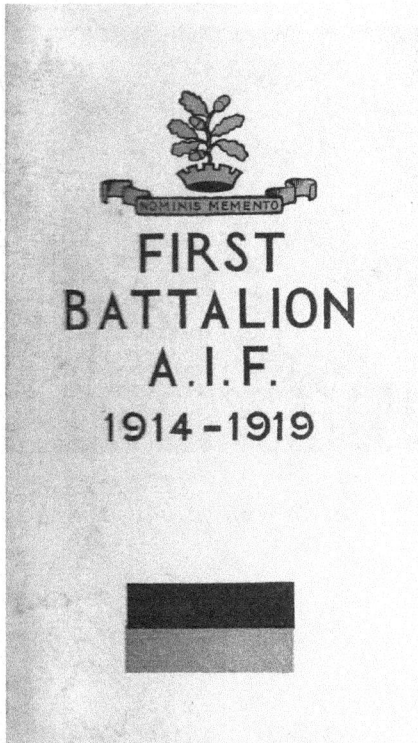

NOMINIS MEMENTO

FIRST BATTALION A.I.F. 1914-1919

His letters after the War testify to the permanent physical and mental injuries Ben suffered. Loud noises and rain storms thrust his minds-eye and emotions back to the crackle of gunfire and the rain, mud and blood of France.

1st Battalion's original colours are permanently on display at St Columba Church, Woollahra, Sydney and a Battle of Poziers church service is held there every year on the Sunday closest to 23rd July.

Lest we Forget

Penny Ferguson

November 2018

1st Division AIF memorial plaque

Acknowledgements

Ben and Frank's daughters Ruth Dolman and Mary Wheeler have given permission to use Ben's copyright material.

Publisher Ian Gordon A.O., (Major General Retired), Publisher of *Echo Books* and *Barralier* Books who turned my enthusiasm into a reality. I thank him most sincerely for taking on this project that became a much greater endeavourfor all than expected initially. His advice, patience and continuing interest was paramount for the completion of this book.

Due to circumstances out of our control and because of Ian's interest in this book I was most grateful to accept his offer when he suggested that he officially launch *Ben and His Mates*.

Peter Gamble Graphic Designer, who turned my typewritten and scanned photographs into the beautiful book it is. This was a very large enterprise so I thank Peter for his perseverance and also his interest in this project. He spent much needed time and expertise, scanning very old photographs to his satisfaction. Peter has had to put up with a lot of tribulations. Peter and his pertner paid a visit to the Somme in 2017 whilst doing the book and visited some of Ben's mates.

Dr Robert *Bob* Breen, OAM, Associate Professor. In using his professional expertise in military history and writing, Dr Breen helped to make this book more cohesive to read as a story for the general public. My sincere thanks.

My husband Neil Ferguson for just letting me get on with it over far too many years and providing help as asked. Without his backup and patience this book would not have eventuated. I thank him very much for his support and perhaps we will have some more free time in the future. I am most fortunate in having his support and love.

My daughter Claudia Liebenberg who encouraged me to keep going with the book and did some editing and proof reading, much needed as a fresh pair of eyes. She has also been a great help in marketing the book. Claudia has learnt a lot about her family and with her interest I hope she will continue to be a family historian.

Friend Jill Bailey my thanks for her invaluable support to me and her encouragement, help with advice and editing, to see this project finished. Jill and husband Nick, through reading this book were interested to pay a visit to the Somme and pay their respects to some of the men who were Bens mates. As it is said *ask a busy person* ...

John Caligari A.O., D.S.O. (Lieutenant General retired) and his father Barry Caligari, (Lt Colonel retired) both ex Commanding Officers of the 1st Battalion and Mr Michael Waldron OAM–1 RAR 1st Battalion website. Organiser of the church service for Poziers at Woollahra each year. They read the original print out of combination of diary entries and scanned letters and gave encouragement and advice on how to proceed further

St John's Uniting church on the corner of Stuart and Coonabarran St Wahroonga. Rev Suzanne Stanton for her help in getting permission for the launch of *Ben and his Mates* to take place in her

church and hall. This was previously Wahroonga Presbyterian Church which Thomas Sydney Champion attended.

The Hornsby RSL sub branch. Mr Terry James AJCM JP, President, for his help and enthusiasm to launch *Ben and his Mates* as a 100 years Remembrance Service on 13 November 2018.

Chloe Estella Smith for giving me permission to use her poem, which she submitted to *Anzac Live*. She wrote this when she was 13 years of age. She has written other stories, poems and continues to maintain her interest in knowing more and supporting those who serve our country.

Ancestry trees to help find family of soldiers mentioned in the Book.

Ancestry.com: Photographs from public trees for the Austin family; Geoff Johnson.

Lorraine Nelson, daughter of Ray Carroll, for her photos of Bert and Ray Carroll.

Jean Cattanach, daughter of Gertrude Champion and Rupert Bergelin, for her information on photos.

Neil Champion, grandson of Arthur Champion for advice on photos.

Helen Watling, granddaughter of Arthur, for providing photos.

Margaret McAlpine for photographs of her parents Dorothy née Champion and Alfred Ernest Smith

Kaye Champion Spence and Gary Champion for photo of Roy Edwin Champion, son of Bert

Andrew Warwick-Champion for photo of father Lindsay Warwick-Champion

Phillip Gurney-photo of Esme Warwick Champion married Colonel Kevin Gurney

Trish Leon nee Fell-Smith, daughter of Ian Fell-Smith and granddaughter of Donald Smith for photographs and encouragement for this project

The Champion Family

Ben's family of Jura Stuart St Wahroonga. Photo taken 1906 approximately.
Left to right back: ,Edith (Edie) 1889; Ben William 1897; Thomas Sydney Champion; Gertrude
Elsie 1891; Jessie Mary Champion nee Holt; Herbert (Bert) Sydney 1894, Arthur Leslie 1887
Front left, Keith Henry 1899, Dorothy (Dot) Jean 1903 and Eva (Marjorie) 1900
Tom Wilfred born 1907 is not in this photograph. He would have been about 11 when Ben returned
from the war

Thomas Sydney Champion.

Jessie Mary Champion neé Holt.

The Champion family home, 'Jura', Stuart St Wahroonga.

Other members of Ben's family mentioned:

His brother Bert, wife Vera nee Barlow and children Jean born 1914 and Vera 1918.

His brother Arthur, wife Althea nee Gentle and family.

Melbourne Aunt Eliza Emma Hirst nee Champion and dentist family.

Uncle William Champion, bachelor, compositor at *The Sydney Morning Herald*, who helped T.S. Champion buy *Jura*.

Spinster great aunts Eliza and Emma Dunman with connections to Singapore. Grandmother Louisa Cottam formerly Champion nee Dunman.

Cousins Morgan KIA and Eve, both AIF.

Revd. John Dykes, born Scotland, *Pioneering Parson of Jerilderie* retired in 1915 to Wahroonga and was a member of the Church Session in 1930. He has a memorial glass window in St Johns Uniting Church in Wahroonga. He married Jeannie nee Holt, sister to Mrs Champion, who prior to her marriage spent some time as a missionary in India after the death of her father Benjamin Holt. She was an A1 grade teacher and a great help to the Church.

T.S. Champions step brothers were the Cottams.

Thomas Sydney Champion was to become Secretary of the Public Service Board having started as a messenger boy with the Technical Education Department, aged 12 years from Fort Street School. He was appointed to the staff at the inauguration of the Public Service Board in 1896. His wife to be, Jessie Mary Holt was a pupil teacher at Fort Street School. They were both strict Presbyterians and attended Wahroonga Kirk where T.S. Champion was a highly esteemed member of the Kirk Session and a member of the church from 1908 when he and his family came to live in Wahroonga. Thomas was interested in history and wrote *The Wahroonga Presbyterian Church History from 1898-1930*. This became part of the book *St John's Wahroonga-the first 100 years*. He was on the Committee of Management for the New Church, St John's Presbyterian Church Wahroonga, inaugurated in 1930. He was given the honour of opening one of the two doors to allow the congregation of parishioners and visiting dignitaries to enter the new Church. He was an inaugural member of Masonic Lodge *Renown* Turramurra and wrote the history of *The first twenty five years of Lodge Renown.* On his retirement he became a freelance journalist writing articles of historical interest. He was a long-time member and councillor of The Royal Australian Historical Society and wrote many letters to newspapers (Trove), TS Champion was a member of Warrawee Bowling Club. He was an enthusiastic advocate of Pitman shorthand and was interested in his neighbours Marconi wireless and the first transmission to Australia. He was a strong temperance advocate.

> *O, these are voices of the past,*
> *Links of a broken chain,*
> *Yet God forbid that I should lose*
> *The echoes that remain.*

A A Proctor, poetess

Chosen by T S Champion at the end of his History of the Church.

Jessie Mary Champion née Holt, Mrs T.S. Champion, spent 20 years as a teacher in the Sunday School and took part in training the children in the Band of Hope. She also held office in the Women's Missionary Association and Women's Christian Temperance Union. It is said in family lore that she worked amongst the Chinese women immigrants and attempted to learn Mandarin.

Ben's brothers Bert and Keith were also AIF men, and youngest brother Tom served in RAAF Pacific in WW11. See family photographs for Thomas Sydney Champion grandsons who served in WW11

Two of Ben's sisters married AIF men. See index

The eldest son Arthur was injured prior to the war and could not take up service. He was involved in farming in the Riverina region and then was a surveyor He moved to Roseville with his family.

The Niland Family

Frances Julia Niland-Frank

Her family

Mr Niland- John Andrew Jack, Mrs Niland–Fanny Clara née Carroll of Windsor

Mary Elise 1898,

Frank Frances Julia 1899,

Ruth Caroline 1900

Agnes *Claire* 1903,

Kitty Cecelia Catherine 1906

Oaklands Tarro near Maitland NSW AUS

Archdeacon Charles Capel Greenway built *Oaklands* previously known as *Howard*, on the original grant to his father the Colonial Architect Francis Greenway on the Hunter River.

Jack Niland purchased the house *Howard* renamed as *Oaklands* plus 23 acres in 1898. He was away from the farm a lot during the war years. The family thought that he was occupied in surveying and building the roads in northern NSW and to the tableland. His extended family lived in the Grafton area and he may have been overseeing their lands and farms. His father died in 1913. He was dux of Grafton High School, went to University and became a surveyor and was with the Lands Department prior to retiring to *Oaklands*.

Jack was an avid reader of Macauley and Shakespeare. He was forward thinking and built the first silo, telephone Tarro 1. He was passionate about flood mitigation. Jack was a representative for the dairy farmers in the time of the dairy troubles and was a Councillor of Tarro Riding on Maitland Council. He died in 1933 and it was said he died of a broken heart having lost his life's work on flood management and his extensive library when *Oaklands* burnt down the year before. (source; taken from his obituary–editor)

Mention is made in this book of the men who helped on the farm, such

Fanny Clara Niland and 5 girls pre- 1915 at Oaklands Tarro near Maitland

John Andrew (Jack) Niland.

Fanny Clara Niland neé Carrol.

as Ponty, Joe, the Andersons, Goolah, Killeys, Woods, Jimmy Lacey, Delaneys and Otto. Usually they were unsatisfactory and the reason Frank, (Frances Julia) second eldest daughter, as the outside daughter, was required to help with the milking until the first milking machine on the Hunter was installed by Jack Niland. Frank took the milk to *Tarro* station in the buggy and also took her younger sisters to the train to go to school at Tighes Hill in Newcastle.

Mrs Niland (née Fanny Clara Carroll) was a governess to the Tindale family at Ramornie near Grafton and this is probably where she met Jack Niland. They were both of Irish descent, one was Roman Catholic and the other Protestant. They spent years courting until Archdeacon Greenway married them in the drawing room of *Howard/Oaklands* when he retired. She came to Tarro and was a school teacher at Howard it is thought in the old barn, home of Francis Greenway. Jack facilitated the building of the Roman Catholic church at Tarro. Illustrating that *Never the twain shall meet*, Mrs Niland and her daughters attended the Church of England.

Some other members of Frank's family are:

Grandfather Peter Carroll, patriarch of Windsor, son of Irish Defender convict of the same name, died 1916.

Uncle Will Carroll, school teacher brother to Mrs Niland, and his three boys, Bert AIF, Philip and William Ray.

Aunt Emma Rumery née Carroll at *Denbigh* Riverstone and children Fred and Marjorie.

Aunt Lucina Harding née Carroll,

Cousin Carrie Carroll, school teacher

Cousin Cecil Harcourt AIF

Ben Champion and Art Felton met the two Niland girls, Mary and Frank when they were on a bicycle trip to Krambach, Buckets Way, Pacific Highway, S.W. of Taree NSW.

Creamy, Blackie and later Belmont are horses at Oaklands and were Frank's responsibility]

The Felton Family

Arthur Art Alfred Felton born 1896

Art enlisted the same day as Ben and was the next number to Ben with 7th Reinforcements 1st Battalion. He was noted as an analytical chemist when he enlisted and his address was Junction Road Hornsby NSW. His parents were **Maurice Ernest Henry Felton** and **Diana Maxfield née Butcher** who died in 1902. His Father re-married and there is reference to the littlest Felton, Noel, born 1912 and Frank known also as Todd, born 1905. There are references to the family until 1920.

Art and his sister Didie Muriel D. Felton were especially close. Didie became friends with the Niland girls and Mrs Niland and she and Todd spent time at Tarro.

1915 Standing l-R Frank 1899, Mary 1898 and Ruth Niland 1900
Sitting Didie Felton, Arthur Felton and Claire Niland 1903 in front Kitty Niland 1906

Ben in his 19b cadet militia uniform

Liverpool Camp

This was written retrospectively and separate to Ben's war diaries.

'From physical drill and route marching, we graduated to dummy rifles, and at last came the day when proper unifoms were issued.'

Wahroonga
11th May 1915.

The bearer, Ben W. Champion - aged 18 years has his parents' permission to enlist.
Jessie M. Champion
(mother)

Permission letter from Ben's mother

When the news of the Anzac Cove landing came through to Sydney accompanied by the huge AIF casualty list, my Dad at last—unwillingly—gave his permission for me to enlist. I had tried to enlist in the AIF previously when the Rabaul Force [Australian Naval and Military Expeditionary Force] was being organised in 1914, but could not obtain the necessary parental permission without which, as my age was then 17 years, I could not enlist.

For some time previously I had been carrying on drilling, rifle duties with a local militia unit, 19B Area Compulsory Training Force, me doing my best to make up for the loss of Captain Concanon and Captain Jacobs, who had enlisted in the first contingent to leave Australia.

One after another my old pals were leaving with AIF contingents. I had received letters from two chums—Bruce Rainsford and Harold Kershaw, both of whom left very early in the War, and their experiences no doubt hastened my wish to enlist. I felt my unenlisted position very keenly, so I was delighted at last to have Father's permission. Quite a good deal of wangling was necessary as I was indentured to Donald Smith of Macquarie Street as a dental student. Arrangements had to be made for the future taking up of my articles when I returned from the War.

After enlisting at Victoria Barracks, Paddington, with my best mate, Arthur Felton in fear and trembling that I would be culled as too young or not fit by the Medical Officer, we became *Arthur Alfred Felton 2481 and Ben W. Champion 2482*. We went to Liverpool Camp, where we were stacked 18 men to each tent for the time being. As we marched into camp, we were greeted by 'marmalade' from all the old hands, who had lined up to see if any of their chums had come into camp. You may be sure that next night we lined up as old hands, and shouted 'marmalade' as well.

They call the recruits marmalades here as they always issue them with that jam at first. About 130 came out today. They are sleeping 15 men to a tent. The tent holds only nine men comfortably.

We were a 'sorry crew' that lined up next morning; some in hybrid uniform, but mostly civilian clothes. I well remember one chap who had a bowler hat, a straw hamper and an umbrella, but he soon shook down and became hardened.

The first few days in the wilderness of dust and humanity were misery for the average boy. No privacy at all; washing and other conveniences were appalling– so different from the later days at Liverpool, when huts

Group photo of 19b Citizen Militia with Captains Concanon and Jacobs

were used, and even warm showers were possible. Dungarees were soon issued, together with a white washing hat, but there were no boots for some time and several of our men were almost barefoot before they came. What a good lot of chaps those tent mates turned out to be when we had learned the rules of 'give and take'!

Billy Hunt, dark and tall, mates with Rupe Neil, short thin and fair. Brewer and Goode, teachers who soon proved a godsend to the staff for very early clerical duties; McKenna a Scotsman with his strange phraseology; Whitfield who became our Sergeant Major; Bryant, a railway man. I think we had almost every calling and profession represented in our 7th Reinforcements to the 1st Battalion.

Our officers were E.I.C [Edward] Scott, an elderly Boer War soldier (aged 42 on enlistment!) and R. Moag, (aged 34), a dashing unknowable martinet. Scott had solid lovable characteristics and supplied the fatherly care necessary in training and for looking after a lot of boys. Moag, on the other hand, was a mystery. He wore ribbons; I was too young to remember them then, but he did not inspire confidence, although he punched our reinforcements into something like soldierly shape. Two more opposite men could not have been found. I afterwards wondered if the authorities placed them in their positions knowing their different characteristics.

From physical drill and route marching, we graduated to dummy rifles, and at last came the day when proper uniforms were issued. These were all shapes and sizes and issued anyhow, so that we had to trade one with another until we had suitable sizes. Oh! What a mess when our webbing equipment was issued: each strap separately– marched from heap to heap, collecting as we passed. What a task for the new hands to put it together and make a whole! Finally we got through and assembled them and what a simple matter to strip and reassemble once we were used to it.

A tidy square pack was a problem. To make it tidy and neat for parade purposes, the corners had to be stuffed out with socks and clothes, of course thus making it heavy and like a ton weight at the end of the day. There was Moag, trudging along full pack up, as fresh as paint at the end of a day's marching. The secret came out later that he had an air cushion and small pieces of three-ply board in his pack to make it appear the right thing.

Of course we had some old soldiers among our lot. O'Shea and Devlin are two I bring to mind, wearing ribbons and, of course, wangling their way out of all dirty jobs as old soldiers do, and getting leave passes where we couldn't.

Days at Liverpool passed slowly enough to us, but too quickly for our parents, who visited us at the weekends; bringing parcels of dainties [food treats].

Thought to be Scott. Probably taken on Parade Day when other photographs were taken by Ben at Liverpool

What a happy family our tent was! These mates from the bush and whose people couldn't visit shared in the one big picnic party and lifelong friends were made among our different folks. After several false alarms we really did have our final leave, I mean the actual last one, and settled down to pack our belongings.

I have always admired a military pack for the quantity of goods it can hold, but several parcels had to be made up. On the morning we marched down Macquarie Street I am sure a more unsoldierly looking body of men could not have been seen, but under their bag-like appearance beat some wonderful hearts. Some of the reinforcements were to become very trusted senior officers and one of whom was to obtain that highest honour, the Victoria Cross.

One of many photo that Ben took of Troops parading at Liverpool Camp

———

Pte Ben Champion c/—Salvation
Army tent, Liverpool –
22 May 1915

My dear Frank, I am fairly miserable here in a tent with six shearers
and six non-sorts. We have not yet received stripes; they appear in
the dim future. The stew is so tough it cannot be cut with a knife but
has to be torn with the fingers. Nine men in camp died today from
pleurisy or pneumonia. I hope neither Art nor I get stricken. It's just as
well that I had plenty of flannel shirts.

Dear Frank, keep Art and I supplied with news or I'll peg out, as
one feels as if one is in a jail not being able to go out of bounds. Leave
appears to be very strict, so if we can't get off to see you and Mary, I
will very nearly die to get out or else I'll break bounds.

A hoary frost on the ground this morning for first parade nearly
froze our feet off. Art and I were sworn in this morning, most men (or
rather scallywags) thought it a great joke to kiss the Bible. Another
instalment tomorrow Frank, Art gives all the news– read his and
thinks it comes from me.

Love to yourself and all at home and Creamy [Frank's horse],

Ben

Monday 24.5.1915
3rd letter to you. Salvation
Army Tent, Liverpool

My Dear Frank, so far have not yet received a letter from you but hope our letters will cross in the post. I'm not very happy, Frank, as I've met with one mass of disappointments here. But please write every second or third day. You cannot imagine how we look forward to your letters. As the Scriptures saith, 'Variety the Spice of Life.' What do you think of this for mealtimes and menus? The times are very roughly put in.

6.10 am. Coffee water sweetened with salts.

7.10 am. Greasy water and tough horse meat and if there is any bread left over from the night before have that.

12 noon—tough horse meat, spuds and greasy dish water and perhaps bread.

5 pm bread jam and tea. I spend about one shilling five pence a day on etc etc ers. I'd love you to see me as I have not had a shave since I left you. And I've only been looking in a looking glass twice; those are the times I did my hair. As you think, just the opposite to our Newcastle trip.

On Saturday and Sunday lots of visitors came to camp but all our relatives were conspicuous by their absence. I think it is going to be hard to get away to your place.

Today we were issued with dungarees which had to be washed at least 6 times before wearing. The blue indigo dye runs and rubs off on to skin otherwise. There is an extra good Presbyterian minister here; he suits the men right down to the ground. I suppose you wonder why we get our letters addressed to the Salvation Army tent, well Frank, if addressed to the company or to any other church, there is a chance of us not getting them but the Sal-Army people look after them well for us. It is a pity Tarro [Frank's hometown near Maitland] is not closer.

Frank, merit does not count in this camp–it all depends how much cash your father has. The concerts in camp are extra good, all things considering. Local talent in the plenty and choirs up from town. You'd be surprised to hear all the men in camp singing, some have such good voices.

It is awful drilling under a man who knows no drill and, goodness knows how he got his job. Don't think I'm home sick but I'm only disappointed. Your soldier boy.

Ben

———

Tuesday 25.5.15
Address Sgt Ben champion
c/—Salvation Army tent, Liverpool
Camp, Liverpool

My Dear Frank, I am in a totally different mood tonight Arthur and I have become Sergeants and have gone into the Officers' Instruction camp. There we sleep four men in a tent and all are gentlemen. I received your lovely letter tonight and shall be overjoyed to receive its duplicate often thereafter. Please thank Mrs Niland for her kind note. Regarding the parcel she wishes to send, we cannot get to the station and, as the parcel cannot come by post, I don't think she had better send it just now. Perhaps in a few weeks we can come to some arrangement.

Tonight we attended a lecture given on the Northern Territory by Reverend J. Flynn in the Presbyterian tent; no doubt more could be done by the combined churches there.

What do you think of this joke?

Two wounded soldiers were in hospital, one a German and one English. The German said to the Tommy, 'All the English men fight for is money, we Germans fight for Honour.'
The Tommy scratched his head and then said, 'No doubt we fight for what we lack.'

The 20th and 19th Battalions are ready to move off to the front now. Today they did a route march of 16 miles loaded with their kit and only about four men fell out, jolly good wasn't it?

Six men died of pleurisy today and were buried at home by their own people as they did not wish a military funeral. We were issued with one suit of dungarees, one white hat, two singlets, mug, knife, fork, spoon, three blankets, and one waterproof.

I suppose you enjoyed yourself at the Tarroites picnic.

You'll excuse my writing to you so often but this is a good tent. Only decent chaps come here. I know our time will be more fully taken up at night now the school is on. In our tent is a corporal who went to New Guinea and Rabaul with the Australian Naval and Military Expeditionary Force. The tales he tells, all vouched for by other men, about the officers looting makes one ill. No wonder that the Court Martials in town create a scare.

One Captain, I won't mention his name, although everyone in camp knows about it, crawled up a concrete drain pipe when the shooting started, so the men in ranks gave him an awful time. When marching along near Captain N----—one man would say intending Captain N to hear, '*He didn't crawl up a pipe* etc.' Then another would say, '*I bet you he did*' and so on. They even made up a song about him.

The troops there were half starved; someone sold their stores to the Chinese. No wonder a riot nearly occurred. I wonder, '*Do I charm away your tooth ache?*' I want a small painting all right and am extra glad you like going to art classes. You ought to do well at it as long as you don't do yourself, I'm pleased. You know I don't like pretty girls. Any colour will do, I'm not fussy about scarves, if you knit one.

Colonel Legge the officer replacing [General Throsby] Bridges (deceased) is a fine man and all here say he is as good as General Bridges. We can't afford to lose any more leaders. There was a man in our late tent who died, married, wife living and four children. He was giving them 21 shillings a week. What a shame they accept married men.

Good bye for the present, Frank, love to yourself and family again. Thank your mother for her nice little note.

29.5.15 *'Jura'* Stuart St Wahroonga

My dear Frank,

I suppose you can see by the address on the back of the letter Art and I have gained week end leave. We squared the Sergeant Major to let us off extra early and so got home at 3.30pm. Liverpool is only two miles from Central Station yet it took us from 11.10 to 12.45 pm to reach it. About every second station we stopped to let a train pass.

What have we done to deserve that glorious box of food, toiletries, and stationery delicacies? How can I repay you? I suppose by visiting you again (giving more trouble) when we can. We left before the letters came today, so am sure I will receive a budget by Monday. We have leave until 12.30pm on Sunday night.

Please thank all who participated in the preparations of the box. Everything shows thoughtful consideration from soaps and towel to writing paper, books and eatables.

If we pass the School of Instruction at Camp we will try and get into the next School to be held at Marrickville, then we will be prepared to accept senior Non-Commissioned rank and go immediately to the front. You can bet your socks we'll see Tarro before that occurs.

I've had a close crop on top so as not to be bothered much with hair brushes etc. I've also taken to a pipe and calmly await your opinion. How our two tent mates appreciated with us the brown chutney biscuits etc. Which did you make? They wanted to know were there any more cousins of ours near Sydney.

I notice Mrs Niland in her letter headed 'Dear Bonnie Boy' asked us to take care of ourselves. Well I believe I'm getting like *'Jessie at the Zoo'* savvy?

What does *'Oh well Mum, that was the first time he ever put his arm around me.'* What does this mean? I really don't catch on. I'm quite excited, Frank, about the heading of my letters from you.

We got a quarter of an hours leave to get your box and can do so in future, so just address to Railway Station. This camp runs away with cash, all mine is mortgaged yet I do not receive it until Tuesday.

Give my compliments to Pontie [a farm hand working at *'Oaklands'*,

Frank's family farm near Maitland]. I trust he is in a better frame of mind than when you wrote last. Don't forget Uncle Ben when speaking to Miss Smith about painting.

We were issued with full equipment on Friday and take on soldiering in dead earnest when loaded with rifle, pack, haversack, entrenching tool, rifle cartridges and belt, water bottle and mess tin—the whole weighs 53 pounds and 83/4 oz. The entrenching tool is like a shovel one end and a pick the other. It is used for digging in medium soil making trenches The only use the bayonet is at present is opening jam tins, but it gets one used to handling it.

Evidently you didn't stamp the letter as the stamp was on ok. What is the meaning of that Eh? What a glorious night Thursday night was. I awoke to find my head and shoulders outside the tent and as I was perspiring, I suppose I shivered so hard that must have caused it.

General Birdwood has been slightly wounded in the head. How that occurred is hard to say for no doubt he was surrounded by his staff of officers. Most of our NCO's at the front have been replaced by more highly trained Imperial men. In the next tent to ours is a sergeant who was in India and went to Egypt with our first contingent, but he was sent home on months sick leave with malarial fever.

All today in town. The Red Cross Society have been collecting and selling goods for the benefit of the sick returning Australian soldiers.

Arthur and Ben at Jura Wahroonga.

There are sure to be a lot. Which is correct? You have been at school more recently than me– 'is sure' or 'are sure' in the above sentence.

Picket duty these nights is not to be envied as there is generally a frost on the ground when we go to physical training in the morning.

How are Goolar Cow and Company progressing now Mr Niland is away? Any tricks on the part of any of your faithful henchmen? Have you had time to read the *Wood Carver* or does dropping stitches get you down like it does my sisters. Gertrude [Ben's sister] has started the mandolin. The house now resounds with such sweet strains!

Sydney had not altered whilst we were at Liverpool I thought it might have *picked up its bed and walked* like some of the Belgian towns have done. Well, Frankie, I'm in the mood for writing tonight and hope you are also. This morning we had no parade but had to tidy camp up a bit. I'm sure it knocked some here off their high horse and considerably lowered their dignity. Love to all at Tarro. I'm going to run for the post now. We have no nice Baker boys to post letters here. Good night dear.

Ben

Once more thanks for the box from 2 very undeserving soldier boys.

————

Salvation Army tent Liverpol
Camp 31.5.15
–no 7 letter

My dear Frank, I received your two last letters this morning and was agreeably surprised. Just what I wanted. I'm sorry you had toothache, what a pity I wasn't there to stop it like last time. Why don't you say, *Open a little wider pet?* Poor old Art was muchly cut up about Mary [Frank's sister and Art's sweetheart] being ill. Yes, we have the food, toiletries and stationary parcel but it is nearly all gone now. You notice I'm using your paper so I bought some ink. I'm afraid somebody has wept into it.

You'll be able to wear that new skirt of yours before a month's out so take care of it. Glorious weather here in the day but like the South Pole at night. I feel rather groggy tonight as if I'm getting a cold.

Who told your Aunt Em [Emma Carroll Rumery of Riverstone] about your goings on, it wasn't me I'm sure. Now I'm starting your other letter. You are improving with practice in the letter line, more chatty etc. There are no doings since Saturday night when I wrote last, except we had skirmishing through the bush today in battle order.

At Camp here we have started a mess, six pence per day for extras and these six pence mounts up when about 130 men pay at once.

We'll see you within a month now so keep up your pecker [spirits] till then. Poor Clarice Muncaster. I'm sorry for her—why doesn't her husband go to the war.

In drawing ones bayonet today one careless mug in the ranks cut his next man's arm not deeply, but such a nasty cut. We have bayonet fighting tomorrow morning but we have the scabbard on then.

It was so lovely getting into a bed again after camp, for the first time in a week I was warm. Some poor fellows are out on a picket duty now; it looks like a wind storm by the peculiar clouds. I have a throat like a lime kiln now.

The 27th list of casualties is out in tonight's paper. I think that so far Germany has won the war on points. We have in the next tent a man who was a Lieutenant Commander in charge of a destroyer (discharged for being drunk on duty I believe) He has five medals, China, Zulu, Boer wars and Edward V11 and George Coronations. He is going for the same position as us and yet we have the audacity to compete against him.

I'm going to bed dressed tonight to try and get warm. Yet, I'm not grumbling. It's a glorious healthy life for a change. About 140 new marmalade recruits came into camp today. I'm meeting every day fellows I have known at Fort Street School. Art and I thought we would be on our lonelies but such is not the case.

Don't you think I put too many I'm in my letters? If I do please mention it as you know I can't write a sensible sort of a letter. We worry the Salvation Army man so much that he says every time, *Felton three letters, and Champion two.* You won't recognise me when you see me. I've almost had a shave on top. My hair was too much a nuisance to keep in order so I got it cut off.

Lots of love Frank,

Ben

3.5 [6] 15 Liverpool
Camp

My dear Frank,

Your pleasant surprise to hand tonight. Just what I wanted. It's you alright, you without your specs. I'm sorry I can't give you a very good one of his nibs [me] but I'll get one taken some day. Won't put anything in about writing, it takes up valuable space which you could fill with some news about yourself.

When and where will I see you in Newcastle some time tomorrow? I can't understand you're not receiving a note on 1 June. I've written every each day. We'll have to interview the postal authorities. Get some horses ready won't you. Give Claire [Frank's sister], many Happy Returns of the day for me dear. I suppose she will feel quite ancient when we meet her. I'll soon charm away your cold. Don't let it stop you going into Newcastle on Saturday. Until I see you, Ben.

8.6 15 [says 14]

My dear Frank,

I received two letters today. One posted on 3rd, on 4th. The one written on 4th is the best I've yet received from you. (it is going to receive a special frame with your photo) All leave is now stopped for a fortnight. There is a lot of talk of the whole camp walking out in a mass. Why should we all suffer if a few get drunk and rowdy?

I would like you very much to read your letters over a couple of times carefully for sometimes they are so ambiguous and I have to search for the meaning. Your postscript, I cannot write here for the space required but I cannot make head nor tail out of it xx

What a glorious heading your last letter started with and I'm sorry

Frank (Frances Julia Niland)

I can't reciprocate on paper. We had such a rum trip as the train was absolutely crammed and didn't start until 7.30, travelling the whole time, we made Liverpool this morning at 12.50. I slept most of the time but the trip was easily worth it. What do you say? Thank your mother for her kind note, she is most considerate and she evidently thinks you want educating. I'm sure I'll have no hand in it. Everyone here is most disappointed with the State of Affairs. Some men have been here since November. One can't get leave unless under special circumstances. Your Ma's cake is going extra well. I believe she thinks we care for nothing but our Little Marys.

You mention wondering how you will keep on writing. Don't you stop or you'll get a telegram asking you to explain yourself. There is a parcel for me at the station but I can't get leave to get it. Our camp cakes are dough. Mr Felton and Di came up to see us on Monday. Isn't this a soapy letter, yet I can't help it. I have to put the curb on when writing.

How do you spell emphasis? Art and I have been wondering for the last half hour and tried 'Emmphatesis, empetes, Impehetis and all sorts of ways. I'll have to write home tonight or they will think me dead. We finished a steak and kidney pie for dinner, Art supplied it. Have you heard us talking of Ginger Smith, my boss's son? He came up yesterday.

I wonder how your photo will come out? I'm not satisfied with just one from you so let's hope it will turn out well. Love to all and extra to you dear. How can I end off? Can you suggest something mild. Your

Ma says I can't write.......letters. I can't if I know anyone but yourself reads them. Burns says *'Tis a sacrilege committed for a disinterested person to read another's letters. '*

Give me plenty of news. Have the natives been talking yet. How is Mrs Turner's toe and Net's cows. Mrs ....née Muncaster and has Joe turned up yet? If so how did he explain himself?

I posted your Pa's letter ok. We shifted today into a big iron shed. We are immune from the wet but by Jove it's cold. Good bye duck,

Ben

Camp 9.6.15

Dearest Frank,

Your letter to hand today at 12 (noon). It started to rain here last night and has done so ever since. You are not the only one who felt strange yesterday, Art and I had to wash up our mess table things. It was a dreadful job without any help from the gentler sex. Surely the onion was not necessary for you. In the tear department I'm sure it wanted something stronger than that to bring you down from the heights you climbed into while on the drive.

Give Ruth a bad time for me, she deserves it. (Frank's little sister) Pontie is ok. I don't mind you writing in anything as long as news filters through. Only one letter a week is now allowed (aloud if necessary the rest silent). Catch on.

Last night we heard a very good concert in the YMCA tent. One man gave a step dance and mandolin solo. (the sweetest I have ever heard). It was put to words by an Australian author, I forget who, perhaps you know. It was entitled *Not understood.* It went on to say how a jest or fancied slight often sets 2 persons apart who before were great friends *Not understood* was the refrain.

People generally speaking, are very good to soldiers one notices when in the train, boat etc, coming all the way from Sydney to give concerts. Don't you think Creamy is important enough to spell with big C. 'Go on You .... ', .says Arthur. Can't our person go well out on the drive?

Art and I this afternoon are detailed off to carry a sick man up to the hospital (incidentally we get out of Parade). He has 6 blankets on him and is still shivering so we thought it best to get him to hospital. (Since found out he is down with pneumonia, temp. 106 degrees). Very thankful to be in barracks instead of tents this wet weather. We tried to scale out of camp last night, to get our parcel, but as no passes were forthcoming, other than our weekend ones, we were quietly and firmly turned down. Coming home on Tuesday morning we were blocked by a sentry guard with fixed bayonet, and when he saw Art and myself he said *'pass officers All's Well '* so we might as well think we are officers while we can.

The ground under the influence of feet and rain is developing into a slushy duck pond. How are your ears and face? Did I improve it at all on Monday afternoon? I'm always bumping into old pals. Today I received an unexpected salute and found one of the NCOs from Hornsby. He marmaladed yesterday. He will have a glorious time beginning in this wet weather as it appears to have set in for good. As long as we don't have to parade in it, I'll be satisfied.

Another funeral today for a man who had been here 4 days and he must have developed pneumonia when he came here. Have spent/ wasted 3/4 hour cleaning wet rifle and equipment. One of the joys of soldiering. The new camp Commandant Kirkland is greatly disliked here. He issues orders in the morning which are cancelled at 12 and come into force again at 5. One doesn't know what to do.

Love, to see me mending clothes with a darning needle, cotton coarse enough to tow a ship—If you have two buttons this size (drawn) you can enclose them in the next letter. Is this No 10 or 9 letter? You seem to have given up on numbering yours. The boards were like ice last night and as we have no overcoats, Art and I have been wearing our water proof sheets as capes. Please try and understand this letter as I have written it under a cross fire of chaff from all sides. Love to yourself and family.

Ben xxxxxxxx (many x) the real thing .

Liverpool Camp 11.6.15

My dearest Frank,

(I won't take a mean advantage and start with Julie), Yours to hand at 12 noon. I must tell you of a peculiar dream I had last night. I dreamt I was in a cellar up to my waist in water picking up shillings wholesale. They had dropped through a grating into this water and no one thought to get them. I believe it was in the Hotel Metropole and the money came from a Hospital Saturday Collection. I can still picture the cellar.

When I come up again I will shew you your letters and with your help try to understand numerous phrases and P.S's. Leave the camera, it will be a good excuse later. Be good in Newcastle tomorrow and come home with a good painting. What's the next going to be? *Creamy*?

There is no news today except we braved the elements and had a shower and after it I felt good and clean enough. That man who is in hospital with pneumonia lent his bed to us but I gave it up to Art as I consider it warmer on the boards. No one here has read your last letters, I've simply told Art the news and I hope you either burn or put them away safely. Heaps of love, Ben

We had jelly blanc-mange tonight for tea. You see we get paid shortly and the Cook wants a tip. It went down well. I hope when I develop your picture tomorrow night it will be a success. Do you think that next time I come up you'll be well, you generally get a bilious attack, toothache or ear ache. I'll think of you at this time tomorrow night when I'm in the Dark Room and perhaps your portrait will appear on a picture plate. Have you been on horseback since we left?

I'll have to knock off the pipe slightly, I nearly smoked myself silly yesterday. It doesn't do one any good. Cold day threatening here today with peculiar inky clouds. If you saw them in a picture you'd say them unreal. We can hear men counting the picture show *out*. The engine has gone bung and the men have paid their six pence's.

I'm sorry we left our old Company. They have received their uniforms and equipment and will be off shortly. I suppose you say fate was on your side. I see how hopeless it is to get a commission and will be content with a permanent Corporal as one can't expect men to follow a nipper.

Are all well at *Oaklands*? Art and I have slight colds. I was extra warm last night. I rolled myself in my blankets and then shoved myself into a bread sack so it was impossible for the wind to sweep under me. We went to tea with our hats on as the mess tent continually sprang leaks.

Has Pont been behaving himself since we left? I know you won't receive any education from him. What can I say more, we heaved the cheese away, by a majority vote, much to the disgust and disappointment of several table mates. There is no account for tastes. We look forward so much to the Tarro letters that even the Salvation Army man noted the keen disappointment on our faces.

I'm afraid I can't say any more, Julie dear, you know I would have Plain Ben from you duckie. I'm used to it and only like Bennie from Ma and then only on special occasions and Willie sounds like the Crown Prince. Is there any resemblance between Willie 11 and me, if so I'll commit suicide. The Scripture said *There are more people alive that dare not die than people dead who dare not live.* Had jaw ache for about 5 minutes tonight and it shook me up some. Have you been to Mr Parker yet? I wonder will I live to fix up any more teeth. Yours lovingly, Ben. Continue to be good pal Frank

Do you really mean xxx or is it only writing—on your answer depends a lot. If 'tis earnest you have changed around a lot from last time. I hope so. 'tis a strain when one does his best to influence you and does not succeed. I wonder if you could lavish on me as much care as you do on Creamy.

Give love to Mrs Niland from me and tell her we appreciate all her goodness and are sure her daughters will follow in their mother's footsteps. See you for sure.

Jura Wahroonga 20.6.15
Sunday 11.45pm

We arrived at Wahroonga OK on Saturday. Life is made of partings, but I hope ours will only be a short one. I felt pretty crook when I saw you and Creamy disappearing in the mist and I waved until I saw no more. How did you take it? Well, we have the whole of our lives in front of us now. I wonder what tomorrow will bring, further good luck or otherwise?

I wonder what you are dreaming of now, pleasant or otherwise, or perhaps sleep is banished and you are worrying about the war. How did Mr Niland take our going? Pleased or otherwise?

Today I was farewelled from the Church. They presented me with a small pocket Kodak camera in a leather case and so someday I hope to be able to amuse you with experiences and illustrate them to you.

I wonder will we leave on Friday, – so many chaps have had a couple of final leaves. If not could you have us at Tarro again? They said such nice things about me at Church tonight (mostly soft soap) that I wonder why I'm going. I'm such a God fearing pure young man. (So they say– what is your opinion of the devil in me?).

Will I ever forget the bosker afternoon we spent when your mother went to Maitland? Tell me, did I deserve all I took or was the fault or otherwise on your side. I don't mind Mrs Niland reading these letters she won't mind I'm sure. How are you keeping since I left? Any of your usual complaints?

Art's cold is not better but worse I think. My hand is rapidly healing thanks to the kind ministrations of the gentle sex at Tarro. I wish you were here, I don't suppose I will clasp your gently capable hand for many a day to come now.

What's done is done and cannot be undone. I'm not sorry, but I wish we were away from here.

Tonight I made my will and found I would have more to give away than I credited. Bike, camera, books, tools (curiosity killed the cat---) etc. I had my phizog taken on Saturday.

Would you care to correspond with Gertrude? She is a sport. I'd like you to do so anyway—not much time lost yet perhaps a good friend gained. Did I act the good comrade? I'm still stiff from that ride but I think it did me good to see you sit Creamy so well. 12pm love. I have to be up at 6am. Till next time love.

Camp 21.6.15

Dear love.

Camp again at 9.30am such is life without a ....what must it be like with one. Well camp just the same old hole, cold and bleak as usual. Final leave up. Work is a farce. None today. The O.C. told Art and I to clear out and enjoy yourselves. My people came and Mr Felton so we met them and had a pleasant time together. No rank as usual at present, but some looking in the near future as father spent the afternoon having tea with the Camp Commandant so something is sure to turn up. Of course the Corporals kicked up a row as 2 privates messing the Sergeants tent is against rules but we told them (walk off face of earth in pleasant language) so perhaps they will leave us in peace.

I suppose you noticed that I left off the beginning of my last letter, well so many people were around at home that I was going to put in an extra nice one but duckie I forgot. Better luck next time. The *Orsova* is 11 days overdue so I'm afraid we won't be off as soon as we expected. Three letters today, old ones so I can't reply to them as you know my news. Do you think we will see Tarro again before we leave Australia?

I had a letter from one of our pals in Egypt he says the wounded are coming in wholesale and all beds are taken. He happened to mention Wahroonga to one of his patients and discovered the patient also knew me and so they were friends immediately. What a small place this world is. (Do you think so?—Newcastle seems fairly hard to get at)

How is Jimmy getting on? I saw my photo today. (proof only) Never saw such an ugly picture in all my life. You won't be satisfied with it I'm sure. How is Mrs Niland keeping? She is not a shadow for worrying about us I'm sure. I hope and trust you now get to sleep early of a night time otherwise you'll lose your beauty sleep. Read Art's letter for news. Mary won't mind I'm sure.

Have you painted lately? It seems weeks since I left yet it's only a few hours.

No expeditionary uniform yet everything in the far far distance and I don't suppose we'll go for a fortnight now. I suppose you're glad. It's only natural for your sex. Art is going 19 to the dozen but I can't shift.

I saw some machine guns in action today. Fine little tools they are, 450–700 shots a minute. It is cooled by a water jacket containing 8 pints of water which boils after 600 rounds and the steam generated gives the show away to the enemy. Sometimes the bullets jamb and the men are so expert they can strip the gun in 2 minutes. It stands about 2'6" off the ground.

Have you driven Blackie yet? Isn't he a goer for horse back. I'm still stiff. It seems pretty certain we go to India---the O.C is a sport. He rather likes us and told Pa we had whips of personality to lead men and I don't know what not. I'm writing this in the Officers mess tent, someone is singing *I want to be* and opposite Euchre is most fascinating.

We had a railway warrant to come from Tarro to Liverpool but we got out at Hornsby. This morning we tried to scale through on those old tickets but were had up by a fat old boosey looking ticket collector and made to pay 1/5 !!! Rough isn't it. Why can't we travel half fare?

Be good, Ben.

Kind regards to all at Tarro. I'm telling Art to tell Mary to give you a kiss for me.

That Australian who got the VC, well Hunter the boot man is going to give him 7 pounds a week for life. Why wasn't I there sooner.....

Camp Tuesday 22.6.15

Dear Old Girl

Received your letter this morning. I was awfully sorry to hear about Mr Higginson. What is wrong Frank? No terms of endearment and such a small letter. I know you are cut up about Chris and quite forgive you.

We met Mr Morris today at dinner time. He told us about you all at Tarro. We were today issued with two complete uniforms and innumerable small articles and a big great coat. Two tunics, two breeches and puttees, one cap, one hat, one great coat, kit bag, comb, brush, tooth and shaving brushes, two towels, hold all, two belts. We won't be long now. Am looking forward to our trip to India with great expectation. First post is just sounding 9.30 pm and all good soldiers should be in bed.

Remember me to your people, love. Musketry instruction this morning was very interesting. You'll have to forgive this scrappy letter we've been going the whole day long at full speed. Good night love, Ben

Camp 23.6.15 Wednesday

Dear Old Girl

We ought to have been ashamed of ourselves for sending you such paltry letters as we did the last time but I've been going the whole time. I'm orderly Sergeant today and that leaves one little spare time. We will be off shortly. I haven't tried my little camera yet, I hope she will be ok.

From where I sit I can see the Company being kitted out with kit bags. I know there are men here who have never owned such good clothes before. You say we are mad, but you know yourself, although you don't say it that we are only doing our duty. The bigness of the war is being brought home to us now, that friends are being killed and wounded. The Government is sparing no expense to fit and equip us. You won't care for our photos. I look like a convict. If I go to town again I'll have another taken.

We have rather a decent Company. Your father is off today I suppose. What a pity I can't be with you. Nothing startling has occurred lately but an atmosphere of excitement pervades everything that is done. A sailing order may come at any time.

Mail just been delivered. A Corporal mounts on a rifle case about five foot high and the company gathers around him and he sings the names out and shots the letters in the air and the men generally get them. There have been a lot of men from Newcastle and Maitland gone or wounded. Strange how it should be cold up there, the days and nights here are nippy but not blowy, thank heavens.

I've never seen such a mess up as in our lines. There are about 33 separate straps and parts in the equipment which are rather ticklish and each fool seems to have mixed his with the other chaps, consequently Art and I have to be constantly running about fitting them together for them. The other NCOs are worthless. Please love, don't get to thinking we won't come back. It's not as black as it looks and certain percentages return. Look on the bright side and hope for the best. If we don't come back you have done your part in cheering me up.

Why don't you kick Goolah right out the door, I wish I could. That means I wish I were there to hold your little hand. Yes Ginger [Smith] is very mournful he has to stop and drill with the Rookies as about 120 came up today, rather a superior class of men. Won't they feel miserable tonight and tomorrow? You're like Jessie [Ben's mother] calling in the youngsters.

I think you would love a garden so why don't you try and start a good one. All those roses and other plants ought to make a good start. How are all at home? Pretty perky now that Mr Niland is away? What do you think of this? One man had a duty pass to go outside; well he met three cobbers outside who had no pass. The trouble was to get them inside without getting into trouble, so the four of them marched up to the guard and presented the one pass. Of course, the Sentry called out the guard, but this chap said these men have no passes but you don't want the camp to know they have only just carried a coffin out, so the sentry let them in. Those men had pinched out and were half drunk but such a good excuse on the spur of the moment.

Look out you don't give Creamy the gripes with so much corn. You haven't your pa at home to give him 12 packets of salts. Did you get your purse back again? You wanted me there to gently assist you. Why don't you put the kisses in, then I can turn them into ones when I come back from the war.

Good night, Love, Ben. xxxxxx

24.6.15 *Jura* Stuart St
Wahroonga

Dear Love

I'm at home for this afternoon as you can see by the heading.
By Jove its great having a hot bath or rather a soak—that what's I've
been doing and now feel as good as a new pin and clean enough to
meet you.

This morning I got into town. It took from 11.30 to 12.30 to fix
my teeth at my *open a little wider pets*. He did shake me up, four small
cavities. Now they're as sound as a bell. I don't know any news except
I suppose that Art will be enjoying himself when you get this letter.

I have to be Orderly Sergeant on Sunday and so it squashes the
trip on the head. The devil only knows what excuses I will have
to make if Art's people come up on Saturday or Sunday. Gone on
Route march–gone with Provost to Staff, to Barracks–Gone to
town–Gone to see a man about a dog etc (the Lord will provide–
eh!).

When I arrived home I found a parcel containing a khaki
handkerchief and a fountain pen, quite appreciable gifts I assure
you. How do you think the pen writes? Inform Art that Archie
Thompson was found drowned at Manly. I pity poor Mrs
Thompson. One boy at war, one dead, one married and one a
scallywag. My people are coming up to camp on Sunday so I'll have
to invent some excuse for Art. I wonder when we will at last shrug
off. This suspense spoils a man's appetite and you know what that
means to me.

The school we were attending is in quarantine. There was a
case of Scarlet fever; we left the school a week before so there is no
danger. The 18th Battalion is leaving tomorrow morning for certain.
I'll try and get some photos. We have been so busy issuing uniforms
I've had no chance as yet. What are you going to do for letters when
we go away? I missed one day and you threaten to stop a week's
supply, how dare you, you little puss. I go back to Camp by the last
train so I won't get your letter until tomorrow. Are we mad to go, do

you think so? Especially after the fall of Lemberg. Soon I am afraid Compulsory Service will take place.

Haven't you any spare xxxxxxxxxxxxx? You needn't give them to Art for me– he has enough and don't you believe what he says. Creamy doesn't care for them but I do. Say that you are pleased to see we are not hiding behind our mother's apron strings, and that we are going to prove we are men. I'm sorry you will be lonely, but I really can't get away from camp. I really would love to see you again. Poor sick Ben on the sea trip. What will I do? What will I not give to be at your place safe on Terra Firma at *Oaklands*. Are you going to have a cat farm, if so, you had better start a rat one, so as one will feed the other. Like they do in America.

Marjorie rode to Ryde, tell Art and she feels nearly dead. It's a good ride for a girl.

Our garden is pretty soapy looking, nothing but violets and jonquils, your favourite flower. Frank. Mr Morris looked as gigantic as ever the other day, especially his chest?

Have you had recourse to that bucket and onions yet? I really pity you women folks; you can take no active part in the war except as helpers, sewing etc. You can only look cheerful yet I'm sure in your hearts you feel the opposite.

Good bye, old Pal, I will look after Art and make sure he behaves himself.

Your only Pal

Liverpool Camp,

Friday 25.6.15

Dear Old Lass

I caught the 11.44pm train last night for Liverpool and, as you imagine, rolled into bed this morning. Never in all my life have I seen so many drunken soldiers. I believe I was the only one in the carriage sober. Of course they became rowdy and more than one window was broken. The poor pickets were helpless. The 18th and 19th Battalions left today for the Front about 2, 300 in all, they

Marjorie and her bike

looked so well.

Tell Arthur all will be square if any of his people come up on Saturday and Sunday. We will be out at the rifle butts all day. One of the Sergeants in the Company is developing cold feet i.e. he is becoming funk. He has transferred, or is going to transfer, to the School despite the experience of Arthur and myself.

Such a day as today I do not want to meet again. Wind and dust stuffing every crevice and cranny down fore neck etc, and on top of it all came the rain. I was out with a party of six men, on visual training. I left one man as a marker per each 100 yds. so at least 650 yards away when down it came. I cleared into a cottage for shelter and they provided afternoon tea. Then, when the rain had abated somewhat, I made a bolt for shelter. One of the Sergeants and the Colour Sergeant had a bit of a fight in the lines.

Last night I was presented with a gold mounted Waterman's fountain pen and a silver wristlet watch engraved. 'Presented to Lieutenant Ben Champion from NCOs and cadets of H Coy 19B Area on his departure for the front with the AIF.' Very considerate weren't they. So glad to get rid of me no doubt.

Look out you don't give Creamy the gripes with so much corn and don't go doing too much hard work on the Sulky and harness. It doesn't agree with your hands or constitution, and you must take care of yourself now I can't do it for you. Gertrude posted me some tooth apparatus last Tuesday, but I haven't received it yet. Father sent me a telegram yesterday at 9am. I haven't got it yet. The Postal authorities ought to be shot. I received your mother's letter card and have just managed to decipher it. I don't understand the allusion to Mrs Green.

Art isn't here for me to hear about her from Mary's letter. Anyhow she is a sport. Do you run into Tarro every day? Yes, love, I have a baby Ensignette camera, but have been unable to use it as yet. This issuing of uniforms takes up such a lot of time and then the light is not suitable. Just saw the parade hours.

Yes I'm very sorry for Mrs Higginson and you also, love. [son died at Gallipoli] Your mother says you feel it very badly. I think Didie wants being shook up also. It's a disgraceful thing not to answer a letter especially if one is indebted to the other, like Di is to you. Fancy you bringing out Di like that the first time. If Mrs Niland thinks Ben is such a shy boy I don't know what you'll do to amuse him. How I would have loved to have sat around in the sewing room or on the porch. Never no more for a time.

How is that scarf? One has wanted it here these last two nights. I shivered all last night and had to roll two men out of the way before I could go to my bunk (six man tent). You can imagine the atmosphere after I shifted them. What a pity you only put 2 xx in a box. I'll have to increase when I come next time (after the war, we will see).

From your lonely devil, Ben

———

2.7.15 Liverpool Camp

Dear Love,

I'm awfully disappointed in not receiving any line from you today. None since I left your *Oaklands* so you can imagine how I long for news from you. As you know I've had a very busy time lately. I've not had my clothes off for about 48 hours. That tells you how busy I've been. Mr Felton and Di came up tonight to see Art. Di wishes to be remembered to you. She appears to be growing fast. While I was on duty yesterday I saw an action between some improvised Turks and some Light Horse men for the moving picture shows. It's to be entitled *The Hero of the Dardanelles*.

By Jove it was cold last night. I cut the ice off the rifles at 4am
to go on the beat. Our Colour Sergeant's father died today and
the Company is today to supply a firing party over his grave. I just
slithered out of the job and so did Art. Rather an unpleasant position
to march behind the hearse in slow time for a couple of miles.

Since I wrote the last letters, such a lot of startling things have
taken place. The camp in general has been attacked by an epidemic
of measles. The cases reported about the same time from different
quarters of the camp. Your scarf came in handy last night. I blessed
you and it and often wished you had knitted some gloves as well. We
are never satisfied we men are we (especially on horseback eh?).

When it comes to xxxxxx [kisses], 'what ho' by the second paddock
rails. What do you think of the photo, like yours truly [me] or not?
Plum pudding today four days old, yet it was most acceptable, you bet.
Art goes to the rifle range tomorrow. You know he missed his musketry
by paying attention to Mary last Friday and Saturday. Good Bye. Please
don't forget a letter. I'll do my best to write, but one is so unsettled. I
haven't cleaned my rifle for three days and it should be done each day.

Love and kisses to you, Ben, –remember me to all the Family and
dear old Creamy.

Sunday 4.7.15

Dear little girl xxxxx.

You know I've been rather miserable towards the end of this week.
No letters from you and practically no sleep but yesterday I received
three letters, so I was overjoyed. It's not your fault; I notice the letter in
pencil was written on the 30th. Fancy taking all that time to reach me.

So the deed is done you are at last confirmed into Church of
England. You have taken a step that I can't. [Ben is Presbyterian] but
I'm sure you won't be sorry for it. But love, you'll have to act up to it.
It's rather lonely here without Art but I'm having a good rest, ready
for picket duty or guard next week. Such is life, work, sleep, and eat,
amusement. Last time my people were up visiting they gave Art a box
containing razor blades and a pair of scissors inside a bigger box of

Ben in civilian clothes in July 1915 before leaving on the troop ship Orsova

cakes. Well somebody must have opened the big box and taken out the smaller one as it can't be found anywhere now.

Now I'll answer a few of your questions. Yes, the train played the same trick on me it always does but the trip up and seeing you was worth it. Art told my people I was on picket duty when they called and so I let them believe it. Ruth wouldn't care to know Keith [Ben's brother] as he is too quiet for her.

I told you Pontie had gone to the sports, but I didn't dream for the moment that Joe [another farm hand] would do Jimmy in for his money. The little thief. Did Jimmy give him a thrashing or what? I would have wacked him in the horses pond right enough. Now I suppose the State will fix Joe up about time too. Will Amy go too? Poor old Miss Morrow. I also wish Hell to be filled up before my time comes.

I'm sorry I gave your Ma the impression about Pontie, for I think he is the best man you've got. That is not saying much though. It's strange how you girls talk about us, well Art and I do the same when we sleep together. (There is generally guard or something to do). Yes I have all the bits of hay off my clothes though it took me all the time to do it from Newcastle to Strathfield.

So nice of you on the 1.7.15 after confirmation ceremony to sit
by a fire and write to loved one [me] at Liverpool. At that time dear,
I was shivering on guard with an icy rifle and bayonet. What a bosker
letter. First you write, that's the best of having plenty of nothing to write
about. How do you like turning out to drive Creamy to the station of a
morning? I'll have to see into it. So kind of you to remember your letters,
keep it up. I'm thankful to say you don't put a sheet of blank paper in your
letters like Mary does. Have you anymore REEL kisses for me yet?

Whereabouts is Wansey? (Wangi) It's the first time I've heard the
name. How is it that Art can get off to Tarro and I can't? I've tried my
hardest but Mr Moag says he must draw the line somewhere. Do you
know he can't tell the difference between Art and me? He told me off
to accompany him on Friday to the Contact Camp and half way there
he started addressing me as Felton. Of course I objected and he then
wanted to know the difference between us two. At last he came to
the conclusion. Art has a bigger nose than I have. Could love tell the
difference between us two?

Paspalum grass is growing on the tennis court at home. They say, it
is easy to see I'm not at home. By now you ought to have that post card
picture of me and I also expect father to take me in uniform before I
leave. Our identification discs came yesterday. Circles of white metal
the size of a penny, with regimental number and battalion to which you
belong. Somebody sent to mother a boot-box full of homemade lollies
for me. We don't know who it was.

Art and I had a mob on the rifle range yesterday and Art made
rather a good score. I shot before and so just looked after the men.

The first hospital ship has touched Fremantle. She has on board
some of the wounded from the Dardanelles. Tomorrow Monday I
suppose your father will be home. What a glorious day it is here and
what a more glorious one would be out on Blackie with you for a
scamper on the river bank.

The breakfast yesterday was so bad no men would eat it. The meat
was like Indian rubber and vegetables like wood. Anyhow a complaint
went in about it and we are sure to get better tucker in the future. The

men are going to duck the cooks in the river if they don't. We have
in our company a solicitor, the medium-weight boxing champion of
NSW; the champion cyclist of Australia and a champion Sergeant
named Ben. Not bad record is it. No more news just now.

From a very lonely Kiddum soldier, Ben.

In the finish of your last letter you say, *Everyone sends their love but
Ruth,* and she won't say anything. So don't include her until she says she
is sorry for treating uncle Ben so...

Love to all at *Oaklands* bar the cats.

---

10 .7.15 Camp Saturday night

Dear love.

No letters yet but could hardly expect some yet. We are off on
Wednesday. What luck? Yet my gladness is mixed with sadness at
leaving relatives and friends behind. Never shall I forget the time I
spent at Tarro amongst you all. Should I not come back love, you will
know my friendship with you has done me good. The many kindnesses
your mother has done me have left a mark on me which can never be
effaced. I'm going to do a man's job in this war though only a nipper.

I would like you very much to keep up a correspondence with
Gertrude. It will keep you in touch with my family and news that
filters through to them will also reach you. When far away, my
thoughts will be constantly on you and, my dear, I expect you to do
your part and write and write and even pray for us all. Perhaps it will
do some good eh?

Putting aside the mournful part of it, should I come back, what an
experience to have. A very few marmalades came in today, Saturday, as
usually more come in on Monday than any other day. Just imagine me
on aboard the troopship. Oh my. What do you think of my pictures in
camp rig you received today by letter?

All my people are coming out on Sunday. How I wish you could come
but wishing won't help. Art is on leave tonight, so no other Sergeant is
present. I'm extra lonely. No gazettes yet. I'm living in suspense. This is a
true Irishman's Company. Fancy a man being through Boer, Zulu, Tibet,

Arthur Felton
'With Arthurs farewell wishes July 1915'—before he left on "Orsova"

and China wars and being a private in my section. His nibs [me] who has never seen an action commanding him. Doesn't it seem ridiculous and absurd? Yet he is drunk every night.

Private Reading another in my section. Five years Oxford University, four years Miles End High School, seven years engineer. Been all over the world, speaks seven languages fluently. He is a remittance man from England with ships of cash and yet he is in my section. Of an extra good family and has probably been tipped out of home for something. Shickers up a lot also.

Tomorrow night NCOs go to a dinner tendered to the Officers. Bayonet fighting all this morning. Beastly and realistic–explaining the best way to stake a man. Lieutenant Moag borrowed some bagpipes and drums, and the Company went spanking down the road to the admiration of all bystanders early this morning. How many will answer roll call three months hence? Art has had some socks pinched from him. I can forgive a man for most things, but I can't for stealing personal belongings. He's going to get killed when found out. Dear little girl, I wish I were at Tarro yet I know I must act the man. I hope for the sake of my friends I do not show the white feather. Give my love to all at Tarro, Mrs Niland, Mary, Ruth, Claire and Kitty, that is if any is left over from your share. I haven't got those pictures developed yet. Good night love, be good, Ben

Dear Frank,

Excuse the pencil, the ink is too faint for sure. This morning 7-8am bayonet fighting, 9-12 drill 2-4.15 Battle order. Hard at it the whole time. I am jolly tired. I'd love to be able to cut my feet off at the elbows and put them in my pockets. The pretty uniform is here but there is nowhere-with-all to clean it until pay day. When that will be the Devil only knows. Compliment Joe for me upon shooting the possums. I didn't think it was in him.

I believe the letter writing is what has broken me—never in all my life have I written so many letters in a fortnight and hope to increase or keep going as long as you 'reciprocate '. Art was out at his grandmothers last Saturday night and was fortunate (the wicked boy) to win a raffle, a cake, it came today and is nearly all gone, mock crème inside, eh what. Last night was not so cold but my sore throat has not yet disappeared. Sorry you are suffering from tooth ache. Such a little thing but doesn't it nag at one so. Have you caught on yet as to what the letters on the back of Art's letters to Mary are? Just today three weeks ago we enlisted—it seems months ago. We all cheered the marmalades again today. Why doesn't Ponty join, can't he shoot possums also? Short letter today dear, am nearly asleep now. For tea I ate four complete rounds of a tin loaf and yet I'm hungry, being in the open air makes the difference. Love, tons to you.

Your Kiddum soldier boy, Ben.

Vera, Bert, Mrs Champion, Marjory, baby Vera, Gertrude and Dot

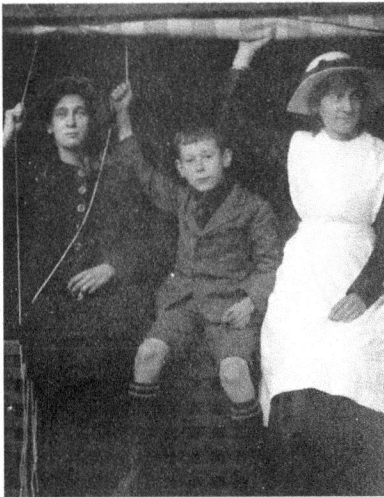

Dot, Tom and Marjory

Journey to Egypt

The poor old chap is very sea–sick because it is pretty rough.

The journey for a young Australian to join his compatriots on the Gallipoli Peninsula was by sea on ships that had been converted to cram in thousands where formerly hundreds had journeyed in comfort. For Ben Champion, his adventure began in the early hours at Liverpool camp on 14 July 1915, a proud member of 7th Reinforcements, 1st Battalion. Gertrude and his father joined hundreds of parents, brothers and sisters, relatives and friends to farewell the best of a generation.

For clarity, diary entries are dated, justified, indented and in grey text, letters are indented, ragged right and in black.

14.7.1915.
> Left Liverpool at 4.30am on Wednesday 14.7.15 after a crowded train trip. We passed into Macquarie St from King St and were met by Gertrude and Father who helped me to the Quay.

Boarded *Orsova* below the water line. No going on deck to wave Good Bye to our people. We were battened down and out deck port holes were on a level with the sea. Herded below with hundreds of others the air foul and clothes blocking up ventilation ways is not conducive to comfort. The awful odour of hundreds dressing and undressing in those confined spaces will never be forgotten.

We left the quay at 12 noon anchored on Double Bay until 4pm when we left Sydney Harbour. Moag and Scott O.C. As we went on the boat Moag used some frightful language and poor old Dad was nearly sick at the thought of his Ben being in his charge.

Being picked for guard duty was a relief, as it meant fresh air, but first of all sea sickness had to be conquered. Here Moag's martinet ways were good; *Keep that head up! Don't let it get you down* etc. did some good and the Guard was not quite as bad as it might have been but for him.

Ben wrote his first letter to Frank at sea on 15 July 1915

Off Victorian coast

15.7.15 S.S. *Orsova*:

Dear little Frank,

I suppose you have heard that the *Orsova* left on Wednesday afternoon? On Tuesday I was home when we broke camp, well we got

H.M.A.T. "ORSOVA." A. 67.

Postcard of Orsova

back to camp at 1am on Wednesday and packed up and doing numerous duties we had no sleep and we left Liverpool somewhere about 5am. A special train took us to town whence we marched to the quay. The mothers and sisters soon broke the ranks on the march and it was all the sergeants could do to keep the troops going.

Father and Gertrude came to the quay with us. Gertrude tried to carry my rifle down but didn't succeed. We had a roll call on the wharf and found had only 3 deserters—a very good record. We had some excitement on the boat before we left the wharf. A Corporal and 2 men became rather drunk on Tuesday night and rather ill-treated a private cutting his face. This private had a very strong mate and the next day (on the boat) caught the 3 together and smashed them about rather badly, broke 4 teeth out of the corporals mouth etc No doubt these 3 blackguards deserved it. Fight on board. C.S.M. Whitfield strained back when he slipped when separating parties.

As soon as Mr Moag found out he sent the 3 ashore and now the company is rather a good one. This strong private is greatly respected by the men now. The men sleep in hammocks (canvas) slung from the ceilings (I don't know the nautical terms for it). My word it is stuffy there, it is just as well Art and I have a cabin to ourselves so far.

By Jove love I have been sick. Oh Golly, I thought many and many a time I would peg out before the morning. My insides are all gone on strike and don't I know it. Can't stand upright yet. Head like the milk separator when Ponty turns it for ¾ hour. Whizzing like Billy ho. Every now and then we get the signal to rush on deck and there is sure to be something on. Boat drill this morning. On a certain signal being given everyone puts on their life belt and rushes up on to the boat deck and *stand firm* is given. Tomorrow we are to be given boat stations.

While we are on parade this afternoon 5 blasts of the whistle went and we saw all the crew rush up to the boats and in about 50 seconds, 2 boats were out after a man who had fallen overboard. They cruised around for ½ hour but he couldn't be found and he was drowned. Hard luck. He meant to fight for King George and before he was 24 hours out he was gone. Only privates pay so far love but hard luck.

We will get back pay some day. We have on board Mr Donald Smith's former mechanic before I went there. He is a good chap and I have met him at Smiths. Also 2 cadets who used to be in my company at Hornsby.

It is getting rougher now; I hope I can stand it. We are off Wilson's Promontory somewhere. There is to be no leave given in Melbourne just when I wanted it to visit some relatives. By Jove it is a peculiar feeling to have something throbbing the whole time under your feet. I was on 2nd relief at guard last night, of course I was too ill to do the job properly and of course, bumped the officer in charge but Mr Moag came along and he sent me off to bed and arranged for someone else to have it.

Lieut. Tyson has measles on board here. I hope I don't have it. The most popular game here is gambling. As Art and I have no money to waste we don't go in for it. You ought to see the mob scatter when a military policeman comes along. It is 9pm now and we all have to go to bed. Good night, pleasant dreams and may you never have to come to sea.

Love to all at home Ben

16.7.1915.

Friday. Dull, reached Port Melbourne 11.30 am, very long pier. Port seems very shallow. Not impressed with sighrs from deck of ship of Queen City of South. Felton orderly Sgt. Loaded leather and provisions for troops. 400 Victorians came aboard mostly Artillery. The Siege Artillery men are very big, mostly 6' and 12 ton men. Met Ratcliff, who was late mechanical dentistry teacher at the United Dental Hospital. He had been appointed a staff Sergeant attached to the Dental Corps. Letter from Aunt Eliza, couldn't meet her at the Quay

---

Sgt Ben Champion
7th reinforcements 1st Battalion
C/O S.S. *Orsova*

Dear Frank, We are here at Port Melbourne but no leave is being given because so many men would abuse it so we have to stop on board.

They are coaling now and the dust from the coal flies everywhere. We went down to the Sergeant's mess today for first time and continue in the future to do so. It is so different being waited on by a slick steward in clean clothes. Last night I had a hot sea water bath so lovely and refreshing after the sickness.

The Aberdeen liner *Demosthenes* is lying alongside with a lot of troops aboard. Port Philip, is exceedingly wide, land being out of sight yet is seems rather shallow. The sun rose through grey clouds and looked so pretty. One sees such glorious sunrises and sets on the water.

The barber on board the boat pays for the privilege to do his work and he sells all sorts of curios at ridiculous prices, because he is the only man on board to do so.

I wonder when I'm going to receive a letter. The mail is so precarious. You had write care of HMAT SS *Orsova*. We don't know where we are off to next—we don't know nothun and we don't care for anythink. I suppose the censor will open and read these letters. Let us hope he corrects the spelling etc.

The spare men are loading the officers trunks and one man dropped one overboard but after a lot of fishing about it was found and brought to the surface. I wonder what the chap will say when he finds out.

We have not heard the war news yet. I hope they are being walloped as they should be by this. Although away from home and friends I find it hard to put my thoughts on paper, but you bet you are not absent from my mind for 1 second. A lot of men from the motor transport are on board, they wear bather caps. My aunt is down at the pier gate and I can't get word to her no matter how I try. Later I received from her through a friend some fruit and lollies.

The big *Demosthenes* has just pulled out crowded with Victorians, some up the mast, in the boats and everywhere.
The police only let the people come alongside when the boat had started to pull out. They might have let the people say farewell to their boys. Girls came alongside our boat and distributed wattle to those who wanted it.

When we were in Sydney Harbour, girls came out in launches but Frank, I didn't care for any, they were all too pretty and you know what pretty girls are like. 'Tis awful bother keeping our rifles clean—the salt air rusts the barrel and spoils them if you are not extra careful.

Apples are at a premium on board and very scarce at that. I've sent word to my uncle here to send me out some. I hope I get them.

The artillery men are such fine men, big and brawny like young giants. There is one man in our company who takes size 13 in boots. Of course we had none that size to issue him so Lieut. Moag sent him ashore to buy a pair for himself. Good of him wasn't it.

By Jove the Sgts mess is a different affair to mess with the men— Soup, fish, meat, vegetables, pudding, cheese. We feel like being in prison on boat in part as not being allowed on shore. Gertrude packed a box for me and when I opened it today found 2 boxes chocs, 2 boxes toffees, 1lb barley sugar, sultanas, Ruth Niland Almond cake. By Jove she is a good sister.

Our 8 bunk cabin is rather spacious for only Art and myself but we manage to untidy it alright. Art is continually acting the fool–he is now talking about a little girl with frizzy hair and a forelock who would like to hear the tramp of 2 soldier boys. I wonder who he means. A little time ago he was reading the Bible aloud so disturbing me all for foolery.

Have you received the Girl's Own Paper (GOP) for June yet. We do practically nothing all day and am longing for a route march or something lively. Bayonet fighting and boxing would do. How is Joe

Demosthenes leaving the wharf, crowded with Victorians

getting on and what arrangements has Mr Howard made.

I wish we had a case of oranges or mandarins like those your father sent down last time he was in Grafton. I suppose he is at home now. Have you finished the winter's supply of corn on Creamy yet? You ought to have by this. We've just finished dinner and I can hardly move. It's just as well we don't have to go to sea tonight or I'm afraid I wouldn't come back alive. Just imagine being on Active Service and getting this, soup, fish, 2 meats, 2 sweets and tea. That's what I had for dinner tonight.

I took some pictures to day, 5 in all of the trooper. I hope they come out alright. I wonder could I make a plate now or a gold crown or back a Logan. We have on board some passengers as well as men and nurses and they don't like having to go to bed at 9 when all the lights go out. There is a mutiny on at present, about 120 have broken ship and cleared off to shore.

Good Luck to them. I think the authorities ought to give some leave or else a route march through the town so as to let us see it. Goodness knows what will occur when these men return to ship.

It was 124 degrees at Alexandria last Tuesday. I wonder what it will be like when we go through. I like hot weather but I hope it won't be as hot as all that. Oh well, good night love

Keep smiling. All's well so far. You won't receive a letter for about 5 days. We don't touch anywhere until about Albany or Fremantle. Your loving Pal Ben

Siege artillery being loaded onto ship at Melbourne

Sgt Ben Champion
7th reinforcements, 1st Battalion AIF Egypt
17.7.15

Dear Frank,

We sail shortly and so I thought I would write you while I had the chance. At present I'm troop deck Sergeant and have to look after all decks used by the 7th of 1sts. By Jove I have a task. About 150 men broke ship last night and Art and I had the job of collecting all the names of those present.

Melbourne seems a soapy place. The piers run out ever so far into the water and the *Orsova* stirred up the mud, so shallow it was. If actual service is like this I don't mind it except ones friends are far away and the only thing a person can look at is a photo. I can't see my people here as leave is so strict.

The Salvation Army has redirected a letter to me here that you wrote on 11.7.15. No doubt by this you have spoken to Aunt Hannah. Please apologise to your Mother for me for not writing but really love when I have written home and to you there's nothing more to say. Please ask her to forgive me. I owe her a few letters.

Fancy a rubber tyred sulky. Oh Golly, what will Creamy think.

Good Bye love Ben

I think we are bound for Isle of Lemnos.

[Too sea sick to write, Art sent a short letter to Frank]

At Sea 20.7.15

Frank in the sulky.

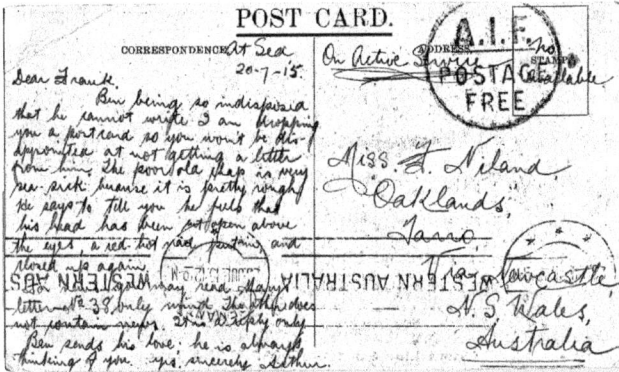

Art's postcard to Frank 20.7.15

Dear Frank, Ben being so indisposed that he cannot write I am dropping you a postcard so you won't be disappointed at not getting a letter from him. The poor old chap is very sea-sick because it is pretty rough. He says to tell you that he feels as if his head has been cut open above the eyes, a red hot nail put in and closed up again.

For news you may read Mary's letter No 38 only mind, the others do not contain news. It is a reply only. Ben sends his love. He is always thinking of you. Yours sincerely

Arthur

The XXX was code devised before they left Australia to denote where they were going

22.7.15 On board *Orsova*

Dear Pal   XXX

It seems a long time Frank since I wrote to you but I hope you understand it wasn't my fault. The horrible sea has upset my digestion and I have been completely *hors d'combat*. Being away from home the shortage of fruit is the most noticeable thing. There are men here who would give 10/—for 12 apples. Not stretching it a jot. I'm feeling better now. I haven't had a smoke since I left camp. I have two bosker new pipes and lots of tobacco but the bare thought of them turns me up.

Gertrude will explain what the 3 x on top means as space won't let here. We tumble out at 6am and generally mozee around getting things shipshape till 7.15 when we have a scramble called breakfast, the men call it a different name not to be put in here. Then generally there is some work in connection with the Company until 10 am when there generally is a lecture by the OC then 'til dinner at 12.15, then parade at 3.15 or thereabouts and then tea at 5.15 and lights out 9pm.

We have on board a wonderful lot of voices. The favourite songs are *Annie Laurie* and popular recent ones. *Mother, Girl left behind* etc. The Captain of the ship one night extended the lights out for a ¾ hour in order to listen to the singing. As usual on board every troopship we have a certain % scallywags. One Corporal from another Company was found stealing money from the men and was fined by courts martial to 90 days cells and dismissal from the forces with ignominy. Serve him right, a man who thieves from a mate ought to be shot. We haven't had any war news for some time but we know the old flag is flying. It seems so strange seeing the sun in different places. At least we are turning around and that makes the difference.

We had a sort of re shuffling amongst the NCO and now Art and I are Lance Corporals i.e. Sergeants on Corporal pay 4/– a day more than formerly.

Such glorious sunsets we see here, but I haven't seen any sunrises yet as its been foggy every morning since I've been better. The swell on the new ocean we are in seems huge but the waves were not choppy like when I was ill.

It's strange to have a life belt parade. One is provided for each man but we haven't been put in boats yet.

How are all at home? If I don't feel too well when we reach where we are going I have a chance of transferring into the Dental Corps. Mr Ratcliff who used to work with me at Smiths is sick of his job and would like to swap and I'm certain it could be done. Yet I couldn't leave Art now as I've promised Mary I'd look after him.

The waves are curly with peculiar white tops which blow off and soak our uniforms and we are covered in salt spray. Cigarettes

2d a packet, on board tobacco 5/6 per pound. I've used my camera rather freely and hope to be able to send home shortly some films. Have you got a copy of Joe and Ponty, if not get Gertrude to post one up.

Shaving on board is nearly as bad as coming down in the Brisbane Mail but we prop ourselves in a corner and there do the deed. I don't know how Art writes 10 pages. I can't, I'm blocked for news. Its rolling like billyho now and the wind is humming and the rain (or sea spray) I can't tell the difference, is sweeping all inside.

Art and I have just been roused on for having our cabin untidy. We hadn't touched if for days. This is a teetotal ship yet strange to say, liquor sometimes flies around and makes it hard for NCO's to control the men. The Officers for the main part are good fellows but there are a couple of staff warrant officers who make lives of timid NCOs unbearable. Art and I have learnt a thing or two and don't take any notice of them.

At our next port of call no leave as usual is to be given. Hard on those who have friends there. All the men hum *My little Grey Home in the West* and others are asking what's the name of some street in .... because I want to have a sick Aunt living there. This writing is just as big, about, as yours Eh?

How are all the talkers in Tarro doing, anything more? What did Mrs N say when she received her first On Active Service letter for you? It's getting rather warm here now yet I suppose you find it cold enough when driving the kiddies over to the train.

When in rough weather the ports of the troop decks are closed and that makes it practically unbearable, for the stifling heat nearly drives one mad. I bet we all sleep and mess on deck when we near the Red Sea.

How are our sox progressing, we'll be in the firing line when they reach me. What about those split hoofs of Blackie are they any worse or will they get better? What else can I say; I'm about stuck for something to write about as there is no letter to answer.

Some of the men in the artillery on board have been stationed on Thursday Island. Have been there since September last and haven't seen any service yet. Art and I have been in about 8 weeks and will probably see action before 6 weeks are out.

The Canteen here is a ridiculous farce. It's intended to satisfy the wants of the ships passengers but when these hungry and thirsty soldiers go for it, only 1/3 gets served and then it has to close down until more stores come out of hold. I think it's you who will have my diary (through the letters) for I can't write about anything when it comes to the point.

They keep putting the clock back every day (your pa will explain) and so each night we have a longer sleep. How I would like to be going home to England to see all the places familiar to our forebears.

Don't look at the spelling. I'm getting horribly rusty on it as you can see. The men term the nurses Florence Nightingales and all salute when they approach. It livens the color scheme up some to see ladies in grey dresses, scarlet capes and white caps on board and it raises the tone of the boat. Men tend to become careless when no ladies are around.

We are just 3 hours off port now, Fremantle, I wonder what it will be like. Love to all at home

Ben

─────

22.7.1915.

Off Fremantle. A tiny Pilot Boat tossing about so much (I felt ill again) came over to us as we passed Rottnest Island. On the island is an internment camp for Fritzes. Posted several letters home, it seems absurd to start the censoring business so early but they are doing it from the boat. Fremantle seems a dirty place, plenty of dust and coal about. As no leave was given men are taking *French leave,* shinning down ropes etc. but I didn't go as I felt too weak about the knees. The nurses however were given leave and they brought lots of fruit on board for us. Nurse *Lemon* brought oranges from shore for me.

─────

23.7.1915.

Spent an awfully stuffy night at Fremantle no breeze to clear the ship out but we left at 2 a.m. As we passed out we left a few men behind and when they saw the boat leaving they jumped in boats to try and catch us but the skipper would not let them come on board as it was too risky. I don't think anyone really wanted to stay behind. Have been Orderly Sgt today and very busy. Everything clean, then following the C.O. [Commanding Officer] and M.O. [Medical Officer] around on inspection.

24.7.1915.

Sea like glass (Good job too). Three whales sighted. Billy Hunt slightly better on deck reading. Talked to Art, both of us leaning over rail watching sea, very calm, decided to sleep on deck. Evans and Young make cabin dirty, squared Paxton to clear it out. Discussed with Art if life is mapped out for us. All rifles and equipment mixed up but after a few days sorting cleared the matter up to our satisfaction but not to satisfaction of Siege Battery—we got all the new rifles. You can notice the weather getting hotter each day. Moonlight night. Frank and I first went down the river bank before we started again for Krambach.

25.7.1915.

On board 11 days now, seem to be getting on well with the men. Had a chat with an old NCO, Beyers, an old K.O.Y.L.T. man and we are not above taking wrinkles from him in the finer art of soldiering; so that when Canteen goods are hauled up from the hold several cases of soft drinks manage to become *broken* and the bottles disappear. There is no doubt that the old soldiers would live and thrive when we would starve. He also said to keep a good duty roster so that the men can see they are getting a square deal. I intend to do so. Church service *Pearls of great price* Finished F's chocolates, very nice gift. A few letters from NSW would make a big difference to us now.

July 1915

[probably *Orsova* which has been censored]

Dear Frank

I suppose this letter will be censored at your place as it will be on board this boat. The sea is medium now but there is a huge swell which makes the boat roll awfully. I'm not so ill now though I suffer terribly from headaches caused by a close stuffy cabin. When we are closer to the equator I will sleep on deck and only store my clothes below.

We haven't heard any war news lately but when we do get it you bet it will be fresher than yours. We will see the beastly realistic side of the question. Do you still think it will be over before we reach there? We have been handed out little books on the German Army and if we could, it would make interesting letters but we cannot say much though. Art will probably write another 21 pages to Miss Niland.

We had a parade today of all hands in full equipment and you'd be surprised to find how much they had lost. At the last port I invested 3/9 in fruit and had a good feed. I had about ½ the fruit over and put it in my cabin under some blankets and when I went to see it again in an hours' time, it had disappeared. We have an awful lot of pinchers on-board. They would take the shirt off your back if they wouldn't disturb you. The example made of a corporal who stole money has made no effect. At our last port 2 of our men wanted to desert and had everything ready on shore, room engaged, civilian clothes etc. Now one of them had lent one pound to another man and he wasn't going without it so he (a) came and woke up (b) who happened to be rather merry and had to be pulled and kicked etc. Then b) kicked up such a row that by the time the money was handed over their engaged boat had moved off and that's how you have 2 good men still with us.

The fascinating game of 500 is played to a great extent here. I cannot understand men who start at 10am and finish at 10pm with only breaks for meals. *Housey-Housey* is all the rage and we pass a considerable amount of time playing it. The Number Caller introduces quaint sayings for some numbers I suppose they have been long used but I hadn't played before, 'Clickity—Click for 66, *Kelly's eye* for number one, etc. and until you get used to it you run the risk of the wrong number.

Tonight the sea is very calm and the phosphorous on the water makes it shine like a mirror. No sharks have yet been seen and very few porpoises and 3 whales (small ones) We were looking at the Southern Cross and wondering if you 2 girls were looking at it also. Claire used to be the best at finding it.

Does Ruth still make jokes or has the date for the qualifying exam made her thin? You would think some of the men were convicts to see them with heads practically shaven and dungarees on. Couple cases of measles in isolation ward, one an officer, I tackled a tin of preserved fruit today and finished it on my lonesome. I intend to make up for lack of vegetables somehow.

Lately boxing has been going on and often the men would get a blow in just as the ship rolled. If the other happened to go down the boxer was given the credit but most likely it was due to the roll of the ship. Today I had the misfortune to catch the roll of the ship and a slippery floor as well and went skating about 30 feet until brought up very sharply by a board sticking out but this wasn't as bad as a mess orderly dropping the whole tucker belonging to the mess down the stairs. He got sat on properly.

The weather is warming up considerably. I slept on deck again last night and it was so different to our cabin. We have been tipped out of so to make room for the hospital which is overcrowded. Lucky our brother sergeants let us leave our gear in their cabin and its lucky the weather is hot so in future on deck we shall be . We get allowed 1/0 per diem on board and the rest when we arrive in ports. This is a satisfactory arrangement as it is quite enough to spend and the men gamble it mostly.

This morning the sea is like glass, even calmer than dear old Sydney Harbour. I feel grand. If you could only see me in dungarees. Much cooler than uniform and it doesn't matter if they become tarry from rubbing on the deck.

We had a good C of England service yesterday and it turned my thoughts back to the Sunday you escorted me to Tarro Church. Wonder if I will appear there again. The men being cooped between decks most of the time invent all sort of games and they skylark worse than nippers. I heard a commotion down stairs last night and found all men out of their hammocks shooting bags of water at one another. The deck was like a lake. This morning they are all cleaning rifles.

Early morning hose ablutions—Ben's photo

Orsova men wearing white hats—Ben's photo

I seem to have grown much older since sailing. Though only 12 days out, we are nearly in the tropics now and may strike a monsoon at any moment, though to look at the sea at present it would appear impossible to be rough. We have no facilities for drying clothes we have washed and we have to hang on to them ourselves for fear someone will pinch them. The canteen is sold out. Everything except Sunlight soap, chocolates, Sarsill (a drink) and cigarettes 2d packet.

What a pity I have no letter to answer that would make this letter longer. Then I suppose I will receive about 6 when we reach port. I've just had afternoon tea, quite a luxury, sardines, onions, lettuce (tinned) bread, butter...bosker.

Bayonet fighting for 2 hours this morning, rather rough when we haven't had any exertion for some time. I've had a very tiring day being orderly sergeant. I had to post two guards and get deck sweepers to arrange for extra food for guards in addition to the bayonet exercise.

Sea like the Hunter River only rippling but of a very deep blue. Not a cloud in sky, very hot, order not to go on deck without hats—wonder the next port we are bound for. Compulsory Parade under the hose of a morning. Very, very, funny to see some men shirking it.

It's going to be a hot night all right. A very good concert is now being given by the A.M.C. Violins, flutes and piano blend well together The moon making the whole very pretty looking. The ship is going a good 14 knots per hour today and we have to be careful not to go anywhere without a hat.

The orders last night say we have to go without boots. So today one sees a ragamuffin mob with nothing on their feet. We have rigged up a boxing ball in the cabin and have a go now and then at it. Doing nothing all day is becoming a bore. Programme 5.30 am reveille 7am breakfast, 9.30am parade to 11, 12pm dinner, 6pm tea, bed 7.30 pm

Bosker Programme isn't it! I can't write any more news and Frank dear, there are no letters and we simply repeat the program every day. Plenty of flying fishes can be seen at any time skimming the water. They seem to leap and then plane for about 30 feet. There was an

operation for appendicitis on board yesterday The ship was stopped
and then the operation was done. Successful I believe. There are such
a lot of nurses aboard, all solid looking nurses that wouldn't knock up
no matter how hard worked. We were all lined up on the 1st deck and
all the nurses trooped round to have a squize at us. Strange to say they
were taking statistics and so they heard the history of each man. How
many children, where and when wounded, age, church, where born,
widower, single, married etc. It appeared to be very amusing to them.
One of the nurses remarked to another when they were calling the
ages, Sgt Champion, Presbyterian, single, age 22 years.(Ben was 18,)
Doesn't he look young for 22 then the other replied *just look at the size of
his feet* So I immediately moved down the other end of the line. I didn't
want to be regarded as if I was a horse.

Good Bye love. For the present,

Ben

PRIVATE

I expect to see a mighty lot of painting when I return. Do you
remember what Ruth said about those paintings when your mother
wanted to hang them and you didn't. I do remember it. Is she still as
funny?

Hunkle Ben indeed.

Be sure love and don't worry at all. You can be sure it is decided
elsewhere whether we are to come back or not. You ought to have
received 4 letters or cards from me by this. One cannot imagine the
phrase *Alone on the (deep Blue) Sea* until you have seen it away about
there where we are.

Has anything been said about the Aunt Hannah business or as I
hope, everything died down as soon as we left. We were inoculated
again this afternoon. What a bother washing is when no space is
allowed for drying. I wish you were here to wash for me! Aren't any
of those Haile–Hale–ale–ale—ale boys going to volunteer?

This concert is the best I've ever been too. To think we should
have such a lot of artists aboard. Miss Fazzardines took the cake. She

completely took me in. After the first song I thought her arms appeared extra strong and brawny for a lady, then I looked at her feet and saw she wore about No 8 in shoes so it then came to me, she was a man dressed up. She was good. Then Sgt Woods (he used to do exhibitions at one of the Theatres) performed. He jumped over the piano, sat a man in a chair and while jumping over took a cigarette out of the seated man's mouth with his feet and numerous other items.

They serve out lime juice to us now so as to keep us in health in this hot moist region. The sea is as calm as your Hunter River. There appears to be a heavy layer of oil over the sea which prevents the swell from breaking. Doesn't' stop flying fishes from jumping out of and skimming the water.

Boxing tournaments, wheel barrow races, potato races and pillow fighting on a greasy pole have been causing a lot of amusement and you can be sure the 7th of 1st didn't come near the last.

This is the last day Kaiser Bill reckons to make his big dash. I believe the war started just a year ago and how many good men and women have gone under during that time. I hope we eventually have a holiday in England won't it be great seeing all the famous old places we've heard people speaking of.

Church this morning. Good singing Church of England style of together. You would be surprised to hear what England and allies are doing on the battle front, converting chaos into order, bringing Britishers across to run the affairs of the Belgians and French.

No more news about the confirmation of our rank but

The slippery pole competition on the Orsova—Ben's photo

Programme

Overture	"Sweet Briar"	R.A.A. Band
Song	"The Veteran's Song"	Cpl. Larkin
Recitation	"The Irish Fire Brigade"	Gunner Brown
Violin Solo	"Intermezzo"	Cpl. Clarke
Humorous Song	"Telemony"	Bandsman Aitken
Patriotic Song	Selected	Nurse Burkitt
Fancy Jumping (Champion high Jumper of the World)		Sgt. Woods
Vocal Chorus and String Band	Plantation Selections	

Absolutely the first appearance on the high seas of this unique and talented combination of Artists.

Recitation	"Gunga Din"	Gunner Ellis
Song	"My Old Shako"	Gunner Kelly
Character Sketches		Mr. R. Colton
Song	"Ragtime Melodies"	Capt. Cohen

Male Quartet	"The Soldier's Farewell"	Cpl. Larkin, Pvts. Ryde, Lucas and Baker
Trio with Violin Obligato	"I'd like to live in Loveland"	Mrs. Malloy, Mrs. Money and Miss Holdsworth.
Serio Comic	Selected	Mdlle. Fontaines
Dramatic Soliloquy	"Denver's Dream"	Cpl. De Lacey
Violin Solo	"Cemetirine"	Sgt. Jeffries
Song	"The Rosary"	Gunner Jamieson
Humorous Song	Selected	Private Jago
Instrumental	"The Larkies' Dawn"	String Band
Song	"Ragtime Melodies"	Private Lamont
Song	"Sally Horner"	Private Hook
Song	"Was I a Fool"	Private Lewis
Cornet Solo	"Good Bye" (Tosti)	Bandsman Mouchmore

God Save the King.

H.M.A.T. ORSOVA.

A 67.

PROGRAMME
OF
CONCERT
IN AID OF
Australia Day Funds.

By kind permission of
Commander A. J. Coad, R.N.R., and
Lt.-Col. Walter A. Coxen, O.C. Troops.

On Friday, July 30th, 1915.

Programme from the Orsova Concert

I hope to become permanent as soon as we land. I wonder if you are driving to church this afternoon while I'm writing this or if you are writing to me as I hope.

We have 2 Courts Martial in our Company and a Corporal who come from Newcastle has been reduced to the ranks. Good Tucker. There is no news now; if we were attacked by a submarine or something like that then I would be able to write for I can't now.

I'm not wasting films on views on the boat. I'm waiting on land scenes. If you know of anyone coming, load them with books and magazines, they will want them on the boat.

I'm sorry I took none

Love Ben

2.8.16

Life Boat Alarm and as we were not told only practice, so doubled up quickly. Stations gained quickly all in order. Man buried at sea, leaves 7 children and wife, burial seems to me more impressive than on land, with the liner still, engines stopped etc.

Page, one of our men, had an argument with a 3rd Battalion man and although Page had no idea of fighting, a grudge boxing match was set up which developed into a ding-dong fight. Page carried on; although he had a bad beating he punished his opponent sometimes and earned the respect of all on board. The Captain stopped the fight after the 10th round—it was a gory affair right through. Seventy pounds was collected in all and will be sent to the Australia Day Fund.

6.8.1915

Nearing a Port we passed a small collier which was the first boat seen since Fremantle. About 4 p.m. as we neared land we saw it to be precipitous and very barren looking. The cliffs being bare of all vegetation. This proved to be the approach to Aden.

Stopping while we picked up a Medical Officer and Pilot; we saw for first time a bum boat manned by natives. They were a poor class of natives, very skinny and underfed. They afforded us great amusement diving for coins and never missed collecting them. The atrocious price asked by the natives for wares was ridiculous but the Australians weren't to be gulled and soon beat them down.

The garrison composed of about 5000 men were absent as fighting. An enemy force was expected 15 miles away. It only rains here once every few years and the people and troops live on distilled water which is the only way to cut down the dysentery which was rife. We were not allowed to buy fruit there owing to dysentery germs being possible.

Saw a camel train of 40 camels loaded with ammunition. This main station being close to the water and peaks towering about it, so that communication with other parts was established by a chain of signal stations, high upon the peaks. In Port was the *Empress of Asia* a converted passenger boat; the crew lined up and gave us a cheer as we came in.

Left Aden at 4 a.m. after taking on board 300 tons of coal, the dust permeated every inch of the ship and we were black. Passing through Bab-el-Mandeb into the Red Sea, we passed an island on the Port-side. Also a pretty lighthouse on the starboard side. Another good concert at which the nurses were present. Pleasant fatigue bringing up cases of soft drinks from the hold. Broken cases entitle handlers to the contents—unofficially of course. The water on board is a bit high and sanitary arrangement horrid. Line up in a queue and wait 30 minutes for a wash.

Sighted the Brothers, a lighthouse on flat rocks. Africa in the distance, very hazy. After dinner sighted a big island also Mount Sinai. I pity Moses climbing to the top, he must have been warm. We must be close to our disembarkation Port as we are ready to move off at a moment's notice. Continually passing high rugged mountains.

11 August 1915

Dropped anchor in Suez, lots of shipping in the Harbour. Arab Dhows etc. but the town still a long way off. Anchored opposite huge mountain, good sunrise through clouds.

Arabs selling grapes and melons. We leave for Cairo tomorrow, so it is said.

Disembarked and we had to be fumigated. We all dumped our clothes

Suez - L'Entrée du Canal

X marks the spot where we did out Salome dances.

and put on nighties made of unbleached calico. We must have looked weird. Many a Salome dance was performed. Our woollen uniforms were fumigated but we didn't like putting them on again after the cool calico slip over the heads. Slept the night in sand, very cool towards morning.

I thought desert was just sand after sand, but every now and then comes pretty little green spots with palms. Silly little donkeys not much bigger than large sheep, by the dozens, and the riders sitting well on the rump instead of on the back. Tel-el-Kebir has a wonderfully well-kept cemetery. Peddlers sell their wares in the streets and each has a different and peculiar cry for his wares. Water melons were very cheap *en route*.

Preparation in Egypt

'We can see the Pyramids from here, looming in the distance.'

13.8.1915

We arrived at Heliopolis Camp at 4 a.m. It was a long hot train ride. *'Carriage de Luxe'* consisted of cattle trucks with the remains of the late occupants still on the floor.

Ben's scene from the Pyramids of the Camp-Mena Egypt

Men of 7th Reinforcements in cattle trucks

Heliopolis is about seven miles from heart of Cairo and is built on the far edge of ancient Heliopolis. Brilliant white buildings, big and varied designs, wide avenues, shady trees electric tram four stops to Cairo. Clean little towns, white washed three stories houses, chiefly drinking fountains I think. It is the residential part of Cairo. It's a clean town as Gippo [Egyptian] towns go. There are native bazaars with medley of sounds and people, gorgeous eastern shawls etc. Natives are very quick. They do cushion covers of the Australian Imperial Force badge design worked in colours on cloth in a few minutes.

Natives talk about five different languages, but are in general miserable specimens of humanity. Quite a majority of the natives here have runny eyes and the kiddies make me sick, the way they allow flies to rest around their eyes. A few phrases of the language we picked up like, Talla hena, 'come here', Ruh henak, 'go there', Thank you 'Katter Kheirah', Imshi 'Go away'.

As I've told you no doubt before, some customs and implementation used by the natives are perhaps 2000 years behind time Fancy crushing corn and wheat by means of hand mill stones as that is what most natives do. Round and round the natives turn the [round milling] stones and can earn about 2 ½ piasters per diem. Just image the fortune a native would make if he could afford a small oil engine to do the work. But somehow they have no initiative, no go, just like huge babies.

Ben's drawings of the stone mills used to grind corn and wheat

Each man has brought a cane bed for five piastries and on this a mat is laid and then a blanket. After the hot day, at night time it is very cold and, if sleeping outside, heavy dew falls. Mess huts with tables and forms are used for meals. The Australian or British Government allows each man a few piastres a day, known as *disasters*, for an extra messing allowance and this buys a good addition to the Army rations. Every morning at 4.30 a.m. we go on Parade after having a cup of coffee and a biscuit and after various breaks are free by 11 a.m. unless a special parade or duties keep us in camp.

The buildings here at Heliopolis have opened my eyes. I expected a squalid place and instead find big white buildings, turreted and with minarets, mosques etc. All showing an artistic taste and the carving even on gates would surprise you. Cafés in town have picture shows to amuse their patrons and as everything is in French it's just as well I learnt it once upon a time.

Cairo itself has many quaint quarters. I was fascinated by the 'Old Cairo'. The natives and bazaars of streets were so narrow that often a man could step from the balcony of one house across to the balcony of the house opposite. Behind latticed windows you could see curious women peeping down but no clear view of their faces could be obtained—they were either wearing a veil or the lattice was very close. But think they had a good view of us.

A Native Burial is very weird. As soon as a person dies, wailing and shouts commence, the mourners really seem to become frantic. Raising their cries and then letting them die away to quietness. Then commencing afresh again. All the time trying to get as near to the coffin as possible. The coffin has no lid and has four handles but it is never buried with the person. The corpse is tipped into the grave and the coffin taken away to be used again. Some of the people tore their clothes but not in places where it would show much and mostly tore them at the seams. The cries are very weird and often they break into chants with no rise or fall and it gets very monotonous. If a funeral is going along a street where there are people, often someone would go and give the bier or coffin a lift along even if they did not know the occupant.

CAIRO. - El-Tabbaneh Street

Old Cairo with little donkeys

15.8.1915

This is the 2nd note today. I didn't feel inclined to write when I posted the cards. The YMCA building is made of reeds and is very nice and cool and can seat 500 at least.

The heat is stifling already at 7 am. I'm due for Cairo this afternoon to see Bruce Rainsford, ex Wahroonga area, he is with Australian Army Medical Corps (AAMC) in No 2 Gen. Hospital. I am also enquiring for Harold Kershaw.

To see the wounded, it nearly makes me howl yet is has made me feel more anxious to go to the Front. So I haven't gone into an NCO School as I expected. The money gets me tied up =1/2 piastres and 1 piastre are practically the same. [5 piastres to the shilling] At one minute you seem to have a handful of coins and the next 1 or so 'tis most confusing. The Palace Hospital here was originally built for a Monte Carlo sort of place costing 2, 300, 000 pounds. It is gorgeous to look at, and has some 3000 bed rooms. A few troops paint the town red yet on average the quiet element reigns. Expect letters from you very shortly, hope come thickly.

Guides take you from here for 15 piastres to the Pyramids practically 3/1 ½. I bought two mats this morning for our tent, each 10 square for 6 piastres, woven with reeds. I shouldn't care to put as much work in for 1/3. (one shilling and three pence). We wear Khaki shorts cut off 6 'above the knee for coolness and freedom, besides it feel much cleaner than when gathered in at the knee. We all carry walking sticks (swank) really to wack arabs if molested.

YMCA building made of reeds

19th September 1915.

Dear Frank

I kept the answering of your letter till the end of
the week when there would be a probability of word from
Ben per "Moldavia". Imagine our excitement when on
Saturday morning the kind postman actually brought
us 4 letters from our soldier boy. They were from
shipboard, Cairo and Heliopolis which place they
reached early on the morning of 13th August —
our "violet" day. Ben said he had never felt better
in his life and asked if we had heard from Jack
lately. He said they were expecting some mail short
and that he would "peg out" if there shouldn't be
any for him, but as we have been writing regularly
to him since 19th July and have also sent newspapers
and 3 parcels I think that he should have some of it
by now. One reads of so many soldiers who, in writing
to their people, say they have received no mail since their
arrival in Egypt. That last week I asked the clerk at
our Post office if registered letters would be more sure
to reach the soldiers, he said the men travelled about
so that in the trenches it would make no difference.
I said Ben wasn't in the trenches and so registered
that one. So the Post Office man said the only remedy
was "keep on writing". I have just written to Ben and to a
soldier I write to through the Lonely Soldiers' Guild. I
suppose you have read of it in the paper.

I am quite over the measles and expect to be
back at work tomorrow. It will seem a long day
and I suppose I shall be glad to go to bed early.
I had a letter from the office gentlemen enclosing a
limerick they had composed. It was in shorthand as
they were not "game" to write it in longhand —

"There was a young lady named Gert
who went up the mountains quite pert,
thro' sketching on eagles
she captured the measles
and now she lies prone and inert."

I cannot sketch a scrap. I suppose you are making headway
with your painting. Hoping you are all well
I am Yours very sincerely
Gertrude

Gertrudes letter to Frank

A Coy 1st Bn. 7th Reinforcements, with pith hats and swagger sticks

The drinking water is extra good I think though it is brought all the way from the Nile. Sergeant's mess is good, not up to boat's dinners, yet no one could grumble. Though grumbling and rousing are the only ways open to you if you want the natives to look after you. The more you bullyrag the more they like you.

The big parade in the morning from 6-9am is a killer, especially on an empty stomach. Our officers shewing themselves to be men as well, liked more and more every day, men would follow them anywhere. Great joke about Lieutenant Moag's legs. You know the short trousers shew at least 6 'above the knees and putties are below knee so this leaves big space for the sun to touch. Day before yesterday the Company cleared out and Mr Moag, Art and I, went out as a picket to collect them. Mr Moag's delicate white legs went absolutely crimson and that sore he could hardly walk. Yesterday he was orderly officer and that meant riding a horse all day. Last night he came and borrowed my Hazelene snow. His legs are a picture. No one rides here with leggings on. Everyone uses shorts and putties.

The mail closes tonight and the tent is crowded—everyone is chaffing the other about the Christian name at heading of letter. Such as Dear Catherine, Dear Molly etc I'm glad yours is an uncommon girls name. I'm left severely alone. One poor fellow had his nose broken in boxing the other day and as it's crooked he says he won't go home to his girl any more.

The journey from Suez in horse boxes was crook before we got our water melons at Ismalia. The Bengalese Lancers are fine little men and are just the sort to fight the Turks. Art and I paid a visit to Harry Smith a friend from Wahroonga in the 18th Battalion and blow me if I didn't strike in his tent a fellow I used to go to Sunday school with. What a small place the world is but isn't Tarro a long way off. Both watches are gone bung, mine and Arts and my fountain pen disappeared out of my pocket. I'm getting some films developed in Heliopolis so perhaps will be able to send some prints if the beggars do not spoil them.

Nothing definite about our appointments but will go as Corporals rather than go with another company. Have you had a letter from my home lately? Seems like years since I left. That bugger of an Art is writing like a steam engine 2 pages to my one. He has *the gift of the gab* orl rite. Ever since we came to Helio there has been a ban on Cairo 'tis the Mahommetan Christmas and they fast for a few days before and then go absolutely mad with drink so the soldiers have been kept out of the town. The ban is lifted today so I'm going in. I'm sorry to say an Australian was hurt in Cairo not long ago. His own fault and mates rushed in and when they had finished 5 houses had been burnt to ground.

All natives and Egyptians are absolutely dead frightened of Australians and rightly too. We can see the Pyramids from here looming in the distance. The discipline here Frank dear, is very strict. Not jumping quickly enough to an order given by an NCO = fine 5/–. Headquarters is very slick and nothing like Liverpool. I was regimental orderly Sgt yesterday and was never so shaken up in all my life. How different all this is to compulsory training. The flies here are awful (one keeps walking on my pen) biting one and by the million. Men here are getting used to them but I can't stand them especially when they try to get up your nose. Our mess rooms are the coolest of all places and there we take the men for musketry exercises etc. I rather like this hot weather as I have said before but I wish grass grew here. Such a lot of deserted tumble down buildings can be seen with goats roosting in them mainly. Good bye love. Mail closing now. Ben XXXX

24 August 1915
YMCA Egypt
from a kiddum soldier

Dear Frank,

By last mail Frank dear, I sent you a couple of small keepsakes which I hope you received safely.

Last Sunday after church I went to the Pyramids right on the edge of the big desert. It was the best trip I've ever been on except 3rd visit to Tarro. Art and I left about 11am on 22.8.15 and reached Cairo at 11.20, so you can see a very quick trip about 3 stops only, fare ½ piastre. We spent about 20 minutes there waiting for a tram and occupied ourselves drinking lemon squashes and scrapping with boot boys.

These little larrikins if you give then any encouragement at all will follow you for miles. I generally get my boots cleaned free (Baksheesh) by looking sourly at them. In the tram to Ghezirah Palace Hospital where we picked up Bruce Rainsford. He then conducted us through the Palace Gardens (pomegranates galore) to the tram for the Pyramids. The road leading to these was built by some big gun high in the Emperor's favour and leads from the Palace Hospital (which was built as a harem) up to Mena House ½ mile from the Pyramids.

This road is as good as Macquarie St and is lined with gum and acacia trees with the river on the left. Somehow the gum trees don't seem the same, perhaps the soil or heat does not agree with them for the foliage is slightly different–but a gum tree is a gum tree and reminded me of home. For at least 5 miles this road runs straight as a die and as it

Young Arab boys looking for 'Baksheesh'

Avenue des Pyramides - Heliopolis

Heliopolis—Road to the Pyramids

is lined with these trees and river, the place looks delightfully cool and refreshing. This strip is really on the edge of the big desert and it is the garden of Cairo and surrounding towns. Corn and cotton, tomatoes and practically any crop that needs heat, soil and water will grow in this strip, the irrigation is perfect. The dhows along the river give it a very quant and charming appearance but when one comes close to them and sees the filth encrusted around them the enhancing appearance is destroyed. Such is the same everywhere here nice only in the distance. While on the camel one feels up in the clouds, the jerky motion is not unpleasant but not so easy as Creamy. The next was a visit to a tomb at least 100 feet deep. Here an Englishman named Campbell found a couple of mummies. We paid a native 2 millemes to go down and sit in one of the sarcophagi (coffins). The side of these granite boxes at least 18 'thick. The pyramids next claimed our attention, only one climbable and that one we didn't tackle as too hot and 350 feet is a long climb. The big pyramid was the one we walked completely around, quite a route march. The surface was once coated with some preserving paint but time has worn it out like steps. I wonder how they built them. We saw other pyramids in the distance as we came along but none as big as these particular noted three. We clambered in the entrance of the big Pyramid. The floor slopes down at about 30 degree and is as slippery as ice. The guides won't take you inside unless in bare feet (no place for ladies) so we didn't tackle it as time was creeping on.

An American professor is finding a lot of fresh treasure near here
so we tried to get there but were blocked by locals with military passes.
Weeks and weeks want to be taken to explore this place as the whole
district is one mass of historical records. We went to Cairo, had tea
and after a while we went back to Camp. I'll write again this week. Love,
best wishes, write, kind regards to all at Home. Bugle now going, love
Ben, By Bye How is your painting getting on--Route march tonight
6pm—10.30pm 12 miles

25.8.15

Dear Frank (Frances Julia)

I wrote yesterday but feel inclined to do so again. We are continually
hearing news fom the *nellies* (Dardanelles) which you wouldn't get
and I could write all day for a week on them but of course it would be
squashed by the censor. I wonder what you are doing now, let's see Cairo
is about 8 hours behind so 'tis about 4 am and I hope you are snoozing
in bed. I haven't had any letters yet but I hope to get a mail about
Friday. Many of our chaps went up the Pyramids and into some of the
chambers.

At present the chaps in the tent are arranging a sport meeting for
Christmas, that's just to shew their contempt for the war. Walking sticks
are ½ piaster–what we'd pay 1/6 in Sydney. Such bosker horses and
donkeys for such awful prices, 300 piastres each, proper Arab stock too.
The birds of prey kick up a row in the park that they drowned a band
which happened to be playing.

Rows in Cairo start so easily, an Egyptian looked at an Egyptian girl
who objected to this and 2 Australians saw this man and gave chase and
soon 20 Australians were after him. Cutting him with canes and if the
military bobbies had not stepped in he might have been seriously hurt.
Tucker not so bad today but the natives probably washed their sox (if
they wear any) in the tea water.

Dear Frank, I would like to be at Tarro for 2 hours or so just to see
you and spend a little time in the buggy and make those Tarro natives
talk. Art is in camp, quarter guard with 21 men and I'm on tomorrow.

Night operations on Wednesday night, skirmishing entrenching etc.
The water here is ok but it gives some men trouble, but hasn't touched
me yet. Thank heaven you don't have to wear the veil like the Egypts
women do, they look horribly miserable and it would completely cover
that forelock of yours.

Is much water lying at the farm now? No rain has fallen here for
ever so long. Our topee or helmets are 6 ozs in weight and the air
comes in between the pith and the head piece. Esticelalia is a hospital,
one of which there are many full here. I got some films developed
here but all practically failures you bet. More men in camp today. No
blankets have been issued as yet. I don't know what that means but
it is cold so we use our overcoats. I wish we could have our slap and
have done with it. Either come through or go down. Eggs though for
breakfast but 2/3 bad . *Sargeant maaffan boots cleeene saor* Then I say
Bakseesh you cleanem and sometime they do.

17.8.15

Extra hard parade today 6-9, very hot then 10-12, we had a lecture
by Major Clinton on discipline. One little incident he vouches for, you
can have it for what it's worth. 7 British (I won't say Australians) were to
be shot for some very serious breach of discipline. That night the Turk's
attacked in force and as every man was required, the prisoners were give
a place in the trenches. The remainder next day were granted pardon.
They had fought as well and had saved a position. This major says the
Germans are not brave but fear officers and iron discipline makes up

for it. He was in the retreat from Mons and is transferred here suffering from nervous debility.

Out little puppy Roger (christened after our Lieutenant Roger Patrick Moag) is suffering from bad eyes. The lads are very sympathetic and are over feeding him. He is like a balloon. The natives call all soldiers *mackenzie* and the arab women who can't even speak English have learnt to wink and say *Kiss me Sergeant* The natives are as cunning as could be if you do not ask for change on the street when due, you will not get it.

A double company in the Nellies every officer and NCO done for. A private stepped forward led the company and captured the position required. He is now in hospital wounded. He was offered a 2nd Lieuts job and he wouldn't take any position except a corporal. He was awarded a D.S.M. and made so that he can never be reduced below the rank of Corporal. These little stories and thousand others all true from reliable sources are quoted all day long. I haven't written up my diary since Aden. You will have my diary in your letters

Ben

We stopped at Mena House (now a gigantic hospital) and were immediately pestered by hordes of brigand like looking fellows with camels and donkeys each saying he was the best guide to the pyramids but a total disregard for them and bored expression did wonders. Bruce as guide and mentor, Art, Newing (the armourer), Rupe Neil, Billy Hunt and I trudged 1 mile over the sand to the Pyramids which we passed, to reach the Sphinx. Very disappointing I thought. The cannon ball marks made by Napoleon disfigure him. What famous men have marched through this amazing country, Alexander, Hannibal, Napoleon, Nelson, Wolfe, Kitchener and who knows Ben Champion and Art Felton. We visited the temple of the Sphinx. How on earth these Gippos raised such blocks of stone I don't know. Dozens of pillars are scattered around. One part of the court yard is composed of Alabaster which scintillates in the candle light and shows that delicate pinky tinge peculiar to the stone. Becoming tired of this place we had a camel ride and photo taken.

Ben on left standing in front then Rupe Neil and Billy Hunt.
Back on camels in not identified order, Bruce Rainsford, Art Felton, Sergeant Newing the armourer and
possibly Young. Same group who went to the museum and zoo

YMCA Egypt

Darling Frank,

I must tell you about the experiences I've had since Monday last. The Battalion has been for some time past practising up ceremonial Drill, Guards etc. and as we were so good we were placed as guard in the Citadel at Cairo. Kits were packed on Monday morning and about 8 am we set off on a route march 8 miles long—now I've done a few route marches but this one is the cruellest I've ever been in. Full marching order (80lbs in weight), full dress and helmets with only two eight-minute rests.

The Citadel is the place to which in times of peril the inhabitants retire and naturally it is extremely solid and build on the highest and safest part of the city. The walls in a number of places less than 4 foot thick and in many places three times that thickness. It is one mass of concentric rings of walls, each fortified and the only man who ever captured it was Napoleon who built the fort on the only piece of rising ground near and bombarded it. We saw some of his cannon and cannon balls and one ball embedded in a wall.

The officers' quarters are one mass of relics of ancient fights around the Citadel. Shields and spears as far back as Rameses 11 and guns up to the last encounter on the Suez Canal between Australians and Turks. Alexander evidently was a huge man; his sword (2 handles) is at least 4 foot long and heavy as well. The room Napoleon slept in was washed by 20 men from my platoon for the Major.

We were relieved at the Citadel by a Middlesex Regiment detachment after ten days duty. Didn't look much as regards physique, but drilled like clockwork.

We were inspected by General Spence yesterday who complimented us on our work and behaviour. The Sikhs and Gurkhas who have been wounded are here and fine men they are. They have fought side by side with the English Tommy and have had no opinion at all of him, yet they laud Australians up to the skies.

The Citadel Heliopolis. Ben paid for a copy from the AWM decades ago.

The view from the Citadel is lovely just at sunset, when the sun dying spreads his rays all over the city and transforms it from a dirty horrible place to a fairy city. The minarets and domes throw off the light as if looking glasses. The streets near the city are so narrow that it is quite possible to shake hands from balcony to balcony. On the outskirts of the city the streets have been laid by French and English engineers, with the trees on either side, and are first rate. I was unable to see the wonderful mosque that is next to the Citadel but I'm told the walls are made of alabaster carved; one carpet cost 400 pounds and took ten years to weave. No wonder they make you wear slippers when you enter the door.

There is one circle of electric lights 80 yards in diameter. The next Biblical place I visited was the well they put Joseph down which is about 30 foot across and at least 100 feet deep. The stairs wind round and round the sides. It is not dry now like it was in Joseph's time. His coat of diverse colours was not present.

Moysey Adams, Art and I saw place where criminals are killed. Outside the Citadel is a weight, say one tonne, raised on two poles, this used to be dropped on the heads of criminals. It's much after the style of what I should call a Guillotine would be like only it squashes instead of cutting.

The Grand Mosque Heliopolis

2.9.15 at Matereih

Last Sunday (day before we went to Citadel) I went to the Virgin's
Well with Sergeant Newing. We wandered through cotton fields galore,
date palms and gum trees to an ancient town which we ransacked, walking
into shops enquiring prices and then walking out again without buying
anything .Quite enjoyed myself.

Cotton fields as far as the eye could reach. Irrigation is
wonderful. It is interesting to watch them planting date palms. They
dig a hole about 6 feet deep and revert the sides with wicker ware to
stop the sides caving in and plant the palm at the bottom. The date
palm therefore is in partial shade and gets any soakage. There are
cotton fields in their white blossoms which look like a field covered
lightly with snow. Egypt has a charm inexplicable which it exerts on
one. It has glorious sun rises and sunsets and cool nights. It seems to
say 'Poor generation, what do you know of life—we flourished 2000
years ago and have forgotten more than you ever learned'.

This Well is the one (supposed) from which Mary and Joseph
drank when they fled from Pharaoh and the Massacre of the
Innocents. The Well is in the midst of a beautiful garden and the
Sycamore tree under which she rested is half tumbled down through
generations of tourists cutting their names on it.

I'll first of all put in the Guides language.

'Shentlemen, Mary, she rest her under tree and drink out of well and she and
Joseph wash the baby Christ. All dee wells around here salt but dis one now him
fresh coos der baby Christ's wash.'

Guides state that the Virgin's Well turns into fresh water from
brackish. It is hard to believe but it is really the only fresh well among the
dozens around.

This is a marvellous old well, Frank, even taking away the
supposition about Mary, Joseph and Christ. 30 feet deep, lovely and
cool. I had a drink. We went into an ancient Jesuit Church (French)
and saw the marvellous paintings around the walls. Christ's entrance
into Heliopolis, under the tree, the halt on the edge of the Nile, the
flight into Egypt, The order to depart from Jerusalem, The slaughter

Sgt Newing on way to Virgins well taken by Ben

of the innocents. All the above titles depicting the flight of Joseph and Mary from Jerusalem. The faces and halos shine out like phosphorous and give the whole pictures an uncanny appearance.

There is a granite obelisk which was brought from Aswan 66 feet high and has four inscriptions. It is supposed to have been erected 2000 years ago and is similar to one on the Thames embankment.

Once a man's a soldier he is no longer a man and vice versa.
Only a machine'
Good Luck Frank love, be home in a couple of years.
Ben

———

4.9.15 Orderly Sgt.
Wrote to Mum Frank Gertrude. Greig and Art on Guard
Left Sydney 14/7; Left Aden 6/8; Left Suez 12/8
Still in Egypt inured to Egyptian climate by now. Sergeant Neil ill. 26th /27th /28th Battalions left for Gallipoli

———

The Obelisk taken by Ben

6.9.15 Musketry.

Minature range practice Company drill by Mr Moag –very solid from 5pm—7pm. Plenty of swearing by him and no rest. Walked to Heliopolis after tea with Art. Heliopolis is about 7 miles from heart of Cairo and is built on far edge of Ancient Helioplois.

Dysentery—try to avoid salads, lettuce etc where food is exposed. Flies light on filth and then on to food and spread disease. Oranges, bananas and any skin fruit safe, figs grapes unsafe. Most drink is adulterated but bottled beer is generally safe. Drinks in native quarters unsafe.

Natives in general miserable specimens of humanity

YMCA 9.9.15

Dear Little Girl

Still here sticking in the sand waiting for the order to shove off. Still strolling around sightseeing, things which are really strange and picturesque are losing their glamour and becoming monotonous.

I can't fill up in answering your letter as it hasn't come yet. I wonder will it ever or is some other reading it. Lots of lots of letters go astray and are lost as are many we send.

Last Sunday a party of us, Newing, Young, Hunt, Rupe Neil and Art, visited Cairo Museum and we only had a little time there. It takes a good week to study the place decently. We saw mummies galore in every stage of preservation, wrapped, half un wrapped and stripped. Rameses 111 (I believe the person who made the Israelites be chased across the Red Sea) was half unwrapped and his cruel mouth and talon like fingers make one believe in his cruelty very easily.

The sarcophagi (coffins) made of marble, granite or some other good stone are cut out of one piece and have engravings on them in picture writing the deeds of the person buried. Only those who are skilled can read this picture writing As you enter the hall you are confronted by 2 figures 30 feet high of an ancient King and Queen, yet the Queen has her arm around the Kings waist in just the same manner as it is done today, So fashions haven't changed. In Cairo you seldom see young couples out together. The parents fix up who is to marry the girl. She has no choice at all. Rather bad luck Eh What!. Just as well those things don't happen in Australia.

Lots of boomerangs have been found in tombs. Just the same as the Australian ones. The idols used by the old Egyptians are very similar to those used by Hindus except the Egyptians are made of stone and Hindus are made of wood (similar to those bought home by Aunt Jeanie Dykes—missionary in India).

Cleopatra's diamond necklace was on shew, given by Anthony to her, when she wore it, it must have made her neck one blaze of light. Tons (by weight) of gold and precious stone are on shew and most exquisite is the work. One can hardly credit such good work with such tools as are on exhibition. The doll of the white child has its double in the Egyptian doll for many dolls exact replicas of our style of dolls are shewn here all botched about with weather but dolls for all of that.

Leaving the museum, everything was just too old, we went to the Zoological Gardens. The exchequer being run out we had tooth picks and a glass of water for dinner and then entered the gardens. Most of the animals have been presented by military men of many famous names and Regiments are referenced as Regimental mascots had to be left behind at the Zoo. The Gardens are laid out well, animals are separate and trees and grass grow everywhere. Tigers, lions, leopards, giraffes, 15 foot high, crocodiles, alligator, zebras, gnus, gazelles, monkey, hippopotamus, rhinoceros etc. The Keeper has trained one hippo who comes out of the water when called by name *Said* to be fed.

We became tired of animals and went in to the Grotto. Here maiden hair fern grows in abundance and water trickling everywhere makes a very cool rest house.

The 2 pontoons in which the German tried to cross the Suez Canal are in the gardens and are a mass of shot holes.

Good Bye. Just now. Your old pal, Ben. Keep writing I won't be able to shortly. Give my love to all at home.

A paper (the *Sunday Sun*) came into my hands yesterday from NSW addressed to the troops in general but it came to me. In it were 2 names I wonder if you know of them. Anyway the paper gave great enjoyment. The names were Ethel Kayne, Newcastle and Marion Jauchan, Pinshipp St Hamilton Newcastle.

The Grotto, Cairo. Newing, Rupe Neil and Billy Hunt

10.9.15.

Oasis No 2 Camp out on the desert Rifle range, practice.

There, six miles from any water was where Napoleon had a huge Camp, his watch towers are still standing and we used one as a Sergeants Mess. How difficult it must have been to bring water in carts to this place. It shows what an organizer he must have been.

Sudden call for 10 men from our reinforcements to go off to the peninsular and as everyone wanted to go I didn't stand a chance. Wonder will the war last long enough for me to get a cut in. Ten men picked out to go with Moag to Peninsula. Although no one trusted Moag, pinning our faith rather on Scott, everyone admired him a little. Even the way he learned to ride a horse whilst in Egypt pleased us. He couldn't ride at all to begin with but he just stuck on and managed although at times he couldn't walk for days.

Still out on the desert shooting. Scored 10 bulls and 2 inners at 600 yards. Have had so much firing it's hard to miss any sort of target, but we particularly like the targets which look like a man's head and shoulders.

To Heliopolis 11.9.15

About 150 men left from 17th, 18th 19th 20th AIF Battalions off to Peninsula; six of ours among them. 8th Reinforcements of 1st, 2nd, 3rd, 4th Battalions arrived.

24.9.15

out at Bulls Rifle range

My dear Frank, we are camped 2 miles outside Heliopolis near the rifle range. There is absolutely no news to tell you, none at all. Writing this in the dugout behind the butts and the bullets are smacking the targets wholesale. When a miss is signalled a red and white flag is waved and sometimes 24 flags are up at once making it look like coronation day. On the top of range mounds, one can see on one side an old tower built by Napoleon and on the other side the Pyramids looming in the distance. Napoleon after he defeated the Mamelukes at the Pyramids camped in the district and built watch towers every 5 miles along the maid road to Suez and this tower we can see is in a good state of preservation. What a marvellous man he was. We have water laid on in pipes but he had to carry all his water by carts.

We have had an awful shortage of food here, I didn't think before I was active in the trenches, I'd have to have for dinner 1 slice of bread and tea, so we all marched in a body to Sergeant's mess in Heliopolis and demanded an explanation. Evidently someone has been pocketing cash. That always goes on in the Army.

Last Thursday I went to Abassieh Barracks to inspect a rifle range there and was cordially entertained to morning tea by the Canadian troops stationed there. There is a marked difference between Territorials and Australians. If I had charge off Territorials I'd send half of them home to school where they should be—mere nippers most of them though I must say any of their sergeants can beat ours as most are old Imperial Men.

I've done my fair shooting out here, though the glare of the sand makes the foresight misty. Did your father form a rifle club? My father still attends 1 parade a week, I believe, for no letters have yet filtered through except that one from you. We were paid today, such a relief after being a week without a cent in my pocket now I can get a few necessities of life, tinned fruit etc.

The average horse used here is a regular outlaw. I don't know if the Army riding and feeding them makes them so but they are out and outters, only good men can ride them, Our OC Mr Scott is riding one now which is supposed to have lamed half a dozen Light Horse men.

Have you been communicating with family lately. It is awfully strange having no news about ones other, for all I know they might all be dead and buried by this. The natives here when they fight, fight anyhow feet, nails, head etc. No honour at all—they would as soon knock a man with a stone or knife as kick him. This morning two had a fight and while it was fair the boys let them go but the instant one drew a knife the lads rushed him and gave him a bad time, he can't sell tomatoes here anymore.

Mena Camp with horses in foreground.

The men have a long mess room with tables all ranged around the sides and its nice and cool in there so they gather there for amusement and lectures but they aren't allowed to sleep there. It is strange how you can sleep in any position here now that you're hard. I always sleep on 2 forms placed side by side both not wider than 2'3 'and sleep right through the night. I never wake up till Reveille goes. What an awful call that Reveille is. *Get out of bed, Get out of bed now then you skulker*s All our calls have words to them. Officers Mess: *Officers wife have pudding and pies whilst we poor chaps have skilly y y* Guard call: *Come and do your duty lads, and do your guard If you don't you'll find it very hard d d.*

What do you think of those Post Cards that Art sent to Mary of us on camels?

The camp is cleaned by eagles or vultures. The place abounds with them. As soon as some refuse collects, there dozens will be and if it wasn't for them the refuse and fly questions would be a very difficult one to solve. I suffer from that tired feeling lately so you can't expect long letters but I expect long letters from you, Been having much milk lately . I hope you've had a good season since we left. Not too much rain.

Do you know a chap called Peacock from your district? I was searching the attestation papers for some errors which had crept in and found his name as coming from Raymond Terrace district. He is clean shaven solidly built man and is in the company.

Major Lazarus has a very peculiar toast for the 5th Battalion *For King and Country and the Girl* when he gives this, he rises in his stirrups and give the first part and then let the men thunder out *the girl*.

Our Sergeant Major went for a ride with our 2nd Lieut and came an awful cropper hurting his chin, knees and elbows so much that he has been in bed a week The horse is hurt also, knees busted and shoulder sprained. The Asphalt was greasy as he went to turn a corner and down horse and rider went.

We have rather a musical company and often sing songs, though we often sing items more than once they are seldom stale. When we get back to Heliopolis camp we will have cane beds to be on, just like those crates they bring fruit from the Northern Rivers and South Islands. They are very good and clean as one is right off the ground.

Had a donkey ride not long ago around Cairo and back—half piastre for one hour. Well love, no more to tell you with tenderest thoughts.

Ben

26.9.15

Yesterday rec'd letters, 3 from Frank, 2 from Mum Today Recd 1 from Mr Walker and 1 from Frank. Happy now.

27.9.15

Heliopolis

Dear Little Girl.

I'm orderly Sergeant today—all the rest of company are out at the rifle range. 'Tis lovely as yet 6am the sun is not too hot.

Well love, I received some stray letters from you during last week 25.9.15. The bulk I suppose will come on at intervals extending over some time until all are here. Your letter lifted me for news from dear ones you don't know for the want of letters. We just repeat the same routine day in and out. One day Art is at the Batallion and I'm in camp and vice versa next day.

Our band has progressed so far that we seldom see it now as the heads generally collar it for their own units. You still mention Mr Morris as being a busy body. One would think that as soon as were out of sight we would be out of his memory too.

The only news I rec'd from home was about Australia Day—surely NSW must have done magnificently when even the tiniest little child seems to have denied itself something for our benefit. A man in our company received a letter from an unknown lady in Victoria. She has sent him newspapers as he has no friends practically in Australia and as we were all receiving letters they came in very handy. Anyhow, what a nice spirit that lady shewed. It cheered the chap and made a new man of him.

You are continually teaching me something about The Land, I didn't know calves would kill themselves if they drank too much milk? Nature ought to tell the calf when to stop and so Jimmy let them have too much milk? He ought to be made to pay for them . Have you any fresh riding horses down at the farm? Potatoes seem to be flourishing. I wish we had a few here or even some of your delicious pork or some cake. A decent meal here costs 8-10 piastres (commonly called disasters as it is such a calamity every time one is spent) for that, one can get fish meat and ½ potato pudding and coffee. I wish the war would end and let us be back doing something rational.

So Gertrude wrote to you. What do you think of her? She is such a sport and the more you know her the better you will like her, I hope you are receiving those Girls Own Papers they have such a lot of lovely thoughts too and reading matter in them besides practical advice on such subjects .

I'm sorry Creamy has something wrong with him. What a lot of drives he took us on not to mention the best morning ever spent up there when we rode down the Maitland Road with motors continually passing and sat down and talked in the paddock beyond the culvert. Do you remember how you couldn't get off and how you came out of the saddle? What a glorious morning that was, didn't everything seem pleased to see us even great fatty Green. In the afternoon we rode down the river bank and found those men camped there fishing and how I with a bit of bluff made them sheer off. I suppose they thought I was a mounted bobby or something like that in those military pants. Didn't we go up often? Your mother WAS good to let us stop and to trust us to out with you girls. I don't think the privileges were misused do you?

If only those swamps were here. One would coin cash. The ground here needs nothing more than water and crops will grow like wild fire.

You won't be too old and grown up (when I return) to come on similar scampers and rides will you love?

Poor old Pontie. What a pity it is some men won't leave booze alone when they know they can't touch it without going too far. Have any of those great loafers around Tarro enlisted yet? What does your father think of the conscription idea?

You say you would like a good chat with me and you can't put down on paper your thoughts, well neither can I. Art writes page after page and I can't.

You ought to see the sand storms here. Suddenly a cloud of sand rises say 300 high in the air and moving forward picks up stones, sand etc. until it bursts. I saw a tent carried away 60 feet in the air one day. They move just as rapidly as a huge bush fire and you've seen that. That man who came around collecting bottles and said he was returned from the front because his teeth were done in is evidently one of those healthy maligners who plead rheumatism and all sorts of complaints allied to it. Such a lot of men funk the front after going so far in Egypt.

Wish I could only see those hedges one mass of golden balls, wattle reminds me so much of *Jura* where we had so much of it. That nice pressed piece goes inside my bible thank you muchly Frank.

Do you still call me chicken? Well Mary ought to call Art that, he has grown so big

What a difference in the writing yours and mine. Don't you think Ruth glued that music of Mrs Ling on purpose? I wouldn't put it past her. Those little verses under separate cover have not yet come to light and I will treasure them most highly for I know if Mrs Niland wrote them out they must be good.

You are the only person telling me about Father going away with Mr Felton. Art hasn't received any letter from home yet and is taking it better than I thought he would.

It is not necessary to be at Tarro to hear cat concerts. Some of our lads are bad enough when they are singing though on the whole our company is very musical. I can't imagine you moving cats on at all. How could you be so cruel?

Art with pipe outside reed hut.

Do you always polish those buttons when you have the pip? If you rub those black metal badges with any metal polish they will go nice and shiny also. You know we are patiently waiting at the front for Achi Baba to starve out as it is recognised we will never storm the place.

It is a difference when we climb into uniform we wore on our departure from Sydney. We nearly suffocate. I wonder will it be the fashion in Sydney when the troops come home to wear short trousers and puttees. I for one wouldn't mind a bit. When are you going to Sydney again?

Our Company 7th of 1st supplies the markers for the Range and of course they are superior to other companies as they have a flying column and can bear any other company out here at marching quickly with compactness. It's a good scheme to match one Company against each other as then they take pride in their own and soon both companies come to a high grade of perfection until one beats the other. The no 1 works to return their position etc. As a matter of fact the Australians are better than the Territorials simply because of this rivalry. Here comes our company so I won't be able to write ay more just now.

Figs are very cheap here. They dry the figs then shove a reed through them piled high. They have a nice spicy taste different altogether to those bought at home. I haven't tackled the dates yet simply because I can't find a shop which looks clean enough to buy them from. There are not too many places you can get food cooked in English fashion. The Arabs cook most of their food in horrid tasting oil. Hen eggs are the size of bantam eggs and cost 4d a dozen to us I suppose about 2 1/2 d or a piaster to the natives.

Do you remember those heavy military boots we saw at Tarro, well I've just worn a pair out now. How are you all at home Kitty, Claire, Ruth, Mrs Niland, Mr Niland. Do your eyes still hurt and has the dentist cured your toothache. What a time we had trying to make that filling stop in and I was easily satisfied with the reward, you bet.

Have you done any painting lately I expect to see a fine lot of paintings when I come home. Remember me to all at home. Good bye.

Ben

2.10.15.

Back from the Range. Went to see Bruce today and went to the Hospital and met Harold Kershaw, he is suffering from dysentery chiefly, looks very thin and worn out. Went to the Pyramids at night, there has been a flood and with a good moon in the back ground shining on the water the Pyramids look absolutely pretty.

6.10.15

The Young Men's Christian Association with H.M. Mediterranean Expeditionary force in Egypt

Dear Frank.

I've been for last 2 days out on a post a few miles from camp guarding stores and have had a good time being my own boss and only 15 men under me. I didn't write last week Frank as it is just like now, practically no news at all. On this post the chief stores were Dhura and Drees. Dhura is only maize taken just as the corn is forming. You would think this style of food would play havoc with a horse but it is mixed with hard foods and is counter balanced. Also used for donkeys and camels.

Ben's postcard of the Pyramids by moonlight

Drees is all sorts of crops and grasses dried and then baled up. It has the appearance of Kooloos or Eel grass. You ought to see the Ships of the desert laden with Dhura. I took some pictures of them and hope they will come out good.

The little Arab boys lead these great camels around, make them lie down and they crawl on to their necks and get the brutes get up. The camels grunt and groan like wild fire and then get up on hind legs first, then on fore legs, so for a moment the rider is almost on his nose and then he is square. It is worse than a sea trip to ride a camel.

A little donkey is worth about 150 disasters and when they are young their owners tattoo designs on them so that it is quite common to see donkeys with patterns on legs and sometimes they appear to be wearing stockings even.

You know we have cane hospital beds to sleep on, well now every morning they have to be put on end causing a lot of bother as when the orderlies have to sweep the floor when the beds were down there was about 3 feet between the ends of each bed that could be easily be kept clean by tossing the bits under the bed. Now all that is put a stop too.

I hope someday to be able to get all these letters I write to you & from you so that I can write up a diary as I've given up all hope of ever keeping one here. I possess that awful curse of vice namely tired feeling.

The Arabs and donkeys are very cunning. I'm certain donkeys have brains. An Arab took 1 donkey out of the car and when my back was turned the donkey ate some dree-—when I looked again the donkey was quiet its jaws weren't even moving. I turned my back and the donkey ate

Camels laden with Dhura and wagons of Drees

again. I soon hunted the beast away but is just shows how animals take notice of your movements.

How is Creamy and the chickens (They will probably be in the pot long before you get this letter) but that doesn't matter as long as I enquire after them does it ? Do you consider I'm as nice as the chickens you mentioned in your letter of the 12.8.15 I notice you head your letter in like terms anyhow.

Art and I went to Church last Sunday the 1st time in a building since 11 July. Now doesn't that shock your nervous system. I brought back a souvenir in the way of an appeal for cash. Such a nice old Scotch minister preached. As the church closed he stood at the door and shook hands with all. I saw he had nice delicate white well-manicured hands so I mentioned it to Art and we squeezed that mitt of his like a vice. I felt the old chap wince and felt sorry for him. I suppose he thinks Aust. soldiers have a grip of steel; he doesn't think it was a special grip for his benefit.

You don't seem to think XXX means Egypt. You little sinner it does perhaps seem ambiguous. I don't object to you taking it otherwise not in the least. How are all your beloved sisters? I hear plenty of Ruth and Mary. A nice way to end a letter 'love from all, from FN 'Don't I deserve more than that.

This morning I received a letter from you dated 11.8.15 the longest you have ever written to me and it took a long time to digest, so now I will do my best to answer it. After you relating your adventures with Blackie and the storm I wonder if you are allowed to drive after dark. By Jove, Frank you have had a narrow squeak and ought to be very thankful you are alive. No doubt it was merely good fortune that took Blackie through or else intuition made you guide him correctly. Were the splash boards belonging to the new buggy from Grafton—those you broke? What has happened to Creamy, in each letter I receive you mention something about him but no news about his accident. I hope you didn't get a cold after your wetting, seems funny to have rain. Our last rain was at sea.

Are our letters censored, or not? Why Frank don't you try and learn music? I'm sure if you stuck at it you would easily beat Mary. The only reason why I didn't learn was I was frightened of going cross eyed through reading bass and treble at once. But that reason shouldn't apply to a sensible person like you. Poor old Ruth and her maps. Why doesn't she trace them like I used to do once?

A garden in front of that spare bedroom would certainly improve it and would please weary town dimmed eyes if looked upon. Let me congratulate your father on having water laid on for the cattle and horses. I suppose your dairy will be three times as big now. Do you still send only cream to Raymond Terrace or does the milk go over to Tarro Station?

I'm so sorry love to read you had aches in your back. I hope you are better now and that you will take better care of yourself in the future. What would I do if I should come home and find my little pal ill or in any way hurt.

It is very foggy here now, if on guard you find yourself wet through when you awake at morns first approach. Poor little Kitty, Art and I are very sorry indeed and hope it will heal up quickly and leave no scars but accidents will happen, I remember having my fingers jammed in a shed door at school and they weren't right until fresh nails grew.

Hard luck that boy and man being struck by lightning out Minmi way. It was far from thundering when we went down the Minmi Road. Eh Frank? Perhaps Creamy would not have gone so quickly without attention had lightning been in the air.

I wish I could go to Church with you again. Who knows perhaps someday? You seem to be putting in praties. 'Tis many a long day since I tasted one as we only get yams here.

Do you know why so many people rub me about sea sickness? So far I have not opened a letter from anybody with some words re sea sickness being in them. I see Claire gave your parents plenty of notice re Miss Bodily, slightly more that you gave them about Didie, the first time she came out. Do you know Frank that coolness is one of your chief characteristics and no doubt it is a very good point to possess? I only have a little of it worse luck. I can't imagine your mother taking me for over 18. At present it is a compliment but at home I would always like to appear my own age 10 years 2 months.

Yes Frank, I do think wattle day is too late in the year. At Wahroonga the wattle was always practically done but after all we must consider the other states. I like the big African wattle best of all and then the silver wattle. You have a couple of nice trees down by the swing .

What do you think of the *Lonesome Pine* (book, still in the family) I like the chief girl character very much indeed, but the *Wood Carver* is an excellent book as well. You would like *A Rough Shaking* by MacDonald it is about animals and farm life mainly.

All here are ramping about keeping us here so long 'tis sickening. At first we were told not to unpack as we would be off in a few days and here we are still stuck here. Hard Luck, you know we haven't got cold feet to hear some of the men talk who have been over to the front. I wish we could go. Remember me to all at home

Love and kisses from Ben

14.7.15 to 9.10.15

A good spell without a letter isn't it? But I'm happy now, 37 letters in all. Met Moore from local Govt Dept. Brewer, Youman, Goode and Black all teachers, fine fellows. Cpl. Brewer life of camp, funny as a circus. Sent home films to father of Camp Oasis No 2 camp. Charlie Moore, Davidson, Hampden in Crown Solicitors Office. Due out at range again tonight. Art left in Camp. Went to Pyramids Pub last night not a bad concert Moysey Adams shouted drinks, have been broke now for 4 days. About ten gone to Abassiah out of our Company now.

11.10.15.

Went to Hospital this morning. Got chafed with light trousers. I can hardly walk but will only be in for 3 days or so. Can't march, want to be get well before we go. A nice spell in a cool reed hut doesn't do anyone harm. The 9th of 5th arrived.

14.10.15

Dear old Pal,

I'm out on the rifle range and have had no opportunity of writing to you before. During my stay out here I suppose Art has been on his usual 10 page stunt to Mary. I'm sure I don't know where he gets his news from perhaps he writes the same thing over 3 times in different ways. Well F I'm still well and so far our chance of getting to the front is as far off as possible, who knows where we are bound for, Dardanelles, Salonika or Hades. All the same to us perhaps the first before either of the other places. Now new troops coming and going but never Moag's 1sts. We seem doomed to spend our lives in training and there seems no chance of fulfilling the purpose for which we enlisted namely to pot Germans I recived a week ago some letters from you Old Girl and a letter from your Mother which I will answer in due course, when I feel there is some

Rifle Range.

news in the air. The vultures are becoming so fearless they swoop down, right between the tent lines after scraps. If you throw a stone up into their midst one is sure to catch it and after finding its not food drop it again. They have such big wings. Underwings outstretched a man could easily be protected from the wet if he could bring himself to be near the bird for being carrion........?

18.10.15.

On return from bivouac at Oasis No 2 Rifle Range for over a week put through about 700 men, Victorians best shots owing to being trained by Rifle Club men, at least 30% better. Tattoed snake on arm. To town three times. The Vultures have been making a nuisance of themselves so a couple of us told to get a few, which we did. Horrible looking birds. Dug out a Jerboa or animal like it. Sergeant Grange very decent–wrote to Frank and Mum, no letters as yet after last big batches.

Postcard 17.10.15 do you know if any of my films arrived at home? Plenty of grass hoppers have made their appearance around our camp being blown out from plantations by huge dust storms. Vultures are having a good feed on them. No news here out at Oasis Camp so can't tell you anything except about 500 horses belonging to Light Horse and supply

Mena Transport Lines.

transports have mouth disease and are quarantined out here. The vets are at a loss to know what is wrong as it is not ordinary foot and mouth disease

---

19.10.15.

We have had leave stopped to Cairo or to any village inhabited by natives. The feast of Bairam is taking place; the natives fast for 3 days (Ramadan) then gorge and drink for 5 and its best to keep out of their way in case of any trouble. Hurray! We expect to be off next week. Mumps broken out, about ten down.

Gallipoli Service, Malta and Suez

'It's strange living like a rabbit in a hole dug in the ground.'

20.10.15

Well we are off at last. Orders to move came out. What camels we were! It is astonishing the number of seemingly absolutely essential goods you collect when you stop in a spot for some time. Immediate bustling. Hurried to Heliopolis for some last minute purchases I thought might be handy, such a chlordane, toothbrush and a pocket knife. This time in Heliopolis has been good as it has built up an *esprit de corps* and we know each other now. Also bought some native cushions, shawls and trinkets to send home.

21.10.15

Reveille 4 am. Never have I humped such a pack, everything possible to go in, even after jumping and stomping on it couldn't get all in, so remainder had to be dumped. Train started at 8 a.m. and off we went to Alexandria. Never saw such unbridled intoxication nor ever dreamt of it, practically every detail on train drunk.

We were covered in cinders from the engine and no food on train apart from buying oranges and melons as we stopped to let other trains pass through. It is really interesting country. Passed cotton fields, the woman working in trousers, I do like the green palm trees and the maize.

What a wonder this land becomes when it gets water. At last Alexandria came to us and we were embarked on the *Borda*, Boat absolutely crammed and very verminous and had no sleep. It had been carrying Indian troops and the lice are awful.

48 films with me and hope to take them all. In Alexandria roadstead troopers and hospital ships galore. The Hospital boats at night time with their green strips and Red Cross and many lights look well and couldn't be mistaken for any other type of boat. 2 French warships in harbour.

We slept on deck that night and next day set out for Lemnos Island. As we passed out we were beaten to the entrance by the *Patros* a boat laden with Greek Reservists. We gave them a cheer and they did likewise. We felt very happy. How many of us will see Alexandria again?

Troops on Quay, Alexandria.

24.10.15

On S.S. *Borda*. Last night a wireless message from a destroyer was received and now we are zig zagging all over the place. We must do hundreds of miles more than is necessary to escape the submarines. Lemnos is only 36 hours run from Alex, yet, here we are still zig zagging about dodging submarines.

We are all wearing life belts by order, such a nuisance as soup etc, always seems to trickle down between it and your tunic. Many were

SS Borda

the scares given by the submarine guard.

Wouldn't it be lovely to have a hot bath and sleep between sheets and sleep and sleep and no reveille, We are sleeping on the decks as it's so putrid down below.

26.10.15

At last at Lemnos Island, we entered the harbour laboriously. As we came up a tug appeared and towed aside a huge submarine net, then closed the entrance and moved on and opened up the next one. These precautions were necessary as this is a huge base. Monitors, warships, troopers and every class of boat that ever went to sea. And what a base! Every branch of warfare is represented here.

Lemnos is a peaceful little place, very hilly, the hills clothed with green grass on which goats and sheep graze. The hills slope to the sea making many ideal camping spots. For the last day or so we have been circling about in the Grecian Archipelago. They are fine noble looking islands, some cultivated but the majority very bare.

We felt very safe, for slippery looking little destroyers kept buzzing about, now in this direction, now in another, churning the water up. Chief war boats here are the *Lord Nelson* and *Agamemnon* with lots of smaller patrol boats. Troop ship sunk somewhere.

27.10.15

Very pleasant job today, mail fatigue; was loaded into a motor launch driven by a baby midshipman with several other chaps and every bag I handled I felt sure contained 1 letter at least for me. Moag, Adams, Johnston on board for mails.

———

S S *Borda*
27.10.15

Dear little Pal

I can't make any excuses for not writing sooner but somehow or other I possess the tired feeling. I'm always thinking of you Frank and I can see you now though a few thousand miles away with your frizzly little forelock that always takes my fancy so. It's too late now to get cold feet and most of us have set our teeth and have determined to see it through to the end.

Dear old girl what times we had together just before I came away. All the travelling, so new to me after that workshop in Macquarie St. (dental apprentice) Little did I think once that I should sail through the Grecian archipelago and see the same sights as the old patriots of Greece.

There is Art now scribbling away like wild fire yet my thoughts do not come to my pen. If they did I'm afraid Mrs Niland would square the Censor not to pass the letters for they would turn your dear little head.

How is Tarro treating you? (It will be 10 weeks before an answer can come) God only knows where I'll be then but keep up your little pecker as I'm doing and as I'm doing my people are doing for I haven't had news much from them.

We've had a bosker trip through the Mediterranean Sea. I wasn't a bit ill thank heaven. Alexandria, all we saw of it, seemed a very up to date place indeed. Railway running right down on to the wharves so that it is no trouble to load and unload cargoes.

We have a man on board by the name of Lane. His youngest son is on board with us and he met two sons at Alexandria and such a joyful cackle you never heard and the old father seems 10 years younger since.

Keep up your correspondence Frank even if I drop it for it's fairly easy for you to write, yet it is mighty hard for me with no conveniences. Art is getting as fat as a Christmas duck and we both feel very well indeed.

I've smothered my rifle in oil as the salt air effects them so. Such a fine lot of destroyers and boats here. Such slippery rakish looking craft but all the guns as clean and businesslike as the ships look wicked.

Well Old girl, I'll close now, remember me to your Mother and Father and the girls and a letter from your mother would be highly esteemed along with yours.

Ben

30.10.15

Tethered Zeppelin [Observation] Balloon. Ben's photo.

Ship terribly lousy (muchly so). We are so cooped up its impossible to keep clean, but we all had a few swims here off the boat but it's rather a long dive from the main deck. More Tommie's left today for Anzac— *Bloody Hell* as they term it. Very interesting sight today, a big balloon shaped like a sausage, a zeppelin, was loosed from a neighbouring troop ship, the observers in it were equipped with telephones and I think they were scouting for submarines which can be more easily seen from a height.

Every day, 2 of our submarines patrol up and down outside the nets.

The 5th Battalion is resting here so today some Sergeants came off in a native fishing boat and met several chums from their home districts.

The native population here seems a very indolent lot; they look very picturesque from a distance, if the wind happens to be blowing from you to them. But if it is visa versa, they are not nice to know. They have exceptionally baggy trousers, velveteen jackets and gaudy ties, sealskin caps and turned-up toes on their shoes.

Our vessel continually being paid visits by Staff officers so we must be off soon.

Just gossip. The Gippo as a worker in my opinion is worthless and appears to be divided into 2 classes, lazy indolent ragged mob and the very rich. There appears to be no big middle class who make a country, the rich seem to spend their days in Cafes smoking, playing draughts and tossing dice, always with a cup of coffee alongside. Lower class herds with the natives and are no better off. The shop and Cafes owners are Belgium, French or Italians. Egypt is a mass of smells, yells and plagues, but it exerts an irresistible charm. At Lemnos the fishermen spear fish by torch light in the shallows

Mail lighter cut in two outside Suvla Bay and 500 bags of mail lost.

1.11.15

Orders came along to disembark into lighters and then into a fast turbine boat, the *Osmania*. We packed up an extra 200 rounds of ammunition and were about to leave when we were told to stand by for some hours. Monitor No 18 alongside, draws very little water for its weight, it carries 9.2 forward and 6lb quick firer aft, with several maxim guns alongside. Saw the biggest boat I've ever seen—*The Mauritania*! it is here as a hospital ship with 6000 beds. Some boat too. Sister ship to *Lusitania*.

Soon we were off on our biggest adventure—off to Gallipoli and a creepy feeling started to trickle up and down my spine. We were packed in like sardines and if torpedoed not ¼ would have been saved.

The front of the above postcard from Ben. The HMHS Mauritania.

ANZAC COVE

Postcard, Landing at Gallipoli.

2.11.15

1, 200 on board. At dusk passed the Island of Embros (General Staff Headquarters) and at 7.30p.m. came to anchor in Anzac Cove. We showed 2 red lights and soon some iron lighters came out towed by man-o-war pinnaces. Each pinnace in charge of such a boy, yet each held the rank of midshipman. These lighters were like flat tanks and we were shut below like rats in a trap. Anywhere open it wouldn't have been so bad, but down below it was terrible.

The pinnace towed us to a pier where we disembarked in a heap on a narrow beach smothered in walls of provisions. Tiers and tiers of cases of biscuits, ammunition etc. so that the beach was walled across time and time again. So here we were on the Peninsula at last.

We struggled along the shore in the dark, loaded like camels for about two miles past the original landing place. We had the impression that everywhere were men with muffled voices and that we had come to a place peopled by voices for we could not see any living people but ourselves. We stumbled on into communication trenches which seemed as wide as lanes and about 12 feet deep until we reached a fairly level piece of land under the lee of a large hill. This was we were told the edge of Shrapnel Gully and we were warned not to go away from the edges as enemy gun fire swept the middle area.

Our quarters for the night were oblong holes cut in the side of the hill and partly covered with waterproof sheets. It is no wonder the 1st Division was *towelled up*. I cannot imagine how they stormed the place. They must have been as agile as monkeys to do it. Then we went through wide communication trenches to Shrapnel Gully where we camped and had our 1st casualty by a spent bullet.

3.11.15

Too cold and cramped to sleep so out at daylight. No green grass as all torn up or trampled. New arrivals met up with old friends and made new ones. Surely these men were not the spic and span soldiers we had seen leaving Australia a year before! Nearly all had beards or had not shaved for weeks; all were dirty, their breeches hacked off at the knees and few were wearing puttees but they seemed happy, cheerful and full of joke.

Visited the cemetery and saw graves of several chaps I knew. Also saw the Turk's trenches in the distance, the trenches and supports were so numerous that it was called and looked like a draught board. In the afternoon we joined our battalions and were allotted to companies. I went to A being claimed by CSM Barber.

The hill has an entrance to the front line through a tunnel and at the entrance is A Company's cook house, being ministered by 4 of the blackest greasiest cooks imaginable; good tucker though. Passing through tunnels we came on the Regimental Aid post and a cheery Sergeant hoped he wouldn't be binding any of us up. His name Ford. Then on through more communication trenches to more tunnels through the next hill and we were in the front line.

Saw several Turkish planes but they turned about when fired at by anti-air craft guns from the war boats. First introduction to *Beachy Bill*, supposed to be a big German gun loaned to the Turks, he fired, but fortunately we were all in a tunnel and his shrapnel was harmless to us, but he caught some chaps from other battalions who were working on Shrapnel Green a noted spot for casualties.

Received letters from home. The place is split up by communication trenches like deep sunken lanes, wide enough for 2 chaps to walk abreast. Our guns don't fire until they make sure of a target, the R.C.O's say they have not much ammunition. One gun I know only allowed 15 shots to 24 hours.

We are in Lean's Trenches on the right of the infantry and on our right again stretching down to sea, run the Light Horse regiments.

The CO, Medical Officer, Capt. C Thompson inspects each day and straffs if any food is about as it attracts flies and they are already here in millions. Immediately a tin of jam is opened they flock to it and smother it. No wonder dysentery is rife and what would it be like if Thompson didn't growl and make things be clean.

Read letter from Miss Smith and mother. Spoke to Pvt Johns he is very pleased about receiving parcel from Miss Smith, Gert's friend. All night guns booming away.

4.11.15

At daybreak on 4ᵗʰ we bustled out of our holes in sides of communication trenches and lined up for what is called *Stand to* It is found that the Turk usually attacks at daybreak. We were issued with S.R.D. Rum capital R It warmed the cockles of my heart and made the stand too worthwhile.

5.11.15

Stood to arms early last night. Light Horse opened up new trenches. Turks charged and got 2 of our chaps. Had a good time last night. Don't think I hit anyone, but I bet they kept their heads down below the level of their trenches in the sector just opposite me. Last night our gulley was as bright as day. 2 monitors stood off and turned search lights up it and they enfiladed the Turk trenches with gun fire.

This morning with glasses we can plainly see the damage done, yards of their trench blown in, but I wonder if the damage done was equal to the money spent on shells etc.

We have to carry water from large tanks in Shrapnel Gulley to the battalion cooks or *babbling brooks* as they are named. The water is doled out, and my ration is 1 mess tin full for each day, so I drink it and forego a wash. I've a glorious beard and moustache.

On Holly Point where Lean's Trenches are, there is a good observation post and it's quite plain to see Gaba Tepe and Achi Baba in the distance and Olive Grove in the middle ground. We can actually see the damage done, as our shells burst. *Beachy Bill* is supposed to be in the Olive Grove and so that is paid particular attention. The Turks rarely fire it at night as the flash can be too easily seen.

It's impossible to say Jacko is frightened for he is not and takes risks to get a good shot at us. We throw all our jam tins over the front of our parapets so that if Jacko comes over at night time we will hear him coming. Of course he knew our exact position, so there was no chance of the glare of the tins giving the show away.

Running down in front of our trenches are 2 tunnels terminating in a T with 2 bomb thrower possies. The men in these advance posts when not on duty sleep in these trenches and to go out into the trench you have to climb over sleeping forms, getting a few good natured curses as you go.

What wrong ideas we had about trenches and fighting. Stripes had to be taken off, same with numerals. Wire out of caps and here we find men who have been here from start with all these badges etc. What awful times the first men here must have had. Our daily orders, Saps etc. 4 Platoons, 1) Firing line, 2) 2 x Fatigues, 3) rest

Gallipoli. From Ben's photo album.

7.11.15

Today had a treat. Three monitors and two destroyers stood close into the land and firing over the heads of the Light Horse pasted the Turk line, support and guns and they must have done some damage as no retaliation took place. It's good to see the Navy at work.

Parcel from home, chocs, very good parcel, very acceptable. Men here simply dead tired of work. General Sir CC Munro now in charge of Mediterranean Expedition.

7.11.15

Dear Frank,

Well old girl we are here at last and not sorry either to start to do our little bit. It is altogether different to what I thought the trenches would be like. I've been on duty in the actual firing line only 24 hours and have only seen 2 turks heads. I fired about 35 shots at the loop hole but of course can't tell what happened.

Out little trip from Lemnos was in the *censored* a very fast packet boat ..... on board. It's strange living like a rabbit in a hole dug in the ground yet here where there has been a bombardment every night. I haven't heard a sound.

This is a very pretty country, very mountainous of course, but there are places on hill slopes where cotton and many Australian crops can be grown and has grown, for now and then there is an area with no scrub on them only green grass. Achi Baba is to our right front and many, many are the shells planked there by our navy.

We landed at Anzac cove the night of 2nd November and climbed up the mountain and around another to Rest Gully which we reached at 11pm. Next day 3rd we stopped in the gully until 4pm. All the morning shrapnel and bullets were exploding and sometimes rather close.

I rec'd a couple of mails from you Frank and very acceptable they were too, thanks, we all read them. Aeroplanes continually flying over us, chased by shells and look very pretty in an azure sky. I received a parcel from Gertrude just as a piece of shrapnel burst overhead. By Jove

Poppy Valley, Gallipoli. From Ben's photo album.

Frank it's a peculiar feeling being under fire .... shews search lights on the tunnels all night.

You wouldn't know the Jackies trenches until they were shewn to you, all cleverly concealed. They are also experts as sappers, Dig, Dig, Dig, when not firing so we are doing the same. Well I'll close now with best wishes to all at Tarro

Yours faithfully Ben

8.11.15

Light Horse on our right made a slight attack last night gaining their objective; we all kept up a rapid fire on our sectors so that Turks could not send reinforcements along. Saw several dead Turks. They don't wear socks but have long strips of calico wound around their feet. They are very verminous.

9.11.15

Several chaps down with mumps, water supply cut down to 1 mug full. Had a wonderful wash with a shaving brush. Met Padre Mackenzie (Salvation Army) he is well liked. He was behind the cook house where he was stripped to his pants catting his shirt and he called out his score of 47 lice for the morning's catch. Teacher Billy Goode was evacuated with mumps. There is an old hand here in the Battalion named Clarke. He is like an old bushranger, at night on Patrol he looks for dead Turks and gets watches, money etc. from them, and you can imagine how his dugout can be heard some distance away. He calls it his museum and it is quite smelly too. Corp

Madson got ringing watch from dead Turk on our parapet. Been deepening trenches. Think I must have put the whole peninsular in sand bags, by the aches I have in my shoulders. Impossible to underestimate Jackies bravery. One Turk crept up to our parapet, jumped over, gave up and kissed our Sergeant.

10.11.15

Rumored that the Turks may use gas against us so that we have been issued with funny flannel bags to put over our heads and tuck down our Tunics. They have two eye pieces to peer through and we are issued a small tin of anti-dimming paste which we rub on and then polish off so they remain clear. The helmet is guaranteed to give one a headache for a week if used for an hour. Our first death of the reinforcement; F.R. Morris, looking through a loop hole. Darky was a good chap. We had an issue of mustard, it goes well with bully beef, and I like it. But of course it's nice and hard now. Rum issue and cigarettes too. Arthur Felton's birthday, couldn't write him Many Happy Returns of day.

14.11.15

Sunday. Heavy bombardment by us today. My first experience in the advanced bomb possey. The tunnel down from the front line is about 5 feet x 4 feet wide. The bomb possey is not known to Jacko—we lie doggo all day observing through bushes and at night we are in the *Qui Vive*. Only a dozen Mill's bombs are allowed and the rest made of jam tins and iron bombs like balls. The Turks line is only about 50 yards away. Sneaking my camera out I took a picture of Brewer and Davidson in the bomb possey. McTackett is in charge of my section.

It rained very hard as we left the front line and soon the line and dugouts became saturated and some of the latter started to crumble in. Some assistance was needed to dig out some men. Slush is over the knees, all food wet and blankets muddy. No fatique—only to get water.

Achi Baba one white ring of smoke. A very pretty sight, it looked as if it had a Halo.

14.11.1915

P & O Service paper

Dear Frank, A Merry Christmas and a Happy New Year. I'll get
in early as I don't know when this letter will reach you. I think the
mail boat must have gone down as letters haven't been seen since we
landed.

This is a bosker place I wouldn't mind living here for good if all my
friends and relatives were here. It will be 6 weeks before you get this
letter and I can't fill up by asking you how you are. Well I am quite well
despite the nerve shocks etc. Whips of shells are knocking around and
if you don't cling like a limpet to your dug out you take a lot of risks.

The Turks had bacon and onions for breakfast yesterday we could
smell them and we thought of charging just to capture it. We boil
cocoa and tea in the trenches and some even cook bully beef and make
porridge of biscuits .

The ground here is full of germs which do as much damage as
Germans. [This before antibiotics–Ed.] A little scratch often leads to
a poisoned hand etc. They intend to inoculate us for Tetanus germs
shortly. What a lot of inoculations we have had. 3 for smallpox, 3
for enteric and now for Tetanus. I wish they could inoculate against
shrapnel.

The people at home know very little about the war and Mr Censor
will cut out anything we put about it, so they will still remain in
darkness.

How has Creamy's leg got on? Has her knee all dried up as you
expected? Do all those men still go to Browns at Hexham or can you
notice a difference in the numbers?

We want more men here so as to give some final clashes and reach
97 and Achi Baba. The ceaseless roar of naval guns on Achi Baba is
like thunder at night and the search lights make the trenches almost as
light as day.

I've finished dinner–the cocoa we made was too strong, the
spotted dog ok, the biscuits slightly mouldy but I don't grumble as it
can't be helped.

Davidson with Brewer's head in front.

Oh well Frank be good. I wish all at Tarro a Merry Christmas and a Happy New Year and a speedy finish to the war

Yours Ben

15.11.15

Trenches a big lake. It rained last night and is very cold. We are slush right up to the hips, each time we move we slip in the mud, but our rifles are well oiled up.

18.11.15

Thursday. Flooded out, blankets wet through—what a nice thing war is. 6 casualties today caused by a broom stick bomb. We can generally see them coming but these chaps were not quick enough.

18.11.15

Gallipoli ANZAC

Dear Frank, I had a pleasant gift on Tuesdays last, 2 letters from you and 2 from home. You put in a couple of pages in each note which you can see I am using now. All the Christmas mail we posted from here is in Davy Jones locker. The packet boat was torpedoed out of Mudros Harbour, so you won't receive your Christmas letter as I know I couldn't write another like it. One little thing I've noticed is that your handwriting is getting older and possesses more character.

I don't know what my people would do if they had so many visitors. Your mother must be very fond of company. Poor Old Phil if it is so as you say [Philip Carroll] You've never kissed him. He has missed a lot as I know.

You could not have given me a better gift than that muffler. I use it now every night and morning and sometimes right through the day. So you have at last started some sox. Claire must possess a lot of patience to have almost finished a pair. I am writing this on a Dixie lid balanced on my knee so the usual scrawl will naturally be worse.

Yes it was lucky that that black snake didn't make it up .... in the hay shed when you were acting the ass. I might have seen 2 heels making a lot of dust towards *Oaklands*. Gertrude has had German measles and has been isolated for about 9 days so I received a couple of letters from her.

Last Christmas sat down to a good dinner at home. This time, greasy stew and biscuits. What a lot of things I have learnt since last Christmas. Why I didn't know you even, your frizzy hair had never been pulled or teased and what a lot of letters you and I have written. Could you count them? Art and I chanced to be on a post together last night for the first time and we talked and talked so that the trench officer had to come around and complain to us that perhaps John Burke (the turks) might possibly hear us

The dates of your letters 11.10. 15 and 2.10.15 and 2 mails about the same time I'm sure there must still be mails missing as the thread in letters has been lost and can't pick them up. I'll have to do that Maitland trip by road in the sulky if it is so long and I have as good a time as I had last time I went down the road. You seemed to enjoy that picnic you all went to at Thornton, a picnic or like that or down to Lake Macquarie when we come back would be ok.

Have you any fresh horses? Blackie and Creamy seem to have plenty of work what with the trips to the station and saddle nags for friends. Those two have a bit of graft. There are no horses here only mule trains manned by Sikhs, great big chaps, some with red beards bleached with washing powder. The mules go only where a man can walk upright.

How are the Girls Own Papers going? Any useful little hints or Pretty Pictures to copy or stories etc. From what I read meningitis is rather prevalent in the recruiting camps. Do you understand what it is as I don't. Of course if you know?

When we joined our battalions we reverted to the ranks so I am afraid I have no chance of getting any strikes' till after the first rough and tumble and of course there are casualties amongst the NCO's practically every day but no casualties among our company's N.C.O.s. We are in A Coy 1ˢᵗ Battalion. Well old Girl, wish you a very, very Happy New Year and Christmas. I've wished it you in 2 previous letters but they are at the bottom of the sea. I hope all at *Oaklands* will keep well and have a good time at Christmas, Good Bye Old Pal

Ben

19.11.15

After stand down on the 19ᵗʰ the Turks got Drummond-Uncle we used to call him. He got it behind the ear as he turned around to belt clip of cartridge. On 20th Chas Higginson killed. Enemy had been repulsed at Johnsons Jolly. Few dozen Turks in some dead ground shot from heights above. Sun out, lakes subsiding and we are busy scraping mud from our persons and trying to dry out clothes. The track from the cookhouse tunnel to the green is a mud slide and up this we have to carry rations etc.

Gallipoli

22.11.15

Dear Old Pal,

.. day before yesterday I received about 12 letters from you and I didn't know if I was standing on my head or heels I also received 9 from home and elsewhere. You want me to put more variation on the headings well *Copal* is about it, best brand I think, that whether it is dearest ducky or any other conglomeration all have the same meaning from me, you ought to know that.

Glad to hear you are using both Blackie and Creamy now. Don't let any more horses down for goodness sake. You evidently had a narrow shave with your fathers new horse jumping on you. Hope you had no after effects.

Pleased to hear your painting is going ahead, don't you think animals are rather hard to do? A I F and? are just the same only Art leaves out the Expeditionary in his address.

Very, very cold here, use your scarf. Absolutely best present you could have given me. Receive mails regularly and pass them on after I've finished with them. You and all at home were evidently taken with the latest little Felton. He is rather a nice little chap especially as he now can talk, slightly. Did you say you were 5 foot 4 ½, well I can give you 4 ½ I think.

The ground here is very, very bad for cuts and grazes, they immediately start to swell up. Have you ever gone 5 days without a drink of water? We haven't had an ounce now for a week.

Ruth's note in Arts letter, hope she gets through qualifying exam. You ought to go and do her geography. I feel inclined to writing now but here comes a wretched man to put me on fatigue . I think I have received all letters posted to me from you now. I didn't think I could ever read the last bunch but I soon got through them. I am keeping well and trust you are all doing the same and Art is as well.

Gertrude writes often as well to us 2. Hope she isn't overworked. Wouldn't it be nice to get the measles or some other little complaint just to go to bed for a while. This paper I am writing on has seen Tarro before. You are indeed very thoughtful. How does the new sulky go?

Haven't received a letter from Kitty or Claire yet. Ruth was very funny selling Noel by auction. What did Mrs Felton think of it? Nice little note from Mrs Niland only she seems to think I'm nearly dead. That sea sickness did a world of good to me. I won't be ill again you'll see. Must go on work again now. Love to all at home

Yours Ben

Australian dug-outs, Gallipoli

22.11.1915

Had a stroke of luck today, went on beach fatigue and coming home met a party of Sikhs and mules coming along the sap when *Beachy Bill* opened up and caught the mules but missed us so we went back to see if any damage done and found all the mules on the ground and the Sikhs gone It seemed a pity to see the loads of cheese on the ground so I snaffled one, laboriously lumping it up to the Battalion. Didn't know I had so many friends but gave each a lump and kept the rest. It's a great scheme to go on beach fatigue as you can generally get something or other like that even if it is a water bottle of rum. A gimlet here is priceless. The Tommies here (Royal Marine Light Infantry) will sell their souls for a few bob. The chaps christened them Run, my lads, Imishie (Gyppo for clear out) They are not permanent RMLI men but mainly school boys.

24.11.1915

Wrote Frank and Mum. Very quiet. Great shortage of water as due to rain and storm water lighters have not been able to land their water. 3 days without. Managed to steal a bottle full when on water fatigue.

26.11.15

Friday. Reg Cook killed today. H. McKenna shot through chest and arm. He died through the day. Supposed that as McKenna was helping Cook over parapet, McKenna's rifle went off and shot them both.

No shots fired. Today an Army Corps order came out that everyone had to be quiet, no movement, and no shots. Silence right from Suvla Bay. It's O.K we don't have to do any fatigues in the day time and Jacko doesn't shell much at night. Wonder what the meaning of this quiet stunt is?

This was a precurser to the evacuation of The Peninsula. From the Diary of the 1st Battalion:

> 'the health of the troops who had been on Anzac for some months was at this period so bad that it deserves mention, as never again was the physical fitness of the men so low. The majority were wasted and thin and suffering from shortness of breath and diarrhoea. Lack of variety in food, unremitting toil and the unceasing strain of living constantly within gun range had undermined the strongest consititutions. With the advent of Winter the general health improved slightly but brought worse living conditions. On November 28 the thermometers did not rise above freezing conditions and at night registed 7 degree of frost Next day many of the Battalion saw snow for the first time '.

27.11.15

Saturday in bomb possey with Billy Goode and 4 others when 20 Turks came over bombing. Remembering that we were not to fire unless absolutely necessary we let them come to within ten feet hoping they would miss the possey but they stopped and talked and then came right forward. As there were too many to capture and they would crowd out the small possey, we let them have it, one rifle and bomb but before they ran they threw one bomb only into the possey and got Billy Goode. 19 dead Light Horse outside in view.

27.11.15

Dear Frank,

I wrote you a couple of days ago but as I have a few minutes off will spend it writing to you. We always have to start and say whether we are inclined towards letter writing, then the weather. It is very cold, although I wear two pairs of knitted sox I suffer with cold feet. (not the cold feet you might hear soldiers talking about) but through cold and not fear. We have had a few attacks and fusillades within last couple of days. Two more 7th of 1sts being put out of action, one Cpl McKenna. You might have seen his photo with two other NCOs I took at Liverpool, when uniforms issued.

I suppose Ruth is sitting as I write this, (if I remember the date rightly) for her qualifying Certificate paper. She will sure get through this time as the Yankees says.

I can't answer your letters one by one as Art has been doing as I have had to get rid of them quickly. Somehow by fine points or otherwise he got yesterday off from the firing line but the heads knew and while he slept he was pulled out and made go as reserve to the firing line (His lagddwwidge was dredful).

In the 23 days we have been here I have seen only 3 glimpses of (Jack Burke) Turks but several bodies of them in the distance. It is strange how you get used to guns, bullets aren't noticed much now but when *Beachy Bill* gets going I'm about the slickest runner on the Peninsula.

You all seem nice and jolly at home, pleased to feel you are not worrying about us at all, for if there is a bullet labelled 2481 you can't help it at all. You say you have been thinking of Sgt Higginson lately, well I met a Corporal who was with him at Johnsons Jolly when he met his death and If I get a chance I'll get a picture of his grave. It is about ? miles from where I am at Holly Spur but I'll try and get a chance.

You ought to hear *Beachy Bill* as I write this, he is screeching like a good un. When Mary goes to bed and she thinks of Art, poor girl, you, like a sensible common sense girl go to bed to sleep. I turn in about 6pm and that is about 1.30am in Australia when all good people are dead to the world.

Your friend Miss Adamson is you say as big as Art. Why are all your friends bigger than yourself? You want to put some paper in your shoes but good things are nearly always done up in small parcels aren't they?

I suppose the hot days are coming fast now with nice long evenings and lovely sand flies and mosquitoes to worry you. Do you remember sitting out on that front verandah with the mosquitoes making merry overhead. What lovely song they sing. Interrupted by a bang, buzz buzzy bang! (got 'im) Buzzy Bang. etc.

Has *Goolah* been at *Oaklands* lately? There are hundreds of his compatriots here, though mostly about 24 years old The Sikhs are such dignified looking men and the Gurkhas, small boyish looking jovial little fellows who have no time for Kitchener's Army. I've seen Gurkhas sit down with Australians and eat bully beef which is an unpardonable sin in their religion. This shows how well we get on with them.

I'm getting used to not have a wash, it's convenient even if it is not good for the constitution. I wonder if the Gov't are going to supply the troops with sheep skin vests. Art and I will have them if they haven't gone to Davey Jones Locker but what will all the other poor fellows do?

29.11.15. I'll get another move on now, Jack Burke has kept us so busy the last few days. Well Old Girl I'll tell you of a little affair that took place on 27.11.15 at 3 am. The Turks attacked us. I was in No 4 bomb position whilst Art was in No 3 just to my left. Two bombs were thrown by Turks into No 3 possey. Luckily Art was away sleeping, meanwhile

Ben and Art with Corporal McKenna.
Ben wrote 'To Frank from Ben'. Taken at Liverpool Camp

Major Davidson in bomb possey with snow and ice.

the other chaps and myself were pumping bullets into the Turks and we threw some bombs. Well only one chap got hurt which was very miraculous. Well next night it started snowing and has snowed ever since. 'tis very cold, More anon

Love from Ben

28.11.15

Sunday. Quiet. Came off post, miserable time with the cold, snowing everything, which looks nice and feels cold

29.11.15

Fatigues (Silent stunt over) Down to the Beach for biscuits and to the gully for water. I felt so dirty that although it was bitterly cold and there was no fun I had a swim.

Tuesday 30.11.15.

Today ended my short stay on the Peninsula. I was on cook's fatigue and whilst in Gun Lane, an 8.2 ' shell came through the top of the cook house tunnel, killing several chaps and got me, little splinters entering left leg and side of face. Killed Chapman who I was talking too. Knocked his head off. Concussion awful—everything black and the next thing I knew was smiling face of Sergeant Ford who reassured me by saying that I'd only got a little crack and was lucky as he had been there since the landing and couldn't get away.

Turkish Coat of Arms on a gun at Lone Pine

31 11.15

Evacuated to the Light Horse Ambulance where I received anti Tetanus injection then off to the beach. Transferred to Emergency clearing Hospital where cold intense. Doc fears for left ear–hope not permanently deaf. As a walking wounded hobbled down to pier with the others at dusk and put into a small rowing boat and on to a hospital boat which came in closer at night fall. Had a hot sponge by orderlies and a nice warm bed. It's like heaven to be away from the snow and lice and frozen feet. Slept and slept.

Thursday 1.12.15, on *Karapara*

Woke up nice and refreshed but side very stiff. Orderlies told me that Jacko pasting Lone Pine heavily. Sure enough later on we get our full complement of cases and out we went to sea. They looked after us well. Especially Nurse Souter. My wounds listed on tab of linen sewn to pyjamas says *Wounds in face and thigh, superficial burns, shock and deafness left ear.* My letter written to Frank in my pocket burnt by the shell. We seem to be getting hell on Lone Pine now.

Another Hospital ship taken from HMHS Karapara *at Malta*

MALTA

Saturday 4.12.15

At Saint Elmo Hospital, Malta. Had rather a bad time on boat. Temp 103 each day. Doctor said I must have had a touch of malaria. Early this morning on the Hospital Boat I was awakened by hearing strange cheers and sitting up in bed saw that we were in Valetta Harbour, in Malta.

The cheers came from French Dreadnoughts, war boats at anchor in the bay. The *Karapara* was a very fast boat and she was landing the slightly wounded at Malta before going on to England. Was glad to be put off here as lot of AIF in Malta. This is evidently a Tommy hospital. Malta is known as The Nurse of the Mediterranean, as there are so many hospitals. At lunch I was surprised to see one small bottle per man of Stout. (Some hospital!) I have not been able to sit up since Tuesday 4 days ago. I must have developed malarial fever so the Sister said.

Approach to Malta is very stately through walls 100' high all of stone, the whole place is stone. All along the harbour except for landing places huge walls keeping back the land. One is immediately struck with the age and strength of this place against that of Sydney. We were landed in motor ambulances.

St Elmo Hospital 5.12.15

Dear Old Girl,

I'm seeing a lot more of the world at Malta. Now I'd like to go to England next. A shell threw me out of action for a while. It is only a miracle I'm even here instead of having a good grip of Shrapnel Green.

I know you are all busy right up to your eyes in making the home look Christmassy-like. I'll have a better Christmas dinner than Art. I'll be able to walk before then with comfort.

If you only had the snow and ice we had on Gallipoli for your Christmas at Home you could image yourselves in England. By Jove it was cold. I had 2 frozen toes that had to be dressed as I did my 24 hours on Ordinary then 24 hours extra and the whole time it snowed.

You have read about and seen pictures of high cliffs with castles on top, the entrance gained by narrow entrances up through gloomy steep narrow stone blocked streets. Well that is like Malta. The Island juts out of the water and the harbour sides are all blocked with stone.

I'm a nice individual! You can't have an interest in the place, yet Old Pal I write so often, I can't scrape any news up. I'll cease now. The Sister is looking towards this way, she means to have another fiddle around.

Love Ben

One of many postcards sent home. This is a pre-war image.

Another postcard. Pre War image, Malta Saluting Battery

10.12.15

Getting near Christmas. Granted a pass and struggled just outside the main door and sat in the sun and wrote some letters home. I'm glad I'm over the stage of getting an orderly to do everything for me.

Sunday.

Went for a stroll up the Strada Reale, all cobble stones, very narrow streets, so narrow that 2 good sized motor lorries could not pass at once.

Monday

Went as far as the Post Office and from the height saw the city of Valetta. I have no money so borrowed some to cable Dad for some. The goats here are funny. All goats graze outside the City walls and are herded at the gates by their masters in the early morning. Being driven through the gates they all disperse and go and lie down outside their respective houses where they wait until milkmen come and milk them into the housewives jug then they go and wait at the gate again. It must be awfully convenient having no big cans to wash out. It's strange how each goat knows which house to go to. We were ordered not to drink the milk as strangers develop a rash after drinking it.

I have made a good friend here in Company Sergeant Major L Teitzel. He is from Warwick Queensland and is in the 25th Battalion. We often dine

Milking goats in the street in Malta

out together for an extra large afternoon tea. He has the money—I have none as yet. Teitzel and my self paid a visit to the Chapel of Skulls. The following is an extract from a letter written from Malta':

> ... what a horrid dream; and as I the patient sat up in bed and glared around me muttering words about skulls and pirates the experienced nurse at Saint Elmo knew that another one of those Naughty Australians had wandered out of the Hospital gates and visited the nearby Chapel of Skulls.
>
> As my temperature gradually went down to normal, the nurse bit by bit drew from me the story of my wanderings, the result of which had turned me, almost convalescent soldier into a sick-bay patient once more.

Ben left back row behind Sister with + on pinafore;
possibly Teitzel in wheelchair on right

I had seen some horrid sights on the Peninsula some time before, but in my weakened condition caused by trying to help with some other chaps to stop a Turkish shell, the sight of the bones of a few hundred dead and gone Maltese had been too much for me.

Bed is a lovely place, but as days drew into weeks it became very monotonous and a desire to be up and see a little more than 4 walls of a ward and to hear something else besides 'Hello choom want a Woodbine ' took possession of me, and I decided that as soon as I could I would see a good deal of this quaint old fashioned and historic Malta, one of the Keys to the Mediterranean.

Leave Passes were out of the question to an open wound man but in places other than Malta, money had been found to be a sufficient passport. So passing a coin to the sentry, Teitzel and I found ourselves outside the Hospital gates hobbling up the narrow well paved and clean street. As hospital patients are not supposed to be wandering about the streets without a pass and seeing a very well beloved Red Cap waiting to pounce on any small man he could see, we ducked into a little alley way, which led down steps to a queer sort of a chapel half crypt and half erected above ground.

Out of curiosity to know what it contained, we knocked at the iron bound door. A cowled head presented itself and a rusty clothed emaciated looking priest enquired my business. Making him understand signs that we desired to see the chapel, the priest extended his hand and for the second time in one morning a coin proved to be the *Open Sesame*.

By the way, I may state that Saint Elmo where I had apartments (?) was a Tommy Hospital and as the weekly pay was the large sum of

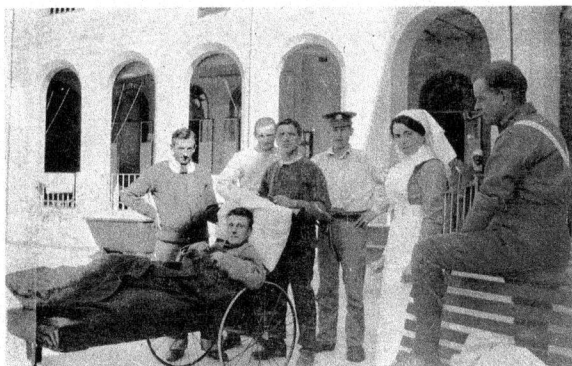

Louis Teitzel in trolley bed and staff of St Elmo

2/—the coin handed to the Priest was not a very handsome one. However, he seemed satisfied and allowed us to pass in.

As the door clanged behind us shutting off most of the daylight, I was staggered to find that the Chapel contained little else but human bones. We were in the famous Chapel of Bones (also known as Chapel of Skulls) erected to perpetuate the memory of the soldiers who fell in the defence of Valetta against the Turks about year 1550.

I shall never forget the sight; ranged around the walls in all kinds of gruesome and fantastic shapes, in mouldings, arches and scrolls were nothing but skulls and bones. It reminded me of the tales about the huts of the cannibal head hunters of Borneo. Not that there was not a wonderful amount of methods and ingenuity of a devilish kind in the groupings of the skulls, thigh bones, etc.

We escaped as quickly as possible to the clean fresh air outside I travelled as quickly as my legs would let me, back to the Hospital. Never had I appreciated it so much. My little experience caused me a night of fever.

Tuesday.

Touch of malaria fever 105—confined to bed. Sister gave me three cold baths and quinnine . Had a visit from 2 Victorian ladies who distributed papers and cigarettes.

Thursday.

Temp normal, out of bed. Again, paid the magnificent sum of 2/—a week. This is all that is allowed, isn't it absurd, but get over the difficulty. Major Mifsud, our CO is a Maltese.

Art Felton, Harry Brewer, John Aylwood, John Drummond (dead), Reg Cook (dead) Charlie Moore, Joe Chisolm, Sid Hampton Davidson, Eric Funnell, William Hunt, Rupert Neil, D.K. Young, Leno Young, D.Taylor. Note written at Malta, presumed to be notes in A Coy at Gallipoli.

19.12.15 Sunday.

Wrote to Frank, Temp 105 Malaria very bad 10 grains Quinine have to take 5 grains regular each day—side quite healed, left ear still deaf

---

22.12.15

Last batch left for Convalescent camp. I have now been in hospital 4
Dec1915–22 Dec 1915=18 days

New nurse, our previous nurse put on night shift. Heard yesterday
troops had evacuated Anzac and Suvla. Wondering did we get all
provisions and guns off or how much sacrifice. Still in bed, hope to be
up tomorrow. As few days longer in bed preventing me for some time
from going on any more adventures.

24.12.15

Preparing for Xmas Day, we didn't want any leave but set to and helped
decorate the place. We have hundreds of different coloured streamers
and connected them in front of the electric light globes Christmas Eve
night we had a most wonderful tea, even to cakes and *hundreds and
thousands* sandwiches. Afterwards we had a splendid Carols concert
some of the English carols very pretty, most I had not heard before so
the Australians not to be outdone got together and sang some songs
for them.

25.12.15

On Christmas morning we found our stockings filled with chocolates,
cigarettes, trumpets, and as we had in our ward only cases who would
not be worried by noise—we made it. Ham and two eggs for breakfast
(a marvellous thing for the Army!) Then we set too and straightened
up the ward.

We had a Church service and for the first time sat down to a dinner at
a table together instead of eating it at the locker beside the bed. The
nurses waited on us and afterwards at their own Christmas dinner
several chaps who were fit enough helped at theirs. It was a happy
time.

The doctor looking after me has ordered a special diet with chicken
as he says *growing boys*, but believe it is underground (rabbit) mutton.

Carotchie cabs, Sliema, Malta

25.12.15.

After a tour around the city in (Carotchies) cabs we came back to a concert and in the middle of it in came Father Xmas and gave out more presents. In all a nice Xmas Day.

28.12.15

A treat for me as we were taken to see an Opera at the Valetta Opera House by Sister Harris.

This is a fine stone building, seats are mainly in boxes shut off by curtains and it was very hot though. *Lucia de Lammermoor/Nancy of Lammerenoor* was the show. We enjoyed the acting, the singing was all in Italian, of course but we enjoyed the music too. It appears that Nancy is married against her will and it drives her mad and her lover to suicide.

Right in the centre suspended from the dome is a huge cut glass chandelier—an 18lb shell would make a mess of it.

The Maltese women seem bigger and stronger than the men. The women wear a black hood and are never without it even when in the streets.

30.12.15.

I had the kind of day I liked. At 10.30 a.m. the Red Cross Motor Car picked me and a few others up for a spin. Went up the Strada Merchanti and through lots of solid stone arches into fairly open country beyond, passing the inner harbour the many coloured Gondolas making a pretty scene.

Postcard, Royal Opera House Valetta.

The fields are divided by rough stone walls—wood seems to be very scarce. Most of the fields are tiered and there is no depth of soil and if it was not for the wall the soil would be swept in the gulleys. Even the farm houses are of stone I wouldn't like to storm this place, each house is a stronghold. It was a beautiful trip and seeing that we were really pleased the man in charge of our car asked Teitzel and myself to lunch after he had dropped off the others at the hospital.

After a nice lunch he took us to the Valetta Palace Armoury. Entering through a courtyard filled with palms and ferns which made the place shady and cool and cute little fountains were playing among the ferns. Receiving tickets (Buckshee) passed into the building. Hundreds of suits of the most wonderful armour, all worn by Knights of Saint John. Then on to the Spanish and Moor section. Over each suit was the Knight's shield with his coat of arms on it. There were some bosker dints in some suits of armour. But the suits wouldn't fit the average Australian. They are short, yet they were very wide. I suppose that means we are growing a bigger race of men.

The show armour was inlaid with gold and silver. One chamber was devoted to Tapestry, some of it in shreds though, this was done by Napoleon's soldiers in spite. Hundreds of British regiments must have been stationed here at various times as there are hundreds of banners and war flags preserved.

I bought many Malta postcards.

Have to go to St Andrews for ear specialist.

31.12.15.

Went for a trip to Sliema, this by a Ferry trip for a halfpenny. This is the fashionable quarter and the sea promenade is good. It would open their eyes to see Manly though. Had tea in town, blew my weeks money 2/—in one go——steak and onions.

St Elmo Hospital Malta

Dear Frank,

It seems very strange to write 1916 but we will get used to it I little thought we would be here in 1916 but now the end of the war is further off than ever. Through being on good terms with the head sister, her little baby boy went out on a long motor drive on the 29th.

We left the hospital about 9.30 and came back in time for dinner. The Island is mainly rock and there isn't too much soil so on sides of the hills they bank the soil up in tiers with stone walls. In my pictures of Sliema you will see that. Ask Gertrude for a couple.

We caught glimpses of *Dysers* or Gondolas being rowed about by fishermen and they stand up to row and face the bows. The better class of people have such pretty carts drawn by ponies. The car is just a flat floor with rails around it with a mattress in the floor, they either squat or lie down to drive. They must be very comfortable. The country streets are very narrow. We nearly had a collision but a friendly policeman lifted the approaching cart and horse-like donkey into a side street for us to pass.

I saw such a pretty yellow car with cream ponies and a girl driving it yesterday. You know the kind of cars I mean, like the Irish people use without seats. The donkey here are very much smaller than the Egyptian donkeys are and just like big St Bernard dogs.

At the Valetta Palace Armoury the walls were fine paintings, by gone famous Johnnies some of whom I had read about. One wants to know more history to be able to appreciate all these Old World sights. Weapons there were by the thousands, from huge double handed swords of 7 feet to delicate rapiers. Guns with barrels 10' long and old cannon that fired stone cannon balls some of which I saw there.

An old stage coach with huge coat of arms and sedan chairs to match. Dotted over this Old World Island are lots of tiny gardens all heavily fenced with iron railings.

Where perhaps 2 streets enclosed a small triangular block we would perhaps be inclined to put a sky scraper, there the Maltese authorities put in a tiny garden.

I wish I could get some letters from you and home. Of course I will get the lot in the dim future but they would be more appreciated now that I cannot find a mate on the Island. I've searched through the wounded lists but cannot find a name I know. Perhaps they have gone to England or Alexandria. Gooda bye old Girl Love to all at Tarro

Ben

1.1.1916.

The Scotch orderlies kicked up a row last .night celebrating the New Year. In bed again—have been overdoing it and my leg has gone stiff on me. Trip to Barraca and San Antonio Gardens, Teitzel being the host. I

C.S.M. Teitzel and Lt Holcom

took a picture of Teitzel and a friend of his in front of a bush house in the garden.

At every street corner, set in a niche of the angle of the building, is the statue of some Saint or other. The sculptors must do a good trade.

The Barraca lift is a huge lift which takes people from the water's edge right to the level of the top—say 100 ft. From our hospital we overlook the entrance of the harbour.

Last night we had a good view of all the proceedings. About midnight every search-light in the place switched on and all focused on the entrance—there was a scare—subs were expected but nothing came of it. Bobbies here are funny and all they do is to worry the boot blacks to see if they have a license, no traffic people at all, of course, it's not necessary as there can only be one string of traffic each way in most streets.

Marsa or old Valetta is in ruins for the Knights of Saint John walled in Valetta and left Marsa out in the cold and people wanting protection came inside Valetta.

2.1.16.

Went to the ear specialist at Saint George's Convalescent Camp, a nice motor run. Talk about pain. He pushed a probe up my nose into throat and up the inside ear, it was lovely, as good as eating Ice Cream on a hot day. Said something or other was wrong through the shell concussion, but that time would fix it up O.K.

My face is much better but I still look peculiar owing to the Picric Acid they smothered it in. My hair too is yellow through it. You would laugh, Mother, to see me NOW. We are dressed in hospital Blue Flannel suits and red ties.

My coat lets the wind up and my trousers have 2 folds in the legs, but the folds do to hold Camera and cigarettes. Teitzel 25th Battalion, ? Mitchell. Had tea in town, took picture

3.1.16

Went with Teitzel to Barracara and San Antonio Gardens. Took several pictures.

Dressed in hospital garb

In Antonio Gardens, Governors late residence, big stone walled place very bare looking. Had afternoon tea in Hotel there. Met Lieut. Holcom. S.M. Teitzel in trouble re German origin. Father came to Australia 45 years ago and naturalised. Mother Australian. Blocked him from commission.

In afternoon walked town with Teitzel. He bought lace 27/6. Linen lace more valuable than silk. Silk when washed goes woolley. Linen improves with age and washing.

C.S.M. Teitzel and Holcom in the Antonio Gardens

5.1.16.

Major Mifsud, the C.O. of the hospital, asked me if I would like to visit his home for afternoon tea—and off I went with a couple of others. He is a Maltese, but his wife is American I think. The house was nice but we liked the flat roof best, where we had nice cakes and a meal. Good music, good tea, home to bed. Feel good.

7.1.16.

Paid a visit per Carotchy—see photo of them in picture of Sliema—to the Gardens beyond the Opera House. The terrace commands a fine view of the Grand Harbour with its war boats at anchor. Here on the terrace are old fashioned guns only used now for saluting purposes. But one end of the terrace is built off and sentries were on guard, so surmise that big modern gun was behind the wall.

I couldn't get any pictures as the Policeman was mooching around, worrying small boys as usual. Behind the garden is a cemetery and in it are tablets to many famous men including one to Sir Thomas Maitland.

The Barraca lift is most handy, for by it you can descend directly to the water's edge and save a laborious descent by very round-about roads. Teitzel and I walked through the slums of Valetta, but even here every street is regularly swept and sanded.

Teitzel too tired to do much, as its only 10 days since a couple of his toes were amputated (frost bite). Under certain parts of Malta there are giant caverns for storing grain. They were once used as a preventative being

Teitzel

The X marks rows of huge stones which cover the entrance to wells for storage of grain etc

starved out in a siege. The openings are covered by huge round stones. I've some pictures of them if they turn out well.

Today I was put on the convalescent list

17.1.16.

Went with Sgt. Maj Teitzel to the Marsa Polo Ground. We saw a Polo match between some Permanent Navy Officers and some Maltese gents. Fine game, only I felt sorry for the horses they seemed so knocked up. There is no doubt that some navy men can sit a horse.

In the afternoon we went to the Museum. Here are life sized models of some Phoenician tombs which were found at Citta Vechia. It was strange to see the mummified cats. I believe these cats were sacred to the Romans and when one died it was mummified.

19.1.16

Then off to Saint John's Church. The floor was too pretty to walk on. If a Knight of Saint John died at home he was buried here—consequently the whole floor is a mass of tomb stones—not just plain ones but the chief battle the Knight was in was depicted in different colors on the stone, underneath his coat of arms.

There were 3 altars in marble with silver and gold fal-de-rols and candles etc. The carvings were wonderful, especially those which supported by their heads, tablets to the memory of some knight or other. There are

2 gates in this Church, the original ones made of gold were stolen by Napoleon and they have been replaced by silver ones. The arched roof is painted with scenes of Christ's childhood.

22.1.16.

Sergeant Major Teitzel, Warwick, Queensland no. 768 age 29, 25th Battalion. True Gentleman supporting me during period had no cash. Hope to reimburse him later. Wish a few letters would only come, rather lonely without any news from home. Leaving Hospital 24.1.16 after 7 weeks 2 days wonder how soon now can join Battalion. Now I am well I'm hankering after joining my unit. All chums doing a service and I'm not. Suppose if I come through I'll only receive a nominal medal without bars. Sister Harris could not have done more for me than she has. Kind, jolly, always ready for fun. Wish I had the means to give her a little gift but afraid exchequer won't stand it.

Q.M. Sergeant Brewer left for front day afore yesterday, wish was with him. Rumour yellow fever broken out in Egypt. Hope not for our troops sake.

Saturday. First time in a train in Malta. We went to Notabile, fare 2d. Immediately on leaving the train we were besieged by boys who wanted to guide us to the Catacombs. Entered the old city, once capital of Malta. Through crumbling walls some 30' thick, all built of stone solid, and from this high part saw the whole district from Citta Vechia to Valetta and halfway between them standing alone is the huge Musta Church and Dome.

The grounds all marked out by stone walls—looked like green draught boards, and San Antonio Gardens could be picked out by the trees, everywhere else they were stunted but there they flourished.

We simply had to tear ourselves away from the view to see the Cathedral. Immediately struck by the wealth of it and the care and labour of love bestowed on it. Here we saw the original cross brought from the Isle of Rhoda by the Knights of Saint John. It was of solid silver and the head gilt. The floor was of marble with mosaic pictures so cleverly done that until I examined it closely, I thought the pictures were painted on. Bishops etc. were buried in the Crypt and some parts of the floor were made of tomb stones let in, with coats of arms and the history of the person buried below engraved on them.

The altar of marble studded with gold and silver and 20 candles each 4 feet high were burning in silver candle sticks. The arches of the roof were supported on black marble cut out to resemble figures, I think they are called Caryatids.

The arched roof was painted in scenes and the priest who showed us around said the figures were 30 feet long. They were done 500 years ago and are still in excellent state of preservation. Next visit was to Saint Paul's Church. We didn't bother going into the Church, but saw the cave where Saint Paul slept when he came to Malta.

On 25th January there is a Public holiday and feast day in Malta. It is to celebrate the anniversary of the conversion of Saint Paul. In fact the Museum was built around it. Mosaic floors, Doric Pillars, and dadoes around the walls, the chief pattern was ⌒𝒆𝒆𝒆 The statues, of course, were broken, but the pots and pans were still O.K.

24.1.16.

I was struck today by the way these Maltese continually have before them some painting of Christ. Even the barrow men in the markets have a picture, chiefly the one with Christ in the arms of Mary, and each picture has at least one candle in front of it.

At every street corner is the statue of a Saint or a Crucifix. The most appealing piece of sculpture to my mind is *Les Gavroches*. One elder boy with rather a horrid look on his face is dragging a younger boy and a girl with cherub faces towards something he sees in the distance. The figures being beautifully proportioned and the faces don't seem stoney, the expressions are there.

There are quite a number of Maltese Mummies said to be about the same age as the oldest Egyptian ones. This afternoon I went on the most interesting trip I've been so far—to the Catacombs. Took a train from Valetta to Citta Vecchia and entering the old city, paid 1d. to go down the tombs, arming ourselves with candles and a guide. Long continuous underground passages with niches cut here and there. In some niches were human bones still as a person died, he was buried in the niche he slept in and a flat stone placed on top of him, then an inscription was cut in the stone.

Every now and then the passages opened out into rooms some 40' x 40' where I suppose the folks came together for worship as I don't suppose they had concerts much in those perilous days.

There were stone corn mills identical with those used by the Gippos of today. These Catacombs once led to Valetta 6 miles away, but the passages are now in a state of bad repair. It was interesting but tiring. Many of the bones in this place went to form the 'Chapel of Skulls '—another gruesome but interesting place. I wouldn't like to sleep there every night.

St Elmo and Chapel of Skulls were destroyed in WWII
Patients and staff upstairs and in front of the building.

From Arthur.

Dear Frank,

I have been hearing all sorts of unfavourable news about my old friend, you. No not from Mary only, but from others as well. As far as I can understand my comrade in arms, now in hospital has been neglecting to write to you so often. Well, Frank never mind; buck up, you will hear from him sometime I expect. I am sure Ben thinks of his pal, (you were his pal you know) but being a lazy fellow is too tired to write.

He has only written to me once in nearly two months now and I hear that his people at home sometimes get such brief news that they go up to our place to hear my letters I write a lot to Mary because—well you understand how it is with us. I simply have to write long ones to her—but because she gets long letters from me don't you be disappointed if none comes for you sometimes. And if you feel you would like to send me a letter occasionally I am sure I will only be too pleased to write to you sometimes when there is time and when I can.

I expect you are becoming regular adept at painting now Perhaps someday you will honour us with a master piece from your brushes There is no telling what may happen is there? Remember what I have been trying to tell you.

Your sincere friend,

Arthur

While Ben was in Malta at least 75 men from A Coy on charges for December January 1916 in Egypt—Source Australian War Memorial

---

25.1.16.

Hospital previously a school—upstairs verandahs also wards. Believe my stay in Malta is coming to a close, my only regret is that I couldn't send Mother any lace. But 2/– per week won't go far and although some used to sell the hospital blankets to the Maltese for 5/– a pair—I can't come at it. I was sent off to All Saints Convalescent camp today to get a little hardened for the trip. Dreary place. Got out of it as soon as possible and went long walk with Luck

---

26.1.16

Marched with a draft to the Customs House having been refitted with Tommy Uniforms and black boots and put on board the *Bornu*; we set out in a glassy sea for Alexandria,

We were accompanied by the *Acorn* a snappy looking destroyer which would now and then whirl away into the distance to interview some suspicions—bottle or a stick floating in the water to see if it was a submarine or not. Generally not.

As usual sanitary arrangements shocking. We are just herded and there

HMS Acorn.

are only 6 washing basins and no washing water. Ship also very lousey.

27.1.16.

A naval Lieutenant came on board today and had an interesting chat. He was a decent chap, and didn't mind talking to us—not like 99% of English officers—ashamed to talk to a Private. He told us that they thought the German Submarine Base was somewhere around Crete.

28.1.16.

Had an interesting day. At 6 this morning the *Blenheim*, another troop boat started firing, and a distant boat replied so we cracked on full speed and managed to do 10 knots. The *Blenheim* signalled submarine and soon we saw distant white waves, which in 20 minutes or so appeared to be destroyers converging on us in a circle. It was a great sight to see, these Bull pups with spray being thrown right over their funnels and a wake of bubbles behind them.

How they appeared on the scene so quickly amazes me. But nothing more was seen of Mr. Sub and we slept in our life-belts that night but the throb of our engines making us do 10 knots prevented anyone from sleeping.

Teitzel gave Luck and myself some bread, jam, butter, gin, a tin opener and candles a piece.

29.1.16

Some rock scorpions, natives of Gibralter, on deck today kicked up a row. Alexandria: Last night one of the submarines guard dropped his rifle over board. Housie or Lotto greatly played on troop ships, and Banker about fairest of gambling games. Sea like glass.

ALEXANDRIA

30.1.16.

Disembarked at Alexandria, the land of Sin, Sun, Sorrow and Sand and without any kit were put into trains at 9.00pm and arrived at Abassaiah on 1st February.

I am in the base detail at Zeitourn. This is the dumping ground for the A.N.Z.A.C. army. As we were just loafing around I requested leave to Cairo and met up with some of the old Battalion and they told me that they are now at Tel-el-Kebir.

Cairo has changed for the better since I left in November. There is a large canteen run by Australian Ladies in the Esphegai Gardens and there I wended my way for a feed and a rest. I am becoming fitter and stronger each day and more used to the hard food.

Applied for issue of AIF clothing to stop chi—acking from others. I'm a wreck, puttees frayed at the bottoms looking like whiskers around a draught horses feet and short trousers, breeches being cut open when I was wounded and a Tommy cap which is no good for the Gippo sun.

3.2.16

Route marched out into the desert but had to fall out as was too soft—chicken diet in Malta doesn't make good marching muscles. I must write to Sister Harris who was so good to me there.

TEL-EL-KEBIR

5.2.16

Lieut. Kellaway, a reinforcement officer to 1st Battalion, whom I knew

Ben having a hair cut at Tel-el-Kebir .Bill Hunt standing

at Liverpool came along and collected details for 1st Battalion and we entrained for Tel-el-Kebir. I entrained by wheedling the Sgt. Major and giving him 20 piastres. He didn't want me to go back to the Battalion but it is no good messing around, the Battalion seems a home. There were miles and miles of tents there; it seems as if the whole A.I.F. was encamped.

Re-joined the old Battalion and back to my old A Company. Reported to Sergeant Shaw and between us I was reclothed once more as an active service soldier. Back to the old Battalion—you might say back home! As tents are crowded, for those who wish, they have permission to make a nightly temporary reed bivouac. Art Felton and I did this with reed mats against the Quarter masters shed.

YMCA 6.2.16

Dear Frank, Art has been giving me an awful shaking up about not writing oftener to you. It appears you seem very disappointed and down in the dumps through not receiving more letters from me. You know Arthur is a marvel at letter writing and writes often as he is a very high state of perfection which I could not ever hope to attain.

Don't let yourself imagine my regard for you is growing cold. Since

leaving home I have found out the value of friends and who are my
true friends. There is not an hour in the whole day that I think of you.
What is SHE doing now and I reckon back 8 ½ hours and knowing
your customs can fairly trace your doings though thousands of miles
distant. So now little Pal don't be hard on me. I'll write more oftener in
future and don't you worry or grieve if no letter comes for I'm always
thinking of you and of Tarro and your home where perhaps I've spent
the happiest days of my uncoloured existence.

Egypt, the land of 4 S's, Sun, Sand, Sin and Sorrow, after all is a kind
of home to the Australians. I felt like coming home when I disembarked
from the *Bornu* at Alexandria Do you remember Frank, that night I
came late at night from Liverpool Camp. You had a cold and were in
bed with a rosy fire at your head and we drank coffee and ate cakes until
late at night. How good your Mother was to Art and I those times and
how little we deserved it after all. I'm afraid she thinks I'm a good boy
like Art. I must write to her but really I use up all my news in writing
my infrequent skimpy letters to you. Even my people at home go up to
Feltons when they require news of my doings.

How is your frizzled forelock—for goodness sake don't alter it. It's
you alright when I see that. I think I'll have to grow one so as Peter can
pull me up to Heaven by it for this trip hasn't improved my morals I'm
sure.

Don't you have revenge on me by not writing for I look forward to my
little Pal's letters just as much as I do those from my own Mother. One's
best friend is our mother. I've proved that over and over again since I
started this tourist trip to the war.

By Jove, it is a peculiar feeling to be under fire, especially if anyone is
hit alongside you. A little shiver goes down your spine and that is all you
feel. You feel as if you own the world. And when you are hit thoughts of
everyone you love crowds into your brain for an instant. I wasn't like the
chap who when asked what it felt like to be hit he said *Oh I remember a
streak of lightning, then "Sit up and take this"* it was the nurse who told him
to sit up.

Keep some good horses handy should we come home before

Christmas will you and condescend to come out riding next time. You know you seemed scary last time. Do you remember how Blackie tried to roll in your father's saddle out in the lawn in front of the house.

Did Gertrude go up to Tarro? Tell me straight out your impression of her. Am I at all like her in any way, speech or habit. She is a real good sister to me, always writing and she savvy things others don't. I hope she didn't see any of my letters or that you didn't say much about me while she was up there. I saw by last mail I rec'd some more Newcastle boys in the columns. What did you think when you saw my name in the paper, shivvery?

This scribe is a bit longer than usual isn't it but what about Art's 16 pager? It is just as well we go and get our letters signed ourselves. One of my brother Sergeants of 7th-1st and great pal of mine, left for the front a fortnight before us and I had the job of destroying his letters etc, has now received a commission, a 2nd Lieut. so now he signs without reading them. We just say there is nothing injurious to military affairs. That saves us a lot of time doesn't it. He has been using his eyes and sometimes when in private calls us respectively Miss F and Miss M. He is also going to count Art's letters to Mary for me.

Today we received orders to pack up as we are evidently going to some other camp a short way off. Art won't destroy any of Mary's letters so he has several HUGE piles.

Are any of those painting yet adorning the walls at *Oaklands*? They would doubtless enhance the place. How does the Sulky brought from Grafton run, have you taken any gate off with the hubs of the wheels yet.

Can you always understand my writing? We are very crowded here, the chap on my left is writing to Dearest Lottie and on the right the other chap is stringing yarns to his father. What a lot of good these YMCA have done in this war. Half the letters written home would never have been written only for paper, ink and places to write supplied by them. Immediately you enter the door there are couple of placards:

WHEN DID YOU WRITE HOME LAST

and

"A" Coy blanket inspection

DOESN'T SHE DESERVE A NOTE NOW

and the chap in charge always helps you when they can.

How did Joe get on about that cash? I still hear of him being at Tarro. I suppose you all have given him another chance. In my last scribble I enclosed a maltese 1/3 farthing I hope you get it.

Egypt is a great historic place. We do our drill and battle formations over a battle field famous in history when an English General turned, what seemed like defeat into a glorious victory and utterly routed the Malide. There is a great grave yard (out of bounds) where all the English soldiers who fell are buried and it is kept well in order. We passed it when coming here in the train and it is so green and cool.

Thank you pet, for all you did to make my Xmas more home like and your mother and the girls—who helped in parcels. It is just like your Mother to help in doing anything for the good of others and incidentally Art and myself.

This is what I call a spanking letter. That note that Claire wrote to me some time ago came just as I was having my worst time in hospital and it cheered me up a lot. My honourable marks are well out of sight, thank heaven. I wouldn't like to have been marked in some visible place.

I think I will close now Old Pal. I never mind your Mother reading my letters Frank but I don't like others doing so. For often meanings are misconstrued when they don't know what has gone before. Besides I always have the tired feeling I'm sorry to say and it saves me a letter to her as I should do.

Your Soldier Boy Ben....Take care of yourself. Give my best respects to Mr Niland—my love to all royal chicabiddies at *Oaklands* Ben.

6.2.16 Tel—el—Kebir

Dear Frank,

I re-joined my Battalion yesterday and met Art and all my 7th of 1st friends. I was handed 2 letters from you, all the rest are chasing me round somewhere. I hope you are not thinking hard of me, little pal, but you know whilst in hospital I had rather a rough time and did not feel inclined for writing although your presence was always in my thoughts, don't make any mistake about that.

18.12.15, Tuesday night are the 2 dates on the letters so you can see they are fairly recent. It is very kind of you to give Gertrude one of you precious pictures, I'm sure she doesn't deserve it.

If I even said in any of my letters that it doesn't rain in Egypt I made a mistake. It rained cats and dogs and small sized butcher boys here last night and only for one Briton getting out of the tent and digging a trench around it our clothes would have floated away. Only a little wet came in though.

'Tis glorious seeing new peoples and customs, all strange etc. My diary ought to be worth reading when I come back.

It is quite possible we might all be home for next Christmas. I hope so anyway. The mud around this place is awful today. I hope the

Ben's photo of Tel-el-Kebir camp. Camp tents in the distance.

sun will come out hot so as to clear it away.

Art is on guard today. I rec'd some photos from home and they were just what I wanted. Did you hear of that awful accident in Wahroonga with a rifle in which Harold Dean was shot? I read about it today and it is too awful to think about. I enclose 1/3 of a farthing, a Maltese coin.

Please remember me to all at Tarro I hope to spend many good days there yet.

BC

7.2.16.

Route marched and skirmished out into the desert, picked up cartridges used by Arabi Pasha's army. This desert has seen more than one British Army but this is the first time Australian troops have been here–Sudan contingent also of course. Nearly dead with fatigue and my new boots are too stiff yet. Wrote home to Frank explaining why not writing. Art writes every 2nd night. Full pack parade this afternoon.

9.2.16

Great trouble getting cubby house erected in the rain/skirmishing and shooting. No more targets using tiles or tins but pieces of wood shaped like heads, good fun and better practice than targets. Art and I curl up and sleep like dead men in our demountable bivouacs. I'm getting hard and very bronzed. Short trousers are a comfort.

In Sgt Gorry's Platoon..

10.2.16

A wager was made today between Art, Ben, Rupe and William Hunt. If Arthur does not marry Miss Niland within the period of one year from the above date, he will treat the aforesaid gentleman and their partners to a Dinner Theatre party and supper. If Arthur Felton does marry Miss Niland, Ben Champion pays for Dinner, Rupe Neil for Theatre and Billy Hunt Supper. All three signed

11.2.16

From hammock behind camp, fine view across canal where barges sail all day long. Green country beyond with waving palm trees in distance, then desert again. Miss A Smith sent me book for Christmas, wrote home thanking her on 9.2.16.

11.2.16.

Colonel Heane from Dubbo has taken over the 1st as our C.O. and already is making us a unit worthwhile. He doesn't smile, has a very dour look but he is fair and just towards everyone.

Dolly Rowland lost us in the desert on a night march and although many could have found their way home we did a perisher out in the desert without blankets or food. We came home at daybreak and routed the

Ben at Tel el Kebir.

Battalion drills. Tel el Kebir. Bens photo.

cooks out.

We have ceremonial drill and it breaks the monotony of form fours etc. Detached for duty on the sweet water lakes. The Canal and banks are very green but anyone found swimming in the canal is crimed. Something is wrong with the water and boils come out on the skin and after bathing—

Possibly Ginger Smith and Fred Thompson

what a nice country.

Paid a visit to Tel-el-Kebir cemetery. It is beautifully kept, the shady palms are nice, I wrote home from there today. Not forgetting that buried around me were men—real men.

Met Ginger Smith and Fred Thompson today, both look very well, especially the latter, who has been looking after artillery horses since April 15 at Alexandria.

A cinema show was put on and though it was poor we enjoyed it very much ... It doesn't take much to amuse the troops.

13.2.16.

The dear old Battalion was split into 2 today, half of the old hands going to form the 53rd Battalion, so they took over their share of the Laurels the 1st Bn gained.

Col. Heane, said we had in future to consider the 53rd Battalion as our blood-brothers. Fortunately I was picked to remain in the 1st Battalion. Geldhard, H Brewer, Arch Black, Lt. E.I.C. Scott and Rupe Neil went to the 53rd. Art (Felton) to B Section 53rd Batt but asked for transfer back to original Batt. The two Battalions now up to full strength.

Letters received today. We were all on railway fatigue today, so got our share of the good jam and left the A.S.C. to mourn over their Apricot remainder. The Apricot is awful muck, it isn't necessary to cut the tin open all you have to do is puncture 2 holes like in a milk tin, and it runs out if it doesn't spurt in your eye when you puncture the holes.

The cigarette issue is looking up and our canteens have everything required. It's a blessing I don't have to live on 2/– like at Malta.

———

19.2.16.

Received sox from V. Lansdowne.

———

YMCA 19.2.1916

Dear Frank,

I have received 22 letters within the last 2 days not a bad score only they should have reached me long ago judging by the different post marks and the dates in which they were written. Between October 4 and December 30 were the dates.

You still seem to be making plenty of life out of the inhabitants of Tarro or the Tarroites as you sometimes call them. Why do you want Miss Forrest to call me Mister? I'm still only a kid worse luck, not yet 19, just imagine it and here in Egypt and have been potting at Turks on Gallipoli.

Pleased to see you took an active part in Welcoming, was it the Wallabies or Cooees. You'll have to take a very active part if I come home (hang that if). All day long out enjoying ourselves. What a time the quartet will have.

What do you intend to do with that blind foal, will it ever be able to do work like other horses. You will look flash in that painted Sulky. Don't let it be damaged before we come home.

There seems to be nothing doing on any front at present and no hope of anything in or around Egypt. We struck tents today so the sun could get at the sand and kill any microbes—also microbes with feet.

Have you seen some of the pictures I sent home? Father writes

Frank and the blind foal

to me, said that if you come to Felton's for a stay you might perhaps visit our place for a while. It is hard to imagine Didie looking at the masculine gender at all. Perhaps you all thought about her as you did about me at first. Didie *Oh Mrs Niland, Ben is such a shy boy*. Yes I am very backward at coming forward when the ladies are about eh!

So Mary is no longer a flapper. I heard accidently from Art that she has her hair up. I can't say how he feels on the matter, only it will be awkward now if ever you want to swop dresses like you used to do. I suppose hers are slightly longer than usual.

There must be very little work done when the Egyptian mail comes in. I can imagine it very well. How is it that you and Mary don't hit it off very well together? I'm continually hearing about one or the other.

The boys at Liverpool seem to be very rowdy. Why don't the authorities knock a little discipline into them like what has been hammered into us. The army can do anything to you and one can't wink.

That little bit of Xmas bush you put in your letters reminds me how I used to go out in Wahroonga, in the heat and gather it by the arm loads. Is there any particular meaning in Xmas bush? I know Mary often puts in violets and wattle or some bouquet.

We can't say a thing about our future plans or else our letters will be 'mafish 'and that is no good to anyone. We've been enlisted 9 months now and that seems a long while to us here.

Motor Cars in Tarro! Eh! That's something new. How does

Rev John Dykes, pioneer Parson of Jerilderie.

Blackie act now when a motor goes by? It hard to imagine the swamp dry. You must have had a dry Christmas indeed. Though I suppose there was plenty of fodder for the Beasts as my Uncle calls them (Scottish Rev. Dykes) If there was Mutton or Beef on the table he used to say in the rough slow voice *'Now Bun what will you haaave Beast or Mutton?'*

How dare you address me as Bennie, that's forbidden or else you know Juli .... How is Phil getting on? Enlisted yet like his brother Bert? Ray is the one Ruth likes isn't he? (Franks cousins, the Carroll brothers) How is Ruth? Just as large as life I suppose. Did she pass the qualifying certificate?

You don't like kisses or used not too so I seldom put any in but you deserve a dose now. Give my love to all at home. Keep all my letters dark Xxxxxx to be paid in reality someday

Ben

22.2.16.

Just drilling etc. Cairo leave given, but seen enough of the place. More rumours re France. Mr Mackenzie taking A Coy. Beavis seems to be 2nd in Command.

Received papers and mail from Frank. Can't make Frank out, while I'm away, she seems to be as good as possible to me. When at home appeared to have tired feeling. Billy Hunt very cut up about having very crook letter from his girl. Getting dont give a damn feeling like I have now.

Harry Brewer, Arch Black and Geldard and Rupe Neil all recommended for commissions. Thank God I am no longer in Capt. Rowlands company, he was nicknamed Dolly, typifies the man. On the peninsula he put fear into the men more than he inspired them by his actions in the trench and the ridiculous way which he kept the trenches clean. One night 11.30pm he woke Tom Mackley and told him there was some loose paper outside his dugout.

The latrines on the Peninsula really seemed so clean and comfortable in comparison to those at Liverpool. Those in authority evidently knew what it is that caused sickness, the flies and so all latrines had lids on.

23.2.16.

Skirmished over the desert and ended up by charging the old trenches of Tel-el-Kebir. Saw Bruce Rainsford and Harold Kershaw.

24.2.16

Went to Cairo with Art on 12 hours leave and spent all my money. 7 successes; Pictures, 3 of inspections and 4 groups. Obtained suit of clothes from Bruce. No money yet in Cairo.

Wrote Mother, Frank, Miss Landsdowne, Field Service A Macdonald, Post Card Grandma, note Kitty, 53 Battalion sports. News came through to pack up.

25.2.16

Dear Pal,

I received more letters from you this week with some mails and a little parcel with the paper in it on which I am writing. Pleased to hear all well at *Oaklands* but very sorry to hear your grandfather not too well. He must be a fair age. (Peter Carroll of Windsor).

If this letter is somewhat disjointed just blame my tent mates who are playing a rowdy game of cards. We are sleeping rather a lot per tent now but I believe when I get to sleep you can stand me up against the tent pole, I can sleep anywhere.

I don't know if lately our letters have been coming through, some trouble at the base in connection with our Battalion but Art and I have been using our knuts so perhaps they creep through.

Art and I had 24 hours leave so slipped into Cairo quite a long run in the train. Some money was sent to me to Cairo and after waiting some 2 hours was told it hadn't yet come back from Malta. I had it transferred there when I was crook.

With hats, Carl Waugh , Billy Hunt, possibly Newing and Rupe Neil in front

Without hats, Ben (top left), Billy Hunt, Newing and Rupe Neil in front

Art is getting lots of papers from Tarro and we all enjoy then muchly The run into Cairo was through the pick of irrigated Egypt and the growths looked so green, a real emerald green, just like the country around the Patterson River.

I met a chap in the tent who lives not far from Krambach and he said we were fools cycling over the mountain, so we were, but if it hadn't been for that trip, Yours truly would never have met a young person whose initials are FJN

27.2.16.

Reveille 4 a.m. Packed up and moved per usual cattle truck covered with the manure. Train started and soon got on to Suez Canal Bank after going through some beautifully green country. Oranges 2 for a half a piastre

Tel-el-Kebir railway station

seems O.K.

Passed several camps, one Gurkas, one Sudanese, Sudanese fine big men around the shoulders but have skinny legs. About 2 p.m. came to Serapeum the other side of the Suez, over which we passed by pontoons made by the Naval Brigade. Now in Asia.

Pitched camp about mile from the Suez Canal. The Canal was lined by sand bag trenches among the fir or pine trees on the bank so that if attacked the defenders had a beautiful field of fire. Canal seemed about 100 yards wide here.

Birdwood says he is keeping the Australians here until they learn discipline. I suppose he means drill discipline for there is no lack of discipline under fire.

Monday 28.2.16.

Usual fatigues when building camp, then marched dawn to the Suez and all Brigade lined up for swimming parade.

Some of us swam across to the other side, but I was too tired to swim back my leg being stiff, and had to walk about 2 miles and across by the bridge. In the suit of clothes I was born in I did feel a fool. Art swam from Asia to Africa and back again. There is a big current setting towards Suez in the Canal.

There is a small grave yard near here, full of Turks. They were killed trying to get across the Canal in steel pontoons which they had dragged or carried. I don't know how many hundreds of miles.

Suez Camp with pine trees

Just before we came the graves had been robbed—it was traced to the Military Police. My blood boils when I see those Red Caps. I can't understand why, but they are such a low lot and the things they do to get their own people into trouble are awful.

29.2.16.

Today we had kit inspection and all surplus clothing beyond the exact issue was confiscated. We are only allowed 3 prs of socks so from the look of things it won't be long before we move.

Notice the date; leap year! Have had no proposals yet.

A large Argyllshire liner passed through the Canal today.

Sgt Maj Pegg picked me to be promoted to the glorious rank of Lance Corporal but hope it's only the first step up. Lance Corporal Cassidy now Sergeant. I take Cass's place. I've a good section, all good chaps.

Capt AC Mackenzie is our new Captain and Lieut Beavis is 2nd Command. Australians too cute for officers and buried all spare kit under tent.

Took 10 prints and 5 films in at Opera Square. Wonder when will be able to get them. Had another swim in Canal-very cold.

Alice Eve's birthday

1.3.16.

Shivered all night, very cold. In the night saw the *Franconia* pass up the Canal all ablaze with lights. Marched to a new camp called Fairy Post—seems to be a good joint. A company on its own has an easier time. Our job is to supply picquet posts out in the deserts.

Swimming parade, Suez Canal.

Picquet duty in the desert. Ben's photo

Trenches in the desert Ben's photo - tents in the background

One scheme is to tie bushes and a blanket to a camel's tail and drive him up our sectors front, then we can easily see on our patrols if anyone crosses it in the night.

These outpost stations are to stop individual Turks creeping through our lines and causing havoc on the Canal works.

At daybreak we march back to camp for food, a swim and then sleep. In all, a wonderful military holiday

———

2.3.16

Parade this morning very sandy....Major Roberts proving himself worse than Dolly Rowlands. Something tells me something going to happen, either action or home.

Wrote Mother and Bruce, he to send films home and prints to me. Last thing called out to outpost. Rather a beastly night, very fine sand which continually blew down our clothes.

Guard over portion of canal over which Turks advanced last year. Grave of Major von dem Hagen who was shot etc. Someone evidently dug up his body for what the clothes contained. Lots of boots and bandages, bits of clothing etc. Bones lying around.

Took photo of our trenches here.

Lent Mr Beavis 3 films –hope get them back, must remind him re them. Received letter Miss Smith, 4 from Home, Sent Field Service Card to Smith and home. Innoculated against Typhus. Went to doctor to get quinine, slight dose of malaria.

The *Mooltan* went through and we swam out towards her and people threw down tins of cigarettes and tins of Cadbury's chocolates to us. Nice gifts, greatly appreciated.

We are as brown and as hard as nuts now. I'm putting on weight. Can't tell if the moustache I've grown makes me any heavier but I can stick the ends with bacon fat now in lieu of Pomade wax.

Wonder if we will go to France, there are rumours of India or France. Hope its India; I'd like to go there. Last night we swept across the desert and this morning found a native had crossed it, so we hunted his footsteps down and got him and handed him over to the A.P.M. I don't think he looks intelligent enough to be a spy.

Some of us sewed our blankets into a bag and wriggle into them at night, but found we couldn't turn out of them quick enough.

5.3.16

Dear Frank,

Letters date 21.1.16 to hand Tuesday. Am all alone in the tent tonight all the others are on duty, outpost or picket etc. so I ought to be able to write you a long letter.

For the last few nights I was so overworked, so that is why I'm here on my lonely. I had 4 letters today, the first for 15 days and feel quite overjoyed. It is miserable here now, though we have a swim each day.

A couple of big naval cargo boats passed today with some native craft. That was all the extra life we saw. The war seems to be progressing favourably though. I'm afraid we will never see any more action, worse luck.

The fine Arabian sand penetrates our clothes and tucker so that often we have to heave out our boiled meat and only drink the gravy. But you must not think I'm growling at anything except being kept here and doing nothing. Why can't we have a smack at the brutes in Europe—that is what we are all dying to do.

Now I'll take your advice and not mind the censor xxxxxxxxxxxxxxxxx will those do you until the next note? You have changed. For the better it seems. Why do you only put Tuesday or Monday—please old girl put in the date as well on your letters.

Who is Reg? Where did you sit him at the table and where Didie? Said she is coming out of her shell 'Masqiuish 'very. Are many men enlisting now the fighting is over?

We have 4 camels with us on this outpost to carry water and provisions and they cause such a lot of bother. The driver is native and can't understand English so you can imagine how we have to gesticulate when we want anything done. They are really savage brutes and make horrible gurgling noises when they get up. They seem to have 4 joints in their legs.

Brough bottom left and four camels.

I still have your big scarf. I couldn't leave it after you made it though it takes up such a lot of room. The swim each day is of great importance in our lives here; if we didn't have it we would feel we had missed out.

I'm sorry you have been getting indigestion—it is rather nasty complaint—Have you tried drinking a cup full of hot water for it? Do you remember how I used to take a cup each morning out of that big fountain when up at your place.

Besides all this rot stopping in doing guards etc. we sometimes run up against a snag. Another Coy caught a couple of spies lately. The only suspicious chap I've ever bumped is the Orderly Officer and I soon made him put his hands above his head although I knew him.

So Blackie has a sore back. I hope you gently gave some advice to Mr Daley. I've just been looking over a Sydney paper and saw some hospital ship pictures. You cannot know what it is like to go home. I wish Art and I could return now. Just imagine us walking up George Street again. I wonder what it would be like. Will I ever settle down to dentistry again or will I what?

Have many changes occurred in Tarro? It seems years and years have passed since I left though it is not even one year yet. Don't let them at home know the length of this letter as I'm sorry to say I've only sent skimpy letters home lately.

A fox terrior trying to preach instead of Mr Mather in Church. Did you never see such fun? I bet you girls giggled like wild fire. How good to go to bed instead of doing your work, do you know when we get back I think I'll hire a boy to blow *Reveille* and then you see, I can throw something at him and tell him to bag his head. The getting up of a morning is the strain *Oh it's a fair cow*(as the chaps say).

Art and I have not yet gone up the scale as regard to NCO or Commissioned rank and there is not a hope either. Didn't we dream things once? We have both had broken hearts and spirits, since in a way no letters for Art today and I know there should be some for him as mine came.

I see Gertrude still sends you the GOP(Girls Own) that's right. I hope they are quite up to the mark. I often used to read bits of them when I came home from work. What soft times I used to have then and what an ass a man is to enlist.

I'll have to close now Pet, Love and all that you wish yourself, Ben.

———

5.3.16

Before we went to the Peninsular one of our men Cunneen deserted. He was sent back yesterday for identification. He was caught in Shepherd Hotel dressed as an officer and for 3 months has led a fine life. Don't know how he got the money to carry the game on with though. Found out today that Johnnie Sheridan was killed at the landing. Wrote Mother, Gertrude in her last letter put Champion after her signature evidently thinks I write to more than one Gertrude.

———

6. 3. 16.

We are going to France and all five Australian Divisions will be fighting together. Won't that be good!

Had a lecture by Col. Heane when we re-joined the Battalion giving us a fine talk on France; its history and tradition, and he made it quite interesting. He asked us to remember that we were going among men and women, some of whom had lost all their property, and most of them had some relative killed at the war. We were to be polite and to mask our language when we get there. Some of the chaps are a bit lurid, but they don't mean what they say, some of the phrases are funny though.

He suggested that we should start a box in each section and the person who used certain words being fined by the tent. The collection to be used for some entertainment which the whole tent could enjoy. We have started something similar in our tent; the person who used ... word was to be punched until he counted 10. Scotty got first punch.

Art seems very miserable, indeed seems sick, same old Cowans cough. A balaclava cap posted on 1ˢᵗ July 1915 reached me 6 March 1916 not bad going—just eight months.

Some excitement happened today to relieve the monotony of existence. Some Red-Caps (Military Police) raided a harmless Two Up School right away from the lines. The news spread like magic and soon hundreds of chaps were around them-exit the Military Police. Everyone thought some damage would be done to them. But they chose discretion better than valour and left calmly.

7. 3.16.

On patrol with Sgt Tindale—more rows of Turks were dug up, some chaps must be gruesome. Pity where Turks had fought so hard their bones should be left in peace. Several big boats passed in the night. They go dead slow so that their wash won't disturb the canal banks.

Our Major Roberts is the Major who used to command the 19ᵗʰ Battalion.

8. 3.16

Another lecture—this time by company officers telling us to salute when we address a French girl or when we enter a shop. Our rifles taken away and new high velocity rifles issued, but they don't seem to be finished off as well as the old rifles. I like the desert life, the heat agrees with me and we are harder than any nails could possibly be.

9. 3.16.

Am now a Lance Corporal viz a baksheesh corporal. Instructions about rations today. Menu: Breakfast, Bacon 2 'x 1½ ' 1½ x 3/18 ', M Tea, bread and apricot Lunch, stew half filled with blowing sand and then bread, Tea cheese, tea, bread and apricot. (I won't say Jam)

The Gippos have different rank or so it seems to me. Some raise hand to forehead and some halfway and some bob their foreheads and so on, according to caste I think.

We have a fine team of Officers who pull well with the men and inspire confidence in themselves. They are Prior, Bootle, Beavis, Gill, Mackenzie, Major Roberts, many tales told about the latter re him being the *Galloping Major*.

10.3.16.

Issued with cigarettes, in packets instead of tins. Cigarette cards are little books with French and English words, clever isn't it and handy too.

Sunday 12.3.16

Church service, the chaplain spoke most strongly against strong language. Only too true. The language is awful consequently we had a discussion, very heated one, afterwards in the tent. On quarter Guard. Inlying piquet called out re some stranger footprints across the swept tracks. In a sand storm, after dismissal rushed our tents and closed all doors etc. A couple of hours later when it had died down found that sand was banked up to height of 18 'around the tent.

Church parade.—Ben's Photo

12.3.16

Dear Pal,

A couple more of your welcome letters to hand yesterday (Saty) addressed as Sergeant. A Coy 1st Batt. Please don't address them like that again for I know I wrote you stating that I had been placed in the ranks like Art. (Split of 1st Battalion) You cannot understand the mistake but Pvt. is quite sufficient.

I've just come in from church parade, rather a solemn service as we know not where our next service will be. We will be idle no longer in a few weeks' time.

In the issue of cigarettes is a little French dictionary and they are coming in very handy. Little bits of doggerel French are being shouted about. Well the camp we are in is an awful place ¾ bottle of water per diem, and no place to wash. We are all dirtier than pigs, and the dust! Battalion tactics this morning A being a flank Coy and had all the doubling to do

This spot is to be a permanent camp later on I think for they have been cementing a place for showers. It is funny to have a bath with a Dixie of water Had bully beef today for dinner, supposed to be no fresh meat in upper Egypt through transports being taken up with troops.

What about the 1 ½ page letter I sent you some time ago. I think the censor must have taken some off the bottom. Was my signature there?

I also got a note from Claire and Kitty, thank them for me and I'll write from our next destination. Alas no more shorts and pantaloons as we have to conform to British Regulations.

You headed your last letter Dearest and Best. How many dearests and worsts have you known since I left? Well Didie has had a long stay at Tarro. I'm pleased about it and so is Art. She must deserve a holiday.

There is a peculiar insect here, its shell is very, very hard and as soon as it hears a boot it curls up and scarpers under the sand and you can't see its legs moving.

Thank heaven I've good teeth, bread is so hard and crunch, crunch goes the sand and pebbles as you eat. What will it be like to come home? I'm sorry your Mother gets knocked up with the hot weather; she wouldn't like living here then on one half bottle of water.

My face is alright, no shell could hurt my dial. It is as hard as iron on the shell itself. I'm sorry you objected to my showing one of your letters to a chap on Gallipoli but there was nothing in it not fit to be seen.

If Mary is going to learn the Organ, why don't you learn the piano, now do, just because I want you too, that's a good pal. I can't play and I miss it a lot.

You must have had a lot of hay if you have sent 18 tons away to Newcastle. I'd like a little painting just smaller than a Post Card. You say you ought to see the Tarro lassies out on a Friday night. I only want to see one Tarro lassie and she is good enough for me when she is nice and affable. She has a curl right in the middle of her forehead.

How would you like to be in the middle of desert miles from anywhere and the dust as thick as pea soup? We are always talking about what to do when we get back into civilian clothes. I wish the wretched war would finish and let us get home. We are all waiting in suspense to go somewhere. I'll close now Pet,

love Ben

Please put date as well.

13.3.16.

Inspected by Birdy, after which we went to Musketry. Nasty accident occurred; an N.C.O. was killed so we were marched home. Oh, if only we had the nice cool reed huts we had at the Heliopolis I could stop here a long while. We were very comfortable in those days. Tuesday Heane said we ought to be moving in a couple of days.

14.3.16

I went this afternoon for a spin per the electric train which draws dozens of trucks every day out towards the trenches further out into the desert Beyond where I went are lines of trenches garrisoned by Indian troop in case of a Turkish raid They extend 9 miles right across the Sinai Peninsula. They are in turn, covered by our Light Horse. Garrisoned Indians, Tommies, Australians. Ten miles out from Seraphim. There is also a good solid road the whole way made by engineers and Turk prisoners.

Miles on miles of camel trains come in from nowhere every day. Indian Camel Corps saddles built for 2 men. Bite of a camel supposed to give wound. Ryan and Kennedy field Court Martial. Lynch up for murder. Pioneer Battalion formed.

Glorious horses here. Seems pretty certain we go to France. Hope men behave themselves. Mr Bootle had Scotty up for orderly Room 27 days. CB Special Brigade machine gun Corps formed and now to Battalion. Received nice cheerful letter from Sister Harris c/– Cammerata Valletta Malta.

15.3.16.

Inoculated against typhoid fever again.

16.3.16

Billy Hunt first Corporal. Letter from Malta saying money in Cairo.

Light horse, putting horses into train

19.3.16

Visit from the Prince of Wales and Staff. He seems a nice little chap, rode well, very high horse, escort of Generals, seemed about 30 of them. He looked about 17. He ought to be able to catch the girls. He had a colour like a red apple, has a good figure and is quite pretty. He gave us a day's spell so we hoped he'd come again. I had hard luck. I took out my camera to snap but it was choked with sand. Kit inspection, surplus taken away. Wicked to see socks etc. being burned instead of being stored.

21.3.16

Full pack, moving off, marched to the rail head and entrained in open trucks, 42 in mine, awfully cramped, as night fell, moved off. Gee it was cold and no blankets. Our legs were cramped sumthink hawful. How I wished then that they were detachable ones so that they could go in pocket. When day light and the sun came we were glad.............and then didn't we get roasted.

Prince of Wales speaking with Col. Heane

23. 3.16

Boarded the old *Ivernia*, a huge Cunard liner, whole Battalion aboard, we are over strength too. The troop decks were fitted with bunks so we made ourselves comfortable. Had to give up my camera, not allowed to take them on board with us, hard luck but I'll get another somehow when we get there—wherever it is. Our Band gave a display for benefits, and it brought a good number of whites and natives to the boat so we had a good farewell. Drummy Downes was funny.

Inoculated again, very calm. Actually had Australian butter for breakfast but all other meals rotten, the rice seems blue, the bread is not sufficient and the frozen meat badly thawed so that it is tainted and no sugar. We were in a state of mutiny but our officers could do nothing as the old tub had nothing else on board.

24.3.16

Skirting coast on Port side Suppose it is the Northern part of Africa. The boat *Minneapolis* that left after us was sunk. Every day a mock alarm to get us used to alarms.

25.3.16

Sicily sighted. Usual routine

26.3.16

Passed Algiers with prominent light house. Passed 4 steamers and can see our consort of destroyers now and then but know they are looking after us. Boat stations today. We are miles and miles out of our course if we are going to France.

Sergeant WR Yates on Ivernia

Egypt has gone with its 4 or 5 S's It is indescribably dirty but charming—what will France be like? The army is a wonderful organisation. Look at us in the desert. One day sand, in a few days a comfortable little town with rations etc. going like clockwork and even water laid on.

Passed a big 5 masted American ship with all sails set. First time I've seen one at sea and it looked well. How blue is this Mediterranean Sea and at present so calm.

27.3.16

Yesterday we were quite close to Sardinia. It has a very bleak look towards its peaks but in the hollows is vividly green. We dipped our flag to a French packet boat, then getting dark we lost sight of it among the islands around Sardinia. I don't know if we passed in between Sardinia and Corsica but there is land on both sides of us.

About 12 m.d. today we sighted land directly ahead of us and of course speculation ran rife as to what the place was. By 2 pm we could see a red submarine nosing around in front and as the skipper didn't run, knew it was an allied one. Soon we came between headlands and knew what the sub had been doing

This port is guarded by submarine nets and the sub was giving the skipper his course in. The course is changed every now and then. Found that the Port was Toulon. We entered through low breakwaters with old fashioned cannon mounted on them and anchored ½ mile from town.

A fussy little steam launch came alongside and handed the C.O. his orders. It is such a pretty place, every house had a tiled roof and none were mildewed, preserving the new red tiled look. Close cropped lawns were plentiful and if did our eyes good to see such homeliness after sandy gippo land.

The harbour is not deep, for the old *Ivernia* churned up the mud on the bottom. Only destroyers and submarine chasers were in port. I like the look of the chasers. They are about 40' long and built for pace more than sea worthiness and skippered by boys it seemed to me.

Trains came right down to the wharf, loading apparatuses all over the place The trip over took 5 days

Rupe Neil, Billy Hunt and Art Felton

Some members of A Company

France

Tuesday 28.3.16

MY BIRTHDAY 19 YEARS OLD TODAY Stood out to sea and hugged the coast. A big swell running and we were broad side on to it. The *Ivernia* rolled like a porpoise and I was sick—a nice birthday present for me.

About 2pm we came in sight of Marseilles. First thing that met my eyes before entering the harbour was a big church on the summit with a golden angel holding a torch. Railway running around coast crossing solid stone bridges arch style. Marseilles Harbour is artificially made and when we entered we received a great ovation from the French man o war men anchored there. Of course we played *La Marseilles* as we entered to which we all stood.

They replied with *Rule Britannia*, not correctly but heartily played. Plenty of big wharves and machinery with railways handy that is similar to what we are used too in Australia, railways to the wharves.

We got fed up with some Tommies (who came down to see the New Chooms) owing to the fact that we threw coppers down to the French gamins on the wharf and the Tommies would snaffle them.

Women acrobats on wharf. Saw some German prisoners for the first time; they were working on the wharf. They seem awfully clumsy and not quick at all—too well fed. Not sorry to leave boat as starvation on board. Feel sick still. Latrine rumour that we go to Loos.

Left the boat at 9pm and marched through cobble stone streets Oh! Our poor feet, used to the sands of Egypt and boarded the train at 12 m.n.

The French soldiers we saw, who turned out to be old reservists, we thought looked peculiar with red trousers tucked in at the boots and the Royal blue coat turned back and buttoned on the side pockets to give their knees a chance when marching. We never march in overcoats— generally waterproof sheet wrapped around shoulders. They have a very long rifle and bayonet, must be unwieldy I think.

29.3.16

Wednesday We were not too crowded in the train and made ourselves as comfy as possible with blankets and overcoats. The country we are traversing is intensely cultivated up to Tarcasmor and on to Arles. Most buildings tile roofed and in the parks are plenty of cypress pine closely planted forming hedges.

The apple and pear trees were in bloom and really this is about the best time to be here. As we passed through the people were so different to the Gippos and welcomes us right royally and the kiddies thrived on the biscuits we passed to them and they in turn gave us now and then bread The vineyards are fine and we have a lot to learn with regard to cultivation. Here cultivation extends right to the top of the hill tops. Tarcasmor seemed to be the end of the plain country for it started to get very hilly and here were the vineyards. Lots of women working in the fields, wearing bloomers instead of skirts. I suppose they are taking the mobilised men's places.

Often we would come to break—winds of reed fences. The roads are bordered by hedges and there was snow on the distant mountains. Avignon was passed but we stopped at Orange for rations. Huge tubs of coffee were prepared for us and we did enjoy it. Soon we came to the Rhone and passed over dozens of bridges 'til we reached the Chateau du Rhone with a neighbouring very old Chateau right on the top of the mountain with walls around it.

How we appreciated the kindly gifts by the French people. French, very very polite, ladies and gentleman, much appreciated after Egypt. Quietened our chaps down a lot. Women when we get home will be better treated with more respect than they had been before the war.

At noon we came to Valentia, another great welcome, French ladies blowing us kisses, not bold, just doing it out of kindness to us. More coffee royal and bread. At 4pm Lyons came into sight and we proceeded over the many bridges which span the approach. Very cold now and snow often seen on the mountains but also plenty of roses and fruit blossoms. Here were a number of women washing clothes on the river bank.

At 6.30 had tea at Marcon where they put cognac into the coffee to warm us up for the heights trip. German prisoners were on fatigue at railway under escort, dopey, clumsy, uncouth, too solid, cannon fodder.

30.3.16

Flogany was welcome as it broke the monotony and dozens of people turned out to see us pass through. Here on the station were some Australian civilians who had been living in France for a few years and between them they had brought 300 loaves of bread and gave them to the quarter master to be distributed to us.

Very pretty to see acres of primroses and daisies and fruit trees all in bloom Towards 4pm, after passing through Laroche we came towards Paris and we thought we were going to that wonderful city but we circled away towards Versailles.

For the past 20 miles, school kiddies waved and asked for souvenirs and staid looking old men and ladies waved to us, Oh we had a great time. Passing through the Forest of Versailles we came to a glorious lake with a castle overlooking it, here the ill-fated Marie Antoinette lived some time.

Getting tired we settled down for sleep and were awakened early on morning of 31.3.16 at Abbeyville for more coffee. The whole of yesterday, balloons, planes and big guns were seen.

Ben's Photo–The train from Marseilles

At Boulague Sur-Mur we actually saw the North Sea so that we had passed from one sea to another, South to North as tourists. The people here somehow did not seem to be as nice as the Southerners. Hundreds of Huns working around here but they are well guarded. The Guards say they wouldn't run away even if they had the chance, they are too well fed.

28.3.1916 Marseilles. Entrained

We are fed up and depressed—have had enough of travelling and want a spell. Calais next halt and we came to realise that we had crossed France from South to North as tourists. The traffic on the roads around here is marvellous. Lines of lines of motor lorries carrying goods and we saw a battery of anti-aircraft guns mounted on the roadside.

St Omer we detrained. Most of us so stiff that we could hardly move. It was bitterly cold especially for us all coming from Egypt. With our packs up we stepped out our best pace, headed by the band but soon we were straggling—the hard cobble stones after the training on sand in Egypt were our downfall. We sparked up and marched into a pretty village named Wallon Cappel.

31 MARCH 1916 WALLON CAPPEL

1.4.16. April Fools Day.

Billeted in a big old barn with straw on floor and were very cosy. The people are so poor yet clean. Very cold, nevertheless It is a funny affair; on the ridge pole outside are Geraniums and cabbages growing, evidently getting some nourishment out of the straw thatched roof. There is no drunkenness, I'm surprised, after being on the chain so long too I suppose it's because there is so much drink that they don't bother. We can hear the guns all day from here 13 miles away as the crow flies. Had a shave by the village barber who was a lady. Her hubby is at the war so she is carrying on, ordinary yellow soap and a razor like a saw. Old lady and Mademoiselles came and chatted to me. People have a good opinion of us. Went to Billets and had another shave.

Sunday 2.4.16

We can hear the distant continual bombardments going on and last night we could see the occasional gun flashes. Had a good sermon today. *Nothing could take away the love of Christ*. Mohammedanism grounded on a book ie: The Koran, also Christianity. We all marched to a field enclosed by trees and the Padre talked well.

This Battalion looks well and solid and Colonel Heane said he was quite satisfied with us. After church parade, Art and I visited Hazebrouck which is about due east from here. Struck by this pleasant town there are only 2 damaged houses. Made a few purchases and came home tired out.

3.4.16

Had a good bath this morning in a pond down the paddock but Madame went crook when she found out, as she reckons her cows wouldn't drink it afterwards—but she is a nice old soul. In the living room of her farm it's so cosy.

The floor is of red brick and there is a huge stove in the centre so that you can sit all around it. There is a shelf running around where a dado should be and on this are several pieces of china and she is very proud of them. They have religious scenes on them.

We had a gas helmet parade and we marched some distance and were made to don them and enter a trench filled with gas. We have got used to this style of helmet before, but they are superior to the Peninsula ones.

5.4.16

We have been drilling and route marching and are now fairly used to the horrid cobble stones. Today I took a party to Brigade Hqr. at Ebblinghem, west 2 Kilometres from Wallon Cappel.

The roads here are very straight and lined with poplar trees and passed an old Chateau which was moated, we had a good look at it and at the shrines on the roadside. Each family here seems to have a family shrine with statue of Virgin Mary or Baby Christ.

6.4.16 France

Should this reach you about your birthday I wish you all the compliments of the season, hope your next year will be happier and free from all cares .

Ben

Dear little Pal

Well here we are in La Belle France, the culminating point for which all Australian have been aiming. Truly we are 6 shilling a day tourists, the Tommies were right. I've been on 3 continents since last I saw your welcome smile, Africa, Asia, Europe. Africa represented by Heliopolis etc Asia and Europe by good transcontinental tour.

The people here are so polite and kind. They look on us I believe as would be saviours of France and really we have a glorious reputation to keep up. My little French, the amusement of mother and a great stumbling block in my poor school career, has come in very handy. I can understand most of their speech and by their actions and expressions of surprise they can savvy me.

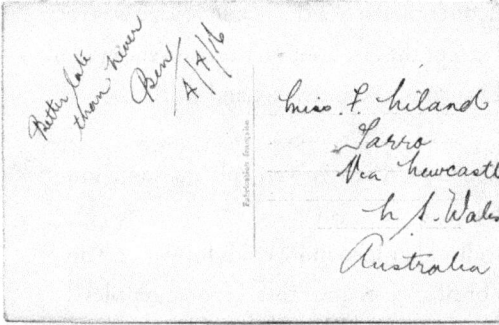

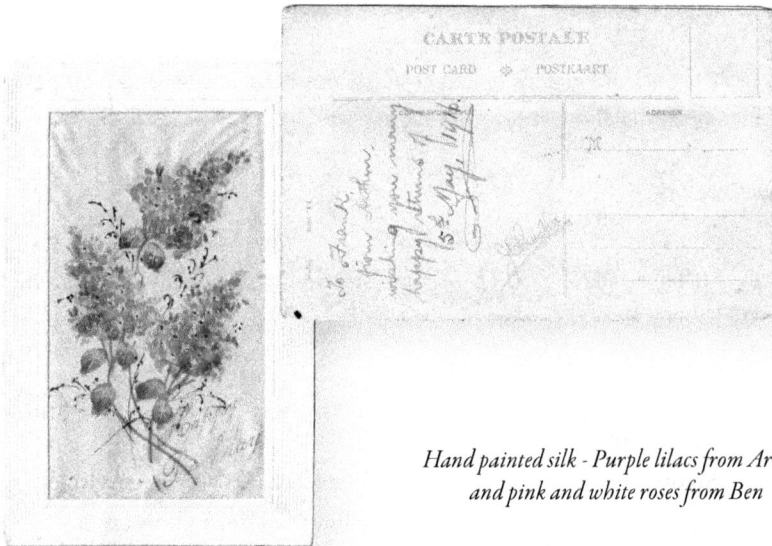

Hand painted silk - Purple lilacs from Arthur
and pink and white roses from Ben

Beer, wine and cake all most superior brands cost only 1d. They seem surprised at there not being a special Australian language. Now if we were to run a few words such as Maroubra, Warrawee, Wahroonga and Tumbarumba etc and someone said Yugilbar as an answer then that would be Aust'n language. They expected it and the Tommies (some of them) were the same.

There is no novel or pretty sights such as at Malta. I wish I was there now. Coming across the Mediterranean Sea the whole voyage was very peaceful, the sea like glass, except the last hour on the anniversary of my birthday and then the boat began to rise and heave and so did I, worse luck.

We are all a jolly crew here now, when we were split up, somehow the rowdies were left behind.

I hope all at home are well, old girl, no more colds for you and no more busters with Creamy or Blackie or any other 4 footed reptiles. I have written another letter but I do not know if it will pass the censor

Love Ben

7.4.16

Dished out with an extra blanket per man—we needed them. New gas helmets tested, no failures.

8.4.16.

Sergeants Brainwood and Cassidy and a few other NCOs were taken up to the line to see things. They came back O.K. and told us all about it. We'll be there shortly now.

8.4.16

Dear Frank,

An opportunity offers to send you a note in Art's green envelope. A couple of days ago I wrote you some lines so I don't know exactly what to say. I rec'd 2 birthday cards, one from Mary and one from you. Thank you to Mary for me will you please and accept same for yourself.

Well old girl I got two letters from you dated 17.2.16, so far none have turned up from home. You said Mary had passed the Intermediate exam, good girl. I failed you know. I'm such a young mug at all clerical and brain work. That exam meant such a lot to me too.

The dogs here are made use of, there are some Belgian refugees who sell chocs etc and they make the dogs pull little carts. Hope you have a good birthday. I was terribly sea sick on mine.

All your last letters mention how hot it is at Tarro. I wish it was hot here. Our cold toes each morning make us creep around like bandicoots.

I'd like to meet all these cousins of yours. I'm getting quite jealous and anxious for your safety what with Reg and Joe. I don't know what to think. Never mind, if they have as good a time at Tarro as I had I don't mind. Sorry to hear of Mr Black's rifle accident, handling one every day as we do there are sometimes accidents.

Your roof leaks you say, well why not get on top and mend it. Oh, what is the use of Reg being up there if he didn't do it. Tiles always were a nuisance and old painted iron is as good as anything I think.

Art says Mary's letters are not up to the mark recently. She used to write such long letters too. You said: I am going to get myself looking pretty. Well I tell you that's no good to me, I've often said I don't like pretty girls and I don't, so stop as you are.

How is your hair. As frizzy as usual? We've all had ours scalped again preparing for action, you see. How is it you always say you are tired. We can't say that in our programme. For last 48 hours. Friday rise 6.15 clean up, breakfast 7.20am, fall in 8, strenuous parade, come home 12, dinner 12.30, warned for guard so have to be extra spruced up and fall in 4.45pm and guard ever since and no sleep at night. We come off guard at 5 tonight. Night parade at 7, sleep 9.15. Such is life for us.

Can I imagine myself eating any of your glorious pork again at a white table. You know everyone thought we would be home by Christmas but our coming to Europe settled that. Yes old girl you did behave crookly that night in Newcastle, but you have made it up and will do more should I come back. Let bygones be done with.

Tomatoes are good this year are they? In Egypt they were very cheap indeed.

If Kitty is learning music why don't you? Painting, dressmaking, music would be indeed another string to your bow. If you become so skilful a dressmaker as your mother, you'll do 4 pairs of sox all for me, *Voila tres bon.*

The only fires we see here are in grates. It is too beastly cold for one to start anywhere else. I'm sorry you hurt your leg. Don't do it again until I tell you. What a shame I wasn't there to pick you up.

Had to give my old camera up. We all had to, otherwise we might be taken as spies. The Belgians are becoming much disliked here, through so many being spies. Even amongst the Belgian refugees in England spies have been found. The Frenchman is a lot bigger than I thought he was. There are two mountains of flesh here too old to be to the war.

2481 l/Corp Ben Champion A Coy 1st Battalion, AIEs British Expeditionary Force. That is my address, no more sergeant, reinforcements or Egypt. For goodness sake put the date on your letters, Tarro 6.6.16 or some other date. It's awkward to get a letter with Saturday on the top.

We get the English papers 1 day old, that's not bad and when the Tommies get 7 days leave they can spend 6 at least at home, by fast train and boat only 10 hours from here to London. All alive and kicking,

love Ben

———

9.4.16.

Into Hazebrouck and bought a few souvenirs which I sent home. Handkerchiefs for Gertrude and Frank, also pair silk stockings for Gertrude. *(see letter 23/4)*

Told we trek tomorrow. Leaving a good home for what?

———

10.4.16: 7.45 a.m.

We left Wallon Cappel with full pack up—terrible route march. Two blankets are nice to sleep in, but not much good to carry. We ended our march at 5 p.m. 1 and 2 platoons. Feet very very sore, boots too narrow ...

Light boots may be quite O.K. for ordinary parade work, but for mine I'd like to see an extra sole on the bottom. This sole to be renewed as soon as it wears and so the x boot would never be spoilt by ripping off the original sole.

Close to Bailleul. The Hazebrouck—Bailleul road simply thronged with traffic, guns, wagons, men, all are strictly adhering to the rule of the road and enforced by military police who are cusses of men.

Saw shrapnel burst over one of our balloons, the first burst in France. Though tired and the cobble stones hurt our feet, most of us paid a visit to Bailleul and saw the roads leading to Ypres and Lille.

Went to YMCA for tea. Told to be careful what we say as German spies still here.

People talk Flemish mainly. Can't understand French although they say they are Francais. Gun boom heavier than ever, sounds crook.

11.4.16.

Drizzling rain set in so no parades. Was told off by C.S.M. Fowler to report to Battalion Headquarters where I was conveyed with 1 N.C.O. from each company in a motor bus through splendid scenery to Cassel—this place I think is our Army Headquarters. There are Staff Officers galore and planes are constantly coming close to a big field on which is pegged out a large T shaped sheet and they drop small parachutes to which I imagine are fastened message containers.

The school is a gas school and instruction is given in the use of the P.H. Helmet and Vermicide sprayer. From Mount Cassel, a splendid view is obtained on a very clear day—with a telescope the front line area may be seen. The farms surrounding the Mount look like a chess board and appeared very fertile, or just like toy land, truly the Frenchmen are industrious workers.

Beautiful mansions and grounds are here, truly chateaus. Peculiar shaped trees cut to represent figures birds etc. Glorious beech trees. On our motor bus the tips of the trees used to sweep our hats. The grounds thronged with pheasants and deer but the absence of men is noticeable—women doing most of the farm work and every French boy has some part of a soldier's uniform for continual wear; it may be a Frenchman's cap or a Tommies jacket cut down.

Billets very good. There are trams in Cassel and plenty of military policemen (how I hate them). The cemetery seems ages old and well kept.

12.4.16.

Went into Gas Chamber with helmets on. Gas thinned out, cautiously lifted front and sniffed. Choking sensation in back of throat, chlorine gas. The masks are efficient if uncomfortable. The O.C. a small Scotchman, says a new type of helmet, a box type, is on the way to the troops.

We learnt the use of the Vermoide sprayer to commence with. In front of the dugouts in the front line in trench systems which have been well established, is a blanket which fits snugly against the sloped doorway. This blanket is lowered when the gas alarm goes and is wetted with an anti-gas solution pumped from the sprayer.

Sunday 16.4.16.

Rejoined Battalion at Bailleul.

18.4.16.

Marched from Outtersteene to Saille in all muck and rain. It was boot-deep all the way and soon it splashed from the wheels of passing vehicles onto our overcoats which became as heavy as lead and flopping about weighed about ten tons more or less.

Saille very fine little village, plenty of troops. Had fine talk in an estaminet to daughter of house who told me Germans there on 11th October 1914, and people say the officers paid for what they used and took but regular men—pigs paid *rien* (nothing).

At 7 p.m. we left here and marched towards the line. The road was not so brilliant and some Labour Corps men were busy repairing shell holes in the road. We were very wet when we arrived at the line, instead of trenches; they were built up too as the ground was low-lying to dig down much.

Mch. 19—Inspection by H.R.H. The Prince of Wales and General Birdwood.

,,   22—Entrained for Alexandria. Embarked on T. *Ivirnia* for Marseilles.

,,   27—Arrived at Toulon.

,,   28—Marseilles. Entrained.

,,   31—Billeted at Wallon Capel.

1916.

April 10—Marched to Outtersteene.

,,   18—Marched to Sailly.

,,   19—Entered trenches for first time in France—Laventie. Fromelles Sector.

May 11—Fleurbaix.

,,   18—Relieved by 10th Battalion; billeted in Sailly.

June   1—Address by Mr. Hughes.

,,   10—Fleurbaix.

,,   28—Raid under Capt. P. L. Howell Price.

July   3—Relieved by 47th Battalion. Moved to Sailly—Cul de sac Farm.

,,   9—Marched to Outtersteene.

,,   10—Entrained at Bailleul for South.

,,   11—Detrained at Doullens. Billeted in Domart.

,,   12—Marched to Vignacourt.

,,   13—Marched to Allonville.

,,   16—Marched to Warloy.

,,   19—Albert. Relieved the 12th D.L.I. in trenches at Contalmaison.

,,   23—First Battle of Pozieres.

,,   26—Relieved by 2nd Brigade. Marched to Bivouac at Tara Hill, via Albert.

,,   29—Marched to Vadencourt.

,,   28—La Vicogne.

,,   29—Bonneville.

,,   30—Halloy.

Aug.   9—La·Vicogne.

,,   10—Toutencourt.

,,   13—Presentation of medals by General Birdwood.

,,   14—Marched to Vadencourt.

,,   15—In bivouacs near Albert.

,,   16—In support at Wire Trench—La Boisselle. Fatigue duty at Chalk Pit.

,,   18—Relieved 3rd Battalion in Front Line. Mouquet Farm Sector.

Excerpt from 1st Battalion diary

An early form of gas alarm

On right of Armentieres we relieved some Bantam Regiment, there are none over 5'1 '. but were nevertheless splendid sturdy men. Their dialect was peculiar.

Needless to say the number of Bantams per dugout would not fit same number of A.I.F. because our men on the average are about 5'10 '. It seems funny to see the long and the short of the Army. It is a case of cutting our legs off short at the elbows isn't it?

Duck boards are extensively used, the water collects below them and they help to keep the feet dry. There are rats here galore as big as cats. Fritz seems to be about 200 yards away and his snipers must know this ground well as the loopholes are seldom used—he has them ranged as well. We were glad to work all night as it kept us warm.

DIARY OF 1ˢᵗ BATTALION-

On the 19ᵗʰ April, the Battalion took over its section of trench with HQ at Rifle Villa. It was Petillon Sector near where the Laies River (LYS) passed through the front line. The trenches were different from those of the Peninsula, but merely breastworks made of sandbags piled on on top of the other to a height of 6-8' with a thickness of about 6'.

THE WESTERN FRONT

This part of the line had remained in the same place since the very early days of the war. Every inch of ground was known to the enemy and well-marked down by artillery of both sides. This area held no key to important position in the rear. For this reason it was treated as nursery in which to train new units which explained our presence there

20.4.16.

Stood too early this morning, very cold, no life in feet at all. Water, fatigue rations issued in bulk, no consideration for mucky trenches—why not cut up into decent size for troops. Rotten tucker, meat big and stringy, 4 to loaf of bread.

Duck boards blocked up above level of water. Rum issued, very good scheme this rum issue. In these trenches Michael O'Leary won his V.C. and parts of them are called after him.

Rusty barbed wire marked Fritz's line with grass knee high in No Man's Land. Colonel Heane says it's to be our land and arrangements have been made to constantly patrol it to get superiority over Fritz. Captain Mackenzie wants to start the war here and we are waking things up.

21.4.16.

Got a dose of shrapnel this morning. The 9th Battalion. had stiff luck last night, a shell caught supports in a barn with a company in its billet and 73 casualties resulted, 26 deaths. First casualty in France to 1st Battalion. was a man in C Company—he was killed.

This morning several Taube planes overhead fired at by dozens of guns but not hit at all. Very pretty to see the planes and background. Blue sky and all white fleecy explosions around.

22.4.16.

We didn't get any Hot Cross buns this morning although it is *Good Friday*, instead our heavies engaged theirs and a heavy duel resulted, but they didn't bother the poor wet mortals in the line. Our sheep skin mittens very warm, pity B1 they didn't have a finger made in them for the trigger finger.

Easter Sunday. Rations light today, bread spoilt before it reached us, so 6 biscuits and eight to a tin of jam. Took party into Saille for a bath so augmented our rations there. Bread 4p for 10d. Still in trenches.

Today shells, rather too close for comfort, started busting around like on old Peninsula. The graves of the English soldiers are well looked after by soldiers who are temporarily unfit for service.

23.4. 16 France

Dear Frank

Ten pence=1 Franc. It's a long time since I wrote to you old girl and entirely my own fault. I certainly have been busy, some of the time at a school learning how to combat various shells and gas. There are a lot of ways of killing a man besides shooting him aren't there.

I received some letters from home last night, the first for at least 5 weeks, where they have been I cannot say. I received some of yours about one month ago. How are the sox getting on Frank. I have no pair now that I came away with. I hope you know how big my feet were. Any way you ought to know considering the number of times we've played tootsies under the court and breakfast tables. I wish I could play now anyhow....*It's a long way from, is it Tipperary or another T at* ....you know the rest.

By a mail, I sent some time ago, I sent you a little birthday gift I hope you have received it. Like it, Art and I took one whole afternoon picking them out. I know you liked cream and white better than coloured. I sent Gertrude some too, also a pair of stockings.

Art wanted to send ultramarine coloured ones but I sent black. We've come to our present possey by means of 16 mile route marches. The last march was a terror. Slush and mud right up to the thighs. And we have never had our feet dry since worse luck. The Australian boots are not made for wet slushy weather and ever since we lobbed into the trenches it has rained. Does it always rain in France in April?

We are seeing some country all right. I wonder will you ever have a chance to see this part of the globe? Perhaps Cooks will run trips to Gallipoli and the battle fields. By Jove, the rats are big, they charge us

Cooks Tour, London

even when we have bayonets, they're as big as possums. Last night some rats in the roof of the dugout started to throw dirt into my mouth. To stop the villains I got up and lit a fire and smoked them out. They're just as big and strong today.

Coke is supplied and every night a brazier glowing. Oh the weather is dreadful here, no comfort at all—rather be on old Peninsula for its much safer there not so many whiz bangs.

There are so many desolate farms, sheds and barns. The French have had a bad time from the Germans especially the women. Nothing to report old girl at all except military matters and I can't say anything about them…miserable weather. Next war I will march down to the boats in the harbour and wave good bye to the boys and come home. Wise man says once bitten twice shy. I wonder when this war will end.

All the chaps have named their dug outs Ours is *the overcrowded one* 6 of us are in it 12 x 5 x 5' high so you'll see me with a huge bump in the back of my back through continual bending. How is your dressmaking getting on? Made many stitches successfully yet?

The big top boots have run out so we have bound sand bags around our sodden puttees. Winter is getting close on to you now pet and I don't want you to get so many colds this winter. I saw most of you during the cold months of last year. How we used to steal away from camp to visit *Oakland*—10 months away from home; and how long will it be before we get back.

Please address letters 2481 1/ Corp Ben Champion A Corp, 1st Batt A.I.F. British Expeditionary Force ... Don't put Sgt or reinforcements or Egypt or France just the above plain address.

Your photo is getting a bit rubbed now and faint but I can still tell its meant for Frank

[Page 5 and 6 missing]

[p 7] don't you think we ought to be sent home for a holiday, it's about time. Art is well and perky in a dug out opposite to me with 2 mates; he is not in my section worse luck.

About two months ago I took some photos of Art and myself and some mates from 7/1st but through shifting about from Town to Town now they are lost until I can get back some day to Cairo.

You needn't bother (when we come back some day) preparing that room. Art and I can sleep anywhere—on the top wire of a barbed wire fence if necessary. You ought to see some of the places we have slept in since leaving Sydney, under seats, tents, Egyptian houses, open, dugouts and in many cases in places where Art wouldn't have let his old dog Nip sleep.

Well Old Girl, I'll close now. Remember me to all at Home. Good bye for present.

Ben xxxxxxxxxx etc

25.4.16.

A year ago since Anzac attack. Letters from Mrs Niland and Frank and Mary. All seem well and happy. No news. Rec'd lock of hair . Not asked for don't know how to carry it. Some Pioneers killed along V.C. Avenue last night and couple from First Brigade. Received 6 letters from Frank and chocs from Gertrude.

27.4.16

Had a gas scare last night. Capt. Mackenzie (AC) ordered helmets out but nothing came, sorry. A few dopes couldn't find helmets at last moment, taught a lesson though. Very anxious night indeed. Our 18lb shells got onto Germans and smashed them wholesale. Barbed wire pinched by German B Coy. Very clever patrols. Terrific 4 hour bombardment in morning of 28th. On our right the South Welsh Borderers were tickled up and a few came down into our area. Comical chaps, got some badges from them. Left of Levantie, Firing Line.

28.4.16

A new weapon of offence was introduced to us in the form of a Trench Stokes mortar. This is a secret weapon as yet and is carefully guarded, so the officer in charge told me. A small sand bag emplacement was made at the back of the trench and this small stone pipe gun was inserted and fired.

We treated Fritz to a few shots. 1 whole section of about 10 feet of his line was blown up. Mortars make an awful crump. These bombs weigh 60lbs or twenty, very efficient. They look like red hot fishes at night, hurling through the air. Gorgeous sight the bombardment, bombs bursting, guns shelling hardly hear speak .

Last night Fritz put out a notice board saying General Townsend had surrendered with all his troops, don't know if it's true of course.

31.4.16.

Received 4 letters from home. Very good letters from Gertrude and Mother. Mum seems extra worried about me. Plenty of Taubes over yesterday. G's supposed to be massing for an attack. Suspect will use gas again shortly. 2 Fritzies gave themselves up last night, they were trotted off to Brigade Hqr. They were Saxons, not military class. Don't like this breast work trench, too much back—burst from a shell liable. A shell lobbed in Company HQ. No lives lost, a dud fortunately.

3.5.16.

Heavy bombardment mostly on supports though. We marched out
of the line in small batches, being relieved by the 3rd Battalion. They
seemed pleased to be right in the line and not in support—said further
away from the line the more shells. So we found it.

We repaired to Weather Cock House, residence of Major Dumant,
Mayor of Levantie. This was a large two storied house which had been
hit by a few shells but was still intact enough to offer shelter from the rain
and the wind.

*Ben's photo of Weather Cock House before (top)–note some damage to roof of house before
shell attack.*

5.5.16

Dear Mrs Niland

I'm afraid I have neglected my duty in not writing even after
receiving so many letters from you. Well, Art and I are still in good
health touring France. We've done a little turn in the firing line and are
now out resting. Our work is not as strenuous as on the Peninsula and
we receive more comforts.

Our health is considered and we are often given clean change of
clothing. You will see us come back dressed as Tommies most possibly,
as the Australian uniform is twice as expensive and hard to obtain
here. Of course we are all sick of the war and wish we were home and I
know everyone in Australia wishes the same.

One can notice the Spring here more than at home. Here, one week everything is dead and perhaps the next, trees will be green and the sun shining. The fields are covered thickly with daisies and buttercups so that it is impossible to walk without stepping on them. It's such a shame as much land is idle and so many houses desolate, razed to the ground.

There is hardly a farm without it's little graveyard in one corner, either of German, English and French soldiers and now some Australian have been left here.

The whole day long aeroplanes soar overhead looking so stable in the air, but I'm afraid I'd be the same as on water if I rode in one.

The Belgians are becoming utterly detested and the whole place is over run with the spies. The part of France where we are stationed, the people are a mixture and there is no set language only Patois, partly German, French, English and Flemish.

It is rather funny about Mary's curl. I hope you curled it up before it was sent. Don't let your front be made untidy with Ben's block of wood, only we were tired after Krambach but I think we could have done it easily enough only for Tarro. Why the wheels wouldn't turn around—such a magnet drawing us back. We have done thousands of trips worse than that little pleasure jaunt since we left Australia and will do million (?) before we return.

I won't be able to look a pig in the face some day. We have had bacon for breakfast ever since we left the Shores. One of our chaps named Jones or rather *the poet* he is always talking about the Englishmen and how they polish their buttons. Well somehow he came to get the name of *Shiny Buttons* At our lst billet all the chaps were calling him Shiny Buttons, the people around thought it was his real name so one farmer had to ask him a question and addressed him as *Monsieur Shinney Bouton* now Jones walks around all day with his head in the air.

He wrote a little piece about a little occurrence which took place here and its very good. I'll put it in Franc's letter next time I write. 10 months out of park now, it seems long to us. There is a chance of the old hands receiving 8 days leave for London. What a chance, perhaps if I'm lucky I may go some day. Six shillings a day tourists all right.

Someday it will be hard work starting work again after this. The people on the Belgian border look on us with nothing but black looks, they don't want French Government it's easily seen and every 2nd man and women is a German spy. It makes it hard for strangers in a hostile district. Everyone is against one and you are in turn suspicious of everyone.

Frank by her last letters seems to be all right, well etc. I hope this letter will find you all the same.

I'll have to close now, Yours truly

Ben.

4.5.16.

In the middle of the morning we got it. The first shell bashed into the house and we cleared into the open. Then more shells. Fortunately for us the lull for five seconds or so in between the first and next shells saved many lives. We got into the open as quick as we could and Lieut. Prior looked funny with one side of his face lathered and the other shaved, running with a razor in his hand. Capt. Woodforde couldn't get out quick enough and he was wounded in the back and Sgt. Tindale got it in the hand and 5 others wounded.

Soon as shelling was over we went back to get our stew but the *babbling brooks* had left the lids off the dixies and it was spoiled by dust and dirt, so we repaired to the fields. A shell bursting in a house makes a horrible disconcerting row. Major Woodforde being evacuated—A.C. Mackenzie took over.

Fritz must either have observation on this place or someone must tell him the best time to shell the place. Suspect taken before Col Heane. Didn't hear the result, only the froggies immediately opposite Weather Cock house vacated and took their bedding away 20 minutes before the shells came.

Our planes got busy searching for their guns. Buttercups and daisies galore around here. Grass 6 feet high. Wish we were back on at Firing line. Billet past 2 Tree Farm around 2 left of Weather Cock corner. This bombardment is in retaliation for us smashing Fromelles station, the German railway base tit for tat.

English plane has 3 colours under its wings red white and blue. Germans Taube has black cross under its wings. Slept out in the open, better than in that murderous building.

5.5.16.

Weather Cock House after shelling

Orders read, even on active service when out of trenches must salute. We dug some trenches close to the House in case of further bombardment. There is an Australian mobile 18 lb.gun that fires around here then moves off. Most audacious places for guns around here. There is one quite close in a hawthorn hedge, well covered over and camouflaged.

Of course the Coy. Poet one *Shiny Buttons* or Jones, made up some poetry about the shelling, sung to the *Boys of the Dardanelles*. (See also original diary note sung to *If those lips could only speak*) The reason the doggerel was composed was that the Brigadier was at hand and saw us scatter from the house; he thought we were needlessly alarmed but he acknowledged afterwards that some words were ill chosen.

Ode to "A" Coy
by Pte Jones (Shiny Buttons)
To the tune of "If those lips could only speak"

The shells they have scattered our homestead
The guns they are blazing away
We'd mortgage our chances of heaven
To be in Australia today
We knew our old homestead was settled
So away to the trenches we fled
'A 'Company's awfully frightened
Were the words that a General said.

Chorus

If that chap would only wait
'till those boys are under fire
Then he'd see that he was mistaken
And he'd know that he's a liar
For the boys are not afraid
And they are surprised that he
Should throw that insult at Australians
And the boys of Gallipoli

The boys of 'A Coy 'are waiting
For that General to lead them to fight
Or will he just sit in his dug out
And say that we suffered from fright
That General he may be a hero
Or he may be a dug out king
But when he says we are cowards
Just lift up your voices and sing

(instead of chorus sing 'Boys of Dardanelles ')

To Frank from Arthur

France 5.5.16,

Dear Frank

Your letter came the other day as a surprise to me but I received it with none the less pleasure. At first I thought it must have been a mistake when I read all the terms of endearment and that it was meant for one Ben, but on close examination I found it began with my name alright and that all the nice pretty little terms were in the third person and not addressed to me at all.

Certainly you talked about *poor old Chaps* the *darling old Ben* etc. in a very nice way. No doubt the fact of his being incapacitated and in hospital aroused a lot of sympathy and with it another virtue which may not and yet may have been dormant or undeveloped. Anyhow I should say if Ben writes about you to anyone as you did about him to me and meant it, my previous few letters and post cards to you will have all been in vain and will have found me barking up the wrong tree. I hope it is so.

Thank you Frank for the unselfish sentiment displayed when you said you should like to see Ben and I come home together as we went away together. I sincerely wish that both of us may be spared to return home again and on the same troopship, and that the time won't be long either because I am sure that we are every bit as tired of being *somewhere in France* and want to get back to good old New South Wales, as you are of knowing us to be so far away. I do look forward to happy days spent with Mary, your mother and yourself in the not too far distant future.

You want to know news about Harold Kershaw and Sergeant Hunt. I think I told Mary about one in my last letters; if so she will READ out to you what I said and what I didn't (and am not quite sure). I might say that I have not seen the former since leaving camp in Egypt before going down to the Canal and that the latter being one of our fellow sergeants was reduced to the ranks like the rest of us on joining the Battalion in October last but has since been given the rank of corporal and that only recently.

He is at present in C Coy where he was first taken on the rolls of the Battalion. I am glad you accepted the love I sent you; there was not very much of it you know—someone else has all that. Well I accept yours too and before that you will not 'jib 'at having what little bit of mine that I have to spare.

Yours very sincerely

Arthur

PS Did not give you any news as I expect Ben will have told you all that in his letter and he has a happier knack as a raconteur than I.

PPS Just dawned on me that today is the anniversary of your birthday Allow me to repeat my congratulations.

6.5.16

Dear Franc (tenpence)

I've written to your mother and a little note to Claire so it's up to me to drop you a line. I'm writing this, all amongst the butter cups and daisies, I wish you were here to see them. When 37 shells lobbed on our billet of course we vacated it and our General said A seems afraid. I'll just put in Shinys poem [see elsewhere].

By Jove, Frank, we were wild when he said that. Next time we are in action you see if A Coy is 2nd. I'm putting in my note a few little butter cups just to shew the size they grow to here.

We came on a few moles the other day, without any eyes, they have baggy claws for throwing out the dirt they dig and snouts like shovels. You know how soft a horse's muzzle is; well their fur is much softer than that.

We were very lucky when in the firing line only a few casualties. This paper you sent me has come in very useful indeed I think I told you I rec'd one of your curls, I'm sorry I can't reciprocate with one of mine. I'll have to tell you about a very funny dream I had not long ago. I was in uniform out riding to ... our last billet town with the section, what infantrymen were doing on horses I know not. Well we had steak and kidney pie in town and then rode home. I remember dismounting, leading the horse inside and he suddenly shrank and I hung him up on a huge nail. Next morning when I awoke I remember distinctly looking at that nail to see if really there was a horse there. The dream was vivid I can tell you. Any how I haven't tasted that kind of pie for months.

The fruit over here is getting ripe only a few more weeks to go. How are the Tarro people treating you? The English people call moles moudy—warps (?!) Some of the shell holes made by a gun called Jack Johnson can hold two horses and riders without being seen. It's enough to make one cry to see the mess these shells make of the farms. Hundreds of farms are smashed about no one living in them.

I wonder if I'll be home before your next birthday. I was thinking of you yesterday all day as we lay out in the support trenches. I hope you receive those hankies I sent you from one of our billets, for your birthday. You know General Townsend had surrendered, well that night the Germans put out a notice board with that news on it and we heard 3 days later from our own side that it was true. They are brave chaps and splendid fighters.

There is a notice put up on a German's grave here, Erected in memory of a valiant German soldier who after helping a wounded English Officer was accidently shot. Erected by the Royal Sherwood Foresters, so you see all Germans aren't bad but they are going to be considered bad by Australians.

The aeronauts are very brave fellows, sometimes there are shells all around them but they simply swoop or rise and so escape as calmly as you like. Please forgive this skimpy note but there is absolutely no news. They are bombarding again now.

How do you like your dress making? You must have finished a quarter by this time. How is Kitty getting on with her piano lesson.

Good Bye for present

Ben xxxx love

7.5.16

Corp. Nielsen gone to England, taken letter to Father for me. Wrote Olive Crouch. Shrapnel bursting today brought through mobile gun. Messing with Corporals, separate room. Sermon by minister. Gave Mr Beavis his chit for his films. Tom Brown made a Lance Corporal.

8.5.16.

Still doing fatigue work up towards the line each night and resting during the day. Our latest job is burying a telephone cable 18 'underground; at this depth it is lying in water in most places and the digging is very mucky. Carrying up A-frames is an art in itself. These huge frames shaped like the letter 'A 'are used in forming communication trenches. The narrow end goes into the earth and the cross-piece allows the duckboards to be supported clear of the drainage which flows underneath.

13.5.16.

Lot of old Peninsula men re-joined today and 5 men gone on Blighty leave. Wonder will the Russians make it easier for us by keeping Fritz occupied elsewhere. Glorious weather, its Spring.

14.5.16.

Received an air cushion from Gertrude. Very kind of her. Mr Felton agrees with me re Mary and Art. Wrote Mother, Miss Lansdowne—not on fatigue tonight.

15.5.16.

Picked up our packs at Weather Cock House and trekked towards Sailly, new billet, horribly crowded, but can't be helped. 3 German zeppelins bought down.

15.5.16.

Word *Retire* cut out of British Army, for time being to be move back *Go Back* etc. but not retire owing to it's common use in German Army. Wrote 7 page letter to Gertrude. Sneak into baths at Sailly. The change of underclothes is a relief for we are nearly as lousy as we were on the Peninsula, the front line trenches having been in constant occupation for so long.

The time out of the front line is spent organising; having lectures and becoming shipshape. Each turn in the line puts back drill discipline and the spells out bringing it back to is previous pitch.

Fatique to the Bac Saint Maur where we loaded and unloaded for the division passed quickly and on the 18th we moved to fine billets near Estaires ½ kilo from Doulieu.

———

17.5.16 France

Dear Pal,

Well I received from Tarro a fine large mail yesterday, generally a good score, 1 from Mrs Niland and 4 from you and 2 from Kitty and Ruth. The dates were about 5th of March as I saw from the stamps as you still forget to date the letters. You were very anxious about not receiving many letters from me and you even said you had a weep.

Don't worry or be sad about letters old girl and try to cultivate a habit of not expecting a letter each mail or letting your feelings get the best of you, for weeping has a nasty taste. If there's anything I hate is to learn about any girl crying, it upsets me.

Well everything in the garden is lovely here. I'll try to answer your questions now. There are several subjects you mention and tell me not to say anything about them. I'll save them up until our next meeting. No pal, I don't think you are an un reciprocating girl now. I know now that though young, you possess a deal of sense more than any other girl in your house, though some people don't think so. Oh Girl, I wish we were home, this miserable shifting life, always carrying your house on the back, no comforts, no congenial companions, no home. And yet sometimes one feels like not coming back until all the Germans are wiped out. But there are thousands of decent fellows amongst the enemy.

This is an extract from one of your letters dated 5.4.16 'Your last letters brightened me up wonderfully Ben, I thought you had deserted me for ever. 'Don't let a thought like that ever cross your mind. I'll be your friend so long as I can be of any use at all to you and I guess someday a man friend will come in very handy Perhaps later on, may be of assistance to you and repay you for all kind thoughts conveyed in letters etc to me. Of course, anything other than friendship should not be thought of at our respective ages.

You ask me how I got on with the first parade when I re-joined the Battalion. It was a route march and well I remember it. Every 10 yards I would say to myself *will I drop out or not* and then my pride would say *no stick it you coward* and on I'd go for while further. I saw Noel Smith a couple of days ago. He is well and enjoys touring France just as well as we do. By Jove this is a glorious country just like up beyond Maitland, Patterson way.

Now don't you mind my dummy finger it's ok and it doesn't do half as much the other fingers. Instead of saying do I miss the Malta Sister? You ought to be thankful to her for getting me through. I believe you are the only one who has ever said Gertrude is like me or vice versa, quite a compliment to me I'm sure. And I say you are like no one in your family at all.

I wonder will I go back to dentistry or something else. The land would be a welcome change. I've known you a little over a year and it seems as if we have known each other for a life time. Gertrude, if she said that Art and I came back from Kempsey in a hurry instead of going on is not far wrong. I wouldn't like to see you on a bike, I don't think it looks too nice. Now horse riding is just the thing for all and there is no bother at all about getting off.

When will we be able to have a decent hand to hand scrap with the Bosches? When we do, Peace will come all of a sudden. Such a sudden finish I believe. Dear old Girl, I hope you have not changed much. I'm afraid I have, slightly taller and thinner. That malaria and wound took more out of me than I thought at the time.

It seems years since I saw home and you all. I look on *Oaklands* as a sort of 2nd home. That's if you will let me. No news at all. I hope your new station master is a different man to Mr Morris, only old Pal don't become so familiar with him as with Mr Morris. It is best for yourself and for your mother. *lots of cross out* .. The crossed out part is something I should not have said at all. I hope you are satisfied with this letter girl. I can't write letters like Art can. He is cleverer than I.

Yours truly Ben

18.5 16.

We had hardly settled down for the night when terrific bombardment from enemy woke us up and before long the news came to get ready to move in Battle order leaving blankets behind. Then the news came to Stand Down. Chocolate girls come around our billets selling sweets.

Hutchison goes to England tonight to Plaistow near London. Last night our guns opened up and Fritz replied with 4.2 of 13lb shells, nearly skittled, one lobbed very close indeed. Weather glorious. Cuckoos, thrushs, especially bright.

19.5.16.

Football, physical drill, really spelling, new bayonet exercises. March last night comfortable. Heavy bombardment last night. Good Oh, occasionally drops an egg into Bailleul making things unpleasant for those around.

21.5.16.

On Sunday we had a church service at Headquarters Sailly. The Prime Minister Mr W.M. Hughes and General Smythe attended. The whole Battalion being drawn up around the hedges and leafing apple trees on the lovely green grass. The Sermon was Garden of Eden—very appropriate. Orders were given that if any enemy aircraft was seen we were to remain perfectly still. Colonel Heane, Major Lindeman and all officers except Captain Woodforde were present.

After the Service General Smythe talked to us and he appealed to us as a straight soldier, who wouldn't get us into any mess he couldn't get us out of. He is such a smart man and is liked muchly same as Gen. Birdwood but very few care for Walker. He called A Coy cowards.

21.5.16

Dear Frank,

I received more letters from you yesterday dated 20.3.16. Well done old girl you are writing well to me. But pal you are taking life too seriously I think. Treat everything as a joke, we are not old uns yet, not even young uns but kiddies.

Photograph signed by General Smythe

We have a scotchman in the section he is always talking about windeys (windows) and that's a *good gun* etc. he is the life of whole mob of us.

Thank Claire for her little note when some news turns up I'll write to her and to Ruth. I'll return Art's PC. I wonder at his audacity, I hope you took it as a huge goak. If not I'll have to walk into his affections.

What do you think killed the chooks, measles, mumpts, double hyonia or what?

Art reckons does he, that I wouldn't have been hit had I been writing to you, well I'll retaliate by saying he might have received a stripe had he attended more to his business and less to his girl.

You are entirely forgiven about sending my letters to *Jura* but pal you ought to possess a little more tact. The same about your father, I really don't like you slinging off at him. He is a fine old chap. Besides you owe him a big duty you know.

Fancy Old Art telling Ruth to write me a dilly note to make me laugh. What was he thinking about I wonder? Did you use up the 3/— worth of stamps your father gave you for holding his horse for him at that funeral you had the misfortune to attend. (This would have been for patriarch Peter Carroll of Windsor, Franks grandfather) There is no news at present. We are billeted in a fine old house, plenty of ground but kilometres away from any towns worse luck.

Wait until after our next move then I'm sure there will be something to say. The prices of goods have gone up a lot since one lobbed here. The French people are continually saying *Australia plenty mannaie* so eggs boiled have jumped to cinq sous or 2 ½ each, 1st chocs to 2 pence, so we have boycotted some of them and I think the prices will climb down. One can't buy a good meal here. It is generally the custom to buy the meat then take it too a restaurant to be cooked so a meal takes anything to 40 minutes to prepare.

Have you altered at all pal? A little bird just told me that you have been hard to get on with lately (keep quiet about it) and I'll listen for improvement.

The swallows are pretty especially when mating together. Do you know the bush called Spirea or May. Well there are hedges of it here, some trunks 9 inches thick.

After Church we had a cricket match A beat B Coy by 9 runs, a very close one indeed. Fancy playing cricket on the Peninsula or attending church there. I believe there used to be a church but it must have been in a very quiet part of the line.

What a bother washing is. I've just thrown a flannel shirt away as I had to wash it had I kept it.

We ought to be able to pinch some fruit shortly as the orchards are looking fine now. We are strawed just alongside the Quartermaster stores so often a baksheesh tin of jam disappears. Of course no. 5 section knows nought about it.

I am well, thank you in every respect but Art has not been too good last 3 days, seems like dysentery. He has been attending the sick parade and doctor has placed him off duty.

I saw Bill Hunt from C Coy yesterday. We NCOS of 7th of 1st are unlucky not getting decent stripes on joining up the Battalion.

Do you still remember how Art and I returned from Krambach and how you would make us a cup of tea and how you utterly squashed us when we tried to remonstrate with you, And what a wreck we were Ah 'twas a magnet at work awll right. You must have had very little faith in our physical capabilities if you thought we couldn't reach

Kempsey. Sheer pride would have kept us going had there not been an attraction.

Marmalade jam and marmalade bread and marmalade jam ...for tea always the same.

I hope you receive the letters posted in England for you. A mate went on leave so do not think I'm there will you. I'll have a good time if I have the luck to get there.

Did you see the photo of your little boy in the hospital group at St Elmo Hospital?

Now you say, *Will I come down to the boat or not.* When the boat comes in I'll let you know all about it. All the same I'd rather come up to see you, you know, and the family. Just imagine the crowd on the wharf; Father, Mother and Royal Fambly, Aust'n uncles cousins, 2nd and 3rd cousins by the thousands and then city friends. Oh Goodness don't suggest it. I'll have to kiss them all I suppose, generally the way, isn't it?

Awfully sorry about your indigestion old girl please don't get it again till I tell you please. Thanks for Sydney Mail, I wondered why I hadn't been receiving them and was blaming the military authorities.

You say you wouldn't trust a Turk out of your sight, well I would, I think the way he has carried out the game on the Peninsula, fine. But as for a Prussian we won't leave 'til we wipe them right out.

Now I'm going to close now pal, don't forget what I said about slinging off at your father.

Always your friend

21.5.16 cont...

Returned to billets and we were spoken to by Colonel Heane and raiding party was formed 5 Officers and 60 men were picked for the job. The whole being in charge of Captain Phil (Howell-) Price.

Doulieu is a pleasant little village and possesses a large church. The village barber being mobilised I was again shaved by a lady, his wife, who, armed with a very blunt razor tore off a slight growth. Yellow home-made soap doesn't do very well for shaving.

Quite a number of Highlanders billeted here, their wet kilts in the line make the backs of their legs sore through chafing.

Captain H. Jacobs joined up—remembered me from old 19B days. [Ben joined as a student 19B Hornsby NSW height 5' 8 ½, 'weight 7 stone 11 pounds and in 1915 he was 5'11 ½ 'and 10 stone 5 pounds. Had been promoted to lieutenant which stood him in good stead when he went to Liverpool training camp]

We are all very verminous though we try very hard to keep clean I find it impossible, the billets cause the beggars to come. The raiding party Price, Moffat, Prior, Little and O.R's are all working hard—deserve success. Lieut. Walker was shot through thigh last night evacuated wounded; I think he must have been reconnoitring for the Party.

Fowler brought the cooks out into parade today; they are easily seen to be cooks. We were all pleased to see Tom Brown made a corporal. He gets on well with everyone. Len Hesketh also got his 1st stripe and is very keen. Billy Hunt is still going strong, as dark as ever and Oscar Madison (Olof Madsen) went on blighty leave.

A pay of 40 francs came in very handy and Art and myself went into Steenwerck to blow some into souvenirs for home We came home in time to bid *au revoir* to Ponto McKenzie and Joe Errod both off on leave-lucky chaps. Joe to bring back my watch when he returns

Aunt Jeannie and Uncle Dykes in hospital sick

—◆—

24.5.16

Billy Hunt on view, went to see a French girl near Estaires. Complaints about soldiers black over green being seen there.

—◆—

25.5.16

Wrote to Mr Smith, Walked to Doulieu, a one horse little town but with gigantic church with good stained windows untouched in the only remaining wall which Tom Brown Billy Hunt and myself explored.

I like poking about in these places; prefer it to sitting down in the estiminets. Went into private house with Tom Brown, very fine little girl refugee named Alice from Armentieres speaking perfect English. 3

children Marie, Michel and Marcel. Majority of people here have very bad teeth—must be the water. Fine looking girls spoilt by very crook teeth [Ben was later to be instrumental in having flouride added to town water PF] Came home across the fields, Elder, Willow, good shade trees

---

29.5.16.

Went to Estaires—nice little place with its main square and cobbled streets. Still very lousy. Pity someone couldn't invent an acid to wash to kill the vermin. Very jolly after dinner, CSM Fowler very much so. Practising, crawling, creeping with rifles over ground, similar to no mans land. We hear that Quinlin who was hit at Weathercock House with Captain Woodforde died of wounds.

---

30 5.16

Dear Frank

Received two bosker letters from you last night. All well here. It has been a good war since we came to La Belle France, only a few wounded or killed. We are going to have some sports this week which seems so strange having sports during a war—so different from the Peninsula.

So another man is going from Tarro to the war. He will be here just in time to go home again. I had a shave and hair cut by a lady hairdresser the other day. So funny I thought. France is a strange place so opposite to Australia in many ways.

Are you sending any sox over. Please let me know as I can look out for them.

I can't make up any news pal. You write fine letters but you know I can't answer many of things you mention as you know about them a long time before you get the note.

That Casement of the Irish Rebellion is a cur and shooting is too good for him. We get the English papers daily here. The French kiddies are very quick at picking up the English language and Egyptians kiddies also.

The chaps who come back from England say that the English ladies and girls meet you in the street and cannot do too much for

Australians taking them everywhere and letting them pay nothing, *sol riete* isn't it. Shows a nice spirit and shows they appreciate all we've done.

They took this particular chap I mean around so much he had an average 3 hours sleep out of 24. Well I really have to close Old Girl, forgive me this short note but there is actually no news, nothing doing.

Ben

———

3.6.16 France

Dear Pal,

Didn't write last week as I had to give up my only green envelope etc. to one in the sector who lost his. Now the answers to your notes about end of March-stringing them out as much as possible. Well, one day we went for a long route march in full marching order without blankets.

I didn't see the use of carting all my goods so I blew up the air cushion that Gertrude gave me and stuffed the corners of my pack with strays and to all appearances I had a good heavy pack. Everyone wondered why I finished up the freshest.

It's no use doing something solid when there is no use for it but you bet I'll be there when there are whips cracking. I've sent home a few postcards of the little town we visit frequently. I can't mention names but find out from Gertrude and look it up on the map.

The kiddies here are getting as bad with their cry of *Souvenir* as the Gypos with *Baksheesh*. Especially here they flock around Australian knowing they won't hurt them and clamour so much that sometimes it costs a few half Francs to get away from them.

Although prices are high, the people are so honest and for that reason they are not taken down. If you don't understand how much the price is, just pull out some pence and coppers and let them take what is necessary, trusting that the people will not rob you.

In Egypt, in a shop there would always be a gypo looking on to see nothing disappeared and you could tell by his sardonic glare that he was up to all capers. A few men went into a post card shop here for some views. When there, with goods all around us, the women's baby began to cry and she left us and we were in that shop for 20 minutes at least with no one looking on and nothing was touched because we were trusted. In Egypt it was their duty to take every gypo down for they robbed us right and left.

We've been seeing air fights galore the last few days. In the morning Mr Hughes spoke to us and a Taube fell burning to the ground. The German aviator was only dazed and taken away in a car. There are some lovely planes about now. Big and stable looking and on a clear day it's great to see them being shelled.

The horses we bought from Australia are becoming fine looking with regular green feed and the climate agrees with them. When they came from Serapeum in Arabia Nile of canal they looked awful, only fed on Tibben, fodder just the fine shavings.

You have no doubt heard about the fuss the English are making over Mr William Hughes our Prime Minister. Well last Thursday (1.6.16) in the morning the whole Brigade massed and we had a fine stirring speech from him and Mr Andrew Fisher from an ASC lorry.

Mr Hughes looked very ill indeed I thought and has become deaf. I expected to see Mr Fisher and Mr Hughes dressed well as they hold high positions but no, Mr Hughes came in light grey suit and slack trousers tucked into legging. Mr Fisher wore military pants and boots but a white coat. They looked typical outback Australian farmers and not the Prime Minister and High Commissioner of Australia. Gave Australia three cheers.

Prime Minister, Billy Hughes addressing the troops.

Hughes spoke well, said didn't know how long war would last but very pleased with the stamp of man who is going to see it through.

Of course our chaps were there with their staff and even if we don't look soldiers they do. They are General Walker and last but greatest of all our Bird or General Birdwood KCMG etc etc he deserves all his titles. I'll never forget the time he trod on my neck. A bit of a Turks advance took place towards middle of November and I was down in the bomb position—my two hours off and I was sleeping in the tunnel and he came round inspecting the post and didn't see me and trod on my neck but he soon heard me utter and I found out who it was, for he apologised to me. I believe I'll let him walk all over me now if necessary. [Ben changes his mind-Ed.].

In the afternoon Major Lindeman judged the Battallion drilling squads and our Coy. won. Ponto McKenzie, Hutchinson, Tom Brown, Frank Warne and myself formed a party with some Seaforth Highlanders and went to local concert in the night.

In the evening all the Battalion Officers turned up and we rendered them a fine concert etc. Plenty of comics and fancy dresses etc.

This seems too good to last. Wonder what we are in for. We are fit for anything.

No wonder the Frenchies are drunk a lot when they start as babies. A little kiddy in arms was yesterday being given some champagne to drink and I looked hard at her but the woman evidently thought no wrong to it and went on. The kiddy drank about 1 dessert spoon full in all. I've seen also a little chap about 5-6 who couldn't walk straight through drinking rain water out of a beer jug.

The country is one mass of hops at present. The vines being trained up to a great height some 40' high. The grape vines some 3 'thick run all over our present billet—in leaf it must be a glorious sight to see. This is the prettiest country I've seen. I've never in NSW seen such pretty green fields, hedges, trees etc. Australian scenery seems to me to be too sombre all together.

The cuckoos are still busy. The English men with us say they are very late in the year. It makes such a deep throaty call. The thatching

Street scene near Havre.

over our barn didn't keep out the wet the other night, only over one corner was it dry and into this space 20 feet by 10 feet about 50 of us herded. I won't say anything except we were fine and warm.

I'm on guard at present in France. This day 1915 I was up at Tarro. What a difference in occupation and location. Close now, with best of respects to all at *Oaklands*. Sincere friend.

Ben.

1.6.16.

Marched through to Steenwerck. Main bodies of Tyneside Scottish and Seaforth Highlands Queens Own Royal moving towards the line rumoured to take over the AIF section. All very merry but not as merry as we were, Hutchison, Ponto McKenzie, Frank Warne, Tom Brown and myself all singing for all we were worth. Passed also some African Scottish in Kilts on cycles.

3.6.16

Capt MacKenzie went on leave last night. Sorry to see leaving the Unit Capt Street (son of Justice Street) resigned position as Adj of 1st Battalion through preference being given to new hands and not to men who have been some time on the Peninsula. He is going to Staff Appointment with another Division. Lt Prior to take over as Adjutant. Yesterday 1 Taube and 1 British plane brought down

5.6.16.

The 3rd Brigade seems unlucky, as last night the 9th and 11th were subjected to a terrific bombardment and many casualties resulted. The whole horizon was lit by flashes and there seemed to be a dead silence for three minutes then it broke again with renewed vigour. We all stood too at the road ready to move off but once again we were not required.

4.6.16.

At Church Service today Gen. Birdwood (he seems fond of 1st Brigade) told us about the Naval disaster off Jutland and mentioned that P.P.C.L.I. (Princess Patricia's Canadian Light Infantry) had refused to budge when its 2 flank regiments had been driven back. It left Canada 1126 strong and refused to budge at Ypres during the gas attack and only 93 came out fit men. Reinforced up again and now half wiped out again.

He also told us of 6 of 20th Battalion had been taken prisoners and how well 1st Battalion had stood ground when heavily bombarded and then lined the parapets with bayonets fixed. This may only be talk as Birdwood likes talking, not like Smythe, he's the opposite.

5.6.16.

Had Brigade manoeuvres. The battalion split up to represent the Brigade. My section captured 1 whole Battalion when we got Lt. Everett *Pull Through* (he's awfully tall and thin) and he took us on fatigue road mending as far as Bac St Maur filling in shell holes. On the way back I asked to drop out for a few minutes to see Ginger Smith—he is here with a mobile gun crew.

7.6.16.

Fatigue 8.00am right through Bac St Maur and Fleurbaix, road mending (Some navvies) Returned about 6.00pm very tired indeed. Saw more trees cut to fantastic shapes. Armchair, horse and like a sun dial. Writing letters in little estaminet near Doulieu. Tom Brown and Hutchison sported bottle of Champagne 5 Fcs.

8.6.16.

Met Ginger Smith at the Tubs. He told me Dr Walker and Mr Smith had dissolved partnership and heard facts of case. Very sorry indeed. Hope Mrs Smith didn't hear facts. . Huns shelled Bac St Mur but missed the Railway Station where our supplies come to.

9.6.16.

Left at 7.15 p.m. for the lines and after a tedious march we reached them, relieving 5th Battalion. on the left of our old position near Fleurbaix . Communication trenches are very long and much same as before, sloppy except now about 2 miles long.

Shiny can't help it—doggerel comes from him like water from a tap. He keeps us amused with his sayings, polished Tommy buttons and dirty black unshaven face.

> Somewhere in France
> 13.6.16 Trenches

Dear Frank,

Your letter dated 3.4.16 to hand this morning and very pleased to receive it too. How dare you have indigestion without me telling you to have it. Don't do it again until I tell you so.

No green envelope so only a short note. We had a good route march to get here, full pack up too we are the human camels.

We have a regular poet amongst us. There are just outside the dugout door some graves of unknown soldiers so Shiny Buttons said as he saw them

> They buried him just where they found him
> and now he is sleeping alone.
> They just wrapped a blanket around him
> and wrote on his cross Unknown.

Not bad is it for a make up in a hurry.

Well so Marj. (sister) has been up to your place. Did she enjoy herself as much as I did.?

We had some battalion sports last Thursday and of course A Coy won all the chief events. Cricket match, football, high and long jumps. I had the honour to play in football semi-final but not the final.

Our rifle drill squad couldn't possibly be beaten. The funniest item was the catching of the greasy pig. It was all greased with dubbin and B Coy who won the competition deserved the pig which they received as a prize. Of course the winner was covered in fat from head to toe.

Hope all at Tarro are well. What do you think of 21 eggs going in one pan at once? 3 of us went into a little estaminet and ordered 7 eggs each and the women put the lot in one pan. You can imagine how nice each egg looked.

Our march of 11 miles full pack up was rather solid and I was glad I carried no luxuries at all, only necessities. That is the worst of infantry for me. A.S.C. or artillery. It is thundering terribly, just like 15lbs shots out of a machine gun. Have to close now.

Ben

———

Made Gas Warrant Company Officer whilst in trenches.

Sunday received letter Frank, 4 from Home all well. Harry Jones left for France on day of our battalion sports. The Germans put out a notice board to Battalion saying 'Hope 1st Battalion enjoyed themselves at the Sports. 'Still stoushing at 4.15 pm each day.

———

1ST BATTALION DIARY

The Brigade went into the line again on June 10. The 1st Battalion took over the right sector of the line near La Boutillerie.

———

12.6.16.

On with gum boots, the trenches horribly moist. Woods, 4th Platoon received shrapnel in abdomen and heel—severely wounded. Tom Brown, bullet across nape of neck, nasty wound, as so near spine and all nerve centres. Both in my Platoon. We are re wiring the front line to make it more difficult to raid and so covering patrols are sent out to guard us. Otherwise very quiet. Raining solidly. Very, very sloppy and wet. German 13 pounders very busy along Devon Avenue.

15.6.16.

Stood to arms at midnight whilst the 2nd and 20th Battalions had raids. Our guns opened up and formed a curtain barrage around each raid sector and both raids successful. We had a few casualties, perhaps Fritz thought the whole line was coming over.

The machine guns captured had to be blown up as they couldn't be pulled through barbed wire easily. The mortars and bombs going off were O.K. The mortars looking like gold fish in the air and the wallop when they came down and duck boards went up is good to hear. A bit of a dust-up occurred earlier in the night between two of our own patrols, but no casualties happened. (Forgot to draw the pins when threw bombs).

We now have control over No Man's Land. Last night Frank Foster shot through eye, died today. I went out in No Man's land last night on listening post—very quiet—saw Hun patrol in distance. German working party kicking up awful row. Our party on wire silent. Our barb wire in awful state very rotten indeed, stakes snap very easily.

Letter home to mother in Mac's envelope

15.6.16

Dear Frank

I received a fine lot of letters from you at mail day-what a fat lot. Last date 16/4 so there are still a few floating around. It can't take a whole month to come here.

I'd like to be put in the post box with a stamp on my forehead delivered by Mrs Burton into the hands of a young maid with frizzy hair named Frank. It will be a long time till I cast my peepers o' you but never mind, —time flies (slow flies here too).

It's about one year since I left Sydney now. Not quite as bad as some of the contingent. I'll never forget the sight of you maidens as we steamed out of Hexham.

Here 3 loaves of bread and 1 candle for 9 men. What do you think of that!...no jam or butter or meat. I'm thinking of writing a recipe book with directions how to turn candles into puddings. Quite often we get that bill o fare. Just imagine the differences in the menu from home. Oh well, such is life and we all are a happy crew although we do spend a lot on tucker when out of trenches.

Did you go to town this Easter? You very seldom tell me much of the doings, —I have to pump Art and Mary's letters for news. Have you made a blouse like Mary of minon over minon.

So you saw how poor old Roger Moag was discharged. I'll tell you someday when we do not have to do all our talk on paper. I'm going to get my phizog took 1ˢᵗ opportunity. You want to know how much water a dixie holds well a large cookie's dixie holds about one gallon but the small dixies at mess time that we use ourselves to eat out of hold 1=half pint.

So Pontie has the bottle fever every now and then, well there are lots of chaps here who have the same and they are just as good fighters as ever.

Some boys from A Coy showing a food dixie

Do you know Pal, I think you get indigestion through jumping up from the table every now and then like you used to do when I was there, so be a good girl and take plenty of exercise riding, walking, working.

Thanks for the mails old girl. The last issue was very fine indeed, worth saving. Such a fine lot of photos too of you all......

Remind me to all at *Oaklands*.

Ben

15.6.16

Germans very quiet last night until 12.15 when they started on our left to send trench mortar bombs over. The air turned a lurid red color. The bursting force of these huge bombs is terrific. A 30 lb bomb makes a hole 18 feet deep and round. The aerial torpedo about 6 feet long are only a huge bomb.

Put the clock on one hour

Trenches so slushy, Shiny Buttons wrote a piece of poetry about them.

There's slush on the floor of my dug out
The trenches are muddy and wet
And my thoughts wander back to Australia
The land I'll never forget
But I'm trying to write you a letter
In spite of the roar of the guns
And the shells they are bursting around me
May the devil set fire to those Huns
Mention the singing birds in your note
Sweet is the voice of that songster
Singing his song as he goes
Over the farms and the trenches
Singing to us and our foes
Had you a voice like this songster
Look at the joy, you would carry
Into the heart
Of the man who will part
With his freedom and ask you to marry

16.6.16

—Terrific bombardment on our left 2nd Division position. 12.14 Gas alarm and klaxon horns, shell cases banged. All stood to arms with helmets on 12.30. Heavy whistling came from Sailly = gas there, steam whistle kicked up awful row. Several people in Sailly gassed and about 10 soldiers also. Very jubilant over Russian victories.

17.6.16.

Very quiet all day. Lieut. Burstall and 5 men went out on patrol reached as far as German barb wire, lying down watching wiring parties when 2 German officers clothed in roundish caps without peaks, big capes, pistols in hands, practically trod on them. Burstall fired, Mackley fired and 3 bombs thrown, —scattered and made for a rendezvous near our wire.

Sid Wilson was missing. Searched and searched but found no traces. Saw big stretcher party out after wounded and bombed Germans.

18.6.16

Last night I and 3 men went out as a covering party to the Patrol looking for Wilsons body or any trace of him. No luck. At 2 minutes past 12 furious bombardments towards Armentieres followed by gas attack, wind blowing in wrong direction for it to be swept on to us. Germans using a fair quantity of gas lately.

After searching thoroughly no trace, came to conclusion that he had been blown to pieces by Huns bombs. Lieut. Burstall signalled a washout to Fritz who had a pot at him over the parapet. He is still wild about losing Sid Wilson—he has been lost for 48 hours now and if he has been captured Fritz knows the unit opposite in his sector.

19.6.16.

At 4.50 a.m. Sid Wilson wandered back to our lines. We saw him crawling across No Man's land and went out to get him. He said the second night out he watched flares put up by Fritz and started to crawl back when he found a strong Fritz patrol in front of him and he couldn't move so he waited all day in a hole. He was dazed very weak and done up. All this didn't agree with him so evacuated to hospital.

He said that Fritz comes down to his front line in hundreds and then goes away again at Dawn. The Colonel was glad to know this as Brigade had often suspected it.

Went to sleep in Signals Dugout and slept through stand too then right up to dinner. Very tired indeed. Speaking to Mr Beavis, he said he saw a slip in Gazette about Brewer, Goode, Youman and Beavis. Father must have put it in.

4 gas flappers. Good for dug outs. Air cushion very good indeed. To me if warm feet and comfortable pillow I sleep well.

I've just been watching a few of our light trench mortars at work. Have terrific exploding force, blow yards of hun parapets down. Colonel very wrath at Capt. (milkman) MacKenzie ordering 14 batteries to play on Hun trenches. Our Capt (Baker) AC MacKenzie is very sober man not likely to do things like that.

Great system of Gas alarms here. Claxon horns, sirens in trenches. Big steam whistles in neighbouring towns. French parapets here very thick, no loop holes. My belief is that lines here are held by artillery and not by men in trenches. Rifle grenades being sent over very frequently from 6 Bays. All our bays have been named; Botany, Rose, Woolloomooloo etc look fine, 53rd Battalion supposed to be in Wallon Cappel.

———

20.6.16.

This morning was sent into Fleurbaix on Gas duty. Not bad little town at all, fine Church and cemetery. Big shrine with crucifix in it. Noticed crucifix and figure untouched but big shot holes and cracks in shrine. Came home 3.15.

Bill Hunt hit in 9 places with trench mortar backwash. We blew in their parapets wholesale and they did likewise. The whiz bangs fairly frequent. No one could possibly imagine the demoralising effect of heavy artillery fire if they haven't been through it!

My nerves gone completely shivered like an ashen leaf before bombardment and wrote to Mother, Frank, Mrs Hunt, Rupe Neil, 53rd Battalion not far away. Learnt that a mobile 60lb, a Stokes trench mortar was operating in our sector and so we got it in the neck.

Terrific bombardment by Germans in reply to breaches we had made in their trenches, 8 inch shells, all crouched in close to parapet. Shook the earth, jumpy and nervy as could be. Feel ashamed of myself.

Lot of damage done. Some casualties but could have been many more but for the C.O. making us build sand bags and backs to the breastwork and we stood in between. Fritz working hard, since the Australians came, have put in several new communication trenches.

Wish we could have a proper belt at them instead of these racking bombardments. Vermicide sprays in use, spraying blankets covering doors of the main dugouts. The mixture hypo 1 ½ lbs, washing soda 3 lbs and water 3 galls neutralises the gas and prevents the gas getting inside. Hope gas proofing works!

Have been in trenches 10 days.

21.6.16.

Terrible stoushing up in the afternoon. We started it with 60lb trench mortars They started putting mortars and 5.9 'shells all down our line. Nearly deafened. One man 3rd Bn working with 1st Battalion killed. Lance/Corporal Butchard in the neck, George Golder 2 feet knee and arm. It took 1 ½ hours to get the doctor down from Hd Quarters. To AMC—shell proof steel arched with 15' of dirt on top.

Sometimes wish I was in AMC. Look at Bruce Rainsford, has not been in danger at all unless over eating is danger.

Fritz retaliating to our rifle grenades sent over by Sergt. Allen of the bombers. Whiz bangs shaved the parapet—we are thinking Fritz wanted to see how close he could go without hitting them.

Think the whiz bangs were meant to cover the report of a much heavier gun they were using on the roads.

Glad they made us wear steel helmets; the 1st time in the line we didn't have them. They seem about 6' across when wearing them on Parade and about ½ 'wide when shrapnel comes along. Private Salkeld has a huge dent in his. Something struck it.

A dud 5.9. lobbed on our dug out burying our things, but Ponto McKenzie, Brownlie and myself were on duty and missed it. Being Gas

N.C.O., inspected helmets, found 5 out of 40 defective mainly through incorrect folding creasing the rubber valve and perishing it. Shiny Buttons to keep us smiling hatched an ode entitled *How I Won the V.C.* awful doggerel but might amuse someone at home:—

HOW I WON THE V.C.

We were standing to, as good soldiers do,
At the close of the day and at morn,
The bullets were humming, the Germans were coming,
And our trenches with shrapnel were torn.

We greeted the Germans with good nickel sermons,
They're sermons that take great effect.
Their lines thinner grew, but our comrades went too,
And most of our dug outs were wrecked.

How Captain MacKenzie flew into a frenzy
Of rage and he gave a wild shout,
Saying *'Come with me Shiny* then over the briney
To Blighty we'll go or go out '.

I grasped at my rifle,
Though I felt just a trifle upset by those murderous Huns,
But I dashed to the Stunt and the Captain in front
Killed old Fritz to the roar of the guns.

The Huns were defeated and wildly retreated
And loudly for Mercy did cry,
But our brave Captain fell, he'd been struck by a shell,
I'll save him, I cried, *or I die.*

I rushed to our leader;
He cried 'You will need a strong muscle to carry me through,
I replied with a laugh 'I'm a man of the staff,
With muscle enough! for the two.

The bullets were flying, and brave men were dying
As I staggered along midst the slain,
And the boys wildly cheered as to them
I steered my way to the trenches again.

When Captain MacKenzie recovered his sense

He cried 'Shiny, you're one of the best',
How the Captain you know won the famed D.S.O.,
and I've the V.C. on my chest.

I'm going to Blighty, for they've heard of the mighty
And glorious deeds that I've done,
And in Petticoat Lane, I'll meet once again
All the maidens and kiss every one

By 'Shiny Buttons 'who is the sanitary man. (Private Jones)

If First Battalion is home by Christmas I promise to buy
BW Champion a 50/–(fifty shillings) hat signed, J Farlow

22.6.16

Heaviest bombardment ever experienced 5.9 ' trench mortars and whiz bangs, 77's. C. Thompson, Fletcher (cook), E.C. Parish, A. Teaze, Stedman (seriously), Martis besides others in 12th Battalion. Donnely, Thompson, Fletcher, Stedman all playing cards when a mortar burst and they copped it.

Teaze was hit inside a dug out. Doctor came down very quickly this time. All night we were anxious about gas. Cylinders have been seen in their trenches and as wind very favourable we were on the alert but fortunately nothing came of it.

23.6.16

Bombarded in the morning no one hit at all fortunately. 3rd Battalion relieving us to right just as well we are absolutely sick of it. Swopping over with 3rd Battalion billets. I wonder will we be home by Xmas. I really don't expect to be alive then. They are heavily bombarding our old position at V.C. Avenue very hotly. Relieved in the sopping wet. Wet through we marched with many tumbles to Fleurbaix in supports. Bed, stone flags in stable at 1.15 am Pulled out again at 7 am.

24.6.16.

7 a.m. marched to firing line on fatigues but only to be marched back again as fatigues were cancelled. More bungling somewhere. Sopping wet. Visited Fleurbaix. Wrote to Gertrude, mother, received photos of home.

25-7.6.16.

Rumoured Austria surrendered, hope it's true. Sunday went on Fatigue to the supports and while there our raid under Capt. Phil (Howell-) Price took place. Very grand sight, the crack of our flying Pig (60lb) Trench mortars solid, the ground seems to crack. They replied likewise.

Then Fritz put up red lights to say they were being attacked and onion bags and red rockets again and their artillery replied but the curtain fire by our own guns was good. We were all up the Top of Dead Dog Avenue watching it.

Raid very successful but it cost us some good men + 6 men captured and 40 killed. Prior and Little out of action permanently. The Australians have made a name for good artillery. We have made this place Fleurbaix a veritable hot shop.

Wrote to Tom Brown. Went for a walk and visited big ruined church and Fleurbaix cemetery, very carefully tended by an old man in charge who says *apres la gueure* England will pay for the upkeep. England is paying. Each cross has the man's name, regiment and number on it. Canada, Middlesex, Royal Irish Rifles, Queens Own, Royal Lancs. Royal Scots 1st afoot, right of line and pride of British Army, oldest regiment.

Raining very hard indeed. On guard, very good guard indeed, no equipment needed when on duty. Cylinder of gas seen going down to the trenches. Hope we gas the square heads. We bombarded heavily... we Australians have been singularly successful with the raids. 2 prisoners brought back, all rest killed. 2 very big shells probably 10 'lobbed in Fleurbaix.

26/6/16

Dear Frank.

Five nights ago I received a fine bunch of letters from you. We were in the trenches and I was on duty so they nearly burnt a hole in my pocket all morning. The last date towards end of April ie after Anzac day.

We've had a rough time in trenches this time—cold slushy and wet dug outs, *But such is war* well there are big rumours that Austria has thrown in the sponge—hope it is true. It means a lot to the Russian troops having strategic railways running into Germany.

I received a letter from Mrs Niland, thank her. She writes a very nice motherly letter. What a lot of troops have left Australia within the last 8 month. What a pity we didn't all land on the Peninsula and march to Constantinople.

Well, I will answer a few of your latest notes. First of all last mails I wrote and Art forgot to enclose them in his letter. Hope you have been receiving my letters—some say here that the mail was closed for 6 weeks whilst we moved from Arabia to France.

We are now billeted in a little town where a lot of street fighting took place—everywhere are bullet splashes and loop holes commanding streets etc. Most of the houses were mined by the Germans before the British took it.

New Methodist church has been built in Wahroonga since I left— seems strange and hard to picture it. Am very pleased you are going to learn music for you will get a lot of amusement out of it and please others as well.

I don't like the idea of the name on back of envelopes pal for everyone to see. You always tell me where you sit so that I can picture you. Well you can picture me sitting in a ruined barn on cold stones resting my pad on my knees. Every now and then the rats in the roof scurry about and knock pieces of mortar and bricks on my head.

Like you, there is nothing to write about except that news the censor would cut out. A note from Mary accompanied your last Frank...I'll have to close.

Ben

Tell Ruth I'll write an answer to her note later on BWC

THE 1ST BATTALION DIARY

On the night of June 27, a successful raid was made by a specially trained party under Capt. Phillip Howell-Price. Casualties among the party were one killed and nine wounded. The party had been taken out of the line beforehand to practise their training on trenches modelled on those to be raided.

The strength was 5 officers and about 60 other ranks. There were 4 groups consisting of two trench parties of an officer and seven others, a supporting group and another group in reserve. A heavy 'box 'barrage was laid down by our artillery in the portion of enemy trench to be raided, cutting it off from support. Difficulty was experienced in getting through the enemy's wire which appeared to be untouched or almost so by our previous fire.—

29.6.16

We all marched from here through Bac St. Maur to Sailly baths. Long march but the bath was well worth the walk. Met a chap who said he knew me at Stanmore School. His name Cunningham, strange he should remember me after being 8 years away from the place.

3 big shells just dropped about 100 yards away in Fleurbaix, don't know damage yet. We are shaking Fritz up a lot here. He used to bring his troops from Verdun for a rest but he doesn't since the Australians came.

Have been seeing a lot of 5th Brigade here. 17, 18, 19, 20 Battalions, same colors as 1st Brigade but diamond shape different. (Ben does drawing of them all) Lots of colors about black and green they are 3rd division— some completely new Battalions and some recruited new battalions in Tel—el Kebir.

Australian Army Medical Corps now use circles instead of oblong and diamond. Sgt Dewar going into line tomorrow we follow very shortly. Any amount of letters from home. Letter from Arthur Champion, Frank, Gertrude, Mother, Miss McCoy. Replied to Art, Billy Hunt, Miss Vernon Tom Brown. Received tin of chocs from Gertrude.

The Germans use Fleurbaix church as a sight. This church built by Spaniards. In our back yard is the place where the Germans stood last in Fleurbaix. Better type of trenches than ours. Smaller firing bays i.e. to localise shell or bomb burst. Well drained and sides of trenches done up with osiers [basketry—Ed.] turgs etc. ours are done with wire netting hurdles There is also a machine gun position well cemented in 9 ' concrete.

Our raiding party says the Hun trenches have dug outs 9 feet underground and well cemented in. Electric light in dug outs. The German shells have a fair percentage duds, don't explode. Suppose this is through women workers in factory.

Sergeant Shaw has re-joined No 2 Platoon. Corporal W. Allan has been given his other bar and a M.M. He deserved every bit of them both. One of the quietest and bravest men I've ever known. In charge of the bombing section.

Whole sale bombardment on all sides. Can easily tell size of shell by row it makes. An 18lb gun has a very big roar for its size. An alien aeroplane has just had a close shave. Flying low as our aviators do, taking risks in order to see clearly the Hun anti-aircraft guns, got on to it and made the plane rock perilously in the air.

The Taubes and Fokkers fly very high and must use very powerful glasses. A brick wall is usually hard enough to explode a 5.9 '.

There are many soldier graves in Fleurbaix, mostly September 1915. The Germans on the march buried their dead. This accounts for absence of German graves. There will be many brave chaps gone when the fruit becomes ripe.

Cherries, Pears, apples and raspberries already ripe. Had a feed yesterday. Sooner this war over the better for Australia. Fleubaix—9 ' shells. This is a fearful drain on a young country's male population. Another dud just came over.

3 of our planes in now looking for the gun. Wish I could get some news about Corporal Will Hunt. Once a man leaves his battalion no one knows where on earth or how he is. We are superior in Artillery as proved last night during the raid.

Vic Fowler acting as R.S.M. for a while and Fred Hodge acting C.S.M. of the Company. The French girls call Vic Fowler the 'Petit Noir Sergeant Major 'and nothing used to get him so wild.

30.6.16.

Paid today 30 francs on Pounds 1/1/—= 8 6/15d is equal to one franc i.e.: we are gaining on the French Govt. in money. Raining cats and dogs. Water, water everywhere.

Went to gas lecture. Wind favourable for gas tonight. 23 of our planes up at once tonight made a raid on Lille which is practically opposite us. South Wales borderers made 3 trenches in an advance last night towards Gavinche way on our right. Expect we advance here shortly.

Gas already in some of our trenches. AAMC already been seen cutting linen into patches for armlet pieces for backs so as our own artillery will know when to stop firing when we reach enemy trenches. Last night we loaded engineers trucks at Dead Dog and shoved them down to firing line. Tonight on fatigue on firing line. Last night 3 x 18lber batteries opened up not far behind us and made our ears ring continually with their barking.

All platoons filled 12 bags each, this to keep us fit for no other earthly reason, why we should do it. To bed at 2.45 am and pulled out at 8.am to tidy up.

Inspected Vermorel sprayer down at Cains Post. Fleurbaix 3rd line of resistance. Ammunition galore in case of necessity. Stedman had to have his leg amputated. One raider went into a dugout where 5 Germans were (Bavarian Regiment) demanded surrender. All seemed so stupefied that he shot the lot.

Rum issue tonight Yesterday 4 men to loaf, no jam, butter only candles. No reason at all why we shouldn't get full issue whilst out of trenches. 6 ' shells still lobbing Fleurbaix. Fleurbaix to Nouveau Monde.

30.6.16

As usual on fatigue, more heavy bombardment whole day. British advance on the right, bombardment terrific In front of our 18lbs wind nearly knocked one over.

2.7.16

Still on fatigue. Mr Horniman 3rd Bn, Mr Kellaway 1st Bn hit in hip. Sunday Rev. Ashley Brown back again, fine missionary sermon. Francs down to 8 8/15 but we received 10 d for it from people. Peas and cabbages and lettuces galore. Last night 9th Battalion made a very successful raid,

20 prisoners and 2 officers, 2 machine guns and 1 trench mortar. 3rd Brigade again very fine lot indeed.

3.7.16.

1st Battalion relieved by the 47th Battalion. Last night billet shelled only 1 hit. Old couple shivering like jelly in middle of shelling. In the middle of the shelling Sgt. Shaw brought word around that we move off early. So we started to get ready.

At 4.36 a.m. we started—no breakfast no bon (good); myself and 6 others are to take on a support line at Nouveau Monde. Moved through Bac St Maur to Sailly on to Nouveau Monde 4 kilos from Estaires. We relieved a garrison of South Wales Borders and settled down to a good loaf for at least a week.

Drawing rations from Ambulance Station near Estaires. Our duties are to repair clean and generally look after these lines. This is a beautiful district, the poppies are out and the fruit trees in blossom. We often walk to Estaires. We met some of our boys from the Battalion also now out of the line, drilling etc.

There is a large canal and it was interesting to watch the boats and barges going towards Armentieres. What a job these inland water sailors have. Received 1 letter Mother, Mary 1, Marj, 1 Franc 2

4.7.16

Wrote to Mother, F Service Card to Cliff Gentle, rainy very. Light Horse Brigade here, 24 hours given to people in Levantie to clear out. More Victorians captured Somme way.

Went into Estaires with Hutchison. Met Art Felton and Lance Corporal McTackett there. They wanted me to go with them and visit an old acquaintance Madelaine Lecompt, Rue Jeanne d'Arc, Estaire but I persuaded Hutch to come home, away from guard too long already.

July 4th

Dear Frank

I've received no mail from you this week so now I'll get a double batch when it comes. I received a very nice letter from your Mother and will reply soon, until then I hope this letter will suffice.

Well, you can now address your letters to Corporal. Being fortunate enough to scrape through when others didn't so I got the job. Art is fortunate in being away in a good hospital having a rest. I hope he never comes back but continues to have a good time.

We all are poked away in a little pokey town where there is nothing to do, to see, to eat or drink, so the sooner we are on the road again the better. The people at home found out where we were by the postal address on the stamp of the parcels.

Did you tumble to it at all? I hope we go away for a holiday somewhere. You know the Battalion has been away from home two years by the time you receive this. If I were to tell you all the rumours one hears you would be as bewildered as ourselves.

One second the Battalion is going to England, next to Australia, so we are going somewhere in the dim future. You know there is no Battalion. left, only a few remnants and they are all nerves and jumpy.

Glad the kiddies liked the cards from Hazebrouk we sent them on the off chance from the 1st big town we went into. We would have liked to go into Amiens when we were went so close but now we are moved right away from it. There is no chance.

Give my love to all at home there's no news.

Ben

7.7.16.

Still at Nouveau Monde, big clearing station here quite a number of 52nd and 53rd men coming through.

The above rough diagram is a plan of a farm house that 2 platoons were billeted in when we first came to France we lived in the barn for 12 days. The waste matter is put on the gardens after fermenting drying a summer or so in the pit, often the heap overshadows the kitchen and bed room windows and smells badly.

The pump is very close and the soakage must go into the well. We used to have the water chlorinated by the A.M.C. and it was often necessary to spread chlorinated lime about to cover up the smell—this used to lead to trouble as the chickens used to die after eating it. I feel sure had we not been inoculated so often, some fever would have broken out.

Saturday

...orders came through and my party marched back to the Battalion. Sunday, (We always seem to move on that day) We moved off at 5.15 a.m. having had breakfast as advanced guard, to the Battalion who moved to Bailleul.

Monday 10.7.16.

Stobo and myself saw quite a bit of Bailleul as we were in the advance guard and were struck by the splendid buildings there, Bought some post cards.

The Battalion arrived and from Bailleul we were put 40 to a truck and started off on a jolting journey towards Candas. The trucks were filthy. Route:—Hazebrouck, Berquettle, Ham-en-Artois, Lilliers, Marles, Callone, Pernes, St Pol arriving at Candas at 12.50 p.m.

As far as Choquettes, country purely agricultural. At Choquettes we entered mining districts and then on to manufacturing districts. Pernes Camplain, huge works for making fibro slates and sheets.

At Candas we detrained and a weary march in the dark started, but Fowler, Shaw and Jones etc. started up a song and it cheered up the mob so that at Domart, our destination, we lost not a man, much to Col. Heane's pleasure.

We were the first Australians at Domart and goods were awfully cheap. Our Bethune notes were no good so most of us had no other money. It's absurd how one community won't cash another's notes. Here we heard that Spinks and T.R.B. Wilkinson got Military Medals, Price D.S.O. Little and Moffat the Military Cross and Good Luck to them, they deserved it!

12.7.16

Marched to Vignacourt. Stobo and myself again billeting NCOs. We report to the Mayor in the new village and find out the accommodation and when the unit arrives guide them to their new quarters, splitting up the Companies into the smallest number of houses so the platoon leaders will have their platoons handy for training purposes. No A men dropped out. Capt. Street and Capt. Price used their horses as pack animals for their respective companies, but Capt. MacKenzie didn't, his as it was not necessary.

From here Brainwood and Tate had to go to hospital. Tate's old shoulder wound from the Peninsula played up with him and Brainwood had very high temperature from boils and couldn't march.

From Vignacourt on the 15th we moved to Allonville. Rotten March as we only had 5 to a tin of Beef and 1ft loaves to 14 men. When we got to Allonville our billet was miserable and the owner locked the pump, but we lifted the door off and let down the transport buckets.

On the way we passed through Fresnells & Longchamps. From Allonville Amiens can be seen, but we were too tired to visit the place. The march was rotten and quite a lot of A's boots are not too brilliant.

Col. Heane complimented the Coy. on none falling out. A Coy, O, B Coy, 6. C 14, D 4 fell out. This record due mainly to a steady even pace set by Fowler, Shaw and Lieut. Bootles. It was a pretty march, trees lining the road and poppies and flowers ablaze in the fields.

12.7.16 Wednesday

Dear Franc

I suppose within a couple of days I will have word from you, in reply to my letters from France. During last few days we have been touring again and are very tired indeed. Mail closes today so instead of sleeping I'll drop

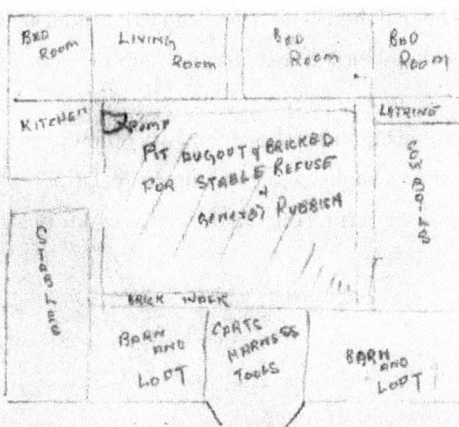

Typical French Farm plan:-

you a line.

Yesterday we marched a few kilos and this morning some more. Down South the country is prettier than the north. We stopped in such a little village last night. We were the first Aust'ns to go through and didn't the rustics open their mouth when they saw our hats and many bare knees.

There is a church built in 1633, some age that, with magnificent glass windows and beautiful pipe organ. It seems strange a village a little bigger than Tarro should have an RC church as big as Newcastle church.

We are in glorious country quite different from the last style. This is all hilly and heavily wooded. I saw some family picture taken at Art's place, and I'm surprised how Didie Felton has grown.

We've just had 2 Lance Corps of A Coy given military medals. A military medal is between a DCM and a VC. The 2 lucky men are Spinks and Wilkinson who is from Maitland West way, they deserved them. I cannot let you know what they did but it will keep till I lob home.

I think you'll see us by Christmas if not I'll be disappointed indeed. Just wait until we swing into the quay. All our rifles are in a crook state through travelling. I'll have to get on to mine. What do you think of a Frenchie who locked up his pump so we couldn't get any water, well the company had revenge by eating all his spring onions and lettuces.

I thought the poor chap would go of his head but he thought better and unlocked his pump and we took up a collection for him. Please forgive these short notes but pal there is no news I can write about at all. Some of my family had photos taken and they all appear just the same except Mum. She looks older.

There will be some big stunts shortly and who knows a chap may be lucky enough to strike a blighty and go to the Auld Dart.

How is dressmaking getting on. On the bias as usual? Plenty of love Ben

———

14.7.16

Boots fixed up. Amiens built in a valley looks O.K. but no leave is given. In this place is a large aerodrome with any amount of planes. There are many types, each for its own job, from the fighter for protecting the bombing planes, to the slow buses they use for directing gun fire.

The handwritten receipt for Frank's dressmaking course.

16.7.16.

Marched to Warloy about 15 kilos—like pack camels with full pack and tin helmet and rifle. Feet parade-astonishing so few were knocked up.

17th.

Gun fire in the distance just one continuous roar. Big dressing stations here and wounded coming in by the dozens in motor buses and ambulances. Estiminets out of bounds. Everyone in the unit realises what we are in for and I was astonished at the voluntary attendance at a Church Parade—fully half the Battalion was there.

18th

Packed up in 16 minutes ready for moving off. Standing too, for immediate action.

POZIERES

FROM THE 1ST BATTALION WAR DIARY

Pozieres itself was a small village some two and half miles from Albert, along the Bapaume Road and was one of the strongest points of the German defence. It had already been attacked by the British troops without success. The village similar to most French villages in that area had one straggling street, and it had been very strongly fortified. Our actual entry into the battle was on the night of July 19-20 when we took over the front line from the 12 *Durham* Light Infantry. The relief was carried out in dense darkness and was completed about 2 in the morning—the whole operation being harassed by a continuous gas shelling from which we suffered many casualties. Among others Lt Everitt was wounded and died while being taken to the dressing station.

The trenches we found to be exceedingly poor. They had been adapted to requirements of the smaller men of the English regiment, the firing steps, for example, being much too high for the Australians, while all the trenches were narrow and deep and not connected up. Our CO and the *Durham* Colonel were forced to get out on the top every now and then and were fiercely sniped at by the enemy, 250 yeards away so that both did some fine sprint championship training.

To take over the relief, the Brigade left Warloy at 4.15 am and were met by guides at British Brigade Headquarters, where our men were taken—A and B to the front line and C and D in close support around Casualty Corner. An attack had been planned for the 20th but was postponed in favour of a bigger offensive on July 22.—We were told that the capture of Pozieres was a necessary part of the operations which aimed at wresting Thiepval from the Germans, who, on their part recognised its extreme strategic imporance; so that the struggle, we knew would be keen. This was soon proved in no uncertain fashion, for as C and D Companies came into position a rain of gas shells came over. This, we at first thought was only tear gas, but we were soon painfully aware of its asphyxiating character, our throats were badly affected and gas masks were hurriedly donned.

Among our casualties, in addition to poor Everitt, our Adjutant Lieut White and Lieut Graham had to be evacuated with about 30 men and both the C.O. and the Brigade was sadly handicapped by the loss of the adjutant in this, the first big engagement in France.

All day on Saturday, the company commanders were with the Colonel, while every unit was busy preparing for the onslaught etc etc and all day long the enemy shelled us a proceeding which resulted in the death of Major Lindeman, one of the saddest events of the period at Casualty Corner along with Lieut. Yeomans who was killed at once.

Night came and with it the battle that will ever live in memory. Zero had been fixed for half an hour after midnight and 11.45, A and B companies left our front trenches and took up a position that had been selected by patrols in No Man's Land. To permit identification in the dark, each man wore his sleeves rolled up to the elbows, and A and B Companies wore White Strips of cloth, six inches by one inch, on the back of the right shoulder the remaining companies wearing a corresponding strip of blue.

A and B were the first to take the first objective and after they had occupied it the other companies were to pass through them and get as close as possible to the second objective and to rush it as the barrage lifted. As soon as the ground was clear C and D Companies followed into No Man's Land.

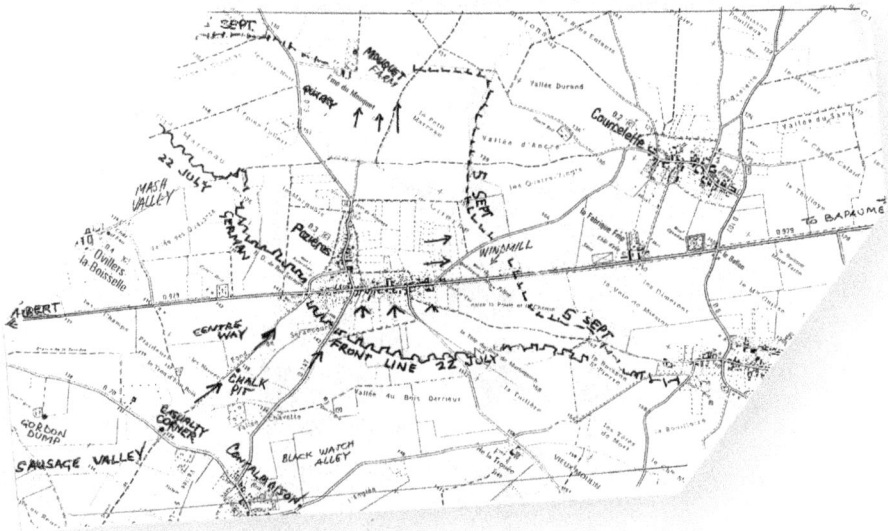

Map showing Pozieres and the German Lines

The main street of Pozieres after heavy bombardment by British and Germans looking towards Bapaume Between the 23 July and early September 1916, the 1st 2nd, and 4th Divisions between them launched 19 attacks on German positions in and around the ruins of Pozieres. The Australians suffered 23, 000 casualties while advancing two kilometres, British and Australian artillery were no match for German artillery and machine guns. The German bombardment was the heaviest and longest lasting experienced by the AIF during the First World War

19.7.16

After several contradictory orders, the final order was given-battle order only. Issued with pink squares of cloth which we sewed on our backs; for recognition by aeroplanes I imagine. Only allowed to take in overcoat and water proof sheet. Passed Henencourt and halted at 6.45 p.m. ¼ mile from Albert.

There is a big church with Madonna and Child leaning over, almost falling. Dozens of our observation balloons up, can't see any of the Fritz's. Issued with an extra 250 rounds of ammunition two sandbags and two bombs per man.

Postcard from Ben

Had a very impressive church service today. Everyone quiet. Possibly the great adventure tomorrow. Don't expect to come out of this stunt. They wipe out a Division in days. Hope and Trust will be alright for sake of people at home. Have resolved to lead a better life in future.

Poem

I see across the shrapnel-seeded meadows
The jagged rabble-heap of La Boiselle;
Blood-guilty Fricourt brooding in the shadows,
And Thiepval's chateau empty as a shell.

Down Albert's riven streets the moon is leering;
The Hanging Virgin takes its bitter ray;
And all the road from Hamel, I am hearing
The silver rage of bugles over Bray.

4 p.m, Marched under the shadow of the church and on 4 miles to the trenches with English regiment guides leading the way. The ground we crossed was most difficult and often as we passed the guns would roar out nearly knocking us over with the noise of the discharge. We realised that the Northern sector was just a nursery to prepare us. What a pickle! A few dead men about. Germans and British mixed together; some half in and some out of the mud and everywhere broken guns, equipment and war waste, picks, shovels, sand bags, everywhere huge dumps of empty shell cases, hundreds of thousands of them. To make matters worse we went through valleys of gas and gas helmets had to be used. So laden with equipment, sandbags, extra 250 rounds, provisions, we stumbled on not caring where we went, blindly following the man in front; till we got there. Half A Coy had a trench to go to but the remaining had to set to and dig. This, after a day's march, laden like camels was hard, but in emergency a reserve strength seems to come and we manage it. In the part that was dug were some old German dug outs—not ordinary affairs, but concrete ones some 50 feet deep.

20.7.16.

Half relieved for a 4 hours' sleep and we dropped where we worked. Awfully hard job stopping platoon from broaching their water bottles, somehow we did it, partly by reasoning partly by threat, but everyone was too tired to argue much. First time I've seen shell holes of good size, some 20 feet and a diameter of 30ft but I think they were done by our own guns in ousting Fritz. We took over these shell holes as nucleus for a starting line and connected them by short trenches they were particularly handy to hop into when machine guns started. Souvenirs galore, German helmets with big eagle and brass spike and badges, bombs equipment etc enough to stock a large museum. Their rifles are very good to snipe with. This place looks to have been heavily garrisoned and the men must have been blown to bits. What's the use of burdening oneself? Stench as usual awful due to bodies decaying in the open. Continuous gunfire. Fritz had his own late trenches marked off to a 't 'on the maps and can shoot back on them with accuracy. Bombarded continually the trenches caving in and we were digging each other out all day long. Soon our beautiful trench was nothing but a wide ditch, each caving in making it shallower and wider. Men going back wounded and our garrison became thinner and thinner. Intense bombardment. Huge guns rocking the earth.

21.7.16

They have found out our new line although we kept low, Martin Neilsen hit this morning, enfiladed gun fire too from our right. Fritz line 350 yards away, but pieces of our shell fly back on us. Orders came out about the attack. We are to get our direction by a line of telegraph stumps. All sleeves rolled up, 1st Battalion for a distinguishing mark. Water bottle and haversack on back. An intense bombardment will start we double slowly forward and lie down until the barrage lifts then hop in for our cut. If man drops no notice to be taken but get forward and leave him to A.M.C. All wounded who can to crawl back to the old concrete dugouts. Attack in 2 waves, 3 & 4 platoons leading 2 & following at 10 paces. Every 4th man to carry pick, every 3rd man shovel, every 2nd man sand bags. 3 bombs per man and N.C.O'S smoke bombs for big dugouts. 3 lines of trenches to be taken, other Coys of

another battalion to go through in leap frog fashion. Village is Pozieres.
It has been attacked before but failure resulted each time.

22.7.16

Letter from Tom Brown, he is in clover in Lady Northcote's private
hospital in Kent from Evington Military Hospital.

POZIERES

23.7.16

Hopped parapets at 12 midnight. Oh! Those anxious minutes. It affected
men in different ways. I couldn't stop urinating and we were all anxious
for the barrage to begin and when it did, it opened up with a crash. The
ground shook and trembled and the concussion made our ears ring. It was
impossible to hear ourselves speak to a man lying alongside. It is strange
how men creep together for protection. Soon instead of 4 paces interval
between the men, we came down to lying alongside each other and no
motioning could make them move apart. We crept from shell hole to
shell hole and when the barrage started we made our lines, just like on
Parade, got our direction and waited—teeth chattering and frightfully
cold but hot with excitement. Hell opened up; Bootles with his trench
mortars made the earth rock. Surprising how few of our men hit by our
own shells. Asked Capt. Mackenzie how close we were to go to barrage, he
said so close that a few of our own men may be hit by pieces of our shells.
At 12-28 our artillery fire increased and looking back, the heights around
Sausage Valley were one blaze of our flashes. Huge mortars glowing red
in the air like gold fishes. In meantime their machine guns opened and
got Capt. Mackenzie, Sergeant. Carter and many others. Bullets seem to
split in front of you. Sergeant Cuddeford passed out alongside me.
At 12.30 we rushed their line and fixed 'em up. This was the first time I
ever got a bayonet into a Fritz then I wondered why he was so quiet and
found that he had been dead some time before I reached him. He was
leaning against the parapet and his big feet wouldn't let him fall over.
Immediately set to and organised men to reconstruct the line, when
another battalion moved through us, and being over anxious quite

a number of our boys went through with them to be in the fun and caught up to the barrage. In their turn hopped into Fritz. 3rd Battalion rushed the Pozieres wood itself. How the sterling qualities of the men stood out! All our Officers and N.C.O's killed or wounded—only junior men left. Yet they worked with a will using their own initiative and the lectures that had been given and thought forgotten came to their minds and they acted as if on a parade ground, only difference was they were joking and making fun and laughing at each other the whole time.

We were badly knocked about on 24th, it was Hell, but other units, Pioneers and Engineers dug a communication trench back so we were not isolated. And so day passed away. Continuous gunfire all the time where we were being continually bombarded, the trenches caving in and we were digging each other out all day long. Soon our beautiful trench was nothing but a wide ditch. Several Fritzes were caught and one chap in particular was in a shell hole with one of our men bandaging him up.

A German Doctor came in but as he was wearing a saw bayonet we treated him as an ordinary soldier. 4th Battalion are in the village itself. Rations hard to get yet they came up. The Babbling Brooks' forming the parties, cooking the bacon all day and bringing it up at night. It's a pity it was so salty though as water was so scarce. Losing men right and left— just sitting down getting pasted at. Trench caved in several times and our cobbers dug us out before we suffocated.

—

24.7.16

More shells, mainly 5.9 ' and they are very demoralising. The concussion affects different men in different ways; McTackett went dumb, but carried on although he couldn't speak. The day consisted of heatching ?, getting hell, losing men, digging each other out and wondering if we would ever get out. There are Fritz souvenirs here galore, but we are too tired to pick them up.

Made Corporal.

—

25.7.16

More of the same—us getting hell from shells and 3rd Battalion getting it
from bomb and bullet fire.

———

Philip Howell-Price later wrote....

... The Huns simply poured high explosive shells into our position.
Trenches disappeared like paper in a storm. Where there had been trenches,
nobody could tell. The place was a series of large shell holes, some 30 feet
wide and 20 feet deep.

Shells were so thick that they obscured the sun, smoke was so intense
that one could not see, the row and noise was so terrific that men went mad,
men simply stood and shook, their nervous system one entire wreck. Shell
after shell planted itself in our lines, man after man was blown to pieces and
yet not one man faltered.

Explosions buried all the men at least once. Some were dug out. Some
weren't. ...

———

26.7.16

Our worst day ever. By then we had word through by provision carriers
of the casualties and we found out that Yeomans, Lindeman, Burstall,
Graham, White, Everitt, MacVean and many other officers had either
gone west or were wounded. Today we lost more men than in the hop
over. The 4th 6th and 3rd Battalions were having a bad time time, so we
had to go over the top in daylight and help them consolidate and help
them in any emergency.
This was a so called wood called Pozieres. Lieut. Beavis took charge of
A company and under him we did our best, but casualties were high. Of
course Fritz shelled us unmercifully absolute murder infilade fire, dozens
buried alive, most awful sights I've ever seen awful. Trenches on Trenches
of mutilated bodies. Digging one another out I was buried twice.
Reg Oram lost nerve—shellshock—was buried. Donnelly wounded.
and charging over the ground and walking on corpses of our own AIF

The Main Street of Pozieres from Centre Way trench near Pozieres Church –
AWM EZ0095 also From the Australian Front, *Shrapnell and Smiles 1917*—Ben's copy.

men gave us the creeps. The ground was so churned up that the line
we dug continually fell in, but we relieved the tension on the 3rd and
accomplished our errand.

Lieutenant kept us busy which was the best thing. If we sat down to
think things through, it seemed impossible. It is estimated by roughly
counting the men when we were relieved that our company was only 67
strong. But others may have turned up later on. Throughout the whole
business Heane walked around unconcerned and R. J. C. McGregor
was worried because he had lost his walking stick but was one of the
coolest men there. He walked about in the open, unarmed, supervising,
swearing, bullying or coaxing whichever served the best purpose and
instilled into many a wavering man something of his fatalism.

We were relieved on the evening of the 26th by the 7th Battalion and
straggled to the Chalk Pit. What a scarecrow battalion we were! We
felt very sad for the look of it we had lost more than half of our men.
Lieut. Moore re-joined the company

On the morning of the 26.7.16 we marched out of the firing line to a
little place close to Albert.

27.7.16

All day we rested. There were fully half the packs unopened. Wounded
and killed men's packs examined. Took letters out of pack and destroyed

Chalk Pit. Schrapnel and Smiles

them, no good carting them about. Mr Beavis taking over the Company with Mr Moore.

I was made Orderly Room Corporal and Lance Sergeant. We moved to Contay, or rather should say stumbled. We are in rotten shape, still, what is left of us. We saw the splendid 13th Battalion march through on their way to the line. I didn't see Harold Kershaw but wrote a note and gave it one of their boys. Vadencourt Wood. Here all the Ruberoid huts are in amongst trees and Aircraft can't see us but everyone slept outside, 19 reinforcements joined up. Rested until afternoon of 28th.

28.7.16

Sent on in front of Battalion as Billeting N.C.O. ASL Lorry hopped to Halloy and got places ready for everyone. Our Brigade is here and our Division HQ also. Halloy is a pretty farming town, near the train line in a hollow, big hills surrounding it, poppies and cornflowers everywhere. Harvest nearly ready to bring in. Surprised to get a letter from Art Felton who is in hospital in Bolougne with a sprained ankle. Saw 3rd coming to relieve 2nd who had relieved us the 1st. News came through that Bayliss and Purcell had died of wounds.

30.7.16

Rest, good food, good billets, etc. made new men of us. Lieut. Beavis is to have the company permanently. The men like him. Throughout the

Lieutenant Beavis

whole show Vic Fowler was everywhere at once helping, advising and cheering the men, I don't know what we would have done without him. For some reason he was turned down for a commission just before going into action. Whether he offended a senior officer or not no one knows but if anyone deserved it he did.

Some of the officers who were killed during the Pozieres engagement were:— Captain MacKenzie, Major Lindeman, Lt. Burstall, Lt .Atkins, Lt. Blackmore, Lt. McShane, Lt. Yeomans. One of the most striking things to me during Pozieres engagement was the way rations, rum and water came to the line. On several occasions ration parties coming up, were blown up, but the rations were brought up by any working party coming towards the line; and not one of the carrying parties broached the food, keeping it solely for the line men. Sometimes on parade or during a lecture N.C.O's and Officers would get so sick of talking and seeing the men not seemingly taking the lecture in; but in action those men knew as much as their N.C.O. and acted as it they had been soldiering for a decade. This is the only example I can think of. Say Bill Smith appears not to be listening, he only does that to make Joe Jones down the ranks think he is not listening and the blasé look on his face is all put on. Smith is listening and in action he puts the lecture into force. The men of the A.I.F. are wonderful; I have compared them with the lot of English Regiments. and know they are superior.

1.8.16

Made Orderly Room Corporal just for a time to try and fix up the mess for Pozieres. Lieut. Beavis never seems to go to bed; he is writing to the parents of the boys killed. A job he doesn't have to do, but I'm sure he will be repaid by the blessings of the people when they get his letters. The official Returns from the Orderly Room are Pozieres we lost 7 officers, 110 other ranks 4 officers wounded and 50 men missing.

1.8.16

Dear Pal,

I suppose you have heard that we, the 1st Brigade have been through hell and back again, Thank God. We have charged twice now and both myself and Art have come though scott free. Art has of course a strained ankle but is not wounded at all.

Thank you all for writing so often and freely only I wish I could do likewise. On the night of the charge whilst waiting shivering in the cold, not knowing if in 30 minutes our spirits would have fled or not, I received a note from you and one from your father and I must say it put a lot of heart into me. Your lavish affection which perhaps I don't deserve. If I don't reciprocate in writing I do so in feeling for ...

[page 2 missing]

... little village which is situated in centre of concentric ranges of hills with town as centre. The approach is very gradual and on either hand are various greens and browns as far as an eye can reach. I saw a very pretty sight about 400 glass domes about 3' high, under each some choice little plant and women (all men at war) in dresses like riding skirts so as to give freedom attending them.

We are continually having trouble with old dames about water. They actually refuse to give us the water but nevertheless we wash, generally Dixies lowered on supporting straps. Our cooks got drunk last night and killed a pig so this morning all hands had pork galore, no one has missed the pig yet.

I sent home today my diary, hope Father gets it. When Art went to hospital of course his pack didn't go with him. The only things I was allowed to take out of it were Mary's letters. Such a bundle.

I've been made a corporal, another little step and it means a bit more cash of course which is not to be sneezed at. There are such a lot of Company records to be kept. I'm doing that until they are in hand. Then to hand over to another man and retake my section.

More sore feet in the Company as the average march with pack up is 12 miles per day, not so much on paper but some on the feet when it has to be done.

I have not yet seen any delicious fried snail or stewed frogs legs but am on the lookout for some. I believe snail pie is great. I'll be ashamed to look a pig in the face when I get home after having bacon every morning practically since 14 July 1915.

The wheat and barley are in ear and soon will be reaped but where are the reapers to come from All men at war and only women left and surely they can't swing a scythe.

How are you all getting on. I think of you all at *Oaklands* and *Jura* all day long and wonder how you all are. So good to keep up such a correspondence. In the trenches for 6 days without sleep. I used to reckon back the difference between the times and try and guess what each and every one of you are doing. Let's hope we come through this war, then I will have to pass my exams and make some money to use later on. There will be a lot of study necessary but if I come through the war I'll do them ok.

We have built up a name which is a pass word anywhere. Now not so much have the living done but the way to success has been paved by those who lay down their lives for others to walk over them. The bayonets and implements of warfare as your father puts it are truly *Devils machinations*. Saw backsaw bayonets etc. bombs that do not kill but shatter the nerves utterly. We were on to the beggars so quickly that they couldn't throw too many in their excitement they forgot to ? them off.

What do you think of the machine gunner chained to his machine gun? I vouch for it as I saw the man and gun. If only we could snatch their guns. The Germans themselves are nothing.

Well old Girl. Good luck attend you and keep you safe and sound waiting for my return. Remember me to all at home.

Your friend Ben

2.8.16

We had a long route march out near Permois keeping us from getting soft. We are getting plenty of wonderful tucker. Lot of reinforcements and old hands came back, amongst them Company Sergeant Major Barber who has been in England before the Evacuation of Peninsula with Jaundice. Each afternoon we route march to Permois and have an hour's spell there. We often go in for a swim in the canal.

Wrote to Mother, Mr Niland, Edie.

3.8.16

Wrote to Art enclosing 20 Fc.

4.8.16

list of Australian casualties in todays English Paper Handed over Orderly room to Bingley.

3.8.16 France

Dear Mr Niland

I've been receiving letters from you all but so far have not been able to reply much. I'm in the best of health. Once again I have come out of a scrap unscathed. This was SOME battle I can assure you and relief was never more welcome to the boys when it came on the 6th day. Our battalion was in it from the word go and came out with flying colors. Many decorations will be awarded to Officers, NCO's and men but who they are or how may I cannot at present state for all these kinds of things are shrouded in mystery until such times as they appear in General Orders.

For a few hours after the capture of P. things were fairly quiet but Fritz became busy with his artillery and shells of all sizes from wiz bangs to coal boxes simply trained upon the captured positions. Owing to

This photo included as it shows some of the mates named by Ben.
General Birdwood addressing soldiers of 2nd Australian infantry Brigade at Vadencourt Wood after their first tour of duty at Pozieres.
AWM EZ0085

the weather being against aeroplane observation our artillery could not effectively reply but as soon as the weather cleared they got to work with the result than many of Fritz batteries are now on the scrap heap and many Fraus and Frauleins are weeping for their departed relations now in the happy hunting grounds of their forefathers.

This bit of a mix up has easily shewn Abdul's superiority over Fritz. Abdul stands up to anyone but when Fritz sees a body of British troops rushing forward to meet him with the bayonet he suddenly remembers green fields well to the rear and out of danger; he generally loses no time in his frantic endeavour to get there. All the Hun's work is done by machine gun and artillery. He has no bomb to come up to ours either for demoralising or killing troops. The German star is setting and the *Day* not the day, to which they drank, but the Day of the Allies is coming when they shall be driven right over the Rhine defences into Berlin and will have the pleasure of seeing their own land laid waste by us in the same ruthless slaughter of life, land and stock was done by them. Of course the losses will be heavy but must be borne if Germany is to be put in the one place she has earned and be forced to be kept there.

I forwarded my diary home to Father, hope he receives it safely. The Germans my platoon captured were typical, some young, tall, fair eyes and light straw coloured hair, all looked knocked up. We also captured a Doctor, although he carried firearms we didn't kill him for he was very careful in handling our wounded and many a man in the Front line of trenches owes his life to his treatment. He was stockily built, square jawed and headed, with big spectacles and I would not have been surprised to have seen him pull a lump of sausage out of his pocket and start to eat it.

I was glad Arthur went away with a sprained ankle the day after the charge for he didn't see the solid fighting or murderous slaughter when we went over the parapet the second time. One of our Pioneer Battalion men was found 50 hours after he was hit in a shell hole. In this huge hole 20'square and deep was a live German. The Pioneer man said this German had bandaged him up and taken care of him since he was hit.

When our stretcher bearers (wonderful men) came along with a *do* this German would insist on takings turn at carrying. (no joke when high explosive shrapnel is flying about).

The German and Australian swapped addresses and as many of us as could, shook hands with the German much to his surprise. We all thought that he was a man. This episode does not look much on paper but it appealed to us at the time.

German bully beef and biscuits both labelled 1914, was far superior to our own and we enjoyed it after our strenuous operation. Despite the serious predicament we were in we could not restrain from laughing at one another. We did not charge with overcoats and as the night was bitterly cold we soon slipped on the dead German's overcoats and with their little round caps we found ourselves comfortable for 1/2 hour until the beggars started to shell again. It was continuous shelling during the 6 days in the trenches and none of us had more than 1 hours sleep. I was surprised to find, how in such emergency, sleep was not required but we sure slept when out of danger.

The gas shells caused us considerable alertness as they burst with very little row indeed as some found out when it was too late. 'Tis cruel this awful war. During our second charge the trenches under foot were springy and were we understood, our comrades killed. There were more on top—no time to bury then. Arms, mutilations, legs. God it was awful. This is not war but wholesale slaughter. Soft flesh pitted against shell and explosives. Rifles, equipment and dead Germans buried in the parapets, anything put there so as to give cover. Many men were buried by the big shells and nothing known about them.

This wretched war which spoils mankind. I've seen some men here with the blood lust in them. One man in particular reported to Officer...... 'no more left to kill Sir '. His eyes glazed ... and his face ghastly. Oh well ... Hope to be home again ... once this nightmare is finished ... nothing but a nightmare.

[This last section of page has been torn off so meaning indistinct.]

7.8.16

Still at Halloy, concerts are got up among the Companies and generally try to liven up the Battalion. New Australian clothing issued. I was nearly killed in the rush. Plenty of mail. Sgts. Steel and Lanser made 2nd Lieuts, and Phillips AMC given a commission. There are wild rumours we are moving, but while so much Australian transport moving towards Albert there is little hope of anywhere but in that direction.

9.8.16.

Trek once more, this time to Halloy and back to La Vicogne.

10.8.16.

On to Toutencourt, Headquarters of 4th Reserve Army and a few brigades of 1st Division artillery. Had several long chats with Fred Thompson QMS of Artillery, same battery as Noel Smith. We are at the HQ and consequently can't move from billets without a web belt. It's an awful bother stripping equipment each time. 13 mile march, feet blistered. We passed miles of artillery; we have thousands of guns in this sector. There are plenty of apples on the trees and some have made themselves crook through eating green ones. Wrote to Tom Brown day before yesterday, wrote to Frank and posted paper to Gertrude.

We lost our poet, wounded at Pozieres and we miss his cheery unshaven face.

AN ANZAC'S MORNING SHAVE.

13.8.16

Big Church Parade. Decorations given out by Birdwood. He said, rubbing his hands together in a pleased sort of way. *Good news for lst Brigade, very good news. You will all be in action in a few days time.* All down the line you could hear:— *The old b..................* etc. Birdwood must have heard it too but he didn't bat an eyelid. He is and looks a splendid soldier.

Moved back to Contay, actually saw British nurses there. Came in contact with Padre McKenzie who was attached to 4th Battalion. His cheery bluff personality endeared him to everyone.

15.8.16

Marched and bivouacked Brickfield area near Albert, and as it rained we naturally got 'wet'. Saw Osborne from Old 19B Area. Sent Art a F.S. Card. Lot of Light Horse in town doing Police duty. Pity they couldn't be put into a scrap as they simply tour France. Chaplain McKenzie says Prieste has fallen with 30, 000 prisoners

l6.8.16

Off to Tara Hill outside Albert much safer than our last turn in the line and here we spent a frightful night, wet through. 1st Battalion in Reserve. 3rd and 4th in Line, 2nd support and fatigues. Line no quieter than on 25.7.16. Next morning Ted Sparke, Bootles and myself left to see the line and to guide the Battalion in. Sent ahead to Pozieres on a bike. Went up to Front Line to learn the way to guide the Battalion in. Had an awful time going up *Centre Way* right through the heart of Pozieres village. The stench was

Sign at Centre Way, Pozieres.

awful, dead everywhere even sticking out of the sap. Our party, Sparke, Bootle and few others had a rotten time. They kept blowing in the trench in front and behind us but didn't get one of the party. A squelch meant we had trod on a body. Corpses everywhere and we saw a row of heads and upright tips of rifles where a trench had caved in the men had been smothered and then their heads had been cleared only to find that they were dead.

Reported to Colonel Price of 3rd Battalion brother to our Phillip who gave us a tot of rum apiece and cursed authorities who had sent us in during broad daylight. Over his possie was a big bronze bell 3' high all engraved from Pozieres Church, now used as a gas alarm. The Fritz trenches very good, all riveted with wicker work. Every now and then runners would come in reporting from 3rd Batt.

Lieutenant Colonel Owen Howll-Price DSO, MC, 3rd Battalion.

We found *Centre Way* completely blown in when we were about to come home, so had to wait until dusk and come back via 'Wire Sap '. Wire Sap was a communication trench now totally devoted to wire telephone lines. Oh! What a tangle. We started too early and were observed and were chased with whiz-bangs right back to H.Q. Back for a meal & sewed on pink patches and then back on fatigue. 7.30 pm. Led a large working party under Bootles up to the line going by way of Wire Sap instead of Centre Way. Had a hard time keeping direction, guiding a party in day time is different to doing same job at night, especially as the face of the country is continually changing under heavy gun fire. When we reached the line a slight counter attack was going on, so we couldn't do any work 2.am, nothing accomplished. On the way back we had two casualties; being a great loss.

All night the eighty pounders roared ceaselessly. Fritz replied only once or twice but down near the old Brigade HQ there is a continual barrage of shell fire through which all fatigue parties have to pass. Sergeant McKenzie had a big dent in his helmet where lump of shrapnel had caught him. There are plenty of those huge bosch dug-outs boarded and concrete. Poziers shelled beyond recognition absolutely Several Taube's over today, spying out the land, but our planes are continually up. On the night of my coming into the trenches, the night we stopped at Albert, I rec'd a pair of sox and tin of chocs from Gertrude.

17.8.16

Usual bombardment, towards 6pm it rained and the Germans counter attacked 4th Battalion positions inflicting heavy casualties for which they dearly paid. At 10 to 8 pm Mr Bootle took A and B Coys on fatigue. First we halted on tram line in the open when shrapnel forced us to take to saps. We were 3/4 of time out of the broken down saps 'till we reached the firing line. With Pioneers and engineers we went through the line practically to Mouquet farm. He asked the engineers if they knew their directions and they acknowledged they were lost so Lieut. Bootles spread us out at 4 paces lying down and sent forward two men to find out where we were. They had not gone 50 yards when they were fired on by Fritz and his flares for artillery support went up; He barraged 60 yards in front of us. By this time we were well down in shell holes and no one was hit. We had wandered right through the line by mistake and pulled up in middle of No Man's Land. On retracing our steps we came to the front line and on asking the NCO in charge of the post why he let us go through unchallenged he said he recognised from a distance some of our chaps and thought we were going to do a stunt. Shelled so heavily we could not work so came home via 4th Battalion lines. Heading back to our quarters was very hard going. Young mountains of soft powdered earth flung up

8   **REVEILLE**

"Fighting Mac." Honoured

Commissioner W. McKenzie ("Fighting Mac"), of the Salvation Army, who visited Narrabri recently, was accorded a civic reception. Because of his splendid record of service with the A.I.F. on Gallipoli and in France, Diggers everywhere have been always anxious to honor him. At Narrabri many Diggers attended the civic reception, and in the evening a party of returned men marched with their old comrade to the Salvation Army Hall, where they were joined by other Diggers, one of whom was accompanied by his wife—an ex-service nurse. Narrabri District Band headed the procession.

"Fighting Mac."

There was no body associated with the A.I.F. more universally respected than the Salvation Army, and no one held in higher regard than Padre McKenzie, said Mr. J. M. de Lepervanche. The Salvation Army helped when to all appearances "help may seem useless." Mr. W. J. Mulholland declared that, as a returned soldier, he regarded the Commissioner not only as an outstanding example to the A.I.F., but also to all of the present generation. Mr. R. C. Piper, who served in the 4th Bn. with Padre McKenzie, recalled incidents, demonstrating the cheerful spirit of "Fighting Mac" and his ever-ready help to the Digger.

The Rev. A. G. Wood, speaking on behalf of the Churches, said they had a tremendous admiration for the Salvation Army and for Commissioner McKenzie.

In his reply, Padre McKenzie said he was delighted to meet the people of Narrabri, and particularly his old friends, the Diggers. He was proud to have been with them overseas, and of witnessing what they did. His mind was full of unforgettable scenes of heroic endeavour, heroic endurance and invincible spirit manifested under difficulties such as might have daunted the stoutest heart.

They all thought they were fighting a war to end war, but not a year had passed since peace was signed that hostilities were not reported from some part of the world. The war, he declared, left a trail of debt and destruction in many countries, and they would continue to bear the burden unless the leading nations decided to abolish the whole of the war debts. Fear had gripped the heart of many nations, and unlawful ambitions had gripped the hearts of many leaders. Any day we might wake up to find certain nations flying at each other.

"Fighting Mac" saw in the present world position a challenge to the Churches of God, and explained that we had not finished with the results of the Great War, as since their return to Australia 33,000 soldiers had crossed the Great Divide.

"One of the great lacks of Australia is home training," said Commissioner McKenzie, and added: "It is not riches, goods, guns, or gold that make a nation great; it is a strong, virile race of godly men and women."

Extract from a 1934 edition of Reveille *about Padre McKenzie.*

by shell bursts. Our legs ached and rifle and shovel seemed ton weights. Picked up an engineer guide, did our job on a communication trench and started for home when the racket started.

Mouquet Farm was being slightly shaken up getting ready for a big attack so we had to come home. Lieut. Bootles and Joe Shaw, were standing on the parapet of an old trench when one of our 18 pounders burst right overhead. Barney Marr was badly hit by it; both Bootles & Shaw were knocked over but were unhurt. Handing over the fatigue to the next Senior Officer, Bootles and Shaw had to report to Battalion, H.Q. for some reason or other. We moved homeward and reached there 3 hours before Bootles & Shaw turned up. They took a SHORT CUT. We were awfully anxious and several of us were just turning out to look for them, when they came in, done up.

SONG

Sang to Advance Australia Fair

1. On 25th of April in year nineteen fifteen,
    We landed down at Anzac, and many sights were seen,
    We braved the shots of Beachy Bill, and though he scored some hits,
    We made a mighty charge, my boys, and gave old Abdul fits.

2. On 19th day of May, my lads, the Turks made their attack,
    But we were not caught napping and drove old Abdul back.
    Three thousand Turks were slain that day, a
    A vile stench filled the air, and we had won another scrap,
    Advance Australia Fair.
    And we had won another scrap,
    Advance Australia Fair.

3. On the 6th of August then, my lads, we charged for Lonesome Pine
    We shelled them for an hour or two and captured their front line.
    It was a glorious charge my boys, the finest we had made,
    The honours of that day, my lads, were with the First Brigade,
    The honours of that day, my lads, were with the First Brigade.

4. Now we have left old Anzac's shores, and we'll go back no more.
    We sneaked away at dead of night, before the break of dawn;
    We failed to capture Beachy Bill, we failed at 971;
    And now we do not know, my lads, if we have lost or won,
    And now we do not know, my lads, if we have lost or won.

5. On the 23rd July, my lads, in the year nineteen sixteen
    We charged for Pozieres Town, my lads, through Hell on earth we'd been;
    We took the Trench, we took the Wood, at last we took the Town,
    The blighters couldn't knock us back, although they mowed us down

---

TEN COMMANDMENTS OF A BRITISH SOLDIER

1. The Colonel is thy only Boss. Thou shalt have no other Boss but him.

2. But thou shalt make unto thyself many graven images of officers, who own the earth beneath, who fly in the heavens above, of submarine officers who are in waters under the the earth. Thou shalt stand up and salute them for the C.O. thy Boss will visit with field punishment unto the 1st or 2nd degree on those that salute not and shower strips on those that salute and obey his commandments.

3. Thou shalt not take the name of the Adjutant in vain, for the C.O. will not hold him guiltless who taketh the Adjutant's name in vain.

4. Remember thou shalt not rest on the Sabbath Day. Six days shalt thou labour and do all that thou hast to do, and on the 7th day, the day of the C.O. thou shalt do all manner of work thou and thy officers, thy non-commissioned officers, thy sanitary man.

5. Honour the Army Staff that thy days may be long in the Corps Reserve, where one day they may send thee.

6. Thou shalt kill only Huns, slugs, lice, rats and other vermin which frequent dug-outs.

7. Thou shalt not adulterate thy sections rum issue.

8. Thou shalt not steal or at any rate be found out, but thy Kit willy nIlly must be complete.

9. Thou shalt not bear false witness in the Orderly Room except against Red Caps.

10. Thou shalt not covet the A.S.C's job, nor his pay, nor his motors, nor his waggons, nor his billets, nor his horses, asses, nor any other cushy thing that it his.

MOUQUET FARM

18.8.16

In broad daylight at noon was the time we started to take over a new piece of the line. After going for one hour at a snail's pace, blocked up shoulder to shoulder in a communication trench, we finally came to a dead stop. It was thought it likely that this trench would be enfiladed by Germans. Our lines are very hard to understand indeed. This stop lasted for 20 minutes when we moved along again. As five men reached an officer of the 3rd Battalion who was stationed just on the crest of a hill, he told us that the next 50 yards was in direct view of Fritz and to wait for the next shell burst and then to run for our lives forward to the lee of the next slight hill. This we did passing a number of our cobbers hit by previous burst of shell. Naturally under the lea of the hill those in front did not hurry and soon all available space was taken up and still groups of five kept coming. Joe Shaw called for volunteers to go back to the 3rd Battalion officer and tell him to wait and not send any more men across the gap but finally he went himself as he said he couldn't let anyone else go. This he did and was fortunate enough to cross between bursts and then to recross again safely.

Soon all were over except for casualties; Major Moore sniped in the shoulder in front of me. We moved to our new line reaching there at dusk. All night we dug fresh positions. Col. Heane personally, seeing to the work, but the soil too soft and churned up by shells would not stand and it was often after an hour's work to see the trench cave in and after working all night the trench was just a broad gutter. To make matters worse our shells started to fall short, about 20' in front of us, and several casualties resulted before we could make them lengthen their range.

Communication trench Centre Way looking towards Mouquet Farm
AWM EZ0100

19.8.16.

Daylight showed us Courcelette in the hollow & Mouquet Farm further on. Len Hesketh was sniped so the position of the sniper was marked and on reference to maps we found he was behind our lines. Here the trenches ran so awkwardly that it was practically impossible to tell which was front and which back. Col. Heane came down and on seeing the position of the trench ordered it vacated so we moved to another and by doing so improved our direction.

Most of the day bombing and rifle fire was coming from the direction of Mouquet Farm and by night it had warmed up considerably and another attack was in full swing. The 10th Battalion, I believe made the attack which was then relieved by 3rd Battalion. We expect to be relieved very soon. Quite a lot of incomings chaps buried. No rest last night after finished digging as it rained heavily and our possies went mushy, burying our blankets.

Rifles in a frightful mess. Fritz used to allow our stretcher bearers to go overland here carrying a Red Cross flag, but when the chaps had to jump into a communication trench, that communication trench was marked by shell fire later on. Over towards Thiepval there is one solid wall of fire, red glare from bursting shells. We must be attacking there. Hope it's successful.

20.8.16.

Snipers very busy. Rum issue. Communication trench from which we dug the 10th Battalion. Men again blown in this morning, another job for us tonight.

———

21.8.16.

No rations up yet, 10th Battalion seems very careless as regards leadership of men. Still digging new firing line, sap blown in leading to hill trenches. Courcelette shelled, can plainly see the big howitzer shells falling. Rum issue, cold, smelly, knocked up.

———

22.8.16.

Mail from Frank, Fine newsy letters. Fritz still very jumpy. 10th Battalion got 2 trenches of his toward Mouquet Farm last night, the casualties had to pass down our trench. Buried Len Hesketh and erected a cross. Bulmer killed—sorry for his people as remember seeing his brother's grave on Peninsula. As the 23rd were coming in to relieve us Fritz saw them and pounded the same communication trench they caught the 10th Battalion. Hell on earth, howitzers whiz bangs shrapnel etc sap completely blown in. Fortunately 23rd hadn't reached that part, so they waited further back until he had finished. During this relief, we were awfully scared. We took over the trench with a very short handed company. The communication trench was so narrow, only in places could 2 men pass. It looked as if we would have to go over the top to run the gauntlet but we all blocked up shoulder to shoulder down a small sap and let their full sized company take over the area our shorthanded company had. As it was A Coy had to bend and run, run overland to escape the shells.

In the trench met Major Woodforde, first time back since Weathercock House, recovered from his back wound. He commenced to regulate our numbers for the dash across. The moment a salvo of shells burst he would say to a few crouching figures waiting for the word, *Go* and off a party would go dashing through the fumes of the just exploded shells. It was a hectic time and most of the chaps came through roaring with laughter and swearing how they had tricked Fritz; it was real hysteria.

Away on our flank you could hear Thiepval being pounded to bits and we wondered what unlucky unit was going through the mill. The Battalion got out except the bearers for the Lewis Gun Panniers. They were laden and came so slowly that Captain Beavis sent back a party to help them on.

Poziers very difficult place to get too. Poziers Wood now only stumps remain.

24.8.16

Left Warloy and marched through Contoy, Herrisart, La Rosel, Beauval. It was good to be leaving the Somme area. General Walker *Hookey* inspected us as we marched into Beauval but I don't think he was too pleased with our appearance but the Battalion was on its last legs. Pozieres then Mouquet and the march.

A very beautiful church in Beauval with stained glass windows, bigger than Hazebrouck.

25th Left Beauval 4-15 and marched to Doullens when we entrained and journeyed north; the beauty of the Army is that you don't know where you are going next, nor do you care; all night we rumbled on in a northerly direction detraining at Hopoutre, a few miles from Poperinghe in the Ypres sector. Canadians in this sector made us welcome and supplied us with boiling water for tea and did not charge us like the English.

Brigadier General J Heane, 1st Division

Map of France and Belgium show major conflict areas.

27.8.16

Sunday no service, The Canadian Scottish were moving southward, full pack and I expect they will take over our old sector. Poor chaps. A Company was put on divisional fatigue and spent a rough time juggling guns and limbers off the trucks but when we came to the A.S.C. Department we made several hauls, of good jam and cheeses and tucker generally.

28.8.16

Rejoined the Battalion at Eyrie Hut Camp behind Ypres and found number of old hands including Art Felton and reinforcements so our battalion didn't look so funny. We are in Nissen huts and are generally comfortable. We are all happy to leave the Somme.

29.8.16

Battalion went on to Bath Parade to Poperinghe. The slush was awful and if we had stayed at camp and taken off our clothes the rain would have given us just as good a bath as we had at Poperinghe. Having soaped ourselves and a few being fortunate to be quick, got a bath, but the water was then put off, and so we had to wipe the soap off and have a dry bath. Poperinghe is an active little town quite a number of shops are still open for business and there is actually a cinema there. Tom Brownlie, Priestly, Art and myself had passes and saw a cinema—it was a nice break from army routine.

Poperinghe street view.

1.9.16

Wattle Day. Rec'd wattle in letter from Gertrude, very appropriate indeed. Go into either line or supports move out of here. 3rd Battalion O.C. Coy sniped yesterday when visiting line. Just learned Syd Hampton DOW 1.8.16, buried Warloy.

Moved by train to Ypres, (half the size of Sydney). No complete building intact, all smashed, such an eerie feeling being in a large city, not a sound from it and everywhere smashed buildings and shell holes. Marched to the support line.

Sydney Victor Hampton

Ruins of the Cloth Hall, Ypres.
Shrapnel and smiles

YPRES HILL 60

We marched through the supports behind the 3rd Battalion position at Hill 60. Next day a fatigue party under Lieut. Moore worked, deepening cleaning and draining a communication trench behind the front line but very little work was done as gas alarms were continually being given, making us break off work. We are working alongside the Ypres-Menin railway cutting which has formed some lakes and the gas seems to stand around the water. The whole area is dank, greasy and unhealthy.

1916.

Aug. 21—Attack by 3rd Brigade. 1st Battalion holding the Line.

,, 22—Bivouaced at transport lines near Albert.

,, 23—Moved to Warloy.

,, 24—Beauval.

,, 25—Entrained at Doullens.

,, 26—Detrained at Hopoutre (The Salient). Eyrie Camp.

Sept. 2—Relieved 3rd Battalion in the line. Hill 60 Sector.

,, 13—Devonshire Camp, near Brandhock, by rail from Ipres Asylum.

,, 22—Battalion Sports at Busseboom.

,, 26—Relieved 6th Battalion at the Bluff.

Oct. 13—Relieved by 13th Battalion. Moved back to Devonshire Camp.

,, 14—Billeted in Steenvoorde.

,, 15—Billeted in Oost Houck.

,, 16—Nordleulinghem.

,, 20—Entrained at St. Omer for Longpré.

,, 23—By motor lorry to Buire. Thence march to Fricourt.

,, 24—Mametz Wood—Bivouac.

,, 26—Unloading sleepers at Quarry Station.

,, 30—Relieved the 1st Essex in line via Delville Wood.

Nov. 5—Attack on Bayonet and Hilt Trenches—3rd Battalion co-operating.

,, 7—Relieved by 11th Battalion. Moved to Bernafay Wood.

,, 8—Pommier Camp.

,, 12—Marched to Dernancourt.

,, 13—Billeted in Buire.

,, 17—Embussed for Flesselles. Marched to Fremont.

,, 18—St. Sauveur (in billets).

Dec. 1—Route march to Vignacourt. Train to Ribémont.

,, 6—Marched to Mametz—Melbourne Camp.

,, 23—Bernafay Wood—Fatigues.

1917.   Relieved 2nd Battalion in the

,, 31—line—Possum Reserve.

Jan. 3—Relieved 17th Battalion—Gueudecourt.

Jan. 8—Moved back to Bendigo Camp.

Excerpt from 1st Battallion diary

2.9.16.

Slept until dinner time Went with Lieut. Moore on fatigue towards Hill 60, 1800 hours to clean out communication trench at 8.30pm shifted to left side of salient just to left of big dam and deepened and widened trench until 2 am. Continually being stopped by a gas alarm. Ypres is a very gassy place, and in the big cutting formed by the Ypres-Menin railway, regular lakes are formed and around this the gas hangs as it is heavier than air. Back to supports when the Sirens and Klaxons went again. Three times during the night it did this and at last we went to sleep.

3.9.16.

Mr Moore's party on fatigue. In afternoon we went to old German trench leading to the dump and 3rd Battalion Headquarters. Minenwerfer barrage; trench mortars and howitzers kick up a devil of a row. These have a range of about 500 yards and are like huge rifle grenades or mortars. We couldn't work but watched the bombs coming over—from a distance of course.

4.9.16

In the night time we reported to Marshall's Walk and worked from 6 till 2 a.m. deepening, widening and generally improving. Tommies and Canadians only go into the line for 4 days; consequently they cannot do much work. We come in for 16 days, consequently when we leave the trenches are in a good condition. Down by 3rd Battaliion Headquarters which is behind the dump and next door to the railway cutting, is a huge dam blocking up the cutting and forming a lake which flows under our line and between us and the Germans. Once Huns came up in a boat and bombed the dam. We dug up old German duck boards below the dam and cleaned muck away. All this time under shell fire, luckily we had no one hit. They were also slinging a few shells over our possies, there has been too much troop movement. Both sides digging in well for winter. We are mining Hill 60 again, our own men are here. The line A is to occupy is known to be mined in more than one place.

FRONT LINE LEFT OF HILL 60

7.9.16

Left supports and took over the line, rather a ticklish position, as it was known to be mined. We held the line very lightly and had crater snatching parties ready in case a mine went off. They were to rush and occupy the nearest lip because Fritz was sure to be on the other side. Our men had worked well and A's sector spread over the cutting, half on each side. Each evening you could hear the windlasses being worked evidently bringing up soil from the mine shaft, but we never could locate the sound, Sgt. Black and Lt. Sparke went out on Patrol but returned without finding out. So we listened and located 4 or 5 windlasses working. Fritz was so close we could hear them talking and Sgt.Brownlee forgetting this was rewarded by a piece of a rifle grenade in the thigh and the company mascot, an aboriginal named Punch was wounded in the head. There are rats galore here, great big coves, we used to put pieces of bread on a bayonet, wait until they nibbled it, then pull the trigger and finish rat. This line has plenty of Lewis guns and they in turn are covered by Vicars guns and they in turn by 18 lbs. etc.

It is a most uncomfortable existence to know a mine might blow up under your feet at any moment.

RIGHT OF HILL 60

9.9.16

The mist lifted early this morning quiet unexpectedly and we saw a dozen Huns pushing a trolley and turned a Lewis gun on them. I think we got 1 or 2. Fritz is working hard, but so are we. 20 Canadian miners came out of nowhere today, they are nearly ready to make a blow; they state they are right under Fritzies line. Snipers very busy under the culvert. L/Corp Liefermann wounded, piece of bomb in hand. Gas alert on Fritz working well today. Received from home letter from Dot and sketch of the pup. Letter from Gertrude, Mr Walker Lieut. Millar. 2nd Battalion friend of Mr Pendreans friend of Gertrudes. Dr Archie Collins, 2nd Casualty station (Major) Glorious last two nights—too good for fighting. Fine if out with a girl.

10.9.16

Mumminwerfers came over today, no casualties; Whilst a carrying party was on the way to the dump we happened to strike a bad piece of luck. We were shelled unmercifully losing Mick Wray and 8 wounded. This area has wakened up considerably since we came and there is a nervous tension. We will be glad to be relieved when someone else takes over this possey. Relieved by B coy and we moved back to supports.

12.9.16.

Spent a crook night, raining, myself and 10 men sent out of line to prepare billets near Bussellboom. Very one-horse town and the Battalion came down next day 2 am in trains. The camp was very slushy, the huts covered with stuff like ruberoid, leaked, but being once more away from the line we cheered up.

Near this area is a nest of our observation balloons. They are huge affairs to which are attached baskets containing 1 or 2 observers. These men are connected by phones to Artillery headquarters and range and report on activity and guns. Each man has a parachute strapped to his back and should the balloon be attacked by a plane, if he is quick enough and jumps at the right moment he can generally escape. They fall, it seems about 100 yards and the parachute opens suddenly and their fall is stayed; they land somewhere according to the direction of the wind. We saw one man blown over our own lines one day, to be safely taken Prisoner of War!

13th.

Huts very draughty. Wrote to Gertrude, Mr Donald Smith, Mother enclosed cigarette case in Cpl. Bingley's parcel for Bert c/o of Father. Cold wet miserable, pains in knee joints.

17.9.16.

The Sgts. of A went to Poperinghe and had our photos taken. Tea etc. and custard cakes galore. Several Belgians around selling Cartridge souvenirs bought a couple. Copper bullets are French, Heavy dull pointed Belgian, rest English. Marched to Hopoutre and had a change and a bath, very much appreciated, came back and were issued with the new box respirator—more comfortable and feel much safer in them. We are to keep one P.H. helmet in case of emergency. Lachrymatory gas chamber fitted up. Passed through with our new helmets. Soon told which were the bad ones, not more than a dozen in the Battalion New ones are modelled after German ones but ours last 12 hours and theirs last 20 minutes. Dick Marsden, great trick, cleft palate, can't breathe through mouth at all.

A finer group of men couldn't be found in a bunch anywhere. (Ben, writes later that the moustache came off the next day!)

The Sergeants of A Company, 1st Battalion 17.9.16
Back left: Sgt Black, QMS Bubear, Ben
Front left: Sgt Marks, A Shaw, W.V. Fowler C.S.M., Sgt Wallen.

21.9.16.

The 1st Battalion Sergeants and 2nd Battalion Sergeants were always more attached to each other than in any other two units in our Brigade. 1st Battalion Sgts gave 2nd Battalion Sgts a dinner. Decorated No 45 hut. Erected tables and forms covered with blankets and water proofs. Very enjoyable evening indeed only too much liquor to my liking. When the 2nd Battalion Sgts were leaving they ran into a newly erected barb wire fence and several nasty cuts happened. It appears that Capt. Price had his wiring party out practising putting up wire and entanglements. 2nd Battalion vowed we did it on purpose.

21.9.16

Dear Franc

I've had a slight touch of bronchitis for the past week and have been exempt from duty, that's the reason why I have not written to you. Please forgive me. I've been trying to sleep it off. We have been doing some extra fine work down South with those armoured cars; they are great animals and carry rather a handy sized gun on them.

There was a terrible cannonade here last night. The vibration woke us all up and then kept us awake and we are 10 miles from the line. So you have been having a shot with your Dad's rifle. Did you manage shutting the left eye successfully? I would have liked to be behind you when you pressed the trigger.

Have you all been keeping well, the cold must have gone by this. September is a nice month in old Australia. When we come back in 1918 you will be surprised to see how filled out Art is. Getting more and more like his dad every day.

The following Ruth will explain to you. A chap who knows a few words of French sees 2 cows eating a woman's cabbages so he goes inside and then is nonplussed for words at last he stammers out *Madame deux laits dans garden cabbage* Madame compreed.

Yesterday our hut became flooded out so we bored holes in the floor for the getaway for water, we put so many holes in it that instead of a floor it looks like a bath mat. I had my picture taken with some brother

Sergeants. I hope it comes out good, if so you will have one and if bad you won't get one. I'll get another taken.

Do you remember me talking of Rupe Neil, well he is missing, poor fellow and he is the only son too which makes it worse still. You will have to be content for next month with very little news, no opportunity will come to write. Mother rec'd a cable from me but sent from London; naturally she thought I was there. But you see we send cables etc. to Anzac Hd Qrts in London, they write them out and charge to our deferred account, that's the reason they are posted in London.

I wonder will I ever do any work when I get back. If I feel as lazy as I do at present I won't. You ought to see the harvest of hops (practically finished now). The people erect some poles about 30' high in form of a square and run wire along (Ben did a drawing) then they run wires to the earth. The hops run up these, so when vines are full grown they are very pretty.

There is a banquet in 3 night's time, hope it stops raining. We have made great preparations. We are entertaining the Sgts of 2nd Battalion. (purple over green) We expect to have a good time. By Jove Pal, wish I was home again it's no bon sleeping in slush with boots always sopping. Our new respirators are exceedingly bulky but we can slip them on in 2 seconds after adjusting gadgets etc to 6 secs final time. It is very amusing here sometimes, when you can't tell the name of an article, we always call it a GADGET which answers very well.

Well we received some very hard thinkers to day in shape of reinforcements. They thought a long while before they came to the war didn't they? When are you going to send me a photo of yourself? I didn't like those you had taken before we came away. Have a smiling one taken', *Si'l vous plait*.

Our band has gone bung, at least all players are either wounded or otherwise and there is no one to play. There seems to be no chance of one ever getting a commission here. They like AMC privates and hard thinkers before those who have seen some service with the Battalion. Let's see, enlisted in May, left Sydney July Wounded, November 29 re-joined, Jan 1916 and been with them ever since.

Well, I hope you are still at loggerheads with Tarroites. You didn't have to take milk in boats to the station this time. Hope you don't have too much rain. It rains here practically every day and the local people say the rainy season starts next month. Oh Golly. This is the life. A chap ought to sing *I want to be back to the farm far away from harm with a milk maid etc.*

You know when I heard Billy Hunt was wounded I wrote to Mrs Hunt, well I received a reply from her; my letter was the only one bar official notification she had received. Billy was too bad to write and my note must have cheered her a lot for she thanked me very warmly. I was so glad I wrote.

We hear no birds now, lately all birds have been flying southwards to a warmer climate, I wonder how many rests they have on the way and if they take their full marching order with blankets and 48 hours iron rations. It is an awful nuisance carrying emergency rations, we always do. Small biscuits and bully and so far we have only once had occasion to use them. That's when we were in advance possy and no rations could come up to us. (down South)

Remember me to Kitty, Claire, Ruth and Mary. I owe each one more than one letter but really cannot find time to write. A big concert down at YMCA night under supervision of Chaplain McKenzie. He is a fine man and probably most popular with 1st Brigade now Birdwood is so detested. We know him properly now, due much to our Casualty lists.

The cows here are very meek. They are milked in the open without bails and leg ropes are unheard of. But shoeing a horse they put them in a cage and pull their feet outside when wanted to shoe.

The chaps here are playing 500. Do you remember Art and I trying to teach you at Tarro? Did we succeed or not? Mr Felton plays often. That big dog of Art's *Nip* is one of the best I've ever seen. All the dogs here work hard for their tucker, pulling carts, turning butter churns etc.

Do you ever catch sight of Goolah now; wasn't he a funny old chap. He must have been a good age. The Indians do not keep well in this country and are not much use in this kind of warfare. They must see first of all their opponent.

This sitting down and waiting till the opportunity offers is no bon for ghurka soldats. Well I've 3 candles alight to write this letter by and they reckon I'm extravagant but then I say I'm writing to you and they say *Oh carry on', we mustn't stop such an important operation.*

They still have same wall paper and gadgets on the mantel piece. In fact everything is just the same with exception of the dog. I haven't seen it alive yet, a fox terrier it is. When I come home and they send a guide down to the boat to show me the way home, I wonder will it bite or bark or will it be able to smell that I'm a Champion.

70% of the population have gone from here, just a few old men and women about but in the town great hulking cold footed traitorous Belgians can be seen holding up the lamp posts. Funny thing these people have electric lights laid on but not the water. There is generally only one large public well and women and kiddies of all ages and sizes can be seen drawing the water. A pretty young lady is generally not allowed to draw the water by herself, smiling graciously some soldier generally winds up the bucket.

It was funny when we had our pictures taken. An old Belgian with whiskers like the Kaiser said something which sounded like *Apple pudding garochie* which made us all laugh. The poor beggar meant to say *Look pleasant please.* But I believe we will all have a grin like the hole left in a water melon after Ruth has taken a slice out. Some grin. I had a week's growth on my upper lip. I didn't know it was there 'till after the deed was did. You won't notice it please. Just imagine it's not there.

You know I must look older considering the positions I hold now Ahem? Our rifles get very rusty here, we always have to keep a coating of oil over them. Rum has been issued now 3 nights running, it is so cold we need it. By Jove a tot goes well when in the trenches, it covers up the cold and stench at the time but it soon goes away.

This Battalion has deteriorated during last 2 months, all the casualties etc. Things have gone to ruin a lot. I'll have to go to school again when I come back. Oh well old girl I think I'll close now. Kindly remember me to your father and mother.

23.9.16

2nd Battalion Sgts. gave us a dinner, put decorated boxes covered with blankets for tables. Spent a good time.

THE BLUFF

25.9.16

Moved into firing line—Train as far as Ypres—new sector called *The Bluff* on the right of our old position. We relieved the 6 Battalion, A Coy being in supports. Here are 3 big craters, all occupied by us. Place well tunnelled for supports; communication trench, good bunks made of wire netting ranged in tiers of three being provided; well revetted and to the right of it connected by short trench is a fire trench over-looking the right, down a big gulley. Canal at the bottom. There is a Klaxon worked by a cylinder of the compressed air. It would awaken the dead in case of gas alarm.

26.9.16

Accompanied Capt. Beavis around our sector, checking S.A.A. bombs and gas alarms. While doing so a shell lobbed into Thames Street, on a pile of bomb boxes and exploded 50 bombs. Our mine craters connected by tunnels. In crater nearest Fritz is a lot of water. Coming up through the water were lots of air bubbles and Canadian Engineer Officer said it was a sign that the earth was being moved below. Fritz mining, well, so is we. There is a Canadian Tunnel Company continually working under the Bluff.

29.9.16

Several bombs over into 1 mine crater today. All night we were throwing out loose wire to catch Fritz should he come over. Crater snatching party forming in case of need they are ready. Across the Canal Fritz towelled the 11th Battalion up there. I think it's the 4th Brigade. Very heavy shells!

29.9.16

trenches

Dear Frank,

Many thanks for the huge parcel I received last week, the sox are very good now that the cold weather has set in. The cake was soon finished, so was the toffee and peanuts and the other goods were very suitable indeed.

Well I told you I had my photo taken but before I went I forgot to have a wash, that accounts for the black upper lip. Art had his taken also but by himself so I suppose I'll do likewise. It is only 13 weeks to Christmas. Last Christmas I was at Malta. I wonder will we still be *somewhere in France* this time.

The sun is trying to peep out so off comes the overcoat and gum boots and as usual the place is rather sloppy. It seems impossible for the ground to properly dry up. Two German planes came down yesterday, a Taub and an Aviatic, both brought down by our battle planes. Its easily seen we hold the mastery of the air and soon we will hold the championship of the Terra Firma.

Our bread came up to see us today in the sizes you usually have it for bread pudding, someone had evidently been sitting on it and using the jam for a foot stool. How is your cooking and dressmaking getting on. I expect your court is grassed by this. I hope to have many a game there. I think we could easily beat Art and Co being such athletic people (I don't think).

This game is no bon for the knee joints or any joints at all. You being so busy at the Tech College, Old Creamy must be running wild, too fat for sulky and too lazy for riding purposes. Wait 'til I get home. What about getting another photo taken. You know 14 months is a long time. You may get a natural photo this time not like the last with a stiff chin etc.

All the digging, revetting etc that we do has made us all first class navvies so we will all have something to do when *Der Tag* comes ie: when the ship comes in. Remember me to all at *Oaklands*.

We have a canteen ½ mile from 1st line, fruit etc can be bought. Golly I had a pain under my belt last night through eating tinned lobster and prawns. They evidently did not agree one with the other. Fancy on Gallipoli a canteen near the line. This warfare is something different to there.

Gen. Birdwood. Gen. Walker, Gen. Smythe and Andrew Fisher Esq., were at Church parade last Sunday and they gave away several sandbags full of military medals chiefly to runners and batmen. The paper (English) are saying a lot about the zeppelin raid. Reading between the lines I think more damage than is said has been done.

What do you think of the advances on the Somme? What do you think us starting them though, a great honour and it shews their faith in 1st Division and us.

Well Old Girl. I'll have to close now,

Ben.

Enclosed please find photo

───

30.9.16

In night time silent raid took place by 8th Battalion going through 2nd Battalions lines. In subsequent shelling Major (Dad) Rowlands and 3 Sergeants of the 2nd killed. At Poziers Major Rowlands said *come on boys follow your old dad* The raid was very successful.

20 dead in trenches with those waddies, entrench tool handles with a cog wheel on the end. They looked ferocious enough with faces and hands blackened; they brought back 3 prisoners for identification.

───

The Bluff

31.9.16

Dear Frank,

I'm writing this in a dug out, in which the bunks are built ship fashion one over the other and I wonder will we ever be permitted to see the old home and folks again. We've been away some little time and the anxiety is *no bon*. Once we get out of this game we'll go mad absolutely. Of course there is none of the hardships of the Peninsula and one has plenty of people in the big towns. One wants to come home too. To put it in a straight, way. I believe I am a bit home sick.

This morning is bright clear and sunny. Just a splendid day for aerial observation and our planes overhead are whirring daring the Aviators and Taubes to come out, which they won't do at all. One German plane yesterday (when none of ours was about) tried to conceal himself by climbing up the suns wake, but the sun shone on the aluminium and gave him away, even after one of our planes came humming and Fritz cleared out much to our joy, for whilst an enemy plane is about we have to stick in the dug outs.

I would so like you to see an aerial fight so interesting and to be terminated by the Fritz coming down in flames. One minute he might be soaring like a dove and the next, dashing to earth in flames. One chap today picked up a nose cap of a shell with his regimental number on it; he will evidently be safe for duration of the war now that his shell has exploded.

The trench insects are very bad indeed. An old doggie about 3' high came into the dugout the night before last so we christened her *Anzachia* in the middle of the night we thought the Allemandes had come but was only the dog chasing the rats which live in our abode. Have you seen the Anzac Book? It is fine, after the same style *Fragments of France* which is very funny also. There is a paper printed by Commonwealth offices in London called *Anzac Bulletin* issued free to troops, it contains very little news but it is fresh.

William Joseph Punch.

We have an aboriginal who goes by the name of Punch, he was wounded slightly about one month ago so the saying went around, 'the S.M. has lost his punch 'but he re-joined and now everyone is complementing the Major on regaining Punch.

There is any amount of water lying about; it is good to be able to have a wash each day. On the Peninsula the only water was the beach and that meant a long tramp.

I received a fine large parcel you sent, thank you very much Old Girl. It had a better fate than the Xmas parcel you sent didn't it? That cake soon disappeared.

Did you know the Australian mail is a week overdue so next time it comes in I'll be able to reply at length. The wind whistling through the larch trees last night reminded me of Newcastle Beach (not the first time we went) but the time when I was in uniform and those shops in Newcastle trading with an enemy name were broken open.

I've seen many cake shops broken but generally by shell fire. Aren't the boys following well in our footsteps down South. We had the stoutest nut to crack in starting Fritz on the go. Pushing is not good at all, no sleep, all in the open, wet and fine and so many comrades going but it is good going hand to hand with Fritz and proving that you are the best man. That is good.

All Fritz pocket books and letters we took all seem to prove that Germans as a nation, thinks this war a Holy One and caused by Britain. Some officers we took expressed surprise about Australians being there. One said English bombard 20 minutes, Canadian 10 but Australians only 3 and then they charge. Some of us even forgot to fix our bayonets we rushed so fast. But as old Caspar said *Twas a glorious victory* There is a good canteen here once every 2 days, it is sold out 1/2 hour after opening time.

You'd better get your photo taken again. Give my respects to all at *Oaklands*. I hope you liked the phizog I had taken with the other Sergeants. It was very funny as there was a crowd at the door and although we had 3 taken only one was a success; the beggars at the door tried to make us laugh and succeeded twice. Do you remember how I used to try to get pictures of you under the wattle tree? I still have some copies in my pocket book, also a copy of the photo of Art around by the Porch. We must look strange in Civie clothes. Mother looks after mine but I don't think they will fit later on, the boots might, that's all. One good thing they can't make my feet any bigger. Think I'll close now Frank, Ben

1.10.16

October ushered in by a very cold snap and we are thoroughly frozen. East Wind directly head on to us—on the alert for gas. Ypres is a grassy sector. Canadian engineer brought around the news Fritz digging heard directly under our position. He heard them and said 'While they are digging you are safe '. Very cheerful man. I thought. Canadian miners if they find a German mine, get 14 days leave, a case of whisky and 20 pounds. Easily worth it if it saves front line men from being blown up and down. Raiders made row fit to wake the dead. We have to rub our feet with whale oil, and a fresh pair of socks are issued immediately afterwards. This rubbing is to prevent trench feet; we have lost a few men with this horrible complaint already. When you are numb and sodden from the knees down day after day its no wonder the circulation stops. This time last year in Egypt ready to come over to Peninsula.

Brigade gas officer inspected lines. Strombo Horn erected in Canal Street. Dug up Canadian and Hun in No 4 crater both smothered. Art gone away to a school, probably England. Wrote to A.C. Hollingworth Esq. short note. Germans very jumpy indeed, machine gun rattling whole night long. Our dugout leaking Very few Minewefers over today.

3.10.16

Fritz seems to be getting jumpy. All day today we have been continually shelled and there is plenty of work building up the communication trenches and line again.

4.10.16

Arthur Felton went to an officer's school in England today. Lucky Chap! He certainly missed the bombardment which took place when Thames Street and Canal Street were practically filled up by the continued shelling of one large gun. Unfortunately at 10.00am Pte Murray who occupied the same dugout, as Arthur was buried by a 5.9' shell when his dugout collapsed, both legs severed, subsequently dying of shock. Thankful to say Art had gone as it was his dugout that Murray was in. Murray was 16 ½ but gave his age as 18 and came away without his people's consent. At 5.15 he commenced to bombard and finish by blowing in 70 yards of Thames street and burying J.P. Brough of Wingham, smashed legs and stomach, death instantaneously. Eade, his brother in law naturally badly cut up about it. Immediately stopped shelling. At 7.30 pm had big fat fatigue party on and by 3 am had cleared trenches sufficiently to have cover. We offered no retaliation whatsoever. It must have been an armoured train that was bombarding for same guns came from opposite 15 & 16 Battalions later on.

5.10.16

This morning we heard that 15th Battalion had been raided by Hun with 9 of our lads dead. All troops withdrawn so that our trench mortars cut up a raider party, but did not manage to regain Hun Lines. At 7.30 a big mine went up under 15th Battalion burying ½ platoon, about 20 men, we occupied the crater. Colonel Heane complaining about non retaliation to heavy bombardment. Our 18 lbs open up and close like a factory whistle. The sock question is a bother to all concerned. Whale Oil is a good scheme as it makes the feet feel same as usual and really softens corns Hope no one goes away with Trench Feet.

8.10.16

We are now down in Tunnels under the Bluff very cramped and stuffy and hot but a happy mob; only two casualties this times so far. A cross has been erected over J.P Brough's grave. Note received from Mr Bayliss asking particulars re Walter's death Very quiet since we left the craters, probably 3rd not doing so much work as we used to do. 52nd Battalion on other side of canal, they relieved the 16th. Read *Daddy Long Legs*. Good Book

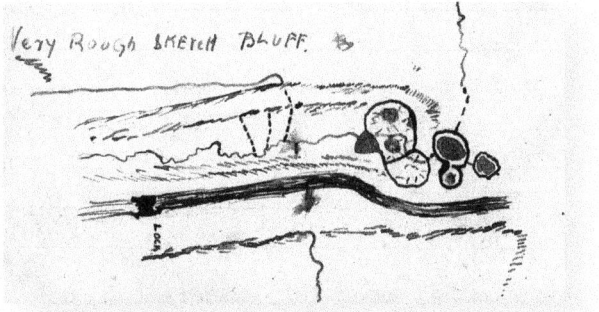

Ben's rough sketch of The Bluff.

8.10.16 France

Dear Frank,

I suppose you have heard that Art has again left the Battalion, this time to go to a school (probably in England) probably for officers. How he managed to be selected no one knows. Lucky isn't he. I believe he will miss the Winter in France. It is still sloppy, wet and growing colder each day. We are living in tunnels at least 30' under the ground and they are very stuffy indeed. You know how I like the fresh air so I live outside as much as possible and live inside of a night only.

I received only one letter this mail from you but I was satisfied as I had not written as often as I ought to have done. Who is Ivy and to whom was she married? It is usual for a girl when she goes to a wedding, to describe what sort of a dress so and so wore and did you wear minon over chameuse or what, I'm a beggar for details.

Well Art's away and half my pack is full of letters to him, mostly from some young lady in Tarro, do you know her at all? The sooner he can send me his address the quicker he will get them. If he is studying hard doubtless he won't want them. I sent away 39 of those Filled Service cards last mail. They are most satisfactory of all letters, 'I am quite well and am going on well 'etc.

Talking of leave to England there is no justice at all in this Battalion at all, they send men on leave etc right out of their turn and give commissions in the same way, the Sergeants have to advise the new subalterns then when they learn, they are ordered about without any consideration. It is a queer, queer world we live in surely.

So Ruth is writing to a lonely soldier, good on her. You would be surprised to learn how the letters are appreciated. By Jove you will be an accomplished young lady when I come back, painting drawing, sewing and ? music. Don't be too proud for a worn out soldier boy.

You say you have not forgotten one event that occurred whilst I was up at Tarro, well I haven't either, not one word. About how many letters have I written to you? Have you kept them all? We won't be home for some time yet and I wonder what sort of a job I'm going to take, Dentistry, farming, loafing or something else. Gertrude always keeps me well supplied with news etc.

Do you know what I am going to send you for Xmas? A picture of myself, the group I sent you is not very good. Well Old Girl there is no more news. We will be out in the firing line shortly.

Yours truly Ben xxxx

10.10.16

Posted letters to Frank, Mother, Gertrude, Geoff Johnson.

12.10.16

Relieved by 13 Battalion . We are probably going to Armentiers salient on the Somme. Shelled rather yesterday. Heavy cannonade from the coast, probably monitors. At 7.30pm we relieved and marched out to Ypres, caught train and back to rest camp Some stoush.

13.10.16.

Raid going over tonight from 3rd Battalion. Supposed to go to 3rd line of trenches. 1st Battalion , 3rd Battalion trench mortar batteries gone up to the line. 3rd Battalion raided Huns, very successful intense bombardment, to which Fritz replied very faintly.

Just read *A Sentimental Bloke* illustrations by Hal Eyre. Sent to England for some Christmas cards to send home, enclosed 10 Fc. Marched to Poperinghe for change and bath, very cold and draughty place. In afternoon taken off with St. Omer in an ambulance as billeting N.C.O. went to Steenwerck.

14.10.16

Battalion marched here and settled down to a nights rest. Several Coys of 19 Battalion doing farm work here, living with people, doing their farm work, great saving of farm rations. I billeted for Brigade transport, hard, hard job trying to find room for them.

15.10.16

Marched 15 miles to a little cluster of farms, nowhere in particular, somewhere in France, about 7 miles from St Omer. Major Woodforde got us lost several times.

Divisional Baths.
Billjim: "'Ow do yer git into the bloomin' bath, digger?"
Orderly (thoughtfully): "Do yer see that tap? Well, crawl up through it."

16.10.16

On to Nordlunham through Watten, a big town with jute factories and big motor works. Approaching Watten we were on a plateau and descending we had a glorious bird's eye view of surrounding country with its farms so well laid out looking like a chess board. A canal with barges and several watermills and a big Electric Light Power House.

17.10.16

Full marching order parade shortage list. Beer, wine, cognac very cheap. No village main Street, only scattered estaminets, very dead indeed. Just heard from Battalion Headquarters that Germans had blown up 2 craters in our late sector at Ypres, occupied them and only driven out at heavy loss to both sides. We occupy them now.

19.10.16.

Shortage list taken. Clean up parade, plenty of sore feet. I think it's through the use of whale oil when in the line. Carl Waugh our transport Sergeant now Second Lieut. received his commission last night. He did such a good job when Yeomans was killed at Pozieres. He deserves it and it is splendid to see merit rewarded in the Battalion instead of bringing importations from other units.

20.10.16.

Marched to Saint Omer entrained 2nd class, set off, sausages, bread etc. detrained Long Pre via Calais, Boulougne and Abbeyville, awful round-about journey. Finished up at Brucamp and then onto a village named Moufflets where we came on a fleet of French Army buses which held 30 men. The drivers had overcoats of bear or goat skin with the fur outside and looked warm enough to go to the South Pole.

We journeyed about 30 miles in these cars, touring France through Amiens to Fricourt and marched 8 miles and slept in bleak tarpaulins huts, very crowded. After an awful night, after a tiring day and our feet sore and stiff in the morning we tried to get our boots on but found them frozen in the wrinkles in which they were when we took them off. Some Brainy person had some paper which he stuffed in his boots and then lit. The heat thawed them out and everyone did the same—paper being diverted from other possible uses for the purpose.

21.10.16.

So its certain—Somme once again. Lovely place. On Brigade railway fatigue unloading limbers ASC etc. Broke a GS wagon. Also heard that our old possey under the Bluff had been blown up. Lucky to be out of it!

MAMETZ WOOD

24.10.16

Marched into Mametz wood, what an awful hole! It had been raining for 2 days and we were told to bivouac in the side of a hill. There were no huts, tents or dugouts, so huddling together we made bivouacs from the waterproof sheets and slept, wet through in mud. What will it be like after 2 months of rain? 10 miles to the firing line, impossible to bring stretcher cases away. Muck everywhere. Sloppy, ammunition wagons bogged, mud over top of puttees, bog up to knees, I pity the poor horses, moving restlessly in their piquets, had churned up the mud until it was over their knees and they looked as miserable as they felt. Horses down every moment, some so bogged left there. Whole place awful. What a Life. Fritz sent over a few H.E's, but they were all duds, perhaps through the slush.

25.10.16

We dug out a small donkey today, poor little brute, gave him to the transport. Caterpillars pulling a huge 9.2 howitzer passed on towards the line. They are wonderful animals the way they plough in and out of shell holes and doing more work than 15 horses and not getting tired. They heave and rock like ships of sea. The 53rd Battalion is down here, we had a visit from Hawkins, late Sgt. of the 1st. He brought news of casualties at Fromelles and amongst others, Rupe Neil is missing.

We are just fooling around in the mud waiting for our turn to go into the line. Mud everywhere; several chaps have lost their puttees through the clinging slime and we are putting sand bags around our legs to try and keep the puttees whole.

PROMOTED FULL SERGEANT

Tom Brown engaged to Miss Doris Hill, High St, Morpeth. Have been asked to write if he is wounded or otherwise.

26.10.16.

More rain, what a lovely country! 12 horses to a G.S.Waggon instead of 4 horses. Plenty of dud shells through the slush and mud. Quite a number of chaps have gone sick with bad feet despite the whale oil parades and rubbing their feet. I personally do not use whale oil now though I would get into serious trouble if OC knew. I think it makes the feet to soft.

28.10.16

Dear Pal,

Two very welcome letters from you last night, quite a budget from home so I read until this morning before I finished them. Slush and mud everywhere, wet through for 3 days now from the knees down. You can't feel the feet though so dead.

Wish I was home again. I suppose you wish the same. I've been rather disappointed in not receiving letters from you but they came to hand last night and I expect more recent ones tonight. If you only could realise how we look forward to letters from home, being cut off from the world and only allowed to send certain restricted news. Well putting that aside, I don't know if you will receive a letter every day when I come home. I'll be glad to get home and rid of letter writing you know.

Tarro isn't far from Wahroonga and that spare room window is always open and sheets and blankets are extra now so have no need of them whatever. I received a parcel from Tarro about 10 days ago. I 'm afraid I didn't acknowledge it as soon as I ought to have done but you know we've been moving about. I think we travel about France more than any other unit.

We had motor transport of 30 miles one day after a big train trip. Of course we had to unload the Divisions transport, guns, pontoons etc. No small job at all, receiving as compensation a route march to catch up the Brigade. My brains have disappeared (if I ever possessed any) for I can't bring them to concentrate on this letter.

What about getting your photo taken again. I know by your letters you are not the same girl I left behind; you have stiffened up a lot same as I have done. I was pleased to receive Mrs Niland's letter which contained lot of home news you forgot to put in, also a letter from Ruth. She thinks that because I don't write too often to her she has offended me. Such is not the case whatever and I'm only too pleased to receive any letters which refer to you.

Sopping, wretched, with the outlook of another July Stunt. Affairs don't' look too bright. Wish I could receive a little blighty and get to England with it. Lucky Art being right out of this accursed country but what' s the use of grousing.

One old lady whose son had hadn't written for some time wrote to General Sir Wm Birdwood and asked him to please find out the reason why. So last time he inspected us and gave out a few bushels of medals, he told us to write more often. I hope that at Xmas time you have a first class time and during the New Year you have all your wishes. Am closing now.

Yours truly

Ben

29.10.16 Sunday.

Moved up into the trenches. After floundering about knee deep, No 1 Platoon reached what was supposed to be the front line trenches, *no bon* at all. From where we entered trench to front line 3 ½ miles of bog. We were bogged several times on way up but struggled on losing one puttee in the muck.

We struck a Communication trench but as it had 18 ' of slush in the bottom and we had an extra S.A.A. 2 bombs per man and 2 sandbags, we decided to go over the top but this encouraged Fritz to whiz bang us. Brotherton sniped and Limbing wounded, so that we were eventually forced to drop back into the river of mud and stumble on into the line, 3 ½ miles of bog.

30.10.16

We stopped 24 hours in the line and were relieved by another company. The Headquarter is in a sunken road, down this road we had to come and it was knee deep in slush. We reached supports, found some dug-outs and turned in, but in an hour's time the rain came down in bucket fulls and the dugouts caved in on us. So, searching for blankets in the mud we sat up all night listening to the heavenly music caused by the rain falling on our tin hats.

Even in this desolate hole the humour of the chaps didn't desert them and one humorous but pathetic incident amused us in our weak stage very much. During the building of the trench a Fritz was buried under foot but with one hand sticking out of the trench wall into the trench so that each time anyone walked over his body the hand wagged as if shaking hands Sure enough every man shook hands with him and solemnly wished him luck.

31.10.16

Broke as a fine large sort of a day overhead, but underfoot the continual slush made life unbearable. We were too tired to lift our legs out of the mud preferring to stand still or lean up against the side of the sunken road. We have more planes up than Fritz has and more guns in this sector. Guns everywhere chiefly Howitzers, and they are all over the place, not even camouflaged. 10 Huns gave themselves up last night, said they had had no rations for 8 days owing to our continual barrage on his communications. Fritz that were bought in were thin and muddier than we are by far. At present our 18 pounders whizzing overhead like blow flies. Our observation balloons everywhere must be going to be a stunt around here. Every time Fritz puts a balloon up one of our aviators burns it. We are getting very careless how we move overland instead of in trenches. Shelling started again, seems Fritz is getting impudent. Rain, rain and slush. Big push started too late. Real wintery now.

1.11.16

We trekked back to Delville Wood and here were able to see openly some of the carnage brought about by war. The weather conditions were such that all men not in the line were used in carting shells, making roads etc. so that no one could be spared to tidy it up and bury the dead.

Amongst the broken and twisted tree trunks were the remains of guns, limbers, horses etc. in all conceivable positions. If this is the result of our bombardment I'd like to be out of it. Bodies by the dozen, broken guns, mules, piles of equipment from the men evacuated, wounded, smashed rifles and every possible piece of war waste and debris. If only it could be carried away to—say a museum. Captain Kirkwood our medical officer was very worried about the fatigue manifesting every man. No one was allowed to have breeches legs laced up. Putties have been discarded—we now wrap sand bags around our legs.

The object of this loosening of clothing is to prevent any blockage of circulation to our feet. Not withstanding all these precautions, we lost some men with trench feet. A welcome addition to our wardrobes are sheepskin vests or bather jerkins, sleeveless but very warm; the skin side is worn out and the fleecy linings keep us warmer. Smoke and Lachrymotory, Royal Engineers and batteries went into the line this morning, evidently going to advance under clouds of smoke. I'd rather have a night stunt than a day one.

Taube in this morning evidently spotting all he can. We send over 50 shells to Fritz one. Generally have 50 planes up also. Guns everywhere, chiefly 8 'siege guns, more guns than I ever dreamed of, everywhere, not covered up as Hun is robbed of his eyes by our superiority of air. Only take time now 'til we drive Fritz out.

2.11.16

Out in Reserve, we are due back tonight. Probably advance tomorrow. No 1 Platoon on right connecting with 6th Bn. Mail from Mother and Frank, did Art's letters up in bundle and hope to get them away. Sent Christmas cards to Gertrude, Mary, Frank, Nancy Johnstone. Elsie

Knitting socks for WW1 war effort, Marjorie, Didie Felton, Mrs Champion and Gertrude

Hirst and Dot Williams, Postmaster Moore, Jean Austin, Miss Smith, Mr Walker and Bruce, Uncle Will. Slushy wet crook. 6 gone to hospital, 2 pneumonia and rest trench feet.

3.11.16

Continued wet nothing doing at all, very cold.

4.11.16

Posted off letters to Art

5.11.16

November Attack on Bayonet and Hilt Trenches—3rd Battalion co operating, relieved by 11th Battalion and moved to Bernafray Wood.

FIRST BATTALION AIF DIARY

GUEUDECOURT

Flers and the Somme Winter—October 1916—February 1917

The Road to Flers

After their operations at Pozières and Mouquet Farm in July, August and September 1916, the divisions of the Australian Imperial Force were sent to garrison the lines east of Ypres [Ieper] in Belgium. This was a relatively quiet sector at the time.

Ben's photo, Flers.

Because of the losses the Australians had sustained on the Somme it came as a shock to them to learn that they were to go back there in mid-October 1916. The move was very unpopular. One onlooker who observed Australians leaving Flanders on 12 October 1916 noted how grim the men looked 'without the least buoyancy about them'.

The autumn rains had set in by the time the Australians reached the Somme and the whole battlefield had become a sea of mud. Broken ground, easily traversed in dry weather, was a bog. Trenches and tracks were often impassable. It could take relays of stretcher-bearers many hours to bring in a wounded man, the mud slowing the journey to a kilometre an hour.

As the Australians reached the Somme, the great offensive that had begun with such high hopes on 1 July 1916 was nearing its end. The fight now was about seizing suitable positions for the winter during which major campaigning was impossible. On 5 November 1916, the Australians launched one attack near Gueudecourt before dawn and another near Flers in mid-morning. A further attack was made near Flers on the 14th. These actions were made in some of the worst conditions the Australians were to experience on the Western Front.

These attacks were carried out by two battalions of the First Division. The battalion at Gueudecourt, after an exhausting journey through the mud, was seen and shelled and was unable to assemble in no-man's-land. The troops advanced in good order but because of the poor conditions they could not keep pace with the creeping barrage. Similar conditions existed at Flers later in the day and, while troops from both assaulting forces held parts of the enemy trenches for some hours, the partial gains were not defensible and the Australians withdrew. The gains made on a second attempt near Flers on 14 November also had to be given up.

On 18 November 1916, the Battle of the Somme officially ended and for the remainder of the winter of 1916–17 the Australians garrisoned the line east of Flers. From there they kept pressure on the Germans by means of small attacks and raids. However, the main battle was against mud, rain and frost-bite.

The front lines were up to twelve kilometres away from good roads so major efforts were made to repair approach roads to allow supplies to be brought forward. As the roads neared the front they became 'duckboard' tracks', the only surface by which it was possible to get across the sea of mud. Supplies of hot food, leather waistcoats, thigh boots, worsted gloves, dry socks gradually reached the front where they made the awful conditions if not better at least bearable. In the rear, however, both the accommodation and comfort for troops in reserve were dramatically improved.

Four weeks of colder and brighter weather from mid-January to mid-February 1917 froze the land and water hard and improved conditions although new troubles arrived. Bread could not be cut with a knife, hands were frozen numb within seconds if exposed, boiling tea quickly became ice, and German shells, no longer cushioned by the mud, exploded with more deadly effect. This 'Somme Winter' experience was not easily forgotten by men who served through it. One historian of the AIF has described the mood engendered by the terrible losses of the Somme battles and the trials of the winter:

> The world seemed a perpetual round of pain, misery and death, and men seemed to endure ceaseless travail, till their souls were deadened, and they resigned their course on earth to the whims of a malicious fate ... They had come to Armageddon. '

Bill Gammage, *The Broken Years*, Sydney, 1990

An autographed group portrait of five Australian officers. Back row from left: Major Noel Edmund Barton Kirkwood, Captain Hayward Hugh Moffat, Maj Philip Llewellyn Howell-Price. Front row: Lieutenant Charles William Henry Rollo Somerset , *Lt Francis Leonard Flannery.* Source AWM

5.11.16 – Ben's Version

Guy Fox day [Guy Fawkes]. We moved back to line about 8.00 p.m. to Cheese road and are to hop over tonight. An assembly trench has been dug 100 yards in front of our line and into this C & D Coys moved, B in support in the front line and A Coy. in reserve. A the weakest Coy. Fritz must have known we were coming for as C & D moved out into assembly trench, up went his artillery flares and as soon as I saw them knew we were in for a rough time. The time of barrage was changed to 12.30. Fritz started to bombard us before our barrage opened. Our barrage was perfect, a creeping barrage on the trenches and the heavy guns engaged their guns. The shooting was excellent. C and D went over and only reached the trench when they were shot down chiefly by machine gun rounds. Then B was launched and A brought over from sunken road to assembly trench. B also failed. Fritz gave C, D and B Hell.

Casualties 172 of which 71 missing. Lt. Somerset, Lt A'Beckett and Sgt Wells only ones seen in Hun Trench but had to come back when no others

Flers, held by the Australians all winter. From the Front - Shrapnell & Smiles *1917*

got through to help them. Wells killed, Somerset wounded, Mr Phillips, Mr Finlayson, McIntyre killed. Mr Steel missing. Sgt Allan of the bombers, after being wounded crawled forward toward hun line cheering his men on then seen to faint away. After being 48 hours in no man's land he crawled back to our line. Mr Phillips head of machine gunners is a brother of Mrs Read (wife of Dr Read, neighbour of Bens parents in Wahroonga). A Coy got it in the neck too in support, and R.I.C. McGregor was wounded in the wrist so that his arm was useless, came back and reported to Col. Heane who spoke to him as if he had deserted his men. Mac burst into tears and though wounded tried to regain his men when Col. Heane ordered him to dressing station. Lieut. Sparke took charge and we went forward to help B, C, and D. We could see the casualties had been heavy, so a second attack of B, C, & D and part of A went forward and were again knocked back. Our men were trying to fire their rifles but they were choked with mud. Orders from Col. Heane came and we all trekked back as best we could, picking up as many of the wounded as we could to the reserve line and then back towards Delville Wood.

The casualties were very solid. Officers killed: Phillips, Finlayson, McIntyre, Steel, and Lanser—in all about 170 casualties, including Captain Jackson and R.I. C. McGregor, two fearless soldiers. It is quite impossible to tell who was most heroic on that night but Hastie a Beckett , Somerset, Edgley, Jacobs and last but not least Howell-Price were the officers who carried most of the attack on their shoulders.

Gueudecourt pond and Church.

We are the 3rd regiment to sound defeat on that Bayonet and Hilt Trench First time we have ever had a defeat. When a 3rd effort was impossible we were ordered to take our platoons back to Delville Wood.

In my humble opinion, causes of failure were: ·

1. Mud too stiff, not allowing the following of barrage close enough.
2. Shower of rain just before hop over, making everything sticky and causing rifles to jamb.
3. Men used up with 12 days in the open in awful weather.
4. Boy given a man's job. (Col Heane)

DELVILLE WOOD AND POMMIERS REDOUT

6.11.16

We reached Delville Wood at day break in an awful mess.

7.11.16.

Moved to huts out of the wet near railway. Battalion in an awful mess, clothes torn and ruined, boots like brown paper, and arms in frightful state.

Ben's photo.-Flers

8.11.16

Moved into Pommiers redout, slush mud huts wet very cold.

9.11.16

Out on fatigue all day. Carrying sleepers from railway yard near Albert, raining.

10.11.16

Carrying metal. Repairing Mametz Link Road. Met Fred Thompson and spent afternoon with him Fixed me up with boots. Posted letter to Art, Frank, Mum.

Ben's photo Steel and Lanser memorials.

11.11.16

> Harold Kershaw, Miss Smith, Puss Cottam fine. Terrific bombardment by us last night.

12.11.16

> Marched to Dernancourt about 7 miles. On the way we passed the Guards Brigade; Scotch Irish Welsh Coldstream Grenadier Guards. All fine troops about 5'10 ' and very uniform. What a contrast, they wore spic and span uniforms, every button polished etc.

13.11.16.

> Left Dernancourt and marched to Beure-Sous Corbie. Here are German prisoners by the score, working on the roads. They all look so well, and that contented cow-look about their eyes. We had a concert in the evening.

14.11.16

> We marched on fatigue to Dernancourt. Quarter Master fixed most of us up with new boots and by degrees new clothing. Found out we were not wanted so very pleased we got back. The 6 mile march with no equipment making the blood circulate well. It was an awfully slushy march too.
>
> Parade, Meaghan remanded for Field General Court Marshal.

15.11.16

> General clean up, foot inspection, rifle inspection, shortage list taken, and raided transport for horse brushes to clean mud off clothes. Fairly tidy now.

16.11.16

> Billeting N.C.O. in a car to Flesselles. Passed through Amiens and Corbie. Battalion arrived later.

17.11.16.

Moved at 8 a.m. to Fremont, 3 miles from Flesselles, small place, no estaminets but electric light in the village, people seem very poor indeed. Bought a case of Watsons No 10 from Flesselles.

18.11.16.

Marched to St. Saveur through Vaux, better town like Saillee, quite prepared to stop long time in billet we are at present. Old dame very obliging. 2 rooms, one to have meals in, (a fire in it) other to sleep in. Rec'd letter from Mother saying received Diary. Posted note to Father, Mother, Frank.

19.11.16

Saint Saveur. Parades all day This afternoon 2 or 3 men gave Battalion a bad name by knocking over an old dame. Mail from Frank.

21.11.16

Went for a route march to Ailly sur Somme rather large sized town with big factories. Here the Somme is a large stream. All along its banks are two paths where the barges are towed against the stream. Rations 17 men to a 1 lb tin of honey. *Missing part of page.* Poor old Beavis, no wonder his nerves went and he went away. From start of war to now never away from Battalion. Stands to reason must break up after all that service. Leave has started for Amiens. First time in this town on leave. Very fine cathedral, it was being sandbagged up, all statues encased in sand bags as Fritz comes over bombing. 3rd and 2nd Battalions supply the mess and Maltese carts for conveyance of men. Col. Heane and Lt. Bootle gone on leave to England.

22.11.16

Today is a red letter day for me. I was promoted to commission as a 2nd lieut. and have to leave old A and go to C Coy. Stepped out in fear and trembling to go to the Officer's mess. To my great surprise

I was welcomed by Captain Jackson, Graham, Sparke, Webb and Boardman.

After tea Ted Sparke gave me two stars and made me give a speech. I was ushered to a real bed with sheets on it by Captain Jacobs under whom I am to serve. As I had him as an area commandant in old 19 B days we know each other well.

After a chat over old times this being my first real opportunity I went to bed tired and happy. Next day when going on parade I met Sgt Mackie, a very old hand and a friend and when he saw the stars he said *Good God, what will they be doing next?* talk about being taken down a peg.

Soon old Hastie A'Beckett turned up with my new command; he has been on piquet duty in Amiens for some time and I was to take over his platoon.

24.11.16

Move tomorrow, lot of supercilious Tommy officers taking over this billet. They have baggage galore enough to stock officers of 1st Brigade. Trunks, Valises and boxes—how on earth they manage to carry on and play the game by their men, I don't know.

25.11.16

Moving orders cancelled. Pleading the excuse of new clothes, officers kit—and a Sam Browne Belt I went with Sparke into Amiens riding the distance of 11 miles on horse back. Gee I was sore—I can't ride at all. Had lunch at Hotel Dauphin, bought lots of things. Dinner at Hotel du Rhin, very fine place, seating accommodation 500. Cathedral very fine place but not as fine a place as St John's Knights in Valetta, Malta. Rather fine town with Canal Somme running through it. Amiens about same size as Valetta.

1.12.16

Left St. Sauveur marched to Vignacout via St. Vast, arriving there at 5.30 a.m. as we left St. Souveur at 2 a.m. We stopped about until dinner

Amiens Cathedral taken post-war.

time in the Icy frosty weather, when we entrained for Mericourt and detrained there and marched through Buire to Ribermont. Very dirty billets and the people are Jews. Everything must be paid for and at high price. Charges are miles in excess. Then all the trouble at home with J.W.W. shews that this war is being born on a few shoulders only. We clubbed together and bought sports material, plenty of foot balls (20 franc each) etc. Had a few days spell, doing road fatigues and playing football. Made mess secretary.

11.12.16

Moved to Mametz.

12.12.16

Col. Heane badly hit through head. C Coy at Mametz on road fatigue, A.B. & D elsewhere on general fatigue, unloading at railway dumps etc. all in very good condition and fairly happy. One of our men on road fatigue killed by nose cap of anti air craft gun shell. Some good scraps witnessed, there were 14 planes fighting at once over us today. It was so pretty and then Fritz turned tail and got away, they seem to be faster than our planes. Gramophone given by Comforts Fund very handy and cheery.

Parcel from Miss Smith. Note from Frank and Art replied. Cabled reply home to cable received *Sorry, Hope Felton and you are soon well.* Sparke taking over Webb's job.

The hut is bedlam when A' Beckett, Richards and Somerset give a war dance. 500 and bridge are the chief after work entertainments, poker having been given the go-by since someone put on his last poddy calf as a wager. Col Heane is looking after Brigade whilst Smythe is away and things are functioning well.

Somewhere in France

14.12.16

Dear Frank, Your letter dated 4.10.16 to hand today. It is a long time since I wrote to you. I'm sorry you have been ill and more sorry still when it was that young imp Mary who took the complaint to *Oaklands*. Haven't I told you often enough that I absolutely forbid you to be ill or develop toothache until I tell you to do so.

The letter received from me with name 'C C Lambert ' on it was posted inside one of his envelopes to his people. He is a friend of mine and when green envelopes were scarce used to oblige each other *Comme ca.* Thank you for the Xmas parcel, it hasn't come to hand yet but will soon and with each goodie will think of you.

Can't drive Blackie! I didn't know that any horse could beat you and rather surprised for Blackie used to be some goer. Do often go for long rides here, say 10 miles now that I have a star lots of privileges come my way. Won't be sorry to see old Art back, we don't make satisfactory correspondent. Hope your Mother and Claire enjoyed themselves at Riverstone [home of the Rumerys—Mrs Niland's sister]. Don't quite *comprez* Mellie but suppose she is an aunt or cousin of yours. [Probably Marjory Rumery—Ed]

We are up to our necks in slush. Just imagine us staying here in action all the winter. And a chap can't get sick enough to go away to

Taken Amiens.
Carl Waugh, girl from shop, Hasty a'Beckett Front Teddy Sparke and Boardman

hospital. I suppose you think me mad to want to go to hospital but I'm one of the few who have managed to keep their heads up since March. It must be all the thoughts of those at home which keep one safe from harm. Of course one does not know when but someday he must be hit lightly or heavily. One does not know which.

I've had rather a misfortune lately, screwmatiks in the left arm and a nail off on left forefinger The nail was torn on some barbed wire and naturally came off. Worse luck it will take some time to grow again. I'll have to return by post the 8 kisses you sent me 8 x. Luckily I censor my own letters now or else the censor would have a laugh. I can't think of any news at all so will have to fill up somehow.

How is your forelock? You can't possibly think of the plight we are in, for instance I have dollops of mud everywhere, right over my knees went the slush today. Wet feet for a fortnight now and yet I can't go away sick.

Saw 2 German planes come down in flames today. They looked o.k. Of course you mustn't think what happened to the poor

Allemandes inside. The tanks, well I can't explain them at all but I've seen them in action now and a few more blown out.

Love Ben

Enclosed is one sleeve color from my big coat. Green goes to the bottom

15.12.16

A'Beckett and Somerset and R.I.C. McGregor awarded M.C.'s for 5th November stunt. They deserved it! This camp was hit by a slippery-dick shell yesterday, but no one hurt. Have been attached to D Coy for 2 days and now with 30 other ranks making a road and general renovation of camp.

Captain C W H R Somerset, MC

16.12.16

Our working spell came to an end and went to new possie about 800 yards in advance of Gueudacourt.

Gueudacourt is subjected to solid bombardment and no one goes through it at all, always skirt to the right. This new line not *too bon*, mucky and cold, but not a big war on. As both Fritz and ourselves in not too good a position. A certain officer who likes his food very much asked Starkey for some gerty bread. Sgt Page showed him where it was and told him to help himself. Hour later heard a wonderful flow of language, and on enquiring found all the Sgts. bread eaten.

2 Lt Page. Joined 7th Reinforcements—left Bn 1915 as private.
went to Officer School.

20.12.16

Grease Trench, Gueudacourt our new possie, it should be slushy
stench trench. Bernafay Wood in Nissen Huts. Inky Wells our good
quartermaster gave us a scare—he had a heart attack and was evacuated
sick. He and his horse Piastre were inseparable and it was often that
Piastre brought Wells home when he was knocked out bringing up
the rations etc. His organisation ability helped at Pozieres; we were
never short of food there and we had every reason to be. Received a
letter from Mrs Hesketh about Len, wants to write to me. Sent her a
FS card. Have been up to our new position to right and 300 yards in
advance of Gueudacourt. The Germans shell G unceasingly especially
3 mounds they left intact. 3 heavy howitzers there and lot of papers in
dug out . He pours 2 x 9.2 ' shells every 2 minutes into it in hopes of
smashing them. New possey *no bon*. Line runs very roughly like this so
that one can be sniped at left flank by our own men. [drawing]

Lieut and QM E. Webb, KIA Bullecourt, late chemist of Hornsby

20.12.16 France

Dear Fran(k)c

Your welcome parcel to hand today just in time for Christmas, you are a dear. We all send our thanks for the eatables which very soon disappeared. For the last few days we haven't been having such a bad time in huts a few miles from the line.

We have a fire going with coffee simmering on the top ready for the officer coming off duty. Last night we had ice all over the ground and today it started snowing. It is bitterly cold so we will have a real Christmassy Christmas. You are having it bonnie and hot in old Tarro now.

Last night a few planes came over dropping bombs, no damage was done and we brought 2 planes down wallop. Our quick firers are very accurate and once the search light focusses the planes are good night Allemand.

I'm terribly homesick Pal. What am I to do? I'm like a little kiddie, want to go home . This time last Xmas in Malta I was thinking of you and wondering where on earth are the letters but this time all is ok. I'm ashamed of old Australia with all its strikes and won't work or won't fight who are at home. How I wish I had charge for a bit I'd tickle them up. The authorities are frightened absolutely frightened of the chaps who are frightened to come here.

There are Golden A's for Anzac to be worn on the old black and green for all those who have been on the Peninsula. There are lots of fights over it too. Old hands alone wear an A, the others don't. Am always expecting leave which never comes but I believe it will very shortly now. Will see old London etc and will paint it blue. I'll tell you who keeps the pub there when I come back. I believe I'll take a trip to Scotland. Just been listening to a very fine Gramophone, *tres bon*.

Love Ben

ADELAIDE CAMP

New padre joined up Julian by name Seems O.K. Captain RIC McGregor awarded Military Cross for bravery. Xmas parcels coming in galore.

21. 12.16.

Rode to Albert, caught cars to Pont Noyelle 6 kils from Amiens. Bought lot of goods from Amiens. Lots of (Ben's drawing of scabies? or otherwise with many legs) of cases shewing up from St Saveur and Ailly-sur-Somme, now closed to us.

25.12.16

25th Christmas Day. Plenty of tinned pudding. Col. Heane sent some Blighty delicacies; he ordered them when on leave before he was wounded. Very fine Dinner. Wonder what sort of Xmas having at home. Hostilities just the same. 9.2 gun barks continually here and awakens us up at night. Fritz trying to find this gun smashed 2 empty huts in the camp. Our Engineers and pioneers have now laid duck boards right from Bernafay Wood through Delville Wood, past suger refinery on right down to Brigade Headquarters.

Delville Wood still reeks of dead men and horses. There are wagons, guns and equipment galore there. In November you could have collected tons and tons of salvage and even yet, though most of the men have been buried, the war waste lying there is cruel. This Wood was a tough nut to crack, I forget which British Division did the trick.

Last night we threw over a big barrage and of course Fritz retaliated. It was mainly a search for our big gun barrage though. In the middle of the gun fire our 2nd Battalion raiding party hoped over in search of identification and as much damage as possible to be done in the time allowed. They were all dressed in Tommy (English uniform) clothes and had trenching tools with a cog wheel on the end to act as clubs. The raid was very good, very few casualties on our side.

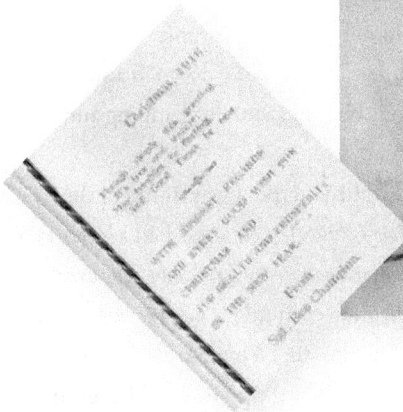

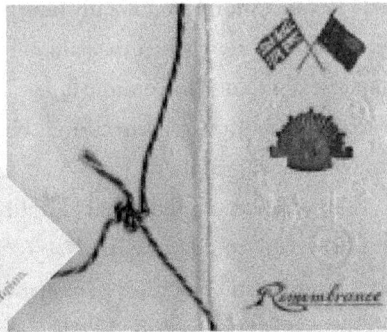

26.12.17

Edgley, Page and Bruton went up to the new sector today to inspect. Will
be glad when fatigue to the line ceases, they are very tiring and the duck
boards make the feet very sore. I have received no mail now for about 3
weeks and the girls parcel has not yet turned up. I wrote to Tarro to day .
Raining like wild fire. Would very much like some mail. Lent Corporal
Snowy Howell of A 50 francs. 25 men to a 16 lb tin of pudding. YMCA
have a coffee stall right at Bgde HQ beyond Delville Wood.
Still doing fatigues to line.

27.12.16 France

Dear Franc

I spent a very sloppy and muddy Christmas and expect a worse
one for New Year. I had the usual pain under my waist coat after Xmas
dinner, except that the waist coat was not there, in place a tunic worse
luck but expect to be able to sit down to a civilised dinner by next
year Wonder when this war will cease, the sooner the better. *Apres
the Guerre finis* as the little song goes lots of things will happen. Even
suppose I will have to work my nut?

We had mutton chops, pudding jelly but our feet and up to knees
were sopping. Talk of glue this mud beats it all. Someday I'll send some
home to sample. Remember you said you liked that old CMF uniform,
well, I expect shortly to have my photo taken and then you will have
the honour of seeing me in a spanking new officers tunic. Saw today
funniest sight outside Tommie huts. a mule sitting down in a shell hole
with water right up to his neck and the mule actually grinning and
enjoying the huge joke.

Did you have a good Xmas? I hope you did. I was thinking the whole
time how you would be saying *How is Old Ben* etc etc. I had a letter from
Art yesterday and a card too asking me *whatever I did to be very careful*.
Me, up to my neck in slush. Oh! but never mind *La Guerre sur finis par
Mars tres bit for soldats*. Won't I go mad then. I'll tear up all the spare
paper thats about. Well old bint (excuse the gippo for girl) I'm going to
a school probably for a month, thats how they give a chap a spell. And
you wont be able to say I'm an unreciprocating little cat, as I'll send a

photo in place of the nice one you sent me. Each time I have a screw at it I say will I be fortunate enough to go home? Suppose if I manage to get through this a crane on Woolloomooloo wharf or a tram will bump me or some such occurrence to stop me from seeing you again. Have you been reading any more good books lately? *A Rough Shaking* forget the author, but Gertrude will tell you is a very fine book. How are your Royal Household? Well I hope and sprightly. Please remember me to your father and mother, Mary, Ruth, Franc I think I met her once or twice and Kitty, Oh dear, and Claire, I nearly forgot her in my terrible hurry. I'm a very busy man now Pal, get up at 8am and bed at 8pm. Not bad for old Ben is it.

Ben

Plenty of barbed wire....the badge on back of envelope is very classy *nést pas*. [PF-havent got this]

1917 TIRANCOURT CHATEAU

29.12.16—1.1.17

Left Bernafay with Cassidy and Dick Price, who joined us before Christmas, younger brother to Major Philip Howell—Price and reported to Anzac Reinforcement camp at Albert. We were sent into billets in Albert and stopped there until morning of 31st December.

2nd Lieutenant Dick Howell Price, Ben's photo..

Picked up by motors, taken through Amiens to La Chausee and reported to 1st Divisional School at Tirancourt Chateau under Colonel Stevens *Sticky* of the 2nd Battalion.

Tirancourt Chateau

Ben's Photo showing snow on the ground

France 8.1.17

Dear Frank,

Haven't had letters from Australia for some time, over a month at least. Some boat must have been sunk for I know they leave Old Sydney. Have been out live bombing today and of course one bomb must have slipped out of a chap's hand and exploded. Of course we cleared when we saw it drop but luckily only one chap was hit and he only slightly.

2ⁿᵈ Lieutenant R.D. Dick Howell-Price 1st Battalion and 2nd Lieutenant Jack McMahon 4th Battalion

Visited fairly large town last Sunday–had rather a good time, two dinners and paid rather well for them. Very swanky place bon. 3 times size of Hotel Metropole Sydney. Our old General was around to see the school today and had dinner with us. He is General Walker and commands 1ˢᵗ Division AIF. A very clever soldier, but wish I was as safe as he is. He is sure to go back. He never visits front line and generally has a 40' dug out about 3 miles from the reserves. Lucky beggar.

Have been rousing on the men for writing mournful letters home and here I'm starting. Well my leg is practically o.k. now with the rest at the school and being away from the mud has made a big difference. Wonder when this wretched war is going to finish–couple more years I suppose. Perhaps when next you see me I'll have a grey beard or a little halo, one of the two.

Had my photo taken couple of days ago but they will take about 3 weeks before I get them, then about 6 more before you get them. A lot happens in 9 weeks war and it might even be over. Would so like to be home even for a week just to see my ain folks *Oakland* is of course included in ain folks.

Some very picturesque barges pass this old chateau each day along the canal. Each one has all the families washing out to dry in the fore peak. Such a variety of colors and patches. Things are getting frightfully dear. And the shortest article is sugar, then corned meat and coal.

There's a fine old church in the village built in the 1700s so it has seen some fighting in its time. Napoleonic wars, Franco-Prussian and World–Prussian. Don't think there's any more news now pal.

Your's truly Ben

—

24.1.17 France

Coldest place under the sun

Dear Frank, For last few days it has been steadily freezing and roads are as solid as iron. We wear all the clothes we have and are still cold especially in fingers and ears. The wind is icy. The paper today remarks that yesterday was the coldest day since the war began.

We had some fine fun sliding alongside the creeks, until somebody fell in and became rather wet so we stopped. The ground is terribly hard. I would much sooner be in old Sydney with temp of 105 degree than here with 19 degrees of frost like last night.

I have promised you from time to time a photo of the ugliest boy in Christendom and here it is attached. Note his scowl. By Jove pal it is a long time since I had a letter from you, can't tell when the last was about 2 ½ months ago I believe but it feels like six.

There are absolutely no flowers of any description to be seen, nothing but ice and snow. This morning there was ice on the inside of the window pane. Shews how cold we sleep at night. Thankfully though we are not in the line where exercise to keep warm would be impossible. Anyhow there is one consideration and that is Fritz is just as bad, perhaps worse.

There is going to be HELL let lose here in the spring. I haven't been to *L'angleterre* yet and I can't say when I will be going. I'm months overdue for leave. I often wonder how you are getting on and do your ears often burn. Mine do, it's then I suppose those at Home are speaking of me.

No letters so can't reply to any questions. Suppose all letters have gone to bottom of Mediterranean Sea. We had a good football match this afternoon. Have you ever seen a good fast game such as Maoris v Australia? It's great. May perhaps someday have the honour of promenading you to see one of the great rugby matches. Wish I was with Art in England. He ought to be leaving there shortly to become an officer here, on the dinkum active service. I suppose he has made many friends there but from his letters they cannot come up to the Australians.

As I have told you in other letters I'm a bit home sick. This wandering unsettled life is *no bon* for Ben. I'm thankful there have been no zeppelin raids in Australia like there have been in England. It must be awful for lot of children and women to be wounded, not so bad for men. Every time I see women or kiddies hurt it makes me feel mad. If there are not more reinforcements coming over I don't know what the Australians will do especially in Spring.

Well old Pal, I don't believe I can tell you anything more and I'm absolutely freezing.

Bon Soir and Bon Chance

Ben

25.1.17

Nothing to write about at the School, very cold, snow continually on the ground. Fine old chateau with quaint nooks and crannies. It overlooks the Somme and the Railway is close. Picquigny is the name of the station; we often run into Amiens. Septic leg has developed and have not been on Parade for last few days, but think it is healing. Snow fights galore and sliding on the ice pools. Near the camp is a big plateau on it, we do manoeuvres. Caesar is supposed to have a fortified camp on it, and in olden days it would be a difficult matter to attack. Will be pleased to re-join battalion, miss my mates. Chief friends here are:–Norris (2nd) Jackson, Morgan, Boileau of the 3rd, McMahon, Agnew and Symington of the 4th, Little 9th, Nanking 5th and Mills 10th Battalion.

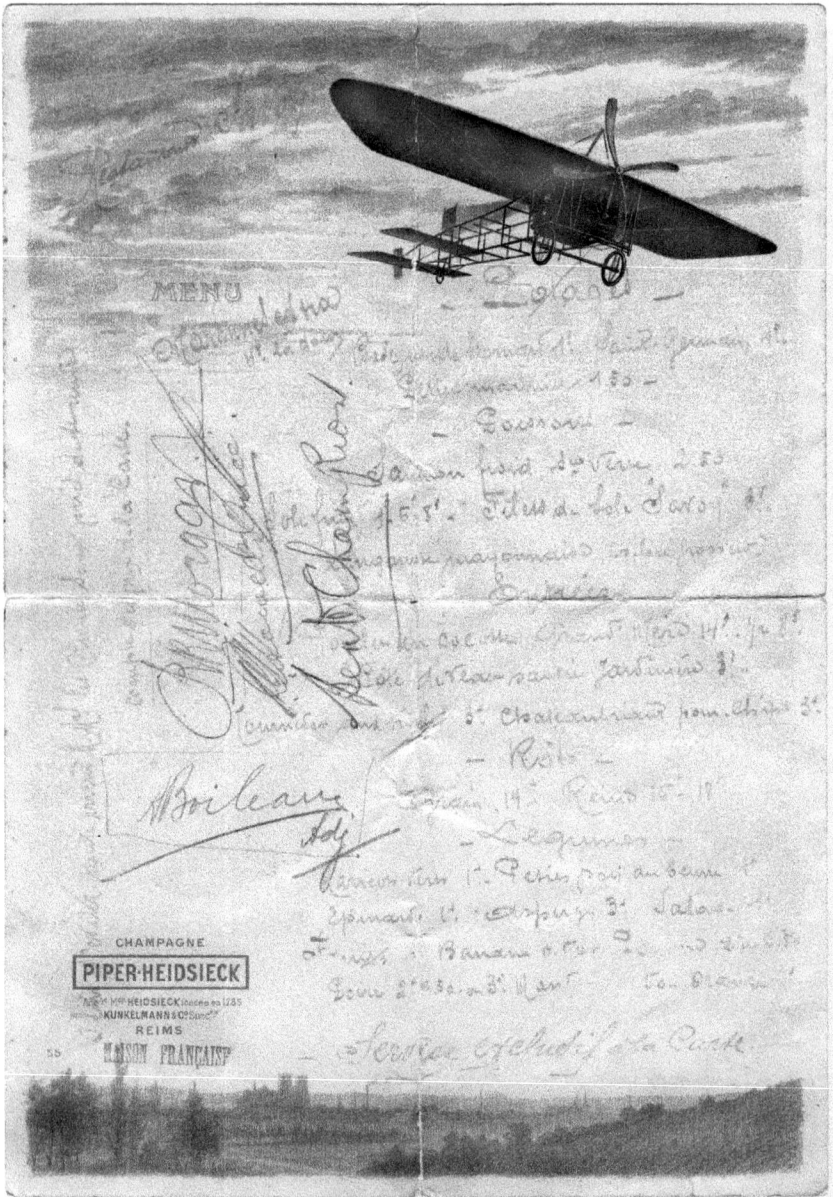

Dinner menu with the signatures of Morgan, Boileau and Dick Howell-Price.

2nd Lt McMahon of 4th Battallion, note the 'A' on the battalion patch.
Wounded at Lone Pine and Pozieres. Died of influenza pheumonia in 1919 after 4½ years of
active service

ACROSS THE SNOW, NEAR FLERS, JAN·1917.

The Duckboards.

From Shrapnel and Smiles

29.1.17

Rejoined unit in front line between Martinpuich and Flers. Very peculiar state of affairs, practically no war on. Either side could make it practically impossible for the other to bring up rations as the 2 lines are in a dip and have to come down long hills to reach the lines. There is one old Fritz like Bairnsfather's *Old Bill* who pops his head up each morning and shouts to us. He is so cool, we can't shoot him. Each side could see on a moonlight night the other side relieving, as both sets of duck boards leading over the hills are in plain view. Bill beckoned us with a cognac bottle today, cheeky old man.

1.2.17

Moved to Eaucourt L'Abbeyee. All that remains on top is a heap of broken masonry but below the ground are large tunnels with little crypt-like caverns cut out. Evidently used by the monks in olden days. There is a long passage leading for ¼ mile underground and then it is blocked, perhaps it went much further once. There is also another passage leading to an underground spring. In the day time we are not allowed out on top, as we are on a hill and over beyond the Butte de Warlencourt, Fritz occupies a wood and from there we are shelled.

4.2.17

4th Division made a stunt last night on the right of Gueudecourt, very successful I hear. Earlier in the night saw how quick our men answer S.O.S. signals. 2 went up and in ½ a minute a barrage was well and truly played in the middle of No Man's Land and our heavies engaging theirs. Yates and Waugh should have been back from leave days ago, but haven't turned up.

6.2.17. France

Dear Franc,

I'm so sorry that I missed the last mail but we have been in a place where is practically impossible to write. Anyhow in about a week's time we will be out resting and then I'll write more often. The snow and ice has been on the ground for about 3 weeks now. It's terribly cold but a lot better than the mud which would be there if the ground didn't freeze.

NOTHING is to be written on this side except the date and signature of the sender. Sentences not required may be erased. If anything else is added the post card will be destroyed.

I am quite well.

I have been admitted into hospital

{ sick } and am going on well.
{ wounded } and hope to be discharged soon.

I am being sent down to the base.

I have received your { letter dated _____
{ telegram ,, _____
{ parcel ,, _____

Letter follows at first opportunity.

I have received no letter from you

{ lately.
{ for a long time.

Signature only. } Ben W Champion

Date 3/2/17

[Postage must be prepaid on any letter or post card addressed to the sender of this card.]

Reply card from Ben

How time flies, it is now 6th day of Feb 1917 and last time I saw you about 10 July 1915. That is a long time away and yet I can see you as plainly as if I'd only seen you yesterday.

We had a note through from Army re America. I believe something will be doing in that line shortly. If America comes in the cream of German Mercantile shipping will be lost to her. It is now sheltering in American harbours.

Hope you received the photos I sent you. The usual number of planes overhead, same bombardments etc. everything same as I've told you lots of time before so no news at all. A chum of mine named Brown has been married to a nurse he met in hospital. I'm very sorry for he was engaged to a girl somewhere on the northern line. I'll give him some talking too when he comes back. He was hit in the head so perhaps that has made him a bit soft.

Do you remember us talking about promotions when Art and I were just about to leave? Well we've been very lucky so far in escaping injury and receiving commissions. (Art probably has his by this).

How are your horses? I'm glad to hear the season has been good at home. I don't know what the Frenchies will do with their land that has been fought over, shell holes, craters, trenches right across fields etc. I believe there is a scheme to put the whole of it under forests and let the trees even up the land. Then there would be plenty of timber too in years to come. That is if this war ever finishes. It seems to be unending. Just fancy the reception the Old Battalion will get when it marches up George or King Streets. You will have to see that sight little girl and it will be one never to be forgotten.

I think I'll go to Scotland as well as London for leave. My, it must be great and for those chaps who have homes over there to see their people once again. How are all the Royal family, Kitty, Claire, Ruth, Mary, Mrs Niland and Mr Niland. I receive very little news of Mary now that Art is away. Am hoping he will be back 'ere long to the old Battalion. I had a letter from your father a week ago and must endeavour to answer it. Remember me to all please.

Your Ben–

The little moustache you spoke about in the Sgts group came off the day after the picture was taken BC.

————

9.2.17 France

Dear Mr Niland

I received a letter from you about one week ago and this is the first opportunity I've had of replying. We have had a most peculiar weather for the past 3 weeks, the snow and ice have been clinging to the ground and it is bitterly cold. Anyhow it is better than the mud and slush as not so fatiguing and miserable. The ears, toes and fingers suffer most.

We have completely cut out trench feet in our Battalion. It is a terrible complaint and often means the losing of a leg or foot. At first we used whale oil rubbing it well in to the feet but now there is a special camphor borax mixture which has proved equally as good and it is not so difficult for transport. Every day that rations come up a clean pair of sox per man comes too. The dirty sox are returned.

I wonder would our evergreen trees gradually turn and lose their leaves each year if transplanted to this climate. I'm enclosing *A Rising Sun* a little AIF paper, the enclosed copy is not as good as the usual issues.

1917.
Jan.   9—Ribemont.
 ,,   13—By route march to Baizieux
          —under canvas.
 ,,   23—Becourt.
 ,,   27—Relieved 5th Yorks in line
          opposite the Maze, Hexham
          Road.
 ,,   31—Bazentin Camp.
Feb.   5—Relieved 4th Battalion in
          support.
 ,,   13—Relieved by 11th Battalion.
          Moved to Fricourt Farm.
 ,,   18—Marched to Bresle.
 ,,   19—Bombing accident, Lt. Dingle
          killed; 1 officer, 12 others
          wounded.
 ,,   27—Relieved 10th Battalion in
          line near Eaucourt L'Abbaye.
Mch,   3—Buried officers and men killed
          in November 5th operations.
 ,,   6—Bazentin.
 ,,   7—Fricourt.
 ,,   18—Presentation of medals by
          General Birdwood.
 ,,   22—Ribemont.
April   3—Montauban.
 ,,   6—Doignies
 ,,   7—Attack on Hermies.
 ,,   9—Demicourt.
 ,,   11—Relieved by 4th Battalion—
          Doignies.
 ,,   16—Boursies.
 ,,   24—Relieved by 7th Staffords.
 ,,   25—Velu Wood.
May   3—Vraucourt—Bullecourt.
 ,,   6—Relieved by 4th Battalion in
          line.
 ,,   8—Vaulx—Vraucourt.
 ,,   10—Le Transloy.
 ,,   14—Bazentin-le-Petit.
 ,,   21—By route march to Laviéville.
June   28—Marched to Engelbelmer for
          tactical exercise.
 ,,   30—Mailly-Maillet.
July   4—Night operations at Serre.
 ,,   6—Returned to Laviéville.
July   14—Moved to Bray-sur-Somme.
 ,,   23—Dernancourt.
 ,,   26—Entrained for the north.
 ,,   27—Wallon Cappel.
Aug.   9—Marched to Petit Sec Bois,
          via Hazebrouck.   Training
          and sports.
Sept. 13—Marched to Fontainhouck,
          near Meteren.
 ,,   14—Palace Camp, Ouderdom.

Excerpt from 1st Battallion diary

Sugar cannot be procured privately now in France and our issue has been cut down so that there is only enough for 2 drinks of tea per day. Then bread cannot be bought either from the people. Each family is given a bread ticket or its equivalent in flour so a person can only buy his share of bread.

Somehow I think we'll be home before next winter, lets hope so anyway. And I assure you sunny New South Wales will be good enough for me. No wonder France doesn't get much sun when we get so much there! Frank tells me you have had a very good season, she writes often.

I look forward to the time when I will be back in Sydney and able now and then to come up to Tarro. But no more bike trips–I laugh every time I think of the excuse we put up to get back to *Oaklands* Too Hot? Could only get as far as Tarro, well—I think I'll have to finish now. Please remember me to Mrs Niland, family.

Yours truly

Ben Champion

11.2.17

George Priestley from Raymond Terrace sniped yesterday. The trenches around the Butte were covered with dead Scotties, so Battalion put on to bury them. Eaucourt L'Abbaye must have been a tough nut to crack, but at least it was taken. It was said that either armoured motor cars or Tanks were used.

12.2.17

Left supports and moved to Fricourt Camp. Had dozens of busters on the way. The roads so frozen that it's hard to walk on its iron like surface. Pitied the Lewis gun pannier carriers, so took it in turns to help carry them.

13/14th

Road fatigues. 14th. Moved through Fricourt past Albert to Bresle about 4 miles from Albert on main Amiens Road. Very comfortable little billet.

15.2.17

Bomb Practice, bayonet drill, company drill, men very fit and hard. Few evacuated with bad feet.

16.2.17

A nasty accident occurred today, resulting in the death of Lieut. Dingle, Pte Lublin and Dwyer and D.Company Lieut. Scales and 12 others seriously wounded. Pte Lublin was throwing a bomb when a premature burst happened. C. Company was just near and we ran to their aid. All these casualties caused through only 1 bomb, so glad Fritz hasn't a bomb to compare with it. Bomb fuse must have been defective. Cast a gloom over the whole battalion, especially missing Dingle, he was very popular.

20.2.17 France

Dear Frank

Mail stopped again, roads too great a state of disrepair so no mail. Rather a nuisance but will get them all in a bunch I suppose sooner or later. By Jove I'd love to jump on a train at Tarro and surprise visit you but worse luck no possible hope for a couple of years yet I'm afraid. Usual state of discontent but then it's a soldiers privilege to to be able to grouse. Snow and frost finished, now mucky and wetness. The country is not worth fighting for, that is my opinion.

We had a bit of a bomb accident yesterday in the Battalion, gave a couple of chaps Blighties which will take them to England. We have the most powerful bomb of all the fighting forces. It is a little beauty. Well Old girl I guess you are just the same only a little older judging from your letters and I hope you say the same of me. There are hundreds of German prisoners working on the roads around here. Very dopey looking but solid. They just loaf around not much work done. I would like to be able to speak German and have charge of them for a bit. Don't cut your fringe off Frank or put it out of the way at all. There no more news Pal This is just a very scrappy little note more anon. Old Pal

Ben

22.2.17

Moved once more to Fricourt Farm Camp, road and general fatigues. Rumours that Fritz evacuated his line.

23.2.17

45th Battaliion secured a lot of prisoners. Huns in charge of wounded men, very funny to see a Hun carrying his guard's rifle and helping the guard along. They seem quite happy to be prisoners.

Ben's photo of Flers

24.2.17

Fritz evacuated the Maze.

25.2.17

Stood to arms, to travel light, to chase up Fritz. Several cavalry regiments passed us going towards the line.

26.2.17

Our line still advancing Patrols through Ligny, Thilloy and came in contact with Fritz at Warlencourt Eaucourt.

28.2.17

Moved to Eaucourt L'Abbeye in support.

Cassidy sent to Flers, place of our 5th November debacle. Bodies of men shot down on 5.11.16 recovered, mostly well preserved by the snow and ice. All buried properly and crosses erected. Finlayson found practically in Fritz line.

29.2.17

Now that Fritz has gone back we can walk about on top of Eaucourt L'Abbeye, and appreciate our position. The building of course is just a mass of masonry and tangled timbers, but down below there is tons of room for a battalion in the tunnels. This place must have been quite a centre as avenues of trees flanking the roads radiate out. Of course all the trees are down, lopped across the roads to make it hard to pursue.

Fritz used this place, and now we use it. Judging by the bodies this place was stormed by the 22nd London Regiment with several tanks. Male tanks have 2–6lb [6 pound] guns and machine guns, and female tanks only machine guns. As a direct result of the evacuation of this salient by Fritz due to our July to September offensive Fritz now only has 8 miles to guard instead of a huge semicircle of trenches which was 26 miles round. His new line is across the base of the semi-circle.

The first withdrawal started from Wheat Trench, Le Barque, Ligny, Thilloy to what is called the Grevilliers Line.

The 1st Division has shoved forward through those villages but our flanks had met with more opposition so we had to dig in and wait for them. This is the first bit of open village fighting we have had and it's a treat after trenches and lice and rats. Around the Butte de Warlencourt (an old rifle range 50´ high) were lying dozens of Scotties and Sussex men with a sprinkling of London Regiment dead. Naturally we fatigued and buried 5 officers and 40 others of the Regiment.

We sent back by a light Decanville Railway hundreds of rifles and equipment as salvage. Our engineers pushed on the railway under fire and every night brought up rations etc. Beside this Butte is Warlencourt Eaucourt and between it and Le Sars stands the remains of huge German workshops of thousands of tons of briquette coal. Our Tanks must have come on them

Second Lieutenant Ronald Finlayson, 1st Battalion. Killed at Flers, 5 November 1916

Gueudecourt Memorial with burial party left rear.

Australian transport returning along the Bapaume Road for supplies for the troops fighting beyond Bapaume. In the background are Le Sars Railway Station, the Quarry, and the Butte de Warlencourt (centre).AWM.

very quickly. The main Baupaume road here is in a good state but before it can be used we will have to clear the hundreds of flanking trees from off it when they had been felled to stay pursuit by Tanks.

1.3.17 France

Dear Old Frank

Was very pleased to receive your letter written from your Aunt Em's at Riverstone last night. For some reason or other chiefly the U Boat blockade we have had no letters so when your two came along and one from Mary I was highly delighted. There was a great reunion last night. I was on fatigue carrying water with 100 men last night when a chap wearing the 4th Battalion colors hailed me as Ben and it was Art. I was overjoyed at seeing him.

You read the papers and find out what the AIF are doing here. Some stoush as usual, always in it. We captured a few villages during last week and gained quite a lot of territory. Surely we deserve a rest after this. The worst of it is the Generals change and get rests but we don't. I am having so much better time as an officer. I'm glad you were pleased.

Dear Pal, officers don't have numbers so you leave out the 2481. This is how to address now; 2/Lieut Ben Champion C Coy 1st Bn AIF and Arts address is 2/Lieut AA Felton D Coy 4th Bn AIF. There is not much news at all. We have very changeable weather but it's not half so cold as it was a month ago. Yes old girl, I remember you at Riverstone and at Waitara at Feltons. It must have been terribly hot at home. It even shrivelled the fruit up at Wahroonga. The flying foxes at home ate quite a lot of the fruit. Mary wrote me a letter which I must reply to in due course. I like your photo much better than the one Art shewed me of Mary. I long for the day when one will be able to walk about in peace for good and not expect every moment to be blown out.

Your old friend Ben

8.3.17

Moved back to Fricourt Farm. New system of attack in vogue for semi open warfare

Bayonet men, Bombers,
Lewis Gun, O.C. Grenadiers

15.3.17

News through that Grevillers line and Loupart Wood taken. Our Padre has been missing for a few days. Think he is off his onion. He was found today (16th) wandering around Amiens by the M.P.

We practice in rifle grenade shooting over the heads of men advancing in front wave. It ought to be very handy. There are many booby traps left behind by Fritz. A German helmet badge tied to something or other and when badge lifted a small explosion takes place. Their bombs left behind only made instantaneous instead of 5 second fuse. Examples string tied to bomb cord and left where possible to trip over and so explode bomb, a loose dugout canister and when pressed on it pulls a bomb string.

The advance steadily going towards Bapaume which is now occupied by us and the 5th Division and 2nd Division.

22.3.17

Marched to Ribemont a very dirty village but possessing good Parade and Football grounds. Major H. Jacobs gone to the 61st Bn. (6th Division). Lieut. Colonel. Stacey from the 4th Battalion took over the 1st Battalion. Dr. Kirkwood examined a'Beckett and found suffering from slight blood poisoning. General parades and manoeuvres and discipline, new attack formations etc.

Ben's picture of Bapaume church

25.3.17 France

Dear Franc,

There has been no Australian mail in now for 3-4 weeks so naturally we are anxiously awaiting letters from all those we love. I've been very lazy lately. I've not been writing as often as it is my duty to do but the cold is intense and we've been in the middle of the biggest advance yet made by the Allies. What to you think of us in Bapaume?

Our goal for so long now accomplished. The days are getting longer but as yet no flowers have appeared on the scene. How I long to be back in dear old NSW. You can easily imagine yet somehow I believe it's some little distance away yet, worse luck. Old Fritz is going to a lot of bother to inconvenience us and our advance. Cleverly concealed mines etc but we generally get the best of him.

Had a letter from Art. He is in a big London hospital. Wish I was with him. I heard you had a big crop at home. Is that so? We have been having some great games of football this last ten days. Only our ground is dotted here and there with shell holes which one is sure to tumble into. They act as a magnet if you run that way and you are sure to go into them. We played the 2nd Bn officers and beat them 3 to nil then the NCOs played us officers and beat us 6 to 3. You see the scores are very low as we are in terrible condition for running. We are hard but to use a horsy term, broken winded.

I'll be 20 in a few days, how time flies. I left Sydney 14.7.15 and its now 25.3.17–only twenty months but it really seems ages. All the transport horses look well although all BEF and AIF horses are on half diet. White head ropes make a lot of difference.

We had a funny competition this afternoon called Grady drill. There is a squad of men and the rule is they are only to act on the order if the word Grady is prefixed like this. 'Grady says Slope arms'. On that order they would move but if you said simply Slope arms and they did

Photo of Frank with her hair up.

slope them then they would be out. Out of a squad of 20 men only 2
remained, and the instructor couldn't get one of them to make a mistake
so he just said 'Oh you're too good for me FALL OUT. One fell out so
the other won. You see he didn't say Grady says fall out. It was so funny
we gave the winner a couple of francs and the loser a chocolate mouse.

Well old girl hope you are well as I am. I can't get sick at all so
that I could have a spell in hospital, I don't believe you could kill me
with an axe now. There is no more news Dear Pal

Ben

28.3.17

20 years old today, 2nd birthday on Service. There is an Angelic Lady
in this village called *Incinerator Kate* from her activities in picking out
from the incinerator any article, food or clothing etc. that might come
in handy. Lofty Buckley who takes about 12 in Military boots went ill.
It was no good carrying about more boots size 12, as he was away. It
was decided to secretly throw the canoes into the incinerator–so far
so good.

At Mess that night we were disturbed by a tramp–tramp outside
our windows. Ongoing to see the cause we found out that Kate was
wearing the boots put in the incinerator and they fitted her like the
paper on the wall. There are other funny incidents about her. Ask
Mervin Blake about the washing he gave her to do. Had a lecture by
Colonel Blamey on Tanks.

30.3.17

Carl Waugh ill–evacuated to Hospital and Dick Price made Transport
Officer. I was tried out but couldn't stick the horse they gave me. I
heard afterwards that the boys had purposely fixed up the saddle so
that it would hurt the horse if anyone mounted. Anyway the same
joke was put up on Price but he managed and carried out his duties
well. We have been just a year in action in France now.

6.4.17

Moved from Montauban Camp across country till we met Bapaume
Cambrai Road north of Bapaume Road. Came to a little village called
Beaulencourt then to Villers au Flos. Here we met with more of Huns
barbarism. Small Church built in 1713 smashed to bits by a mine and
the heads of the statuary just smashed off. Acres of vines and fruit
trees just cut off about ground level and left. They would have been
of no use to us, so why destroy them. Haplincourt Chateau in same
plight and the lovely little church within the Chateau grounds used as
a stable and latrines. More images smashed by hand. There has been
no shell fire over this country. Moving at night through Lebucquire
and Velu we were shelled, so moved into Artillery formation over
the Bapaume Cambrai road to Beaumetz which was hardly touched.
Then on into Doignies commonly called *Dogs knees*. Here we dug
a line around the village behind hedges and made ourselves as
comfortable as possible. On our left is Louverval and in front and to
the right Demicourt and Hermies.

BOURSIES AND HERMIES

8.4.17

Fritz found us and subjected us to heavy bombardment from the
direction of Morchies. Major Mackenzie and a couple of C Coy Hdqr
officers sleeping in the village were buried by their house being hit, but
dug themselves out with entrenching tools. This is the second time that
Major has been buried. They were badly shaken. I slept with my platoon
and so escaped the shaking up in the evening.

Orders were that while the Battalion was stunting for Demicourt,
a fair-sized village on the next rising I was to take my No 12 platoon
and seize Boursies. After reconnoitring the area we got into our new
attacking order putting the Lewis gun on each flank. At zero hour
midnight we crept forward and dug a trench as close as we could to
Fritz line. We were subjected to a machine gun fire but only lost one-
man Pte Landon. We wanted to get as close as possible to a sunken road
in line with Boursies. We hopped over and met Fritz We had such a

swing on that we dished him up but he turned on us after going 50 yards or so and gave us some heavy machine gun fire. We disconcerted him by the rifle grenades, fired as we advanced and the Lewis Gun which did wonderful shooting. The Huns were clearing up the sunken road behind Demicourt so we turned a Lewis Gun on them.'

In the sunken road we got 20 huns, some of them only seemed to be kids. Unfortunately I could only send back a few of them as most were too badly wounded. Whether it was the appearance of the men I don't know but as I came up they appealed for mercy and were very grateful when simply souvenired over and allowed to remain in a safe spot.

Peter Bowling and 3 men went through Boursies to try and link up with the 12 Battalion and found one Fritz dead drunk in a wine vat. Peter said that as long as he lived he would never forget the look the Fritz—as drunk as an owl one minute and as sober as a judge when he saw who were the people awaking him. Boursies was patrolled every hour after that and we were getting some hot fire from the crucifix on top of the ridge and Landon was wounded

Hayward Moffat came up with his B company. What a tower of strength was Hayward, as solid as a rock and every man adored him for his solid personality. Of all the officers that passed through the 1st Battalion, in my opinion Moffat was the King Pin. He took his company forward to embrace the crucifix area and made everything secure. In the sunken road at Boursies were still gathered the wounded Huns well looked after by our chaps who even supplied them with rum and that night we got them back. They thought our Army bread was like cake—their black coarse bread was awful and tasted like sawdust. Their sausage was good though and we enjoyed it. One man had a very narrow escape—he wrapped a Fritz waterproof around him as it was cold and was fired at by one of 'B 'company but fortunately the shot missed.

Sampson had already been into Demicourt with a patrol and had sent word back that the Battalion would occupy it but there was so much delay that by the time it arrived Fritz was back there in force and the Battalion was driven back. Finally the Battalion came on and with the help of Sampson in one spot and Price in another and with my guns into Fritz at the rear, Demicourt was finally taken.

The Battalion. attacked Demicourt but there were sufficient men and machine guns to give them a bad time coming over the ground without any cover. Eventually they got the place.

In the evening B Coy relieved my platoon and Capt. Moffat consolidated in a more advantageous position beyond the one I had chosen. He also sent a platoon beyond Boursies, making his flank secure. Near Boursies was a small brick pit and in this tunnel Coy. Hq. was established.

Dick Cassidy was killed by a shell on the Demicourt road. Lance Corp Bayne was wounded in both legs. Pte Whatman offered to get him in and he crawled and dragged Bayne in. All the time under machine gun fire from behind Demicourt. For this action I recommended Whatman for a decoration.

Rejoined the rest of my company in Doignies in a sunken road. It snowed and we got wet through.

This was the best stunt we had been in so far. We lost about 69 men in the Battalion among whom was Dick Cassidy, a splendid chap who got his first star at the same time as I did He had been an original man and saw every bit of fighting up till the time he was killed. The casualties in my platoon were 13 out of 45 men engaged.

10.4.17

Sent back to transport while my platoon got over their Boursies stunt. Congratulated on getting my position in Boursies and the prisoner taken, but Stacey didn't know he was too drunk to walk until he saw us. Carl Waugh showed me a short cut back. It was so cold that Waugh, A'Beckett, Sampson and I slept together, bringing all our blankets in one pile. I drew the centre position so was lucky.

11.4.17

Brought back the 50 reinforcements to Battalion Hdqrs between Doignies and Beaumetz. It is still raining. As I was away the night before no one had made provision for a dugout for me so crawled in alongside Whatman and kept ourselves from shivering into a sweat. The casualties

"I say, cobber, got 'ny room in there
me an' another bloke?"

"Schrapnel and Smiles"

and sickness in my platoon have been 13 out of the 35, so was very glad when I had some of the reinforcements allotted to me. This has been a most trying time for us all–very poor tucker too. 3 to a loaf of bread, tea, and that's all, no jam, butter, bacon and very little bully beef.

13.4.17-

Had all my kit taken by some other Battalion but Sgt Eather saved some for me. Capt. Mackenzie looks funny; he has had a rough time. So unusual to see him unshaven, he has been buried twice. Russell, Baker, Bowes, Patterson and Whetten some of platoon's casualties. On night of 14/15 terrible bombardment took place and Fritz counter attacked 4th Divisional Sector on our left and it caused the 4th Battalion's left flank to be cut up badly.

The Old Battalion did splendidly and wiped out 5.11.17 failure of Flers Guendecourt. Rifle—grenades splendid for attacking work.

Captain A K Mackenzie - 1st Battalion Diary

Firing from the hip when advancing is also very demoralising. Official news came through on 14.4.17 that 4th Division had met with serious reverses losing ground. 4000 casualties and 1000 prisoners and missing. All day 15th we stood to, not knowing to which sector we would be sent, eventually we moved forward in open order over the ground. We attacked and rushed the last piece reinforcing the 4th Battalion (Major Sass & Lloyd). Got there in time (at Crucifix on top of hill near Chapel) to see Agnew carried out badly wounded in back.

At 4 p.m. we moved away from the 4th and our Company in ones and twos crept through Boursies and then ran the gauntlet over open ground through machine gunfire. It was really a marvel more were not hit (only 1 or 2) We relieved Lieut. Bennett who had been wounded through the mouth and was hanging on until someone turned up. In front of us on a white chalky slope we could see Fritz in groups working away digging. Sent back word but from where our guns were they could not do much damage. We worked all that night putting out wire and getting dugouts ready and before morning with the aid of iron from Boursies made ourselves comfortable. But we ran out of smokes. One of B's men was accidently shot, as he failed to answer and as we heard later was deaf but I'm afraid the events of the day had made us jumpy. This affected us very much.

16.4.17

> After working hard we were relieved by A. Company. Dick (Howell)
> Price came up with a working party and helped. Marched back before
> daybreak to sunken road at Dolgnies. Had a glorious sleep and wash.
> No shelling at all, everything peaceful. Turned in with Sampson.

BATTALION DIARY

Some of the heaviest fighting that the Battalion experienced
throughout its career took place during the next few days There was
continual bombing attacks and counter attacks. There was a fierce enemy
attack with flammenwefer but Capt. Somerset jumped out of the trench
hurling bombs and they departed hurriedly leaving 5 of their companions
dead. All the time there was a heavy rain of shells and sniping and bombing
went on without intermission. By means of our bomb attacks the line was
extended to the left by both the 1st and 3rd Battalions and bombing blocks
were established, many of the enemy being killed and 16 prisoners taken
etc etc Corporal G.J. (Snowy) Howell awarded Military Medal (Later to
receive V.C. at Bullencourt).

Our casualties however were heavy. the Battalion losing five officers,
including Major Woodforde, and 44 other ranks killed and 8 officers and
2232 other ranks wounded. The command of the Battalion then near
Vaux Vrancourt was resumed on May 7 by Lieut Col Stacey and on May
9 we left the forward area for what proved our longest rest.

19.4.17

> Came back to line A had worked hard and we finished their job by putting
> out the remaining wire. [Ben now in C Coy] Some wounded Fritzes must
> have been out in No Man's Land, but we couldn't help them and their
> cries were horribly weird.

Major Woodforde - 1st Battalion Diary

19.4.17 France

Dear Pal

I'm so pleased you have been having such a good holiday away from home. You would enjoy especially meeting folks for you don't see too many people at Tarro.

It is still very cold in France especially in the line where we are now. The usual slush over the boot tops so that I cannot feel if I have toes at all.

Rations for the men have been very short of late, 4 to a loaf of bread, short commons of biscuits and bully. All the lads say it is because of all the prisoners we have captured recently so amongst themselves they have decided in a jocular way, not to take prisoners.

My platoon and yours truly had a bit of scrap with some huns. Ending up by leaving the Fritz's on the green grass toes upward. We also found a hun asleep in a barrel in a village. I think he had been drunk but sobered mighty quickly when he saw we meant business. He said *And will I go to England some of my relations live there.* We soon shewed him the way to the clink.

I'm looking forward to the snap shots Gertrude took of you and Mary. I believe you have grown quite into a woman since I left old Aussie shores. I had a good feed at Huns expense a few days ago When we took the village of course a lot of tucker was left behind, garlic

2nd Lieutenant R. "Dick" A. Cassidy-killed Demicourt,
wounded Lone Pine and Poziers
(Written on back in Ben's writing)

sausage, blood pudding, cake made with honey and lard in little tins like Rexona comes in. I secured a lovely little German automatic service pistol and I intend to send it home as a souvenir.

The same day I lost one of my best chums 2/Lt R A Cassidy, he and I were lance corporals, then Sergeants then Lieutenants. He was a good chap, death was instantaneous.

We have some lovely artillery now, quite as good as Fritz. Pal, these huns are curs they way they spoil everything. Acres and acres of fruit trees and grape vines I passed 3 days ago all just cut off at the roots for devilment also a lovely avenue of fir trees all cut down and spoilt, statues pictures crockery beds perambulators all strewn about ... (incomplete).

19.4.17 France

Dear Mrs Niland

Your very welcome letter to hand yesterday telling me all the local news and about Franks holiday. Letters take a long while to come these times. I think it is owing to the stress on rolling stock, caused by the big advance up north. We are gaining ground up there all day long and we hear the continual roar of the guns like distant thunder.

These huns, Mrs Niland are running a terrible muck amongst the villages we beat them out of. No building is left standing, mines, shell fire and devastation by hand, go on in each village so that they are of no value at all to us. What we object too is the sinful waste of goods which could be of no use to us at all. Beautiful paintings out of churches, house hold goods all ruined.

The putting of arsenic in wells, the spraying of grass with poison that affects the frog and horses feet and are of no practical military importance and gets us wild. There won't be much left of the first German town we meet in our travels.

When is this accursed war going to end so that once more we can be civilised human beings instead of licensed murderers. Slush, discomfort, dirt, insects all make ones life unbearable.

I suppose you would wonder if I told you that no one in this battalion has been out of his clothes for 27 days. In the forward area such as it is now, right away advance from a base, work like this is bon. Lucky Felton getting a couple of bullets through his foot the way he did. Yet we are winning despite the set backs. I'm proud to say I'm with the 1st Battalion and to say I've come out of the ranks step by step till I gained a commission.

One didn't know what it was to have a home and parents, now I do. I'll never go away from home again should I once catch a glimpse of it.

Well dear Mrs Niland there is no news so will close. Please remember to all at *Oaklands*

Yours truly

Ben Champion 19.4.17

24.4.17

On the 24th I had wonderful news–I was told the Colonel wanted me and wondered what I had been doing wrong. However he smiled and thanked me for job at Boursies and handed me a leave pass to England. I came back to the transport line changed and taking no luggage except a toothbrush and overcoat beat it for Albert which I reached in quick time by means of lorry hopping.

Lieut ColonelB.V.Stacy - 1st Battalion Diary

Then onto Amiens and I caught the 11 am boat to Folkestone and went on to London putting up at the Craven Hotel near Charing Cross.

My first call was to the AMP Society to see Mr Hollingworth. [His son killed 5.11.16] This leave was up on the 6th May and in the 10 days holiday I had inspected London Tower, Buckingham Palace, Whitehall I had seen the Guard change, Mansion House and here at the last named place I met Captain Beavis and he invited me up to Scotland.

I saw Edinburgh and his friends and stopped at the Caledonian Hotel. I also saw Edinburgh Castle, Arthurs Seat, Colton Hill Linlithgow; I went over the battleship *Australia* and was introduced to Commander Walsh

6.5.17

Saturday, Left for Folkestone. Caught train

11 May 1917

Dear old pal,

Coming back from leave I received 10 letters from you, all that old mail which I said I hadn't received turned up. You are a fine little girl to write so often and such length. The Old Battalion whilst I was

Lieutenant Ben Champion, taken The Strand London.

on leave was cut up terribly. In fact, I believe there was some guiding hand that delayed my leave so long. They gave it at that opportune moment.

[2nd Battle for Bullecourt 3-5-17, 7000 casualties]

Do you believe it Pal. Out of all that Sgt Group I had taken there are only 2 left, Sgt Nicholson and myself. Officers were killed and wounded galore. Never mind, Old girl, things are running fairly straight for me at present. The sun is shining very brightly, quite like an Australian day.

As for all the news in your letters, well it's nice to know all about things but nicer to know you are well and happy and longing for the time when I will be home. Won't we have a picnic together. Well I am going to get out your letters and read them over again so I can answer your questions.

Drawing, painting, dressmaking, what an accomplished young woman I'll come back too. Only want piano playing and she'll be too good for me to know. I had my photo taken again on leave as I didn't like the expression on the PC.

You seem very fond of chooks and ducks. I'm glad if you are, that the farm has been let but I suppose you are keeping a few horses and cows for your own family needs.

Mosquitoes were bad in 1915 when we were there, biting ones ankles. Do you remember how we all sat on the grass and I rolled a log of wood over to sit on. Well I can never forget the calm of that evening. In the midst of a stunt, thoughts of home immediately flies through one's mind and its then one feels what a glorious place home is.

If you are pleased old girl when my letters arrive, what must I feel far away from old Australia when yours come. Do you know what I want. Not photo of yourself taken by a professional but every now and then get a girl friend to take one. I believe you had your photo taken didn't you at Wahroonga? Well, so far I haven't received one. Will one come along.

What on earth old girl is my name in Tarro Church for. I'm not a Tarroite neither am I a Church of England man and I was only in the Church once I believe. Anyway I don't mind but it seems very funny don't you think so? [Ben was also on board in Wahroonga Presbyterian Church].

You reckon you are not worth the trouble that Gertrude goes to over you. Well don't let me hear you say that. There is no trouble too much for anyone to do for you. Now pal I will close Yours truly

Ben xxxxxxx

Wednesday 10.5.17

Rejoined Battalion at Beaulencourt, Sugar Mill. Oh! The poor Battalion. I left it strong and came back to find it has been in Bullecourt action. Sadly cut up–seems to be only about 400 left. In the twelve days I have been away the Battalion has been in action under Major MacKenzie and has lost hundreds of men in casualties. According to Orderly room, 5 officers killed, eight officers wounded and 276 men wounded. What a show it must have been.

Thursday 11.5.17

Visited by Birdwood, Walker and Leslie, all complimented the old first.

24.5.17

Was selected as Instructor for General Training School at Havre, being the longest constant service with the 1st of any junior officer. I accepted on understanding that I would be recalled when we went back to the line. Reported there on 25th May and found it to be very decent place, instructing in bombs and German Grenades. The school Commanding Officer is a Guards man and his staff are excellent. Lieut Jacks of Oxford and Buckinghamshire Infantry, Simpson and Vaux of 1/8 Middlesex Regiment, Captain Parvin and Major Mitchell of the Grenadier Guards. They are all a jolly group of chaps with service.

Every day re-inforcements troops come up from their bases and we each take a party for instruction. The live bomb throwing is interesting, there is a huge pit about 50 yards long and at the end is a picture on a tin of a Fritz and the chaps have to throw the bombs at it. As each instructor detonates each bomb himself there is not much risk of premature explosion.

The pit is walled with sand bags and each man wears a tin helmet and the system is so good that about 6 bombs per minute are thrown. When you consider it takes 5 seconds for a bomb to explode this is good going.

[Ben thought that Vaux was killed but he was taken prisoner and spent time as POW but eventually returned to England. I have been in contact with his family and returned coloured original of tank and

Vaux is on left seated.

his portrait. — Ed]

There are some good chaps here, Vaux, an artist in private life did many a drawing for occupants of our hut; some were very good especially one of a tank, coloured in action.

He and Simpson of 1/8th Middlesex, are particular mates.

Havre being quite close, we often slip in there. Very fine concert party, Miss Lena Ashwell is visiting there with Miss Carrie Tubb and they had a concert with many famous people. Met Miss Venn-Brown from Wahroonga and had a yarn over home doings. Met Miss Vidal at the YMCA and made up a party for walks on to Havre beach. She is getting up amusements for the men in connection with the YMCA and I went and watched an old English series of dances.

Many Yankee officers at the school, but it's impossible to teach them anything as they do not think that a knowledge of German bombs could be of any use to them.

Met Sgt. Mackie from the 1st on 28/6/17. He is acting as a conducting N.C.O. from England to Havre. Had an attack of Tonsillitis, sent down to the Divisional Base and marked Base for 1 month. Kicked my leg against an iron picket and it developed a nasty sore.

Some very fine walks around here and the country is very pretty. Every Sunday afternoon the band plays and the French people come along to hear it. Some were invited into the Mess to afternoon tea. Harfleur Mostevidier, Rouelles and Havre all look as if they could do with a wash. Joe Shaw and Northcote are here waiting to be sent up to the Battalion

4.6.17 France

Dear FJN

Only a little note this time. The country is a one mass of flowers and growing crops, it's great. Clover with a deep old rose color top, buttercups, white and purple violets. It is so peaceful too after all the stunts I've been in. I'm longing for a long note from you old girl, my mail somehow or other has become mixed up and I haven't had any for a devil of a time.

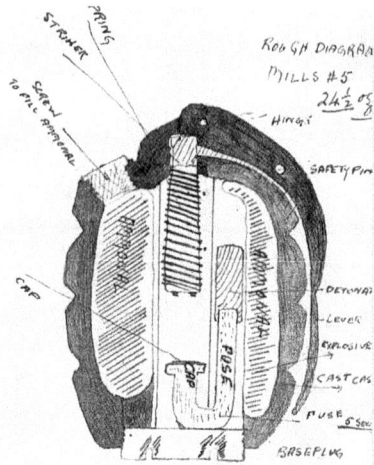

SAFETY PIN WITH DRAWING LEVER
ALLOWED TO FLY, striker comes down
striking Cap. Causing Spark igniting
fuse exploding detonator explode
ammunition bursting bomb

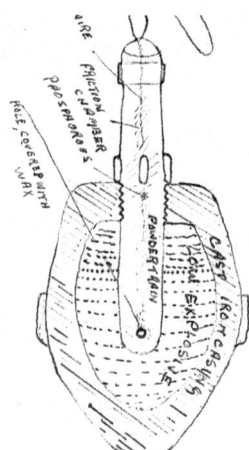

Wire pulled through friction chamber
causing spark which lights phosphorous
lighting powder train which melts
wax over the hole, flame spurts
out igniting low explosive

Ben's sketches of Mills Bombs.

Vaux in gas masks.

Now that your Dad has no farm work to attend too I suppose his time hangs rather on his hands. Your mother wrote me a note some time ago and said the people around Raymond Terrace didn't seem to appreciate his work. It is not good that style of thing is it.

I went into Havre yesterday, enjoyed myself, spent 100 franc and came home having gained nothing for it. These Frenchies seem to be terribly frightened of fresh air and baths. In the many houses I've been in, never yet have I found such as things as a bathroom. And all their rooms are tightly closed up. They are a wretched people I think. Good for nothing more than grabbing money from soldiers.

There are a few decent hotels in Havre. Tortonis and Prettys. I had a fine dip in the sea off the Havre Esplanade. It's only a tiny beach and more mud that sand. Nothing to come up to even our very worst beach. Canoeing here is rather a fine past time. It must be fun, couple of English officers and myself went out in one and not being expert in the use of the blade we had an upset and we had to tow the bloody craft about 500 yards to the beach before we could right it.

21.6.17 Havre

Dear Frank

It's been raining for 2 days now and the parade grounds are very slushy so there is no parade today. *No parade today boys, no parade today* That's the call all soldiers look forward too. We knew that call away back in the Liverpool days and together with the sick parade and Canteen calls they are our favourites.

Well, a wretched lot of reinforcements yesterday counted out a Guards Officer who is a very fine chap. As they were Australians all the Australian officers were called out to drill them. We all got soaking wet. I hope each one gets pneumonia for the trouble they have caused You know a battalion lot of men wouldn't do it but these reinforcements are made such a lot of in England that their heads are turned. They are spoiling our names and are chaps who haven't yet been into the line. Boastful lot of chaps they get us terribly wild with their, *I guess it took us to come over and finish this war for England.* There have been some rather beastly scraps between us and them.

The Russians have rather a neat uniform pale grey not the blue grey like the Frenchies The Belgium are the dirtiest and most wretched troops I've ever seen. Well old girl I can't tell you any more news

Love Ben

I received today a letter from Harold Kershaw. He is still ok and is a sergeant in a machine gun corp. My old OC of the 7th Reinforcements, Scott is now Lieut Commander of a Pioneer Battalion. He has risen quickly hasn't he.

My old pal, what we miss by being away from home and civilisation. I went last night to the best concert I've been too since leaving home. I was in the theatre in Havre given by a concert party formed in England. They tour all the bases and pay their own expenses and all moneys taken are handed over to the YMCA. These ladies are doing more than their bit by giving amusements to the troops.

I haven't heard from Art lately but I would have heard if he was not in good health. He is not sure yet if he is with the 63rd Battalion or only lent to them for training purposes. The instructors here all wear yellow bands on their arms and I heard some very funny instructions being given to a sentry re who was to pass his possie of a night time Sergeant. *Only officers with yellow bands on are allowed to pass here* Sentry *Right all canaries are to pass and no one else*. So they call us the canaries.

There are a few hundred hun prisoners here. Some work on the School area, gardening etc Well one got in the road of an instructor's bayonet when he was demonstrating to his men and the hun was accidently stuck. Then we had a marquee burnt down, so quite an eventful week so far.

There was a big scrap down town 3 nights ago, 10 Algerians fought 18 Frenchies with knives. With the result that 9 blacks and 6 Frenchies are dead, all the rest wounded. Some trouble with a girl, an Algerian said something the Frenchy didn't like and wallop they went for each other and gradually the whole 2 parties were scrapping in deadly earnest. I didn't see it but the newspapers are full of it. Isn't it strange how black and ordinary Frenchies can't agree?

I saw Russian troops in Havre yesterday; their tunics button up the side. They looked smart big chaps alongside some French soldiers. The standard height is going down in our army. We have quite a lot of small chaps now in our London regiments. Lovingly yours

Ben

24.6.17

Dear Old Franc,

Today is Sunday and we had breakfast and lunch in bed. This afternoon we went to Havre and spent the time watching the people in the water. There are no bathing sheds like at Manly, but little wooden boxes for 17c a head, and you can wheel these right on to the water if you like. The sun was scorching and I saw the pattern of more than one bathing suit left behind by the sun. They will be sore tomorrow. I know what sun burn is and can sympathise with them. Have you been badly sunburnt? I remember once up at Woy Woy we had no cocoa nut oil for burns so used butter little thinking of the salt in it and when the salt soaked in didn't we jump.

Do you know you cannot buy cakes in London. I mean fancy ones. Sugar is so scarce. I wish I could paint, there is in my room a chap named Vaux who is an artist when in civilian life and he turns out most beautiful portraits of people. He gets the natural color to a T. You haven't stopped it have you?

The last letters from you were dated 23.4.17 so you see it is over 2 months now and all that mail has gone astray for I know you write. Every time you write I can tell by a feeling inside and I say well Franc is writing to me now so I must be respectable. You know there are lots of choices to sink below the pale when you are away from home and every time I feel like that I say to myself would you like me to do it and more often than not it brings me home to bed instead of stopping in town.

Oh, by the way cut out of the address the 2/ Lieut, I am now Lieut. Was promoted on 5th of the month. Hope Old girl you are well. I am at present, it's not a bad war when you are down at the base and have some good pals here.

Remember me please to Mary, Ruth and Kitty. Your mother and father and when I come back I'll be up *toute suite* to see you. Has the letting of the farm caused you any inconvenience?

I was absolutely soaked a few days ago and felt just like a washing up rag very limp and sticky. What do you think of the last air raid, abominable of them to be hurting women and kiddies. I once saw a nurse wounded and I went *berserk* for a while.

Carette of Sark and *Maid of the Mist* are 2 very nice books by John Oxenham. I'd like you to read them. Havre is just one mass of geraniums and standard roses and they look *tres bon*. As there is no more news now Your loving Pal

Ben

28.6.17 Havre

Dear Mrs Niland,

It is quite a long time since I wrote to you isn't it but no doubt you hear any news I send through Frank. Havre is quite a change from the line and I appreciate it but it's an awful place for spending money– everything is so dear I'm frightened to see my pay book since I came here.

There are quite a number of troops particularly the young soldiers, those under 19, too young for the line training here and these young soldiers do all the guards and sentry and so relieve the older chaps for the line.

Strawberries are very cheap so are cherries but bread and vegetables are practcically un obtainable. Potatoes cannot be bought for love or money. But one article you can buy here and you cannot get in the British Isles are fancy cakes. There sugar and flour are the chief shortages

Dreadful casualites from those air raids over London. I'm very glad Australia is so far away or I'd be fearing Wahroonga and Tarro might be bombed. So sorry Art has decided and written to you re his affairs but it will make no difference to Frank and myself...

Vaux's watercolour of a tank in action

[no further pages so probably censored by Frank or Ben. Art apparently became engaged to marry an English girl when he was in training school there.]

12.7.17 France

Dear Old Pal, Franc,

Isn't it a beastly shame that the *Mongolia* and *Mongar* have both gone down. Our letters to you from 11th to 30th of May are being read by Davy Jones in his high seas locker and worse than our letters going down is the fact that yours to us have gone also. I hope he enjoys the note addressed 'My Dear Ben ' in large writing. My, the pains I spent over that Blighty letter, the mild reproaches I had received from you and now Frank old girl I'll try to make up lost time.

Went for an hours walk to a little village, just the usual dirty type of village with the gamins calling for pennies and souvenirs. How I wished you were here to enjoy it. On the road dainty solid little chalets nestling in one mass of green trees, with perhaps a cluster of magenta colored roses climbing over the side balcony. Then miles of bright green vegetables, all shades of green, spinach, sugar beet, French beans, peas, turnips and other vegetables that I can't think of. Raspberries as big as

Ben's photo observation balloon Havre

plums. And all owned by the dirty squalid people of the village I walked through.

On this walk, Pal of mine, there wouldn't be frogs to jump on to your shoes but nice short grass with grass hoppers dancing about in it. Isn't it strange how these Latin races get old so quickly. Now at 18 most girls here are women yet 30 they are old and infirm. It's good that the Australian girl is the same practically all her life.

Two whole years pal since you waved adieu at Hexham station, off to the war. We didn't know what to expect. We know now. It seems a hundred years age at least. If this very big next stunt is successful there is a possibility of this war being over by January, but if it isn't successful the war will last 'till 1919.

It's a very pretty country, is France, especially in Spring and Summer. But in Autumn when the leaves start to fall then everything starts to go dead and in winter it is really desolate. We came across a snake, gorged, lying in the middle of the road and killed and opened him and to find out why he was gorged and found he had swallowed a frog about 5 'long and could hardly move. Talking of frogs, do you remember our first walk as far as the river and you didn't like the frog jumping on to your shoes, quite a nice walk that was.

Have you done any painting lately or has all your spare time been spent on dressmaking? I have quite a lot of repairs to my togs to be made but am not game to do them myself. Wish you could come over in a plane while there is no scapping on and then skoot away as soon as they start to declare war again. You must have quite a lot of spare paintings. Have you ever tried portrait painting? Someone sits for you for a while and you put them on canvas. I didn't know I was so ugly until I saw my own picture done. When I was at the School I had an Englishman friend who was really a marvel with colors. If a picture of a tank ever gets home ask them to shew it to you, it is very good indeed.

There are quite a lot of little birds twittering in the trees. Yellow hammer. A small greeny yellow bird, honey suckers which get their food and their wings keeping them poised while they get it. Sparrows, thrush, starlings and dozens of crows squarking in the paddocks.

I was speaking to an English officer and said *what a fine paddock* pointing to a good grassed paddock, he only stared and couldn't understand me at all. They call them fields or meadows.

Trench art of Ben by Vaux.

Ben at Havre

If I get back what will I try to be, a farmer, dentist, soldier, waster or what.

Think I'll close now Old Girl. Please remember me to all at home.

(as much barb wire as you can manage)

Ben

13.7.17

Met Morgan in Havre. [Ben's cousin John 'Jack' Morgan, KIA] Had lunch overlooking Southampton Packet boat, also with Richmond 'Dick' Howell Price, then came from the city up on to the big plateau in the Funicular, a tram sort of a lift, it rose 1' in 4' and is on 4 cables. Then we walked to Rouelles Camp, through village of San Vic into Foret de Morchy and on to Rouelles. Forest is 3 miles square and well provided with carriage drives, they are perfectly straight with hardly a bend in them. In the centre of the Forest on which all drives converge is an old Oak tree, supposed to be 300 years old.

14.7.17

As my leg did not improve was boarded and will hear verdict in few days.

John 'Jack' Morgan, Aunt Eva's boy.
John Philip Morgan Gunner 36th Australian Heavy Artillery

18.7.17

At the base but address letters to the Battalion

Dear Pal

I'm still down here. Feeling no good at all, Doc says I'm run down and all my nerves are out of order. It seems hard to imagine that I should have nerve trouble. I went up for a medical board a few days ago so far though no verdict has come through.

We had a band concert last Sunday and I asked a French family into afternoon tea. They were very funny, continually watching us to see how we ate and following suit all the time. The old lady asked me if we put the cup and saucer on the plate or keep the plate for bread and butter. Then the tea spoon worried her, you see they usually keep the spoon in the cup so thought to ask and couldn't understand why we took the spoon out of the cup after stirring the tea and put it in the saucer.

Anyhow we went home with them and had a bit of musical evening. Treated us to wine Bordeaux, then coffee and then a little cup of cognac and sugar and my mate was rather rude and ate the remaining sugar in the bottom of the cup and *toute suite* the Frenchies did likewise.

I met Miss Venn Brown from Wahroonga here in Havre. She has been a YMCA worker since the war began. She is about 40 years old. Well she asked me to come to see a dancing exhibition given by the YMCA girl workers. They were all old English dances, some as far back as 1600. The Morris dance, Peas pod, Barn door. sword dance and several others. They were very pretty. Girls in different old costumes of the period. After the exhibition Mrs Dakin who was in charge called for volunteers and several stepped out, Yours truly among them and she taught us several dances. They were really only romps but I did enjoy myself.

The best evening I've spent in France so far. Then it was too late to go back to camp without being bailed up by the Military Police so I went to the old Central Training School and slept there the night coming back to camp this morning at 5.30am. I cannot get out of camp very easily now for I'm looking after 2 officers who are under arrest.

The weather is delightful here, simply glorious, especially down on the beach of a night time the flare off the water with sitting hearing only the swish of the waves as they come in. A few nights ago I was there and the phosphorous in the water just made the pebbles blaze with light. Then to see all the black shapes of the destroyers creeping out to sea with their tail lights, the only light aboard.

One can imagine quite a lot of things about you all at home. Don't believe I can write any more. Hoping you feel quite a lot better than I do.

Yours truly,
Ben

19.7.17

Up before medical board and recommended to proceed to Dieppe convalescent home. Caught train at 11.30 a.m. It went very slowly picking up French soldiers as it went with the usual emotional scenes as they left their home people. Very flat country and went close to the sea in many places and had tea at Faucamp then on to Dieppe, getting there at 10.30pm. Country passed through was magnificent, wheat and oats ready to be reaped and amongst it masses of poppies and corn flowers. Even the railway embankments were masses of flowers, and in the flat meadows buttercups galore. Not too many Australians have been through here, for I was an object of curiosity. Funny to see French soldiers kissing one another as they met.

20.7.17

A motor Ambulance met me and took me to Lady Michelhan's Convalescent home for officers. It is the old Hotel Metrople of Dieppe and is right on the beach. Hot and cold water laid on bath to every 2 bed rooms.

Had supper, a bath and into bed. Reported to M.D. who said I'd stay 3 weeks, gave me a blood tonic and dressed my leg. Being guests we pay nothing, and magnificent meals and wine provided.

This place, Dieppe, mainly fishing, each day dozens of boats go out and return laden with fish. Boats look very picturesque with their different colored sails. Perched up high on the cliffs is the old Chateau of Dieppe. From it tunnels run down through the cliff to the beach and it used to do a great smuggling trade. Town built on several islands as well as on mainland, the islands connected by fine bridges. Each day the English Veterinary Corps bring down horses and the horses love to swim about in the water. The beach is very pebbly and here the best flints in the world are found.

23.7.17

Took a motor spin to Martin l'Eglise, through Arc Forest. Leaving town steadily climbed to a plateau, passing such picturesque little farms and peasantry out hay making. Descending into a valley of Bethune where good trout fishing can be got. Large battle fought here between Henry IV. and the French. Through miles of planted trees occasionally catching glimpses of deer until reached Martin l'Englise where we had afternoon tea by the river. Came back to a wonderful dinner.

MICHELHAM CONVALESCENT HOME

Menu   Dieppe France

CONSOMME PAYSANNE,

MERLUCHE SAUCE BRUXELLOISE,
POMMES VAPEUR,

FILET DE BOEUF PORTUGAISE,

CELERI DEMI-GLACE

CREME EUGENIE,

FRUITS.

Metropole,
Diner,23/7.

Menu

390 DIEPPE — Le vieux Château

Postcard of Chateau Dieppe

Light Horse taking the sea–Ben's photo

Flint girls

28.7.17 France

Dear Franc

Thank you so much old girl for ever so fine a batch of letters, 8 in all. I love to get them all and to hear how you are getting on. I'll try to answer all the questions first then tell you any news I may have for you.

Am glad old fatty Ruth is on holidays and when and where are you going too? I suppose you want to visit the horrid old city and do some shopping. It must be nice to be able to make dressess and clothes. I've a wretched job on hand sewing buttons of 2 shirts.

These Frenchies generally manage to wash them off the clothes but they wash very cleanly, the things are spotless. It is better to have buttons off than wash holes in the things like the Hindus do. Do you know I nearly became a permanent soldier last week in the Indian Army

Did I tell you Cliff Gentle, Gertrude's friend and who we've known for years has been killed. [He was also Ben's brother Arthur's wife's brother] What a chapter of accident your letters contain, death of Mrs Moran, Mr Nicolls and Bert is wounded [cousin Lieut Bert Carroll–to become ENT specialist].

Lieutenant Bert Carroll

I had a fine long letter from your mother and will reply to her as soon as possible. Art's new address will now be 63rd Battalion instead of 4th as unfortunately he has been transferred there.

You don't write dry letters. Do you remember when I once wrote a letter for you to somebody at Richmond I believe? I don't want you to be gifted in anyway. Just plain Franc I want. Can't you believe all people don't want gifted people as friends? Besides if you can paint, draw and sew, how dare you say you have no accomplishments? Not to mention horse riding. As to beautiful letters written by me home that's impossible on my part, for my notes are terse and concise.

So we'll have plenty of poultry instead of that great pork you made Art and yours truly–fat on. My little sister Dot is great on the sox question. She knits continually and Gertrude has gone to be a nurse. I wish she hadn't as it's too hard for her. I've seen the worst they have to do and believe she cannot stand it.

You are right when you say we get the worst jobs. In proportion to our size we have had more casualties than anyone else here. The Portuguese have a few men in the lines. I'd like to see them scrap. They are terribly rough looking mob, would cut anyone's throat for 1 franc = 3/4d.

Tell you what I think about Fritz? I couldn't on paper as it would make the paper lurid. The only thing to do is to exterminate them all. No return good for evil, kill is the only thing to do.

That picture is very much like you just as I should imagine you.

We'll be starting to get the cold shortly. Just imagine it all over again Pal, slush right to the hips with the numbness and pains when the blood starts to run through the veins again. How can I stand it yet it's not up to me to malinger. It's not in me I must play the game. You wouldn't think much of me if I didn't play the game would you, even if I came back in the long run. Not much news, route march, drilling so this tells you what we are doing.

love Ben xxxx more than you can manage.

Please let me know if you ever received a big photo of myself taken in London and posted about June 1st.

31.7.17

Met a Mr. Davis, an Australian artist, who has lived in Dieppe for 15 years. Spent the evening with him. Met the Devernes. Left Dieppe by early train.

4.8.17

Knew it was too good to last! Arrived Rouelles 11.50. Reporting to Sticky once again and asked for the first draft back to the old Battalion. Here in the mess with Stevens at the head, the food was not so good as at Dieppe but the *esprit de corps* was better. Lieut Gould of the 12th Battalion is here as well as Turner of 25th who told me of Teitzel passing out at Mouquet Farm.

11.8.17

Spent afternoon at Camp 18 with Miss Videl, McGrath, Robertson, Tudelock. Cricket match on YMCA versus Cooks, won by latter. Made a new will as required by AIF. Orders to Dad everything.

12.8.17

Reveille 5.30. Left camp 8.30 marched to Camp Adjutant's office with 100 old hand artillery men in the draft. Reached Havre at 11 and train left at 4 p.m. Several 3rd Division officers had full pack and were in a sorry mess. Renewed acquaintance with the bull rig officers, Vaux, Jacks and Simpson and we went to Havre and had a fine evening.

The chief stations passed through Bachy/Beichy where we had an hour's halt and patrolling men went up town. There is a Y.M.C.A. here. The men were packed 33 in a truck and were pleased to stretch their legs. We left 3 men behind here, they were ill, so we handed them over to the R.A.M.C accepting a receipt for them, to show they had not gone A.W.L. Rejoining the train passed through Boulogne and Calais which we reached on 15.8.17 at 8.50 a.m. English major on the train as OC nearly off his head as to why at each stop men will get off the train. Very funny us going in one direction dead slow, train dead slow going in opposite direction dead slow. Some got off and made tea with hot water off the coming engine.

13.8.17

France is a picture about here, with avenues of trees and crops. Quaint little houses nestling amid trees and flowers. Along the route are poppies galore, but marring the peaceful scene we passed lots of Fritz prisoners working on the lines, otherwise there appeared to be no war on at all. On to Poperinghe or rather Hopoutre, the disembarkation centre just outside it. Marched from there to Remingheist about 5 miles and passed the men over to the C.R.A. I passed back on my own to Poperinghe and stopped the night in the old Convent. While I was there Fritz dumped in some very big shells.

14.8.17

Passed a lot of pale anaemic Hun prisoners trying to work. Came in train down a few stations and got out and caught a light car to the Battalion who were pleased to see me and welcomed with open arms. Went on a 15 mile route march this morning; started at 4 am and finished by 11. It was fine and cool. Needless to say what I felt like after 3 months idleness but my pack was composed of an air cushion and waterproof sheet. Even then my feet are sore.

In this part of the world the roads are cobble stoned and *no bon for soldats*. Quite a lot of crops are going to waste for lack of labour and yesterday the C. O. released the Battalion for farm work. I was in charge of a party binding into sheaves the wheat which the froggies cut. The old froggies supplied beer and a 1/2 holiday in afternoon. We all bogged in earnest.

Played football in evening and were beaten 27 to 3 but we tore a few Guernseys in being beaten. 2 men had to go off field in centre of ring of chaffing chums with nether garments ripped. Yes it was a rough and ready game, 1/2 didn't know the rules but they played just the same. The game was suspended 1/2 way through to permit us seeing a big church procession for Assumption Day or something like that.

All froggies dressed up in horrid stiff collars bearing images etc. Girls dressed to represent different saints, St Paul, Jeanne d'Arc etc. One set of angels with golden paper wings, a tall girl had her wings torn and looked quite comical and her halo too was askew whiff.

We be a fine Battalion now, plenty of trainees but no old officer left. I feel rather strange at present and miss my morning tea and Michelham 15 course dinners.

Hope you are ok No more news. Am in D Company now.

Love Ben

15.8.17

Had a bath while I had the chance and came back to Hazebrouck by train where I met Alick McDonald of Wahroonga and Tibbett of Roseville. Then lorry hopped to Sec Bois 5 miles, where was fortunate enough to meet Griffiths in Hazebrouck with a groom and spare horse so I was set and reached home. Re-joined the Old Battalion and was put in D Company 14 Platoon. Major Price, Somerset, Farry, Holt and Johnstone. Huge rain falls have destroyed crops and famine is openly talked about.

16.8.17

The Battalion went on a 15 mile march in full pack, minus blanket. We started at 6 a.m. and finished at 12.45 being praised up by Walker who inspected us. The route was Vieux Becquir, Neuf Berquin, Merrille La Motte and back to Sec Bois. Not a chap fell out and they sang most of the way. In afternoon played football and were beaten 27-3. In evening received note from D.B and replied her. Wrote to Gertrude and Franc.

16.8.17

Dear Pal,

Here we are again. Reached the Battalion day before yesterday at midday minus a few pounds of perspiration through so much exertion and 3 months of soft living. We marched to Havre station at 9 am and stopped in the train until 4 pm before we started. Only 2 of us in carriage so we slept until Bucy where the valiant YMCA came to the rescue with tea. The poor men (draft I had to conduct to a different division to myself) were packed 33 to a horse truck and were glad of the opportunity to stretch their legs and buy tea and cakes at the YMCA there, which sold like wild fire.

Next day we came to a big town/place where my picture was taken in the Sgts Group. Here we detrained and marched 5 miles to their

Frank with her dog and horse.

headquarters. Handed over men and came back to town. When we reached there we found we were being bombed by a horrid hun plane but no hits were scored. Our Anti air craft guns were futile.

That night I slept in a Convent but unfortunately it was nuninhabited. The nuns had been evacuated except one who was sort of Mother Superior and she waited on our slight wants such as shaving water etc. I made a horrid mess of my face shaving in the train. Anyone would have thought I was trying to commit suicide by the gore the shaking of the train and razor caused.

17.8.17

Today the 3rd Anniversary of forming of lst Division to be celebrated by sports. We came 2nd in drill competition. Most amusing event was boat race, 6 men astride a pole with backs toward the goal and 1 coxswain facing the goal. On the word Go, coxswain had to guide the men who were carrying the pole. Turning around the pole everyone got tangled. I was beaten in the 440 yards by Lieut Symonds, who is a fine runner. and Lieut Boyer (clergyman in civie life) who can sprint and jump too. The four legged race was a scream.

Captain Somerset was one side, I was the other and Major Price with his back towards the winning post and his legs strapped to our inner legs making 4 in all. Came 3rd. Wretched bandage cut into old bullet wound in ankle, no bon.

Miss Vidal writing to mother asked for address. Lieuts Bull and Bennett back from Nice today.

The Battalion is changing–Col Stacey on Paris leave. Boardman Training Battalion in England. Phillips, Lanser, Steel and Finlayson were killed Gueudacourt. Of the mites who came to us from the Field Ambulance as officers–Dingle killed at Bresle, Phillips killed 5.11.16. West died of wounds from Bullecourt, Millar leg blown off at Pozieres, Richards wounded, in England, Sparks is the only one remaining with the Bn at present–(another version says has gone to Australia, see sergeants picture).

At 9.50 p.m. Fritz came over bombing and came around us. There is a wretched Tommy labour Battalion near us who cannot see that lights

Train at siding.

in tents are good marks for Fritz to drop bombs on. We didn't have any casualties but a farmer's cow was killed, and the farmer seemed very disgusted to think that 1 cow should have been hit when there were so many soldiers around who could have been hit instead.

18.8.17

Paraded, then tried out on the football team, then marched through Bailleul to Outersteen and had a bath. Saw Ryan of 9th.

Came back to dinner in afternoon and listened to gas lecture. Then Coy soccer match. At night time we had 5 visitors from other companies to dinner–Captain Moffat MC, Captain Griffiths and Major Kirkwood. We had an evening of bridge. I am learning to play.

20.8.17

Wrote to Miss Cottam [Puss Cottam, *Ferndale* Bago near Batlow], Alice Eve, [cousin], Albion St Annandale. Rec. letters from Father, Mother, Frank. Practiced bomb parties working down a trench, Planes once again tonight making 3 nights in succession. The undisciplined labour battalion with their lights in the tents got it, 14 killed and 45 wounded. Wrote Dick Eve [cousin]

Cousin Richard (Dick) William Eve, B Coy 18 Battalion

27.8.17

Route marched to Outersteen for a bath and change of clothing—we needed it. Tom Richards and Captain Somerset came back from England leave. Latter going to NCO Brigade School.

———

30.8.17

Practising Rapid wiring. Battalion officers are C.O. Colonel Stacey, Second In Charge Major Mackenzie. Coy Commanders Edgley, Moffat, Withy, Price, Q.M. Forrest, Adj Flannery, Assistant Adj Bull, Presnell is Intelligence Officer.

The Company officers now are Major Price, Johnson, Richards, Holt, Farry, Jensen and myself. So are a happy crew.

———

1.9.17

One officer from each Coy sent to Armentieres to learn route as it is thought likely to reinforce that Sector. Passed Estaires, Sailly, Bac St Mur and on to Erquinhem where we reported, Armentieres now cleared of inhabitants and the place is awfully smashed about, valuable articles lying around because no one will touch them—looting to be severely punished. 1 house looked very funny, the entire front wall blown away, and there were beds, and a piano and a table set for a meal. Armentieres fairly safe if you know the crook spots. At certain times each day they

Menin Road near Hooge, during the battle on 20 September 1917. The wounded on the stretchers are waiting to be taken to the clearing stations. AWM E00711

A pillbox known as Anzac Strong Post, captured by Australian troops in the attack of the 1st and 2nd Australian Divisions, on 20 September 1917. AWM E023421

baste certain spots and we gave those a wide berth. Saw Hun shooting at a Brasserie chimney, they had 7 shots to bring it down, I wondered if there was any one observing from it at the time. Learnt all we could and got home on the 4.9.17.

5.9.17

Beat 3rd Battalion at football–11 to 3. Received note from D V who has gone to England.

6.9.17

Solid bombardment in Ypres sector today, two balloons came over from Fritz containing letters to the French people, propaganda work. Examination on Lewis Gun and bombs.

7.9.17

Today was one of the most interesting I have had in France and what we saw shows what progress has been made and with what thoroughness the next offensive has been prepared. We went to a piece of ground hessioned off from prying eyes and saw a large scale model of the area we are to attack this month. Everything layed out to scale, strong

Battle Planning on a large scale.

points marked and wire trenches so that when we attack we will know exactly where everything is. Came home via Bailleul and Strazeele, both towns have suffered badly from bombs.

9.9.17

Tom Richards diary: This afternoon Ben Champion and I rode to Outtersteen and had tea and several bottles and rode around back to camp.

10.9.17

Having plenty of work re expecting stunt. Played football this afternoon. Wrote 5 lines home and to D. Vidal, practically saying, Good Bye as this is going to be the worst stunt we've ever been in. Major Price and Moffat on leave to *Gay Paree*. I had the Company for the time being whilst Major on leave. And as I couldn't ride a horse it was quite a task to sit on one in front of the Company.

11.9.17

Battalion moved to Remingheist.

14.9.17

Chateau Segard–Major Price re-joined.

15.9.17

Moved towards the line. Before we started Fritz shelled us and smashed A. Coy's cooker to bits. Past Shrapnel Corner up the main Warrington

A Company travelling kitchen. Ben's photo.

Road past Hell Fire Corner to Hooge and on to Clapham Junction. We were on sky line the last 500 yards and Fritz basted us solidly, 14 casualties. Don't know why the Tommies we are relieving couldn't dig a communication trench. We left Jensen at half way house with Number 13 and 14 platoons, so I'm platoon less. Clapham Junction is tunnelled out and these tunnels used to run a long way but now they have been blown in places. I reported to Stacey.

I was detailed to take over from Tommies (7th London) a Strong Post near Menin Road in advance of our line which had been captured the night before. As we were about to get over the top to go to this advanced Strong Post, Fritz shelled solidly and we lost our English Guide. Stumbling on we reached the place and took over, the cove in charge got away as soon as he could and didn't bother to show me around.

In this Strong Post is a huge dugout to hold 50 men if necessary with 15' of reinforced concrete. We were having Barrages each day getting ready, I suppose for the hop-over, and one of these barrages just managed to skittle a lot of Fritzies which I think were coming to worry the Strong Post.

This Strong Post has been attacked twice in 24 hours and there are wounded Fritzes and dead Tommies in a large deep concrete dugout whose doorway unfortunately faces Fritz. Clow and I had the horrid job of clearing the wounded Huns out of this dugout but we simply had to get room for our own men. To put them out in the open was awful but we simply couldn't carry them back. Having orders to leave Lieut. Clow in charge during the day time, I came back at daybreak and turned in with Presnell.

Had gas masks on for 2 hours.

17.9.17

Went out again to Strong Post and took tapes to mark communication trench, as it was quite likely for a ration party to get lost going there. Had 3 men hit by one of our bombs, he put his pick through it. Managed to get them away. Potter's leg practically blown away—2 ligatures to leg and then bound it up too–it took 2 field dressing to cover wound. Other chaps not so bad. Spent the night deepening and strengthening position. Returned to Hdqrs.

18.9.17

Brought out Coy to Chateau Segard, our Pioneers having dug a good communication trench we lost no one by wounds. Between 15th and 18th the Battalion lost 40 wounded.

19.9.17

As leg and arm slightly septic, went to Dickebusch for anti tetanus injection, intending to re-join, but was sent to Remy siding and boarded hospital train and got out at Etaples. With Boyer (gassed) and Bull (appendicitis) sent to Duchess Westminster Hospital at Le Touquet.

20.9.17

Fine Hospital. The dressings tickled me up a bit, felt very *de trop* owing to old clothes and no hat as thought I was only going for a dressing and left everything behind. Managed to get a loan from Wilkinson. Doc pulled a piece of shell from arm and gravel from leg. This hospital used to be a huge casino. Very pretty sight female Voluntary Aid Detatchments and such of us that could walk grouped around the piano.

21.9.17

News came through that the Stunt successful, so it ought to be, the organisation was perfect–every officer had a small message map and everything went like clockwork. Tom Richards and McLeod wounded just before attack. 3rd Brigade on left 2nd on right we were supporting them.

Lieut. Clow and Lieut. Bruton wounded at Half-way House prior to moving into support.

Ryan of 9th Battalion

Major Phillip Howell-Price, MC

Captain Hayward Moffatt, MC

22.9.17

I ought to be discharged, should never have come here, my wounds are practically better, I heal so quickly.

———

23.9.17

Dear Old Franc

I'm having rather a good time. I told you in my last letter how I came to be in hospital. Well I am ok practically and will be leaving in a few days' time now as a batch of wounded men are expected in. Take care of yourself as I'm doing with myself.

Last night the sisters gave a concert. The Duchess of Westminster was the principal figure and she can sing splendidly. They gave pieces out of *Chu Chin Chow* and spent quite a lot of money over dresses and they looked gorgeous Some gave humorous sketches and there was a splendid string quartet. The whole show was a grand success Then in the afternoon I saw a baseball match between some American Troops and Canadians and the former won. I don't think much of the game as compared with football, (Rugby)

Today is Sunday and all civilian population are out in their glad rags. These Frenchies dress very well indeed. Our hospital barber dresses so that you would think he was a Doctor or some high knut like that but he earns his living collecting tuppences from patients for a shave. I haven't any clothes at all so I feel very awkward in dirty trench stained clobber and my hat is 6 sizes too big but *c'est la guerre*.

The sisters are nice but you need have no fear at all. I rather like the idea of your hair on top but it won't spoil that little characteristic fringe in front will it?

Had a visitor this afternoon a beautiful old wrinkled Bull dog with only 2 teeth. He walked in and licked my hand as if to say *Glad you've a Blighty* when is it my turn?

Nights are getting darker. Its dark now at 8 instead of 10. Autumn leaves falling and cover all paths with a multi tinted carpet. I wish you were here to paint it. I believe I'd let you dab the paint brush in my eye. I'd be so pleased to see you.

I'm learning to ride well. Before I left Battalion I used to ride quite a lot. You see the Officer in Charge of Company was on leave and I had his horse. So don't sell all your good ponies, I'll want to have something nice to ride and I'll guarantee to beat you in a race along the river, near the spot we shooed those men off who were shooting.

Will write again shortly.

Love Ben xxxx

24.9.17

Went for long bush walk saw the fishing boats putting out to sea with their multi colored sails.

25.9.17

I'm in bed again-developed an anti-tetanus rash and it is all over my body and is most uncomfortable–temperature.

26.9.17

Still in bed, ditto 27th, ditto 28th, ditto 29th, got up out of bed.

Sept 1917, an Australian surveys the bombed city of Ypres (AWM).
Ben purchased this copy decades ago

Menin Road, near Hooge. AWM E000762

30th

Ordnance tunic and pants bought. Met Tindale and Holt coming back from school at Aveloy.

4.10.17

Sent to Etaples and on to Havre. Discharged with Captain Sutton out of Kings Own from Hospital. Met Blake, Bitmead and Wells. Usual camp life went to Havre a couple of times.

THIRD BATTLE OF YPRES
ALSO KNOWN AS PASSCHENDAELE

5.10.17

As I missed this stunt through being wounded, it is most difficult to get an exact description from anyone; Head Quarters Signaller's diary (A.E. Smith) was given to me with the description of it as follows

[Transcribed in the writing of Thomas Sydney Champion so probably given by his son-in-law Signaller Albert Ernest Jeffrey Smith]

On the 3rd Oct we were in front of Anzac Ridge. We had nothing to eat, excepts biscuits and bully, and most of the water in our bottles was done. We went out and salvaged the bottles from dead soldiers to carry on with. At 1am on the 4th., we were fortunate enough to get some hot tea, which we surely needed, as we were without overcoats or waterproof sheets, these having been dumped for the sake of lightness but we missed them sorely, and in their place was issued an extra 220 rounds of ammunition.

Our Headquarters is a large square pill box, our first experience of a pill box, which is a reinforced concrete structure, with sufficient concrete thickness to stop a 6' shell. We moved to 50 yards behind the 2nd Battalion front line. At 5.30, Fritz opened up a very heavy barrage and we lost men wholesale. Major Price got a lot of men forward so as to miss the bulk of the shells, but the damage was done. This bombardment lasted 30 minutes exactly, but to us lying in the open it seemed like hours. At 6.am our barrage opened and silenced Fritz completely and we hopped over the 2nd Battalion line and went after Fritz.

The first objective was a row of pill boxes and a small wood. This was easily done but we found in our waves a mixture of 2nd, 1st, 3rd, and 4th Battalions; we were properly mixed up; still, all the merrier, and we settled down to wait until the barrage lifted from the 2nd objective. This was to be taken by us with the 4th Battalion. We formed again, untangling ourselves from the men of the 3rd and 2nd Battalions, and when the time came and our barrage lifted, we went for Fritz hammer and tongs before he could get up with his machine guns. This objective taken, we consolidated. We altered some of the positions to get a better field of fire. It rained slightly during the stunt, and we were all wet through, there is no doubt that being unhampered by an overcoat is conducive to speed.

During the whole action, hundreds of prisoners were taken, and all were very much shaken from the effects of our gun fire. We were all miserable at losing Major Phillip Price. Fritz commenced to barrage us at 4pm., searching right back to his old original line, and at 5pm., he heavily counter attacked, but we drove him back, the Lewis gun doing exceptionally good work.

All day long, from sunrise to dark, Fritz bombarded us and the men were falling wholesale. We were relieved at 1am., on the 6th and we commenced to move back in the slush and mud. The pioneers had laid down duck boards, and the comforts fund had a hot coffee stall at Westhoek Ridge. This was the first hot drink in three days, and it went down well. We didn't mind the condensed milk tins as mugs with their lids turned to act as handles. We had only iron rations for two days, as our limbers were blown up when being brought up. We marched to Chateau Segard, which was about eight miles in all; we got there at 6.am nearly dead with fatigue and we slept where we fell.

Next day, Sunday, after stacks of food, we moved at 2.30pm past Shrapnel Corner, over desolate stretch of country strewn with mules, men and war waste to the front line where we relieved the 2nd Battalion, rain all the time but as we were not to attack, we carried overcoats and waterproof sheets. We were only here for 24 hours when the 58th battalion relieved us, and we came back towards Ypres, and detrained out of the muck and slush at Hopoutre"

Portrait of Alfred Smith. Source, Margaret McAlpine, his daughter.

BATTALION DIARY
THIRD BATTLE OF YPRES

1st Battalion Diary says: '... that section of the front on which the 1st Battalion operated was 1000 yards south of the village of Broodseinde itself. A road follows the ridge down from the the village of Passchendaele to Becelaere where it turns south–west to join the famous Menin road.

Night of 3/4 4am. The depression between Anzac ridge and Broodseinde ridges was an absolute quagmire and very difficult to negotiate even in the day time. 1st Battalion casualities also were heavier at this stage then in the attack itself. Included was Major Phillip Howell-Price D.S.O; M.C. together with several of his men and 2nd Lieut Farry. buried by a shell and bodies was never recovered or at any rate identified (Menin Gate).

The casualties sustained in the capture of Broodseinde Ridge was very severe. The number of the 1st actually engaged was little over 500 and of these 299 became casualties. Two officers killed, 2 reported missing and 2 reported wounded. Of other ranks 58 men killed, 41 reported missing and 191 wounded.

> *It seemed a heavy price to pay for a few hundred yards of ground. No doubt the "Heads" knew what they were about and had weighty stategicaal reason to advance.*

5.10.17

> We lost more today by shell fire than in the hop over. Time and time again the line was blown in burying men, who had to be dug out or they would suffocate in the mud.

6.10.17
1st ADBD

Dear Pal,

I hit the base yesterday after a 15 hours train crawl. I am perfectly well though the arm is a bit stiff. Would like to come home but no go. I'm dying to see you all again but another 18 months will finish this hectic life and see me back in old Aussie. Our Battalion, after I left did a splendid work and I can see they can carry on the war very well without me. We'll be off to the Battalion in a few days now. Had a good time in Hospital. Direct your letter to the Battalion still. Unfortunately have lost all kit so have to buy some more. Will cost me 20 pounds at least. I received a letter from your mother with the last batch and enjoyed it very much. Rather cold here now. Winter is setting in and is very mucky too. So sorry I missed the stunt, they have done excellently.

No more news. Love Ben

7.10.17

> Left at 2.50 p.m. and went via Shrapnel Corner, a very slushy track, road strewn with dead horses, limbers, motors, stretchers, rations of dead men.

We relieved the 2nd Battalion in the wet. Blake left for line. Wrote to E Vernon and Lansdowne.

8.10.17

Heavy shelling and as the Brigade is done up we are all going out. We were relieved by the 58th Bn.

Ypres Howitzer - **Shrapnell & Smiles**

11.10.17

Entrained at Ypres and detrained at Hopoutre. Losses in officers–Dead:– Price, Farry, Holt, McKell, Bennett. Wounded:–Stacey, Backhouse, McCleod. MacKinnon, Richards, Tudelope, Judd, Bruton, Boyer, Johnston, Clow and myself. A Company musters only 70 men.

Holt of D Company KIA 4 Oct 1917—Ben has written that a piece of shrapnel got him on forehead under a tilted steel helmet

Pioneers of the 1st Division preparing a duckboard track over the muddy waste near Zonnebeke, the day after the Australian attack on Broodseinde Ridge.
AWM E00837

12.10.17 with the Battalion

Dear Frank,

I joined the Battalion after a terribly weary trip. Such a dreary trip too. We made such detours. I'll just drawn the shape of the trip [lot of squiggles]. Of course it is a miserable stunt coming back to a Battalion at present moment when all the fresh pals you've made have been killed which is the case. You'll see by the papers. Anyhow I was lucky being only wounded. It is cold, rainy and miserable and the accursed country is not worth fighting for.

The mud around the trenches is ankle deep so you can imagine the state of inside coming from outside in so often. You are a love writing so often and my conscience smites me when I think of the short skimpy letters I send you. How you managed to go for 6 weeks without a letter I cannot say how that happened. I write more often than that.

Such a nice letter from your mother. I like her letters. Aren't those railway men curs; what is the Government going to do about it? Quite fun for some people to walk some distance before catching a train, do them good. Down at Paris Plage in hospital was fine.

I say Old pal this is going to be a dreadful winter, send me some sox please if you can manage it Your letters were dated about 11.8.17.

Glad you like the photo of your ugly wun and on comparing the civie and military pictures can't find much difference. Well I hope not much change has taken place. The water color you sent is very home like. I can imagine those trees down by the swing in full bloom. Only 6 days ago since I had a bed to lie on and bon things to eat. People at home seem very interested in the Battalion, getting up fairs etc.

I am glad you did some little article for it. Gertrude has quite a lot of go in her to try and become a nurse. It means terribly hard work and she had a good position in her office. I went for an afternoon outing to a fair sized town which has been bombed very regularly of late. It rained and we got wet but had a decent feed and drinks which at least put us in good humour. We stoked the fire up till the pipes at the rear became red hot and the proprietor had hysterics saying *You're using up my winter supply of coal* in politest Flemish, which is a most heathenish language. All clacks and guttural tones.

Goods are frightfully dear of course as transport is bad but they rob us right and left and don't want your custom at all. All shops are the same, goods if for a private are 1½ Fcs for English officers and 3 Fcs for Australian officers.

So the time for melon jam is come and gone. Mary made it this time did she? Well last time your mother did and I helped to cup up the melon. I met Bruce Rainsford, do you remember me talking of him, yesterday, he has swopped from his base hospital and is with a field ambulance, but a very safe job still. I'm sick of this game now. I want to get a safe job but don't suppose I could stick it after such an active life here. But pal, the casualties and chaps being blown to pieces alongside you all make one sick and sad but you have to keep going on. Perhaps bandaging up a hopeless case and all that sort of business. But cheer up there a .... Old Fritz got a terrible hiding.

One little chap in my platoon, I asked him how many he got and he said *well Mr Champion you know those lectures you used to give us, well after I'd shot the 6th Fritz who didn't put up his hands I was sick of shooting so let them go to the rear as prisoners* Everyone has a record like this and souvenirs galore.

Next time you go home to my place see the photos I sent home. No More news from your kiddum soldier boy .

Ben.

Frank's watercolour painting of Tarro swamp.

12.10.17

Met Alick McDonald, 35th Battalion, on Hazebrouck Station, and joined Battalion at Wippenhock near Hopoutre. Poperinghe not shelled now, though it is bombed often. Miserable sort of a Battalion—so many old hands gone. Killed, missing or wounded.

14.10 17

Went to Abeele, Poperinghe met Sgt Hedley out of machine gunners now a Lieut in Flying Corps English.

17.10.17

Yesterday Presnell and Captain Withy went on leave to Paris. Played Machine Gunners union rules and beat them by 2. 50 reinforcements and details to Battalion. Wrote to FJN and Mother. Received note from Mrs Alfieri. Expected to be inspected by General Walker but it failed to come off.

21.10.17

Padres gave an awful sermon dry as dust and he says we must bow our heads and say amen otherwise we are cut out of the prayer. Did anyone ever hear such bosh. Wrote 5 + pages to Franc. Presnell and Withy back from Paris leave, enjoyed themselves very much indeed. Bootles went on night of 20.10.17. Withy met Moffat in Paris. Moffat is at rest camp near Paris and had leave for 2 days. Went for a ride on *Nigger* to a spur 10 miles away. Very picturesque old wind mill on the top. Can see Wippenhoek near Hopoutre.

22.10.17

We are at Wippenhoek near Hopoutre. Today all the Passchendaele Ridge maps were distributed, spare gear collected etc. Cannot make it out, don't like the look of it. Court martial promulgated. Brigadier around. Asked by Pte Cox and Pte Ellis to go as evidence as to character. Both good boys and sorry for them. Booze in each case made them desert temporarily thereby missing the stunt. Few long lost letters turned up, been chasing me around France. Had a glorious rum issue. Chidgey and Robinson went on Calais leave today–hope it is my turn soon. This time last year we were trekking to the Somme. Can anyone ever forget the fatal Guy Faulkes night of last year. Absolutely the worst I've ever experienced. Wrote 5 pages to Mother, rec'd letter Miss Smith, Frank, Art, Mother, Father.

25.10.17

Moved to Chateau Belge in motor cars, ground sloppy and uncomfortable when we disembarked at our huts and it got worse, and to make things better we were bombed by huge Fritz planes, the bombs could be seen dropping–glowing red. These huts are sandbagged up three feet on the outside–quite enough to stop splinters from penetrating and only a direct hit would cause many casualties. No lights were shown but Fritz must know that this is a starting-off place for the line. When the bombing was over we went out and saw distinctly six huge Fritz planes over Ypres.

26.10.17

We are for the line all right, there were so many senior officer casualties last stunt, that every 2nd Company Commander is to be left out of the line, the next senior taking his place. We do miss Phillip Price. Those to be let out this time in are, McConnel, Presnell, Bitmead, Lee and Mortlock.

27.10.17

Fritz bombed again whilst tea was on at 6.30pm. He got six of our chaps. He then went on to the 2nd Battalion and killed 14, wounding 60. Nothing is as terrible as the awful detonation of these bombs and they don't penetrate into the earth, but have a great lateral burst.

28.10.17

He got Ypres tonight, his huge planes looked so pretty in the moonlight. 6 huge Gothas. The rum issue is very good, 6 to a pint. Mant gone to Signals School for 7 weeks. Chidgey to Intelligence School. Wrote to Post Office re packet not yet delivered and posted by Sgt Archie Barwick at Post Office Lark Hill in August. McConnel and Mortlock gone to Paris. Edgar's funeral today (killed by bomb) O Company frightful sights.

Archie Barwick - AWM.

29.10.17

Sent map of Flers by Reginemtal Sergeant Major to be posted home from England Rec'd 10 letters, 6 from home. Blighty Concerts going in huts, men sing well in a mass, Rum issue, moving tomorrow.

30.10.17

Moved to Ramparts at Ypres in reserve. Town had a moat all around it and inside wall of moat is built up with bricks and cement. In these walls are tunnels built by our engineers. The whole place is like a warren. Fitted with gas proof doors and may rest in comfort. There are plenty of rats though, and if rations left in a haversack or pack, there's a large hole in it in the morning.

Sketch of Ypres showing fort and moat.

1.11.17

Last night Fritz bombed Ypres solidly, the concussions were terrible. Canadians stormed in conjunction with 1st Battalion of our 2nd Brigade and 5th Army and captured most of Passchendaele Ridge, rumoured that Brig. Heane has substantial eye witnesses that when Canadians retreated to their former positions they had been fraternising with Huns, probably

November 1917 After Battle of Passchendaele 1st Division soldiers in vaults under city of Ypres.
Ben chose this picture decades ago when still in copyright.
[I think Ben may be one with cigarette in centre. — Ed]

Battalion of French Canadians. Big row now going on between 2nd Army and 5th Army. Official photographer came around and took several snaps of the boys in the tunnels and dug–outs. Wrote to D.V. No mail from England for 4 days.

2.11.17

Misty day, no planes over and very little shelling. Colonel Stacey back from England. wounded in last stunt. Strength is only 91, organised into 5 platoons.

3.11.17

Symonds and Intelligence Staff went on reconnaissance to line.

4.11.17

Company Commanders visited the line this morning. Lieut. Bitmead and 50 details marched in and were very welcome as my Company is only 91 strong, organised into three platoons. Les Barwick and Cpl Pont amongst them Pont has been away for close on 9 months, he used to be a runner, now a Corporal made in 6th Division. 1st Division concert party the *Kookooburras* giving a shew in Ypres today

5.11.17

Left for line at 9.30 this morning, carrying 6 sand bags and wearing 2 instead of puttees. It is thought that tight puttees stop circulation to the feet. Also an extra 250 rounds of ammunition. Relieving 10th Battalion. Near Roulers railway.

6.11.17

In dugouts closer to the line, had 5 casualties getting here through Ypres. Gassed for 2 hours, 1 man died as casualty, clearing through it. It was a most unpleasant camp–we were constantly drenched with gas shells and our clothes reeked ot it.

AWM ONLINE

Australian Divisions participated in the battles of Menin Road, Polygon Wood, Broodseinde, Poelcapelle and the First Battle of Passchendaele. In eight weeks of fighting Australian forces incurred 38, 000 casualties. The combined total of British and Dominion casualties has been estimated at 310, 000 (estimated German losses were slightly lower) and no breakthrough was achieved. The costly offensives, ending with the capture of Passchendaele village, merely widened the Ypres salient by a few kilometres.

View of the swamps of Zonnebeke on the day of the First Battle of Passchendaele. October 1917. AWM EO1200

Chateau Wood Ypres, Battle of Passchendaele 1917 - AWM

7.11.17

Officer per Coy went to line through Zonnebeke via Helles Track. Church in ruins, the only building standing is the Gas Works. Passing Church was surprised to see a battery of 4-5 howitzers in amongst the ruins. Rushed for my life over Zonnebeke Cross Road which is a hot shop for enemy shelling. Came back to Railway Dugouts, did about 8 miles in all. Had tea when word came through that I, with small party, had to go to the line again and take over.

———

We were sniped by gun fire right up the track, broken duckboards in front and behind us were blown 20-30' in the air. Fritz must have an observation there on Helles Walk.

Reported to 4th Battalion, and was told that I had to go out on Patrol to learn the Route, so went out and had a wretched time; took a party through Zonnebeke and took part of the 4th Battalion line. Patrolled with a 4th Battalion officer, Billy Hunt, as far as Birma Copse. We were three hours out on this patrol, mostly up to our knees in mud so our rifles were useless as sometimes we had to crawl, so we had only bombs. In front of us is a swampy position which Fritz won't occupy as he is too sensible. Every now and then we would come on what looked like a lighted dugout, we would carefully surround this in the yellow mud and then find out it was a huge shell hole filled with yellow water and with the moon shining on it, making it look like the lighted mouth of a dugout. A back bearing had to be taken by compass, as there was no outstanding feature of the ground to recognise and the whole patrol was done with compass. Lost 1 puttee in the mud. Lovely gripping yellow mud.

———

8, 11.17

Battalion marched in at 6 o'clock to take over from the 4th Battalion B and D front line: C and A supports. Camouflage the posts in daytime and lie doggo.

———

9.11.17

Burrin went out on Patrol with Billy Hunt as I was too knocked up; had 5 casualties in my platoon today. The Copse in front is reeking with gas and it hangs over the swampy ground.

10.11.17

At 6 p.m. relieved by Lancashire Fusiliers, awful mob, poor beggars so tired they could hardly keep on their feet and instead of the officers seeing the men fixed up, they sat in H.Q. dugout and yarned, leaving us to set posts and generally nurse them into shape. They could hardly walk but staggered along and collapsed on the top of the trench. Instead of allowing men to travel light, they carried full packs and blanket all the way.

Where to put these full sized platoons was a problem. We manned the line with about 90 men all told and they had about 200 with all their packs etc. Finally the relieving officer and myself packed half of them back to the support line and when I was ready to leave, he was astounded when shown his new dugout. He almost expected to be able to spread out his valise, I think.

Moved out, only one casualty. All the way out the road was ankle deep in slush and dead horses, mules, limbers, rations, wire etc. all over the place. Australian Comforts Fund supplied coffee. For trench efficiency our Brigade (and A.I.F.) probably can beat these regiments hollow. We consider our men before anything else; and C.O's always see that the men arrive in the line in a condition fit for fighting, travelling as lightly as possible and officers equipped as the men.

Time and time again I've seen Imperial Officers heading a column, marching without packs while their men were laden like mules. The Australian Comforts Funds cannot be praised in too highly a manner– keeping the men well up in spirits by supplying them with hot coffee and biscuits when they went into and came out of the line. The stall was well in the zone of gun fire and served hundreds of mugs of cocoa, each night. The water being boiled in huge boilers and tins of cocoa and milk emptied in and the tins then converted into mugs. Men told to report back to canal dugouts near Ypres. This they did in 3s and 4s along the Potje Road and not a man failed to turn up.

11.11.17

Moved to Halifax Camp near Ouderdon. The Medical Officer said that 67% of these men were not fit to march owing to gas and sore feet through the slush line. The transport relieved us of our blankets, pack and tin hats.

12.11.17

9.30 We marched in battle order, 11 miles to St. Jans Cappel near Berthen. Last time here 9.9.17. Took over billets from Duke Cornwalls Light Infantry.

12.11.17

Dear Frank

I've had a hell of a time since last I wrote. The conditions were awful. Do you remember me writing to you about this time last year, well it rained the whole time we were in the line and mud was too dreadful for words. I was sopping wet for 4 days. The last day was the worst. The rain brought in all the dug–outs and we simply were swimming, We couldn't move as Fritz planes were constantly over and at the least movement he shelled tripe out of us. We took off our tin hats and sat in them until the water over flowed them, then we simply had wet behinds and waists for the rest of the day. I had a few amusing experiences though.

I was taken prisoner by our B Coy one night and had to submit to the indignity of being searched for my pay book. One of your letters came to light with my address on it. Then I was allowed to go free with many apologies. Steel helmets are put to many uses, seat, candle holding, stoves, baking, dishes and wash basins besides keeping off shrapnel.

Patrols here the order and as we were in a marsh you can imagine what it was like.

November 14 at home, November 15 Peninsula, 1916 Somme, 1917 here. I'm sick of this pal o mine and when will it finish?

No News

love Ben

13.11.17

Marched via Castre, 2 miles near side of Staples. 100 reinforcements joined up, Major Jacobs, Walker, Lieut. Moffat joined up with the Battalion. Very good billets, whole Bn and 100 horses in 1 farm. People selling goods at normal prices, not inflated prices because we happen to be Australians, like some people do. Met Art Felton at Caestre as we passed though, no one fell out.

Major H Jacobs - 1st Battalion Diary

15.11.17

Marched to Heuringhem where we were joined by the reinforcements from Caestre including officers, Sampson, Booth, Clarke, Mortlock, Jensen, Steens Lee, Brownlie, Walker, Hamilton, Presnell, Davis, McConnel. We were very pleased to see them.

16.11.17

Marched through Belques. Lubers to St Pierre.

17.11.17

Battalion rested at St. Pierre. I went into St. Omer for Canteen goods. Calais canal flowing through St. Omer, saw Bertin Abbey which was burnt years ago.

18.11.17

Marched to Becourt via Campagne les Boulluois, beautiful undulating country, everything vividly green. In 6 days we've marched 70 miles, including 1 days spell. ·

19.11.17

Moved from Becourt to Menty, 10 miles from Etaples and 10 miles from Boulogne, where we expect to be training and resting for a while. Platoons being split up and making things bad for administration. Rotten billets, terrible mess everybody is in.

20.11.17

Clean up parades.

21.10.17

Jensen gone to a School.

22.11.17

Art Felton from the 4th came over to see me. Vic Fowler [see pic of sergeants] reported back with a commission, posted to D. Company. Col. Stacey, Blighty leave. More men back. Boulogne leave given.

25.11.17

One month to Xmas 3rd from home. Church parade very cold wind, dopey parson. Yesterday officers played against each other rough game. Colonel gone on months leave to Blighty. Major Mac in charge. Sports committee started Battalion going up in scale. Rather cheery billets, fine old girl and family. Nippers funny. 3½ parade in morning 1½ hours recreation training in afternoon.

30.11.17

On the 30th my leave came through. To Paris at 11.30 and I dressed and caught the 12.30 motor bus to Boulogne going straight to the train with no lunch. On the train I picked up Jarvis of the 3rd Battalion and

Ben, Jensen, Brownlie and Beale taken Amiens
On the back Ben has written (Pioneers) Jensen and Brownlie and Beale–4th Bn
Photo taken at Leon Caron studios Amiens

we decided to visit together. The train trip was via Abbeville Long Pre Amiens Picquigny—where the Divisional School under Sticky Steven was—and then onto gay Paree itself.

From Amiens to Paris we had company, in the person of a commandant of French Forces, which is about rank of Major in our army and he was a most interesting person. We gave away no information at all-just listened to him telling us tales of Verdun. What an awful shambles that place must be! He stated that his troops were becoming dissatisfied with their conditions but that their fears were sound; the reason was Verdun itself. Trenches were taken and retaken to be battered out of recognition and then taken again; bodies unburied and unearthed after every bombardment.

He wished us luck after inquiring if he could do anything to make our stay in Paris comfortable and said that the Elysee Palace hotel was catering fully for the needs of Australian and British soldiers and officers.

We reached Paris at 8pm after a run of 6 hours in misty rain. Paris in her war dress of no lights was a very dismal affair on the outside. We took a fiacre to the Hotel and as we both had plenty of money, we got two bedrooms with a bathroom in between being charged 16 francs per day, meals included. This cost us actually 8/–per day on exchange.

After a thorough soak in the bath, we ate and sat in the Hotel Lobby till late; we were too tired to go out and we had a beautiful glowing feeling. Partly due to food and partly due to our new surroundings.

1-12 17

We sallied forth.

[Pages of description and visit to Versailles etc]

9.12.17

Caught 9.10 am train from Gare du Nord in Paris and arrived in Bolougne at 3pm. Caught leave bus at 8pm arrived billets at 10pm 9 Officers in Company now. Lieut. Graham back with Battalion. Photos taken with Flannery. Symonds.

10.12.17

Played A Coy football, D Coy a surprise packet won 4 to 2 points. No tries at all, all kicks. Walter Thompson with the Battalion now as a permanent sergeant, has been instructing at Hurdcott.

11.12.17

Wrote home FJN Mrs Alfieri, D Vidal, 13 letters from home Attack for semi open warfare practiced this morning. Lieut Kellaway rejoined this day. Jensen went on leave to Blighty & took over old diary to Mr Fisher of AMP Society (now that Mr Hollingsworth gone back home).

11.12.17

Dear Frank,

Beaucoup lettres from you old girl to hand today on my return from Paris. Thanks you're a dear old bean. So sorry you've been ill, now I told you before I went away not to be ill until I told you to do so. What do you mean by being ill. You musn't be so at all.

Well old girl, if Ruth says I can't spell your name it doesn't matter, Frank will do me. Well had a glorious spin in Paris. Wish you and your mother could see the place. It's the most beautiful city I've ever seen. Gardens, buildings and people are so pretty, just like in a picture book. They seem a dream now I've come back to mud and slime and bare realities again.

You all don't seem to be having too good a time at home, strikes, weather and rain, one on top of the other. Well I'll tell you a little of Paris. I had 9 nights and 8 days there. Caught a very fast train. In peace times its the fastest in the world but goes a little slower now the war is on. I stopped at the Elysee Palace Hotel on the famous Champs Elysees near the Arc de Triomphe. This arc is in a circle where 12 boulevardes meet each other. Boulevarde is about 30 yards wide, foot paths on each side with double rows of trees. In summer it's a glorious sight. The Arc has all Napoleons battles on it and his General's names. The sculptural work depicts his battles.

When the Germans took this place in Franco Prussian war, out of coutesy they didn't march through it. Next the Invalides, a fine group of buildings other side of Seine River over the Alexander Bridge. Here are war trophies dating back past the Revolution and one British flag which the French captured. Here is also Guynicmers plane the famous air man. It's covered in wreaths. Napoleon's tomb is a gorgeous spectacle and here I saw Frenchies praying before it.

Versailles, an hours run in the train cannot all be seen in a few days Here Marie Antoinette lived The gardens which stretch for miles are beautifully laid out. Before the war there were lots of fountains playing with different colored jets of water. There is a huge marble staircase from grounds of the Castle to the gardens 50 yards wide. Inside the Castle is one mass of scintillating glass and gold ware. Beautiful carpets, robes and pictures, poor old Queen, she must have been sad at leaving such a place. Red marble staircases, everything shows no lack of money or taste.

The clothes of the men are magnificent, all colors of rainbow instead of drab khaki. Hats ornamented with feathers and jewels.

Have you heard of Madame Tussaud's wax works in London? Well there is a similar place to that here. War pictures and revolution deeds all in wax. Very life like. I was taken in once, I spoke to a French Officer to be received by a stoney glare, a bit annoyed I spoke again then I found out it was a wax and didn't I laugh. People thought I was dotty.

Customs here. Coffee and rolls for breakfast, light lunch, dinner then supper. Everyone didn't get to bed before 1a.m. any morning and often much later. Oh it's a lovely city and as light as day in the night time in the main places. Opera house is very beautiful, saw *Mignon* staged enjoyed it although in French, music superb. Disappointed in Notre Dame Cathedral not as good as I expected. Glass windows are good, each spout leading off the roof is different. Animals, humans, insects, birds, fishes etc. Gargoyles they are called. I liked Valetta Cathedral Malta better than any Cathedral I visited in London or Paris.

I like Paris better than London. Easier to get about. Suburbs run in concentric circles and are termed arrondissements. Don't expect many letters in next few mails, we'll be terribly busy, *Comprez?*

What a frightful disaster that was in Halifax such a huge explosion. Couldn't go on top of the Eiffel Tower but it's a fine piece of constructional engineering. We'll tell you more later on. Enjoyed myself immensely. Won't be able to now for some time.

Yours, Ben.

barbed wire galore xxx

SAMER

12.12.17

Wrote Mr Hollingworth, Fiston, Daverne, Paris, Eves. Route marched to Carly attack formation. Played 2nd Battalion beat them 17-5. Capt White on Divison came to see D Coy. Flannery gone as learner to Division. Somerset Adjutant.

13.12.17

Went to see a rocket demonstration. New message carrier range 1200 yards. Makes a siren whistle and shows a light to attract attention. For sending messages from front or support lines to Battalion headquarters if attacked.

14.12.17

Left Menty at 9am to move beyond Samer 15km from Boulogne. As we met main road was told to report to Div Headquarters. Detailed as Camp Commandant at Mount Kemmel. Caught Lorry at Samer at 11.30 passed through Bologne to Saint Omer. Stopped for half hour then through Cassel to Bailleul then to Lindenhock 11pm went to Coy Engineers. They lent me overcoats etc had a sleep and breakfast.

15.12.17

MOUNT KEMMEL Saturday. Reported to Kemmel taking over #1 sub area at Red Chateau. 3rd Brigade Headquarters at Kemmel Chateau. No valise yet, Clephane probably at Baillieul station with it.

16.12.17

Valise turned up. My area extends from Kemmell past Wychete practically to the line.

17.12.17

1st Battalion moved into Rossignol Camp. Bgde. HQ at Chateau Officers Club open very decent place.

19.12.17

Received parcel from Mrs McCleod and L. Edgar both of shortbread. 2nd and 3rd Brigades in the line. Met Art Felton. 2nd pip through today. Art gave me address for Miss Claire Bridges, *Dovedale* 29 Woodfield Road. Kings Heath Birmingham.

22.12.17

Bull reported from Blighty, Chedgey back from leave, Mant and Blake back.

—

24.12.17

Had dinner at Headquarters. Chedgey gone to Musketry School, Downton at Bombing School. Sampson in hospital. At dinner were Doc Somerset, Presnell, Pdre Chedgey, Symonds, Mant and French mortars. a Belgium interpreter whose name is unpronounceable.

—

17.12.17

Dear Frank

Behold me a Camp Commandant for 3 weeks. A cushy job. I don't have to get out of bed until 9am which is a great advantage these cold mornings. It snowed hard to day and am nearly frozen. When coming here I was without a blanket for 2 nights but on each occasion officers took compassion on me and gave me a bunk. It's great how all officers hang together, a sort of chain binds them.

Fritz comes over bombing sometimes but that alone disturbs the monotony of the place. How I wish I was with you all dear people for Xmas instead of being on my lonesome. What a difference here and home, snow and fine hot weather. Discomfort and comfort and being with strangers and without loved ones.

Dear little mate I miss you so and sometimes I wonder will I ever see you again. Thank heavens we can still write but letters though good are very far apart from each other. I nearly went mad last week, lost my wallet with your photos in it but it was returned a little muddy but photos intact. What about another photo pal, one with your hair on top, you know I haven't yet seen you like that.

I saw Art a few weeks ago. To me just the same old Art, full of self-assurance. Pal I'm as skinny as a clothes prop would you believe that. First opportunity that arrives I'm going to swing the lead. I'm sick right from top of head to toes of this silly war game. I'm longing for it to finish so that I can be among you.

As far as occupation you say don't be a farmer or a waster. I'll probably be the latter in any case. Must close now as my box is worn out trying to think of something to say.

love your pal

Ben

28.12.17 France

Dear Mate,

I'm sick of this life. Everything that is possible here goes against the grain. Besides all this wretchedness the unpatriotic curs at home have turned down conscription thereby cutting the Australians here. In the year 1919 I can see a few boatloads of disc's going back, all that is left of the AIF. Why can't they reinforce us. Or put more men into the field so that a few old hands can get back. I'm homesick and dying for the sight of you all.

We had a merry Xmas. The Battalion spent a lot of money out of regimental funds and gave the lads a good feed. Christmas Day menu: porridge, double issue of bacon and and tea Dinner: roast meat, cauliflower, turnips and onions, potatoes, custard and plum pudding. Afternoon: tea and biscuits Tea: rice and figs and tea . So you can see they enjoyed themselves.

One old regimental custom was carried out, the Sergeants were mess orderlies and served to the men instead of vice versa and every one was in high glee. It snowed too very hard and some terrific battles were put up with snow balls. My left eye is still slightly blackened where I put my face in front of a ball.

Besides all the tucker the men had several issues of rum to make them merry. I wonder if next Xmas I will be home. Wouldn't it be fun.

Old Fritz is very quiet on this front can hardly believe it. The quarters for the men too are all dry and well drained which is a blessing. I've a very soft job for a couple of weeks longer and a good canvas hut and a fine bunk to be on and no need to get out of bed till 9am. But I can assure you the Battalion is not being treated like that, it's simply because I've been lucky catching this job.

Pal are you sending me another photo of yourself. You have sent me one each Xmas so far and I have the 2 still you know. They are practically worn out through being looked at and kissed.

No more news from dotty mate for coming to the War.

Love Ben

27.12.17

Pictures last night continued to snow. Snow fights galore left eye bunged, up snow ball too hard.

29.12.17

Very Quiet day, hardly a shot fired. Tomorrow Captain H Moffat leaves for 6 months turn in Blighty. Visited Red Chateau and Wychete. Walking along Wychete Road met GOC 1st Division, General Walker. Had I not known him, impossible to see rank. Very ordinary clothes and wearing a leather jerkin over jacket. Wiring in 18 pounder guns. Series rifle boxes in the eridge to hold 120 men. Very comfortable. Fritz plane lost in mist came down to 300'above camp then was lost in mist again. Letter from Davernes at Dieppe.

31.12.17

Battalion moved into the line tonight. Clear night crisp. Last night Kemmel Chateau burnt down. Very pretty sight. Water in moat melted. In the last few days the chaps have been sliding around on the ice.Tongues of fire leaping up through the gables. Today a blackened skeleton of a building set in woods and snow all around it. 1st Brigade saved all their records. Ammunition going off in fire, galore. The latest gas used has a peculiar odour like decaying fruit, it is very effective. Wrote to Mother 8 pages.

3.1.18

No Aust mail in yet. No casualities in the line yet. General Walker made Knight, Brig. Heane made CB ie CB CMG DSO and deserves every

Red Chateau 1913

one, Brigadier Leslie made Brevet Colonel in Indian army. Clear crisp weather, very slippery. Ice all over roads. All horses have frost cogs in their shoes. Bread 7 to a loaf, no vegetables today Now onwards 47% bread 53 biscuits.

5.1.18

Carl Waugh came back from the 2nd Army School. Line very quiet, no mail.

6.1.18

Bob Humphreys to Aust Army Gas School People are being allowed to come back to Kemmel if they wish Parkinson and Davis came back from leave Went to pictures with Griffith and Forrest and *Trench Mortars*– MacGregor evacuated to hospital last night. Cold and old wounds making him so stiff he coudnt move. Wrote to Vidal, Niland, Smith, Gertrude.

7.1.18

Boardman back from Blighty. Went to Ballieul for canteen goods, had lunch at the Club there. Bought a good leather jacket from a Tommy for 1/2 water bottle of rum.

8.1.18

Dear old Pal Frank

No news at all from here but as I must write you a note I'll try and fill you in. For a start we are all terribly anxious because our last mails were end of October. No Xmas stuff at all. Quite a lot of silly rumours going about. Some say we are off to Palestine others Italy, others say no fighting for 6 months but they are only silly talkers no truth in any of them. Some think that the post office has gone to Egypt but there is no true reason about the mail not coming along. How I long to be back Pal. You cannot possibly think how fed up I am with this accursed war. No more wars for me I'd be over age limit next time.

Had a huge bon fire a few nights ago a big chateau burnt down No military importance though. Saw the Divisional cinema on last night, they switched on war views but the house wouldn't have that so Charlie Chaplin was put on. Do you remember the pictures at Hornsby Didie, you, Art and myself? Charlie Chaplin is so ridulously funny isn't he, one has to laugh at his silly antics. Try as I can I cannot think of a job for myself after the war How would a little barrow and a load of rabbits go. Wild Rabee bottlo ...ever read *Ginger Mick* its so funny. Art has been sent to a school for a few weeks, lucky man.

Australian Comforts Fund sent a cargo of rabbits as Xmas box they went very well indeed. Rabbits 6/–each in England. Bread very short here mostly biscuits. Thank heavens I have good teeth. Open a little wider pet?

No more news.

love, Ben

13.3.18

Hunt, Humphreys back from schools. Parkinson gone as acting gas offficer McConnel gone to School—Aust mail in only one letter from Franc Letter from Nancy Johnson. Went into Bailleul very dead place indeed. Received watch from Mrs Alfieri.

14.1.18

Flannery came to see me. Steen gone to Corps school.

15.1.18

Very wet. Some units of 1st and 3rd Brigades relieved by 2nd Brigade. Chedgey came back from Musketry School. Went to *Kookooburras* 1st Division concert party very good, especially the girl who looked and sang her part very well. Could easily be excused for mistaking him for a girl. Today a balloon broke away and sailed over toward the Hun line. Presently we saw 2 aeronauts jump out and parachute to the ground. As they jumped out they dropped like a stone for about 50 feet it seemed then the parachute opened and they sailed to the ground. Lambert of Trench Mortars close to here. He was an old 1st Battalion Sergeant.

19.1.18

Kemmel. Wrote to Mr Fisher asking to cable for 50 pounds. Rec'd parcel from Aunt Eliza. Wrote to A Smith. Lee gone on Paris leave. Lieut Bull took out a patrol, of 8 men and 2 sergeants to get information if possible about a large pill box called the Giant. With him went Sgt Beynon, a solid old soldier who was once I believe a Petty Officer in the Navy. This patrol actually got through Fritz lines and was fired on by his support line and got between front and second line. Scattering as was prearranged they made their way back to our lines only to learn when they got there that Lieut Bull, Sgt Beynon and Pt Bluey Mansell were missing [Prisoners of War].

Patrols went out to look for them but found no trace. Bull came into our lines two nights after, bringing with him some good information. He was evacuated due to exposure. Fowler went to 2nd Army Musketry School at Lumbres.

23.1.18

Dear Frank,

I've only received one letter from you in last 8 weeks. Perhaps they go to the 18th Battalion as so many do. See quite a lot of people just write

1st instead of First and the silly post chaps think it means 18 Battalion hence no letters, then boats have gone down in the Channel which we don't hear about.

A bit of a victory recently in the Dardanelles for us. Not bad you know, the *Goeben* and *Breslau* gone. Wish they had gone long ago for you know it was a naval shell presumably from one of those boats which came through the tunnel on Pensinsular on 29 Nov 1915 and got me. Its been raining solidly the last 3 days and my canvas hut is encircled. I have a chorus of squeeks all night, The rats gather under the hut on the high ground. I'm going to have a raid on them tomorrow night-will tell you the number of casualties. The days are lengthening out quite visably. Am I not to get the Xmas 17/18 photograph of you with your hair up and dresses down? I'm going to blighty on leave within a couple of months. Hope I have good time. I have a light touch of malarial fever again so kept quiet today in bed but the time drags so heavily like that. Thank goodness I'm on a job which does not need my personal attention each day. I have an excellent batman, the way the beggar manages to secure coal is marvellous. He just goes out and then back he comes with a sand bag full. I suppose he pinches it. Am not too good. Good night old pal and don't forget me.

Ben

Frances Julia Niland.

25.1.18

Jensen, Cruise and myself rode to Steenwerck to see Bull but too late he had been moved to hospital. Glorious sunny today so went to Bailleul pottered about the town came back to Danoutre and had dinner with Cruise, Town Mayor and a few others and came home to Kemmel , 21 miles in all. A good day but sore seat from riding a horse.

————

27 .1.18

Dear Frank

I thought you had deserted me but last night I received some letters from you and consequently couldn't go to sleep for happiness. What a funny girl you are, you don't even know the date of my birthday.

Excuse the gap—runner just bought in 2 more letters for me. The post Corporal knows how anxious I am to get letters addressed in large handwriting that he sent a runner 2 miles to me. I don't live with the Battalion just at present. I'm an area commandant or as the Colonel says area comedian. This job just will last another week worse luck then back to the hum drum life again.

I must tell you about a trip I had yesterday. We had a nice little officer who took a patrol out and somehow he got lost and was wounded and without tucker for 70 hours until he was found. Transport officer and myself went to see him It was misty when we started out but came out a glorious sunny day. I was riding a big black horse named *Old Nick*. We did the 7 miles to casualty clearing station but found that he had been sent down the line to a hospital ... talked to a few Australian nurses then made our way to a big town we'll just call B and had lunch there. Hors d'oevres, oysters, fish, roast pork, spuds and cauliflower. Best dinner I've had for months and months and months. Then came home. No accidents but just a wee bit sore from the riding-just 21 miles all told.

A glorious day just like spring but no green leaves of course yet. Today is misty as usual no planes about. An ideal working day for forward area. Well to get down to some of your numerous questions, all of which I love to answer. I'm waiting for that photo of you with your hair up, –getting terribly old aren't you? I'll be 21 in March and only

18 when left home–time flies doesn't it. Soon I'll be home if I'm spared and looking around for a job. Fencing, wrecking stones or selling silk stocking to some young person from behind a counter I don't think. I reckon it's great fun speculating what I'm going to do.

A C O is a commanding officer, generally a Lieut Colonel An O C means an officer commanding a Company generally a Captain sometimes a Lieutenant. A responsible position with 120 men generally under his command Of course in a scrap if all officers are killed a 2 Lieut may find himself in charge of a battalion and very often a Lieut commands a Company.

Beaucoup lettres today so forgive me for rousing in my other letter. I'm overjoyed at receiving them. Now you want to know what we do of a night time in hospital. Most hospitals have a rule you must be indoors by 8pm but of course for our nights fling its worth having to go before the CO of the hospital and being sentenced to two days CB, which means confined to barracks, which means we cannot go out for two days.

Pictures and theatres are the craze as you do not get much opportunity at the front. It must be nice to have a place like *Oaklands* where you can invite friends over for weekends but for goodness sake don't have anyone over in the spare room when I come up or they may think me a burgular coming thru the window and shoot me instead.

Never been to the mountains. You have missed a treat. It's a glorious place in Summer to go down into the cool valleys but the trip would be greatly improved with some electric lifts instead of climbing up and down hundeds and hundreds of steps. I've been there 3 times and will again if possible.

I haven't been in a church for a service since July 1915, of course there are hundreds of times I've been to outdoor parades. Yes, I know Miss Wood. Not well of course just a speaking aquaintance. Yes it very good of you all to have Gertrude up at Tarro and to have her friends too. Yes when we come to France first *Souvenir* was all the cry. Now Australian girls have robbed the frenchies of their buttons, what a shame. Medals are very common in France. A Soldier who hasn't one is called an embuscary? I think that is how it is spelt ie, a man who hides behind his mothers skirts.

Art and I are still good friends although being in different battalions. I see him some times once a month or so. I'm sorry he has broken with Mary. That means I suppose he will not want to go to Tarro again, but I'll have enough courage to go on my own now. No more bike trips up north and kidding our bike broke down. I believe I was the cause of that which bought us back to Tarro but I simply couldn't stop away.

What ho, the time I came from Liverpool Camp and slept all night in the spare room and came around in the morning. I'm glad you don't have to finish that cream skirt and coat. The blooming old dentist might have spoilt it as so many dresses get spoilt from stains from chemicals in a dental surgery. Gee, I remember my dentistry in the spare room.

Your letters are not trash as you say they are, but I do object to one thing in them and that there is no ending. You send a few kisses or barbed wire. I want them all. Just a few are no good.

Yes Cliff Gentle has been killed and another mate Charlie Smith from Wahroonga has been killed also.

We are a very happy battalion just at present. The C.O. Colonel Stacey is a gentleman and the O.C. of my company is too. I was his Lance Corporal when he was a 2nd Lieut.

No more news. Remember me to all at *Oaklands* .

———

.....

I am to hand over my job to a 5th Division man on 1st Feb so I am busy taking stock and checking over supplies. By that time the Battalion will be at Meteren.

———

28.1.18

I went with Forrest our Quartermaster to Bailleul, 4 miles from Meteren. Saw our new billets. Chedgey gone to another school. In the few days since I was here it has suffered by shell fire considerably in the area around the railway line. Returning to Kemmell I handed over my relief and went on to Meteren.

———

29.1.18-1.2.18

5th Division relieved 1st. Fokker came after a balloon 2 men jumped out of it with parachutes landed safely. Could notice differences in speed when the men were high up where air pressure greater to when they came near the ground when is smaller. I had orders to leave here on 1st Feb. We go in buses to Meteren. Have just had (the men) 31 days in line and support. Too long in rotten weather although the front is quietest I've ever been in.

———

2.2.18

Saw Battalion down to hard training with some reinforcements joining us, filling in the gaps in our ranks and spit and polish is now the order of the day. Very comfortable billets, good bed.

Captains Edgley and Somerset have gone on leave and Hasty A'Beckett has taken over C Company for the time being. Football being a compulsory afternoon sport, everyone soon became fit and many famous games were played.

The N.C.O's. beat the officers badly 8-5 and Downton was evacuated with a broken ankle. In the match next day against the 2nd Battalion which we won, Bowes of the 2nd was hurt in the mouth and also evacuated. We have lost more by football than last time in line. Meteren is a nice spot, the billets good, clean and roomy and this seems to be looked on as our own town. The boys have worked the oracle as they say, and are well and truly established in many kitchens, being looked on for the time being as sons of the old Madames pottering about the stove.

Brigadier General Brand 4th Brigade, kicked off in the football match against the 13th Battalion and half time the scores were 6 to nil but our training stood us in good stead and we won 10 to 6. Carstairs full back excellent.

Here at Meteren we couldn't have an Officers mess but we had a recreation room with a fire burning and Morley performed wonders on the piano.

———

7.2.18

Cosey room in full swing well patronised by officers. Lieut A'Beckett came to C Coy as a O.C. whilst Capt Somerset on leave. Carrying on section drill under section leaders.–letter from D V and Mrs Alfieri and 1 from Gertrude.

———

11.2.18

I won the Battalion competition with No 11 platoon. Consequently my Blighty leave pass was cancelled; I was to have accompanied Presnell and I now have to take the platoon to Tilques where each Battalion in the Division will be represented.

12.2.18

A Rev'd gentleman named Elliott gave an illustrated lecture on Africa which was well attended and he spoke well. In the evening of 12th, in the recreation room, the officers had a fancy dress party. A Coy won the prize for the best combination-Waugh husband, Graham wife, Shannon black son, Mortlock as little boy and A'Beckett as the daughter. It was a scream especially A'Beckett's costume. He had a low necked dress which only came to his knees and short socks held up by suspenders. His hairy legs looked very odd. The party chanted a ditty which ended up, *The blighter never was within a mile of Foray Farm*

Doctor O'Shea had on a complete feminine outfit—nothing missing. Tom Richards went as a Toreador. I went as Good Night in a nighdress (awfully cold).

Officers fancy dress party.

13.1.18

Presnell went to blighty on leave without me and in the afternoon we played the 4th Bn football or rather Boardman did as he scored 3 of 4 tries. Won 37-0. Next day the winning platoon left for Tilques to take part in the competition, Major Burrett in charge of the Brigade detail.

Down here at Tilques, going through a small arms school are Tom Brownlie, Mortlock, Parkinson, Wells, Davies and Stobo.

17.2.18

We visited St Omer with Brownlie, Stobo, Yates on the Sunday afternoon. Met Sgt Huchison. Vic Fowler stopping night in Lumbres. After tea the air raid siren signals blew. Immediately from houses and shops, women and kiddies started running towards the Town Hall many of them carrying chairs. They dived out of sight very quickly and not a glimmer of a light was to be seen anywhere in the town. Only soldiers left in the streets. Soon we hard the drone of the engines and the planes could be heard distinctly gliding overhead and then *crash* and the whole town reverberated to the noise of the explosions. The rackets seems to be ever so much louder in the confines of a town. Soon the all clear sounded. There is a fine park and the sun was shining brightly, weather wonderfully crisp and all the people were promendading in the gardens. Band playing. Some streets in St Omer are so narrow and well made of pavestones that 2 ordinance lorries cannot pass abreast. St O cathedral very beautiful. Cannot like our Padre to my mind he is very narrow minded and not a fit active serviceman.

My platoon looks very well. All equipment blancoed and the brass tags shiny. We went over the assault course today and qualified in the shooting. Colonel Stevens came down to see the training. Carl Waugh joined us. He has been appointed Brigade muskety officer. Graham has gone to a short School. Bitmead is running a Battalion school for NCO.

19.2.18

During the attack today for the divisional competition I was beaten by the 2nd Battalion. There were many onlookers and Colonel Stacey congratulated the platoon its effort. But I think I satisfied Col Stacey that I had tried hard for it.

20.2.18

Today we tried over the assault course and I believe the 3rd Battalion will win. Received a letter from Ruth Niland. Platoon looks very well and even if we did not win, it has brightened up them all considerably.

23.2.18

We left Tilques for Meteren later in the day per motor lorry which broke down several times and I was sorry I did not go by train with the remainder of the men. Via St Omer, Arques, Erquinghem, Strazeele, Wallon Cappel, and Renescue. In our C Coy, the officers are Captain Somerset, A'Beckett, Sampson, Booth, Parkinson, Trail, Davis and myself.

25.2.18

Coy Commanders went to the line. Went to a concert given by Motor Transport, Heard *Roses of Picardy* for the first time. Presnell being called from leave on courts martial. David gone to Musketry School. LEAVE for BLIGHTY

26/2/18

My leave pass came through today for Blighty. Col Stacey told me that if I wanted places to go too he would assist me. I caught the 8 am train from Bailleul to Calais, caught 4pm boat from Calais to Dover, 75 minute trip into Craven Hotel by 9.40.

28.2.18

Reported to Horseferry Rd to get a meat ticket. Had lunch with Mr Fisher at his club and given 25 pounds.

1.3.18

Met Matthews, McMahon of 4th Batt and Phillips. Went to Piccadily Grill and on to *Maid of the Mountains* in the afternoon and it entranced me.

2.3.18

Went to Ipswich to visit Vidals who were so good to me when at our base. I found D Vidal with mumps and feeling very miserable. Spent several hours talking–think I cheered her up quite a lot. Bought her a few flowers when I left and sent around. Came home by 10 to 6 train. D V is a good girl I respect very much. They gave me enough sugar for my leave. Sugar can't be bought here in England, scarraine being used instead and it gives the tea a bitter taste. The Vidals had saved up their supply for months going without themselves in order to give it to any Army friends who should come over.

3.3.1918

I went to the Officers Club at 138 Picadilly and there met some chaps I knew. All the so called waitresses are Australian girls giving their services free. That night I went to Edinburgh arriving at 8.30am on the 4th and I stopped at Brown Country Hotel a very old fashioned place run in a comfortable way. Saw Mrs McCleod, Jennie engaged to Capt Beavis.

6.3.1918

I came back on the 6th and went down to Alfieri's at Battle in Sussex. The route is via Charing Cross and I changed at Tonbridge and passed through Tunbridge Wells and onto Battle and taxied to *Horn Lodge*. Very sociable people Love them.

Horn Lodge

Clare Alfieri of Horn Lodge,
Battle, Sussex

7.3.18

Slacks, slippers, comfort. Clare Alfieri engaged–Lucky man

These are wonderful people. They may have their own troubles, with two boys away in the Permanent Army, but they make a touch of home life for me. In the evening, we see search lights weaving the sky Londonwards and the people said London was being bombed by Fritz.

We went off to Hastings in a little dog cart drawn by a pony. There is an asphalt road and their fields alongside are lined with primroses and peonies; it is just a picture! No wonder the English fight for this place and instilled into our blood is the love for it. I had my photo taken. With my meat card I was able to buy a fair quantity of meat for the Alfieris, which they appreciated very much. We came home tired but a different sort of tiredness from that experience in France.

[There are post cards of Ben's time here not included.]

Next morning it happened to be Sunday so we went to Church. This appears to have been built BC for around it were enough plaques to Lord and Lady this and that till the whole of the lower walls were covered with them. This was Church of England so Mrs A had to help with order of service. In the afternoon I borrowed a bike and pedalled into Bexhill on Sea where there was a Canadian Officers Training School. There is a very fine esplanade covered with wounded soldiers out for an airing from a large hospital here.

Battle Abbey Woods were visited next day, especially the avenue where the headless monk walks on Christmas Eve with his head tucked under his arm. The local farmers will not go near the place at Christmas time. Wednesday was my last day and when leaving was kissed. Thought a lot of it. First motherly and sisterly kiss since I left home. I'm still a kid at heart and need mothering. Came to London back to the Craven Hotel where I met Major Alex Mackenzie and went around town with him.

14.3.18

I managed a seat in a restaurant on the train leaving Victoria Station next morning and got as far as Dover. The sea was breaking up on the cliffs, a wonderful sight and the crossing boats have been cancelled for the day. The embarkation officer stamped my pass but I noticed a boat pulling in

at lunch time and sure enough it was going back and as my money was
done I risked it and was sick all the way across and pleased to go to the
Hotel Maurice for a rest.

———

The Australian Club for Officers
138 Picadilly W I

13.3.18

Dear old Girl,

My letters have been terribly skimpy of late. I haven't fogotten you
by any means but I'm all on pins and needles and cannot settle down
or concentrate my mind on anything whatever.

Well, my glorious holiday is at an end worse luck The first 6 days
were hectic rush but the remaining 7 quiet and on a farm which
reminded me so much of dear old *Oaklands* These people I went to
see are cousins of the Gentles I believe, they made me very welcome
and I enjoyed the peace and quiet of it all. There was a pony very much
the same as Creamy and we drove to places around about Hastings,
Bexhill and Battle. Look these places up and see where I've been.

The post cards I sent you will describe the places better than I
can. If your birthday happens to be on the 5 May as I think it is then I
wish you many, many happy returns of the day and hope this wretched
war will be over before your next comes along. We are terribly short
of petrol and to my mind the cars look so funny going along with
balloons of coal gas on top. They look extra comical when the bag is
nearly empty and it sags over the side.

The people here have had one or two bad air raids lately. I have to be
at the railway station at 8.am tomorrow morning. I absolutely hate going
back to France not that I'm funking it at all but the continual wear and
tear and concert pitch is getting on my nerves. You can't settle down to
write but one keeps jigging about on your feet the whole time.

How I'm longing to be back, I'm very very homesick Pal. Hope all
your family are well, no colds or measles. London is such a huge dreary
place too big and lonesome What shall it be Frank, dentist, soldier,
farmer or nothing at all. Why couldn't this war have come a few years
hence when I had some job at my finger tips.

Did you have much fruit last season? Dad says we had a lot of Dixon plums. You know the great big yellow and red chaps. 2 are a meal for a average person. Of course I had to have a meat coupon to buy meat. The Alfierie's for 12 people only got 5 and half pounds of meat last week. just imagine trying to cook that up for all those mouths. Butter is short, Sugar too. Bread will shortly be rationed and weighed out. Just imagine the bother if dear old Australia had to put up with that.

Had my photo taken a few days ago, would you care for one? Primroses, violets and peonies are out in the woods. I picked a bunch a few days ago but they all have such short stalks they don't live long. What must a home be like. Great dairy country all the way down to Sussex, beautiful grassy fields too just like the Hunter Valley.

Well Franc, I'll close now. Love from Ben

15.3.1918

I went to Bailleul where I met Art Felton and we decided to have out photos taken together. We lorry hopped to Conference Corner and reported to Forrest at Ridgewood camp where I slept the night.

Changing into other clothes and picking up a tin and gas helmet I walked up to Battalion Headquarters beyond the line in the ravine and was sent

2 Lieut Art Felton 4th Battalion and 2 Lieut Ben Champion 1st Battalion'

to D Company. Boardman is Adjutant and we talked over the happenings since I left the Battalion 16 days ago. Shannon has been evacuated badly wounded by one of our own 4.5 howitzers and Tom Brownlie has gone to the Training Battalion OC 13 Platoon in England. The front line is about 500 yards in advance of the position held in October 1916.

In Thomas Sydney Champion's writing so he must have obtained a copy somehow from Signaller A E Smith, his future son-in-law.

World War 1 1914-18 Extract from War Diary of A E Smith 1st Brigade Signallers AIF (from 28th July to 29 April 1918

28 Feb 1918

Marched eight kilos to position in the line called Spoilbank, Ypres Combles canal flows past dug out. Dug out under a ridge consisting of tunnels electrically lit.

28 Feb to 26 Feb.

In line Spoilbank. Position heavily shelled by enemy artillery Hundreds of gas shells sent over, causing great inconvenience and necessitating the wearing of gas helmets–about 10% of section casualites from gas, and remainder feeling the effects more or less. Casualities from wounds slight. Aerial combats and attacks on observation balloons nightly. Enemy aircraft often drop small red balloons containing pamphlets. (these state that Germans did not wish to fight against Australians and if we surrendered we would be well treated.) Nightly and daily raids by both sides resulted in small outposts being taken and few prisoners captured. Both sides awaiting developments.

25 March

Section moved out of the line–ten men, Jack and self included remaining.

26 March

Moved out of line to camp Enfordan At Concert in YMCA petroleum lamp burst. One Tommy burnt to death, 12 others badly burnt and few crushed. Jack and self escaped through windows. Fritz over bombing at night. Very cold weather–only one blanket

26 to 1.4.18

> *In Camp N4D – just behind line at Messines, Eyes, lungs , throat, effected by gas*

2 April

> *Left N4D camp – marched short distance and got light railway to Renninghelst – marched to Busse-Boom – camped there. Fritz shelling*

3 April

> *Wallked to Poperinghe; town knocked about by G Shell fire*

4 April

> *Busseboom*

5 April

> *Raining heavily and marched from B via Renninghelst and Abeele, at Paperinghe to Godwaesveldt (10 kilos) entrained at 2.30pm for Amiens*

6 April

> *Arrived Amiens 4.30am, marched through A to Rainneveille, a typical straggling Somme village*

7 April

> *Rainneville*

8 April

> *do*

9 April

> *Marched from R to Montigny. Met many French people fleeing from the line. some few carting belongings in carts and barrows. Camped in fine chateau*

10 April

> *Montigny, G shelling vicinity*

11 April

> *Hurriedly left M, marched part way and got lift in motors in Amiens. G shelling town and G Planes overhead Camped few hours in large hospital. Entrained at 7.30pm for North. G Shelling and bombing train and station Number of Australians killed and wounded.*

12 April

> *Travelled all last night – train shelled at intervals. Detrained at Borre(near Hazebrouck) and marched to the line, met civilians and Tommy soldiers fleeing before G advance. Battalion sent forward to check hun advance*

13 April

> *Borre. British soldiers coming back in small numbers saying the Huns were close on their heels. Tommies quite disorganised. Heavy German shelling. Australia soldiers in fierce combat with the Huns and succeeded in checking their advance. Tommies blowing up railway lines.*
>
> *Burning villages all along German lines. Heavy shellings. Few civilians in towns of Borre, Pradelles and Strazelle. Troops living in farm houses plenty of food, pork, poultry, potatoes, wines, etc*

14 April

> *Australians repel fierce German attack. Hand to hand fighting.*

15 April

> *Germans attacking fiercly Heavy shelling*

16 April

> *Had to shift H Q owing to heavy shell fire. Australians advance slightly. Farmhouses set alight by shell fire*
>
> *Seven German waves of Infantry mown down by Machine Gun Fire Attacks broken up by 3rd Battalion.*

17 April

> *Owing to shell fire had to hurriedly leave farmhouse and lie out in field*

18.4.18

> *Germans still hold. Fierce shell fire and bombing*

19.4.18

> *Continuous artillery ....with MG rifle fire*

20 April

> *Early? and in night attacks repelled with terrible heavy losses*

Ben's diary continues

Ben must have heard it 7 June 1917 5.30am Tunneling Company blew 2 massive mines under the Messine Ridge . The craters were called Hill 60 and Caterpillar. The largest man made explosion in history to that time and was heard in Poland. It opened up the front line and ushered in the next great battle of Passchaendale or Third Battle of Ypres.

Back row: Lieut. K. C. MORTLOCK, M.C., Lieut. R. G. HUMPHREYS, M.M., Lieut. F. A. PRESNELL, Lieut. T. J. RICHARDS, M.C.
Chaplain REDMOND, Lieut. W. H. PARKINSON, Lieut. R. H. JENSEN, Lieut. A. J. H. STOBO.
2nd row:—Lieut. F. P. SHANNON, Lieut. C. J. WAUGH, Lieut. G. BITMEAD, Lieut. F. W. WELLS, Lieut. A. T. H. BROWNLIE, Lieut. H. H. DAVIS, Lieut. R. W. SAMPSON, M.C., Lieut. B. W. CHAMPION, Lieut. C. A. CLARK, Lieut. C. R. MORLEY, M.C., Lieut. D. J. BURRIN.
Front row: Capt. R. OYSHEA, M.C. (A.A.M.C.), Lieut. F. A. GRAHAM, Capt. W. LIONEL WALKER, Lieut. H. F. FORREST, M.C., Capt. C. R. WITHY, M.C., Lieut-Col. B. V. STACEY, C.M.G., D.S.O., Lieut. H. BOARDMAN, Lieut. A. E. SYMONS, Lieut. H. E. A'BECKETT, M.C., Capt. J. C. BOOTLE, M.C., Lieut. F. GRIFFITHS.

Official Photo E. 1630. 1st Battalion Officers—Meteren, February, 1918.

1st Battalion Officers—Meteren, February 1918. From Ben's First Battalion AIF book.

Hill 60 had its top blown off by our miners and the countryside seems altered. The mines we blew at Messines time here took 70, 000 pounds of explosive under Hill 60 and 53, 000 under the Caterpiller.

I am to take Dick Cassidy's old platoon—No 13. He was killed on the Hermies-Demicourt road months ago. With me are Morley, Fowler and Stobo. All rations are brought up on light railways and there is a very little carrying. We are in support at present in tunnels running under Hill 60.

<hr>

17.3.18

St Patricks Day we celebrated by Fritz sending over hundreds of gas shells and Morley and Fowler together with half of the Company on fatique sat for 3 hours in their gas masks by the side of the duckboards. 9 men evacuated gassed but practically everyone is slightly affected and we can only talk in whispers since it has affected our vocal cords.

The duck boards in this sector are covered with wire netting and prevent one from slipping. They are a great improvement on the bare boards.

<hr>

20.3.18

The day of our relief broke dull and misty and we were able to march out in daylight. We were all lined up in the ravine and Fritz couldn't use his observation balloons to spy on us. What a shambles it would have been if it had been a fine day!

The 4th Battalion took over our posts and we marched out to Spoil Bank where we took the light rail to Ridgewood Camp. Here were rested a few days to get our voices back.

<hr>

21.3.18

We were awaked by a terrific bombardement. Guns woke us up, seems to be in the Armentieres sector as well as around Ypres. Rumour has it that Fritz has attacked the Menin Road but was driven back. We seem to have Fritz bluffed with planes in this sector.

There is a nasty slippery 9.2. gun very high velocity which fires over here and it has dropped one or two close to Ridgewood Camp. Ypres is still being smashed. The Cloth Hall gradually going west by degrees. Last night the Battalion had a glorious feed. Generous people in Australia sent over money and some of it was spent on cauliflowers, a sack of turnips, cabbages and a bottle of beer per man.–the vegetables we generally never get or see.

Censoring letters–funny one ending *Good Bye as I have to get this censored with the best of luck* another *I'm up to my knees in muck hoping this finds you the same*

There are horrible rumours going around that one Battalion in each Brigade is to be done away with. There are not enough reinforcements to keep all going and the 3 Battalions Brigade should work well. But which one is to be out? C.O. called an officers meeting to form a Battalion Mess, not a pleasant arrangement to majority of officers who would rather have a company mess. Tunnels if not supported are death traps. 12 ' shell pierced an artillery tunnel breaking it in and burying 23 men.

During the bombardment last night, Ypres suffered from plane bombing; there will be hardly a wall standing in that place. Any of our troops in that area are well underground but there are so many important roads going through the place that traffic is very much disorganised and many casualties occur. Hasty A'Beckett and I are to go to a school tomorrow at Lumbres.

22.3.18

Next morning off we went by horseback as far as Bailleul. It has been knocked about by shell fire since the last time I was here. We went to Ordnance to get some clothes. Whilst there a terrific crash took place; the concussion was awful. We rushed out and saw two houses collapse like a pack of cards amidst a cloud of smoke an dust. The Ordnance clerks pushed us out and we noticed them making out of Bailleul.

In another minute, whilst we were deciding what to do another cloud of smoke and dust and again a couple of houses fell. We were just about to clear out when we heard shrieks and rushing up found some people staggering out and they said their mother and sister were in the basement. Without any ado, Hasty tore of his tunic and pulling beams apart wormed his way in and was soon lost to sight down in the cellar.

There was an awful smell of gas too and in a minute he appeared carrying one woman and dragging the other out into the open. Then an ambulance full of Flying Corps boys came by and they jumped out and commmenced to search for victims of the shelling. One Flying Officer went to thank A'Beckett for helping but in his gruff manner, Hasty told him to *go to Hell* and that is the sort of man Hasty is.

We then went to our battalion store but it was most uncomfortable. Every now and then we would be deafened with the concussion. Up to this time we thought Baillleul had been bombed but we saw the base of a shell, and I am sure it was 11½ inches across.

Finally we went out into the open fields coming into town at sunset and we turned in at the Officers Club. An Artillery Colonel said he thought the gun was set in a Canal thus using water to take the shock of the gun. Next morning we found the club deserted, leaving the place with its stocks of provisions open for anybody to help themselves. Had to get a scratch breakfast. We went to the train early to get a good seat but found the station thronged with men. The train before had not run. We waited at the railway station for a couple of hours expecting to be caught by shells at any moment. If a shell had hit the station dozens would have gone west: but each shell sailed over head and went wallop into the town, the shell exploding made an awful row and each time it hit 2–3 houses would tumble down. We were glad to get out of the place.

Finally, pulled in at 2 and we got as far as Strazeele where another wait took place until a shell hole in the railway track could be made safe enough to cross over. Lumbres was reached that night and we turned in but my valise was missing. Trail had taken mine by mistake and I couldn't wear his clothes. The C.O. examined us and picking on the AIF officers spoke about their clothes. Doubtless we were rough according to his standards but most of us had just come out of the line and he and his staff had not seen any war for years. It was a lovely school, beds, etc and the staff were very keen.There is electric light in the huts and we are comfortable.

Next morning on parade we were told what was expected of us and we were dismissed until lunch time but in ½ hours time the alarm bugle went and we doubled on to parade wondering what was the matter. The Commandng Officer was talking to the Adjutant and anyone could see they were perturbed about something. He then told us that they had had rather alarming news and that we were to proceed back to our units immediately Fritz had broken through on the Somme and all schools were to be closed as this looked very serious.

We were packed into fast lorries and rushed back in a couple of hours. Rejoining the Battalion, Colonel Stacey showed us Sir Douglas Haig's Order of the day:

> "We are again at crisis in this war. The enemy has collected on this front every available Division and is aiming at the destruction of the British Army. We have already inflicted on the enemy severe loss and the French people are sending troops as quickly as possible to our support. I feel that everyone in the army fully realising how much depends on the exertions and steadfastness of each one of us will do his utmost to prevent the enemy attaining his object" AAA 11.35 pm 23rd AAA"

So that is how serious it is. Another official message says;

> "Our troops south of Peronne have re established their line along the west bank of the Somme southward to east of Licourt when they are reported to hold a definite line southward in touch with the French. North of Peronne it is believed operations are developing somewhat more satisfactorily although the situation South of Le transloy is still uncertain."

Frightful losses were inflicted on the enemy. They attacked in dense mass formations. Our intelligence found out 5 successive zero house and guns played havoc on their massed troops. Only weight of numbers caused our failure to retain the line. So that is that. The official news is scant and ambiguous.

Already from this sector the 3rd, 4th and 5th Australian are on the southward move and no fresh troops have come into this sector to take their places. The New Zealanders are off too and the Artillery is also on the move.

MONDAY, MARCH 25, 1918.

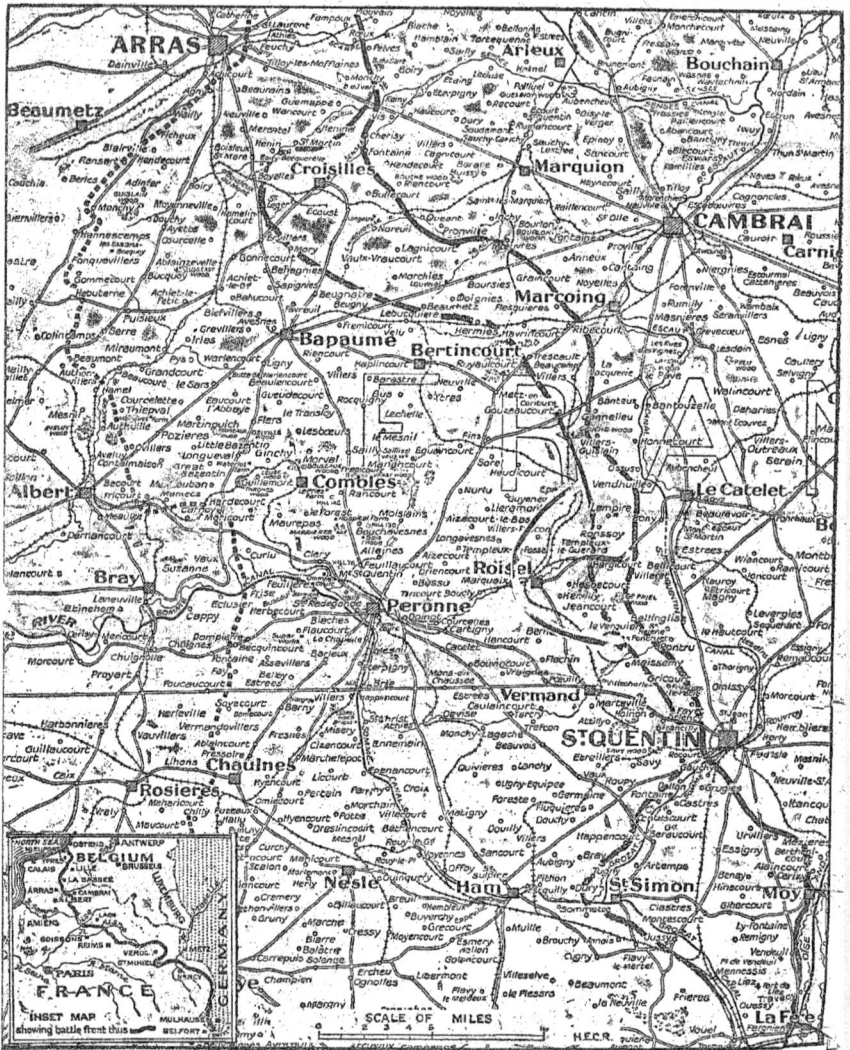

The thick, continuous black line on the right of the map marks the British front before this offensive began. The broken line not far to the left of it marks, very roughly, the new line as it appears at the time of writing; the dent in the middle, including Roisel, is marked separately from the main line because, though the Germans claim it, there is as yet no admission of their claim. It is likely enough to be correct, however. The dotted line away to the left represents the old front before the Somme battle began.

25 March 1918. Ben's map taken from newspaper.

26.3.18

I took over Red Chateau area just for a few days as area commandant until things straighten out. In this sector are only the 1st and 2nd Divisions now, instead of 5 Divisions. It would be a wonderful chance for Fritz to break through here, but perhaps he has enough on his hands down south.

On my 21st Birthday I rejoined my unit handing over the area to no one. Everything seems upside down here. Very pleased to see Major Jacobs back with the Battalion; he has taken over Graham's Company. *Grum* the sport he is, said nothing although he had the Company for a long time.

We are organising and re organising for open warfare; all surplus kit removed to store and our valises are down to 25 lbs max. The official news through is that Fritz is right through Dernancourt and Albert. All the country we once took is gone back to his hands: just imagine the loss to us in dumps of material etc;, besides men and guns! Everyone is back from schools and leave, and we have a fine happy family.

———

29.3.18 France

My dear Frank

This is some war on over here but we are fixing him up splendidly, don't worry there will be a great coup shortly. Pal I am wearying to get home but it's no good grousing. You cannot imagine how I'm longing to be back. I celebrated my 21st birthday yesterday. That makes the 3rd since I left.

There are too may I's but I know how much I long to know what you are doing every day and perhaps you care for the same thing. Seems strange Mary is going in for nursing as you all seem just the same to me as when I left. More officers have come back to the Battalion and promotions seem as far off as ever so I can see myself coming home a Lieut. just the same.

Thanks for the sox you sent. I received them in good condition. We are all in good spirits and very confident about the push down south. Frank is your mother annoyed with me over anything at all, for I haven't received a note since Art wrote last to her re his engagement. At the moment of writing this you are just about to turn into bed,

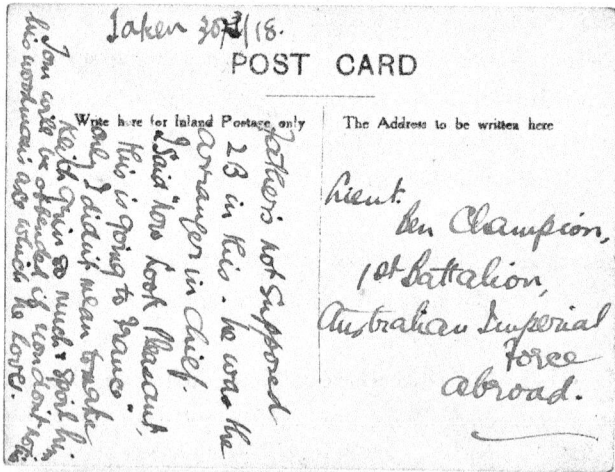

Ben's Photo. Father's not supposed to be in this he was arranger-in-chief. I said now lets look pleasant this is going to France only I didnt mean to make Keith grin so much and spoil him. Tom in front with woodsman axe

hope you have good dreams. I had a horrid one a few nights ago and found myself loading my revolver when I woke up.

Fruit trees are coming out in bloom but I think we will have cold weather yet to come. I left for a school on the 23rd of this month. Spent a day there and were rushed back in cars to our units as Fritz was expected to attack on our front but nothing came of it. I wish he would come, we would towel him up right enough.

Has Bert Carroll reached home yet? Lucky man. I'd give something to be in his shoes. We have in the camp a portable organ. It is in our hut and three blighters can play it, the tunes range from *Chu Chin Chow* to Hymns and rag time.

I had to go to the line this morning at 3.30am on a fatigue party carrying barbed wire. A sticky journey, Gas, bit of shelling and slippery duck boards. All no bon. Chap came to me today and said Mr Champion I've got Vary-coarse vein in my legs. I nearly burst with laughing.

Can you imagine the road in front of our camp. It has the whole main line traffic on it. Black slimy mud ankle deep—Ughhh, appalling or as some people say absolutely hectic. I cannot speak, slightly gassed, wretch of throat. Cough all night before I could get to sleep last night, I had to swallow a cup of whisky then I slept right enough. The AMC haven't got anything for it.

The men who were evacuated gassed were not worse than myself and they reached Blighty. What a chance I missed. No more news, Good Luck, cheeriho Old girl, Good Bye for the moment. Yours, every time,

Ben

1.4.18

Aprils Fools' Day–the long expected move came. We were stripped right down to fighting kit and we moved to Reningheist siding and then to local Camps B Coy and Headquarters being in one, D Coy and Transport in the other. They are really the dirtiest most squalid billets we have ever been in.

Lovely naval gun here 9.2 on a railway carriage when it explodes the shock sends the carriage back several yards Its smoke is very brown. Some of the Battalion got into hots with some Chinamen here but it was hushed up. Throats getting better, marching the gas out of our systems. Back in Company messes instead of being together at a Battalion, merrier and quicker too. Men horribly stiff for cash.

Each day we pester Headquarters for reliable news from the front and each day meagre details are given out—how Bapaume and Mametz had fallen and the 3rd Division had retaken Dernancourt.

Pool old Morley was evacuated with a septic face; only a minor scratch too, which became infected. We have 107 men in our Company and all are fit and proud and give a good account of themselves.

We were treated to a good air scrap today and we had a wonderful view There were 5 hun planes over in boomerang formation only about 1000' high too and there was not a British plane in sight. Soon however high about Fritz right in the sun's rays we spotted 4 British planes and they steadily circled and kept coming down to the Hun's level always keeping behind. To see a British plane come down like an arrow at a Fritz plane firing all the time and then gently roll over on one side away from Fritz and come at him again. The anti aircraft guns couldn't fire as the planes were too mixed.

After rolls, sliding, nose diving etc, our planes forced two Fritzes down in flames and the other 3 crashed just over the ridge near Bailleul— too far away for us to see but I'm sure they were caught. Our 4 planes went up again and they seemed to prance up and down; I don't know if the boys did it on purpose but it looked as if they were trying, like a rooster, to say *Cock a doodle doo.*

5.4.18

Saw us on our way to Berthen and 3am we marched breakfastless in black rain to Goddesvelde siding arriving at 5.30am, There a most appetising smell awaited us from the stew in our travelling kitchens and we hoed into the bully beef stew and the cocoa from the *Café au Lait* tins supplied by the Comforts Funds people—God Bless them.

The train left at 7 and the trip was the dreariest we had ever had. It went via Calais and Boulogne to St Roche a suburb of Amiens where we detrained. Immediately we formed up and marched to Allonville about 10 miles away. What a difference there was in Amiens. It was badly knocked about and people were leaving it in dozens with all their worldly goods on carts and apart from those leaving there was hardly a soul to be seen where only a few months before the streets had been thronged with shoppers.

Amiens station was being continually shelled hence the disembarkation at St Roche. Allonville was reached and the whole Battalion fitted into one barn and the officers of several Battalions into another smaller one. Here the smiling Major Mackenzie met us from his Staff School in England.

7.4.18

Our Padre Prickett had to be reminded that it was Sunday. Lee visited us today. The week has gone so quickly. We are only 11 miles from the line but hear no guns. Here it is unsettled warfare

---

4.4.18 France

Dear Franc

Two letters from you dated 1st and 13th January came along and when I read how you had looked for and received no letter from me for 2 mails my conscience smote me. Anyhow, things havent' been going too well over here and we are on the *que vivre*. Can't settle down and all we talk about is Fritz and his advances. Well here goes for a start. Who are Ray and Bob? I've been away so long I can't place them. Creamy looks fine in the sulky but what mars the picture is I can't see your face. I'm dying for another photo of you like you sent for Xmas 16.

Sorry your mother has been ill, am sure she will be well ere this. Did Pontie come home safely from Sydney after he received the money from your Dad! Just like him to be robbed of his money, he didn't appear to be capable of even looking after himself. Yes I've seen Art once or twice. Strange Mary is going in for nursing. Out here a chap never thinks anyone else is growing up except himself. That's why I want that photo so badly.

Creamy must be growing old now. What Age? I've never yet caught an eel, you will have to teach me how. I believe they get a fishing line in an awful tangle if you are not careful. We never see snakes [live ones] over here but sometimes some of the men dream about them.

If Mary becomes a nurse, don't you become one also. It is dreadfully hard work. I've seen a lot of their work and Gertrude had to give it up. I hope Marjorie passed, she didn't even tell me she had gastritis. You tell me quite a lot of home news. I received a bon pair of sox from you. Thanks very much. We can use them all as Sox wear out very quickly here with the hard boots we use.

The skipper of the Company is not yet back, he went to Rome on leave. We think the lines must be too congested for him to travel. Art and I had our photos taken but the next day a shell got the shop so finished Art's 20 francs he paid for them.

Scene:–D Company officers at mess, enter an irate French woman shedding tears, holding in one hand 6 dead chickens by their necks and in the other hand holding the collar of one of our men who was in the collar. After voluble explanations it came about that he was the sanitary man and was spreading chloride of lime about the place. The greedy chicks had eaten this and were dead. Hence the crocodile tears and a lightened pocket for each officer. We had to part with 5 francs each.

Each officer in turn has to be an orderly officer i.e. inspect tucker etc. Well, he has a new job now. Inspect the sick parade before the Doctor comes and if he thinks the man is malingering, send him on parade instead of seeing the doctor so he is really an improvised M.O. I've had a funny career in the army but one officer I know has a funny job now. He goes around the Brigades now disinfecting blankets. What do you think of that job? This soldiering game is very well when there is no stunt brewing and its fine weather. Now it's just the opposite, wet and cold. There's one consolation Fritz has the bad weather as well as we do. Bath parade this afternoon, an hours march to it but as it is 33 days since the lads had one, they cheered when they heard about it.

Of course officers can get one as often as they like, that is one of the joys of being an officer. Being clean! Get a horse whenever you like and

Foden disinfecting machine for de-lousing clothes and blankets. At the end of the war it was realised that lice caused Trench Fever.

off for a trip somewhere. How do you like this purple ink? Very classy looking isn't it? I went to Church last Sunday. The YMCA allow all denominations to hold services in their huts RC's, C of E's etc.

My brother Art [older brother Arthur Champion was not fit for service due to injury prior to war] is farming up at Yanco. I believe he is making a success of it. Why shouldn't I be able to do likewise?

This seems very greasy paper. It's official stuff. I can't get to a town to buy some note paper but don't enclose any in your letters as I feel so disappointed when I receive blank paper when I think it's a fat letter. *I wonder why you write to me at all.* Do you know the old song *I can fancy anybody fancying YOU but fancy you fancying ME.*

I conjured up a lot of imaginings about you and wonder if you have altered at all. I hope not, for to my mind you were just you before I came away and by your letters you are just the same to me. Cheeriho! Frank. Love from

Ben

9.4.18

Booth and Forrest back from Milan. Left Allonville. We were ordered to Molliens au Bois only to find all billets taken up by refugees and it took 4 hours to get the Battalion under cover. The nervous tension on all hands is high and several have expressed the wish to do something instead of loafing around.

10.4.18.

The Battalion moved in a frightful hurry to Amiens stopping the night in the Blind Asylum. The inmates had been taken elsewhere and the huge building was spotless and clean with large windows and plenty of light but braille books lying all over the place. More like an open air school than a blind asylum. The kitchens in which stood huge coppers barely cold were a pleasure to gaze on as they were so clean and neat. Every man had a straw mattress to sleep on that night and tried to make good use of it only to be be prevented by continual bombing by Fritz.

No lights were allowed so he must have known the Asylum was full of troops from other sources. Next morning we marched to St Roch and then did we guess that we were not for the line down here. The news came through that Fritz had broken through Wychete, Kemmel, Bailleul, Armentieres, etc and we are to go north to try and stop him. The AIF must be thought something of by the Higher Commands when they are used to stem the flood in the north as well as in the south.

Entraining at 2pm we reached the important railway junction of St Pol in the twilight where the engines were disconnected to be watered. No sooner had the engine gone away than over came the Fritz planes bombing and soon we were in the thick of it.

To sit in a carriage 3' off the ground, just at a nice height for a bomb splinter and to know one can't duck or hide and that the thin wooden carriage wall wouldn't keep the splinters out is no good. Lying on the ground, one is very stiff to get a direct hit and unless very close the rise of the bomb splinters makes one generally safe. The worst time is when one can hear the zip-zip of the falling bomb and one wonders where it is going to fall and then the awful roar of the explosion is heard.

To have the whole Battalion in one train and then only wound a few men by splinters, is bad luck for Fritz; that is what happened. A few transport men in the back carriage were hit. Perhap our Lewis guns mounted on trucks and shooting their hardest spoilt his aim, but there was no excuse for not inflicting more damage.

Soon the engine hooked on and off we went on our journey very thankful to be moving, although it was towards the line. At dawn we detrained at a siding and saw how much poor old Hazebrouck had been knocked about. What a difference in the town now compared to when we first saw it I April 1916. We formed column of route and then into Artillery column of sections and advance up the Pradelles Road and halted outside the village. The advance guard was well ahead so we bivouacked at Pradelles. We are living well as owners of the places left some of their fowls and pigs behind and the cooks are doing their hardest souveniring as we go on green vegetables

HQ are in the village and we are outside. Biscuits bread and bully beef. I don't like the possey of our bivouac. It is in a diagonal line behind the church and Fritz will range on the church and we will get the back lash from his shells.

Soon we moved on picking up our guides and that night we dug a couple of beautifully Strong Posts a la text book. We dug all night and had Sampson and Jacobs taken away as casualties. Occasionally a small shell would come our way but they mostly crashed in Strazeele or further back still.

Looking down the dip, Fletre could be seen burning gaily; it was such a pretty village and our Divisional HQ used to be there. I nearly fired on some French soldiers on our left but fortunately discovered their nationality in time. We are pleased to see them for so far the 1st Battalion has never yet fought alongside them.

Wounded

Hit By Shell

UNIT.	On Establishment. Off.	O.R.	Tot.	Hrs.	Attached. Off.	O.R.	Tot.	Hrs.	R E M A R K S.
RETURN NO. 1.			DAILY STRENGTH.				DATE. 16...4...1918.		
Bde. H.Q.	8	19	27	18	3	116	119	42	
1st. Bn.	39	675	714	54	1	6	7	9	*Joined - Capt J McCusker 1%/18 1%-AWL Gone - Capt H Symonds. Ring. 1/Bn Champion 18/wd - Killed 1 An M - Jacobs - wd. 1 On Command. 9 71*
2nd. Bn.	45	757	802	53	1	3	4	9	*Evac - 1 Shellfire, 1 missing 1wd 1 HD wd*
3rd. Bn.	41	679	720	44	1	9	10	8	*Joined - 5 %&x missing Gone - 1 AWL 8 Killed 1 7& 4 CHS Champion killed. 19 wd 1 OC. 1 HD Killed. 1 OC 1wd 1 HD evacuated*
4th. Bn.	32	748	780	55	2	2	4		*Joined - 2 AWL 2 lempst Camp Gone - Lt An Eichler wd 1 ance 3 wd H/H L Montague killed 3 AWL, 2 70 amb*
1st. M.G.									
1st. T.M.	3	43	46			16	16		*Gone. 1 7 amb*
2 Sig. Sec.	2	30	32	6	8	23	33	.	
TOTAL.	170	2951	3124	230	8	185	193	68	.

Brig.-General,

Commanding 1st. Australian Infantry Brigade.

First Battalion Intelligence

15.4.18

At 4 p.m. I finished my Cooks tour of the war. Stobo and I were looking around seeing our platoons were comfortable. We had been resting around the hedges of Pradelles all the morning which were occasionally being shelled when I was hit on the left leg at the shin and knocked over and turned me around the other way. How Stobo wasn't hit is beyond me. Seeing it was serious I put on my tie as a tourniquet. Hasty a'Beckett went for Doctor Symonds who whilst attending to me was hit slightly in foot . He came to see me at the Casualty Clearing Station.

It appears that HQ had been shelled out of their possey as well and were all out in the fields.

Four stretcher bearers took me at once to Borre' dressing station and an ambulance from there took me immediately to Ebblingham, the orderly watching the tourniquet on my thigh all the time. The only thing I remember is an argument between two chaps as to which station owned the tourniquet on my leg and I ventured to hope they would not take it way whilst I was needing it. So one voice said he would wait for it.

Operated on and in bed at 6pm. My next waking thoughts were in the clearing station ward where I found out that my leg had been amputated. Until the time I was operated on, I was astounded the lack of pain–my leg was just icy cold with a numbness creeping up my side but afterward the pain was quite considerable and I found I could not urinate. This was I was told, due to shock and it did not come right for few a days.

17.4.18

Moved to Etaples, admitted to St. John's Ambulance Station. Here Mrs. Vidal and Lois came to see me and overweighed me with chocolates etc. even managed to bring flowers.

17.4.18

Art killed at Strazeele. His body never recovered from the mud. [His memorial at Villers Bretonneaux. Ed.]

Lieut Arthur 'Art' Felton

19.4.18

At 1 a.m. bitterly cold I was carried 1½ miles to railway station, all in pitch darkness, no lights or matches allowed owing to Fritz planes being over, and it was found that there was no room on the train for me so was wheeled back. The train was full of gas cases which are more serious than wounded soldiers.

21.4.18

I was wheeled to the train and had a good trip to Calais. Before we left crowds of English ladies came to see us, asking was there anything we wanted, could they send telegrams etc., had we any friends in England etc. They couldn't have been kinder. Here German prisoners carried the stretchers on to a boat, I asked them not to drop me and in perfect English one said *No fear of that Aussie* The stretchers were lowered down onto a sliding ramp and I slid gently down between decks and into a bunk.

We left at 12.30 mid-day but I do not remember the trip across or the ambulance train to London but I do remember the crowds waiting outside the Railway Station who cheered so much. The Ambulance drivers and bearers who were all women and so careful that soon I was admitted to No 3 General Hospital Wandsworth London and felt at home among so many

A.I.F. men. That night I begged them not to dress my leg but let me sleep, which they kindly did—only too pleased I think, as our ward contained 30 amputation cases.

21-30.4.18

Leg constantly in an antiseptic pack.

26.4.18

Address letters C/–W. Fisher Esq. AMP Society, 37 Thread needle St London

Dear Frank, I haven't written since the wound occurred. I've been too bad. On top of the amputation of the leg dysentery has set in and I'm too weak for words. I undergo my operation on Tuesday and am not looking forward to it at all Although I can't write often, I know you will continue to do so, I have a fine 10 page letter of yours before me.

I can't write Pal, I'm in too much pain. I'll probably see you about Xmas

Cheerio love from old Pal Ben

30.4.18

I was not issued any breakfast and this was the first intimation that I was to have another operation and questioning the sister I found it was so. At 10 am all the boys waved goodbye and off I went. They cheered me up by saying that the doctors often took off the wrong leg or that I really should have my appendix done at the same time etc. The two doctors are Sir Sampson Hanley and Lieut. Bell, an American.

Next day I was sick of course, but I had very little pain as compared to the week before and I went ahead wonderfully. In ten days I was out of bed pottering about on crutches and seeing my friends. Shannon, Richards, and Hamilton are here so we made a 4 at cards and passed the hours away. Captain Page of the Trench Mortars is here, and he is wheeled everywhere in a reed hamper on wheels.

8.5.18

Miss Stobo came to see me; she is an Aunt to Lieut. Stobo and lives in London.

9.5.18

Dr. Thyne, brother to Mrs. Andrew Reid came to see me, he is very jolly and asked me to look him up when discharged. Wrote to Claire Bridges re death of poor old Art Felton [Was she the girl he became engaged too? Ed.]. Major Scott came to see me.

10.5.18

Had a letter from Colonel Stacey which I appreciated very much.

All the way from Sussex came Claire Alfieri and the 3 Reid kiddies.

1/5/18

My Dear Champion,

I just missed you at the Field Ambulance by a few minutes. I was very sorry not to see you say good-bye for a while. You know you have my sympathy about your leg. I know that you are keeping quite cheerful over it which is everything – It's a big loss but nowadays by no means one that hinders people in the ordinary pursuits of life. I am sorry to lose you Champion as I always knew I could rely on you for difficult jobs. I want to thank you for all the good work you did do.

Everyone here is very fit. The Major is with us now. Boardman is having a spell at present, Symons is doing the job for a few days. Booth also is spelling Somerset. We've had a pretty good time since you left & things here are quite satisfactory with a few less Huns in the world than there were – Davis says so anyway.

I asked Mrs Buckley to look you up – she's a real good sort so accept any invitations she gives you if you feel inclined.

Please thank Symonds for his letter & give him the news as not much time for writing these days. Presnell should be in England I know – you may see him.

with kind regards
Yours sincerely
B. Stacey

Letter to Ben from Colonel Stacey

Brought cakes, flowers and eggs. They are such a jovial party that I promised to go down there as soon as I could. Page and wife came and brought flowers.

Head sister–Sister King, Sister Knight, Sister Humberston, Nurses Bennett, Woods, McKenzie, Wordsley.

18.5.18

Was wheeled down to the Red Cross Depot and got a pair of crutches, meeting Colonel Murdoch from Wahroonga who happened to be inspecting the office. Shannon, Richards and Hamilton in hospital.

19.5.18

Tried the crutches and was glad to go back to bed.

20, 5.18

Taken per ambulance to Horseferry Road and was booked to return to Australia. Met Prior at the Road and he fixed things up so that I can go to convalescent home on or about the 27th. Word came through to go to Moreton Gardens Convalescent Home. It is a lovely place in South Kensington, evidently someone's old home. All Australians with Aussie doctors and nurses. There are a crowd of chaps here–all knocked about, Manton, Keightley, Gray were my companions and we got a taxi and toured London.

Sister Kennedy an Australian is in charge of the hospital and as it is a two storied house with narrow stairs we have our crutches at the foot and hop the rest, catching hold of the banisters to aid us. We are a happy party with wonderful food.

They have a funny old pony and low governess sort of a carriage to take us out on drives.

A Mrs Buckley visited the home and made up a party to the Royal Auto Mobile Club for afternoon tea. Here I met Colonel Murdoch who is in charge of Australian Comforts and we had a long chat about Wahroonga and the home folks. There is always some outing catered for by Australians in England and tickets to theatres are frequently given out.

Page in wicker reed trolley

The time flew; there were some places to see; Ranelagh Gardens where we saw wonderful grounds for Polo, tennis etc. Lady Wade and the Misses Wade were there, and we had a wonderful time, ending up with *Violette* a light show at the Lyric Theatre.

23.5.18

Hospital

My dear Frank

Yesterday I received your photo and I like it the best of all. I don't think you have altered at all and although the hair is up on top and you have grown up there's still that glorious bit of fuzzy hair in front which I like so much.

I received 4 letters from you in a bunch and so had a good time reading them over and over again. You villain to remember all those things I used to say and do when first I went to Tarro. I thought you had forgotten everything but I see you still remember every detail, but I don't mind in the least, as you say accidents will happen.

Now as there is nothing to write about I'll have to fill you in with scraps. When I had leave last I had my photo taken. I sent one home and ripped up 23 of them. Most ghastly things, not me at all. And they were all wrinkled and blotched. So that is the only reason you didn't get one. I intend to have some taken and the first will be yours.

Three nights ago a glorious moon was shining so old Fritz raided London. We got the warning, every gun fired one shot and the search

Picture of Frank with note on rear:
To my dear old Ben, –with love and best wishes from Frank

lights went wibbly–wobbly across the sky and policemen blew whistles
and shouted TAKE COVER. Then all the lights went out bye bye,
The 6 'anti-aircraft guns started, and hundreds of search lights pierced
the sky trying to pick up the planes. Soon they were sighted and they
looked like silver doves in the search lights. The latest Gothas are 135
feet from tip to tip of the wings and are driven by 3 motors each, 300
horse power. Can you imagine the size of them? Just step it off on the
ground.

Well our guns got on to them and it was a very pretty sight but they
did an awful amount of damage.

So sorry Frank you have had a touch of bronchitis, do take care of yourself. Glad you intend to start at a Business College. It will be a great change for you and I think you will like it. Besides, you could keep you father's accounts.

Did I read somewhere that your dad was putting in milking machines? They would save a lot of work and fewer hands would be required but do they do the cow any harm? Cheeriho love

Ben

3.6.18

Saw me off to visit Billy Hunt–he is in at 3 Wandsworth with a badly fractured arm and is longing to go back to Australia. The A.M.P. Society was my next call to try to pay back to Mr Fisher some of his kindness to me whilst in hospital. We had lunch together at Frascattis and he took me to Berner's Hotel to visit Miss Stobo.

The bus girls are wonderful the way they help amputees into buses. As soon as you get on to the bus; they hand your crutches behind the steps and escort you to a seat. It is strange for women to be doing conductors and porter's work but they seem more efficient and careful than men.

4.6.18

I saw *A Box of Tricks* with Miss Stobo and next day *Fair and Warmer* two good shows; I find I enjoy sitting them out instead of walking about.

Our rooms and two more you cannot see in this photo.

6.6 18

Saw me booked for Australia and I was given leave until called on to report. I called on Prior at Horseferry Road and he gave me plenty of meat tickets without which it is impossible to buy meat even though in uniform. Prior also had my pay book checked up and rectified a few small errors that had crept in. Lieut Yates came to see me he is at an Overseas Training Course. I'm due to go back on first hospital boat—no more artificial legs made in England.

Harold Yates and Dimmock taken Wykeham Studio,
High Hoborn, Balham Streatham, England

Sister Kennedy of Moreton Gardens knows Sparke and Mills well as they went home on the hospital ship she was nursing on. She arranged for an orderly to carry my bags to the station and in two hours time I arrived at Battle in Sussex and was met by Mr Alfieri. Soon we were bowling along behind a spirited but diminutive pony to reach *Horn Lodge*, their home, passing the village of Catsfield enroute. These good people have two sons away; one is a staff Captain in India, the other an engineer on an eastern cable laying boat. It is only a few months ago since I was here on leave feeling very fit and active and mowing with a scythe in their oat patch. Letters being sent back to Mrs Alfieri addressed to me as undeliverable.

This part of England is like a picture, the farms are like gardens. The only marring sights are the blue—grey uniforms of German prisoners who are loaned out for farm work. At the present they are hay making. I am very pleased to see England at the present time with its woods and lanes smothered in flowers. The grasses are in all colours and whole fields of daisies and buttercups can be seen. Down in Battle near the Abbey, wild strawberries can be gathered and gypsies come around with cute little baskets of reeds full of berries. We went for many drives—these people are so good to me.

One day Claire Alfieiei took me to London and there I met Colonel Stacey by appointment with him and Lieut Symonds and and we all had lunch at Frascotti's and enjoyed the reunion. He looked well and surprised me with his non military talk when on leave. Another day I went to Leicester Square and saw *Lilac Domino* rather a funny operetta. Another day Normanhurst was the goal but never will I forget the trip to Bexhill-on-Sea. We arrived at 10 and I was wondering how I could last until 5pm on crutches all day when to my astonishment they entered a shop and hired a bath chair and attendant for the day and wheeled me about. It was a relief but I did feel a fool.

22.6.18

Said goodbye to Alfieris and reported to Horseferry Road.
A'Beckett has been hit through the jaw. Met Major Jacobs in town yesterday.

29.6.18

I reported back to Horseferry road and went back to Moreton Gardens for the night.

30.6.18

Reported to the train at Paddington Station, well laden with parcels and met Billy Hunt and Chapman. We had 4 good arms and 3 good legs between us so we managed the parcels well. Starting off from Paddington Station and taking on board some more amputees from South Hall Hospital we seemed to wander through England, at last reaching Avon mouth on the Bristol Channel and went on board the Hospital ship *Wandilla* belonging to the Adelaide Company.

HMHS Wandilla

1.7.1918

Pulled out into the Bay and I laid in a stock of food as I knew the sort of treatment I would get once we started moving. There we stopped for a week taking on more patients until we had 600 on board, quite a lot of serious ones too. We averaged 300 miles a day and of course I was violently seasick but only for one day but Billy Hunt was sick for two days.

We entered the Straits of Gibraltar, soon we anchored and I would have given a lot to go ashore at this very imposing fort, but no leave was given. Here one realises the strength of the British Empire and her Navy; dozens of wonderful war ships in harbour with snappy destroyers and the prettiest craft afloat I think, namely the motor boat flotilla, each built solely for speed. They carry a machine gun and depth charge and a few of them a single torpedo. There is one type of boat with a split stern. Through this split is lowered the torpedo. Then the boat heads for her enemy, the torpedo fires and the motor boat wheels out of the way. A depth charge is really a barrel of high explosive weighing about 150 lbs. These charges are lit by fuse and dropped overboard and when they explode either buckle up a submarine or blow some of its machinery out of action. Here also were cruisers and monitors armed with howitzers, a new arm for naval vessels. Many wonderful guns can be seen on Gibraltar. I managed to get a couple of pictures.

The King of Spain has guaranteed that on all hospital Ships the Hague Convention Rules are carried out and we are taking on board a Spanish naval officer to guarantee to any German submarine that might stop us, that we are genuine. The sea is a deep indigo colour.

10.7.18

Several mystery ships pointed out by chief officer, boats which look innocent but full of teeth.

20.7.18

Passed Tangiers with its white collection of square flat houses, looking charming from a distance. Arriving at Alexandria we were not allowed off the boat and it was as hot as Hades, no breeze stirring at all. At Gibralter all films spoilt in developing, gelatine bubbled off.

Our party is a merry one. The kindred spirits were Billy Hunt 1st Battalion who went away with me. Fred Waugh 34th Battalion, J Wilkins 20th; Joe Heslop, R Green 6th; Preston, Fred Hugo 28th; Maughan 5th Artillery; J Cassidy 42 Battalion. We were a happy party despite out disabilities.

20-22.7.18

Reached Alexandria back again in the land of Sin Sun Sand etc and pleased I am to see it again. I love Egypt. We disembarked to Colonel Whisky Dawsons orders after he came on board on 21st. The 24 hours spent on board were very hot; there was no breeze to clear out the ship and the smell of dressings etc nearly drove us crazy.

At 6.am on 22nd a hospital train pulled into the wharf and we entrained and saw the country as first class passengers. Tel-el-Kebir with its deserted camps came into view and it brought back to me many faces and names of cobbers who had camped there with me who had now gone west.

Tel el Kebir will always be the turning point where the old battalion ceased to be and where the 5th Division came into being. Suez was reached and there was the hospital ship *Kanowna*. We boarded. We knew each by now and mateship was very marked.

23.7.18

Left Suez after taking on board 40 nursing sisters who were sick. They had been to Salonika where they had a rotten time. Those who went up into the hills, nursing in the very cold weather felt the snow and ice very much—tent hospitals getting the full blast of the winds.

Concerts mainly got up by Padre McAuliff and Padre Ormes passed the evenings away and the presence of 40 Australian nurses going home on sick leave helped with their voices to make things go with a swing. We had a fancy dress carnival on board. The costumes were weird. The food on this boat is wonderful. Very uneventful voyage, all pulling together and no friction.

Souvenir menu, HMHS Wandilla.
Signed on the rear by some of Ben's
shipmates

6.8.18

We landed at Colombo intent on a good time. We have permission to sleep away from the boat and a party of us intend going up to Kandy. Hunt, Mann, Evans and myself bought some light clothing at Cargilla. We then added Green, Waugh and Heslop to our party, taking rickshaws to the sea front Galle Face Hotel with dinner in a very fine dining room and music and then we set off for Kandy by car.

Leaving for Kandy we were delayed by one member who ate a lot of bananas and then ate ice cream on top; he was pretty sick but wanted to see the place so stuck it out. The driver we had was very skilful and he put the breeze up us the way he took bends—scattering native children right and left.

The vegetation was very thick, palms, nutmegs, bananas, all cultivated. As we climbed the hills to Kandy we met tea plantations with the natives out picking the leaves and bringing them back in flat baskets. The road in many cases is built right on to the edge of the cliffs but our driver sailed merrily on until he came to one particular corner he couldn't possibly get round in one lock, so he had to back and fill until he managed it. As we wound round the hills we could often look up and see the single lined railway, one of the most remarkable engineering feats on record.

The driver killed a dog and a pig but didn't mind in the least. Arriving at Kandy we had dinner at the Queen's Hotel. A trip to the Temple of Buddha's Tooth was on the programme; it is only a stone's throw from the hotel and is marvellous. A guide picked us up and showed us around. The native clergyman still went on preaching while we went about. Their bibles are written on Papyrus rolls and one book we saw had the binding studded with gold.

There is a statue of Buddha about 2ft high made out of a single piece of rock crystal and when a candle was put behind it, it lit the whole figure up wonderfully. There is no lack of gems in this temple. There is a recumbent figure of Buddha 20ft long, also a copy of his supposed foot print 8ft long. It is said that when Buddha sat under a Boa tree a cobra came and reared itself above him and so gave him shade. There is a Boa tree in the garden estimated at 200 years old.

Billy Hunt and Ben on the Kanowna.

Officers and Nurses on the Kanowna. Ben sitting third from right (in bottom Image). Some of Ben's photos

Wandilla Kanowna Officers-
Rail: McAuliffe Chaplain Green 4tb, O'Byrne, Knigbtley, McDowell, Bluett, Cassidy, Parkes, Maugban, Temple, Mann
Form: Schulz, Hunt, Hugo, Preston, Green 6tb
Sitting: Gray, Sutherland, Wilkins, Waugb, Bedford, Champion

Around the walls are painted the Buddhist punishments. For lies a stake through their tongue, an exorbitant tax collector to be burnt alive, etc. There is a wonderful lake here converted from a mosquito swamp, it is so pretty. The rickshaw men get 8d. per hour and gather cinnamon bark or souvenirs of some sort for you as they run. You always want to pick a heavy rickshaw boy for going downhill the rickshaw sometimes lifts the boy off his feet if he is too light. The fire flies down in the gullies are pretty.

7.8.18

Went around Lady Horton's drive at 7 a.m., came back, had breakfast, then were entertained by a Fakir and snake charmer. They did tricks with snakes and sleight of hand tricks which were very clever. Reaching Colombo by car we did some shopping then off to ship and to sea.

Very brave amputees in fancy dress.

On 24 August we arrived Fremantle at 6 am. Disembarked three officers and 52 other ranks invalids. Coaling all day. Leave granted to patients and staff until 6pm. All returned with the exception of one patient. All Hotels were closed ashore. No one allowed to go to Perth. We left Fremantle for Melbourne at 9.15 pm. Light wind, cloudy and fine. North

Photos from Ben's time in Ceylon.

West swell. Received orders to test urine of all patients seven days prior to disembarkation and enter result on back of board papers.

Arrived Melbourne 1 pm on 28 August. Average speed 9.6 knots. Disembarked patients numbering 113 officers, 11 sisters and 153 other ranks for 3rd, 4th and 6th Military Districts at 2.00pm. Stretcher cases brought to deck by Ship's staff and then taken over by shore staff. We left Melbourne at 4pm for Sydney.

On 4 September we entered Sydney Heads at 6.35 am. As long as I live, I will never forget that wonderful blue harbour as we steamed up it to the cock-a-doodle-doos of the Ferry boats. Received word from the Naval Transport Office that patients would be disembarked at 1.30 pm. Lying in Watson's Bay until 12.30pm. Then went to No 1 berth and disembarked 1st and 2nd Military District invalids numbering 13 officers,

5 sisters and 204 other ranks. Stretcher cases carried ashore by ship's staff disembarking completed by 2.30pm and boat left wharf for dry deck at 2.50pm.

Dad came down the Harbour to see us in a Government Launch. He looked so well. I was very glad to get home to my people once again.

A brown photograph album was amongst Ben's memorabilia and it was thought to be his but on inspection it could not be as he was not at Salonika. It is not known who was the owner of the original photographs but The AWM has some similar but not the same.

The specific names on the photographs are taken from the back of these photographs in an unknown hand writing. The town of Salonika was 2/3rd destroyed 19.8.17. How the sister got to take photographs at Karakoy as being part of Constantinople is not known.

Hortiach is twelve miles from Salonika in the hills. It really was a forgotten part of the war and the conditions were worse than any other conditions that nurses had to endure in WW1. Online sources are *Bombs and Bandages. Nurses at War in World War 1*. Also The Diary of Lucy May Pitman is online and she served with the hospital at Salonika including No. 60 General Hospital.

The names of those on board *Kanowna* are taken from the ships indent and log, not online, at AWM. Some were listed as On Duty.

60th General Hospital Hortiach.

Another aspect of tents 60th Gen Hospital.

Nurses tents–perhaps washing tents on hill.

Perhaps toiletry tents, Hortiach, Salonika.

Sister with Bulgar Prisoners of War and tent, Salonika.

Nursing sisters coming or going with suitcase.

Tents 60th Gen Hospital Hortiach, Salonika.

Sister in snow at Hortiach

Sister in snow at Hortiach

Sisters in Kara Coy suburb of Istanbul

Sisters in Kara Coy town in civvies

Overlooking Kara Coy, an old suburb of Constantinople, Istanbul

Damaged Salonika town

White Tower, Thesalonika Macedonia.

Amputee passengers aboard the Wandilla.

ANNEX A

Homeward Bound Press Release

List A. The following have been listed for return to Australia and are actually en-route from abroad. No further information can be supplied excepting the approximate time of arrival which will be published in the press shortly before disembarkation [the rank is not specified it is 'Private'. As there are many more officers in the photo and nurses there must be another press release somewhere. Ben says about 24 officers on board. And total 514 patients. These listed below:]

Champion Lieut. B.W.; Chapman Lieut. W.S.B: Gray Lieut. J.; Green 2/ Lt E.P.: Hunt 2/Lt J.W.; Maughan Lieut. C.W.R; O'Byrne Lieut. G.; Payne 2/ Lt W.R.; Temple Lieut. W.A.; Waugh Lieut. F.M. [MC]; Wilkins Lieut. J.E.; Brownlow Staff Nurse; Hutton Sister M.A.; Murrell Staff Nurse E.E.; Seahill Staff nurse A.C.: [or Scahill]

McAuliffe was the Chaplain Captain: Staff Nurse R.M. Doubleday: Matron J. Murphy; Staff Nurse OCE Campbell: Sister M E McKenzie [many other names mentioned but no ranks attached so presumably privates and if nurses no rank]

The names below from ships manifest in order to try to identify the amputees in the photos that Ben took. These names are only possibilities.

CARNIE Robert Alex, Driver, 6th Rfts. 6th L.H. to 15 F.A. Bde, No 1012.

Born Aberdeen, mother Aberdeen. enlisted Liverpool 6.2.15. farm labourer, aged 25 years. Description 5.6 'fair complexion, blue eyes, brown hair. Wounded 30.12.16 Flers, shattering legs amputated, same day field. Discharge 23.3.19. Died 1958 late of Lindfield. Amp R leg 3 'below knee, Left leg lower third above ankle. Supplied with two legs

BARR Reginald Wallace, Pte, 12 Rfts. 23 Bn, . Enlist 7.2.16. aged 24, property salesman, married with 1 child. Wife of St Kilda Vic. Description: 5.8 'fresh complexion, grey eyes, brown hair. Wounded 5.11.16 France, Rouen Hospital to London 5th General. GSW thighs both leg amp thighs, Discharge 3 M.D. 8.10.18. Died 26 Sept 1951. No 4656

CROUCHER Hamilton Andrew, Pte, 2nd Rfts. 56 Bn, No 1634 enlist 1.2.16, aged 20, labourer of Canowindra NSW. Description: 5.10 '(very large chest) fresh complexion. blue eyes, light brown hair. Scar on right side of nose. 22.5.17 Wounded sent to Rouen Hospital then to Tooting Military Hospital. GSW amp both legs. Discharged 25.3.19. Married 1919. 1946 living in Bondi. Died 1962

LANE Robert Allen, Pte, No. 7288 24Rfts 15 Bn. Enlist 27.10.14 aged 22, saddler, mother of Longreach. Description: 5.91/2 'aged 22, chest 34 ', dark complex., brown eyes, brown hair, Wounded 1.10.14 whilst sick in St Omer Hospital (53rd General Hospital) hostile aircraft bombed hospital. Amp L foot and part R foot with left GSW L eye and buttock. Died 1953.

ANNEX B

Ships log: Of the 453 invalids embarked at Suez the vast majority were convalescent. The only serious cases being three TB, two spine cases and a few septic wounds. The majority of the cases with septic wounds did very well indeed and most of the wounds had healed by the time the boat reached Australia.

Two of the Tubercular cases developed pneumonia and were landed at Fremantle. The heat in Red and Arabian Seas was very trying for the patients and staff. It was thought at least two men would die from heat. Fortunately, cooler weather was experienced after passing Socotra and these men recovered. It is thought that the heat in the above-mentioned places during mid-summer is too severe. It might be better to either delay serious cases in England or send them home via the Cape.

In the tropics men are allowed to sleep on deck. We indeed were very fortunate in having no deaths between Suez and Sydney. Twenty-one operations were performed, mostly for the removal of sequester or foreign bodies causing trouble. The anaesthetics employed in all cases being open, ether was most satisfactory. All these cases did well after operations.

About half of the cases embarked at Suez as cot cases and about half of them had recovered to such an extent on reaching Australia as to be fit for leave. There was only one Masseur on the staff and he could not do the whole of the work thoroughly. Those urgently needing massage received it two or three times a week.

An increase in the number of Masseurs would be of very great benefit to men during the long voyage from England to Australia. Amusements and concerts were held regularly three or more being held each week. During the day the usual deck games were played by those patients who were fit. Deck golf was played by officers. This game was very popular amongst them but owing to the large numbers there were insufficient deck space for the other ranks to play this game. The food was good, but as usual, owing to the monotony of the ship life, some of the invalids became tired of it, but there were wonderfully few complaints.

Ku-ring-gai Shire Repatriation Committee
Wahroonga Branch

To
Lieutenant Ben Champion
Australian Imperial Forces

The Members of the Wahroonga Branch of the Ku-ring-gai Shire Repatriation Committee desire, on behalf of the Residents of the Wahroonga District, to extend to you a very warm welcome on your return to Australia, after having fought in the service of the Empire in the great War which is now being waged.

It has always been a source of pride to the Residents of this District that Wahroonga has been so worthily represented in the Empire's fighting forces, and it is with very great pleasure that the Committee welcome you back, now that you have played your part in this great struggle.

Dated at Wahroonga this 7th day of September One thousand nine hundred and eighteen.

W. A. Parker.
President

J. D. McLeod
Secretary

B. Allen
Treasurer

Home

Jura 12.9.18

Dear Frank

Reported to Hospital yesterday morning and everything in the garden is lovely. Leg specialist, Colonel Gordon Craig said my leg is in good condition and wanted no more treatment or operation. Seeing him in a good *bate* I asked for leave in a kind of sort of a way. He said *Well Champion you know I cannot give you much* (I expected only a few days at most)–*but would a month suit you*. I nearly fainted, thanked him and got out of his sight for fear he would alter it.

So you see I can now accept your mothers kind invitation and spend a week with the royal family at *Oaklands*.

I have a Battalion reunion dinner on Tuesday and might come on Wednesday, but will let you know later on. Drop me a line soon won't you.

Last night I went to see Grandmother, 85 years old and looks like living 20 more. She is a marvellous old lady. [Dunman married Champion, now Cottam]

My kit came home and since then I have been wading through clothes trying to find out what I have and what I have not. Will you let me know if Wednesday is convenient?

Lousia Dunman

love Ben

Jura 10.11.18

Dear Frank

I arrived safely being met by mother at Hornsby. Had a good chat to Chaplain Mackenzie on the way down. That is a great train, its the quickest trip I've made. Found all your letters on my arrival, 6 in all and one 14 page one. I thought you said you could not write long letters, anyhow this was the one I wanted, mentioning all about my leg and saying you didn't mind. There was also a letter from Mrs Bridges, she wanted me to run up to see her, dated day before I left England.

Mother remarked how well and brown I looked and said your treatment must be very good, of course I vouched for it. There is nothing I can speak about as I left you only yesterday.

Gertrude is in bed with a septic ankle she kicked it and the dye from her stockings got into it.

Jura
Saturday 11.11.18

Dear Franc,

Reported to Hospital yesterday, didn't produce my pass so that they didn't even know I was late a day. Deferred for one month then to the

Niland family at Oaklands. Back: Kitty, Claire, Ben, Frank. Front: Ruth, Mary, Billy Nielson,
Mrs Niland.

dentist. He did my 2 front teeth, made a good match and a couple at the
back so that finishes the lot with exception of polishing the fillings on
Tuesday.

In the afternoon I went to the leg factory and they made apologies
of course and said the wood was still wet and hadn't made the leg. I
could have shot them but said nothing aloud as they have the precaution
of having a lady typist in the office. They will ring me up at the end of
the week. Nice sort of blighters aren't they.

On Friday morning a number of brides came in. Rum looking lot,
afraid some of the chaps will be disappointed how they look under
Australian skies. There are some tales going about, don't believe them
of course but I'll tell you as I heard them.

1. One girl, very lonely, was asked her name. She said Mrs
Anthony Hordern [Sydney's largest department store and once the
largest in the world–Ed.] Of course no husband was there to meet her.
Some Bill Jim had evidently married her taking the name of Horden
when he married her.

2 Another lonely girl said her husband had a sheep station 2
miles from Sydney. The name of the place was Redfern–afraid she is
disappointed too. I don't belive the yarns at all.

I was all shaken up last night from the dentist so excuse last nights note. I chased Edie over to get the post this afternoon as no mail delivered on Saturday afternoon, as she came in she said *It's alright she says YES* I don't know what Edie means do you. We all enjoyed those chocs. I gave Gertrude her present from Mrs Niland and she is writing to her. Rupe Bergelin is going up to his place 1570 acres, 18 miles out of Tamworth. It is called *Bective* He is going in for sheep and a farm. His house will be a tarpaulin for quite a long while. In 6 months time, then he is coming down for Gertrude. He and his chum have 2 places adjoining and are running it as a partnership. Don't you know somebody at Tamworth?

Mary Murdoch didn't tell her people she was engaged, she just cabled *Off the shelf* so they were very worried thinking she was married until Geoff cabled out *Engaged to Mary* to his people. Bruce Rainsford calls on me tomorrow night. How are the cows etc doing and does Ruth still milk them? I suffered no ill effects from her cake–that tiny portion I ate could not hurt me. I was so sorry to have missed you this morning, but what were you doing in town? You must be feeling better and have more energy . Keep on with the Clements Tonic. It was doing you good I'm certain. We had a heavy thunderstorm in Wahroonga today, plenty of thunder and only a thimble full of rain.

I'm so sorry old girl I missed you on the phone this morning. I went out for a walk with Tom. We ate a lot of plums. I couldn't eat any lunch. I haven't got Ruth's garter but any old one, 1 yard in diameter would do her. This ink is the limit. Greasy watery and I don't know what. It has sharks in it too (debris in the ink-Ed.).

Father, Marjorie have been looking for a house in Manly today and they are not back yet. Hope they get one. Marjorie is keen on going. Prices are very high there. No more news, Love nice old thing.

Ben.

PEACE

After this, the divison was withdrawn from the line. They would take no further part in the fighting, having lost 677 men in their final battle. In early October, the rest of the Australian Corps, severely depleted due to heavy casualties and falling enlistments in Australia, was also withdrawn upon a request made by Prime Minister Billy Hughes, to re-organise in preparation for further operations. On 11 November, an armistice came into effect, and as hostilities came to an end, the division's personnel were slowly repatriated back to Australia for demobilisation and discharge. This was completed by 23 March 1919, when the division was disbanded. Throughout the course of the war, the division suffered lost, around 15, 000 men killed, and 35, 000 wounded, out of 80, 000 men that served in its ranks.

Jura Stuart St Wahroonga
12.11.18

Dear Frank,

This morning no letter turned up but I'm hoping one will appear this afternoon. *We had great news at 8pm last night and we nearly went dotty. Father, Marjorie, Dot, Tom and myself started parading Wahroonga streets* and after that quite a number of people came out. I whistled so hard, nearly blew out my teeth. Marjorie took out our potato tin and mother's porridge ladle. Dot had a copper bowl. We made an unholy row. I didn't know grown-ups could be so skittish. Dr Read and wife and kiddies roused on dozens of people out of bed at late hour last night. They wouldn't join in the triumphant procession as he called it. They were counted out (Mrs Read's brother KIA).

About 10 boys on bikes riding along with an empty kerosene tin trailing behind, kicked up dust and a row. But isn't the news glorious. Newcastle will be riotious today-would like to see it.

Reported out to hospital yesterday and found out they couldn't do anything for me for one month but have to see Dr Gordon Cráig on Wednesday morning. I'm going to try to work him to fix me up straight away. If he can't, mother and I going down to Melbourne for a little while.

Are you still milking? I do hope you have more labour because you become so tired and have you to get over to meet the girls at the train in the night time?

Young Jeannie was up last Sunday. She is a little character. A few days before, Mother, Vera and Jeannie were in a tram (This is only funny) When Jean said to Vera *Mummie has oo your garters on?* She said it out loudly and everyone inside the car heard it. Vera didn't answer, then Jean turned to Mother and said *Gran has Mummy got her garters on.* Vera said she didn't know which way to look. Jean has a wonderful imagination, she is always telling yarns. One day Mother was out picking beans Jean said *Gran, some people stick on beans with glue* Mother said they didn't but Jean knew better she said *Oh yes they do, they English they silly people.* No one had told her anything about the English at all.

I am going to a social tonight to farewell some chaps off to the war. Sounds funny after the war has stopped doesn't it? Wonder will they go or not. Plenty of butcher birds about so I'm busy mocking them.

Dot has just come home from school. Public Schools closed. Boys in the train basted everyone with throw-down crackers. Pubs are closed. It is of no use you going into town for a drink. Chaps in Newcastle will be dry wont they? I bet Shiny Buttons is not dry though. He is a marvel at getting liquor.

Mother thanks Mrs Niland for those eggs. Only one was cracked, all the rest were ok and I don't think any have chickens in so far anyway. Marjories examinations go on just the same. It will probably be a public holiday tomorrow Wednesday. Mr Murdoch will be home today he is ill. This was the man who visited me in England. He is Red Cross Commissioner (for Australia in England) I know why I didn't get a letter, you have been too busy milking and meeting the girls. Never mind Bon, it can't go on long. Mr N. is sure to be fixed up with some people before long. Gertrude is still away from work with her ankle, so silly of her to kick it. Don't suppose she could stop the dye getting in it though. No more news

Love Ben

Little Girl : " Oh, mummy, do look at this funny
man ; he's got his eyebrows in the wrong place ! "
Do I look. LIKE THIS YeT.

Wahroonga
Saturday 16.11.18

Dear Frank

What a miserable conversation we have just had. I'm certain the girl did not give us 2 minutes. I heard beautifully but I could tell that you could not.

Now, as you did not hear properly I repeat–Last Wednesday I went out to the hospital to see Dr Craig. Well it was a holiday so after waiting all day he did not turn up and I've to go again next Wednesday. I'm not sure what he'll say but I want to be fixed up. If he gives me 3 weeks leave I'll go over to Melbourne to see my cousins as I promised and take Mother for a trip. In that 14 page letter from you I received a photograph of the family, Didie and Norma Davidson. All lying down and I want to get in a similar one when I get up once more to see you. How did you get on when the tyre broke. Did you come home on the frame or did you tie the tyre round again. I am so glad you now have some help. I hated to see you work the way you had too. Especially wood, horses and milking. Loch has become tame rather quickly hasn't he?

New arrivals in our house, a very patriotic cat, 2 khaki and 2 ginger kittens. Gee I'm sorry about you wasting 1/5 over that bit of a talk. Letters are more satisfactory. Don't worry Frank the moment I see my way clear I'll come up. Remember we had not seen each other for 3 ½ years. I've done all my business this last week.

Is this soldier man of yours handy with tools etc I'm so glad you don't have to get up so early to light the fire. I suppose Anderson and Mrs A, and Joe milk now. Then if Amy comes along you will be a bloated aristocrat with no work to do only make dresses for yourself. What about that blue dress? Have you finished it yet and what about the silk skirt?

Gertrude and myself went to town on Thursday to do some shopping She wanted a skirt so took me up into Davy Jones skirt department. I sat down before I noticed ladies slipping off skirts and trying on others, naturally I felt awfully awkward and wanted to fall through the floor. G was only ½ hour–bought a white gabardine skirt 27/6 thats all. Her foot is much better, the hole seems to have dried up She is going back to work on Monday. Father is working in the garden–he looks comfortable in his old clothes. Re; that priest and confession you wrote to me about and the hand. I'd tell I'm sure. Will you remember?

Hope you feel ok. I'll never forget this afternoon and the way you said *and what will I do all that time* Never mind Pal . Cheerio Received your mothers note in yours this morning Please remember me to all the family. Love Ben, Write again soon, won't you

Ben

10.12.18

Dear Frank,

Had a pleasant breezy trip down in the train and Dorothy met me at Wahroonga and so carried the suit case home for me. I grinned all the way down in the train how we had Clark, signal man and Porter chasing us up with tickets. Clarke looked like a monkey and am certain he had a pain through hopping up and down off the station. What do you think of that chap hopping through the window after the train had started? Cute wasn't it. Just the old spirit over again. It was not a question of think before you leap.

Reported to hospital and have a months leave, but during that time have to attend the dentists and get leg fitted. They have made the caste and towards the end of next week, I hope to put on the leg even if for a trail run up and down the leg factory workshop. Expecting a note from you tomorrow.

Several chaps just returned that I knew with lots of news from the Battalion. They say that all the 1914 men will have left France by Xmas.

Did your father see the cartoon on Archbishop Kelly in the *Sun*. it is not as good as his idea. Lindsay is away. I rang him up to tell him about the cartoon but as he was away nothing doing. Its dreadful out on crutches today. Won't it be great when I get my leg and won't I be disappointed if I can't walk properly. I hope I'll be able to ride next time I come up then Joe will be looking for the paddle I'm thinking.

Hope Ruth gets through. Sadly miss your pleasant company all today. I went to bed at 8 last night, nothing to do, no sitting on the verandah hitting mosquitoes. Now dont forget your TONIC when I'm away. No more news. Love Ben

---

Jura
Sunday 15.12.18 2.30pm

My dear Frank,

I was very energetic yesterday. Father, Mother and I built what Ma calls a gazyboo to grow vines over. The sides are made of trellis and the roof rising to a point covered with wire netting. This we hope in time to be covered with passion fruit vines. I had a job nailing the top pieces together but managed it in the very fine misty rain which was falling. I would not go inside as it was such a long time since I felt rain. Have you had any rain at all yet? Mother has

Early dentist's pedal drill—Ben had one he turned into a potter's wheel

not yet made any cakes or pudding. Who stoned all the raisins at *Oaklands*?

Just think of me on Tuesday at 11.30am then I'll be in the dentists hands having my face pulled about. But Wednesday afternoon will make up for it. The Governor General unveils the Wahroonga Roll of Honor. Cakes, sandwiches etc will be there and so will Yours Truly, always believe in turning up if anything to eat is to be provided. I did not go to church today. As a matter of fact, I still have on my pyjamas under my pants and coat. Just about the height of laziness. Vera, Baby and Jean are up today. Jean is just as funny as ever and I haven't forgotten your photo of her yet but can't seem to raise one. [Brother Bert's wife and children - Ed.]

Tom and Dot have gone out into the bush looking for Christmas Bush and Bells. I used to be the great bell gatherer but mafish now. You did not mention your cold in your last letter. When did you get the letter I posted on Thursday evening. Am going to trellis in the front verandah as soon as the timber arrives. I will post the order this day some time, then Gertrude and Rupe will be able to sit there sometimes instead of squashing Dorothy's bed. It will give me something to do also. Do come to town after Xmas Frank, I didn't give you a very nice time last when you came down and want to made amends. I can't make up anymore news so will close with fondest love

Your Ben,

I miss sitting out watching the lights of Newcastle.

Wednesday 18.12.18

Dear Franc.

I'm sorry I haven't written since Sunday. I've been busy. I only had one tooth done on Tuesday and go again on Saturday. All this morning I've been trellising in the front verandah and nearly have it done. It's hard work but I had Dot and Tom holding timber and doing odd jobs for me.

This afternoon was a Gala one for Wahroonga. The Governor General came along to unveil the Honor Roll of Wahroonga. It is a huge affair on marble and will be set in that lobby above the station steps. Dr Pockly gave a magnificent speech and it must have cost him something to make it as he has lost his two sons. Then the Governor replied and Thompson our member moved a vote of thanks. I was introduced to the Governor and shook hands with him so now I won't wash my hands for sometime so as not to wash off his grip. I said *Hullo Ronnie* and he said *Sorry Champ* just like Goolah did. Met Feltons and Byrnes at the unveiling this afternoon, all quite well and wished to be remembered to you. Didie wasn't there. Mr Felton only came home from the Northern

Originally at Wahroonga Station but moved in 1925 as above

Dr Pockley's sons, Capt Brien Colden Antill Pockley, AMC left and LT John Graham Antill Pockley right. AWM

Rivers this morning he looks very well. Royal Fambly prying around when Ma and Pa come home with possible christmas parcels.

Town absolutely packed, quite a number of country people about. Tell them by their hats. Been as hot as the hobs of H....here in town and I've envied the girls their white and light things. Transparent blouses etc. Such a lot of young people around town. Going to the Barracks yesterday Lilias Strang sat next to me and I was absolutely ashamed of her. The gammy talk *How exquisite, Really, How drastic,* I was glad when she got out at Flinders St. Another disappointment about the leg. The factory is closing for a fortnight at Christmas and I have to go on the 20.1.19. Beasts arent they.

Frank Old Pal. I received a 16 page letter from you yesterday, returned from the front, written in June. I suppose it will be your last to be returned.

Bruce Rainsford will come home on Boxing Day or there abouts. Millington, a chap we used to call *billy goat* at school came home last Sunday. He is a petty officer on the *Australia* looks well. As skinny as a lamp post when he went away now 6'2 'and about 13 stone. The Navy is the place for training.

The Governor speaks as if he had a plum stone in his mouth but is very nice and cheerful. Talking of plum stones, we have no fruit,

ripe soon. How are your grapes any riper? Who STONED the
raisins ? Liked to have seen you chasing the fires [grass] with a wet
bag. I take it you didn't have on any crepe de chene dress at the time.

Marjorie plays beautifully although she is my sister I say it. [She
became a music teacher at High Schools] Everyone here is busy
sewing. I marked out the scolloping on a night dress for Gertrude
the other night with a sixpence as a marker. No extravagant transfers
in this house. Varnished the drawing room floor the other day looks-
o.k. Parts of varnish an awful price now.

Had our bath re enameled. You can't have first bath this time
unless you come down *toute suite* as I'd like you to do. Going to
a Soldiers dinner on Friday night with Gertrude, Waugh, Hunt,
Green, Bergelin given by the Womens Clerical Union of Sydney.
Believe they have made it up to give me a 'Cupie '[hat] from the
Christmas Tree but I'm going to ask for an order for a civilian suit.
One for ten pound will do. Much love from me and am waiting 'till I
can see you so do come to town.

Ben

———

                                               ??? Dec 1918
                                               Thursday night

My dear Frank,

I received your letter this afternoon and am very sorry you cannot
behave yourself. If you persist in getting colds I'll have to come and keep
you warm the whole time. Are you going to Bessie Nichols on Saturday?

All day we have had Mrs Hesketh up here, when her son was killed,
I sent all particulars to her so she came along to see me. She is a cheerful
old lady. Since her boy was killed her husband met with an accident
[on the railway] and died also. But she is a cheery old soul and a great
patriotic worker.

Last night I went to a concert in our church given by the choir of
Sunday School children. Had a very enjoyable time, not a bit stiff. A
little boy aged 8 called *Jimmy* had such a small piping voice. On Tuesday
after I posted your letter I heard someone call to me when I was in

Fred Murchison Waugh

Pitt Street and Bert Carroll bailed me up. I had quite a long talk about everything including you then he had to rush off to Katoomba. We parted but before we did so we made it up to come to Tarro together before the University vacation ended.

Met Waugh at the leg factory. His artificial leg is 2 inches too long and they are cutting off a piece each day. My leg will be a different style to his. His leg is all wood, mine is wood and leather making it lighter because I take end bearing and he only takes side bearing.
Sent my watch to the clock hospital and expect to get it when I go to the dentist on 17th. Think of me that day, 13 to do [were Ben's teeth damaged in Gallipoli? Ed.], Oh Golly. So Didie thinks I live at Tarro, well who cares, I don't, so long as you ask me to come along.

All nice roses are finished at the station and as we are forbidden to use spinklers our garden is like an Irishman who wants a drink—dry.

Both Harold and Ray Kershaw are on their way back to Australia. Fred Thompson, a friend of the Austin girls is only a fortnight away. They are hard at work trying to fix his garden up which has not been touched since he went away in August '14.

Mother made some raspberry syrup. Tom and I found it to our tastes and 1/3 is gone. Mum doesn't know it yet. I dreamt that Ruth passed her exam and got Honours in Geography and Cooking. Marjorie passed her yearly exam, averaged B for the year.

Frank have you been keeping on with your Tonic? Do get strong. Father is terribly disgusted with the members of the Board. After beating Holman they resigned, 2 to go out on pensions and 1, Mr Taylor is to be an inspector. No rise for Dad.

Glad to hear you finished your blue dress, I knew you would as soon as you felt fit and I was out of the road. Give my love to all at *Oaklands* including Torsch and Bluie (dogs). Love from

Your Ben

Tuesday 14.1.19

Dear Franc,

I went to the Dentist this morning for last time and my mouth is terribly sore. He burnt the top of teeth around the gum with nitrate of silver and they are black you know, but it will soon work off.

We received a letter from your Mother today, she finds she cannot visit us this time. We would have liked her to come. Saw Mrs Felton today on the wharf with Noel. He is growing every day. Didie will be going up to *Tarro* on 24th Mrs Felton said. Tomorrow all the Royal Family with exception of Edie and myself are going to Manly to stay for 3 weeks. Father has taken 3 weeks holiday.

Hope they have good weather all the time. Mums says she is going in the surf but Gertrude and I bet her a new table cloth she won't. When they get settled down I'm going. The family have a nice cottage at Manly, small you know. Of course Dorothy and Tom will have to come back to Wahroonga in a fortnights time for school. Edie doesnt want to go as she booked for Tugerrah with a friend in one months time. Gertrude sent a bubble pipe to a little boy she knows in the country. His mother wrote to say he hadn't used it yet as they'were so short of water, carting it 5 miles in barrels. That is at Binda near Crookwell.

Garden is absolutely dreadful, have you had any rain yet? Is Belmont home yet? Did Joe ride in the race at Hexham? I missed your letter this week so far. Bruce Rainsford came to see me last Sunday, he looks well. His sister has just gone into Sydney Hospital as a nurse probationer. He says things have changed a good deal there. They have men to do the scrubbing etc if it is true, it is a change to the usual run of things. She waited 8 months to join.

Tom (aged 11) is going to get a spanking in a few minutes. A friend called to see him on a horse and Tom had no boots or socks on and is very untidy and he has gone down near the station so Dad is sure to see him. Did you do much shopping last Saturday morning? I've been sleeping out last few nights on the front verandah And can watch the people going by although they cannot see me at all. I see many little episodes in the moonlight. Miss you quite a lot. Suppose as soon as they go to Manly it will rain. Delaney still down at the farm? We are sorry your mother cannot visit us but it is a long way.

No more news old girl,

love Ben

<hr />

Sunday night 19.1.19

Dear Frank,

We have had awful thunder storm today, absolutely dreadful. Thunder and lightning crashed and shook and then we had a heavy downpour which we needed very badly. Mother came up yesterday from Manly to take some clothes down. Father is liking the place more now than he did at first and Tom parboiled a delicate *vieux rose* shade simply revels in the surf. We are such a small household here. Place seems strangely quiet and deserted. This note is going per your mother tomorrow. Freddy Waugh rang me up last night. He will have his woody towards end of this week. Hope the beggars don't disappoint me on Wednesday, that is all I am wishing. You know I've a beautiful flow of Australian language and am afraid I might let some of it loose if the leg is not ready. My patience has just about gone.

Quite a lot of fruit fly is in our peaches and there is a monkey of an opossum who takes a nibble out of several peaches then off he goes on to the plum tree. He lives in our roof. Mother sees him some times and when she flashes a light on him he hardly bothers to move. Waugh paid 9 pounds for his best blue serge suit. What do you think of that Julie? This beggar can't afford it. Edie started off this afternoon, all in white, shoes as well. Halfway to the station, down came the rain in bucket fulls and Edie returned home, her shoes wet through and awfully mucky. She did not have her Sunday class at Chatswood. More letters from Keith, just as skimpy as usual. No news at all. Read fine book *Michael O'Halloran* by Gene Stratton Porter. It is worth getting. You would like it. Same style as *Girl of the Limberlost*

Beach Attire : Marjorie, Keith, Mrs Champion and Dot with Tom in front

There is a friend of ours, a Miss Barling, she is going to Africa as a missionary. Her family last Saturday went to see her off. At midday the wharf labourers downed tools and won't work over time and ½ hour more work and she would have been loaded. Now they have to wait until Monday. The boat could have been 1 ½ days on the way. Talk about lazy scalliwags. Too much money they have. I'm sleeping out in Dot's bed, side verandah, icy fresh in the morning and my skin seems too tough for skeeters. Days are rolling by–must go to work soon. Great excitement, cat has caught a mouse and has given it to the kitten to play with. The kitten is growling like it's mother. Geoff Johnson has his Commission. He cabled his people yesterday. Went to Church this morning, crowded The organ was played extra well and I enjoyed it. Gertrude was with me. I'm going down to Manly perhaps sometime this week. No more news, love Ben

Inside the old Church as Ben and his family knew it. Source *100 years.*

Sunday night and Gertrude is making preserves. Do you think she will go to Heaven?–have a small boil on my neck. No *bon* at all. Hope you are well and over your cold.

B

22.1.19 *Jura* Wednesday afternoon

Dear Franc,

On Monday, Tuesday and this morning I thought I had been deserted but this afternoon along came 2 big letters from you and I can see by the dates that the wretched post is to blame. The letter posted on Friday was posted at a place called TOMAGO, is that anywhere near you? I will enclose the post mark so that you will understand.

Hope Claire gave you a letter on Monday night? Of course, I've been on pins and needles awaiting your reply as to whether you would care to come to Manly or not. Glad you would like to come. Now to exert all your influence so as to come and let me know at ONCE yes or not.

I'm so sorry abut Creamy and hope you catch the man who did it. Do you suspect anyone at all? If you feel sure but cannot prove it, then let me deal with him somehow or other. I'm sorry because I know what a lot of comfort you get out of him and saving of shoe leather.

(Tuesday) Yesterday I went to Manly and had a good day in the baths. I can swim well, not so fast of course as before but can get along at a fair pace, any stroke at all too. There is a lot of kick left in this one leg of mine. It was glorious in the water yesterday. Marjorie and Dot go in, so bring a costume if possible. Do come, I'll be bitterly disappointed if you can't. Father will teach you how to swim if you like. If Mary wants to know how I manage to get over the stones on Newcastle beach, tell her it would have to be something big to stop me when you come along.

A little chum of Dorothys has been staying with them and I brought her home. Of course we missed the 8.30 boat so had to wait a whole hour on the Point Station. Fortunately Jean (Miss) Austin came along so she told me all about Vic and the influenza. His boat had 245 cases aboard at Durban and 60 died. Vic got over his lot and is now well and in England.

Do you remember me talking of Alick McDonald, well he is home, bullet through palm of hand. Can't close his hand and he is a carpenter too, rather awkward for his trade so he intends to go in for architectural drawing.

Last night before I came home, Edie was disturbed by a noise and going to see what it was, found a baby flying fox so I gassed it when I came home. They are such a pest. The orchards around here have been spoilt this year by them. But they are so pretty. The body 3 'long has fur and the head is like a mouse. The wings attached to legs and body when spread out cover 12 'easily. We are keeping it to show Mother.

The schools having gone back and the trains are crowded with the little skalliwags and their talk is deafening. I hate to see them passing from carriage to carriage as I'm frightened they might fall.

I'm not surprised at Ruth's arm being sore. The elbow is a nasty place to graze. The Manly house is 3 minutes from the surf but 10 minutes from the wharf. Tram passes at end of street though. Bring plenty of fancy work. We can sit on the beach in chairs and watch the *World and his Wife roll bye* Some sights too. I don't think I'll let you go in the surf at all. Too many sharks even in shallow water. Look at that Askell case at Newcastle beach. I think the boy who went in after him was very plucky. it was a brave thing to do and the public ought to do something for him.

Beastly hot here today-have been in town. No news about the leg at all. Ginger Smith is home, he was in Sugar Company with Art. Now he is going to start at the University for Dentistry in March.

Met Waugh, Wilkins, Green and Hunt today. Wilkins, Hunt and Green have each had another operation and are doing well. Wilk's stump is healing. To tell you the truth I think they intend to give me my leg next Xmas as a Xmas box. I'm sick of them but nothing I can say will hurry matters on. Even Dr Gordon Craig says he cannot hurry them and as he is the boss, cocky it's needless to say I can influence them. I'm expecting news in the morning if you can come or not. Did your mother get Mums letter? I thought the girls looked very pale the day you and I saw them off. Perhaps they ate too much fruit. There are still some peaches on our trees so help us to eat them.

Love Ben

Fond remembrances to all at *Oaklands*. Have you put those letters out of sight yet. I'll pinch them If I see them next time I come up, in a few years time. There is absolutely no hope of my coming just yet awhile. I don't know when the leg people will want me. Glad your Dad says he will go to the Tarro *C of E cathedral* (Mr Niland is Roman Catholic). Fine pipe organs and singing. We have a lady in our Church who sings like Miss Vidal–no more old girl.

love Ben

Tuesday night 11.2.19

Dear Franco

Have had an awfully tiring and busy day, I'll 'splain. The reason Father wanted me back was that he wanted to see me about the University. Mr Donald Smith wants me to go there with his son Ginger. The Repatriation Dept are paying the fees, that is providing I can get a certificate from the old school to say I'm fit for the University. So I went with Dad all the way out to Petersham to see the Head Master. The school is now moved to there. Well I got the certificate but I don't know whether it is sufficient. Leaving there I went to the University and found out particulars.

All this was in the afternoon. In the morning I went out to the leg factory and have to leave my leg there tomorrow . Then to Repatriation Department, which is right around Dawes Point and there were hundreds waiting so I knew a chap and he let me in through a window and I got my annual tram pass (silver and available until Feb 1920 when I get it renewed).

Write to me and tell what you think of it. You see I'll be 26 when I get through my exams but then I'll have a degree which will give me a better social standing and will be better off all round. Only I'll be a pauper until I'm through. What do you think of it? You will be nursing. Do go and get on. But don't catch the 'flu. Mary Saunders has it at the Coast but is not too bad. Hope Mary doesn't get it. Tell her I say a prayer each night for all nurses nursing the influenza. Glad Ruth passed her exam.

I can't write any more I'm awfully worried about everything. It is such a rush, Cheerio

love Ben

Father and I have just been to see Dr Purser who is vice Chancellor of Uni. *I'se worn to a shadder*

We are swinging all the weight we can to get me in. Hope they don't tip me in the long run. Think of me all the time and pity me. Forgive me this letter–you'll understand this.

<u>Gertrude is to be married in June</u>. Post down please the tea covers as I forgot them.

18.2.19 Tuesday

Dear Franc, I gave them a surprise when I walked in last night as I was not expected to come until today. Ray Kershaw is home and is coming to see me tonight. Now I got a wretched surprise or rather disappointment when I rang about the leg. Cannot possibly get it to me before this day week. I cannot tell you how I feel about the matter after being buoyed up and excited about getting it today. The result was a sick giddy headache so have been in bed all day till 5 pm, had a bath, a much needed shave and feel a little better.

Billy Hunt is not so serious but is very bad. I'm to see him tomorrow if possible so will let you know. Wasn't it strange about Musgrave in the train. I took off my mask and said *Hows Fort Street* and he recognised me. He was very touchy about the enlisting business, turned down in '15, '16 and '17. Enlisted 3 times. His is a bad case. In 1913 you remember the small pox scare. He was vaccinated. And the lymph had a horrible germ in it which was lying dormant in the calf but when injected into him became virulent and he has been subject to horrible fits ever since. In time he expects to throw it off. He cannot transmit the disease to anyone else. What do you think of that for a horrible case, makes one a little chary of being pricked with a needle doesn't it?

Sir Herbert Maitland says it has occurred before but it only happens in 1 in every 25, 000 cases.

We had a storm today, a few points of rain. Thanks for the nice time you all gave me.

Don't forget your sewing and tell me when you go with your mother to the hospital. What happens? It is not good going in as I told you before if you don't attempt to become a proper nurse. Don't be afraid to tackle the exams. After 4 years stagnation of brain for me, I've to turn 'round and do exams which your nursing ones are only kindergarten work.

I'm writing on your letter tablet which you left behind. Every one here sends their love. Marj. sends thanks for gloves. Here comes Dad and Gertrude home from work for tea,

Love Ben

———

21.2.19

My dear Frank

I received your letter this afternoon when I came home and as Marjorie is going to meet a girl friend I will get her to post this for me. As I write, you and your mother according to your letter will be down seeing Matron McDonald about getting into a hospital. Hope you have good luck which ever hospital you want to get into. I hope you do so. I am sure your mother will make your clothes, she only says that but when the time comes you'll be ok.

Don't worry and stop being miserable over it please. Gertrude will be glad about the tea cosy. I'll let you know what she says about it. This morning's paper says the Newcastle nurses are not going to have 3 shifts, a Mr Alladyce spoke against it.

Now do you remember my last letter I said I would not have my leg for a fortnight or so, well next day, Wednesday, they told me to come on Thursday. Well Father and I went out to the Barracks in the rain and I got it. Caught a tram, came back to the Quay. Father carrying the crutches, ½ way across Customs House Square the foot turned in, the leg had twisted a little I had a fearful job to walk the rest and of course every one looked or rather stared. I didn't like it a bit. By the time Wahroonga was reached I had to hop up the steps on one leg and dangle the woody one. I caught a taxi and came home. Bottom of my stump frightfully red so have been rubbing it with methylated spirits ever since to make it hard.

Oh, I went for a medical board and was recommended for discharge. So today I went (on crutches of course) to the Barracks and am going to be paid off on Tuesday. Received my soldier medals today. The Officer I went to see was an old friend of mine at Wahroonga College when I went there. *He said you look tired and hot Champion,* 'course I didn't

COPY OF TELEGRAM FROM PREMIER TO ACTING PRIME MINISTER,
Dated 25th February, 1919.

Approximately 150 men travelling by Orsova now in quarantine North Head threaten break camp and traverse city.   Orsova definitely quarantined by Federal authority because influenza case on board on arrival and pratique refused.   Case therefore more serious than that of Argyllshire.   Responsibility of maintaining quarantine clearly Federal.   Nevertheless if soldiers attempt land in Sydney, State authorities will be obliged to arrest them.   This may lead to conflict and to very serious consequences.   As Exectuive Government of State we have to make formal application in the terms of Section 119 of Constitution to protect the citizens and public officers of this State against the domestic violence involved in such a conflict should it become unavoidable.   We venture to suggest that full instructions be sent to State Commandants in New South Wales, both military and naval, to take all necessary steps to prevent any such breach.

Signed -   Holman, Premier.
Fuller, Chief Secretary.

Copy of a telegam from the Premier of NSW to the acting Prime Minister

contradict him so he got his typist to make tea and we had it together. You know you are entitled to 7 ½ days leave for every 6 months away ie; I now receive 45 days, that is I'm not allowed to take off uniform until 5th April, but of course I'm getting into civies as soon as I feel fit enough to go into town on the leg.

I'm horribly disgusted with the leg as it gets loose and the toe swings inwards and I'm pigeon toed but I won't make much of a show of you when I go out with you. I brought home a stick from the Red Cross last Wednesday and when I was home fooling about I split it. Serves me right too. I had to buy one and it cost me 10/6, just at the time when I want cash for clothes.

Charlie Sanders, a friends of ours here is coming in by the *Berriman* and I might get in to see him. I'd like to very much as he is a good sort.

Had a letter from Shiny Buttons today. He is well and is a teetotler for 6 months (what do you think of that!) He is learning carpentry at the Tech College. He sent me one or 2 verses so I'll send them, so cheer up old girl. He hasn't an English bride but pretends he has and writes verses about her. Here are 2

My lovely Sue
Is twenty two
and I'm her constant wooer

I've courted Sue
A year or two
And ardently I sue her.

So let me bring
The wedding ring
To bind our hearts together

Her buxom form
appears more warm
as colder grows the weather.

*Send me to Blighty
if there's a chance
For I'm sick of the trenches
and weary of France

and these cursed trench mortars
and shrapnel I dread
And I want to see Blighty–before
I'm dead

*Thats what he put on his medical chart board when he was in hospital in France and he did get to Blighty.

Shiny said he couldn't find a corporal to parade him to me so wrote on the off chance that I'd forgive him. Funny isn't he? You see its a military rule that before a private can speak to an officer he must be paraded to the Officer. He cannot come up to the officer on his own. That's what Shiny Buttons meant.

I've just had to leave to go and put a saddle on Tom's bike. His broke so he took one from my old bike but couldn't put it on.

We have all been hot with a Capitol H. Am not doing more than an hour or so on leg each day as am frightened of rubbing skin off the end of leg.

I want a very long letter from you telling me all your troubles etc. What about that special letter I wanted. Have you done what I wanted about the letters and photos, theres a good sort-put them away. You write véry large and I'm wanting your letters badly.

Cheeriho, Love Ben

Did you leave your toothbrush, here a yellowish celuloid handled one. Gertrude, Mother and Marj are sewing like mad for Gertrude's wedding

Ray Kershaw has been around–looks well. He has an M.C. and very slight wound and is home and only had 3 months in France. Look at this mug.

Billy Hunt is much better. He is up and about the ward, horribly deaf though. Waugh is not going badly on his leg, so he says, but I havent seen him yet with it on. He said I was plucky to go in a tram. He went in a taxi.

25.2.19

Dear Frank,

It started raining cats and dogs and butcher boys last evening and has been doing so ever since, only hope you are getting the same to make the spuds, lucern and corn grow and also to get more milk as the rain will soak through the cow's hides.

It's a miserable day for some more soldiers to arrive as they will think Aussie is as bad as Blighty for rain, but we can do with a lot as the

An advertisement for artificial limbs circa 1919

gardens are awful dry. Stamp upside down on your latest letter. Does that mean a kiss for me or is it only accidental?

Our Asters are holding up their heads at present and our path to them and further over is flooded. We've had buckets of rain.

Tom put his fist through a pane of glass so I had to take it out and remove the putty and Mum is going to get a new pane today. My leg is not too bad–I sway a lot over to that side though–must try to remedy it. Hope the rain clears a little so I can go out to Hospital tomorrow to show it to Dr Gordon Craig who always has to see them before they are passed.

My back becomes very tired and I get a little back ache through straining with the braces to keep the leg on. There is some trouble over the *Argyleshire* men's pay so they put me off until Thursday when I will receive about 130 pounds being final settlement and deferred pay combined.

In your letter written on Saturday, you say you went to a Welcome Back to Haile. Didn't he have one before and is he having 2 welcomes. I've often lost mother in town the same way you did with your mother.

Very glad Cecil Harcourt [Frank's cousin] is coming back, one hears every day of someone else coming back and it won't be very long we hope before Keith is also back. He writes such skimpy letters– plenty of them you know but each about 8–10 lines each. Of course we can't get much news about him at all.

I'm sorry you can't get into hospital as soon as you expected because you were building so on going. I sincerely hope you won't be disappointed once you do start. It would never do to start then leave it off because certain people might say *I told you so*. Any how, more time to get your things ready if she can't take you in straight away.

I've had my leg on all day so far and it is now 3pm . It's comfortable in a sort of a way but one can never forget for a moment one has it on. I'm anxiously waiting to see Waugh on his, to see who walks the better out of the 2 of us. It wouldn't do for him to beat me.

Don't yóu think you ought to say your're sorry for thinking I had a French girl. It will hurt still until I get that and the letter I'm wanting. Tell your Dad I'll be up as soon as I feel confident I can do the trip without knocking myself up. I wouldn't want to do that becáuse it would mean days before I could go on it again. Do you understand Old Girl?

Most people think as soon as you get it you can walk on it, well that is a mistake. There is all the pain to overcome and it touches up my stump painfully sometimes. Then the leg has to get hard so as it won't chafe or blister. Then last of all there is the balance to be got. This is the hardest of the lot, as one feels awfully lopsided. Then there is the braces which support the leg, these make the shoulders chaffed and raw feeling, but I'm walking better than George Norley. Just a weeny bit.

When you see me, please don't be disappointed because those things which I've just told you have to be overcome first. The longest walk I've done is down to my piece of ground to see Kershaw. That was a strain as he wasn't in and I came back straight away.

Do answer all the queries I asked in my last letter. What about that book *Quinneys*. He is a funny character don't you think, but there is a lot of sense in him.

To PLEASE YOU I'll wear my uniform up when I come, so what will be my reward? Our house leaked last night in the verandah over Gertrude's bed and the pantry. This is the 1st wet washing day we've had since I came home in September.

Father seems worried about his work. He gets no assistance as there is no Board and so papers are piling up on their table galore. Compulsory masks might be relaxed next week. They are Beastly Things.

Delaneys been seeing you lately and how is 4 legged Belmont? I've been soaking a pair of khaki sox which went greeny in patches in a mixture of tea, coffee and iodine. Do you think that will make them a better colour?

Most people in Wahroonga don't know I've my leg. I'll give them a shock tomorrow morning won't I? No more news, love to all and yourself.

Ben

28.2.19

Dear Frank,

Hope you received my letter yesterday. Tell me, so that I will know if the letter I post here early in the evening gets to you by next afternoon mail. It is a beautiful day, not too hot yet, the ideal Sunday weather–the sort you feel you can sleep after dinner. Gertrude did not go to bed until 12 last night as she was bottling preserves (quinces) and they look fine. Now that she knows she will have to cook for a home she is bucking too and cooking very well. She says to keep her things until I come up again.

We have a great to-do yesterday. Charlie Sanders came home and I knew he was coming. The Sanders didn't tell anyone about it. So I took the liberty of ringing various heads up who lived in Wahroonga, with the result that quite a small (but very select) crowd gathered at the station to welcome him in. Cars decorated etc. Winnie Wood who lives opposite them I rang to find out the exact time his train came in. She was very excited about it, appeared so over the phone. Mary Sanders, his sister who is nursing at the Coast had 2 days off. Father and I went down to their house in the afternoon. They had an enormous cake 2 feet in diameter with a gun on top.

Charlie is in 3rd Division Artillery, transferred to that out of the 1st Light Horse with whom he served on the Peninsular. He was gassed but is ok now and they have given him 60 days leave ie: 7 ½

DAILY TELEGRAPH, TUESDAY, MAY 21, 1918.

FIGHTERS FROM BILLYARD AVENUE, WAHROONGA.

Left to right: SANDERS BROS.—Driver ALBERT K. SANDERS, wounded; Corporal C. SANDERS, M.M.; Captain ARTHUR L. RICKARD, awarded Military Cross and twice mentioned in despatches; KERSHAW BROS.—2nd-Lieutenant R. N. KERSHAW, at the front, Lieutenant-Sgt. H. G. KERSHAW, awarded Military Medal.

days for each 6 months away. His girl came along with him. She lives somewhere in the country and went to Sydney to see him in.

Have not yet replied to Shiny Buttons but will do so soon. I walked to the station on my leg and of course was standing still when I met Charlie and afterwards when he got home he asked his father where I had been wounded. A compliment to me was it not. He didn't even know Old Art had been killed.

Now I've a bone to pick with you, sorry we can't go on to Kitty's bed to do it. I'm wild with that lady who told your mother *I liked her very much* referring to that French girl. And I did show you her photo. Don't you remember the lady who had a son, a priest and he had a sister. Surely now you can remember? Didn't you want to show it to

Mademoiselle Deverne (R) and her mother.

your Father but I wouldn't let you. I'm sorry Frank that you said you didn't know that I loved her. Well I haven't loved anyone but you all this time. It was reproachfull letter and Mrs—told your mother an untruth when she said that. To make sure this morning I went through every one of my letters to Mother. I didn't say it at all but I'm not a bit surprised at Mrs—she is trying to make that this chicken was just the same as poor old Art and trying to make an excuse for him. I'll bring up her photo and see if you haven't seen it before. Now ' nuff said about it Bonny only it hurts.

Church is at 5 this afternoon, everyone masked and sitting on the lawn alongside the church. Wonder have you been? I'm not going.

Influenza pandemic, 1919
Reason for masks

A virulent worldwide influenza pandemic occurred during 1918 and 1919, in which up to 40 million people are believed to have died. The disease arrived in Australia through Victoria in early 1919, and spread to New South Wales by 27 January. By the time it ended in September that year, more than 6, 000 people had died of the disease in the State.

Leg is much more satisfactory now, end of stump is sore. I rub it with metho. Sorry you have been blushing, they need not question you in front of the girls need they? But some day, I'll be along to put them in their places. I'm wondering if you got on OK down at the hospital. You are going to nurse aren't you? Not just be a sort of go between the trained nurses and patients.

The wretches are playing tennis next door, I hate it on Sundays. Had my leg on for 2 hours yesterday. I'm still sleeping on the front verandah. It's beautiful and cool there early in the morning. There is a couple who say good bye each night at 10pm. Right opposite—awful bad taste in public.

Hope Billy Liddle doesn't count how many letters I send you. Suppose the postal people would like more boys to have girls in the country. It must run the stamp revenue up a good deal. My last letter I thought you might have to pay extra postage on–you did not though did you?

This week I'm going to get an album to put all those little pictures in. I'm always saying I'm going to do it but don't like shelling out the dough for it. 'spect it will cost about one guinea for the 250 pictures.

Some of Ben's photo albums, now in the possession of the author.

Oh Frank, people who have never worn a leg can't possibly understand the pain and awkwardness of it. To be a decent size and active man and have to come down to the standard of old man–it hurts.

I go to get measured for 2 suits next week, grey or navy blue? Doing much sewing? I sewed on 4 buttons today on those trousers I had up there and you offered to do it for me but I was too lazy to take them off and change.

We have a lot of Asters out, we surreptitiously water them each day. Now I want a long letter on large paper in a small handwriting or as an alternative you know the other letter I want written, on small paper in large writing, as you wish. We are having visitors soon, no more news,

love Ben.

Do not leave this letter about with the news about Mrs and the French Girl. How does Belmont look. Is he quiet amd fit for me to drive you to Hinton with. I want to go next time I'm up.

———————

Wednesday Imperial Service Club

Dear Franco,

Wrote you a short note last night when Dad and I were thinking of all the people we knew who could swing some lead, well we thought of about 6. Several Doctors and Professors and I got a note from Donald Smith praising my work etc. Hope I can only get in. You see I'll be 26 before I'm through and that makes me hesitate.

I'm so glad now you are going nursing. Do hurry up and see the doctor and get in but don't catch the 'flu, and be sure you are properly innoculated beforehand. I took my leg in and I am now on crutches. I seem to travel like the wind in comparison to when I was on the leg. They intend to alter it half inch and alter the tongue. I'm to go on Saturday morning about it.

I feel more confident on it but have been advised not to try to do without a stick for at least 6 months and it might cause me to limp a little. I don't have the stick.

Franko, has your Dad said anything about his boots which I pinched. Has anyone written to Mrs Griffin? Try to keep in touch with her, I like her so much and so do you. Had a letter from the Battalion yesterday. Presnell wrote it. Another letter from Shiny Buttons with more doggerel about Brigadier Brand and what he says about saluting. Shiny said he is making a dove-tailed box and the teacher says he should put it in the museum as a curiousity. I 'd love to see it. Billy Hunt is now ok. Saw him today and his hearing quite normal again.

Have been into the Club yesterday and today for dinner. Carmichael's likely to get into a row if he doesn't hold his tongue. He forgets he is still a soldier.

How is Mary? I'm anxiously waiting for a letter from you. Do you want me to go to the University? It will be a long time won't it. Belmont any better?

Wet and miserable today. How is nurse Wood? I'm expecting to hear you are in the hospital any day now. Edie's birthday other day and I forgot about it too (Bad Boy) Don't know what to get her. She has dozens of hankies.

Saw Sparke today here, looks well. Weren't Claire and Kitty terrors on Sunday afternoon. I won' t be settled down until I know if I can get through to University or not. It is an awfully worrying job.

Glad I'm off the leg today. It's sore. Tom goes to Gordon School now. Little Jean has not been up for weeks, until last Sunday and Mum asked her why she didn't come up she said *Oh Gran, 'cos of de 'flu, didnt you know it was on.*

Had an audience on the station, all old buffers congratulated me on way I was walking. No more news

fondest love Ben

Wahroonga
Monday St Patricks Day
17.3.19

Dear Franco

I've just finished the letter you asked me to write to Mary, just a little note as cheerful as I could get it–hope she will be o.k.

Yesterday I went to see Mr Donald Smith. Spent afternoon and had tea. He was very interested in my photographs which I took down. Do you remember the photo in the mail of Snowy Howell's [VC] wedding. Well Ginger Smith was his best man and he was standing behind Snowy. Smith and I had a long chat about Dentistry. A friend of theirs, a Jack Fussell was there (he had his right leg off) so we were a pair. Leg is not going too badly.

Harry Marten Smith from Wahroonga, a friend of poor old Arthur [Felton] is back in Wahroonga. He was gassed.

Today I' ve been busy. Went in by Dad's train to the tailors got my 2nd suit. Then went and bought 2 inverted gas brackets –came home– put them on. Awful job as all our pipes are old and stuffed up so had to clean them out. I could get into a row as only a plumber is allowed to do it but I didn't see why Dad should pay 10/6 for something I could.

Major Donald Smith with three of his five sons on active duty, taken in London. Captain Donald Ian Smith, AMC, Lt Noel Watson Smith and Lt Eric Alfred Smith.
See index – Image courtesy of Trish Leon, nèe Fell-Smith

Write to Bob Bray and ask him who was his dainty little girl yesterday afternoon. I saw Bob, this girl white shoes, silk stockings, white lace dress and white hat trimmed with salmon colored ribbon, an elderly lady and a naval lieutenant walking up from Milson's Point. I was in a tram so couldnt speak to them. Bob was swanking, slim walking stick which he was swinging and lemon colored gloves, his blue suit and a greenish hat. Today is St Patricks Day, lots of green ribbon around town mostly on roughies.

What did your Dad say about 1) the whip 2) Creamy 3) the Bumping. Don't say anything about me now, breaking things . China is easier broken than a whip. *Who Cares* Cheeriho ?

Leg is O.K. I was asked if I would like to join a tennis club so I can't be walking too badly. Was watching Bruce Rainsford and Ray Kershaw play tennis on Saturday when the ball hit my woody a good smack and bounced over the fence (I smiled).

Might be going to Mrs Smith's tomorrow night to meet Ginger, he was week-ending yesterday when I went. Am sure your phone ring was not 3 minutes long today. Can easily recognise your voice through the phone. Just like a dear little mouse speaking, far away and softly. I have some chocs here would you like some?

Tess Byrne bailed me up and asked me how you were. Suppose Didie has been telling her how often I go to your place, alas, that is all finished now isn't it. But I think you enjoyed yourself when I was up there.

Blisters are gone from the leg but it chafes. Now, the skalliwags; Edie, Mum and Dorothy are making me a sock between them. I'll have enough then when you have finished yours. Hope your Ma and Pa enjoyed themselves on Saturday. I've found my tie–inside pocket of light khaki coat. Mum found it when she was washing it.

We have plenty of Snapdragons and Astors. There is no water in our taps so as I've been working, so 'scuse the dirty spots. I wish you had been down. There is a bosker motor drive and launch picnic on 2nd Saturday in April given by Wahroonga Repatriation to all returned soldiers in Wahroonga–leaves here 9.40 am for Cowan Creek, then in launchs for a day's cruise, refreshments on board so I asked Freddy Waugh as you couldn't come.

My 2nd suit is a bosker. Sort of grey, rough with a nice grain going through it. Coat short, 2 buttons, no split and roll collar. All of which comprise latest fashion. Roll of Honor must have been fun. Sorry I wasn't there just to see the fun.

It is a shame, only a week off for nurses after influenza, they ought to get 3 weeks off at least. Any more cheek from the Andersons? I wish I'd been there to see you when the lorry passed.

Put my letters right away Old girl, don't leave them about and I want you to destroy at once that little slip of paper I sent you please. Tell me in next letter if you did it, Don't forget will you. Cheer Up. Let you know soon if I go to University. Get into Hospital soon.

Love Ben

I am entitled to that Gallipoli star ribbon watered silk. Looks well. Rectangle red white blue drawing.

Leave out the Lieut in the address now and put Mr. Ben

Wahroonga Wed 19.3.19

Dear Mrs Niland

Frank has probably told you that I am trying to get into the University. After producing educational certificates and swinging some weight this morning, I received a notification to say I could be admitted without studying for the entrance examination.

Before I accept this offer I weighed well the Pros and Cons and have decided to start on Monday. It is a 4 year course and worse luck although I won't be ancient, I'll be 27 before I can earn a living. The Degree of B.D.S. though carries some social standing which I would not have if I simply became, say in 2 ½ years time an ordinary registered Dentist.

I appeared before the Repatriation sub Committee yesterday and they have not the power to pay fees but passed it on to the full Committee for tomorrow week. Even if they do not pass it, I will pay my own fees, 164 pounds for the 4 years, inclusive of instruments and books. In the meantime I expect to be able to live on my pension.

Mr Donald Smith was very generous in allowing me to go as really I'm still an apprentice. His son *Ginger* is starting with me and his second son will be back from War in 3 weeks when he will start also.

Do you think I did the correct thing in going to University? A couple of years either way before I can earn any money does not count for much.

Frank tells me Mary is still well so I wrote her a little letter on Monday and I'm glad Elsie Daunt is much better. Today is a corker, hot but no wind. I now want to write a letter to *GUG* so will have to stop if I'm not to repeat myself in news.

Yours sincerely Ben

Friday evening
29.3.18

Dear Gug

Well I've now finished my first week at the University and although I feel it an awful waste of time sometimes I'm going to stick it. So far we have not done any mechanical work and if I can't pull off honors (if any are given) in that direction I'm a dutchman. Its very handy knowing

Ginger Smith. I can work a few points as he know's them all at the Dental Hospital.

There are 4 lockers and 17 men. Ginger and I have one each, needless to say. He used to go to school with the Sister in charge and she worked it. Bought a number of tools etc. There is one book on anatomy–am debating whether to buy it or not, a man isn't a gold mine. The term doesn't end until 31 May. I don't know where I got the idea about it ending in April. So nice of you to write so often. I'll be up in beginning of June. If the nurses building is only going up now it wont be ready until then and even if you are at Wallsend I'll be able to see you.

It is a nuisance having to wear masks again but it is for the best I believe. Anyway only wearing them on trams and trains is not so bad as wearing them when you are walking along the streets. So far of course this week has only been a waste of time, but next week things will run smoothly. I returned to roost at 8pm last night. It took me 15 minutes coming from the station and each step felt as if a piece of skin was being torn out. I was chafed so much.

I'm going into town tomorrow morning on business so hope you don't ring up while I'm away. You generally ring in the afternoon. Yesterday afternoon I went before the Repatriation Committee and they seemed nice. I worked the sympathy stunt. Before I went in, I loosened the straps behind the knee so that it clicked with sharp row. When I walked into the room I limped and the knee clicked awfully so they easily knew I had a woodie Good scheme don't you think? I was 3rd man in and they had just had a cup of tea so ought to be in a good humour.

Young Joe giving cheek is he? Some body must have been rubbing him up the wrong way, I'm surprised. Did you hear what he said or did your Dad tell you?

We've fried tomatoes for tea and I can hear them. Isn't 40 acres of lucerne rather a lot to be cutting? I dont know what to tell you but I'd like to be up there, that's all I know. Anyhow I'll try and write you a long letter on Sunday night.

love Ben

Friday evening 21.3.19

Dear Franc

Very pleased to get your letter tonight on coming home from town. You see I go in every day so as to get used to being on the leg all day. The leg is going beautifully, it hasn't twisted the last few days at all. Today I had to buy note books etc. An old piano tuner is in tuning the piano, he is twanging away fit to bust.

Not at all surprised at that divorce proceedings you sent me, there are thousands like that and the papers will be full of them when all the AIF are back.

Franco, I don't like the new tight skirt do you? it seems so absurd to me. I interviewed Mr Smith again today, just went along to see him. (He was frightfully busy too), Just wait 'til I have a following of people like he has. This is a new pen I've just bought and not in running order yet. I've tried several patent fillers but think the good old fashioned *swan* the best of the lot of them.

I'm so glad Mary is able to go out and that she liked my note. Of course you are the Colonel, (didn't you give orders for me to write to her) Dorothy had a birthday today and got a host of things from camisoles to books.

Very breezy in town today and with short skirts you know! Came up with Mr Felton last night. He is well, looks worried though, starts on the Moree route soon. I wouldn't care to travel about like he does, it would drive me silly.

I'm quite excited about going to the University. You will have to remember me in your prayers so that I can pass. The first year is the worst, most chaps fail that year. Do you only dream of me once in away? It's a constant thing with me.

Marjorie sat near a girl at School who was taken away with 'fluenza. Hope she doesn't get it or that will stop me going to the line for a while won't it.

Oh Bonnie, fancy me going for 4 years on 30 shillings per week. Just imagine. Gas is now terrible *bon*, otherwise known as excellent, especially in my room. I've an inverted burner on and a nice globe.

I'm glad there's to be an inquiry about the hospital. I hope Dr ?
Zions has his bumps read. Another hope is 8 hours for nurses, that
would be better than the days off per week don't you think so?

Young Tom is very grizzlifried–he wants a spanking. Mothers pets
him too much. So do you. But he's a nice little chap. Can't get him to
brush his hair though. It grows (like mine too) all roads especially at
the back where it points heaven ward.

Met Snowy Howell, V.C. M.M. yesterday he said *You know Ben,
this marriage stunt is the best stunt out for curing skalliwags I havent
even had a drink since the day I was married* 'Not bad is it He is a good
chap.

Today I met 6 more chaps out of the Battalion. They all came up to
speak to me, called me Ben too. You know Frank its fine these chaps
coming up and speaking. It shows I must have treated them decently
and they like me for they could easily avoid me if they wanted too
couldn't they? I don't think anyone bears me any ill will, not like some
officers whom chaps say they will FIX when they get back into civies.

Dad's train is up. Wonder how much longer I can go without being
disturbed. There is an out-lay on instruments that I will have to part
up for. Gertrude is making, lets see, should I say it, more stepins as she
calls them. She will have enough clothes for years and years and years.

Snowy Howell

Tell me what your mother thinks of me going to Uni. Has she said anything about US?

The bed on Verandah isn't such a bad place. Wish I was there now. Hot, yesterday I was frizzled but it is cold today. Winter fashions are coming in, saw some women today in velvet frocks. Dark green seems to be the rage and black hats.

No more holidays for some time so you get into hospital. Have you fixed it up yet? The *Man of War*. brought 64 cases of 'flu into Sydney Harbour. Our cousins in Melbourne are ok although several people around them have had it. Oh about the sock, Bonnie do what you can, match the wool, if you can't, a dark color doesn't matter. it's never seen you know. I don't wear it outside.

Keith is to be home on the *Euripides*. Have our Buffet tickets already. The Piano man, Mr Danndibicken is just going. He is not a German [enemy nationals—Ed.].

The internees at the Darlinghurst Court have been kicking up a row. We ought to squash them. I think a few bombs would fix them up ok. We are too humane altogether.

Is this long enough ? I write and write until I've exhausted my news. Elva Ward is painted up now. Saw her today. scribble scribble scratched out Going to mention something about poor old Art but I shouldn't should I. I have the fondest memories of him. So have you.

Well Franco, I can't scrape anymore news. Tell me if you get this note on Saturday afternoon.

Cheerio Love Ben

26.3.19

My dear Gug,

I forget who told me your nick name was Gug, dreamt it I suppose, anyhow is suits me to call you that on letters. I generally call you other things when I'm up.

You are a perfect dear to write me so many letters but would like you to continue it. It is great to get a letter from you when I come home very tired because dog tired doesn't express my complaint. I am absolutly

VILLERS-BRETONNEUX.—The Start of the Great Attack 8, 8, '18.

On the night of 24th April, 1918, the Australians made a daring and clever counter attack in the darkness, recaptured Villers-Bretonneux, stopped the German advance and saved Amiens.   This, and the Battle of Hamel, were only a prelude to the smashing advance which commenced on 8th August,

Extract from Australian Corps Order, issued on 7th August :—
"For the first time in the history of this Corps all five Australian Divisions will to-morrow engage in the largest and most important battle operation ever undertaken by the Corps."

85,000 Australians were engaged (with Canadians on their right and British Divisions on their left), supported by powerful artillery, tanks and aeroplanes.   In this battle 7,000 prisoners, 150 guns with an immense number of Machine Guns and war material were captured.   On August 31st and September 1st and 2nd Mont St. Quentin and Peronne fell to the Australians in three days, defeating the flower of the Prussian Guard.

In the centre of the picture a dead German is seen behind a captured gun.   During the months following many important pitched battles were fought and won, over 20,000 prisoners taken, and over 250 guns, heaps of munitions, machine guns and stores, together with over 120 villages.

A GERMAN TANK
Captured by the Australians near Villers-Bretonneux.

AUSTRALIAN COMFORTS FUND.
XMAS & NEW YEAR'S GREETINGS, 1918-19.
"THE GLORIOUS FOURTH."

The Battle of Hamel on 4th July, 1918, was the first occasion on which Americans fought side by side with Australians or other British Troops.

The picture shows Aeroplanes of the 3rd Squadron, A.F.C. dropping Ammunition to the assaulting troops by parachute, (an Australian idea, put into practice for the first time).   The village burning on the left is Hamel, while the wood behind the barrage, in the centre background, is Accroche Wood.

The tracks in the right foreground are made by the caterpillars of the Tanks, the white mound is part of an old trench which had just been cleared of the enemy.

The Battle of Hamel paved the way for the great advance of 8th August, 1918, from Villers-Bretonneux.

CAPTURED BY THE AUSTRALIANS
A 14 C.M. German Naval Gun intact with its Train & Equipment.

Greetings from

Postcards sent by Keith before his departure on the Euripides *for his return journey to Australia.*

dead beat and I'm getting thin too. Each night my clothes are absolutely wringing wet. My waist coat, around the arms the dye has run. This blankety leg will be the death of me yet. Today it started to chafe, as they say in France *No bon pour les soldats*

I told you that article of Kershaw's was in The Telegraph, March 8th *A Soldiers Philosophy* near the cartoon it is. Now that letter your mother read, honestly what was in it? Anything I wouldn't like her to see? I also wish you could give me a shock by meeting me in the train. Honestly there would be no university that day, we would declare it a holiday and mooch off to some National Park or some other nice little spot with a hamper.

I had dinner today with Bert Carroll, all are well but he is under the impression you are in hospital training. We had anatomy today for the first time and rather interesting but awfully hard to understand. There are 2 girls going for Dentistry in same classes as myself. If they can get through so can I. The first year will tell anyway if I go down. I'll simply be a mechanicial dentist but am going to pass.

Spent 3 pounds on books and Practical Chemistry gear, another batch, 4 pounds to go tomorrow on Dental instruments. Kershaw is doing Arts and Science course at Uni.

Don't let Winnie Wood beat you into hospital will you? Are you thinking of charging the Delaneys rent for the chairs they occupy. What did your father think of the tennis winder and posts any good?

That sock you made Frank is just a shade short but Dot is fixing it up for me, but it does excellently. Black hats look nice with green dresses. Quite a number in town, also dresses, ever so many tiny pleats right down which gives them a crinkled appearance. I like them.

There are objections in to the Uni that they treat you too much like kids ! We always let our persimmons ripen inside then the birds don't get them (+2 legged ones too)

Ginger Smith and I are probably going to do some mechanicial work for his Dad and get some money that way. See we have Saturdays off and one afternoon a week so we could do it then. Have to appear before the Repatriation Committee tomorrow afternoon to decide if they will pay the fees or if I'll have to do them.

Ginger Smith in my opinion is going a bit fast around town. He didn't get home last night at all but stopped in town and he said he was too late leaving some friends of his. He looked a bit shaky this morning since he came home. He has only been home to dinner 6 nights in all. A bit rough don't you think?

***

April Saturday.

Dear Bon,

Many thanks for your note today.

I met your mother today at 11.30 and we went out to Mrs Hardings– [her sister Lucina] beyond Mona Vale. Mrs Niland said she would never have been able to find it on her lonesome so I am glad she asked me to come. I really enjoyed myself and we arrived back at the Quay at 6.25. I had time to see her in a tram, then caught the boat and then came home.

So you've been to a Tarro dance and by your letter am glad to see you enjoyed it. I told your mother I might come up this next weekend as a surprise but she told me surprises were not good for people. So if you would like to see Ben William in person just say so–before I promise to come you are to promise that if its fine you will take me down to the river bank. So just let one know what you feel like and if you'll be o.k.

You says *How is my old Darling* well this is how he feels, Run down, rusty wheels in the head instead of brains and wants cheering up. I have had a tiring week and from now onward I must work even harder than I am now to get through the exams, for your sake. Also I've engaged a man to coach me for the anatomy exam and thats going to cost me 15/– per week. Balance sheet; spending–10/–home, 15/–coach, 7/6 lunches, ferry 1/3, leaving a residue of 8/3 for church, smokes, stamps etc . Some gay life I lead. Such a bountiful income–I can afford cigars each day and dance each night. Even in the midst of my studying I haven't missed one letter to you. Now just write the best letter you know how to me. I'm engaged so don't be frightened on that score. Telling me what you wish me to do. I've decided to cut out the Battalion Social if you want me to come as I think a good eyeful of you would do me more good that hundreds of chaps in uniform would.

Am I to cut out the last lecture on Friday and catch the usual 2 o-clock train or attend the lecture and catch the 5.30 train getting to Tarro about midnight or go to the dance and catch the 1.15 am train on Saturday morning arriving Tarro at 7.23am. You see I have thought it all out clearly. Old Mrs Harding asked me where I'm going to live when married. Singie wasn't there but Dickie was. She and her mother are some artists aren't they? They were fulfilling some contract or other and their pictures were wonderful I thought.

I'm feeling as if I want you to hold my hand tonight. You'll have to turn around and answer this staight away so as I'll get a letter by Thursday night. Get Claire to post it in town on Wednesday. Good night old girl, I'm not too brilliant.

Love Ben

Be sure to go for a telegram from me on Friday. If you are rushed, don't come to town. I'd like to catch the 2 trains–just you say come.

Sunday, I simply had to go to bed last night when I did. I was so whirley in the upper story. Ray Carroll told your mother he looked 2–3 times at me on Friday before he recognised me owing to the moustache. I'm going to press my grey trousers this afternoon. Mr Smith hurt like the devil yesterday and the insides of my lip are very sore and bruised this morning.

It is a beautiful day, just the sort to take a motor trip from here across country to Church Point. I saw Emmie Austin and Butcher out in their car

Sam Ward. AWM

as I was coming into Manly with your mother. They are not married yet. Sam Ward and Maud Kershaw are married—will tell you about it when I see you next. He is 20 and she is 19, they are away on their honeymoon at present.

I'm going to work at Histology this afternoon after doing the trousers. I was so awfully disappointed at your letter of 1 ¼ pages yesterday and only getting a fairly short one last Monday and feeling rotten, I decided to be a man and let you wait for one. But I can't do it. I'm o.k. today. Get all your work done so that we have a fairly clear weekend together.

Those cuff links are nice Bonnie. They look too good for a student to wear but I do wear them. Didn't you like last weekends letter? Keith has his bike up for sale and will probably sell it this week. He is only asking 12 pounds for it, just to get rid of it.

It won't be long now before you are 21. I'd like to be 21 again. I'm 2 years and one month older than you. Mrs McClellan was so pleased to see your mother yesterday, I could tell by the excited way she spoke.

I would have painted the wardrobe this weekend but went out instead. We had our annual meeting at the University of the Undergraduates last Friday and we managed to get only returned soldiers into office Which is o.k. for us diggers.

Up 'till the time I started this I was busy staining my light colored brogue shoes a dark tan. I like them much better dark as they don't stain half as quickly. Are the 2 saddles at home now or better still we can use the old trap to go down to the farm, then I can lift down all the rails as we go along and we only need one horse. Do any people around your district ever drive tandem style, horse in front of the other in a sulky?

Naturally you did not go over to Griffins with the trouble occuring but you ought to go someday. I'm going to have a feed of perismmons soon. I put some away for your mother so that she could have some nice ripe ones but she isn't coming up this week and they will be too ripe later on if she comes. She told me that as everyone seems to be getting along ok at *Oaklands* without her she probably will stay another fortnight.

How is it getting along at dress making? Your Ma looks well Frank. Despite her trouble and being a little stouter I think. Oh I wish 1923 was here and I was through. What a time to wait and study, studying the whole time. good by Bon.

Ever yours, Ben

Imperial service CLUB

15.4.19

Dear Franco

This is just a skimpy note to catch you on Saturday afternoon.

Why old girl have you and Ruth to milk? Have Tom and wife left you already, hope not. On Wednesday came to town to buy a few carpenter tools. I've a little job on hand—well Jack planes cost 15/6 now I was not going to pay that so searched the pawn shops and got one for 3/–practically new and will do me.

Winnie Wood came in last night to see Dorothy. Chatted for a long time so that I had to go into my room to rough out the plan of a house I'm thinking of putting up and letting, to make a few bob extra on my pension. The rest would pay off the money and also put 10 shillings in my pocket per week. Good scheme don't you think?

They laughed and talked crochet and knitting all night long. Wednesday afternoon Mrs Donald Smith asked me to come to afternoon tea to meet Eric who is just back Went to the Civil Service. Eric is such a handsome chap. I'd never introduce him to you. *Never introduce your doner [girl] to a pal, its dangerous.*

Went home to their place to tea and stopped the night. Had a long chat to Mr Smith about dentistry. Next morning went to Manly with him and then came home to my place. Today I've been buzzing around the Repatriation Dept. Have to be back tomorrow.

Good bye A long letter on Sunday

love Ben.

Eric Smith. Image courtesy of Trish Leon(née Fell-Smith)

17.4. 19

Dear Franco,

A year ago today since poor Old Art was killed, doesn't time fly. Well I'll tell you what I did after I left you at Tarro. Arrived in Newcastle and went up to the Hospital and had a talk with Mary from her ward. She was on duty until 6pm so I couldn't take her to afternoon tea.

Newcastle Hospital

I delivered the letters and saw Maggie Wood coming out of the home so took her to tea instead. After tea walked to Scotts store to see Bessie Nichols. Saw her and told her you wanted that pattern of pyjamas—said she would send it that night if it was in. She didn't know me at first but sparkled up when I mentioned your name. Wants to know when you intend calling for your suit case which she is minding.

Coming out of the shop met an old pal who once lived in Wahroonga. A Maurice Hawkins, I had a chat with him and then walked to the beach with Maggie. Coming back both waved to Mary again then I went down to the station. The train was packed and I could hardly get a seat. Do you know why? Well the 3pm and 4.45 trains were cut out so I had to catch that awful slow train down and it stopped at every station and I arrived home at 9pm. Such a shame. By catching the slow train it takes 1 hour longer getting home.

Had a honeymoon couple in the carriage from Wyong downwards. Had just finished their 'moon and were going home, both looked tired and wan looking. Suppose they felt a little tired of one another. The gal couldn't leave her rings alone twisting them all the time.

How is the cold in your blose. I have not one.–Lucky it isn't my fault I didn't get one. No more just now.

Love Ben

Franco, do you remember Vera's baby, you'd be surprised if you saw it now. [baby Vera born Sept 1918] It is just 19lbs and rolling in fat and very intelligent looking, can notice things you know. Jean is fatter too. They are living at Concord West now, Ryde way, I think it is.

Do you think I'll have enough brains to go through the course. It will be a frightful waste of time if I fail and I've never passed an exam yet as you know. Thank your Mother for the letter she wrote me and also fat (should be a capital F shouldn't it but I reserve those for you) [Fat is Ruth – Ed.]

Dozens of motors whizzing past reminds me of the Sunday afternoons Art and I used to go for long walks and take Nip. Worse luck those things are past and so also is Nip, he is very old.

There is a St John's Church Social next Friday night to all returned soldiers given by the Church. Am not going, have been to enough already, making myself too cheap turning up to them all. Haven't seen Didie for ages. Mary Sanders is home, over the influenza, only had it in a mild form.

Did your Ma and Pa have a good time at the Vedding? We had Uncle Will [Fathers brother] up yesterday and Vera and kiddies. Quite a house full, all went for a walk in the bush after dinner but had to leave this decrepit old gentleman at home.

Think I'll learn to play with my thumbs. Leg is going excellently. Dot has just finished a pair of thin grey sox for me. They will be better than those I bought in Newcastle. Suits are going well–to see me dressed up you'd think I was earning 500 pounds instead of 75 pound per annum. Enclosed on a slip of paper you'll see your question which you have enquired about.

Went to Town with Harry Jones on Friday. He is well over his gassing. Now that the War is over Jones'people say Harry is going to France and they are awfully worried. Glad Keith will be here middle of April. We are turning out a room for him, painted his old bed and looks O.K. I intend to paint some red lines on the black paint so as to make it pretty.

Harry Jones in front of the Red Cross Ambulance –
On back Bhutpore-Tidworth Wilts 3.4.17

How is Belmont and the buggies and all the stock and yourselves and have you anybody in view yet when the Andersons go? Old Mr Dykes [Rev'd Dykes, Ben 's uncle] is not too well, suffers with indigestion otherwise known to you as the bingie ache. Work tomorrow Eh? Well must start sometimes, only I wish I was going down to the River Bank instead. Ray Kershaw is starting at Uni in about 3 weeks time so will have company and Bruce Rainsford always goes down in that early train 6-8 from Wahroonga.

Gertrudes sox for Bergelin are khaki. You don't have to wash that color so often I tell her. Mother and all kiddies are at Sunday School. It is their Anniversay next Sunday and they are having special hymns. But there are very few scholars. Have you ever read *The Three Musketeers* by Dumas. I'm just finishing its continuation *20 years after?*

There are a lot of those dear little bush doves near here cooing away like wild fire. I think they are so pretty and I'd love to be able to know what they say. I think it would be fine to be able to understand horsey talk and dog talk. Could tell then when they are well or otherwise and understand them.

Made your self your winter dress yet? Winter won't be long now. The nights here are quite nippy, had 2 blankets and a quilt last night. That extravagant Gertrude, the sheets, quilts etc she has got enough to do for a mansion instead of a bush place. They will be wasted up there I'm sure.

Wonder where you are? See if I'm right now—afternoon 3.30pm, you are not at Church. I fancy you lying on the verandah reading in the sun and now and then crocheting. Am I right? answer. Cannot think of anything else to say but I'll think of you very hard instead. Cheeriho

Love Ben

Sunday morning
20.4.19

My dear old GUG

Don't you luv me like you used ta I have not yet received a letter since I came back. How is your cold? any worser cos if it is I'll have to come up to see you. Take gruel regularly 3 times a day.

There have been 4 perfect days since I came home. Glorious sunshine and no rain. On Friday morning I rang up the tutor and he said to come on Saturday morning. I left here at 8 and travelled right out to Glebe to see him. He is a very decent cove, named McGrath. He is a teacher at Morven Catholic College, but he will get me on well. I like him despite his name.

I'm stuck for news already. Oh I did envy the chaps who were taking out their girls yesterday. Such a number and here you are all that distance away. Why don't you live close to Wahroonga?

On Good Friday Mother and I went to Coogee to see an uncle [Mothers brother Holt] Well I hadn't seen Florrie his daughter since I came back and was so disappointed. Fancy trying to be affected with us who have known her all her life. It was *oo noo* you know the style anyhow she must have smelt a rat as I didn't say much to her, anyhow she stopped it later on, then we got on well. I hate that jammy business when it is not necessary.

Why haven't I received a letter? Have you got the 'flu? Sorry to see the late Bishop of Newcastle has died but he was a good age. The Read kiddies did get a smacking this morning like they usually get. It's just a perfect day why can't I take you to Manly? There are a lot of those fine old shady trees in Hyde Park but now they are being cut down. I think it is a shame because such a number of people sit under their shade at dinner time. Now they are no more.

See the 'flu is becoming more serious in Newcastle as the weeks go by. Last week was a corker for cases. I believe Newcastle has more cases in proportion to its population than Sydney has. Gertrude is going to be married (I believe I told you before on or about 31st May). Spent Thursday morning with Ray Kershaw. His place is a picture and coming down the road you can scent the roses. Their perfume is glorious, you can smell it 200 yards before you get to Kershaws.

The Kershaw family, 1908.

I suppose Mary is home today. I'm sorry she didn't have the afternoon off last Wednesday. Did Bessie send down the pattern I asked her too *toute suite*. Have you the new boy yet and is Joe going for sure'? I bet he comes back sooner or later–he knows a good home when he sees one. I think I will get a kit of carpentry tools together again. This tutor of mine made a nice press for clothes out of Queensland maple it looks so nice. The grain in the wood shows up well.

We expect Keith to come in on the 22nd and then go into Quarantine for 7 days. Won't it be fine to have him home once again. As there are no excursion trains these holidays all the trains to Woy Woy etc have been crammed tight.

Mr Felton is home again. I might slip up and see him this afternoon. Will I give Didie your love? Poor old kid just a year ago since Art was killed. More soldiers came in on Friday none for Wahroonga though.

Our little gazy-bo is rapidly being covered with vines and we expect by next summer to have a fine shady nook and we intend to have a few ferns in it too. Tell your mother that Mum hasn't forgotten her Scarboro lillies as soon as they can be separated she shall have a few. Our Loquot tree has tons of small loquots on them.

Can you work the automatic phones? It is so funny. I'd like to know the proper inside working of it. It does away with a lot of telephone girls. How is the chestnut pony going? Give me all the news about the farm. You don't have any one to string your beans now, but get Bert [Carroll] on the game if he comes up and don't let Ruth tell any tall yarns about me. Boo Hoo I was lonely going to Newcastle all alone and that was a cow of a train too, so slow.

My woody is going well, no trouble at all. I was gardening on Friday morning, trimmed those beds under the windows, look very good now. The grass was a foot high so I had to sythe it before putting the mower over it.

There is a piece in this mornings paper about the final exams at the University. Did I tell you the Repatriation is going to pay my fees at the University. They come to 156 pounds.

Be you a going to Church today? Did Mary get her flowers for the Childrens Party and who took them down?

We are going to send Keith a parcel each day when he is in quarantine. Fancy this being the 20th, doesn't time fly. Wonder will you be in hospital this time next month. Don't know whether to say hope so or not Would like the 'flu to be over before you start.

If I pass my first year exam I intend in the vacation to go for a trip perhaps to Tasmania. I think it would be a fine scheme and if I pass I'll deserve a spell.

I love to hear the Church people singing. Two churches have started up. We have to wear wretched masks so I am not going but might go tonight if I feel inclined.

Creamy been shod yet? S'pose not, it is a good way to the blacksmith's. Kershaws had a cable from Harold saying he was on leave in Ireland. So he must be quite ok in the head now. I think that is the hardest luck of all when a man is not ok in his upper storey.

Quite a number of people went out to Cowan yesterday, one van held about 8 kiddies and Ma and Pa. Quite a merry little crowd. Did you fnd any sovereigns in my room? I didn't drop any but they are mine if found. Tom still sleep there or has his wife come yet? Can't write anymore but will send a long one as soon as yours come to hand

love Ben.

Thank the family for the sn'ice time I had.

———

Sunday 23.4.19

Dear Gug

On Friday afternoon we all went down to the Anzac buffet to meet Keith. We waited around seeing the people. We couldn't get a seat. Some dresses. It is evident that most of the ladies had bought a frock, a special dress for the occasion and there were some beauts too. Especially the girls about your age. Georgette blouses and cammies galore. WELL Keith turned up in the first car but we didn't see him come in so Father left us to go to see a better place as to get a better view. Dot and I spotted K and we brought him to Mum and Marjorie.

Then Dot and I went looking for Dad and found him after ½ hour struggling in the crowd.

The sights though, it's well worth going to see them. If a chap could have too many kisses, some were eaten alive by their girls and mothers. Keith is not too brilliant. The cause of the whole sickness was catching the 'flu in England that brought on the kidney complaint. He is like a lath and very round shouldered. He was so weak that often he had to be lifted in and out of his hammock each day. But we will fatten him up in time. He reported to Randwick Hosp yesterday. He has a weeks leave, then will be admitted to hospital for treatment.

I asked him would he like to visit you and said you would look after him like a bunch of mothers but he wouldn't say yes or no. I don't think he would be strong enough to ride a horse and its different when I come up you know. He is wearing my slacks about and he says he feels better than in puttees.

I'm off to Church now. We have to wear masks. People have been asking if I'm away from Wahroonga as I go to Church so seldom. Cheeriho.

We only had a half hour service, everyone was surprised to see Keith of course and everyone congratulated Mother on getting her seond boy home. Vera, baby and Jean came down to see Keith in. The baby is solid and big and smiling all the time.

The minalobata is out all along the side verandah. I'm thinking out a scheme to get you down to Wahroonga before you go into Hospital, so if you are asked and you say not, don't speak to me again. Of course, if you go into hospital before a certain event comes off it will be no good. Don't ask any questions about it because I won't tell.

You can put anything you like in my letters as I burn them as soon as I've replied to them. What a strain it must have been to burn that last long letter I wrote to you, I was very glad you did. I wasn't frightened to ask Bessie for the pyjama pattern as I knew her but I'd have never done it if I didn't know the girl. I caused quite a consternation when I went in, everyone shouted for Bessie and said a Returned S wants to see you.

I've started on my cabinet, planed away all yesterday. I'm sorry today is Sunday as I cannot do any today. I did 3 foolish things, cut myself in 3 places, once with a saw, once with a chisel and the 3rd time squeezed my finger in a vice. What a chapter of accidents.

Keith doesn't know what to do. He is strolling about as if he is on sentry go. Can't sit in one place. Allan Greig is back in Wahroonga. He hooked onto Gertrude going down to the train yesterday and she couldn't get rid of him. He talked all the time and she didn't say a word to him.

All our clocks were fast yesterday. Father left here in time to catch the 19 past 8 train and just missed the 6 to 8 train. Strange for us, whose clocks are always meticulously correct (Some word that, have you had its acquintance before?).

Do you remember that girl in Wahroonga who said I cut her once, you know, told her father I wouldn't recognise her, well she went down to meet a boat yesterday, one of her boys is coming back. She has a dozen to my knowledge. Gertrude says she looked a dream or rather a nightmare–Cream jockey hat, Georgette blouse, salmon colored ribbon underneath, sage green skirt, grey silk stocking with black rings around them and grey suede shoes and done up. I hope she does not kiss Len Robinson or she'd leave red marks on his face. Some flash style what?

Why did you have to milk old girl? I thought that now Tom, Joe and the other coves were there that was finished for you. Hard luck anyhow. Do you get the scented soap to work afterwards Eugh! Don't like my girl to milk.

Eric Smith and I had a nice day on the beach the other day. I would have liked you to have been there–could have searched for another girl for Eric, he knows thousands of them I think by the way they were speaking to him in the Civil Service Stores last time I was there with him and Mrs Smith.

I must have a 14 page letter from you this week and I'll pay the extra postage on it. Don't forget I want that special letter you know, although I don't speak about it I haven't forgotten about it.

The University has been put off and off. Isn't it awful! How can I pass the exam if it is goes on like this?

Dad, Mum, myself, Tom, Keith, Dorothy, Marj and Edie went to Church this morning, some crowd and all the chairs are spaced 3 foot apart so we spread right across the Church. All in masks too. Jean said, I suppose her mother told her to say it, but she said *Is your lady allwright*. I told her yes. I don't think she could remember you, someone must have told her to say it.

Figure 3: The Old Church in Coonanbarra Road.

The old Wahroonga Church, formerly a community hall. Source–Thomas Sydney Champion– The First 75 Years.

Tell Pegg, I thought she was hungry that afternoon as she took the only cream cakes on the plate and I wanted them. But she wouldn't have anymore. Next time I come up Mary, You, Elsie and Peggy and I will have a bun fight to see who can eat the most cakes. You won't win for I reckon you have the most genteel appetite of any girl I've ever had the honour of taking out to tea. What do you live on. Love and air I think.

Don't worry about matching the grey of the sox, no one will see them. I don't float around town in sox without shoes.

Do you hope the mad dog bites you and myself? We are dotty enough as it is, so Kitty says. I'm so glad your Mother takes my going to Wallsend calmly. Of course I will see her too. Wish you would read your letters over again, sometimes I can't make sense out of them because you've written it so quickly and left out some words, *Comprez*. The reason I didn't put up the nets was I thought all the 'skeets 'were done, neber mind. The Lord will provide. Bert [brother] might be coming out in next few boats. We had a letter he gave to a chum to give to Father. He has had pleurisy on top of malaria and it is a good thing as the pleurisy fluid which is trapped brings out malaria germs.

I can't remember to get any new note paper so don't be insulted at getting this sort. It is out of an exercise book which I used at Fort St School 7 years ago. Keith wants to go to the Feltons this afternoon so I think I'll go as well.

Where Jean [Bens niece] stops there is a calf named Ginger. It's horns are just showing through, Jean bumped her head sometime ago and it is still sore. Well, she says her horns are sprouting there. This letter seems full of Jean to me.

Bosker day, what are you doing? Church or River bank, the latter for my preference if you please. Our poplar trees once so nice and green are now browny. The leaves are falling, Autumn is here. Roses on the Station are magnificent. Best I've ever seen them–every color under the sun and plenty of them.

Strange how you can go for a ride down to the farm when I am not there. Of course there was no horse for me. But Oh Frank, I did so want to go and you did not seem keen on it at all.

Don't get a cold next time I come please, don't I feel as if I give it to you somehow or other. Whose turn in the kitchen this week? I suppose you are busy on your hospital clothes. Would you be too busy to come down here if the way was opened for you. Would you? Cannot think of anything else.

love Ben.

Wilkins is walking slowly on his leg. His wife waits on him hand and foot. They are still up the mountains having a second honeymoon. Wilkie says its all right (I had a letter from him)–it is worth going away for a few years to have another honeymoon. Waugh is still on crutches. He uses his leg when he gets home in the evening. So you see I'm doing the best of the bunch. Pat me on the back there is a good girl.

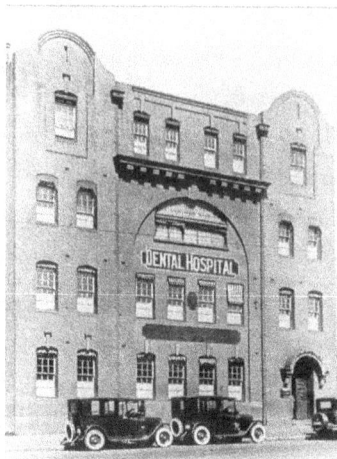

The new United Dental Hospital which opened in 1912–dated 1920–
Sydney University Archives www

Do you think the brown patch of grass down on river bank is green yet? I'll bring you some hair pins next time I come up. There are such of lot of beautiful spots around Sydney which you have never seen and I would love to take you to them. Next time in Anatomy we do Dissection, I wonder what that will be like. I believe we start on frogs first then later go on to proper bodies. They get the bodies from the institutions like Callan Park etc

Don't think Ginger will go back to University, but Eric who is after my style, only much more handsome is sure to be starting so we'll get on o.k. He can help me in some things and I 'll do his mechanical work for him. Mr Smith is trying to get our course cut down for us. But imagine waiting 5 long weary years before earning any money. 27 years old.

Harry Jones is engaged to his Scotch girl *Just imagine*. She must be a dope. I'm wondering will she marry him and will he marry her. Perhaps she feels inclined for a trip to Aussie anyway. Don't blame her, but he is very soft in the upper storey.

Didn't Mr Jones have a hide asking about the piano? Poor simple Enid can't nurse or sew yet she can tinkle on the goanna. Being useful in the drawing room is not like being able to earn ones living as a nurse is it. Nursing for my preference. You'll know how to massage my leg then won't you? It's rotten only having one to work on, but I suppose it is better than being blind.

When I get downhearted I think of those blind coves begging on the street corners and that cures my grouch. There are thousands worse off than myself and a number haven't got a girl like you. Not soft soap I mean it. Cannot think of anything else. Love to all if you like, but all for you.

Love Ben
write me that special letter

Sunday Morning 4.5.19

My dear Franco,

I'm down with an awful cold and feel absolutely wretched. I went to bed about 8pm on Friday night and did not get out of it until 2pm yesterday afternoon but seeing as how last week I received such a lot of bonny long letters, not even one wee note, I have to turn to and do my best for you. Well we'll start with your first letter last week and run through all your questions to the best of my ability then if I can make up any news at all it will be yours. Hope that 16 pages I received will only be the first of a lot I'm to receive. I was so pleased to get it and I appreciated it especially as I was not too brilliant owing to my cold.

We've been having a lot of trouble with our gas since Friday. We have been cooking on the wood stove. It is such a lot of work for Mum and I don't get my cup of tea as they don't get up any earlier like you do. We rang up the gas man and he says the shortage of coal and poor quality is the cause of it which is no consolation to us. Blow those lazy miners.

Now about Heather Adamson, I'm afraid I will have to disappoint you over it, you see Mondays Wed and Fridays, I leave the Uni at 1pm and have to get lunch then go out to the Dental Hospital in Chalmers St Redfern by 2pm so I have to hurry some.

On Tuesdays and Thursdays I work until 9pm at the Uni so there is not a day or an hour off in which I could see her so its no go at all. I'm awfully sorry and all that you know. You are worrying about that scheme that I had to get you down to Sydney. Well here it is, but I dont want anybody to see it at all'.

Gertrude is to be married and when she goes up to your place she is going to ask you to come down to the wedding. There's this about though, should the university start I won't have any time to take you about at all. Doubtless I could squeeze a few hours in though. I'd like you to come even if you could only spare a few days off from your dressmaking.

Anyhow you went out to Wallsend yesterday and probably know when you are to start so let me know. Do you think you'd care to come down just for a week? It will be a change for you and fares are not expensive. That is all you would require so think it over and if you don't think you could manage it then Gertrude won't ask your Ma.

Thanks so much for the sox and book. I think I'll have to give the post man a tip for all his good work The sox are just o.k. I have them on now. It is a pity Heather doesn't know Norma Davidson. You'd better write to each other and introduce them. Not a bad scheme. Eric Smith is in the first year. He hasn't been to the Uni before but he is a horribly brainy cove and is sure to pass without trying. Ginger has gone back to the Sugar Company.

I'm disappointed in not being able to build the house. All the big Societies and Banks have put so much money into War Bonds that they have none to lend so I'll have to wait some time yet until they recuperate their funds.

Keith has not gone into hospital but is going to be an outpatient which to his mind is much better, living at home and going there for medicine and treatment. He is very yellow looking, can't dig or walk far but he gets a huge pain in his back and has to lie down. I'm glad I am ok internally. Nothing much wrong when I got a first class life insurance from the AMP society who are very strict. They have paid out millions over soldiers deaths. The war has socked them to a very great extent. No, you couldn't shock Keith. He says Didie is the best built girl he has seen all the time away and up to when he saw her last Sunday. Will that do you Miss F J curious. You will probably get this letter on your

Birthday. I'm sending you a book by Porter which I like very much. It is very like *Harvester* which you read. Best Wishes and may your 21st year see you well and happy in hospital nursing.

The flu is much worse in Newcastle to Sydney according to population, so that won't keep you away. They will innoculate you on the station if necessary going home. Try to come, for I have not the ghost of a show to get up again. I'd be frightened of offending Dad even if I am over 22. Bonnie you have never gone back in your word yet, don't let nursing influenza make you do it. Honour bright, if you attempt it, some how or other I'll get some influence to work to get me an introduction to your matron and I'll stop your gallop. I'll work it somehow. As the matron has been on active service I could easily find some sister I knew who knew the matron and it could be worked. Don't call me nasty. I don't want to lose you, not even your hair which I think is one of your special charms. Don't forget it

Of course I want your letters, mistakes or otherwise but I was only thinking if you become a matron and have to write business letters. Perhaps if you had a mistake it might cost you the position. *Comprez?*

On Friday morning I had to go to town and met a chap named Marsland, a Returned Soldier who is also doing the Dental Course. Well we struck a bonny place for iced drinks called the Golden Gate. I'll have to take you there. First we had iced fruit punch, then we tackled a Banana special. I couldn't manage mine it was so rich. In the bottom of the dish was a banana covered with ice cream, then a layer of strawberry ice cream, then 4 strawberries then two little dobs of ice cream then a lot of the cream they put in cream cakes. It was so rich I didn't tackle more than 3 spoonsful of it.

We walked down past Farmers store and saw two girls as we thought. Blue voile pleated skirts, (short) silk stockings, shoes, Georgette blouses and nice cammie, hats. The back view was o.k. but oh Lord, when we passed them, their faces, Gee Whiz, they must have been 40 if they were a day and from the back view they were about 18. I got an awful shock.

So sorry the skeeters have been worrying your ankles. You want to wear mens heavy sox over your stockings. You'd look some guy then wouldn't you? Oh Miss Sarcastic, I didn't mean Bert would be on more than one boat unless his kit comes in one and he another. What an awful bore it must be to be clever, glad I'm not. Don't think I'd like Heather. She is sure to be too clever for words and if a chap said something she would correct his grammar.

Won't Mrs Jones give that Scotch girl a time if she is not exactly the thing according to her awfully old fashioned ideas. Ooh how nice, But you must really learn to play the paino. It is hard to write the way she talks but isn't she a goat. When I used to go there years ago on washing day especially she used to forget her jam. That's the worst of the wife having money and the husband none. Mr Jones is Sup't of Sunday School and he always starts his prayers *And now Dear Lord* He couldn't start a prayer any other way.

Good Oh, about the milking machines. I'd like to be there the first time they are put on the cows, some kicking and swearing I bet. That skalliwag of a Joe tho taking Arthur away with him. I thought as Arthur's sister was married to Tom he would stay for good. Franco, it is not use being kind to that style of people. Work 'em till they drop then they haven't got time to think over their troubles.

You won't go to Wallsend until the new nurses home is built, so rest assured it will be the middle of June. Maggie Wood's address is *Billyard Avenue Wahroonga*. We had a visit from her and Winnie last night. They stopped 'till 10pm and seemed glad they came. Gertrude can be very entertaining when she likes, especially as she has just finished counting her trousseau things which she does at least once a day. She is going to have the Wedding Breakfast in the Womens Service Club of which she is a member. It is in Hunter St Sydney and more central for everyone. See Wahroonga is a long way out as all our relations live out Coogee way and towards Burwood.

I think it is a good scheme. She has not arranged the day yet. She leaves her office on Friday. Next Saturday the Girls Fellowship and the Choir are giving Gertude a picnic and a present. Very decent of them I think. Of course most of them do not remember Gertude when she had her hair down her back but some do and I bet they think it is funny giving her a picnic before she gets married Rain, rain in torrents flood our front path and it beats in through Gertudes lattice. Does Belmont jib? I'll take you to the zoo and leave you in the Elephants cage. I 'd like to see the place. I haven't been to the new Taronga Zoo yet at all and I believe it is very nice indeed. But do come down for the wedding.

What is this I hear about George Norley blaming me for telling you to sing out *Hay Press*. I'm longing to hear him chuckle again, he is as funny as a circus. Khaki spelts Khaki and not Khiki. Sir Harry Lauder, some bloke with his Sir.

Sent to her cousin Miss L Morgan, from Gertrude

I have destroyed all your last weeks letters. I am going to do it every week, so you can write what you like, no one sees them. Tell Elsie Daunt I rang up Whitfield but he was out. I'm going to see him on Monday and will let you know.

What is this case your Dad has been on, the Vera Isen or something like that? I couldn't make out the name at all and what about it? Do you know Dad and the children are home from Church. I have been writing for 3 hours and only 9 pages done, but I think I get more on these than you do on your notepaper, wait a shake! I've just counted the two pages. On your page you get 22 words and I gets 50 so I beat you by 30 words.

Had a chum up yesterday afternoon he is advising me about the cabinet I'm making. It looks terribly *bon*, you must know even if I do say so myself. Enclosed is a clipping from the News about masks. Did you give her the piece of paper on which was the Jingle about the Old Woman who always was tired. Tell me if you like the *Daughter of the Land* I think you will. Don't you think the *Mystery of the Sea* a good book and did you bother to puzzle out the ciphers or did you skip them. I think Marjory Drake is a nice sort of a girl.

I'm so lazy I didn't even get dressed tidily when the Woods came, I just slipped my clothes over my pyjamas and have done the same to day also . But there is an excuse, as I 'm so dopey with this cold.

The Woods brought up their crochet and Maggie offered to make a wedding bell for G, out of cardboard and cotton wool. I can't study on my own I 've found out. Dinner is ready. If I can find any more news after dinner I'll put it in, Cherriho, Ben

Well Gug I've had dinner so am going to have a little nap as Bennie Dear doesn't feel too brilliant in the head piece. Blow colds why do we get them at all. 5.30 Had a nap and am tidied up and at last feel ever so much better but am afraid I've exhausted my news. Don't forget about the wedding. I'm awaiting your opinion. Hope you have many more Birthdays

love Ben

8.5.19

Dear Gug,

One letter received on Monday and another yesterday—you are a sport. I'm now awaiting a phone call from you as you said you would ring up sometime. I hope you have written out all you want to say as the 3 minutes go so awfully quickly.

Hope I won't disappoint you too much by not coming up but I cannot go. Father doesn't like me going as he says I float around as if I had an income of 500 pound a year. Perhaps he is a little bit on the right side. I do spend a lot going up there in the train so often.

Hope you enjoy yourself at Bessie's. I've got over my dislike for her completely, as a matter of fact now since I've come home, I like her.

Oh, Gertrude will probably be up on Monday as I want you to wait for a telegram so that we will make her decide what train she is soming on early then wire you. She leaves the office on Friday and THE day has been fixed for the 31st May. Mum and Keith have gone to town to do some shopping. Mother is getting a dress for the wedding and it is going to be black She says she looks best in black but we don't like the idea.

Bert is on *Wandilla* and will be here in less than 3 weeks time. If you have to wash up for 10, like you did the other day, when are you supposed to get your sewing done? I expected to hear what that Matron said to you last Saturday but you did not say anything about it and did you go? You said your Mother had written asking for an appointment.

I've seen Maggie Wood several times. What do you mean about getting Joes 1 pound per week divided up. Is your father paying you girls? Have you always to milk? Do you have any bother about getting wood for the fire now. Don't say that who ever has to do the kitchen does the chopping also.

I haven't seen Fred Waugh for ages but I had a chat over the phone to him and he is able wear his leg again now, but he is going to do it gradually instead of rushing it like last time. I bet when you ring up today I'll be away up in the workshop and so will lose some minutes. If in future you state a time I'll be there on the mark. Do you think I'm a good boy, I've given up cigarettes and taken to a pipe instead.

So glad Mary likes night duty. She is not on her own in a big ward is she? I wouldn't like that much. Do you remember that *Mystery of the Sea* well Dot was looking through it last night and she came on a huge mosquito. Did you put it in as a specimen of what bit you?. It was the biggest I've ever seen.

Don't you dare ever again offer to pay anything for me. Just wait until you are getting your 7/6 per week for hospital work then you won't offer so often. What about another 16 pager this week. I'm waiting to hear what you thought of my last letter.

Next sox Old Sport, make longer in the tootsie and a little wider at the top. Don't forget my one good leg is a bit fatter than it ought to be naturally. Now tell Elsie Daunt I wasted all last Monday going out to Randwick Hospital to see Whitfield and he was not in so I can't go out again.

I'm waiting to see if you will come down for the wedding. Don't bother about a new dress, I want to see you. *Comprez*. Our nice old washer woman has a child ill and can't come so we have this horrid person I told you about. Still kid Ruth about the Jimmy Lacey business? It is great fun I think. So sorry I can't come up. I'm trying to persuade K to go up with Gertrude but I don't think he is much hope at all.

I't s all very well saying if you got the flu you'd recover but if you didn't and I had to come all the way up to Sandgate. [cemetery] So you must NOT. I'm not grinding my teeth but you just dare thats all.

I'm getting on with the cabinet and it is going to be stained rose wood color. It is 3'x 2'x4' long (2 drawers and 2 doors) . The drawers and the doors are the only hard part about it. But it is going to be some job.

Have another nice book here I'll lend you when you want it by E.M Dell. Anatomy bones are very simple. I won't write them out as it will fill up the letter too much but if you want anything in that line I'll write it out and you'll only have to learn it.

The phone just rang but it wasn't you, some horrid man on wrong number. There are a lot of Khaki dresses round town. We'll do the block when you come down and I 'll show you some. Of course, there are some freaks too–I ll draw one I saw, [drawing] waists right up around their arm pits, consequently dresses short and I can't write any more.

Love Ben.

Saturday night May 1919

My dear old Gug,

Have this week received bosker letters from you commencing with an explanation of my last Saturday's letter telling me about you are unsure to say Yes. That's if you want to come you know. Turn on the water works if necesary. We'll all look after you and see you don't get the flu. And if you get SICK, I'll charm it away. I'm a very good talker but when it comes to acting the part. Oh don't mention it.

I believe this is going to be a long letter so just as well Gertrude is taking it up and I won't have to post it or Billie Little will say that is is over weight and charge you 3d. By the way how is old Miss Bedford this cold snap must be hurting her a good deal.

We washed last Tuesday and the clothes are still on the line as it has simply poured the whole week, not an hour but it rained. It's been terrible. Mind FJN, if you come down there's to be no time wasted calling on the Feltons and elswhere. We want you the whole time. Oh do come.

Last week has been a busy one–on Monday, Wednesday and Friday I went down with Bruce Rainsford. He is nearly a full fledged accountant now and sits for his final examination in a few months time. He looks very well indeed. We have booked a seat for you so you'll have to come down to Sydney. All the family 'cept Gertrude have gone for a walk in the rain as they said they felt dopey, but Ben William is keeping the fire warm–but there is no more wood and is on the out run. I'm not going over in the rain to get it–if you were here I'd send you. (I don't think) Gertrude will tell you all about the purchase of her riding boots especially and so Billy Haile is back. How does he look? Douglas Saddington came back in the *City of Poona* today. I haven't seen him yet but I suppose I will see him at church tomorrow. I must go or the people will think I've turned RC.

This morning I went down to McGrath for Physics lesson, he lives at Greenwich now. Anyhow I struck a bad time to come home when all the trains were going right through. I caught from St Leonards one train that went as far as Lindfield, another as far as Gordon and a 3rd up to Wahroonga, rotten wasnt it?

Freddie Waugh is now able to wear his leg but he is having a *Chapter of Accidents*. Yesterday morning getting out of the tram he broke his guide straps. They help the leg swing. Well the leg started to slip off, so he hopped 200 yards to a pub and they rang his home and his sister brought in his crutches. He says the people must have thought him mad hopping across George St and his woody half off and coming further off with each hop, It was raining too so it's a wonder he didn't slip. I'm mighty careful these greasy wet days. I don't want to break anything.

We had such fun moving my cabinet from the workshop the other day. This was the trouble. The door was wide enough but I couldn't turn the thing on an angle to get it out the door–the shed was too narrow. Dad, Keith and myself had to cut away the weather boards on the side of the shed, wouldn't a real carpenter laugh if he saw us doing it.

I hung around the telephone this afternoon waiting for your telephone ring but I think it must have been lost in the rain. It poured all day just like it has done since Monday. I always used to think Australia was a land of Sunshine but if an english (Captial E please) man had landed during this last week he would have thought himself back in foggy London once again. Keith is very disgusted with the weather.

Teach Gertrude how to ride please. Now look Frank, the reason I suggested getting in at Wallsend was that the Coast Hospital won't call for nurses until about February. They only call once a year and they called in Feb last. And I know you'd like to start. Of course I'd like you to be in Sydney. You don't know how I hate the idea of your going amongst all those dirty miners and they have a lot of fun at the Coast. But if you decide to wait, well and good. I would give you a better time if you were at the Coast than if you were at Wallsend. Couldn't I? So do as you think fit won't you. But don't let me persuade you to take either one, act as you think is the correct thing to do.

There are a host of people who are going to be at the *Veddun* as I keep always calling it. Again I say unto you *Do come* I'll make you ill on cream cakes and ice cream do come......

The physics I'm on is fearfully drum. Terrible stuff. There comes the family back again after a walk. Dad wore Keith's heavy military boots and he says he is sorry now. Do you know they weigh 5lbs 2½ each. How would you like to wear them. They are size 7 so would be slightly on the small size for your gigantic tootsies. Why did not you put on shoes when you chased *Spicey* out of the garden the other night and that would have saved you lighting the primus at that unearthly hour.

Do you think you will have that amount of energy for ever. Mum is *cracking hardy* but she has fearful pains in her legs. I'm sick of thinking of Poundals and Dynes and Force and Mass and Volume and pressures. I get all this much in Physics and my nut is a whirl.

I'd give a lot for an hours chat with you even over the phone would do. Did you see how a woman found a mouse in a Sargents Pie she was awarded 25 pounds in damages and from the statement in the paper she could have easily put it in after she arrived home.

I've just *bruk me poipe,* hitting it too hard to get the old bacey out. Rotten luck I paid 4/6 for it. Well I'm stuck for news so I'm going into my room to answer all your thousands of questions which I received in letters during the week. Don't forget to tell me everything in your letters. I feel quite relieved when I tell you all my troubles at the University–you feel as if you pass on your little troubles to some one else and don't have to mind them any longer.

What does your mother think of the book by Stratton Porter I read it sometime ago and I thought it would suit your style of beauty. There's no holidays in June so if you don't come down, what on earth am I going to do about seeing you? Do the trick Bonnie, say we will look after you and make Gertrude see your Dad about it. She said she would. Don't try to keep her longer than she wants to stay, like you do to me, you nice smoocher, for she says she has furniture etc to select.

Don't count the pages, I'm writing small you know. You know Bert and Ray [Carroll] looked very cheerful on Thursday when I saw them. A slice of Ray's brains would do me right down to the ground. His looks simply ooooze brains.

So youv'e a bruise the size of a cricket ball where a cow kicked you, well you know the old remedy, get a black man to kiss it and the bluey blackness goes out of it. Perhaps as you have no blackman handy, George Norrey would do. He is black enough and I'd like to be able to write in phonetics the way he talks *Huh Bath seats all the Barth I need* and he looks like it.

My woody is going well but the rain and cold weather makes the stump jump a good deal. Do you remember one night coming up from *The Man who came Back* at the theatre when we were coming up with Didie, how I jumped and nearly hit you on the chin, well it did the same the other day. Only you can't see it kick as it is inside the woody.

Anatomy is becoming more interesting. We dissect bodies next term rather a gruesome job I think it will be. At mechanical dentistry the other day a chap spilt some acid over his hands and he had to go to hospital to have them dressed they were burnt so much. There are a good number of fools in the world don't you think? Any one knows acid burns and if a chap is careless enough to spill it, says I *serve im right*.

Why do girls wear white shoes and stockings on a wet day so that they become splashed with mud, can you tell me? Such a lot of them are about during the past raining week. I must go to church tomorrow.

My razor has become so blunt it is agony to shave with it. Wish I was a girl so I wouldn't shave. It must be a blessing and it must be nice to get up and know you don't have to scrape your chin with a piece of steel. It is c-c-c-c-cold too.

So the old Cart horse is having an enforced spell owing to spiking it's foot etc She is a good goer when she likes. Has Mrs Griffin ever been to see you? What a pity you were not wearing an artificial leg when the cow kicked you. You see it has some advantages. People can stand on your toes in trams and you never know they are there until they say they are sorry.

Now if you come down you'll be all ok. Do you understand or remember what you told me might happen. Tell me if you remember.

You can't even go to see Norma as I have to entertain you at home so that you won't get the 'flu. Needless to say when Kelly wired, your Dad said *NO Kelly ever wanted on this selection anymore*. What a hide I wonder does he know that your father knows all he told the neighbours about his so called shortage of wages. Waugh is a clerk in father's office, that's how I get news of him so often because I've not seen him for months and months and months or as the Diggers say Donkey years. Keith has such awfully funny sayings.

I've left the ranks so long that I've forgotten the most of them. Some 4 officers from the 1st Battalion came back today. I know them all and Captain Bootle was my Company Commander for a long time.

So you have made a pin cushion and who is the lucky person to get it? me or are you going to keep it for a glory box. I suppose you have finished your sewing if you are making the pin cushion. Is your Ma going to help with the dresses. She could run them up in a couple of days for she is such a quick worker don't you think. I think she is a *rough* bit of a marvel at it to use a diggers expression. The way she joined those small pieces together to make that dress for Kitty was fine. Do you remember the one I mean.

If I cut off the ends of my words, don't worry, everyone else is in bed and Ben William is hurrying up so as to have one early night per week. Four more weary years. I haven't yet received any intimation about my pension. Awfully slow are they not.

The other day I got into a row at home. I'll tell you what is was about—You know I don't care for dolly pretty girls, well I said *I don't like pretty girls*. Mother said *Well you don't speak well of Frank then, don't you consider her pretty?* I said, *No Frank isn't pretty pretty but she is awfully nice* then Ma said *I think she has a very pretty hair*. Then I explained what I meant by prettiness. Do you know what to do to offend this family from Mother downwards and that is to alter your old frizzy hair.

You will only get a very skimpy letter in the middle of this week. it is going to be an awfully busy one for me. *Comprez*? No scandal to talk about at Tarro and has George Norley proposed to you yet? If he does let me now and I'll come up and cut him out. I'd like to hear him laugh—just now what I want is a huge giggle to keep me alive. But I'll giggle when I take you to *Goody Two Shoes* It's very fine I believe, quite as good as *Babes in the Wood* which Claire and Kitty saw when they were down here.

How are the two boys shaping? where do they sleep, Hut or Toms place and is Arthur still there. What Battalion was Buxton in? I got my trouser leg bottoms absolutely soaked this morning. I hate to feel them clammy, it always reminds me of Gueudecourt and winter of 1916 in France. It seems eons ago...scribble out.. Only something I couldn't spell, don't be curious, thats all. Curiousity is an awful thing isn't it?

Talking of curiosity, our cat is a splendid mouser and sits all day outside a mouse hole and generally brings one on to the verandah during the night. Field mice you know. The gill birds have been screeching nearly as badly as Dr Read's children and it makes some noise to beat them. Wonder will they get their weekly wacking. Tomorrow is Sunday and they generally get it on that day.

Well I'm sleepy, I suppose you are too 10.45pm. Pleasant dreams and no more chasing *Spicey* out and lighting the primus to wash your tootsies. Cheerio Ben

Sunday morning:

It rained all night and today it is awful. This is the worst week of rain I've ever seen. All our clothese are not dry from last Tuesday yet. Will they do any harm? I think we are going to have another flood, well I have an ark built, my cabinet will do for one. I call it the family vault as it has so many shelves to put things away in.

Well don't know what to say to you but I'll just meander on and hope you'll think I'm not too dopey. You see it is raining so hard we didn't get out of bed until 10am and there will be no church for us. Hope you are writing me a long letter, a good chatty one. Don't forget I'm to look for you at Wahroonga station at 6pm on Thursay 29th. Catch the 4.45 train down and as I'll be at lessons on Thursday afternoon I won't be able to meet you at Hornsby but 'll catch the 10 past 5 from Town and meet you on Wahroonga Station. Don't forget you simply have to come down. Or when am I to see you again? There are no holidays in June owing to all the holidays we have had through the *fluenza*.

I have not even one letter belonging to you. I've burnt them all. Could you do the same with all my letters excepting those you received while I was away. Could you do that for me Bonnie. I've a sore tongue, burnt it with some bread pudding yesterday, *no bon pour soldats*, is it.

Every boat that comes in brings someone or other from the old Battalion. Such a lot of people have replied to the wedding notices. I've told Mother you will be there and I expect Gertrude will be able to convince your Dad to let you come.

So Billy Haile has been telling you a few things about the war has he? and about the rum. Well sometime the men got too much but it might be once in 200 issues of rum, but due to the men themselves they are great. Give me Aussies anytime for a stunt, they leave everyone else miles behind in the mud. As for the poor old present day Tommy (not talking about the old regular Tommys you know, he is beyond comparison with anybody) he is not much chop at all. He looks neater than our men but in a scrap not much chop at all. I'd swap 6 Tommies for 2 Aussies any day.

I thought Joe had left for Taree? Didn't you drive him over to Tarro one day to catch the mail from Newcastle? I didn't think the Andersons were the style of people to owe money to a grocer. I thought Mr Anderson would pay up at least, even if Mrs A wouldn't. I wonder how she is getting on now. I bet they are sorry they left. They all find out when it is too late what a home they could have had. I had to laugh at the idea of Ruth telling Mrs A to *Shut Up*. Isn't it just like Ruth to do that.

A mate of mine, Marsland had the flu during the vacation and he said it came on him in ½ hour. He sat down, had his tea, smoked a cigarette then had to be carried to bed. They have the phone on now so we've had some long chats. I'm glad all the paths along our streets are asphalted now as when we first came up 11 years ago (on 3rd of the month) the paths were regular quagmires.

What crops are in down at the farm? The lucerne up I suppose, but I think your spuds will have wet feet if you've had as much rain as we have had. It doesn't rain you know. it comes down as if out of ever so many gutter spouts. A good pipe is much better than a cigarette I find and is cheaper in the long run. I'll have to go slow on the cash. Believe instead of buying a hot dinner in the middle of the day I will be content with tea and a pie (not a Sargents one though.)

There is another nice book coming by Gertrude, it is called *Greatheart* and it is very nice. You can return it some time or other. Take a long time over it. I enjoyed it thoroughly and don't bother paying 6d to send it down. Keep it until some one comes up or someone comes down.

Mother has got hold of some of the military songs Keith and I sing. I'm sure she would shock Mrs Strang [a friend] who is president of Temperence Union in Sydney if she heard her. Its funny to hear some of our phrases like *Goodo* or *set like a jelly* coming from the girls lips.

What year and what faculty is Heather doing, Arts or Medicine, is she 1st 2nd or 3rd year. I'm sorry I can't arrange to meet her but in Dentistry we have hardly a moment off during the first year and is extended one year starting this year. All students who entered the Uni for Medicine this year have to do 6 years instead of 5. Bert [Carroll] will of course only have to do his 5 years.

Church bells are going. I like to hear them with their *Come to Church* each time it clangs. Gertrude is dyeing, I mean making my green sox a tan color or thats what I think she is doing in the kitchen.

Have you noticed the price of iron goods, kettles, saucepans etc They are simply an awful price. Dad tried to get an iron kettle the other day and he could only get a small one and the price was awfull. This is an awful place for breaking dishes, someone broke our extra large meat dish and we blamed the cat.

I bet there will only be about 6 people in church this morning, cats and dogs and big sized butcher boys and you know what that means.

I want to get in touch with Vic Fowler who was my mate in France. The only address I've got is that he lives somewhere near Albury NSW so I 've enclosed the letter and addressed it to Post Master at Albury. I hope old Vic gets it. He is a Sgt Major in that Sergeants group which I believe you have somewhere. He has had stiff luck—should have been a Captain by this but he had the unfortunate habit of rubbing up against Senior officers. He received his commission a year after I did and he taught me all my work and then I beat him for a commission.

Gertrude is busy studying a book called the Etiquette of Marriage and she is practising what to do—when to hold his hand etc when to pull off her glove. Do you remember when we were up at Feltons, how Todd said, Would it be etiquity to do such a thing. Sounded funny didn't it.

More rain . Is there anything in this letter that isn't about rain. It is not what some people would call a love letter is it? I'm thankful to say. Well I've reached my lot; I've told Gertrude I won't come to her wedding unless she makes Mr Niland let you come down. So she is sure to influence him. Don't forget come down on the Thursday before and stay a week. That is what Mother suggested so you will have to do it. Its no good coming for less than a week and mother wants to you to stay a week. She says you can take Gertrude's place for a week if you must come down on Thursday Evening, don't forget.

Love from Ben

Write immediately you know whether you can come or better still send a wire so as Mother can get things fixed up. She wants you to come, don't forget that your mother knows that. Ben

Saturday 11.5.19

My dear Gug,

You cannot imagine how upset I am over the last letter I received from you. It was very small owing to you being upset about something which you did not explain and which has worried me some as to what it can be. Please answer these questions as fully as possible. Why oh why can't you go out to Wallsend Hospital. Is it because of the dressmaking or has something else happened? I want you to set your teeth and go your hardest to get it done so that you can get done with the sewing. You can do it you know. Don't let anyone beat you, you are set on going, so go.

You won't be insulted but you honestly couldn't fill a clerical job in an office. You are not built for it and nursing would suit you right down to the ground–so go to Wallsend. Now about the Coast, you have to have 7 dresses to start with but after being there 6 months they (do not give money for dresses) supply you with 12 yards of dress materials so that won't help with the money. Dad says they have a waiting list and you have no show of getting in for 6 months or so. So that's closed to you. Do try to get into Wallsend. You must know I'd love to have you down here old girl, but Wallsend with its 8 hours would fit your mark. I know you won't be frightened of work but you couldn't go home much you know, not more than once every 6 months and you honestly would be home sick if you came to the Coast.

Write straight away won't you as invitations for the wedding are going out and you could make the dresses on your own if you went hard at work now. Even accept your Father's help and pay for the dresses. Get into Wallsend–don't be beaten. I thought you had more pluck.

Now that's done. I start at the University on Monday and will have to work hard to make up all our lost time so won't be able to write you much or often except on weekends.

Yesterday afternoon I went down to the Smiths at North Sydney for tea and afterwards we went to an evening at Mrs Andersons place in Neutral Bay. Had a nice time but they all brought along their girls. Why don't you live down this way so that I could have taken you along. But all the time I was wondering why you were not going to Wallsend.

You must have had a busy week as up to date I've received no letter telling me if you like your book and Gertrudes paper. When you rang up on Thursday you said you had posted a letter. Well I have not received it but got this short one saying you were in trouble.

Do you think the other letter has gone astray? Why did you say *Oh You're a beauty* over the phone. Is it because I didn't come up? Well where am I to get a one pound from to go up. I've been up so often and you've only been down twice. I have other things to do beside chasing up there. Of course I like to come because you are there but I don't get a free railway pass you know and a pound is a pound. Franco I want you to become a nurse. Do you want to please me or not.

Have been having glorious weather recently, strange for May. Your voice sounded so loudly on the phone it is hard to believe you are all that distance away. Did you like the book? Towards the end of the evening last night they had a dance there where Ben William was left out in the cold. Wish you had been there. We had a game called Dumb charades. Half the party goes out and thinks of a word, then they have go in and act it out. My party chose the word Character 1) we pretended we were out in a car 2) Then we just acted goat that represented act 3) then we dressed up and read palms to find the character of a person That represented the word character or caracter you see. The next word was *Bulletin* Some one shot someone else the doctor rushed in a extracted the bullet which was showed to all present 2) we next went in holding tins that represented *Bulletin*.

I'm not in the mood for writing until I get your next letter explaining your trouble. What's the programme today? Have the Douglas family come along or have you gone Churchward. Come down the river bank in the old trap and I'll have a snooze. I've just come home 4pm. Slept last night with Eric Smith and he said I nearly kicked him out of bed with my one foot. I packed a big box full of Gertrude's things on Saturday morning. She has such a beautiful lot. The tea set her office gave her, Doulton Ware is very swish indeed. Green and white. It's really a breakfast set, large cups. She is getting such a lot of things.

I forgot my pyjamas last night so borrowed a pair of Mr Smiths. He is nearly as big as your Dad. I must have been a nice shape in them. All my curves must have stood out to their best advantage, don't you think? I must have looked like an ancient Greek God or rather like Dreamy Daniel in a Comic paper. As we didn't get to bed 'til 12.20 pm, the bewitching hour of mid–night, needless to say I did not get up to Breakfast, which a prim and staid old maid brought to my bedside.

They are very kind. Miss Smith that was, now a Mrs Mackenzie was also there. I like her.

Ginger is all right. At home every night last week. What do you think of that. He is o.k. now. The Fellowship Girls gave Gertrude a nice picture on porcelain and she is going to get those pansies you gave her framed. Mean thing, you might do something for me in that line.

I didn't see anyone last night I liked as much as 1/100 part of you. Do go to Wallsend. Write me a long chatty letter telling me what you intend to do about it. I'm all at sea–cannot imagine your mother refusing to make your dresses. Have you seen the upfolds recently and how is Bessie Nicholl. Maggie Wood was in again on Friday night. Why I had to sleep with Eric Smith was a friend of theirs turned up (one leg too) while we were away and he hopped in to the only spare bed.

Two cousins in Melbourne have the influenza. Harry caught it from a patient and gave it to his wife. A nice sort of a present don't you think?

My beautiful cabinet is finished you ought to see it. It is terribly *bon*. I varnished it in a rosewood color and now it is making the other things in my room look shabby. I've kicked out the wash stand to make room for it. I don't need a wash stand, I always visit the bath room. It is less work for Mother. She'd clean the stand every day you see.

Today is set apart as Mother's day so everyone is wearing a white flower in rememberance. Nice don't you think. Mother's are good the way they slave for their children. Well study tomorrow *Just Imagine*. Did you notice on the paper round that Book that Mother sent when she printed the address, couldn't spell New Castle. If she wrote as many letters up there as I do she would know don't you think.

The little dynamo of an engine next door is puffing away. [Next door neighbour Fisk, had a Marconi wireless] Suppose they intend to send away a message tonight. Wish you had the wireless on to your house. I could send you a message in less than a second, Why I could even talk to you. They can speak now, that is the latest invention. Fancy speaking to the Alfieries or someone else in England, Marvellous.

The Fisk memorial at the corner of Stuart and Cleveland Streets Wahroonga.

I can't write today the pen slides all over the place, do you notice. I'm disapointed over my last letter, make it up to me Bonnie. I'm so glad Eric and I are going through together he is more my style than Ginger.

Some nice dresses at this show last night. Do you notice flounces are coming on again on the skirts.

Thunderstorm is on, black and very large drops of rain and this morning the sun was so 'ot. Will you do your best about coming down–finish your dresses? Fondest love my Frank

Yours Ben

—

14.5.19 Wednesday night

Dear Bonnie,

This is just a very short note for I've an awful lot of work to do. A lot of back work to pick up, so forgive me. I wouldn't write until Saturday when it will be a long one but I know its rotten not getting letters. It's funny I 've never yet got that 6 pager you posted the day you rang me up. You haven't yet explained why you are not going to Wallsend.

We have had soaking rain for 2 days, not just showers but wholesale downpours the whole time, consequently wearing shoes as I do, my socks get wet but it is only the one that matters. The leg is always more tender on wet days.

This poor chicken is absolutely *wore to a shudder*. The Physics and Chemistry now getting me more and more at sea and I can only hope for the best though I doubt that I will pass. Then I'll be a gallant one chance and that is all.

Saw Bert Carroll yesterday and not Ray. Tell Elsie Daunt I saw Whitfield from a tram and his right hand is wounded or rather he has it in a white glove so suppose it is.

We sent you a notice for the wedding. You'll break my heart if you don't come down, don't forget. Though I won't be able to take you out too much at all, *Comprez*. But do come. Go down on your knees to your Dad if necessary. If you buy a new dress for the wedding you'll be spanked.

Today at Mechanical dentistry for some of the chaps the work was hard, as I finished my todays work last day, I spent most of the time faking results for the others and everyone was passed by the boss cockie. Some skalliwag, what do you think I am.

One of the chaps spilled some acid over his trousers. If they don't fall to pieces before he gets home it is a wonder. Luckily he had an overcoat with him. Today is day of Big Schools boat race and it poured cats and dogs the whole time and I bet the onlookers got wet. Did you write to Heather Adamson telling her I couldn't meet her. I didn't get home until 7pm tonight. Blow the university.

All I can think of is you coming down. Do come. Keith is getting on but he only growls at the Military. He went to see Dr Gordon Craig privately. So glad the two boys are a success, but you know new brooms sweep cleanly and they might be bothers later on.

So glad you didn't fix the halter on Belmont. So he pulls away does he? Forgive the short note but it is just a go between to save you being too disappointed, I know you will be. But must study

Love Ben

Tuesday 27.5.19

My dear Gug,

I'm in bed, have been there since Monday night. Got a light touch of the ordinary flu. Its no bon and I feel about worth 6d. Anyhow I'm going to make an effort to get into the Uni tomorrow. I'm missing too much work.

The joint in my woody has swelled through the rain and it will hardly swing. Isn't it strange. I wonder if you have had as much rain as we have had. Talk about raining for 40 days and nights. The Big flood isn't in the running with the rain we've been having. Supppose you have only had a drop compared to ours and Bergelin says they have hardly had any at Tamworth. Mr Adamson's son has a block of land there, he won't be more than a few miles away. Quite neighbours when you think of the Country. Have you any roads left? Ours are like troughs with brown colored porridge in them.

All the beggars are ahead of me now I've been away 2 days. I think I'll be able to come up in 4 weeks time for 5 days if I'm asked and be sure Creamy is shod won't you. Will you be able to come across to Mrs Griffins with me?

Have you written to Matron at Wallsend Hospital telling her you are not coming? It could be nice for her to know so as she can make other arrangements.

I have not seen Peggie or Winnie for some time. Gertrude is ticking off the days until Saturday. A friend of Ruperts is going to drive Gertrude, myself and Edie down in a motor car and on Friday night Nancy Johnson is driving to town with a car full of flowers for decorating purposes. When the people say all the nice things about Gertrude tonight I won't be there. Cold air would be not *bon* for me.

How is Belmont? Fit for driving to Morpeth? Eric Smith's Aunt, a Mrs Tell died on Sunday night the funeral was yesterday so he went. He rang me up to ask if I had yesterday's notes of the work and was surprised when Gert told him I was in bed. Doesn't it seem absurd, all that time on active service and not a cold and now back to Comfort I get the ordinary flu. Rotten I call it. I did not get my chest rubbed with the the rough edge of 1/2 brick. I believe its a good thing though.

Did you start *Great Heart* and if so do you like it. New shoes and sox and dresses. This family will look flash on Saturday. There is some rumour that Greig is going to be married but not a Wahroonga girl, I'm sure of that. My room is awfully dark but not ½ as bad as yours. I think some one had better smash a window through above your chest of drawers.

The passion fruit vines are to the very top of the summer house now and ½ all over it. I'm proud of them and by summer it will look very good indeed. Worst bit of it I can't learn any chemistry or stuff while I'm in bed it hurts my eyes. I thought France was bad enough for wetness but Aussie is just as bad. This is the wettest season I've ever known in my 400 years on earth–or it feels like that.

Well Chum, Old Girl I can't write any more, custard and nutmeg has just been brought to me with instructions to eat it all (quite unnecessary I assure you)

Fondest love Ben

31.5.19 Saturday
after the wedding

My dear Gug,

You can imagine our joy this morning on opening our eyes to see a fine glorious sun shiny day. Of course you know we all booked a fine day for her but we didn't think we could get one. It was just perfect and I'm terribly sorry you were not there. But you know *Spilt Milk* Etc. Your garters came along and they were just splendid. You are a clever girl in the sewing line. That reminds me in 29–30 days I'll be along to see you. We get a weeks vacation at the end of June so if Wallsend Hospital notice comes along, don't go. I must see you. We have a term exam at the end of June and as soon as it is done I'll be along.

Well about the Veddun. All the morning Gertrude was writing letters thanking people for presents and some one said *what a glorious day* and G said *Thanks heavens I don't have to write to anyone thanking them for it*. You just ought to see her presents, magnificent is not the word, it is beyond my vocab. Anyway she has dozens of silver things, one tea set and Oak tray *say no to work* cost 15 pounds and the Church gave it to her Stainless knives etc and linen, real stuff given by Mrs Strang. ½ dozen best linen goods, Table sets etc. You know you don't want me to tell you all the items. Good pictures, serviette rings. It made me wish I was getting married to see them all. Then I supppose I wouldn't get many things, not being as nice or as good as Gertrude.

Mr Hanley, a Government man, said if Bergelin wasn't the luckiest man alive, he doesn't know who is. And Frank, I only hope he is good to her. But I don't see how anyone could be otherwise to Gertrude. Lot of our closest relations were there and some of Rupes and I believe the show went off well enough. I thought it was getting a little stiff once so I acted the goat a bit and things went along merrily. Nancy Johnson sent down loads of white and pink flowers and the Rooms were smothered in them. They were so tastefully decorated. This is the first time I've seen a Presbyterian marriage ceremony. No one kneels down at all. There is a very short service, then the minister joins their hands and asks the usual question you know and then pronounces them married. A ring is not necessary at all. But of course, at Gertrudes wish Mr Dykes brought that in. Talking of rings, Gertrude's latest is a 5 diamond, nice and plain and solid and its [a drawing] better than her engagement one. Gertrude wore an old Rose colored hat, her bluey grey coat and skirt with a fawn lace front and the collar was crimped at back. Navy blue silk stockings and patent leather shoes. She did look nice and I think she is pretty. She had a great colour up too. Berg looked ok but he whispered to me before the ceremony started *see if when I kneel down you can see the price on my new boots* But they didn't kneel so I pulled up his boot afterward and 43/6 was scratched across the insteps. I nearly died laughing.

Quite a number of people asked if you were coming, close relations of course. But I told them some excuse or other to the men and I said if she was here I wouldn't introduce you, then mentioned *never introduce your donah to a pal*? Anything to make them laugh. Afraid I acted the goat a little but it smoothed things over. Just before the family left for the service, Young Tom cut his hand rather badly with the Tommy axe and the silly young prawn fainted. We left him with a lady friend who came to look after the house for us and he did not mind being left behind.

Strange how Tom fainted. Mother ran and caught him and put him on the ground but couldn't lift him. I didn't know I was so strong, but I lifted him with one hand by the trousers and coat on to a bed. The other hand of course I was holding on to my stick. No one knows how strong they are until put to the test. Do you remember the day I made your wrists red. I could have cried when I saw it too. I'll never forget it. Suppose you have forgotten it long ago.

Of course nearly every body had a new dress on and on the whole the turn out was a credit to the Champions. Just a social gathering. I hate things when they are stiff. We wired into fruit salad, jelly and cream etc like wild fire and I was sorry to say we left a lot over. About 35-40 people were there. The cake was a great affair. I thought it such a shame to cut it. A 3 tiered affair with billing doves on top and regular dome pillars around the sides. Of course no confetti was the order of the day but we waited until they were getting into the car and their backs were turned so that none would get into Rupert's eye then we let them have it. I pushed a handful down his neck collar. I bet it's tickly now, something like biscuit crumbs in your bed when you are not well and I reckon that is the most irritating thing one could have. dont you?

Well, do you think I've told you enough *about the veddun*? Of course the bridesmaid was Edie, all in white with a Be-u-tiful bunch of freezias daffodils etc. Rupe gave Ede a silver purse. But I just wish you could see the presents. Rupe said had he known she was loved by some many people, he would never have dared. As we came out of the Club, of course a crowd gathered and some one said *Oh there is another good man gone, poor chap he's married now* Don't you think it's horrid. If Gertrude couldn't make any chap's life happy he wouldn't be worth much of a man. There was an old boot tied on behind the car but Gert spotted it and off it came. But we got even by planting a ½ empty box of confetti on the tail lamp and every now and then some would spill out onto the road. Oh, we've had a splendid day.

Don't forget to keep that week clear for me to come up. No colds or headaches or toothaches etc And you'll have to cheer me up as I'll probably have failed in my exam. It's a hopeless task Franco. The more I learn the more I find out I know NOTHING. Worldly experience or general education is no good. It must be a narrow and deep on on a few subjects that are not necessary in dentistry. I've a cousin out there, a 4th year Med student and she says the same.

I'm OK once again now except a wheezy chest and a bark like a dorg. The masks in lectures are cows of things too. Franco did you do what I asked you with my last Sunday letter? Tell me. Now look, I'm not rousing, but Franco suppose when some night you were coming from the station alone. George Norley got hold of you. I know his type, powerfully strong you know. What could you do. The mere fact of his having suggested something to you shows he has you on his brain. So fight shy of him will you and don't have a word to say to him, there's a sport. He is a maniac of a special class and although he is quiet now, if he had the advantage, where would he go too. I'm not an alarmist.

How are you old girl, did you have a fine day and I expect to hear on Monday that reason, don't forget. I had a welcome surprise this morning, my brother sent me down a cheque for the money he owed me, a tidy little sum and very acceptable because so far, although I've been worrying them I have had no money as a pension yet. Very slow don't you think, only 9 weeks waiting for it.

Tomorrow we start a new month and before it is over I hope to see you. Glad I'm an out door patient at *Oaklands* and can come when I like etc But not go when I like as you generally make me stay a day over my time, don't you? Will you come for a ride this time and be sure Creamy has shoes on his tootsies. I'm glad we don't have our shoes nailed on. I'd like to get a light pair on sometimes.

Thanks for your last letter. Terrible bon and long. Gertrude says she is awfully busy so won't write to thank you for the Garters but I'm to do the trick. We had a scotch lady minding the house and she said *The girl won't be a wee pur bride the now the sun's out and she has her blue garters*

No news at all from Vic Fowler, suppose the letter did not reach him at all. The dashs you ask about represent swear words which I think everytime I think of the University and 5 long years.

What a funny girl you are, all the summer you said it was too hot now you are too shivery. You want a tonic I think or some outside interests. So you like the books I send you, well so they ought to please you. I think I know the style you like and I pick the best books I've read to fit it. You are going to have the loan of another soon. *Lorna Doone* it is a beauty and I think I've read it at least 6 times, after that *Carette of Sark* and *Maid of the Silver Sea* both by John Oxenham. So if you are not a well read young lady by this time you've finished, it won't be my fault or yours either. Sorry I can't keep on the G.O.P.s but I know you, comprez, nuff said.

When you do the tan sox, don't forget to make the foot longer than my khaki or the grey sox will you. My tootsie, horror of horrors is growing bigger with all it's work but it can still keep a grip on old Australia and today was one of the best days. Yes that cupboard or rather minature chest of drawers I had made has a lock and key so now I have a place to put my private papers and any stray cash anyone MIGHT give me. You see it is a very big might. I'm not handsome enough for anybody to die and leave me any money. Keith says he is looking for someone with plenty of money but about 100 years old to marry. He says he would only have a few years misery then he'd be set.

Yes I'm certain Waugh is 34 Battalion. I remember that chap Clouson but he must have gone missing after I left the Battalion as he was there when I left it at Strazeele. I met Didie the other night coming home but she wouldn't let me come up 2nd class with her. She is a thoughtful girl. She knew I would have further to walk at Wahroonga and of course it was raining. She is a well built women now isn't she? Maggie and Winnie Wood went up to see her last night and they came in to see us to find the way before they went.

Didie spent her holidays up at Leura and it rained the whole time except 2 days, bad luck wasn't it but she says she enjoyed having not much work to do. She went up to friends. Mr Felton is up at Casino just now. Isn't the Hunter in flood yet? It would be if you had had the rain we've had. Frank it is absolutely the worst I've ever seen and it reminded me of Gueudecourt on the Somme in Winter 1916. It was terrible and we lived under bivouac sheets and the ground was liquid under us. Any how the soft mud was better to sleep on than a hard floor. I'll never forget the night I slept alongside an old cow to keep me warm and keep some of the rain off, you see I got on the lee side of her and though she moved in the night I followed her around until she stopped and then put my water proof sheet down again.   Now what are you stowing away to rouse on me for, besides lending my trousers to Keith. Your skilful fingers could soon renovate them for me. So out with the scolding. I'm along way away from you so you can't hurt me bodily, *comprez*.

Will Mary be paying us a visit when she is down? She doesn't want a formal invitation and now Gert is not here there is another bed vacant so tell her from Mum we will be glad to see her. Any of Ruth's talkings too would be worth listening too, she has a wonderful flow of language and I'll certainly tell Bert. What about Jimmy Lacey?

Do keep out of Wallsend until after I've seen you, won't you? Just seeing you for a few hours per day and having to stop at a pub is no bon for me. No doubt there is some mistake about Jimmy and the military charging 3/–. It must be for clothes he did not return when he left the area or something like that.

Joe's a fool and I can't understand him sponging on you the way he does. Kick him out and about his business unless your Dad wants another man or boy rather Has he had a 'air cut yet?

Foxes are pretty things. If you can get a skin I'll have it made up for you into a muff or something or other. They make pretty caps. So are our chooks starting again? Train Jimmy to get the eggs each day so there will be nothing for me to do except take you out.

Well I'm about stuck for news. Tom send his love to you. I told him I didn't know if you had any left I had all to be given away. Then I said you always send it down to him and he was quite pleased.

How are you today, breezy and bright I hope as the Comic papers say. I'm going to start and work until 11 each week night now instead of 10 but Oh I feel dopey in the morning, as if someone had tied a lump of lead on the bottom of my woody. It's going rather well lately though the wet weather makes the joint stiff. I'm going to put in a new lace after I've written this. I've almost come to the end of my tether for now, is it any wonder after 10 pages. But a whole 10 pager is not worth 1/2 hours chat is it.

I always am sorry after you ring up because I had such lot to say and I always forget it in my rush to get to the phone. So don't ring up again for some time, besides I don't like you to use the public phone when there there is so much 'flu about. Do as I tell you. You know. Grandfather speaking, –it seems like it, but one word from Ben and you do as you like as the scriptures Saith.

How is your Uncle Will Niland? is he coming back or is he on that job still. I'm going out by the fire to see if I can think of anything else–also to warm my hand. Well I've warmed them and now I can't rake up any more news good enough for you. I'm going to take some Corff mixture and go to the land of nod.

Dreamt a shell chased me round a telegraph pole last night. It had legs and arms and was reaching out for me. Woke up to find head right under the clothes which I don't like. Do you still sleep out? No more news. Keep that week clear the 1st in July for me *Beaucoup* love

Ben

Did you do what I asked you to do with last Sundays letter. I want to know, also that reason.

————

Kings Birthday Holiday
9.6.19

Dear Gug,

I could not imagine why I waited so long for a letter last week. You wrote me on 27th May and the next one I received was on 6th June, an interval of 13 days. But I'm so very sorry you've been ill. I had an idea something must have been the matter because it was just twice as long as I've waited for a letter since I came home. But in future to stop me worrying just address an envelope and put a few lines inside will you please.

Yesterday afternoon I went to the Feltons but Mr Felton is still away in Kempsey. He came home to Hornsby and then went back the same distance and he could only stop one day. Well I went up, and I don't know what to think of Didie. She looks so awfully dismal. I haven't not decided yet but I think its up to me to take her out a bit, ask her down to see Marjorie to play etc Anything to amuse her. You see the trouble was this. A huge box came from Birmingham full of Arthurs clothes and it must have broken her up a lot to see them. Can't a brother's death affect people especially Didie to whom Arthur was all in all.

I did feel so sorry and sad when I saw them. I think it would have been better for them if they had never turned up. All they can do is hold them up and air them and the memory will be just as sharp each time they do it. Poor Old Art, to see his uniform, every crease in it, I know like my own and he is not in it. He was such a good mate.

Just a week and 2 days since Gertrude was married and Mother is the only one who has seen her in all that time She is living in a flat near Potts

Point somewhere. A great chum of mine and Arthur's too came up to see us on Saturday, Tom Brown is his name. He is an Englishman and married over there. His baby is 3 years old and such a darling. Tom's wife comes from Yorkshire. She and the baby have only been in Australia a week last Saturday. She is so very very shy. We took them out on a walk and I think she enjoyed seeing the houses and gardens. We loved to make her talk to hear the way she talks is so funny yet so pretty.

Oh I was glad to see Tom Brown. This is the first time since November 1916 and I sent him on a job he was hit on too, but he doesn't mind as he says I got him a wife and he is happy. Said he wouldn't change to single again for all the tea in China He has improved too. Quieter and more of a gentleman and to see the rough Tom I knew look after his wife as if she was a little piece of china and might break. It is lovely Frank and he is happy.

Edie had her Sunday School class up the same day and one of the little girls slipped and dislocated her knee. It was the worst dislocation I've ever seen. The knee cap slipped from in front of the knee right around under the bend of the knee. I rang up the Doctor. Tom Brown carried her inside and Dr Read came over. As soon as he saw it he rang for another Doctor who administerd Chloroform and so the poor little kid, she was about 11 years old, must stay in the same postion for a fornight and she is lying on my bed so I'm kicked out. It's very inconvenient dressing and undressing in the Dining Room. I'm sleeping outside on Gertrudes bed and its terrible cold during the night.

Well as you told me Mary is coming down. I wrote to her care of Mrs Rumery [aunt] asking Mary to have morning tea with me at Farmers on Friday morning. Didie is to come along too so that will be all right won't it? You say you are not jealous. But there is some trouble about the letter I wrote. I gave it to Dad to post. He did not post it and I can't find out who did. But it is not in the house anywhere that I can see.

Tom Brown is out of work so Dad and I are trying to get him some to do. We are going to ring Uncle Bert Holt Manager of Dobbs Frank and Co and see if he can be put on as a mechanic. Tom's wife is so shy, Mother and Edie were fixing up the little girl. Marjorie and Dot were out so when it was time to go home I lit Mothers room gas and told Mrs Brown it was lit and would she put on her hat. She was so shy she caught Tom by the hand and said *Tom come with me* She says all the Australian men seem to her to have hard faces but she said I was an exception. I told her it was probably because I went to the country so often. And she can't understand me at all so Tom had to interpret for me.

Can you understand this small writing. Hope you won't have to take to specs because of it. I'll be up on 28th or 29th if you'll have me. Make up a programme and be a good comrade to me. I don't want to stop about the house if I can, I want to be out in the sunshine. See that Creamy is shod won't you.

Your 2 pages has just come. I get letters quickly when posted at Tarro as compared with when they are posted at Tighes Hill by the baker. So your old baker is back? Did Palmer ever find his account book again or what will he do if he did not.

What a shame to have all those daughters. What is the name of that man in Maitland who keeps a store there and has ever so many daughters. One of his cars ran away and smashed into a tram some little time ago, I read about it in the paper.

Dad and Marjorie are busy mowing the lawn down the front. It's a glorious day and a shame to be in doors. Why are you not here. What would you say if I took Didie out today? Would you mind? You would still be the only girl but she does look so solemn and miserable.

Look Bonnie I've just rung up Didie and I am going to take her to Manly. Tell me what you think of it. I'm keeping all your letters now they are safely under lock and key, only I wish mine to you were also. Its so awfully inconvenient that poor little girl being in my room. I can't go in for anything at all and she is in a lot of pain. The ligaments of the leg have been torn out, a rotten thing.

On Saturday I went down to Mc Grath the tutor you know, at St Leonards, well coming home as I was walking to the station a chap in a bike and side car haled me and it was Os Andrews, well he brought me right home in the car. It was a bosker trip, only the roads are frightfully dumpy. I had my stick in the car of course and every now

and then a horrid dog would come out barking at us and I'd just shake
my stick at him, and off he would go yelping as if he was hit and I
didn't touch them at all.

How is Blue? Have his paws become all right again after being
squashed under the lorrie. What on earth is Joe doing? Have you all at
Oaklands adopted him. Doesn't he work for his living now at all. But
I bet he gives as much cheek as ever. I've had a rotten week at the Uni,
no chop at all, awfully hard and tedious too. So when I don't get a letter
from yóu I feel done.

Such a lot of troops came back on Friday. Smith and I are right
ahead of all the others in mechanical dentistry I've been helping Smith
with the Dentistry and he has been coaching me in physics. Its an awful
subject Bonnie, and so hard its practically higher mathematics. Oh I'm
dreading this exam on 27th 28th I'm getting frightened of it. If it was
only something where there was a risk attached to it I could sail in and
fix it but being brain work and my nut is like a porous flower pot I can't
do it. But I'm trying terrible 'ard.

I hope I see Mary on Friday. She will probably be able to tell me a lot
about you that you have not said yourself. What about that dancing? If
you learn then you might be able to teach me. At the Ball the other day
there was a man dancing. He has had his leg 10 years though so if you
could teach me I wouldn't like to go to a class you know.

Dot is trying to learn to ride a bike. She is not too sure of it.
Goes down the path a little. Mother is quite upset about the little
girl. Her father comes up to see her. But she has only a step mother
and is not too happy. She told mother she did not have a proper
mother. Sad isn't it.

I'm frightened you may have to take to specs if I write small but
I've got in the way of doing so through writing my lectures quickly.
Suppose your Dad has told how Mr Carroll is, as he went to see them.
Feltons yesterday had a visit from Miss Fredericks. She now lives in
Queensland but came to Sydney for a holiday so came to see them. I
have not had a chat to Freddie Waugh for ages but he is the sort not to
give the show away about Burton at all. He is a fine sort.

Now you always say I'm good to write such long letters to you. Don't you think you are worth them, I do and I want to keep you. I'm supplying Dad with tobaccy today all the shops are closed.

So you like the fountain pen Eh!. I wouldn't be without mine. Gertrude received your telegram and you were the very first to write to Mrs Bergelin and she thinks a lot of it. I'm going to rouse on you when I see you privately. I can't write it in a letter. No wonder you were ill and if you care for me you will have to take more care of yourself. I'll tell you about it when I see you on Newcastle Station.

I'll have to give your Dad a hand at erecting the machine. What news of them? Wait 'till you see my cabinet. I'm proud of it and if I ever have a home it is going to be in it. Dad offered me first of all 3 pound then 5 pound for it and it only cost me 1 pound, fifteen shillings and four pence in materials.

Mrs Turner making you sox and mittens. I'd make them for you only I'm busy (I don't think) How is Belmont? Do you ever drive him. Re the garters, I saw them safely installed in place before Gertrude left. Don't worry. If I know her she has them off and safely wrapped in tissue paper. Did you make them honestly?

Toms hand is better and well. He is like me a cut or a wound heals up in no time. Rupe said to Mother the confetti I put down his neck was a dash side more tickly than Bathurst Burrs or cake crumbs. Old Norley might not be able to run but I know you can when you like, you staid old thing but he could do other things to stop you. Be a good mate to me this time I'm up. I like a girl to do all the things a man can and be a tom boy.

I got all the balance of my pension which was due, about 18 pounds in all at 30/–per week. Some little sum, but books I owed ½ of it on bills etc.

Please remind me to make a catch on that gate so that Creamy can't possibly get out and give you the bother of running round in the night time and perhaps get a chill. Oh you are wicked. To get out of a warm bed when you feel not too brilliant and march out into the cold. I don't want to attend to a funeral. Think of me.

Keith is still looking for an old protestant lady aged 105 years with plenty of money. I tell him they are very hard to find. I couldnt think of one for him.

Don't talk if Tarro roads being bad as ours are as bad too. One main road is just slush and on the main Parramatta road motors have been BOGGED.

Cold hands terrible. Cold heart you know. I would never confess to cold hands, but I know you. The cloth Maggie gave Gertrude was a beauty so neat from such a good linen. Winnie gave her a tea cosy, all crochet and very fine 50 cotton I think she said. Well Bonnie, I'm afraid I've come to the end of my tether, can't write any more but I think is is equal to a 10 pageras the writing at first was very small. Cheeriho love from

Ben.

PS keep smiling, write soon and keep keep your tootsies warm.

21.6.19

My dear Gug,

Only a week before I see you once again. How long is it since we parted on Tarro Station? Can you manage to come down to Newcastle to see me? We have an exam at 12 oclock of Thursday morning and another one at 11am on Friday morning. I'm not certain as to what time the 2nd exam is so I don't know what train exactly but I'll wire you on Thursday. But it is a certain I'll be up on Friday night as long as I don't get 'flu. I want to make as much out of my brief stay as possible.

Suppose while I'm writing this you are driving home with Mary and Todd (Felton). I think I gave Mary a good day yesterday, at least I hope so. If you hear her say she enjoyed it just tell me. You see you have all been so jolly good to me that it's up to me when I get the chance to try and do something isn't it? Oh these wretched exams. Will I ever get through, lets hope so.

Ow I'm a wailing and gnashing. I've lost my dental instruments I used down in the Dental Hospital. They are all gone as far as we know.

The Dental Hospital in Chalmers St was severely damaged by a fire that broke out late on 17 June 1919 in adjoining 8 storey premises of Burnet and Co Ltd, wholesale grocers–

City of Sydney archives www.

A 1000 ton brick wall smashed right through the building and buried and smashed them all. Rotten luck isn't it. Where on earth am I to get another 8 pounds to replace them all.

Well hope Mary gives you good news of me. I've been wearing a bow tie the last few days. Can you tie them. It takes me about 15 minutes each morning to tie it. But I think it looks nicest. What do you think of it? I was so sorry that Mary and I had to leave the play *Nothing but the truth* so early, but Mary didn't have a coat and I think 11pm is late enough to be out in the night time. I'm quite anxious to know how it ended.

I can't write this week there are 4 things putting me off 1) Too excited at the idea of once more seeing you. 2) Knowing that Mary will give you all the News. 3) Chemistry exam on Thursday 4) Physics exam on Friday. By the way are the Carrol boys coming up to see you this holiday and what will we do with Todd?

It has been bitterly cold here, so much so, that I invested in a rough pair of warm trousers so that I won't have to wear my ordinary suit all day. Those trousers I had dyed are so awfully thin, unless I wear a petti the sun shines through. And also a good cardigan jacket. I'm going to look after myself this next week so that I won't be stopped from seeing you.

Oh, I've some news for you and I'm terribly proud of myself. What do you think I have done? All this afternoon I've been riding a motor bike and Os Andrews who owns it, has been sitting in the side car seeing that I learnt to work it properly. As soon as I can ride one I'm going to buy a second hand one. What do you think of that for a scheme. Do you think it is a wise one? The vibration is not as bad as I thought. Of course I did not travel at the rate of 60 miles per hour just about 12! It was very s'nice

The Australia looks terrible swish. I like the cut of her, so clean and neat. I do like that trip across to Manly in the sun as long as you are out of the wind. We have had awful winds here but I believe they blow worser up at Tarro.

What about Jellicoes visit tomorrow. I'm not going to see him as I'm slogging away at Physics. That's the important exam. Eric Smith and a mate left for the weekend up at Pittwater. They have brains and don't need to study hard like I have to do. I feel so discouraged but you'll cheer me up a good deal. Had a shot out of my revolver today just to clean it out. It was quite rusty, last time I used it in the April of 1918. Doesn't time slip by and I've been home 9 months. Today is the shortest day. Do you remember I was coming home from Tarro on the longest day of the year ie: 21 December.

Ginger Smith is going away to *Harvard Mill* up the north coast somewhere and I think it is a good scheme for him to get away from town where it is drink, drink, too many chums. I met an old chum in town yesterday, a Lieut Lee. I pointed him out to Mary. What do you think, I received a letter from Vic Fowler this morning. I executed a war dance on the spot. He signed himself the *Little Black Sergeant Major*. That's what we used to call him in France. Do you know how he got the name? It is like this. He is very fond of kiddies and as soon as we go into billets these kiddes would flock around. One day the mother said she liked *Le Petit Sergeant Major Noir* so always after that we called him by its English equivalent. He is so funny. He didn't get any of the other letters I sent him but received the one posted to the address Tom Brownlie told me of. He is likely to be discharged any day now.

Keith is in civies and the first day he got into them I thought he was a stranger and went to the door to let him in and found it was only Keith. So poor old Miss Bedford is fading away. She is in no pain you say so I suppose she will pass out some night to *that Bourne when a no traveller returns*.

Yes, it's a nice way to Morpeth or rather Hinton and I'm afraid Creamy isn't up to it so perhaps it would be nicer to see Mrs Griffin at your place. But just as you (personally) would like, ONLY take into consideration that night falls quickly and its sure to be dark before getting home. Eh Bonnie, are there any riding hacks among Mr Adamsons lot that we could use for I do so want a ride. I DON'T want you to go to a dancing class where you pay a whole SHILLING. It must be an awfully swish and high class place. Do the men wear dress suits and gloves? Where will I take you to this time? Make some arrangements and I'm not going to stick indoors. I must get enough fresh air to last me another 3 months and you'll have to come with me. Tennis all today next door.

We got such a shock last night, someone named FRANK rang up while I was out asking where Mary was. Dad thought it must be you but as it was a man's style of voice he couldn't understand. Anyhow it turned out it was Todd Felton. Mr Felton has issued orders that he was to be called Frank and not Todd. That is how the mix up came about.

I can't give you any news about Gertrude. We haven't see her since last Monday. I think she may be dead for all we know. She hasn't bothered to ring up. That 1st Battalion Captain you saw in Newcastle was dear old Captain Bootle or as we call him *Old Boots*. I wish I could only have seen him. He went away again on a transport as ships adjutant. You see he'll be drawing 25/ per day and he has no home here at all. So he went away again. If I can see him when he comes back I'll bring him home. He is only 23 and an original 4th Battalion man but came over to us when he got his commission.

If I didn't write so heavily I'd use both sides of the paper but if one writes heavily it presses through and the handwiring on the other side then is faint. I don't want you to strain your eyes do I? I hate specs but am afraid some day soon I'll have to have them. I have a couple of good yarns I'll tell you when I see you.

Thank heavens the results of the exams don't come out in the paper. I'll be able to say I passed even if I don't. To see the Upfolds will be a good excuse for you to get into town.

You are quite ok about engine rooms and sailing ships. I'm quite wrong this time for a change, Oh sarcastic one.

You are very interested in the Strangs. Yes they have gone from Wahroonga to Artarmon and soon they are off to Blighty. I believe you are glad now there is no attraction for me. Just image having a girl who says *Oo Noo How Chorming Won't yer knoo* Wouldnt it be dreadful? She wasn't like that before I went away. Oh, won't I enjoy stopping in bed in the mornings at *Oaklands* I think I will have to learn to milk this time for I'm blowed if I like you to do it. Keith can't come as he is awaiting on a job in the telephone mechanic line.

Look if Gertrude goes up North while I'm at Tarro you and I are going down to see them, *comprez*. That is if you would like too. Will you forgive me if I end now, I'm tired and Sunday I'm working on Physics, Cheeriho. Only 7 days....It's windy, I only washed my hair this morning and it won't stop up

Love B

17.7.19 Thursday
Imperial Services Club Ltd etc

Dear Franco,

I was very disappointed when you rang up last night, that I was so silent. I had a number of things to say to you but being a mug, they all slipped my memory at the right times. I see Bert [Carroll] every day now in the dissection room he looks o.k. Tell Ruth she can reach Bert by addressing it to Second year Medicine, Medical School, Sydney University.

Now tomorrow is Sydney University Commemoration Day and as there will be a lot of *Horseplay* I'm scared of being knocked about so I'm not going. There are a lot of rough jokes going to be played on different people.The Tivoli Theatre has been hired by the University for the afternoon and Stiffy and MO have been given a lot of names of students and they are going to sling off at them. It will be very funny but I suppose crackers will be thrown and I cannot bear a noise like that if sprung suddenly on me. If I'm prepared for it, its o.k., but a shock is rotten.

Over the weekend write and tell me all you and Mary and Buxton did last night and what things they said about me and you. Will you? Last weeks letter I asked you to burn. Did you do that for me? Evidently from what you said about Wallsend last night you do not seem disappointed.

I'm disappointed over the bike business. I can't get a good one cheap and I do not feel inclined to pay 100 pounds for a good one. I saw today a bonzer one but they wanted 100 pound for it. Suppose it will end up by my not getting one at all.

The decoration around the city are magnificent, especially Macquarie St. I'm viewing the procession from Donald Smith's balcony in Macquarie St. Of course I am going in uniform and putting up 3 ribbons, 1914-15, General Service and Allied Service Ribbons. Mother has repaired the seat of my trousers so that it is not seen much.

Keith started electrical engineering at the Technical College but had to give it up, the work was too solid for him and his side gives him a good deal of pain.

I'm at a loose end here this afternoon. Lectures ceased today. Father said he heard just before you spoke some lady's voice in the box and you told them to keep quiet. Hope you caught your train. It was late when you finished speaking. What did you pay for the extension and the call.

Bonnie, you shouldn't have sent me down Arthur's letter. Honestly, as soon as I saw his writing I closed it up and have not read it, neither will I. He might have made a fool of himself but that should be sacred. He died in a manner which aught to have made any of his good sacred in anyone's eyes. Would you have done the same had I been killed? It is not a fair deal. Anyhow I won't read his letter and I'm contemplating whether to send it back or not. Catch On. I'm not sermonising but thats how I feel. If you think I'm silly say so.

I haven't made up my mind yet whether to go to Melbourne next holidays. Arthur and Harry [Hirst, Ben's first cousins] there are at present, both down with influenza. Their dental practices have gone to pieces while they are away. But before Arthur became sick, he wrote asking if I would like to go over and I would muchly.

Last Saturday I went down to Warrawee and had tea with the Johnsons. Nancy is to be married in September. The Wrights were also down. Mrs Brownlie is coming up to see us tonight but I believe Tom is over in Melbourne once again. Dad went to work yesterday for 1st time in 12 days.

How I wish you could have seen this peace procession. It is one of the biggest shows ever seen in Aussie.

Met an old chum yesterday, one Mervyn Blake. He brought out an English girl (to me she looks no bon at all) Don't know how he is going to support her but suppose his Dad will fork out for him. Wish I had Dad who could fork out for me t'would be s'nice doing nothing all day but sit in the sun like a cat.

There are going to be wondeful school picnics for the Public Schools up our way. Tom has entered for about a dozen things including the 1/4 mile but he has no chance at all though. I think Bike riding spoils anyone for running, so I found out. Do tell me the doings last night, I'm terribly curious and about the teasing you received.

Love from Ben

22.7.19

My dear Franco

Got a great surprise this morning when I reached the Uni to find a letter there from you, You may be sure I soon read the contents but I'd rather have you send them home as I always look forward to them then and I m tired in the evening and the letter seems to make me less tired.

Harold Kershaw is coming to see me tonight–am looking forward to a long pow wow with him. I don't seem to be able to find a suitable motor bike and car they are all too dear.

Yes, I'll be along to see you probably on the 9th September. I'll leave the Melbourne trip until Christmas, I'm dropping all my anatomy until then so I really must work in those 3 months to pull up the years work. I have my final Chemistry exam 8th September so have to work, there is no second chance with that exam either. They mucked up in Physics again today so all the kids had no lecture, the lecturer couldn't go on.

What a snice fat letter was yours, hope you liked my weekend one, I wrote small. Yesterday had a long pow wow with Ray Carroll, he has been ill but is now OK.

Mother, Dot and Edie are going to see the illuminations tonight. I'm not bothering as its too much of a strain on the old leg. One of the pleasures I'm to miss. Today I met a chap with exactly the same amputation as myself and he was walking without a limp and without a stick so there is hope for me yet.

Our wattle is just a blaze of yellow and looks snice too. When is Ruth going for her holiday? Can she say the date for I've a mad scheme in my head. Why should I go to Tarro? why shouldnt you come down here. Don't say a word though. I can work it if you think it feasible.

Keith gets 8/–per week pension, magnificent isn't it. Tomorrow I'm probably going to buy a skeleton so that I can learn the bones off by heart. It is the only way.

We've a few sweet peas out. Dot came home and said she had lost her ticket. When the train came to a station she got out and got in behind the ticket collector so that she wouldn't have to pay. Then at Wahroonga she got into the ladies waiting room until the guard had left the steps then she came up the steps. Cute isn't she.

Last Sunday, being practically the anniverary of our sailing for Egypt I went up to see Mrs Felton, found Todd, Bid and Mrs Felton only at home. Didie was out too. Mr Felton is up the Northern Rivers, Casino, I think. Todd and Bid were giving the dog a bath. Bert [brother] is stiff for money just now. He is buying furniture and its an awful price. Did you see Greigs [from Wahroonga] wedding announcement on Saturdays paper. The cold footed coot and I feel like killing him each time I see him.

Tell me if you get my little parcel won't you. I want that special letter in return. I am getting the photos developed–haven't seen if they are any good yet. Do you remember enclosing a letter to me, well, will it do if I bring it up next time or would you let me burn it? Honestly I will if you say so but I won't let it go by post. Have you finished *Young Diana* yet, can you understand it? If your Dad comes to town and doesn't call on us even for an hour I won't be friends with him anymore. If he can come even for an hour just to see us. Hope the bails and machines will be ok. It is a big outlay you know. Are the stones or gravel being put in the yard and how are they arranging for cows to cross the road, Gate across the road?

Did you see in this morning's paper how the soldiers have been mucking up in Melbourne. Perhaps they really did have a cause. The only thing to prevent riots is to give them work–there are 4000 out of work in Victoria.

Have been seriously thinking as to whether to go on with the Dental Course or not. It is a long weary wait and when one is 27 and a leg off most of the best parts of life are gone. Sometimes I think I'll chuck it–sometimes I think I won't. Anyhow 6 months are gone by. Everything about Tom Brownlie's girl is fixed up. She won't be sorry either. Tom is a great chap and loves her without doubt.

We are clockless in the dining room. It is gone to be tickled up. It's funny not hearing the tick tock all the time.

Tom didn't win anything at the Sport but has been in bed 3 days, must have sprained his leg a little bit. Quite a lot of imaginititis about it too I think. No more news Fondest love from

Ben.

I'd rather you missed out the family when sending love to Wahroonga

---

25.7.19 France Day

My dear Franco

I'll send you a letter tonight as I've the whole week end taken up with things I must do. Tomorrow morning I'm due at 9am at St Leonards to do physics with McGrath. In the afternoon some friends of Edies are coming up and in the evening I'm to go to Louis Robertsons place to a welcome home to his young brother.

Well on Sunday morning–church. Sunday afternoon Alex Stobo is coming to see me. He was the officer walking with me when I was hit you know. And Sunday evening I'll be too tired to do anything so there you are, my weekend is choca block but as you've never missed writing to me except once when you were ill, I can't possibly let you slip. Do you know I've had 3 letters from you this week and perhaps one tomorrow if I am lucky. I've got them before me now and I am going to answer the thousands of questions a s'nice girl asked me. Oh! by the way I am writing this in bed as I'm too tired to sit up in a chair.

Tues is the 1st day since Wednesday that I've been on the leg. As usual the beastly thing is always going crook on me and on Tuesday a strap broke and mother took it over to the boot makers to get a new strap put on. It's the the guide strap which comes up over the knee which went. On Wednesday I couldn't do it so on Thursday I didn't go to University. I was too tired and miserable so I went into town and bought the special leather he wanted and he did it. Then went to the University and did dissection all day. We have nearly finished the arm but the names and things we have to learn... Frank, in my opinion there is nothing in the world as wonderful as the human body. It is so complicated too.

One of the massage girls who do anatomy with us, has just come back after 9 weeks 'flu. I hardly recognised her. She was plump and had long black hair. Now she is very thin with black rings under her eyes and she has no hair or rather it is about 1 inch long. She looks a character and so changed.

Keith went back to his old firm as he couldn't get a job anywhere else and now he is getting the same wage as when he went away 25/--rotten I call it.

I have my crutches back and the old tops put onto new legs and they are fine. Believe this writing is too small, you will never be able to read it. Like when that YMCA girl at Havre (that I told you about) used to write to me in hospital. She is an awful writer and I used to make one reading of the letter when I got it but if I read it again I used to get a different meaning altogether.

Mother has gone to take Jean to see the sights in town. There were thousands on thousands in town tonight. The last night of the illuminations you know and France Day also. All the girls are out in their glory looking for money for their bones but I think most of them just go to see if they can hook some chap to take them to dinner.

McGrath has just rung me up. I'm not to go to morrow as he is ill. But in the same breath he asked me to buy him university dance tickets and he would pay me back. He is a nice chap though. I didn't see either Bert or Ray today, just somehow didn't meet them, suppose they were there all the same. Bert the other day invited me to come to watch them dissect the thorax of a body but I was too busy on the arm of one.

Met a chap today *Jippo Green* we call him as he is awfully brown, well he has not yet got a *Woody* and he came home last September with me on *Kanowna*. On the anniversary of my arrival in Australia I hope to be at Tarro. That day of September I came into Sydney, I'll never forget it. The heads looked so beautiful and the harbour so blue and clean.

Do you remember me telling you about *Britannia* on the tramway sheds at the Quay, well in the wind last night her head blew off and when we went into town this morning, there she was decapitated. This was to have been her last night out. Bad thing, she used to stay out all night.

The weather here has been quite hot. Today I'm going to get into some light underclothes. All my light stuff is fairly holey so I'm going to buy mother some light stuff and let her make some. I can't afford to buy the things, they are honestly an exorbitant price.

Dad is going to book a cottage at Manly for about Xmas time. You're coming It's all been arranged by me here. But don't let on at *Oaklands* will you. Had a long chat with Billy Hunt today. Another chap from Wahroonga, Walter Thompson is somewhere about on a transport which has small pox on board and he is to be quarented for 18 days I think it is.

Keith is working on a clock. He is good at getting them to go. Father is out so Edie and I are boss cockies of the ranch. I don't think I could live anywhere else but at Wahroonga. I love the place and all the people know me. I came home with Nancy Johnson and Jack Wright and the train was crowded. I had a seat so Nancy sat alongside me and Jack perched on the arm of the seat so I wasn't playing goosebery was I? It wasn't my fault. They had been into the zoo at Taronga Park. I must take you there and leave you in the yard with the llama which spits. Have you seen the sign *Beware this animal spits*. The zoo authorities put up the notice once *Beware this animal expectorates* but so many people did not know what it was that they altered the word to spit and now everyone knows.

I saw a *Perfect Lidy* today. She had a split skirt on, she must have been a lidy. I don't know what colored garters she had on. I didn't bother to wait and see her get in a tram. I was too busy but quite a lot of gentleman did.

The wattle up and down the line is simply glorious. Never have I seen it so fine before, just bunches of a beautiful yellow. Our station has a row of 15 trees all out.

How is the milking machine going, do tell me all the news. I'm interested in the rows. I'd love to see your Dad go for Jaeger and give him a hiding. Of course I would have to insult him first so he couldn't take your dad to court over it. Wouldn't it be fun. I'm sorry for Mrs J. she seems so slight. Some of the Tarro winds could blow her away.

It's comfy in bed. I do most of my study there now. I've a very good light and it doesn't hurt my eyes anymore than sitting up and reading does. I wear spectacles now you know? Just in the night time when I am studying. I can't see out of them if an object is more than 5' away. They are just to relieve the strain so that I wasn't joking when I asked you to write in ink. Gee Whiz, it is 9.30 and only 2 pages done so far but I'll have tomorrow now that I'm not going to Physics in the morning.

I suppose you notice the difference in the light these mornings now you have to get up at 5.30am. Do you make yourself a cup of tea before going over to milk? Has your Dad anyone in view to take your places. Hope it won't be for long? Just to pull your Dad out of a hole. Wouldn't it be rotten if at a last resource he couldn't and all back on you.

Have the other *sports coats* arrived on the scene yet?

Had my hair cut today, little pieces got down my back, its awfuly tickly. This is first time cut in 5 weeks so you can see I needed one. Dot said she would put it up in papers for me if I wished–a nice hint to get it cut wasn't it.

It seems ages I was up at Tarro but it is really only a few weeks. There will be no need to use masks next time I hope. Even if I get a motor bike, I think the 150 miles to Newcastle would be too much for me–the road is awfully rough . There is a chap in Wahoonga OS Andrews who says the road is very vile indeed.

We had a letter from Gertrude today. She likes the place and 4 girls came across to see her, she likes them very much. She is going to ride across to see them. Berge is very well. She has a nice pony she says but Rupe told us it's an awfully old thing, cannot run away if she wanted it too.

Tom has been playing Bobs tonight so everything is all over the place. Dot is off to bed long ago. We have a new massive clock–our big one has gone bung. This new massive silver clock cost 7/6 second hand. Dad is cute at bargains. I believe he could bargain his way to the *Good Place*. He is more cheerful today as he went to a dinner tendered to the Members of Public Services Board and he was treated as if he is to be the new Secretary, so naturally he is pleased. It will mean a difference of 5 pound per week to his screw which will be very helpful. He MIGHT even say *Here is 10/–per week Ben* but don't spend it all on chocolates, like he used to when he gave me my weekly Saturday penny. How I used to rush across for chocolate mice, used to be my favourite and black gelatine nigger babies the other choice.

There are special trains tonight to bring away the crowds from town. I'd love to have been in but those pleasures are not for this chicken or for you either. How much do you hate *tit pulling* as Ruth calls it. I don't mind you calling me anything at all. As long as you call me up to Tarro at vacation time.

Did you really hurt yourself muchly when the sulky went over your leg. You didn't say much about it but I suppose it hurt. Was it as bad as when the cow kicked you out of the cow bail some time ago. Are you getting the easy cows, share and share about or are the hard ones all yours?

There is one thing and that is that you *would be wasting time gadding about town* don't make me laugh. Have you ever noticed that if you are continually with someone the characteristics of the others writing very often shows? I make a g or y. (shows how) Do you notice the part below the line the twirly bit well, see if you can remember who used to write like that.

Wonder where Jean will sleep tonight? She is coming home with Mother and the spare bed is not put up at all. Suppose she will bunk in with Marjorie and or Edie. Marjorie has a row with Trixie Roberts about twice a day, nearly in pitched battle and 15 minutes afterwards they are all milk and honey and nice as pie to each other. Blowed if I understand them. If I row with anyone properly it's for good and all. I remember I had a row at school in 1910 I think it was, His name is Rebbel and I can still remember the fight and I hate him to this day.

Do you notice what a pair we are for saying *I'm going to do such a thing?* Well now, I'm thinking of buying a camera, post card size so that if I see a suitable bike I can take good pictures. I don't have any really absolute failures but you can't take good pictures with a cheap camera. A bad workman blames his tools but a good bloke can't.

Do you ever enjoy reading my letters? I think them such dopey things. I try to be newsy and chatty and even try to be funny but I fail miserably. Anyhow if you think them ok or could be improved or if they are not the type of letters you want just let me know. I'm to do all you want in that line.

A little chum of Tom's died the other day, a little chap aged 4, Hunter was his name and he died of pneumonia laryngitis–suppose that is how it is spelt..Anyhow this ends the chapter for tonight Cheeriho and hope you sleep well

Ben

6.8.19

Dear Bonnie,

Just a skimpy note. I've to catch the 6.15 pm train back to town to see McGrath about physics. Its rottenly cold too, all the little Sunday school girls are up learning a new song for the Band of Hope. I'm feeling O.K. Had a quick trip down in the train and we had in our carriage after

Gosford that chap Green I spoke to on the Newcastle Station. Well he
had been up to see his girl's people who live at Seaham. Didn't she look
flash with the 7 rings and fuss.

I'm to tell you some news now but don't let on as I haven't told my
people yet. I bought a motor bike yesterday an old fashioned *Excelsior*
with side car. There is no paint on it and it is fairly ramshackle but it will
do for me to learn on, then I'll sell it and then get a good one.

Can you see by this writing I'm in a hurry. The chap who sold it to
me rang up when I was out, hope he isn't going to say he can't sell it to
me now. But will know for certain on Saturday when I'll write a 10 pager.

Did Lacey turn up? Don't box my ears or pay me out for not writing
because of this short note. Bert came back today he has had 2 weeks 'flu
and looks rotten on it. Fondest love

Ben

7.8.19 Thursday
Dear Bonnie
Last night before I went down to Greenwich to see Mc Grath I
dropped you a little note. Well, had a good night at physics and coming
home I missed my tram to St Leonards Station and as there was a big
dance on in Greenwich Chambers I watched it. I think it would be fine
to be able to dance. Everyone there was enjoying him/herself O.K.
and it is even good to watch a good swinging waltz. That song *Roses of
Picardy* makes a good waltz time. I'm to stop in town until 4pm when I'm
meeting the chap and we are going home on the bike. Today is rainyfied
so hope we get home dry.

I met six First Battalion chaps in Moore St so I made the 7th–quite
a nice little group and had a long chat about the old days, never to come
again.

When am I to get a letter?

From McGrath's School, he teaches at Morven Gardens Greenwich,
there a magnificent view of the harbour and he said the lights from the
City during Peace Week were superb. I have just met Billy Hunt in here,
he is o.k. but his Ma and sister have the 'flu and they won't let him go

home. He is staying at a pub in town here. Met Bert Carroll again this morning. He says he doesn't expect to pass his exams in September but that is all nonsense, he must pass. I commissioned Dad to day to buy me a postcard size camera, so that I can take some decent pictures.

Remember me to all and tell me what to do with Ruths button. I'm sorry I brought it away. I remember I found it on the floor and put it in my pocket to stop it being trampled on.

Pollack didn't lecture in physics again today. He doesn't care if we have an exam properly or not. We have missed lots of lectures principally through chaps mucking up but now Pollock is sick.

No more news fondest love
Ben

9.8.1919 Saturday

Dear Bonnie

I'm not in much of a mood for doing anything, much less writing, but if I unburden my troubles a little to you I may feel better. My pride is wounded sorely too, so don't let on to anyone else in the family, there is a dear. This is the first time in my life I've ever been taken down. Even the Jippos in Egypt, The Indians in Colombo or the French or English could not take me down, but this time I've been done, brown to a frizzle and by an Australian too.

All the week I've been in heaven over the idea I had a good bike and honestly it went well when the chap drove it for me, but when I get on it or even the garage man in Wahroonga, we couldn't make it budge, Oh, I feel bad about it especially as it has taken 75 pounds of the cash I risked my life to earn. Risked it not once but over and over again each day.

Last week I was too excited to write, now I can't write for I'm in the depth of despair. I'll tell you about it. I tried the bike at the man's place and all was o.k. We came home on it O.K. Yesterday afternoon I wasted the afternoon from the University to try it but do you think I could get it to start? No, not I. So I took it over to the Garage man, a friend of mine and he took out a couple of important working parts and lo instead of being solid steel they had at some time or other been broken and brazed together again. Do you wonder at my being down hearted and miserable?

Anyhow I sent 2 telegrams to the chap in the hope he'd come up today but he hasn't turned up–perhaps he will come tonight, Oh Blow. Here is Winnie Wood turned up. Well in case he turns up I'm going to ask him to take it back even if I lose 5 pound on the deal. Isn't it rotten luck. Anyhow I'm determined to get rid of it at any price. Have you ever heard yet of anybody buying anything at all second hand to be any good? Oh I wish you were down here perhaps I wouldn't feel so miserable then. It is not the fact that I've lost the 75 pounds but that I should be taken down by an Australian and he knew all the time that I had a leg off. Aren't there some despicable scoundrels in the world. I feel rotten, I trusted him too and he seemed a fair sort of a man. Wish I hadn't paid him but took it on trial. But experience teaches–but it is dear at 75 pounds and my pride has gone to Billy Ho. Don't let anyone know I've been taken, let it be a secret between ourselves and if anyone asks say it's going OK.

There is another disappointment for you. My exam has been postponed 'till after the holidays so perhaps I won't be able to come up for more than a few days. It's rotten, it seems as if fate seems to bump me wherever I go. I had a long chat with Ray [Carroll] Walked up from the tram on Friday morning with him. He is very cheerful isn't he? Oh Blow, here's another friend, a Miss Lockwood, chum of Edies. I wanted to take Mother to Eastwood tomorrow to see Bert now that's squashed. Oh its a fair ..... You can fill in the missing word.

Keith has a motor bike now. A F.N, rather a good style of a bike and in good working order. He has a heart has Keith. He has never been on a bike until Thursday evening when he bought it, rode all through town and up to Wahroonga or rather as far as Warrawee and found when he got home that the petrol had become turned off. Jee, he did perform. Oh I must tell you about a policeman stopping him. He was just going onto the punt when 2 policemen stopped him. Of course he didn't have a license so he just pushed 5/–into his hand and he let him through. Cute wasn't he but just imagine a policeman putting himself in Keith's hands for the sake of taking a 5/–bribe. Rotten I call it. How did that Bobbie know but that Keith wasn't a Police Spy, spying to see that the Bobbies did their work properly.

I think I'm living over my means, must pull in the horns a little bit. But I'm more determined than ever to buy a good bike. Just to beat fate if there is such a thing. It is only a week since I was up. wish I could see you every day. This would be a chance for that special letter as I'm so down hearted, I feel like shooting that man. But I'm going to speak gently to him at first and Father has promised me that he will speak to a solicitor friend of his if he won't give me all or 95% of the money back, Oh he is a ......fill it in again.

We have cut down our bananas as there were soaking up too much moisture and there's one lemon tree to come out, it is almost dead. Tell me all the news. I missed your letter today that I usually get one on Saturday afternoon too. Did Jimmy Lacey turn up and did you milk after I left, surely with Jimmy there, someone could be relieved and are the cow bails getting on? I hope it will be a success for your sakes. Won't it be awful if it is like my bike–sell. I'm nearly bankrupted. I believe I told you before but I'm getting free train tickets so that's some benefit isn't it.

How is the Haile Motor bike getting on? Makes a row like a german tank coming along–I refuse to spell german with a capital G. Charlie Sanders is a bit ill, did I tell you about him? He was to be have been married but something happened which upset him and he became ill but his girl and girl's mother are nursing him so he'll soon get well.

Our tradesman are funny. They are generally about 3' high and a different boy comes around especially with the baker. The boy that came today with 3 loaves could hardly carry them. Did you notice in todays paper that a stone has been unearthed at Windsor in the old church (St Matthews) ever so many years old. Isn't it funny that the Governors in the old days used to put Esq. after their names if they ever opened a church or laid a stone of any kind or other.

Coming up in the train yesterday there was a drunken man eating prawns and lobster eugh! I hated the smell of it so as soon as there was a vacant place I moved.

Didie and Marjorie were going to a concert last Wednesday night but Mrs Felton wouldn't let Didie go as Mr Felton was away. Saw Clive Inch in the train yesterday. Keith is learning book keeping at the Tech College. He finds it a bore but it is good for him. Isn't that horse Belmont ever going to be used or Ego (the chestnut) either?

Bert in uniform.

The Bolets are pretty they are bigger than yours. How have the cats been keeping your feet warm, are they up to the mark. Nights are still cold but the days seem quite warm. We'll have young Tom with a motor bike soon he is assiduously reading up all the books we have on the subject.

Bert is white, the 'flu has brought him down a lot. He will take some fattening to get up to his old standard. The Station master is cute he runs after the engines to get coal for his fire. They make themselves comfortable but I'd hate to have their job especially on night work. Well Old girl I cannot write any more. Give my best regards to everyone but accept all love for yourself. Best love

Ben xxx

26.5.19

Home in bed.. Monday morning...[written in pencil now very faint]
Dear Franco

I was so ill on Saturday night that after I got Tom to post your letter I haven't been out of bed since. I expect to get up later when the sun is stronger..I'm awfully miserable on it. Sent Mum down to the post this morning, no letters. I woke up last night with a start thinking

I heard a motor bike in our back yard but I saw it was the kitten purring on the foot of my bed. It did kick up a row. Mum says I would feel better in the sun so I am getting up.

I'm out in the back now basking in the sun. I've my pyjamas and flannel shirts and cardigan and service jacket on, am running no risks in getting a fresh cold. Keith went away last night. He started work this morning.

We were awfully anxious about Tom last night. 9 o clock came and he didn't come home so Mother and Dad set out to look for him and met him in Burns Road coming home. He had been down to Howells to tea. Didn't think it mattered to tell Mother first.

There was a letter in todays paper about the Uni students, awfully exaggerated of course. The letter said they spoilt a concert at night time in the Town Hall. All they did was to wait for the Interval then to walk through. I don't see that there was any harm in that, do you? Wished you could have seen the procession, the funniest thing I've ever seen. When do I get a letter girl!

How are the cold, windy days playing up with your hands. They must be getting rough. Mum rubbed my chest and back again last night and her hands were awfully rough like fine sand paper. Mine are beautiful hands for a dentist at present, they are all over French Polish which won't come off.

Mother and Edie are gradually getting the whole of the back under cultivation. Edie must have at least 100 carnations plants in the ground. Mother sent up some Scarboro lily bulbs last Thursday. Did you get them and your cotton (let-in work) was enclosed too. You'd leave your wig behind if it wasn't glued on.

Our Minna-lo-Barta is so extra 'specially nice. I think it's such a pretty flower. Mrs Dr Richard Reid died. You remember the old gentleman died just before you came down. They were so attached to one another that everyone thought it wouldn't be long before she followed him.

Here's a catch you can have Ruth on. Say, *do you know that they are stopping all the trams in Newcastle today?* Someone will say no . then you say *Yes to let the people get out* Dot caught me at it yesterday.

A rotten cold and headache combined are very crook things to have. Don't think I've been so crook since I lost my leg. I'm missing a lot at the Uni, especially Histology. We are examined on it on 28 May but I'm not thinking about it as the final exam is not until next year.

Dear Bon, received your letter this afternoon but am too lazy to re-write this former one You are having a breezy time getting up so early in the morning–glad I don't have to do it though I work late I can rise early.

Yes, I posted Mr Mathers letter for you, careless old bean and I hope you received the cotton in the Scarbro lily packet. Re what you told me about the date of my arrival in Tarro. It's always the way isn't it.

So the Doddingtons didn't see us until they were on the track home or they complimented me on the distance I walked. It was a good way wasn't it No more news. Feel much better tonight. Go to University tomorrow

Ben

12.8.19 Home

Dear Bonnie.

It was such a relief to get your letter at last. As usual I was worrying, thought a cow might have kicked you or something, but you will write to me won't you if you ever become sick, just a line will do. Well I've sold that awful bike and only lost a couple of pounds on it. It is such a relief to get if off my mind, but wasn't that man who sold it to me a contemptible creature knowing how I was placed having a leg off. Hoped he would break his neck on the thing taking it home but as there is nothing in tonight's paper he must have reached home safely, worse luck.

Any how it is an awful load off my mind and now I'm looking out for a good one as I must have some recreation. Well your letter has put me in good spirits again, I'm smooching, but that's what it did. Yes, in a way I am unfortunate in having you for a girl, but the only misfortune that I can see and I'm not blind, is that you are not in Sydney so that I could take you out and give you some amusement. What a time we could have. That is the only unfortunate part about me knowing you and perhaps that will be altered next year, who knows, I dont.

What a pity I missed you in that mood you were in the day your mother went to Sandgate. Well you can make up for it later on. Now the Chemistry exam is after the vacation and I'm hesitataing about coming up. I really want too Bonnie, but my consciense says fag up that Chemistry, anyhow we will let time decide Eh?

I cannot see why one of you has to milk because when the Kelly's were there and before that 4 milkers was the most you ever had and now you have 5 milkers. Are there more cows up or what's the trouble.

Today is a blazing hot day and a number of white dresses are out. I like cream best. It's a very good scheme to be sewing mad as you call it and I like the Fugi description of undies. Is that the stuff I'm to get or rather the exchequer is sadly depleted. I'll have to travel 2nd class in train in future when I come up to your place. I'm thinking of selling my war bonds that will make up a little headway.

Was I rather awful with Ina that day or would you like me to be like that, because when you meet anyone you simply have to be jolly otherwise they get an awful impression. We have been having lectures on the nervous systems today, They are wonderful but hard of course to understand.

Eh, Franco what about a photo for me? Oh! before I forget there is a girl doing massage with the dental students her name is Steggles and she comes from Newcastle. We have wee names for them all and we call her Staghorns. Tell me something about her, she is plump, wears glasess and I think she is fair. I'm not certain though. She is always talking about Newcastle so I said I've never been there but on her recommendation I'll take a visit there some day. She said I'd probably enjoy my visit. I daresay I would too, don't you think so.

How does Mary like her work back at the hospital? Was the pink nightie that parcel you took down to be hemstitched? Well I'm sorry about that chap losing his arm but he'd be worse off if he lost his leg wouldn't he. Everything depends on his occupation and I should think legs are more important in the Country. Some very fine ones up that way too. I would love to be around when any of my letters come just to see if you *comprez* all the stale jokes I make. Some of them are so fine you cannot see them until they are pointed out.

Walter Thompson came home last Sunday. He looks well, I went around to see him just for a few minutes. Wonder will he feel as strange as I did. Oh, his girl got married while he was away. Choice isn't she. Walter looks on it in the best way though, says he's glad because she may have made him miserable later on.

So you've a ½ witted chap working, don't make him angry. Is he after the style of George Norley? About Ken Roberts being dead, I'm sorry I wonder does war really make one more susceptible to sickness. Anyhow his girl was plucky. Yes Bray's will feel the loss of Charlie alright. Isn't it a shame after all he has gone through to become a doctor to die when he was useful to to his people, but it is often the case isn't it.

This seems a mournful letter. I wrote to the Alfieries in Sussex during dinner hour yesterday. I couldn't eat any dinner so that is how I spent the time. Dad hasn't seen a good camera for me yet but one will come along soon.

I really don't know what to think about those lectures we've missed, we'll all have to sit for the exam but no one will pass at all I'm certain. Only one week since I last saw you. I don't know if I am mad or not but I ate 18 mandarins yesterday after coming home with no ill effects so I must be. No one in their right mind could do it and not get a pain under his waist coat but I didnt get one. If ever you want a good pain I'll tell you what to do–eat bananas quickly then drink an iced drink on top of them. I tell you it shakes you up O.k. I had that experience in Colombo.

So you like the *Sky Pilot*, look out it doesn't make you cry. I nearly did a weep and do you know every place in that book I've been though dozens of times. And I can see that casualty clearing station at Merricourt as plainly as possible. Only I've never seen any Sisters like those described in the book. Of course when you are ill and perhaps semi–conscious you think the nurses are angels, just out of heaven, but when you get well you find out they are just ordinary homely people, but so nice all the same.

When am I going to write to you as Nurse F J Niland. I believe I write *Niland* oftener than any other word. I'm glad the hot weather is here. I'm changing into light clothing tomorrow. No more heavy singlets etc They are done now and I am glad, I hate to be bundled up.

Did you notice in yesterday's paper that skirts in Paris and London are not more than 16 'from the ground. They will be wearing kilts next. They are absurd of course, but I hate to see girls bundled up in long dresses

Do write muchly as I want all I can get. I'm not greedy but I always like a lot. Fondest love

Ben

16.8.19 Saturday

Dear Franco, I've two letters to answer today and several little mysteries to clear up with you, one of the mysteries is this. There are 2 brothers in Wahroonga called Thompson. The older one is Fred, came home a long time ago and I THINK he is engaged to Jean Austin. Walter came home last Sunday. He is the chap who was in my battalion. Walter was engaged to a girl, I don't know who or where she was from, well she is married now and Walter says Good Riddance. Last Tuesday night I went to a social at Rofe's place to welcome him home, all returned soldiers there and the girls were 1 to 2 boys. Good supper and good games so we had a good time. And I didn't get home until 12.30 but that is the only night off I've taken for weeks so my conscience did not worry me for going. Keith went up to get a bike license today and is home again. Got one ok and the policeman didn't even ask him could he ride. He rode up and is buzzing about every night, so you see luckily he can ride.

Well I lost a bit of money over the other bike but everyone says I'm well rid of it, so it can't be helped. I'm not miserable over it now, I can see that it is no use letting little things worry a chap at all. Sure it doesn't pay, anyhow I'm going to have a try out one tomorrow (don't think I'm wicked) don't tell anyone but I'm paying 130 pounds for it. I really think it will pay in the long run. Never buy second hand unless you personally know who is selling to you. We'll dismiss the subject for good.

So glad your uncle Will Niland is back. Will he be up at Tarro? I tell you what I'm going to do and I hope I meet with your approval. The holiday start on a Friday so I'll come up on a Friday night and will go home on Monday night. I'll only come on one condition and that is you will not press me to stay any longer, for on the result of the Chemistry exam which takes place the day we go back, ½ depends if I can go to University next year. Please understand how essential it is to me. Try and understand won't you? I'd love to stay longer but honestly it cannot be done. Will you be satisfied with Fri night, Saturday, Sunday and part of Monday. Will you?

Here is another disappointment for you, we are NOT going to Manly this year. Father has had too many expenses and I believe he is slightly over the fence as he asked me to lend him some to carry on 'till next pay day. So that is the reason we are not going.

I'm so glad you liked the *Sky Pilot* It is really a fascinating book. For one who has been to every place mentioned there, it is not exaggerated one scrap and I would only wish the story to be altered in one place and that is at the end. I can't think his wife was natural. Anyone who loves a husband like she did could not possibly be too sorry and she may have been but she didn't show it. Wouldn't it have been great had Barrymore been through the war? Didn't the men love him. I know a padre on a par with him and that is Fighting Mckenzie. He is great and we all loved him. Yet he used to talk awfully straight to us.

I went down to McGrath this morning and had 3 hours with him. I'm getting a better grip on the physics now through him. He simply loves teaching physics and says even if he had plenty of money he would still teach physics. He is awfully Catholic Irish and all that but a good chap. I've never yet seen him perfectly clean. He is always slovenly.

Well, I have been thinking of the Heather Adamson stunt. I'll write and let her know some day when I can see her, only this is the trouble, I can't talk and I feel awfully awkward with anyone but you, you see we know each other and can talk on subjects we know but I can't make myself sociable to everyone.

So the chickens have come. Just tell me what arrangements have been made for keeping them shut up. Sorry the new man thinks you are 16 but glad he doesn't think you are older than 30. Perhaps he was trying to flatter you? That's the way to be polite to very old ladies you know. Say they look 20 years younger than they really do.

Mother's sewing machine came home, it's a WHITE and seems o.k. Mother is satisfied with it, it is cheap, that is one thing in our favour you know. We couldn't afford a GIBB.

Dorothy has just finished a cloth, stenciled it, rather's'nice too. Our dental hospital will open after the vacation I'm glad to say. The letters from you are getting more like letters and you'd only have to a go a little way to write me that letter I want you know.

Yours was a very good simile you and I and Barry and his father. Keith might forget his pain now he has book keeping and a bike to occupy his mind. I believe if people have something to occupy their minds they don't feel pain so much. Thats the way I found it in hospital, some one to talk too stopped the leg jumping.

Marjorie has just finished a week of examinations in the music examination. She finished her paper, did every question and 2 optional questions in 1 hour and it was a 2 hours paper. She said it was easier than falling off a log but I find it hard to fall off a log don't you, especially on that white anty log we once sat on.

I'm glad George Norley is locked up–just for his own good. He ought to be put in an old man's asylum don't you think? I was glad when he left Tarro. I didn't like the idea of his hanging áround when you girls had to come from the station of a night time in the dark. I don't know Miss Steggles name but she is fair, plump and wears glasses. I only know her through being on the same anatomy and dissection classes. No trouble with the leg lately which is a terrible good job. The day of the exams I'm going in on crutches to work the sympathy stunt on them. If I can't pass by fair, I'll pass by foul means. Don't know what I put in letters to the Alfieries just bosh and tripe. Pulled their legs a bit, only I can't remember what I said.

Oh Eric Smith went to a dance on Wednesday but came away disgusted. I'll tell you about it some day. He is not fussy you know but he says he objects to have to dance with, as he puts it *a half naked female* those are not my words of course but his. He says the evening dreses are getting over the odds. All the afternoon Dad, Mother and I have been working up in the back digging clearing etc and I've be been putting hinges on the coach house door, only they are better fits than your buggy house doors as mine will close properly.

Ginger Smith finds it very slow at the mill. He has to work too hard but I hope he forgets all about his widow it will make trouble at home yet. Mr and Mrs (especially Mrs) are 2 dears and I'd like to save them any trouble if possible. Mrs Smith is Scotch and a regular boy–mother she is a dear and so hospitable too.

How is Maggie? Winnie Wood is ok and is anxious to go to Wallsend. I told her I heard the place wasn't going to open until June next year and she looked very down hearted. I didn't think she believed me but she did. You see she doesn't know me like you do.

Dad feels sure of his position now. (Secretary of Public Service Board) Of course he will get more money, Dad doesn't want the outside work which an inspector has to do–he is more content in an office.

Ray Kershaw has booked his passage already–he leaves on November 11th and is going via America. I think he is going by *Ventura*. Cheeriho, old Girl–will write tomorrow and let you know if I'm getting the bike or NOT–don't think it will be OR NOT part of the question.

17.8.19 Sunday afternoon

Dear Old Gug,

I've been out on the bike and I've practically decided to buy it. I rode it home from Turramurra, the chap who owns it in a side car and it behaves beautifully. It is what is termed a big x 1918 model. All that is the matter now is that the clutch has to be converted from the left foot (which I can't operate you know) on the the left handle bar.

Excelsior motorcycle with side car.

When he has done that I'll see about buying it! Then we can have some merry spins together when you come down.

Hope you won't be too disappointed about the arrangements I 've made for the holidays–be content–I'm disappointed but it is necessary I should pass the exam isn't it?

I'm sorry I missed church this morning as we had a missionary from China. He is a white man but he came in Chinese dress.

Geoff Johnson is to be home tomorrow and I've been asked down tomorrow night so I'm going. I'm working tonight on my chemistry so that I can go with a clear conscience. It is a dreadful thing having a conscience. If I don't go by mine I feel rotten. I simply must pass this exam and if I do I'll be like a school boy. But don't say anything to me if I don't 'cause I've tried.

We've been having a Nannie goat here. It is is very pretty and playful and we keep it chained up where ever the grass is longest and it eats it very short and potato peelings, it loves them. Muss Butt the human lawn mower Tom calls it and it is a good butter. Marj. is frightened of it as it got loose 3 nights ago and came onto the verandah and poked its face into Tom's so we had to tug it up onto the court again.

When I started the bike today it jumped so much it broke the rope and ran up into the workshop. We haven't had any letters from Gertrude for a fornight. Ma is anxious but it must be hard to get letters from the house to the post office.

Keith is out on his bike again this afternoon. He knocks a good deal of fun out of it and some worry too. Last night he cleaned it in the kitchen. You ought to have seen the mess this morning. Mother performed and only right too. Grease galore on the floor.

Is your Dad's brother married? The one that came home the other day. There are dozens of girls in Wahroonga that own ponies. They pass frequently, all ride astride I'm glad to say. Nothing much in today's paper was there, nothing exciting only Miss Ivy Shilling. Toes we used to call her, the toothpaste actress as she used to have her photo up on the trams as an advertisement for someone or other's toothpaste, as common as mud.

Mother brought 6 chooks last night, white leghorns or legons as some people call them. We gave the others to Bert as you know. He is o.k. and the family too. Ages since I have seen Didie, suppose she is ok. I wouldn't like a travelling job like Mr Felton has. Poor Old Art. We are evidently going to lose the Navy from our 'arbour. It is going to some better arbour somewhere the boats can have better anchorage. I bet they won't get such a pretty place though.

We had stewed loquats last night, our lokies are nice and ripe, only the tree is too big and the birds get the best of the fruit. We've one little apple tree out in blossom. None of the others have yet come to light with any flowers.

Well Bonnie, this letter is not as long as I would have liked to send you but my brain box is exhausted of news. Cheeriho,

love from Ben

...If I didn't put in Ben, perhaps you wouldn't know the writing would you. Write as long as this and I'll be more than satisfied.

23.8.19

Dear Bonnie,

This is Saturday, only 13 days until the horrid old exams. I'm shaky on it. Bert has an exam too and he doesn't expect to pass as he missed all that time with the influenza, you know. As for this chicken I feel as if I won't even have the chance to pass on Knowledge. I'm going to work the sympathy stunt on them by going up on crutches.

You are a dear old thing writing me 3 letters this week and I feel shabby at only writing one but I am working hard so you will understand. Write and tell me if you do please. I'll tell you what I did last Tuesday morning, on Monday night I was dopey, couldn't learn a thing so I went to bed at 9 and got up on Tuesday morning at 3.45 am--honest injun I did. It was a strain, well, I got too and worked until 6am then went back to bed again so you see I'm trying.

I'm sorry now I didn't write during the week. I might have squeezed in a hour for you somehow or other. Now in the last letter you said the Tarroites are having their Peace Affair on the 12 September. Well I'm catching the 2 o'clock train on the 12th getting to Tarro at 6.45. What do you think of those arrangements. I'd love you to meet me in Newcastle but will you miss any of the funny shows? If you will, don't bother about meeting me in Newcastle, meet me at Tarro, only let me know before hand which you intend to do as I need to know whether to look for your nice old dial at Newcastle or Tarro. We'll have to have a lot of fun in a few days, this time won't we, but if you are as terribly s'nice as you usually are I'll stay from Friday night until Thursday night. I don't think it would be fair to you to run away under 5 days, will that be betterish? ('scuse the smudge, it is like me at present, black as the pots).

I'm going to run through your letters now, answer the questions, put in my news. Bonnie, I'm miserable at the idea, you should doubt me. Miss Steggles is nothing to me and I've never said more than Good Day to her ever since I've been there. If you are just being nasty for the sake of writing don't do it as it makes me feel rotten.

Another rouse. You accepted the Dee Why invitation then you said *but I can't understand you all being so nice to me.* Oh you skalliwag, as if anything was too nice and don't you think you will be giving me a lot of pleasure in having you down. Don't talk like that again, anything mine you can have and as for being only nice to you it won't do, it's got to be something more than NICE for me.

Was Mr Massey the man who came about the milking machines? I don't remember him before, anyhow he must be a good sort if he will shake up the machines so that you won't have to milk, are you still doing it? Don't suppose you like to tell me for as usual I'll get wild.

Get the green skirt finished, we must go to a show in Newcastle this time. I've made all arrangements about coming to Tarro on my motor bike some day probably just before Xmas. I'm to bring Tom in the side car to weight it down and I've the road mapped out where to have lunch etc so you see I intend to do the thing properly but I sincerely hope you will have a ride before that date. I can easily pick you up at Rumerys you know, Riverstone is only a 35 minute run from Wahroonga.

Arthur [brother] is down from Leeton for a weekend. I took him to see Bert over at Eastwood. Last time I went I took mother so I had to go fairly slowly but this time with Art I cut the pace out. I did 45 miles an hour in places along a good road. What do you think of that for pace. Of course, I only did it on extra good roads and where there was no traffic or corners and no one about. Oh, it is a wonderful sensation to be flying along like that. Only you go so fast the tears make your eyes very misty.

How is your knee any worser or betterish? Which, do tell me and and answer all my questions won't you. Did you get the white stuff for your blouse, I'm interested in clothes. Marjorie leaves for Brisbane next Friday. She goes up with a friend, I can't remember if it's Tressie or Trixie, I get mixed up, anyway she is going for 3 weeks. Nice trip isn't it. Only I'd rather go by boat and save all the jolts and get in some good sleeps.

Today was simply perfect, hot enough to be warm but with just a shade of wintery spring in the air. Out at Bert's there are such a lot of little birds, more than we have in Wahroonga. It is a fine spot. Of course, you know he hasn't any money and just lives in a little country place but it is fine for his children. Do you remember the little baby– you ought to see the size of it, its Heenormous and has 8 teeth if that is any news to you.

The goat has gone. Mother has got rid of it, it finished a fine crop of sweet peas right off, nibbled jam tins and vegetables galore so it's *parte promenade*. Good job too. It left too many traces behind for my liking.

Dad has just been around with the lolly bag. I scored 3 chocs. Every week he brings home sweets, sometimes barley sugar, sometimes almonds rock or something or other. Can you keep a secret which must not even be mentioned to your Dad, will you? Well now here it is...Father has his new position as Secretary to the Board [Public Service Board] BUT the salary is not yet raised. Don't tell the Dad or anyone yet as it is not official.

Here is another secret, I've been offered 1 pound per foot for my land more than I gave for it. But I'm not selling, I want it for this chicken, but who knows if in a few years I'm offered twice the amount I might sell. I'm not greedy am I?

The bike is simply beautiful I rode down to St Leonards for my lesson on it today and it was fine. There is a tiny little squeak I can't find out what it is.

Now you just get Jimmy Lacey to dig a hole for a post and to get the post for me. Dig a hole in the centre of that little lane beyond the fence so that when I come up I can make you a paddock to let loose Creamy in so he can't get out. Do you think you know the spot? Half way between the fir tree and the gate (red) which leads out into the paddock, *comprez*? Also tot up all the little jobs you want done from making spiders on petticoats to buying you a Rolls Royce like John Browns [the Coal Baron].

Would you like to learn to ride my bike when you come down? I'll teach you. You could easily manage it and if you did, you would then have confidence to drive your own car later on (when you Dad buys one, *comprez*). I bought a big tent fly to cover my bike to protect it from the damposity of the atmosphere. A thing costing 130 pounds needs to be looked after don't you think? There is no balance required for the bike as the side car keeps it up. You just sit on and steer away as if you were in a car.

There's no crook heart about this chicken—that pain I had was your old friend indigestion. Anyhow I don't believe I'm the possessor of my own heart. I imagine some one else has it, otherwise why would I write so often.

Look, you won't get another letter until next Monday, the second last week before the Exam. You must remember I've examinations on the brain. I dreamt I was at one of them the other night and I passed it. Do dreams generally go by the opposite? Hope not anyway or it will be bad luck for you, as I'll have to work through the xmas holidays and no fun for you at Dee Why. You simply must come, come down, if I have to come up and drag you away by the ears. You are coming, get that into your head. If you don't come I won't go, so swallow that. I want you to come and if you get the small wire and boards, I'll make you a chicken run when I come up, that's if you send me an awfully nice invitation. You will have a lot of work on your hands. No Ruth to help you now, I'll be responsible for my own room and sweep all the dust under the bed where it can't be seen.

Father bought Marjorie a beautiful little silver watch demi-hunter style with a closed face but the hands can be seen through a piece of glass in the front. Marjorie has passed so many exams and averaged 80% everytime and as she works hard (no harder than I do now) we all think she deserves it. She is nicer lately but Dot is the best after Gertrude.

They bought a pig (small), in Tamworth last Saturday, coming home they dropped the bag and didn't notice. Suppose Rupe was squeezing Gertrude and driving as well. They arrived home—no piggy and couldn't find it anywhere. Next day the Wollastons drove up in their car and one of the girls brought it to Gertrude. They picked it up on the road.

There are 4 girls in the Wollaston family, all s'nice G says and are regular friends. Whenever they bake they send G some bread in their car and last Sunday took Rupe and Gertrude into Church in the Car. She likes it there and her letter are genuine enough.

I'm so glad I didn't go to Feltons if Didie only wanted to show me off to Doris Cooney. Frank, do you stick up for me when I'm not at Tarro. You didn't let Kitty say *That he could see Miss Steggles but couldnt see Heather Adamson* without backing me up do you. Don't doubt Franc.

When you come down don't stop at Feltons, Bonnie, stop here. I can run you up there often in the side car you know, favour me. You say (speaking about my sticking to you) that you are just like any other girl, well you are not, if you were, would I go to Tarro? It is the funny little ways you have, things you say etc that makes me like you, so you are not like other girls, *Comprez*.

I can hardly keep Mum out of the side car now she likes it so much and doesn't mind in the least paying 1/–for a long ride just to pay petrol expenses. That doesn't pay it all you know but goes a long way towards it.

The nurse I saw wasn't the *Rising Sun* but her mate, such a dear old thing, you'd have to get well, just to please her, you know the sort, all motherly style.

I'll get a snap of myself on the bike. I want one but if you get one you must either give me another picture of yourself or give me back one of the old ones–is that a bargain? Rooting out an old pocket book, I came across a picture of you, one with hair down and a bow. The one printed in white the mate to the dark one I took away. Do you remember giving it to me?

Miss Smith or I should say Mrs Mackenzie now, asked after my girl the other day. I went over to Eric Smith's place and she was there. She seemed surprised at my having the same one for so long. She thinks a lot of me, does Mrs Mackenzie, she always wants Eric to go with me. She says she won't be frightened of him going gay like Ginger did. Quite a compliment I think to know I'm steady.

You would laugh if you saw me dissecting. The way we catch hold of the pieces just as if they were something else but human. I hate the job, so does Smith, so we let the others cut and we read out the directions and parts to them out of the anatomy manual, good idea I think. Saves one from becoming messy and I've so many little cuts on my hands I'm frightened of them becoming septic. One cannot be too careful. I'd love to be alongside you, if invisible, when you read all this tripe just to hear what you think of this letter.

McGrath was so spruce today, he must have been going to see his girl. He is generally so grubby but is a splendid teacher and has no end of patience. I must worry him sometimes as I am so slow but once I pick a thing up I don't forget it for at least one quarter of an hour afterwards.

I've my license for the bike. Bobby Smith gave it to me without even seeing me on the bike. I took young Jimmy Smith for a ride afterward. Oh I was wild yesterday. I came home at 1.30, missed dissections in order to go up to get the license. Well I'm blowed if I could start the bike at all so at 4pm I got a car to tow me over to the Garage and the garage man looked to see what was the trouble and he burst out laughing–wanted to know how long I'd been trying to start it. I told him 2 hours. He fixed it in 2 seconds. One of the magneto wires had become unscrewed, consequently no current could flow and no wonder I couldn't start it. I looked such a fool too'. There was a crowd there. But I couldn't help but smile at my own silly mistake.

Funny about Jack and his girl. I really wonder? has he a girl, don't suppose so, but honestly it is wonderful what some girls will marry. How are the Haile tribe? Does one of the chaps who owns the motor bike still give his girl a ride on the flapper bracket?

I've been out talking to Art, he is planting Soudan grass up at Leeton it grows 6' high, 3 cuts per annum and makes great hay. He expects a lot of money this year providing he gets rain soon. Wouldn't it be fine if we could regulate the rain supply or cause rain by firing a cannon into the clouds or some other silly scheme. I'll have to think of it.

I had a letter from the head factory (Melbourne) about the artifical leg asking how it was going etc. and asking for improvements. I gave them 2 foolscap pages of improvements, chief of them was every strap not only to be sewn, but rivetted as well so that it can't give. My leg is excellent, has never been so well before and I can feel as it I could walk for miles if I had someone to take my arm, dont ya know.

Oh Arthur is shabby, it is such a different Arthur, he came down to get a suit made and he came down in khaki breeches and leggings. As he didn't have any decent trousers, I'm to supply him with a suit to go to church tomorrow. Hope he doesn't split the coat. He won't split the trousers I know that. My right leg is an awful size, growed beyond knowlege, like Bert's baby. This baby loves dirt especially to eat. They have a job keeping it clean and it is never so happy as when eating dirt. Did you ever make mud pies? I used to love to do that and go out with bare feet in the wet weather and feel the mud squash up between my toes. Don't suppose you ever did anything so nice and aristocratic as that.

This is a goat of a letter, please agree with me. My stock of letters is increasing. It fills up a whole shelf in my cupboard but I hope my stock goes on increasing. I would like 3 letters per day then I'd still have a number of questions to ask.

Must oil the leg before Church tomorrow as it's getting stiff. Poor old Keith is crook again. He went to bed at 8 tonight. I'm selling my little vest pocket Kodak to Arthur and am buying his postcard size camera. He is going to send it down to me to try. Gertrude has a small camera now and we expect some pictures of her pets.

Rupe did the baking last week and Gert said he can do it as well as she can. I think she must have improved out of sight if she can say that. I'd like to pay them a visit and be invisible just to see if they have any rows or not. Winnie Wood came around the other night, and I went to buy some petrol off Rod Wood last Tuesday between 6 and 7 after I came home. Gee I was wild the other day about the bike. I think I told you what a goat I was.

I'm going to ride down to Dee Why. There is a good road and can do many nice trips from there out to Collaroy or Barrenjoey for instance. I've been to Barrenjoey by launch from the Hawkesbury. Went fishing, a pack of us from Wahroonga College and 3 masters hired a launch. Oh My! I was ill. I'll never forget the experience–coming home everybody laughing at me too.

Well old girl, I've done my best to give you a nice chatty letter but I am no good at putting nice thoughts on paper. I'll tell you some coming home from Newcastle on the 12th of next month, Fondest Love Ben xo

———

6.9.19

Extra special letter for you this time and no rousings this time
My dear Franco
Many thanks for all the letters I've received from you this week

especially the one you wrote which I received last night. You'd be sorry to see the mess that letter is in now. Keith brought it up to me as I was pumping grease in the gear box of the bike and I couldn't stop to wash my hands before I read it and its filthy, but it can still be read, you know.

Did I tell you I had a little squeak in the bike I couldn't find, well I've found him–he was in the gear box and I stopped him by pumping in fully a breakfast cup of grease. The spot seemed to want a little grease but when I put in a whole cupful I guess it needed grease badly.

Well this time next week I ought to be at your place and the horrid physics exam over. On the 29th is the hardest exam of them all and that is the final chemistry, so you can see me working at Chemistry in between the times I'm smoking at you.

What are the arrangements for next Friday? Am I to go with you to the Tarro Show? If so you and I had better have some tea in Newcastle and if Ina comes out in the train with us, will she go home the same night? We mustn't stop too long as I've tons to talk about and if I don't get it over the first night I forget it.

Right Oh, I do remember, I'll remember about size 6 glove being too small, I suppose 6 ¼ in kid or 6 ½ in silk as your size because they don't make ¼ in silk I knew that long ago,

Glad Creamy is shod once again, Oh what an old slow coach after my bike. It cleared up for a few hours this afternoon and as Keith is very miserable I took him for a run. He reckons he's never been so fast before–just reached 50mph.

Yesterday when I left home at 20 to 8 it was quite sunny but when I got into the train at the Quay it rained small sized butcher boys. It cleared though to let me walk to the Uni and then poured again. Ben W of course had no coat, anyhow I didn't get wet as I waited for the showers to pass then skipped between the drops. The old trouble with the leg chafing has come back with a vengeance and when I put the underpants as stuffing inside the woody, doesn't help it. It is raining again now, we don't want it to be so heavy as such a number of blossoms are being washed off our fruit trees.

Let's hope I bring fine weather to your place when I come. The exam on the 29th worries me. Both Ray and Bert are sitting for the exams. Bert had an anatomy exam yesterday. I didn't see him, though my seat number for the exam is 139. Do you think it sounds like a lucky one? Perhaps it stands for 12 day of 9th month last year when I was at Tarro last year.

Oh you would have laughed to see me in a wheel chair down at Hastings with all the Alfieiri kiddies pushing me about. I laughed at myself. Today I got dressed in old clothes to ride the bike down to McGraths but it looked like rain so I put on my big over coat and went per train. St Leonards is an awkward place to get at from Wahroonga as during the busy times, most of the trains go through going down. I had to change at Killara, then at Chatswood (steps to cross over) coming home, changed at Killara and Gordon (steps) I blessed the rain! If it had not been dull I could have gone down there in 20 minutes and no changing at all.

Oh, I have received my yearly train ticket from the Repat people available from Wahroonga to Sydney so I can travel either via Milsons Point or go round via Hornsby and Sydney. Its very convenient so I've put in my old ticket to the Station Master in order to get a refund of 2 pound on the un-expired portion. That 2 pound will just pay my debts nicely.

I got back the cover for my side car which Scise and I lost on a trip. Some chap picked it up and sent it to Scise's shop. Terribly good of him wasn't it.

Geoff Johnson was supposed to have gone to Melbourne but the day he was to go he caught tonsillitis and he has been very ill with it, delirious at times, wonder what he talked about? The people at Wandsworth Hospital in London say I was the funniest person under anaesthetic they had for a long time. They say I handed each nurse in the place a Victoria Cross. But that was nicer than some chaps. The nurses say that if a chap, say a Parson goes under Chloroform he swears. If a very rough chap goes under he sings hymns. So I suppose being the middle sort of man I struck the happy

medium. General Ryan, a horrid old man and incidently Director
of Medical Services came around the ward one day and a chap was
just coming out of anaesthetic but he pretended he was still under it
and told Old Charlie Ryan better than any bullock driver could have
done and Charlie thinking he was still under chloroform couldn't do
anything at all to him.

I would like to know what happened to the *Rising Sun* that is Sister
Humberstoner. She was a dear old thing and I hope some nice chap with
money married her. You ought to have seen her face. You'd have to smile,
ugly but red and always smiling she couldn't help it she was so fat too.
More than 3 arms full I should say not that I ever tried it you know.

Would it be any good if I made a chicken run for you? Did your
Dad drown ALL Pats pups? I gather from your letter that he did.
Fancy the little beggar bringing them on to the beds. That shows his
Bad broughtings up doesn't it?

Must congratulate you on the writing of your long letter last
week. It's like copperplate writing and I'll give you 95% for it. Have the
machines arrived yet? T'will be handy having petrol on the place when I
ride up at Xmas. I certainly would ride up this time only I've to be back
in town on the evening of the 18th and that wouldn't leave me much
time to take you about. But you'd be too busy this time to come out
much Ruth being away. Glad she is enjoying herself. I mustn't forget to
bring up her little Frenchy button this time.

I haven't seen Didie for ages, nor Clive Inch so don't know how thing
are progressing. Will you have the skirt made by the 12th? You must
make an impression you know at the Tarro do for I'm sure all the elite
will be there including the 'ards. Hope he sings *he drug me around the
room*

Glad you saw Les Holden in his aeroplane but he has not the DSO
as the papers say but the Distinguished Flying Cross, they mix it up. He
is a very nice chap, I know him well. This younger brother that broke
his leg (I think I told you about it) is getting along well. Les flew up to
Warrawee especially so that his young brother could see him from the
bed room window.

Captain Leslie H. Holden MC from No 2 Squadron, AFC. — AWM

I don't want to go out behind Belmont unless I can drive him with you on the trap. It wouldn't be any fun for me just getting someone else drive and I'd have to get out to open the gates, *no bon* for this chicken I assure you. Wish I could get rid of this sore spot caused by the leg rubbing. McLeod, our post master said when I went for the letters today that I get as much mail as any person in Wahroonga. But he a very nice and Scotch and never talks other people's business.

We have a lot of New Zealanders in town too, they are waiting for a boat to take them across. Vic Austin is due on Monday now the boat has been delayed by rough seas. Jean Austin says Em Sutter for name has cleaned out the house from top to bottom every day for a fortnight past. Her boy is on the same boat as Vic and they are due to be married soon after he arrives. He is an officer in Motor Transport (In France like Harry Jones you know) and smuggles extra dainties from the Officers cabin down to Vic.

Don't bother to let Mrs Griffin know I'm coming up as I've only a short time and don't want visitors to see me. That is unless you would like to see her.

I'm feeling blushified when people ask to see your ring. Is it my fault do you think? Am I making the pace too hot and what on earth did your mother say about it? Tell me. I can see I'll have to send some of these people about their business. Tell them I'm only 17 and I'm waiting until I'm 30. One never can tell, can one?

Marjorie left for Brisbane yesterday. I thought, so did Marjorie that as you could only see her for a little while it wasn't fair to ask you to come down. They had a carriage with one lady in it so they will be comfortable. The ladies husband is something or other in Sydney Railway Station and arranged that no one else was to get into the carriage this side of Queensland border.

Yes I can imagine you on a bike. Nothing so ungainly as an ordinary bike as you just sit on comfortably as if in a car and there is no balance required and it is very low and your skirts don't fly like on a bike, not 1/3 as much as on a horse. There is a lady traveller for Griffiths Brothers, the tea people, she rides a Douglas bike around town all day. Nothing lady like about her. I'll teach you, only don't lose your head and send me into the gutter. At low gear, the speed can be cut down to 2 miles per hour thats all right for learning isn't it?

I should think that chap we saw on the Minmi road was doing more than 45 to the hour. more like 60. Wasn't he cutting the pace out. Thats a very good road, don't you think? The motor garage man in Wahroonga did the Newcastle road last week. He has 7 cylinders in his big car and says the roads are quite good, not hard metal roads but good hard dirt roads which I like best as they give a good grip for tyres and don't wear them out half as quickly. A tyre is supposed to last 4000 miles.

No, I'm not going to sell my ground although I was offered 1 pound per foot more than I gave for it. H. Kershaw seems more settled now he has started work. When he first came back he couldn't sit still, he came to see me and wandered about the room all the time. That's how I felt but I couldn't wander. I always heard that grubs liked fresh young things so one bit you on the neck, well all I can say is that it knew what it was doing.

Glad you liked Gertrudes letter, she told us she had written. She is sending down some films to be developed. She says one is of *the young bird taking a bit out of a pork pie made herself* It appears she doesn't always bake bread, most of it comes from Tamworth in the next door neighbours car.

We start our dental Mechanical work after the vacation. Thank Goodness. I hate these waste afternoons per week. Dad hasn't finished that photo for Ben William and his Excelsior yet. Wonder how it will turn out. Bet my face is dirty. I alway manage to get black grease just aound my nose and being a monk have to use Monkey soap to get it off. My nose consequently is red, not through drink though.

Heard of a wonderful operation Sir Thomas Anderson did. If you remind me I'll tell you about it; the operation was on the throat of a man–it would take pages to tell what he did. Do you know how many lines to the page you get? But quantity doesn't count too much does it? I always reckon to lay out 1 whole evening on your letter.

Keith has been in awful pain all the week. Mother has been up 2-4 times each night with fomentation. He has a stone in his kidney and goes to Prince Alfred Hospital Military Section on Monday. If it is a certain style of stone if can be dissolved by medicine but if other style has to be cut out. But Dr Read (over the way) thinks by the peculiar pains Keith gets that it is a stone of the dissolvable style so that there is to be no cutting.

So Jack has gone as well, Good Riddance, just don't you get some peculiar styles in working men but all seem to be of the shiftless variety.

Mother has been away on an errand of mercy this afternoon seeing a consumptive [Tuberculosis] soldier who has 5 children He can't work and he wanted some little baby clothes but can't afford to buy them. Mother said his wife was in bed and a very cheery style. The hubby was trying to manage, so Mother hopped in and made tea etc left the woman comfortable with a parcel of baby clothes she managed to get together from a few Wahroonga ladies.

Tom Brownlie's girl did throw him over for this chap who wouldn't go to the war. I will have to get hold of Tom, he might attempt to drown his sorrows–he might you know. He is back in Sydney now so Mrs Hesketh told me.

Speaking of Tom Brownlie reminds me, I haven't heard of Tom Brown lately, I must ring him up tonight and see if he is on duty as watchman in the Tech museum. He has a nice little wife. Frank, She is petite and Tom is rough and big and they hit if off very well together. Tom said the only row they have ever had was because she said Tom was spoiling the little girl. So he does, that Kiddie does anything with him. Great big Tom, I laughed, the little thing one day just stamped its foot at Tom and he laughed and gave into her. She is just like little Jean. Tom [little brother] and Peter are not speaking, they are just like 2 school girls but it will be all right tomorrow though. They have at least 2 fights each day. What Peter does is this, when he wants to make up with Tom he rings up and says his bike is gone bung and would Tom come down to help him mend it. That is just what Tom likes, messing around with tools and grease. So the row is made up. Tom always helps me clean my bike. That will be your job at Xmas time to help me oil it up. It will take a lot of oil. It is a big engine you know, 9 horse power in a bike is a lot. There are many cars with only 9 hp engines in them.

Well nice old thing, will have to close now. Here is an arrangement now which you mustn't forget. If I miss the 2pm train (it is not likely though) do NOT wait for me at Newcastle but go to Tarro to the concert and I'll come around to the hall. I suppose that is where it will be. The next train is a slow one and meets the 20 past 6 at Hamilton if I'm not on that, I arrive at Tarro Station at 9.30 now dont forget. If you dont remember these I may miss you at one end ot the other. Do NOT wait for me at Newcastle if I'm not on the 2pm train from Sydney. If I catch the train that connects at Hamilton I will walk through the 1st class carriages until I see you, or if I get to Tarro at 9.30 I'll come around to the hall Get me, Steve?

Fondest love, I'm going to sleep well, there is nothing like the bike to make you sleep well, rushing through the air does the trick, it also makes one eat like a horse

Love Ben

Gug I won't write again 'till I see you. Read this letter on Monday and the other 1/2 on Wednesday and you have me on Friday. This letter is equal to 15 pages. Aren't I a s'nice Bhoy, Gug

20.9.19 Saturday night

Dear Bonnie,

I'm terribly tired tonight, the excitement and late hours on Thursday night, getting up early on Friday morning and last night have about finished this chicken. I tried to work tonight but can't concentrate my empty noddle to work. Isn't it wretched having to work for one's living? How is my girl tonight? Did you see the Upfolds on Friday morning and have a good time?

Our carriage was fairly full at Newcastle, became overflowing at Gosford, but the Pommy bride in our carriage didn't object to smoke. The Collector gave me some bother at Gosford. I couldn't find my ticket for some time–after turning out each pocket twice I found it hiding away inside a matchbox, queer place for it to slip wasn't it?

Had a glorious time last night, didn't get home until 12.30. Such a number of chaps there and the yarns we swapped, enough to make one's blood run cold. One chap got tight and swore he killed 20 huns but we all knew he was a stretcher bearer so just laughed at him. Everybody was there from the Colonel downwards. Some chorus troops gave some fairly sickening songs but we wanted to talk all the time so no one paid much attention to them. But there was one of our own chaps there, he sang that song the Clarks sang and he got a hearing and 3 encores. Tom Brownlie was not there and Vic Fowler is to be married soon in Sydney to a Sydney girl. I'm going to cadge an invite to his fatal turn out. What is a good idea for a gift for him? I always think vases, some times called vawses. I think they are always handy.

Do tell me when the machines are running and if those other cases of machinery come to light that are lost. What a relief it will be to you to know no more mllking.

Gee my fingers are sore. Mother has been worried about Bert, no letters, so she asked me to take her across this morning. He is bad, more malaria I think and he is to have a test on Monday to see if his one lung shows any sign of that crook lung complaint, commonly called consumption. Oh this cursed war and what a mess for our family.

I took Tom and Mother across and as Vera is worried with the baby, brought Jean back. Some load for the bike wasn't it? Jean is very forward don't you think and I think she is starting young, she put her arms around my neck and said *Oh I love you my pet*. What will she be when she grows up.

After dinner I took Keith down to Byrnes to see Jack but he wasn't in. Mrs Byrne says he is in love and isn't often at home, well, we talked for a couple of hours until Tess came home and the talk drifted on to bikes and they came out to see mine and it ended by Keith walking home and Tess going as far as the station and back in the side car. Don't be jealous.... You'll have a long enough spin when I bring you down. It will be awfully hot but we'll take a thermos flask and dine often on the way. I am quite excited at the idea and I'll get some expert to go all over the bike to see that is is perfectly o.k. before I start. I can see the old Buggy being tossed out of the stable and my bike going in.

But oh Franco, what am I to do if I fail to pass. I kissed goodbye to a pound note and the one I lost makes me more than broke but the Lord'll provide ..

Do you remember going to see, but of course you must remember, Mrs Jones, well Enid came in for 9000 pounds last week. Someone or other died. Keith says he is thinking seriously of hanging up his hat on their door knocker. Luck some dopes have (I mean the girl not Keith)

Vic Austin is down the South Coast recuperating ahem! What a war he had. I told you about him. Not a line from Tom Brownlie and he is in Sydney too. Dear old Mrs Hesketh was at the Battalion show last night handing around tea, her boy was killed with the 1st Battalion. He was so tall he was sniped over the top of the trench by a fritz. We got the fritz afterwards who did it.

I'm printing some photos next week, post card size of the bike. Gee I'm proud of that bike. Tom and a little boy chum cleaned it for a penny each, some job too. Wait until I give you a go at learning to drive it. Be careful won't you. Down the Minmi road, would be a good quiet spot with no one to see you either. A chum of mine, Piper by name, rode to Tamworth in 2 days. He says the roads are good but dusty. We'll be as black as sweeps at the end of the trip. I'm looking forward so much to it.

Wish this was December and exams finished and I was starting off on the trip up. How are the men? if you had the trouble we are having about bread you couldn't feed them. We have 1 loaf per day and that is brought all the way from Wollongong each day by a chum of Dads. Oh, Dad is in bed ill. The reaction you know from the worry about the job means Bronchitis again.

Harry Jones is due next week or so with his English girl, not married yet. She is on a different boat. Just like him, Pity the girl. I'll go and see them and report to you whether she proposed or if he did. I'll be able to tell when I see her.

Won't Ma be charmed at the idea of having a select English person not a common Aussie girl. Aussies will do me. Mrs Byrnes sister asked me if I'd left my heart in Blighty but some one chimed in and said, *Oh No, It was booked before he went* And did you know I could blush, well I did, so I'm not too far gone yet am I. Well Old girl, Good night and remember this chicken. I've still that good luck black cat Anything said about the shoes? Where will you go to when you die?, but you are not as big a fibber as me yet but I don't fib to you. Best love

Yours ever Ben

It was funny seeing the chaps dance with one another, no girls, so some who had had a bit too much drink tied towels and handkershiefs etc round them to act as skirts. I didn't have a drink all night except tea. See what you do to me.

23.9.19 Tuesday night

My dear Bonnie,

We've had an Aunt from Melbourne up, she is Dad's sister, very nice and all that. [Eliza Hirst] Her 2 boys are dentists and she has been telling, to encourage me, what they are making per annum and truly it seems a fabulous sum.

Many thanks for your nice letter, but Oh Frank, don't go to Cessnock, do come to town for we might drift apart if you go right out there and I do want to see you often and above all it would mean missing the Dee Why trip. That is what I have been looking forward too for ages. If you can't come my spirits will go a wallop, so come.

I've been looking forward to bringing you down in the side car so much since I had your Mothers permission for you. Now about October, do your best to come down so as to get everything booked up for the Coast. I'm sure Dad will use his influence to get you in if I ask him. And I feel sure your Dad couldn't be so mean as to prevent you coming.

If you make up your mind to come down in October and there is no cash for January I know someone who'd give it, just to get you down. I'm sure if you just say you are going and when I come up, I possibly may be able to smooth things over. But come twice if possible and you can if you say you will.

Tell me if anything has been said about the green shoes yet and have you those other stockings. You did look s'nice honestly and if this counts you were the best and most tastefully dressed girl at the Tarro affair.

The train I caught the other day was a fast one, put on especially as the mail was two hours late. Pity there were not a few more Ottos about instead of those other skalliwags, as if you don't slave getting those men good food as it is. I see you are using the paper I left, do you like it? I use it when I don't think I can write a long letter.

Bonnie, I've decided to take on the mechanical dentistry if I don't get through this year. It will be a struggle to live on the money later on but it's just a gamble if I could stand the racket of a practice.

Bonnie, I don't mind if the letters are skimpy while Ruth is away but I must have just the same number. A piece of paper with 3 words on it will do. The amount of work you do and have to do surprised me. Don't you think a small pretty house is best, even if one is cramped slightly, I do. It's no good this everlasting work.

Went down with Jack Wright this morning. I went to town for Dad, he is still ill. Some of the old married buffers on the station were chaffing Jack about what to do to make his wife keep quiet when he gets one.

Tomorrow at 7pm, is the hour, no one knows where they are going, or to what they intend to do. Harry Jones is home. His girl is not coming out here yet. He is going back to Scotland within a year to get married and bring her out. So sorry about you, but you'll be ok soon, buck up,

I know now what you feel like. Well old sweetheart, I'm trying to study. Hope you soon feel better—it is rotten to have a cold. Yours only, Ben

I've made the postman take his cows out of the orchard as they were eating my fruit blossoms. You'll have some fruit about xmas time Love Ben.

27.9.19

Dear Bonnie,

I received a nice letter from you telling me that Ruth was at Riverstone.[near Windsor staying with aunt Emma Rumery nee Carroll—Ed.] during the week, because Dot had done something or other for me. I promised to take her where she liked on Saturday so when I told her where Ruth was, between us we decided to pay her a surprise visit. We left home at 1/4 to one after an early dinner and hit out for Riverstone. You must know that today has been the hottest so far with gusty winds and before we got far we were eating dust wholesale. Any how, after making the pace and seeing some beautiful country we lobbed at *Denbigh*. They didn't hear us come so I rang the bell—no one answered so I went around the back and met Mrs Rumery who didn't recognise me but knew me when I told her the famous Champion name.

Mr and Mrs Rumery on their verandah

She called Ruth who was muchly surprised. Any how, we sat on the
verandah while Mrs Rumery got tidied. I think she was a little hurt at
the surprise I gave them and being in work-a-day togs but you know how
fussy I am about clothes, the older the better I think out in the country.
Dot was awfully knocked up and white, as she wasn't at all well when we
started. After a rest she was ok.

The country was beautiful and nearly every house being smothered
in wisteria It was so nice, and from Castle Hill and Rouse Hill the
moutains looked so tempting, nice and cool and we were baked. Ruth
couldn't talk of anything else but Jim Hamilton and his car and the
times she had. I hope I can give you as good a time at Xmas then I'll
be satisfied. If you can't come I'll come and pull you all the way down
because I want you.

Afte a while, a Mrs Harding dropped in [another sister Lucina
nee Carroll–PF] and sat talking while Marjorie and Fred Rumery
wrangled away for their hearts content. Then we walked up to the
Orchard and filled ourselves with oranges. *Ain't they fine and such a
many* as Grandma says.

I gave Ruth a ride up as far as the Windsor Road just so that she
could say she had been in a side car. She says it was comfy.

Haven't Rumery's got a beautiful little pony. Fred was climbing all
over it and it shakes hands quite snicely. I like Mrs R. very much, just a
second edition of your mother–she made me so at home, with a big cup
of tea at a table so that I wouldn't have to dance it on my knee. I didn't
see Mr Rumery when we came back from the Orchard as he was in the
bath so as we were awfully orangy we had to wash in Ruth's bedroom
and I didn't see Mr R at all. Ruth, Mrs R and family are going to the
Gardens on Monday. Ruth looks well but no stouter. She is anxious to
see the machines going (first milking machines in the district) and I
told her, so were all of us. Won't it be a load off your Dad's mind when
they are thoroughly doing their work. Riverstone looks green and there
is no drought out there.

I'm so glad Wood is going, he is too old and slow for the work you
want done and it would actually be a blessing to have to pay to get rid

of those boys of his. Mother laughed over the porridge episode. I can just imagine how gracious Mrs N would look when she handed over the porridge, one of those smiles, which mean look out for squalls in the near future. Dad is off on Monday night, I hope he has a good holiday with Uncle Raphe [step brother Cottam] but I'm sure it will be hot.

An awful southerly buster has just come and it will cool the air. All our doors and windows are banging. Hope nothing breaks.

Here is the rain, glad it is here. Have you any skeeters up there? a few have wandered in out of the wet to visit me. Young Tom has gone to the *pitchers* with Mrs Lindsay and Peter but he has promised to help me clean the bike in the morning, even a ride that distance knocks me up a little. The strain of keeping ones eyes glued to the road a head all the time. Coming home there were 6 cars ahead of me. The whole distance of the whole column being about 2 miles and they kicked up an awful dust so I told Dot to hang on and I passed each one in turn and got into the clear atmosphere beyond and gave them dust and petrol fumes in turn. Its a beautiful bike, Frank runs *somethink* beautiful.

Between the family we bought Nancy Johnson a nice present, a cut glass flower holder, silver mounted and on a silver stand. It cost a lot but she is worth it. Excuse the roughness of the paper cutting.

Les Holden was flying about again today. He only has an old type of plane though. He is wonderful and only a boy too with no job to go to at all.

Mr Smith asked me to come down to see him tomorrow–suppose he wants to cheer me up about the exam on Monday. He says he'll never speak to me again if I don't keep on with the Dentistry. Suppose he also wants to rouse on me for even thinking of it.

Harold Kershaw was right amongst ½ acre of Stocks when I went to see him late yesterday afternoon. They always cut flowers when the sun has gone down and you can possibly imagine the delicious perfume ½ acre of big double stocks would give. It was just perfect. The sun was down and all the flowers seemed to be giving forth every bit of perfume they possessed. He has planted red and white climbing roses all along his side of my fence. He says, that if I build and live there, I could pick as many as I liked. Next month

Harold Kershaw

is the month for carnations and he is busy planting 2000 plants. He intends to go into partnership with his Dad and has got the 1900 pounds to do it with.

And my cold footed military policeman cousin is on his way back.

Dad got dozens of congratulatory messages for his new position–has been officially announced through the papers. Salary 600 pounds. The message he most prizes is from an old chum, Mr Maiden of the Botanical Gardens, he just sent his card along with his name on it and on the back was the following message, brief and to the point, this was all–OORAY!

Ruth was asking a lot of questions about Otto. I told her he was 6' after your father's style of build. I also told her all the little improvements you were having done. I hope you were not keeping it as a surprise for her.

We got letters and films from Gertrude on Friday. She is well happy and getting stout. She went to a dance and wanted to put on her fawn dress for the first time since she went up and couldn't get the waist band to meet so she let in 6 'of pink ribbon. She danced every dance except one, and for that one she minded someone else's baby. She says everytime Rupe has to go to some part of the place for a day, they get up early, do the work and she goes out with him. Takes the 2 thermos flasks and make a regular picnic of it. She rides on the slide when they go for water. Their rain water has run out and she says they have to draw water for drinking and it's better than taking a pill. I must send you a little snap of her on the slide. I'm glad she has a camera, though I roll of film was completely spoiled by her.

Tonight I've asked Dad for a letter to the Coast Matron for you. Wish I hadn't lost that 10/–note on Newcastle Beach. I'm all behind now.

Can you remember if I wrote to Captain Beavis from your place. Oh Dad says he can't write to the Matron as he has given you a recommendation already. So that is ok.

Is your Aunt Ada a business like person. Dad is getting, he says his *truesaw* ready for going away. He say he is worrying about his mink furs, he say they are sure to be moth eaten before he leaves.

My fingers are now o.k. Perfectly healed up I'm glad to say. I think taking no notice of them is a good scheme as you say. I know you wish me all sorts of luck for Wednesday, Cherriho Old girl

Love Ben

8.10.19 Home

Dear Bonnie

Today is the last afternoon I have off. I start at the Dental Hospital in future in the afternoons so there will be no more spello for me. No results yet about the chemistry examination and we've started dissecting the head and neck, so we feel as if we are actually starting dentistry at last.

About our trip down, the carriage when you left us was naturally full but it got worse at Niagara Park, 16 was the total then until Narara when we had one additional passenger. Were you very disappointed at going home in the early train? I saw you talking to Ruth as our train pulled out.

Look Franco, if you come down during the next fortnight I won't be able to take you out on the bike as it is in dock at present. Nothing wrong at all but I'm getting a patent of my own fitted to the clutch so that I can operate it with my right foot and not bother about moving my hand from the handle bar.

Suppose Mr Gerard is fixing up the milking engines and I hope they will be a success.

We had a funny experience today. An old lady, very well dressed knocked at the front door and Edie went and she said *Oh, I'm nearly fainting, have you any spirits at all.* As we hadn't any Edie offered tea, milk or water.

She wouldn't take them. At last Edie managed to get her away and in 1 hours time she was back again asking for spirits, so I came to the conclusion that she must have developed a thirst.

Marjorie and I have been asked up to Feltons for next Friday night. Mr Felton rang and asked us to come up tonight but Marj said she had 38 little elephants to draw. She has to give a lesson about elephants tomorrow and there are 38 in her class.

I'm feeling very well after my trip to your place but I seemed to get in the road slightly this time. Wasn't Mary funny about getting us that carriage, I laughed. Did I make a prawn of myself in ways or not? I wanted to show Ruth that your boy wasn't altogether a dope.

Saw Bert and Ray today and congratulated them on their successes. They seem glad the exams were over. Well must do some physics now. Will write a lengthy letter over weekend. Ever yours

Ben

11.10.19

Dear Bonnie,

It is only 20 to 9, yet I'm that tired, I'm thinking of getting 2 little matches to prop open my eyes. I thought until this afternoon, when at last I got a letter, that you had forgotten me but its o.k. now.

Keith and I and Mr Rhodes [opposite] have been tinkering up his bike and now its *runnun something beautiful* as Ruth says. Mine will probably be ready by next Saturday, It is ready now for the new little improvements I have to buy on Monday So that when it is fixed, I will work everything possibly by my right foot.

Peter and Tom wangled Mother to take them to the pictures tonight so they are out. Marjorie and I didn't go to Feltons last night, I was too tired so Marjorie wouldn't go on her own. This hot weather, though I love it, plays havoc with the wearing of a woody and I haven't been getting on well with mine at all these last few hot days.

Had a big lesson from McGrath today, we boxed on with several subjects and I think I can do them now.

Have the engines been running at all yet? Glad about the cement but I won't let on I know anything about it at all. But isn't it great, you appear to be getting more improvements as time goes on. Did I tell you that Rupe met with an accident and is in hospital? He fell or a log rolled or something like that and cut his eyebrow from forehead etc so that he can't wear his glass eye. [lost one eye in the war—PF] Gertrude is stopping with some friends which is handy. Rather novel for Gertrude to be stranded on her own isn't it. Write to her now. It would be a comfort.

So Adamson brought home a bride. Hope for his sake she is o.k. Didn't the family know about it at all? What a surprise if they didn't. Do you think you can come down? Waugh says he doesn't think applications will be called for until December or Janaury, but he says they have no regular time and may spring a surprise, but he will let me know.

Had a couple of letters from Dad, he is getting well fast and hardly coughs at all and his cough used to be so racking, --used to be awful to hear it.

Marjorie has been *tennising* this afternoon with a girl chum whose father married again the other day. She said she played 4 sets which worked out to be about 24 games so she is tired. I painted 2 bedsteads yesterday and today and they look much improved. Wonderful what a coat of paint will do even on girls, makes them look like they aint doesn't it?

Weeks go so quickly now that you just have to look at the corner and it is Sunday once again. Expect the results of the exam out any day now so hope I pass. When you come down bring that hankie marked B, I'm short.

Metallurgy pronouced Meta–lurgy is very interesting–smelting up metals etc. I'm to go to church tomorrow as such a long time since I've been.

How long did Maggie Wood sleep after her night duty the day I came away? Nice dinner too she missed. I hate going to McGraths when I haven't my bike.

Sunday morning 12.10.19

Woke up this morning with an awful cold in my head, it is so rotten I can't go to church. I feel so miserable about it. You ought to just see that little garden opposite the side verandah, it is just one mass of colors, poppies and rose and snap dragons.

I've been going down with Vic Austin the last few mornings. He doesn't like work after such a glorious trip away. He only saw a few days fighting and for the remainder of the time he toured France and Italy with the soldiers concert party [also served WWII].

Victor George Austin

It is a glorious day. Hope my bike will be ready by next Saturday. I missed it yesterday. Do you think you'll be able to come down? You'll have to forgive me writing so little but I feel rotten with this cold.

Love Ben

This is the 3rd cut at this letter. It is 6pm Sunday and I've just got dressed. Mr Rhodes fixed up Keith's bike so now he is out on it and happy. I'm afraid you might think things if I didn't fill up this letter somehow. I feel better now have taken some special quinine pills [malarial pills].

Bert and Vera are getting along o.k. She can milk properly now. Have those Woods people been seen since they left and how is Otto behaving himself? Any more spills off the horse? I had to laugh when I saw his tooth out–he looked so different.

We have a plague of moths and they cause endless trouble getting near the gas mantles and they break them if their wings touch. It's been frightfully hot until now, it went up to 90 degree on our verandah. If it wasn't for the woody I'd enjoy myself.

What a day for the river bank, we really must go down there at Xmas. Wonder the Tarro people don't pass some yarns around about me as I'm often up. Bert was surprised when I told him I'd been up there again he said *Oh you must almost live there* I don't mind do you.

Harold and Mr Kershaw have been shooting in this National Rifle Association competition and they have won several prizes besides getting the sport out of it.

Harold Kershaw and the Kings Cup, –Courtesy Jennifer Nixon–Ancestry

Kershaw's roses are beautiful especially my almost black favourite called the *Black Prince*.

I like Ruth Fold Up. I had to bite my tongue several times to stop me saying Foldup instead of Upfold.

Tom has christened the kitten *dusty* as it looks dusty but is really ginger under the black. Am thinking of sleeping out again. It must be nice and I've been getting up at 5.30 and doing an hours work.

When in bed this afternoon I read some of the *Mystery of the Sea*. I like parts in that book especially the place where he jumps over board with Marjorie and swims ashore. If you come down bring the *Sky Pilot* as Mum wants to read it but don't post it.

I'm thinking of making a wardrobe during the vacation and putting a full length mirror in it. Believe it would be simple to make it of some good wood like maple or beech.

It is ages since I saw Bruce Rainsford. He doesn't live at Warrawee now although his family still does but is living at Milson's Point. He says it is too far but I think *cherchez la femme* would be more to the point.

We are going to get some Wisteria soon. Killara station has been a picture, all up the steps leading from the station. Nothing much in the Sun this morning and I looked for the exam results but in vain. You ought to see our tennis court it's just like a paddock with grass 2' high in places. We need an animal lawn mower. How did the cows get on in the new bails much trouble?

Plenty of questions in this. Please answer them, o.k? Don't worry about Winnie Wood going onto Cessnock. I'll give you a good time down here although you will be away from home. I've cut my cigarette smoke down to 10 per diem what do you think of that, pretty good isn't it? Poplar trees look well. I think practically every boy in Wahroonga has a motor bike. There seems to be hundreds pass our gate each day. well Bonnie, no more news. Cheeriho.

Ben

16.10.19 University 11am

In 3 months time you and I should be having a good time at Manly. I've mapped out several good motor spins from there. Out to National Park for one. You have never been there yet have you? It is a bosker place where you can get boats for rowing etc on the river and as we go on a weekday there will be no crowd there at all. Then out to Barrenjoey Lighthouse at the opening to the Hawkesbury River into the sea, right out past Newport where we went that day. I've been there camping with Geoff Johnson and Mr Bruce who was our minister. We are sure to have good weather that time of the year.

After you go home I will have to settle and learn my osteology and anatomy for the coming year. That is if I pass this one. There are no results and I hate this anxiety. The reason I didn't write last last night was because I felt inclined for work. I worked at Physics and Chemistry until 10pm and then I went to bed so that wasn't too bad was it.

We have no lecture this hour so I am out in a chair under the trees facing the Parramatta Road. Such a lot of traffic going by but no dust. The rain has been beautiful.

Gertrude's district had 62 points and all their tanks and water holes are full. Rupe has left the hospital although his head is still sore but he can work around o.k.

It is said the nurses at Tamworth were very good to them looking after Rupe and allowing G to stop long after visiting hours.

Hope you can read this [in pencil and very small writing] as I haven't a book to write on and the paper is just loose.

Have you had Ruth Upfold out yet? Didn't Ina look funny the day we saw her with all that kalsomine lotion on her face. The hair up does make a difference but she hasn't lengthened her dress at all.

I had a note from Bert today and spent the dinner hour with Ray on Tuesday. Both are o.k. I ought to have the bike back on Saturday. I wonder how these chaps manage to get along on one crutch. Some of them go very quickly too. Bert Carroll doesn't smoke at all now.

How is Otto? So you had his father up did you? Did he go down to the farm at all and how are the engines going and was there any fun when they started to milk the cows in the new bails. Look, I want a long letter soon for a week ender. You could write more than 3 pages. I'm not growling 'cause you do write often.

Do you remember how I used to go out to Callam Park? Well Eric Smith takes a couple of mates out there now. I won't go now because I have been so often and it makes me tired with all the standing around.

I will come in for about 75 pounds if they pass this war gratuity business of ⅓ per diem. Won't it come in handy Eh! Just as I'm broke the Excelsior motor bikes have gone up in price. They are now 180 pounds with side car so after all I got a bargain. Well Old Girl, I'm due at lecture on Physics in 10 minutes.

Love Ben.

18.10.19
Saturday evening 9pm

Dear Bonnie,

Many thanks for your telegram I believe you were as excited as I was and that's saying something. Ma says I was excited because I pulled the cat up by it's tail. Something told me they would be out that morning too.

Poor old Henderson, one of my pals didn't pass. A returned digger too and I suppose you noticed that neither of the girls passed either. I really don't think Returned Soldiers were granted any privilges or else Henderson would have been put through.

I didn't go to McGraths as was too tired. Didn't put on my leg until after dinner when I took Roy Saddington out for a ride. We broke the chain while out, but being wise I always carry spare links and soon fixed it up though it was a bother. The bike is fixed but needs some slight adjusting before I call it perfect. Then it will be some bike I believe.

What French did I put in my last letter to you? I don't remember any at all. Anyhow if I did, I knew you would soon find it out. Must have been one of the common phrases we used to use over the other side and it slipped out.

You always accuse me of being sarcastic and I really don't mean to be. That villian of an Edie forgot to go for the mail this afternoon and we have to collect it on Saturday afternoon as the postie has ½ day holiday, so I don't know if there is one waiting for me there or not, so I've slipped horribly if there is one there.

Father came home at 7 this morning and he has lost his cough and says he feels splendid, anyway he is cheerful which is the main thing. Hope your Dad's holiday won't clash with yours. I'm developing a cheek these days, I actually went up and drew my civilian suit, cap and military overcoat from the Barracks. It is just a suit too, you ought to see it but it will do fine for cleaning the bike in. It is sort of rusty blue, you know the style, wear it twice in the sun and it goes a reddish purple or rusty color.

So Ruthie Upfold can't come out to see you huh! Hard Luck but you have only put the pleasure off for a while haven't you. She'll come some day won't she? She doesn't look the sort to break promises. I also received a big certificate from the Barracks signed by Georgie V to say I had been wounded and discharged honourably from the AIF, commonly called the Ac.I. Foo and it is rather a good thing. I think I'll get it framed. It's about 2'x 1'and has an engraving of sailor and soldier presenting arms to Britannia holding up the Union Jack.

Ben's Discharge Certificate.

Hope you are not too fussy about spelling or I'll have to have a dictionary handy, a small one like the one Otto has the loan of, in his bedroom you know. All the family including Dad are in bed but I'm not sleepy. Oh, Dad has grown a small beard and it improves his appearance. He doesn't look so thin in the face now. Tomorrow is egg day at the Church. It is the day allotted by the Presbyterian Church to collect eggs for the hospitals. We generally hand in 100 dozen. Mother had bad luck with two broodies as they pecked the eggs to see if any chickens were coming along before the proper time and I had the job of burying the eggs and I felt like the cows must have felt when the bad eggs were smashed in the cow bails that time.

Marjorie and Tess Byrne are going up to the Feltons to tea tomorrow night. Am afraid Mrs Felton must be thinking something as I generally say I'm too tired. Well so I am, I hate going out at night. Anyhow, my woody won't let me. I made Mrs Saddington laugh today when up there. We were putting the new link in the chain, and Roy and I were looking for something to bang it on–I winked at Roy and suggested my woody, but he said it wouldn't do. Do you remember on the Krambach bike trip I met a chap who knew the eldest boy Saddington, well Roy is his brother. He had stiff luck in not getting away.

He had a weak heart so went for 6 months in the country to get it fixed up and he was then ok. Then they said he had some trifling matter, one toe webbed or something, so he had an operation to fix that up, then they put him into the Siege artillery and he was just about to go when Armistice was signed so he couldn't go, but tried hard, didn't he.

Talking about hard, have the Hards gone from Tarro yet? Hope you're over your cold by this, I am, I can generally throw them off in 3 days. Must go to Church tomorrow morning. It's such a long time since I went in the morning. Have Otto and your Dad gone yet? They were always saying they would, weren't they.

I'm very glad the Military people have decided against compulsory training for men of the AIF. It was absurd to think of making them drill. There is only one more boy to come back to Wahroonga now and that is Maud Kershaw's hero, Sam Ward. Keith is unfortunate, he had a buster on his bike today, broke the front forks. He was just going slowly past an old cow when it suddenly turned and went the wrong way, you know what silly creatures they are. Keith skinned one knee and has a black eye. Luckily he didn't break something. He bumped the cow hard but it walked away, didn't even pick Keith up.

We've got beautiful poppies, larkspurs and roses, quite a good show. They are rambling all over Wahroonga Station cutting too, *somethink booful*. This dusty kitten of ours is funny, it runs after it's ma and swings on to its tail until the ma gets wild and flicks it off. But it is always getting nearly trodden on–it will be trodden on some day. It makes a dash to see if it can get under the bottom of my crutches and I have or it rather has some narrow sqeaks. Now Miss, Wisteria or Wistaria spelt either way in our dictionary, Which in the Niland dictionary because eria it is out in flower our way. Get me Steve!

Have the engines been running yet? Bikes make the hands dirty, mine were filthy dirty until I ran after Clever Mary and she fixed me up. Good stuff that Clever Mary it gets rid of grease o.k.

I'm looking out for a buyer of a second hand chemistry book now do you want it by any chance? When did you get the letter posted on Thursday? I only got yours last night, mails are fearfully slow and didn't the papers give Post Master Webster a time of it. I've been following this Graham case in the paper and from what I gather I think he is a big rogue who ought to be in gaol instead of making the country's laws in Parliament. Wonder which side will get in this time? Mary has a vote this time doesn't she?

What will you do if you can't get into hospital (Coast) owing to the fact that too many applicants appeared last time. There has been great excitement in Sydney, the PSAA competitions are being held. I think North Shore Grammar School so far have won the most events with Sydney Grammar second and St Ignatious College last. Jean Lindsay (commonly called Bingo) took Peter and Tom out there this afternoon they say the Cricket Ground was packed.

Dad is talking a lot about Uncle Raphe. [Cottam] He is 75 and worried because he can't do as much work as he used to be able to

Raphe Cottam and Susan Hartnett —Ancestry tree

do. Dad say Uncle Raphe was scything grass all one morning. He is a wonderful old man and boasts that he has never had a razor on his face. He has a fine beard of course. Wears it in two lots like this (Ben did drawing) old fashioned style something like an old Billy Goat but he is a good old chap and gave 300 acres of land to two returned soldiers in the district. I think, Dad said he did. All his 8 boys are grown up and have large families but they all come home at Xmas time and there seems to be dozens on dozens of grandchildren when I was up there about 7 years ago I think. I got tired of trying to remember their names but he knows them all. They haven't a piano but his daughters are good on accordians and concertinas and dish out some very fine music.

It is 11pm, I don't feel a bit sleepy, suppose you are in bed hours ago. A big day Saturday for you but you have Ruth now to help and Claire and Kit on a Saturday. How are your mother's feet, as painful as they used to be? Look out you don't get blood poisoning if you cut your corns, it's dangerous you know. Harold Kershaw has won about 17 pounds shooting at the Rifle Club Meeting. Rifle shooting and gardening, his only vices, he doesnt smoke, chew, swear or spit. A good chap Harold and I hope this English girl is nice for he deserves a good girl.

Well hope I've expressed myself clearly, legibly and I hope you enjoy this letter as much as I do yours.

Mother won't let the photo of Gert on the slide go out of the house. They are ok now and all tanks and dams over flowing.

Love Ben

---

28 10.19

Dearest Bonnie,

Oh many, many, thanks for your long letter which I received yesterday. it was just what I wanted to fix me up. So Glad you rang up last night, we had quite a long chat for 3 minutes and I could tell your voice quite easily. Ruth was on the receiver wasn't she, wish you had told me sooner as, 'fraid I said something I shouldn't have said about Mrs Bray, catch on?

Now I've put lots of questions in my growling letter of Sunday but I want you to answer them all, will you? And think over that matter I spoke over the phone to you about before I found Ruth was there. What would be best for me to do? I will if you like, it makes no difference to me as I've enough hide for 2.

Saw the *Niagara* come in this morning as I was crossing to the Quay from here. Beavis is to be married tomorrow and mother and I will be there. It is a glorious day for Miss McCleod to come into Sydney and I bet old Beavis doesn't know if he is on his head or feet. So you didn't enjoy yourself last night but wished you were tucked in bed. What a shame. Wasn't there anyone nice for you to talk too and did you feel out of it 'cause you didn't dance. I'll make an extra effort on Sunday to write you the letter you need. Hope everything will be o.k. for you at Xmas time.

Don't disappoint me because it will mean a bed vacant and waste and me disappointed bitterly which will be hardest of all to bear. I'm certain you cannot imagine how I like to have your company otherwise you'd make more effort to help me. I must have a definite answer soon to make my plans. If you are not coming I'll go elsewhere as it will be no good going to Manly with the family, so give me your answer.

I'm so terribly glad that the machines are going o.k. Why shouldn't they, they are well set up and no pains or expense left out to make them a success.

Do you like me still?

Paddocks are beautifully green but you ought to just see our roses, thousands of them and so big and bosker. What is Belmont going to do now he is shod, just loaf around and lose his shoes in the swamps again?

You cannot imagine how this university palls on me after being out in the open and that river bank is so nice and green and cool. Have to buy a present for Beavis today. Poor Ben, (might as well put a capital B for Ben)–who was outside of the telephone box last night giggling?

Answer questions–write like you did last time.

Best love, Ben.

Saturday 1.11.19 11pm

There is a beautiful cool southerly blowing now

Dear Franc,

Many thanks for all your letters this week every one has been beautiful. So don't worry thinking I might like you to write more for you are a perfect letter writer. I'll start by letting you know what happened on Wednesday. Mother and I left here in the 10.30am train reaching St Stephens at exactly at 11.26 am. The wedding was booked for 11.30. It took a long time for matters to be fixed up.

It reminded me of the time I enlisted with all the particulars we had to fill in, even enquiring if there had been any insanity in the family. At last things were fixed up and Beavis went into the church, mind you I had not been warned that I was to be Best Man until I was called in. My duty was to hand over the ring and sign the Register etc.

Miss McCleod came in but she didn't show the strain she was under. Fancy landing in a new country on Tuesday only knowing 2 people in the place Beavis and myself, and being married the next day. She wore just a plain cream silk dress.

She made friends with a girl on the boat and she was bridesmaid, of course the bridesmaid had to walk along hanging on to my right arm so how was I to use my stick? I managed some how. She was given away by a Bob Grant (he has a woody too) Bob knew her brother who was killed with the Battalion in August 1915 at Lone Pine.

After the formalities had been gone through Captain and Mrs Beavis left in a car to get their pictures taken. Mother, Bob and his wife and myself left in another car for Grants home at Concord West. Our car turned up at 2.30 but Beavis and Mrs didn't turn up until 3.30 as their taxi driver got himself lost. So we chaffed them and said they wanted a joy ride and might have told us so that we could have gone on with the Wedding Breakfast without them.

The Mayor's Sons—18 Sept 1915
The National Advocate, *Bathurst*

Lieut Leslie Ellis Beavis (Duntroon College Graduate)
Sge Horace Weston Beavis (Educational Department)
and the late Corporal Edward Bathurst Beavis, killed at Gallipoli,
7ᵗʰ August, aged 23 years, the second son of Mayor Beavis.

Beavis didn't bother asking any of his relations, although he has plenty, just a few chums. What a stiff wedding–2 principal people outside the bride and bridegroom had woodies. Grant has only 3 'of his leg and has an awful time trying to walk about.

Beavis is up at his mother's place at Bathurst but is coming to see us during the latter part of next week. His wedding announcement and Nancy Johnsons were in today's paper. Beavis was sudden wasn't he, it's usual to wait a month after the deed but he did it so as his relations would know. He was as red as a turkey cock the whole time. He had a bother trying to get the ring on her finger, he pushed and pushed and got it only as far as the knuckle, so he has to have it made larger. That was bad management I think.

We had a long chat at Grants and came home at 6.30pm. Did I tell you that Stobo had given me a group photo taken when we were at Meteren in 1918, well I've had that enlarged until the picture and frame are now about 2'. It is so nice I've put it in my bedroom, and all the faces are as clear as possible and I look such a cherub and so fat, a little round face.

Here is some rotten news sweetheart, which I must tell you because I feel awfully rotten about it. Mrs Hesketh rang up mother and told her that she'd received a telegram from Melbourne to say that Tom Brownlie was dead. Poor old Tom he had a paralytic stroke brought about by the sun? Isn't it strange. First Ted Sparkes then poor old Tom. I only brought home the enlargement last night and in it he looks so happy. Mrs Hesketh who thinks the world of Tom is going over to Melbourne to attend the funeral. She leaves tomorrow night, dear old soul, she is so kind and good to soldiers. She is made like mother , just choc a block with kind deeds, nothing is too much for her to do especially for returned soldiers and wives.

I've been getting awfully anxious about Gertrude. In her last letter, was 10th October but then one came along accompanying yours a 6 pager and she is ok and getting fat living out of doors most of the time. She walked 8 miles one day and said she didn't feel tired much and she says also that it is a great novelty driving a horse and dray. She went with the sheep droving when they were taken to be sheared, or shorn, which is it? But Rupe saw she was too tired to take back the 2 saddle horses and came along home in the grocers motor lorry. There's no doubt that city bred girls can make good in the country when they want too.

Today has been a corker, the hottest yet. Tom left our thermometer out in the sun and it can only register 120 degree but of course that was in the sun but I'm sure it must have been 100 in the shade. But I like the heat even with a woodie.

This morning I rode down to McGraths and the road was awful so instead of coming home the same way I made a detour coming home via Willoughby and Chatswood. New houses everywhere, hardly a clear place in the flat parts but Willoughby being so precipitous and rocky in places there are many pieces of land which will never be used.

I was offered an increase of 10/–per foot on the land I bought but want it for keeps I reckon Wahroonga is the most delightful suburb I've ever been in. It is so chummy and the roses so beautiful. I've not walked home from the station once this week, some one always gives me a lift.

There was an Home to Mary Murdoch who is to be married shortly you know to Geoff Johnson. She had about 100 guests. Jeff looks awfully, awfully worried–If getting married were as bad as dying I would understand the worried look. He ought to be at peace with everyone, especially as cash will worry neither side of the family.

Colonel Murdoch has been asking some very searching questions at this wheat enquiry. The things that have come out in the Commission have been astounding. To think that the hard working farmers have been taken down wholesale by these scoundrels is astounding. I'd clink the lot–jail is the only place for them.

Mother is writing a formal invitation tonight about you coming down. Mind you know I'm an awfully jealous cuss and I want you the whole time, no going off quietly with Marjorie now. There will be a revolution if you can't come. DO your best not to disappoint a cove won't you.

There is a family in Wahroonga called Lufft, the father born in Australia of German parents. He had one son killed and the other one came home by the *Euripides* about a week ago. Well a man called him a German and he burst into tears so no one in Wahroonga will speak to this man who called Lufft a German. Quite right, the poor old chap losing one son was hard enough and he will never get over it.

Now tomorrow don't think I'm extravagant will you, but I'm riding all the way to Newport to see Henderson, Marsland, Smith. Allen and Henderson are stopping at the latters house over the weekend and they asked me to come down, so I'm going. Am I terribly bad?

Do you feel sometimes that church is too stuffy and you want the open air, I do. I'm sitting in my room, as Edie has Miss Lockwood down tonight. In the distance I can hear Hornsby Band going full swing.

What about writing to Mrs Bray asking her not to forget to approach the Matron at the Coast about getting you in? Dad said they had miles too many applicants last year but you can only try can't you?

Oh! I must tell you what I did this afternoon. Do you remember the trellis verandah at the back where Gertrude used to sleep? Well outside the back of it, near the back door we have a passion fruit vine in full swing but the tendrils used to glop all over the place so I made a framework and put wire netting on top so that is is now a sort of verandah with vines. Picture it and the passion fruits in thousands over the summer house or gazyboo as Mother calls it. We 'll have plenty for fruit salads and the fruit crop is good despite the dry weather.

Arthur at Leeton has sold 18 pounds of green peas and expects 2 more pickings from them also. I will try his camera out tomorrow and see if is satisfactory. It is a postcard pocket Kodak and I ought to get some good photos out of it. I'm going to rent it as I don't think I can afford to pay straight out for it.

Oh when I was carpentering this afternoon I hit my thumb with the hammer in the same place 3 times. I swore and now without telling a fib there is a blood blister all over the ball of my thumb ½ inch high all over, she's a beaut. I've just been into the dining room and fixed up that blister. I didn't actually prick the blood blister but tunnelled in each side under the skin and let the blood out that way. What with hands that are black through growing grease from the bike (which won't boil out), this blood blister and my dummy finger nail cracks filled with bike grease, I'll look a picture tomorrow. Just as well I'm not going to church or to a dance I have to put on white gloves.

What gave your Bob and Otto the pains, eating too much? That's not possible with you but don't fade to a shadow or else when you come down someone will have to let some inches into your waist band like once before when you were at Riverstone through eating oranges I suppose. Gee Whiz, 66 cows in 64 minutes, some record. Your Dad must be as proud as punch over them . Soon I suppose he will be increasing his herd.

Having any more coves come up lately? I think the *Niagara* goes about the 21th November so Bob still has a little time to get ready. What are his plans Bonnie? Is he going to some University or just to a big engineering show and is it already fixed up for him. Hope he doesn't bring home the gum chewing habit.

By Jove, Frank you ought to see the way some girls get about to business. You know how low the evening dress is these days in the back, well hundreds of girls go to town with backs as low as that. I like a girl to be moderately cool and if she has a nice neck to show it but as low as they cut now, it's really over the odds for decency.

DO you remember asking me about a civilian suit I got from the Barracks. Well every soldier who returns, is given out a civilian suit and believe me it is some suit, they cost 30/-to make. This one I have I use for when I'm cleaning the bike. It's a rusty piece (is that the spelling–like a copying pencil). I dare not go outside with it on and the cap, don't mention the aristocratic shape. Our kitten (socks it is called) usually curls up in it befor I throw it in the laundry. This kitten is funny, it gets lost dozens of time a day and howls until someone finds it or someone takes it to its ma. Also the ma smacked it badly this morning for smelling raw meat. The ma cat evidently thinks it wrong for kitten to eat meat and the antics of this kitten makes us all laugh. It sneaks up behind the cat and makes a flying bite at it's tail and then it scurries away but it is funny. Hope it is still playful when you come down.

Tom and Dot have a fight now and then as to who's turn it is to nurse it. All our big black moths are gone but did you know that locusts have watches on them? Well they must have, for the past week every night, just as we set down to tea, they start and they start exactly at 30 to 7 not a minute before or after and they all start at once. Perhaps they have policemen locusts who go around and warn the others when to start. If you have any locusts near, you just see if they start at the same time each night. It's so strange isn't it?

Eric Smith and I are going up to University in February some time to start to learn up our anatomy which we are at present neglecting in order to hope to pass our other exams. We have physics on 12 December and chemistry on the 8th so I really must start to work harder.

Look here, you've said you've been miserable in the 3 last letters, stop it do you see. Hope Ruth Upfold turned up o.k. Its nice to have a pal out to see you occasionally. Hope you put that photo of me in civie clothes right away out of sight. I hate it. It looks like a dead chinaman.

I won't come to Tarro at all if you say you expect snakes, nasty sneaky creepy things I hate 'em too just like poison.

Yes I'm in touch with Fred Waugh and he is going to let me know when the Coast applications are likely to come due. I want you to get in you know just as badly as you want to come down, for then I'll be able to see you oftener. I don't know what you think about that important question, so do tell me. No one ever sees my letters and even if they did I wouldn't mind because everything I do is honest and there nothing to be ashamed in loving one another is there?

That Scotch lady hasn't written for over 3 months now for which I'm terribly glad. I had a letter from Mrs Alfieri or *Mere de Guerre* as she styles herself to me. They have been down to Brighton for a fortnight, enjoyed themselves but she said she was sorry that she couldn't mother any Australians as there are none down there.

She is 'snice. Hope I have the good fortune to see them again. I must write and tell them about poor Tom Brownlie as he used to go down there with me.

Mrs Beavis is a M.A. of Edinburgh University but she doesn't let anyone know she is clever.

Look I've been thinking over this motor trip down. If they say you can come, well and good, but I think it's a bit risky on your part being a girl. See there no danger of a smash up but suppose some internal trouble with the engine took place–look at the fix I'd be in having you with me. You would have to walk to the nearest hotel and goodness knows where that would be. Of course I would look after you and if your mother and father will trust me with you well and good.

Well, come down all the way and have a fine outing. Have you or your Ma asked Mr N yet about the trip down or do you only think he won't let you come? So Mrs *fold up* likes me does she. it's a wonder. But I had an awful stomach ache that night. I couldn't eat or talk. I thought she may have thought me a funny sort of a boy. I used to think Champion was an uncommon name until I joined the army and then I found out I made the 4th Champion in the 1st Brigade.

Did you notice that my old C.O. Colonel Stacey has been made a barrister. We used to call him Baron von Stacey, a good soldier Frank and one who took you as he found you, not on other peoples verdict thank heavens.

I'm not going to return you the Black Cat until I've passed all my 4 years exams and if you want one when you go up for your nursing exams I know a boy who lives in Wahroonga in a bit of a rabbit warren of a place called *Jura* who could give you one. Dad is 56 in 3 days time. His beard is growing well but must be scrubby for mother.

I'll have to walk into Jack Buxton's affections if he teases you, Does he tease you about me or what does he say? Well old girl, I've been writing for 3 hours now and I can't think of another blessed thing to write about but I've tried to make up to you in this letter for the scrappy and horrid letter I sent last Sunday. Go through this when you write back to me and answer all the questions I'll have worried you over Sleep well,

Love Ben

—

5.11.19

Dearest Bonnie,

Mother wrote a letter to Mrs Niland today and posted it. This day 3 years ago was an awfully anxious one–it was at Guendecourt where we lost so many men in the mud and snow, I'm still here on earth about which I'm constantly wondering after the number of times I should have been killed.

The answer to your question is YES it will be terrible s'nice because I will have finished all my exams. Gee, but I'm stiff for cash, had to borrow 5/–off Major Jacobs in town the other day and have come home with 1 shilling 6 pence tonight.

Of course, all Sydney has been mad about the Melbourne Cup, fortunately having no money I ventured not and did not lose anything, but most of the chaps lost a good deal.

I'm not going to tell you in this letter about last Sundays trip as I want to do it properly and haven't the time now. Only one month to the exams and 5 weeks 'til I see you. Can you put up Tom and I for a few days before we leave for Gertrude's? Perhaps I won't go yet but I've promised to dine with her on Xmas day. You needn't bother writing to say you can put me up because if you can't, I'll go into the milking engine warm room but tell me if there is room for Tom.

Any more news about the trip down in the car? Eric Smith has gone to a wedding today–he was dressed up to the nines. Some class, he did have a nice suit on but a nice price too, 11 guineas. I'd want 2 suits for that money.

Mother is awfully busy getting ready the toys which the Sunday School always sends to one of the islands in the Pacific. Its nice for our Sunday School to remember the Islanders for Xmas and they send us quaint carved things.

Geoff Johnson is to be married on the 12th but I can't afford him a present. Isn't it rotten being stuck for money, not that I should mention it to you if I was a nice boy but I'm not so thats the reason.

It's dusty enough in Wahroonga. I'm glad though we don't actually live on the main road. Haven't seen Didie for some time. I've been catching the 10 to 5 from the Point and she usually catches a later one.

The passionfruit vines have thousands of passions on it and will give you some salads at Xmas time. Tell Mrs Niland that Mother wants you for a month not 3 weeks as she put in the letter. Can't write any more now Old Girl, I'm terribly anxious to see you once again, Say in 5 weeks time that we are to have you for a month don't forget

love Ben

7.11.19
Jura Stuart St
Wahroonga

My dear Franco,

Tonight being Friday night I'm having a spell as I did 1 ½ hours work before breakfast this morning. Well I'm to tell you about the last week–end trip. Last Sunday I left home about 7.15 or so in the morning and started out for Newport. It was a fine fresh morning and no traffic on the roads–left the main road at Pymble reservoir and started through St Ives. St Ives is a very old spot indeed. There are a few convict built houses and the district is given over to orchards, chiefly citrous fruits with oranges predominating. The track is rather a bush road and was dotted for about 8 miles out with these orchards and it looked so pretty.

Tumble Down Dick, one of the steepest and roughest of grades around Sydney lay before me and I climbed the 1st section ok. But on starting at the 2nd section of it, I had the only mishap of the whole day. I was too late in changing to steep hill climbing gear and my engine stopped, so I just let the bike run backwards down the hill 'till I reached the bottom and climbed again like Bruce's spider, try again and again. From the top I was rewarded with a beautiful panorama view of the Pittwater district on the left and away over to Watson's Bay on the right.

The road after here became rough but every now and then I came on this view. ½ hour later I came to a spot called Mona Vale, I was not too sure of my way from here so I noted what I thought to be a nice old man working in the garden, So I called him 'Sir' in my usual style to old people and he turned round and I found out it was a John Chinaman. Mona Vale is close to the Pittwater side of the next village was Rocklily then on to Newport. I easily found the Henderson place and introduced myself to two very wet people. Mr and Mrs Henderson just out of the surf. Alan Henderson and Bert Allan came along so after seeing the bike safely stowed away out of the sun, under the verandah, we made for the beach.

The Southerly wind which we had last Saturday night and which Ruth and you sat in, had made the waves very rough so I took Mrs

Hendersons advice and did not go in. The rest went in and soon Bert
Allan came out, too rough for him and he had a rough mauling and felt
ill. He was badly knocked about on the other side and has 3 ribs missing.

We went back to the house and had morning tea which I assure you
I needed. The house is not bad, more of a bungalow style, 12' verandah
around and no separate rooms inside, just a big room but it is divided by
curtains, which is such a sensible idea for a weekend house. You see they
always have visitors and if there are a lot of boys and only Mrs H they
move the curtains up so as to get more room. What think you of the
idea?

Lunch over, which was cooked outside, the Allans and myself set out
on the bike. 31 stone on it in all for a trip out to Palm Beach. You have
no idea of the view from the top of the hill. We watched where you and
I sat on the beach around past the rocks we climbed over, or rather you
helped me over. Well over the next hill after that you come to a beach
called *Hole in the wall*. This is the spot the battleships have for target
practice. It's so pretty, then another 4 miles along with the ocean on the
right hand of Pittwater, on the left you come to Palm Beach.

This is as far as we went as I was getting short of juice in the bus so
if we had kept along the road eventualy Barren Joey would have been
reached. I'll go out there some day, it's so pretty. The very look of the
ocean on one side and the Pittwater on the other makes one cool. We
got back ok, had afternoon tea then the 3 of us went into Manly.

I'm quite satisfied with the bike, it pulls beautifully under 32
stone. Manly, I dropped Henderson and I brough Bert Allan home.
At the Spit were 30-40 cars waiting for the slow old antiquated
punt and we all started tootlin on our horns to make him hurry
up. I got the 2nd boat load and came home via the Crows Nest
Junction, Willoughby to Wahroonga. A very very nice days run
and not too tired at all. Bert Allan stayed the night here and we had
Harold Kershaw around as Bert used to be the officer of Kershaws
Company. He talked and talked, Kershaw chiefly about his blighty
girl and what he intended to do etc until 9.30 pm so I was tired and
turned in.

Studio portrait of the rugby league team known as the 'Mudlarks'. The Mudlarks was made up of members of the 4th Machine Gun Company. They are wearing blue cotton-knit long sleeved rugby jerseys. Below the opening is a black and white painted cotton cutout silhouette of a bird representing the Australian Mudlark or peewee. The surnames of the members are listed around the edge of the original photograph. An Australian flag hangs on the wall in the background.
Identified(L-R): back row: 2132 Lance Corporal John Henderson Elder; 3233 Stanley Bathurst Tinning "Sam" Allan; 1853 Lance Sergeant Harold George Augustus Kershaw (later awarded a Military Medal); McDonald; Anderson.
Middle row: 2799 Frederick James Creasy; Guildford; Sellers; Chapman; 2695 Private Thorold Toll; 205 Lance Corporal Richard Alfred Overy; 1038 Lance Corporal William Harold Harford.
Front row: 233 Private Ernest Roy Crane; Lieutenant Walter James Clasper; Lieutenant Victor George Veness; 4245 Private Oscar Mullaly (captain); 3232 Herbert Washington Tinning "Slab" Allan (younger brother of Sam Allan). – AWM

Before turning in Mother made Bert a cup of tea and he said it was like being at home again. He lives at Bathurst and boards down near the University and I made him show Dad his wounds. Dad wondered how he managed to move around at all. You can put 4 fingers into the wound in his back where his ribs are missing. He is a nice chap (Ahem!!) as any of my chums would be.

This week has gone by so quickly, too quickly in fact, for although it brings me nearer to seeing you again it also brings me closer to the exam. Give me a good time Franco this time I come up. Today after 11 and before 2, I was floating around town trying hard not to blow up my magnificent salary and became so tired. Eric Smith suggested we should drop into the Golden Gate for a drink so we had a chocolate icecream soda and I felt real refreshed. So he went on to get his teeth fixed up and I went around to the club for dinner. There I met 3 officers from the Battalion for the first time since they returned, Bob Trail and 2 other chaps.

Bob brought his sister out from England and he put in the paper Lt Traill and mother-in-law by mistake and he says everyone is asking how his mother in law is getting on, much to his disgust.

Getting along slowly at the University, 100 years hence I can see I'll have enough money to do something with but I'm sure not before. Bert and Ray, I see them every day, Ray and I are getting on famously. I meet him very often up in the Billiard room during dinner hour.

The soldiers, poor fools, kicked up a shindy last night and there has been great indignation here because a Waratah alderman said *Soldiers are becoming Pests*. But here in Sydney some are singing *Long live the Russian Soviets*, so goodness knows where the unrest and upheaval will end.

Anyway you can depend on me to dig in at *Oaklands*. Did you know that early on in the war the Alfieries had instructions as to what to do in case of an invasion, –drive all their cattle inland etc. I had a few p'cards from Mrs Alfierie and Miss Alfierie together the other day so I'm sending them an illustrated book of Sydney, which will interest them as I'm sure their neighbours (although they don't know of course) think Sydney somewhere in Australia and inhabited by blacks. Strange how little English people know about Australia.

Has your uncle Will [Carroll] made any arrangements about seeing you all at *Oaklands* yet? Tomorrow I'm not going to McGraths. I feel done up with study. Too much is as bad as too little. I want to get my carburetter fixed up. I think I'm using up too much petrol, more than I ought to for the distance I travel, see I'm only getting 30 miles for 3 shillings and 6 pence and I ought to get 45 mile for that sum.

Dad's birthday the other day and yesterday, mother and father have been married 33 years? Some time that, isn't it?

Louisa Cottam, formerly Champion nee Dunman 1834-1922, William Henry Champion, 1853-1921 Jessie Mary Champion nee Holt 1866-1936

Grandma is marvellous for her age and as lively as a cricket except in cold weather when she gets jumping backache.

Tonight is so beautiful. Father, Mother and Tom have been out in the tennis court burning off the grass. Dad cut the other day. The moon is so bright and no sign of rain, worse luck. Aren't things in a bad way out West, no grass, no water.

We could see the flare of the big Glebe Island fire the other night. It was so vivid and lit up the place, it seemed to me for miles. Of course we are very high up in the world. The highest spot on the North Shore Line. I came up with Didie tonight in the train. We got into a carriage marked 2nd class but 10 minutes before the train went, a horrid guard pulled it down and put up 1st Class so Didie and I had to move and there was a rush for seats but I secured one and so did Didie.

I gave the negative for the officer groups enlargement to Stobo and he is getting an enlargement made. They look well and I look so young and such a cherub. Didie says she's been awfully busy with her father away but I told her that was absolutely no excuse for not writing to you and thank you all for the nice holiday. She agreed and said she would write on Sunday night. Suppose she wont.

How is Maggie Wood? Still fagging along at the hospital? You'll never be sorry you didn't go to Cessnock, especially when you go spinning through town in the side car sometimes. Had an accident in metallurgy at uni yesterday. Marsland and I have been working for 3 weeks on refining gold and we had our 3 weeks work in a gold solution in a huge glass beaker. I was frightened I might drop it so I let Johnnie Marsland move it and he dropped it, smash went our work. Don't know where I'm to get any more gold to refine. It is not strewed about the streets these days like it is supposed to be in Australia. It's not the expense but all the work we'd put in on it that hurt me.

Let's hope I get a letter tomorrow, I need one. Well Cheeriho Franco, sleep well it's 10pm. Love Ben

Did your mother get the letter safely and did you tell her it was for a month and not for 3 weeks as she said? Saturday night Today Frank has been absolutely the hottest we've had since I came home and so I'm still in the costume I've been in all day. The folks call it my *ancient Britons costume*. It consists of a pair of white short trousers in which I used to play football and a singlet with my old stump swinging free in the breeze. Its great.

That skalliwag Peter Lindsay is up to night and is skylarking with Tom trying to catch 2 possums in our camphor tree.

I didn't go to see McGrath today. Too hot so put in 2 panes of glass which were broken. The locusts have been kicking up a row tonight, just deafening, but I like them. That young Peter has a locust half out of its shell and is trying to make it stand on one ear.

I slept well last night. Has Ruthie gone home? So tired after the long day yesterday. I like this hot weather though it make me more tired. I'm getting up at 6 tomorrow morning to do some physics. The family don't get up 'til 9 so I'll have a quiet time.

Dad went down to play bowls at Warrawee today for the first time. He says he likes it. Meets some of his own kind there. If I knew as many chaps as Dad, I wouldn't be frightened at not being able to get a practice going.

Tom is chasing Edie–he has a slimy green frog 6 'long and he makes it croak by stroking its tummy. What a pair. Have you come across any snakes yet. Bert killed one at Eastwood in the orchard. He is selling peas now, has made 3 pound out of them so you see peas must be the Champion's favourite plant as both Bert and Art have made money out of them.

I suppose all the RC in your district are staunch adherers to the Ryan Doctrine. Mannix made a speech in favour of him the other day. This Ryan was the man, who, when at the Peace Conference in Perth, wanted Australia to come to terms with Germany. This was in June 1918. What a traitor and he would have done in every soldier still away. Yet we are such forgiving people that he is going for a M.P. for NSW electorate. What think you? Billy Hughes is weak but he is the better man.

Dad was saying how young looking Geoff Johnson was to be getting married. I reminded him that he was 21 when he married, but he says the young people then were older than the people at the same age now. Maybe he is right but still a soldier I think, no matter what age is old enough to get married and he has the cash. The folks at *Oaklands* seem to be giving you gentle hints, but you don't mind, I think you enjoy it in your quiet way.

Tell me about the carburetter, how it is fixed and that it would continually flood. Ask, did they bend down the cork float inside so that it wouldn't float so high? My bike is running well, too hot though to go out today. Though you get a breeze it's generally a hot and dusty one. Still I must take you for a run around the Patterson River, I believe that's fine. Keith's bike is o.k but you can hear it coming miles away.

I'm selling a war bond on Monday. I'd like to hang on to it but can't. I reckon the Tarro trip on the bike will only cost me 5/-more than coming by train and that's not counting Tom's fare you know. The best spot on a hot day at Tarro is the river bank. We'll make arrangements to go, Eh Franco! this time we will ride down. You have never yet ridden with me (is that the correct word it sounds funny to me) down to the farm since I came home and I love getting down amongst those curious horses. Isn't it funny how they all crowd around when you go down.

Mr James, our minister, has a doctor son home from the war and he has been posted to the Coast Hospital. Quite a lot of notable people (ahem! ahem!) seem to be going coast ward don't they?

MILITARY WEDDING

1919

Lt. Johnson and Miss Murdoch

CEREMONY AT WAHROONGA

A smart military wedding was celebrated at the Presbyterian Church, Wahroonga, by the Rev. C. E. James, last night, when Miss Mary Murdoch was married to Lieutenant G. A. Johnson, M.M. The bride is the youngest daughter of Lieutenant-Colonel and Mrs. Murdoch, of "Midhope," Burns-road, Wahroonga, and was for some time attached to the Australian Red Cross in London, where she did excellent work for the prisoners of war. Lieutenant Johnson is the eldest son of Mr. and Mrs. Morley Johnson, of "Gainsborough," Warrawee.

The bridal frock was an exquisite creation of cashmere de soie, trimmed with Limerick lace, the corsage being embroidered with pearls. A pearl girdle was also added. The court train was lined with silver tissue and chiffon, and a beautiful Brussels lace veil was worn with a chaplet of orange blossom. A bouquet of white flowers completed her toilette. A charming rainbow effect was given by the frocks of the bridesmaids—Misses P. and E. Murdoch, Joyce Johnson, and Rene Way—whose dresses were respectively of mauve, pink, maize, and eau de nil georgette, each trimmed with the same colored ostrich feathers. Black tulle hats and posies of pink roses were added by each bridesmaid. Mr. Keith Johnson was best man, and Captain E. E. Johnson, Lieutenant A. B. M'Culloch,

Miss Mary Murdoch and Lieut. G. A. Johnson, M.M.,
who were married at Wahroonga last night.

Mary Murdoch and Lieutenant Johnson wedding announcemet.

and Bombardier P. E. Newcomen were groomsmen.

A reception was subsequently held at "Midhope," where Mrs. Murdoch received a large number of guests in a handsome frock of platinum tissue, trimmed with platinum embroidery, topped by a black tulle hat. Mrs. Johnson (mother of the bridegroom) chose mole crepe de chine and georgette, with a blue silk embroidered waist swathe, and a black tulle hat with a floral crown.

Later Lieutenant and Mrs. Johnson left for the honeymoon, the travelling frock being a smart blue silk jersey cloth coat and skirt, worn with a toque of black and white satin and georgette.

Are you going to answer all my questions as usual? I was rather hurt yesterday, see I'm the oldest chum Geoff Johnson has, he was a mate of mine years ago, well some of his acquaintances gave him a farewell dinner as he is leaving the State of Bachelorhood and I was left out. On the menu, it had a farewell dinner to Geoff from all his chums and I wasn't asked. Geoff came down in the train yesterday with me and asked me why didn't I come? I didn't tell I knew nothing about it. So I can see he didn't forget me but the others did so, I'm alright on that score.

Wonder how is it you don't get my letters until Tuesday? You see they leave here on Monday night. Perhaps they have to go into Sydney Post Office instead of going straight up via Hornsby. I wouldn't be a bit surprised if they went via Melbourne. I wouldn't be a bit surprise'd at anything the post people did. A letter addressed by mother to Tumbarumba near Tumut went to Turramurra two stations down. No wonder Dad didn't get many letters when away on his holidays [to the Cottams].

I'm all mixed up with the number of these pages. I'm feeling excited at the idea of coming along to see you at the end of December or rather about the 16th December.

Marjorie starts to earn 2 pound, 17 shillings and sixpence per week next year when the schools open. I tell her she ought to give me 10/– sustenance allowance for being nice to her. A big wage for a girl to start on. Can you think of any scheme for me to start so as I can make a lot of money in a very little time and do NO work. I heard of one chap making 200 pounds on the Melbourne Cup, wish he was this chicken. Perhaps someone I didn't like could die and leave me a few thou. pounds, of course or I'd take half pennies at a pinch.

Gee, but it's hot still not a breath of wind blowing. I've been out on the verandah on Dots bed cooling off but as I still have my short trousers on, a skeeter bit me on the instep. Doesn't it tickle and it is still itchy but I know it is no good scratching. Don't I put a lot of tripe into my letters, but it's all conversation and I hate a letter where every word is chosen before hand to see if it goes in it's right place correctly and is grammatical.

Well it is practically bed time and I promised I'd tidy up my room before going to bed but I'd like to fill up this page Franco.

Do you mean to say that Pat came home all the way from Singleton? I'm awfully sorry for Ruth. It's hard on her isn't it but she'd hate you to stop writing to me just because she was with you. She is having a nice spell isn't she but I bet she dries and washes occasionally.

Haven't had a satisfactory response yet from you re that question I asked you, think terrible hard. What do you want tell me. I'm due at Church tomorrow–haven't been for 3 weeks, bad boy. Beavis owing to his wife, is now a scotchpretarian.

Met Bob Grant for the first time at the wedding, didn't know him before. Beavis and Mrs have gone back to Leeton. Didn't have time to see us. He was a week over due at his school already and thought he might get the sack if he stayed away any longer.

The rousing, the growling duly swallowed, and we won't do it again until next time but you must read between the lines in a case like that and just you see what a long merry letter from you will do.

Yours ever, Ben.

This is the 3rd longest letter you've ever had from me. See if you can beat it, I bet you can't. Couldn't possibly think of going on to page no 13 could I!

———

15.11.19 Sunday

It's such a beautiful day, after being dull this morning now the sun is out and the locusts are chirping away, but there is a fine breeze blowing.

This morning Mother and I went over to see Bert, taking Jean with us. It is a fine run, there is no dust on the roads at all but the flies were bad. Have you many? We have millions and they are worse over at Berts. Keith rode his Mangle over too. Bert has a lot of fruit but it is very small but sweet. I don't think he will be able to sell much but his pumpkins are coming on well. Harold Kershaw came around to see me before I went and we had a long chat. I like Harold. He is like my style, more practical than brainy. Did I tell you he had patented a pair of pruning shears which catch the flower they are cutting so that one hand does the work for two hands.

Gee, but it is a fine day. Hope we have some days like this when I'm at Tarro down on the river bank. Bonnie will you make an effort to come. I could stop down there all day just to watch the water flowing by. Bert has killed 4 snakes at his place. Have you had any this season? They are bad about here.

I'd like to go for a ride today but no one wants to come with me and I won't go alone. Why don't you live in the near vicinity. We could have some bon time together, but when you come to the Coast, but I'm talking like this but as I haven't had a letter for so long I can't understand the matter. I know you don't want to lose me but perhaps some one else does not approve, but still I know that is silly of me in these uncertain days too. But (plenty of buts) I do want you and you know I'm handicapped. I can't write what I wish to say. Still I can only imagine that the machines have not been going o.k. and you have had to milk, but then there's time for a letter after you have done say at 9 or thereabouts at night. I make awful efforts to make time to write. You promised me on your bended knees as it were, that if very ill you'd still write, but enough of this bosh.

Could you manage to destroy this note for me. I wrote yesterday but I'm miserable, for you know the feeling, just sort of at a loose end. Every one else has their pals but I don't seem to be able to make them for all time like I did with Art.

Allan Henderson is 21 on Tuesday and his people are giving him a dinner and asking all his soldier friends along. I am continually pondering the question as to what to do if I fail at the exam. I'm trying hard but there's that little word IF. To be only a mechanical dentist I'm too ambitious for that. See 4 to 5 pounds is the limit there but even a good clerk gets more than that.

If I thought you could possibly have managed to write to me, would I be writing in this strain? No, Old Girl what ever it was and (I'm anxious for the morrow to come for a letter) it couldn't be helped but it is awful when thoughts are up at Tarro, not to get something in a material shape for them. I'm wondering if to send this or not for can't express myself.

The people next door are playing tennis, lucky swabs. It's about the nicest game going. Hope you won't be too nervous to learn to ride my motor bike because I'm going to teach you. One never knows when it may come in handy and you can wear your riding skirt, no one will see you at all. Will you?

Didie has just come in to see Dad about some business at work but he and Marjorie got into the train (going to Grandma's) that she got out of.

Didie and Marjorie went to a concert last Wednesday night and were supposed to be home at 10.30pm but they missed it and didn't get home until much later. Anyway Mr F being away, Didie felt very sorry of course but it couldn't be helped. Today she is down to see Dad as she wants to be transferred to the typist staff instead of clerical staff.

A chum of Edies, married 6 years ago went to West Aussie with her hubbie, she hadn't any friends either in W. Australia. Well they got burnt out. Lost everything and had no clothes no nothing at all. What an awful plight to be in. And every penny they had was put into the house–a billet of wood fell out of the fire and that did the trick.

We had some information from wholesale people that spuds are likely to be 2d each at Xmas time. How are we to live? Geoff Johnson is down about Bega now, they are motoring right through to Melbourne, what a s'nice trip.

Mr Felton says that at Lismore they haven't had any vegetables for a fortnight or so and very little meat. Poor country, lets go to Russia where the Bolshies live. Did you see what some of those brutes did, nailed a family to their dining room table by their tongues isn't it rotten.

Allan a chum of mine has broken down completely through fagging at the University. Rotten isn't it.

I just had a shave and I did what the froggie women do, they don't wash and they just rub in some powder. Thats what I did, too tired to walk to the bathroom.

Herbert Washington Tinning (Slab) Allan

Oh heavens, it's just struck me why perhaps you didn't write. You can't come to Dee Why and you were too disappointed. Don't say that or you break up the happy home altogether. Can you manage to burn this as there are sentiments in this which no one but yourself should ever see.

Fondest love Ben

Imperial Service Club,
29 Elizabeth St, Sydney
Wednesday November 1919

Dear Gug,

Wasn't home last night so couldn't get your letter anyhow I'm anxious. Allan Henderson's 21st Birthday so was invited with others to attend a dinner given in The Wentworth Hotel. As it was a dress affair and not having any, I went in uniform–put up all the 3 ribbons so I must have looked a Xmas bon.

We went to his place in the afternoon so that I could have a rest as I'm walking rottenly at present. I took the old woody off and had a spell then the others being dressed we set off in the car for the Wentworth. There met other people and had a very fine dinner. During dinner dancing commenced so I sat (being a decrepit old gent) and talked to the old people. I felt out of it but I know Henderson would have been offended had I not gone.

Got home to his place at 1 am and slept til 8 this morning and so went to the Uni. As it was his birthday and we can afford to miss Mechanical Dentistry we are going to the tailor made man this afternoon.

Had a long chat with Bert [brother] this morning and between us only (don't mention it as he asked me) he thinks you all have him set. I tried to convince him otherwise but it was no good.

Souvenered several things from the Hotel in memory of the dinner, namely a copper ash tray and match holder. They are terrible and I don't feel a thief as Mr Henderson said they robbed him over the dinner charge. They will come in very handy for my bedroom.

Raining today. We had a frightful hail storm here yesterday. In town the hail was inches thick on the ground and in such big lumps quite a number of windows were broken and I saw a couple of horses in a lorry clear out frightened by the blows they were receiving.

I wasn't the only one who souvenered last night, several others put ash trays down their coats. The puttee used to be the place for keeping things like that when we ran short of knives or forks, they used to go *restarnats*? to get them, then down south in the puttee they would go.

Well, can't think of anything else. I'm awfully anxious to get the letter which I believe is home. Your telegram came on Saturday saying there would be one on Monday so I stopped home until the post man came thereby missing a lecture, none came. Or, Tuesday I said, Oh it must come this morning and I stayed at home until postman came again. Missed more uni work.

Gee, but I was disappointed.

Fondest love, Ben

Wahroonga 28.11.19

Dear Bonnie,

Just a page to let you know how I am, received your letter this morning Friday. I'm working hard as the Chemistry exam. It is 1 week off on Monday and the Physics is on the following Friday. The University doesn't close until the 21st December now. It has been altered but haven't yet decided whether to stay on or not.

What would you like? It's awfully sad about that little boy who is blind and can quite agree with you it feels like a crying matter. So glad you liked your change at Merewether but you ought to have written from there. I like the Tuesday morning letter best of all. What an awful stop out girl you are, fancy going home in the late train.

Glad you are getting used to going to bed later–too much sleep–no brains. Are the machines going ok? Franco, Reply to this question. I may be not allowed to go to Tamworth–find out if I stayed at your place all the time would I be in the road? Because I'm set on going up there before Xmas I don't want to go up again to bring you down and remember you are to stay one month.

What was the slip of paper I enclosed to you and what about the telephone ring last Saturday? We have tons of fruit on my land too. Gertrude and Rupe are suffering–down to bore water now. No rain water to drink. Cement trough must be some class, big enough to have a swim in.

Cheek of you are enclosing the stamps. Suppose you only did it to make me bite. You needn't put any stamps on at all, they are worth the money to me. Apricots outside my window, some feed soon. Bike going well. If it wasn't for these exams I'd be terribly happy, yet funny isn't it I can still smile.

Best love Ben,

It's as hot as mustard, what a day for the river bank in the shade. Caught any snakes yet?

—

29.11.19 Sat Afternoon

Dear Bonnie,

Have the pleasure to inform you that last Tuesday afternoon I sat for my metallurgy examinations and that's another goal passed by. I posted a brief letter to you yesterday so as to console you a little over the weekend but what's the matter? Again waited until Friday for a note from you and not even one today. Any excuse?

I'm home all next week fagging. I went to McGrath last night–went straight from work, stopped until 10 then went to a train home. At last

I caught one and reached home at 11.20pm in the rain. It rained hard last night and today its simply soaking. I got my big military coat wet through coming home.

It was a fearful strain getting up this morning. My throat was awfully sore—must have caught a cold in it some time last night as I had to console it with several draughts of tea before I felt any better. I cannot do without a cup of tea in the early mornings. Please note for future reference.

It's awfully wet, the rain has been coming down just in sheets all day. I got into the train at St Leonards this morning but I couldn't sit alongside Jean Austin until I'd my coat off. She is a good sort but I don't think she will ever marry. All men are her chums. But she doesn't let them go any further. She said if she had been left a widow instead of an orphan she would have kept a public house. Says there is good money in it.

Continually bailed up yesterday by collectors. It was a great day I believe, though too late to see it. The war orphans were taken around in cars, about 100 cars in all. Slab Allan is probably getting the job he wants as a weights inspector.

Marjorie has 3 girl chums up this afternoon. They are singing or squawking away as hard as they can go. One girl can't speak to anyone without blushing. The blush starts from her neck and goes up. She must feel awfully awkward.

There was a political meeting here in Wahroonga last night and in this aristocratic suburb there were some interjector strangers to Wahroonga evidently paid by the Ryan Push to cause trouble.

And now, here is a disappointment for you, Father won't let me ride up to Tarro but is making me bring the bike up in the boat and riding from Newcastle to Tarro, but he doesn't say I'm not to ride home.

Don't forget to reply to that query in the last letter about stopping, cause I don't want to be a nuisance and Gertrude won't have me up at Tamworth. I've got an idea as to the reason. It is not shortage of water but Tom and one of Rupe's nephews are going up so Tom won't be coming to Tarro. Isn't it a host of disappointments but I don't care what happens (so long as it doesn't affect you) if I pass my exams. You'll have to cheer me up next week, Monday, Wednesday and Friday well, they are my fatal days. McGrath says I'll pass the Physics.

I wish you could just hear this wretched rain, its abominable. I am finding out all the pleasure spots by degrees to take you too. Found a nice one out last Sunday. I went to Berowra and turned to the left down a long sloping grade 4 miles long with a couple of hair pin turns in them right down to the water. When we go we'll get a boat and go up the creek. I couldn't get any pictures as the day, though promising well, turned dull. Several batches of Christmas bush and flannel flowers on the way but some vandals had dragged the bush up by the roots, taken the flowers and left the remains.

So far (I'm sitting on wood) (also my head is wood) I've not had a puncture and I've run it over 300 miles too. Anyhow Gug, I want you to find out some of the trips around your place–say 70 miles there and back. Find out and jot them down and we'll do them when I come to Tarro.

Do you remember Dodger Rhodes who lived opposite, age 11, well he DIED last night. He was only 11 too, of appendicitis. They operated but it was too late as the appendix had burst and he died of peritonitis.

Gee–but these girls can talk. They are in the drawing room going hammer and tongs. This rain is good for the gardens but why does it rain when we all want to use the roads on the weekend. Is every thing going merrily at your place? Where will I put the bike and you haven't yet told me how the sulky came to be broken? Cheek of you enclosing the stamps.

Have you heard the date of the Haile wedding? I suppose everyone is loved by someone. We can't separate our duck from an old hen with chickens. When this Rhode Island red clutters for the chickens the duck runs or waddles along too and the chickens get under it at night time too. Quite a foster father to them. It makes short work of snails and lettuces too.

My land has some beautiful fruit on it. Harold Kershaw came around the other night. He must go somewhere to talk to someone about his girl Frances. I didn't suggest he should call her Frank.

You got me some stamps and they are all stuck together. There are so many things I ask you but you don't reply too, you villain and I'll be starting to thinks things soon. Was Mr Nielsen away at the war? [Sister Mary was eventually to marry Billy Nielson who was a vet to Phar Lap—PF]. I knew a Nielsen in the First Battalion who was a chemist I think. Could it be the same one?

Keith is off to Dubbo on Friday. There will be no boys home here for Xmas time if I can stay so long at your place. Have had an awful pain in my left eye. I know it's too much study but I can't help it. Wonder if it's because I write such a small hand.

Marjorie can play some these days. Tess Byrne I believe has sprained her ankle and is in bed. Harry Jones is busy clearing some land next to his place to build a house on it. What it is to have plenty of money. Judging from the prices I think I'll furnish a tent. One advantage, it would never be stuffy. Do you remember the time they erected tents for people at Daceyville?

McGrath is riding to Moss Vale this afternoon. I bet he is wet through by now. Haven't had a letter from Beavis since he went to Leeton with his wife. Suppose he is so taken up with her that he can' t think of his old chums. I've written to Vic Fowler; expect a reply SOME day. He is a bad hand at writing letters.

Arthur might have to throw up his farm. He has been ill. And Thea is not well and with 3 kiddies what a picnic for all hands.

Who is this young lady, you Ruth and I are going with to Bruggies concert? I haven't heard of her before. Did you book seats for it and am I to be the only boy, Ben amongst the maidens sounds well, but won't feel well when I'm there.

You ought to have seen the chocolate wheels going last night in town. You miss more than you catch at Tarro. Geoff Johnson isn't back yet. Living will be dearer still soon, is it worth keeping on filling the profiteers pockets. It is sure to go up if they bring in this child maintenance bill.

I'm writing around that Black cat you gave me, it's sure to be good. Speaking of cats reminds me of ours, we gave away the kitten the other day and on Thursday night there was some awful meowing so Ma thinking the cat was lonesome went out to see it but it had a rat and wanted to show it. As soon as she saw Mother she stopped meowing and went away contented.

Have you had anything to do with the black pony lately or is one 'perience enough. What is in your garden—we've 10 cabbages, actually with hearts The duck got the lettuces and we've had 3 dinners from beans and tomatoes coming on well. Tons of roses too, Mother says she is sorry about the Scarboro lilies. She left it too late and they are flowering again now so later on you'll have them.

Father intimated that he and mother were giving no presents this year but the Dee Why trip instead. We haven't got anyone to mind the house yet. *The Rose of No Man's Land* is being whistled and howled by all the cats in Sydney now, a nice song spoiled now. Remember the night we heard it. Wasn't there a crush there.

What about the *lidy* with the teeth, has she been over to see the machinery yet? Sure to have a lot to say about it. Marjorie has an exam on Psychology on Monday. what an awful subject to be tackled by a girl. Trixie Fairfax hasn't a bad voice but she squeaks on the upper 'C 's, Has Ruth started to learn music again?

I have a couple of games to teach you all at Xmas time. I'll bring up the big camera post card size. I'll never forget how opportune the arrival of your photo when I was in hospital. The nicest thing I could have got.

Have you had that bonfire of my letters yet? Keep the war ones and any you like but let the common ones go up the chimney. I got a pair of leather laces with buckles for my shoes. They look classy and no more bother over broken laces or tucking the ends in, do you like them? I've had that first pair of shoes since November 1918 and the right foot has had 4 soles and the left one, the original sole outer is not worn out.

The Woodie stunt is saving on boots even if it is rough on clothes. Will you get Ruth to come for some picnics: If someone could sit on a cushion on the carrier I could take you and someone else you know . Do you think it is a good scheme coming by boat? It's a save in money too. Don't believe it is going to rain any more now. It's made the roads too mucky for tomorrow, rotten isn't it? But I'll go to Church tomorrow now. Are you going? I like going.

This time 3 years ago I was made 2nd Lieutenant, seems a long time ago. How long is it since you put up your hair. Can you remember? Wasn't it about the same time? Well, I've come to about my limit now, old girl, this small writing takes a lot to fill a page. If you don't think it enough, let me know but I always write one long letter per week and I like mine to reach me on Tuesday.

Cheerio Old girl, Please remember me to all the family and answer the questions won't you and write.

love, Ben

4.12.19 Thursday morning

Dear Gug,

Sat down to write to you last night but didn't feel up to it. I've had my leg off for some days as it has been causing me intense pain. Well, I was due at McGrath at 3.30 yesterday, so set out on the bike, anyhow at Gordon I struck trouble, had a puncture and after mending it I got to Killara and I am afraid I've stripped one of the teeth off the gears so I had to be towed to a bike man to have it repaired. The bike is down there now and I don't know when it will be done. So after that chapter of accidents, failing to see McGrath and my leg hurting worse than the hot place, I don't feel too good yet. Anyhow if I fail to bring the bike up will you be disappointed? I will be anyway.

Mother is going to town so will get her to post this. Keith is going to Forbes tomorrow. I've fitted him up with my sleeping valise so he ought to be comfortable. Exam on Monday. I don't feel confident about it at all but think I'll pass the Physics on Friday.

Yesterday was a fearfully windy day. The worse I've experienced in this part of the world–but it can blow up on your district, I know.

The Alfieries sent me out a souvenier copy of the British Daily mail. Peace Issue, it is o.k. Saw Vic Austin yesterday in another new suit. Thats about 5 he has had made since he returned. Had 2 teeth filled last Monday by Mr Smith and I'm nervy, they hurt a great deal.

Thea, Arthurs wife will be comng down after Xmas. You will see her; she is coming down to a hospital.

Went around to the land yesterday. I've tons of peaches but I must get some horses in to eat down the grass, its 2' high in most places.

Beavis is getting along o.k. with his wife. What do you think of the glorious rains around Tamworth, will that make Adamson stop from selling his horses?

Mother, Tom and Dot went to see *Daddy Long legs* on the pictures last night, they enjoyed it so much. Our duck ate 3 baby chickens which were just hatched so I killed him and had him for tea last night.

Tom Brown and his wife and baby are coming up on Saturday. We'll have a house full. I must do some Chemistry now for the exam. Sorry this is so small but I have to work

Love Ben

All my envelopes are stuck down with the wet weather.

———

6.12.19

Dear Gug,

We had Tom Brown, wife and child here today I think they enjoyed themselves. Took Tom up to see the Feltons as he knew Arthur so well, we were only there 15 minutes as he had to come back to catch the 6.45 train home.

Am thankful to say that my bike is now ok and giving me entire satisfaction. I'm to let the man have another look at it tomorrow to make sure. Went to McGrath today for the last time I hope as the exam takes place on Friday afternoon from 2 'til 5. Remember me then and also on Monday afternoon when we have chemistry. I've worked solidly and I hope I pass. It means everything to me as you can imagine.

The bike has to be on the boat at 6 but it doesn't go until 11pm– what a dreary wait. We'll take a book and read the time away. Gug you are not writing as much as usual, perhaps you are doing exactly the same as myself. I am looking forward to seeing you and I find I can't write so much. Today has been City Mission Day and people have been around with boxes. Also there was a big fete on in the Inches place on behalf of the Fund.

Tom, Peter and Dorothy assiduously worked this afternoon at collecting locusts. They collected over 100 and yet there seems to be hundreds more judging by the din they are making.

After the locust hunt the children went into the bush and came home with 3 arms full of Xmas bush and xmas bells. I like the bush bested it seems more graceful than the bells or flannel flowers.

Will you be prepared to come down on the 1st January and stay one month? Mother wants you down a few days before so there will be no rush.

Here I am writing to you when I should be working. You have something to be blamed for. Read's next door are in full swing playing away. Didie said she wrote to you the last few days ago but Mrs Felton says she hasn't heard for some time now.

How is Ruth Upfold? You didn't mention her in your last. Eh Gug, will you have to help with the cows when I come up and have you thought about the trips we are going to do?

Went down with Bruce Rainsford in the train this morning. He has give up the Beulah flats because they were too lonely. His sister likes Prince Alfred hospital, though she told him she was thoroughly knocked up after her days work, well what nurse isn't.

I'm taking that black cat on Monday and Friday. Say a blessing for me. Had another look at the fruit on my land today. Don't think now it will be ripe by Xmas but is sure to be ripe when we are at Dee Why. We'll come up for some. I intend to take you to Cowan before we go to Dee Why. Must get a boat and explore some of the old spots I used to know. So, how well can you row because I'm not much good at the game with my gammy leg. The leg is still giving me tripe no comfort until Woody is right off.

Have a number of second hand books now to sell .. if I pass. I ought to know about Xmas time. McGrath had a class for the matriculation exam just over and the pupils asked him to guess 15 likely questions so he worked 15 out for them in full detail and they had 12 of them for the exam. Lucky, eh! They all ought to pass now.

Mr Felton brought down some beautiful stag horns from the Rivers, they look so green and are picking up very well indeed. Did you know they are supposed to live on the last years growth? I think they must live chiefly on air and water. You have some down the paddock haven't you?

Has anyone spotted any more bees nests? wasn't Joe funny about it. Have you ever heard from him or Amy lately? Is the latter still around Maitland way? I don't mind a bit riding in traffic now, quite used to it, Crows Nest Junction is a busy place with Mosman, Chatswood, Lane Cove Spit trams all intersect.

Must get some good photos of you when up there, one on old Creamy especially. I always associate you and Creamy together. You look after him so much, especially when he is such a nuisance. Well, am I to get two letters from you this week or are you saving 'til I come?

People in the district must have a lot of friends up as I can hear several groups singing. I do like to hear people harmonising, the *Rose of No Mans Land* is going strong over at Collis's opposite Dr Read's place. It's been a splendid day after the rain and the roads are in good condition too. Don't intend to go out tomorrow after I come home from the bike mans, must fag. It will soon be over thank heavens. Dr Read has bought a new car, an Essex 8 cylinder, its a love, just purrs along as if it had tons and tons of power behind it and so it has I bet with all those cylinders.

How is Otto? Is there any talk of his leaving or is he satisfied. Have you had any need to call Mr Upfold about the machines. Has he independent means as he never seems to work, wouldn't it be glorious to be like that. Does Ruth still worry about her boy? I suppose it never really leaves her mind.

An old friend of Dad's died the other day, a Mr Timmis of Batlow. I remember him so plainly teaching me how to make cats out of paper which you blow along the table. Like to see the Austins when you come home? (Edie Austins boy is back from the war).

We have a new railway timetable book out. The trains for this line run very frequenty now, every 16 minutes in busy time and every ½ hour during the day time not bad for this countrified district.

Keith is kicking up a row. Tom put 50 locust in a box on his bed and they have crawled all over the place. Nice isn't it the idea of them crawling on you during the night, but I know your pet aversion is frogs. I'll never forget the walk down to the river bank before I went away. There must have been dozens we walked on.

My stump is awfully cold yet I'm hot. So Maggie Wood has gone from Cessnock–are you glad you didnt go? the train service is so bad and it would not be nice to be stranded in Maitland.

Uncle Jack [Holt], the parson bloke, mothers brother and family are coming from Tasmania in February. I haven't seen him since 1909. well old girl Cheeriho.

Love Ben

Wilfred John (Jack) Holt.- Ben's uncle

1920

From Franks memo diary

2   Jan 1920 left by boat Oh My!

3   Jan Sat. Arrived Sydney crossing the punt Oh My!

4   Sun Church. Jones store–wet

5   wet and 6th went to the Austins

7   Wed to Cowan Creek

9   To Woods at Turramurra for petrol. Piggies brothers

Piggy

10   Sat To Dee Why by side car

12   Train or Tram–had a wait of only 2 hours. Met Ben at tram, home with Mum, Ben waited 1 ¾ hours for me at Manly

13   Tuesd Night heaviest storms ever experienced First swim of the New Year–got a mouth full. Spin to Manly on bike

14   Wed Swim at 6.15 am water cold wet my tootsies only Saw Mrs Harding Miss Mullholland at Mona Vale

15   Thursday..Manly..dress arrived

16   Fri No Where–hit baths rained in night, dress

17   raining baths wrote Tarro more rain

18 Sun Rained all day walk with girls

19 Mon Ben Tom and I went for ride down road (I rode)

20 Ben and I went to Church Pt Pittwater I rode Manly in the afternoon

21 Wed Dot and I went into Surf, we both got a ducking

22 Thur I rode bike out to Stoney Creek

23 Ben and I went to see Mary Pickford in *The Hoodlum* had to leave before the finish

24 Sat Mr Brown Mr Champion and Ben went to Great Mackeral beach were away all day

25 Ben and I went to Palm Beach, such a pretty place would like to go again some day.

26 Went into Manly had a nice day Fresh water Procession Girl drowned Dee Why

27 Tues Stayed at home and read, love book. Went to Manly

28 Went to see Nellie Grenwell rained all the time we were out

29 Raining like billy ho

30 Back at *Jura*–Marj, Mrs Champion stay till Saturday to tidy up. Jean staying too

31 Sat went to Hornsby pictures saw *Within the Law*

1 Sun All went to church except Ben and I. Went to Feltons in the evening

2 Mon left for home–had a long dirty trip up

3 Tues Mary came home Stayed at home wrote to Ben

4 Went to Tarro for mail

5 Wrote to Ben. Got a letter from Ben. Peggy Wood here

Ben spent time at Tarro and Frank came to stay with the Champions so no letter neccessary–Ed.

Wed 4.45 PM Feb 1920

Dear Frank,

Sorry I slipped writing you last night but Aunt Eliza died. [Dunman 3 Feb 1920] and I didn't like to appear interested in anything when Dad was so grieved. Grandma's 2 sisters have now died within a fortnight of one another. [Emma Dunman] Neither could have lived without the other I'm sure.

What sort of a trip did you have, hope you were met by someone O.K.? No news about the Coast at all. Yesterday and today have been wretched days for me. Yesterday so hot and my leg played up with me and I was more than dead beat when I reached home. Saw the Repatriation today only took me 4 hours getting an interview with the Doc. Anyhow, I'm to have a new leg made so that's not too dusty, is it?

Drove the bike into town today and left it to be entirely rejuvenated, then I'm to sell it. Don't know how much to ask for it–might ask 130 pounds and be lucky if I get the money. My patent clutch has to go and it is to be reconnected back to its original style.

Am dying for a letter from you. Have missed you badly the past 2 days after having you for 7 weeks but hope to give you a good time when you come to the Coast. Do come Bonnie.

Did anyone remark at all on the packet I gave you upstairs at the last moment and tell me what was said about the white shoes? I'm due at McGraths tonight but am not going home to tea and back to St Leonards. It is too far and I'm dog tired now. Have been wet through with perspiration all day.

I'm going to write you a long letter on Saty night, so you do like wise. Why did you have to go home? Eric Smith and Henderson are still smiling. They wanted to go out to an evening last night but I was too tired. Marjorie rang Didie last night about some tennis club or other and Didie says she'll send up the blouse pattern.

Fondest love, Ben

6.2.20 Friday

My dear Franco,

Must explain why I've been so slack over the letters here, it is simply I've had an undiluted portion of hell treated out to me by the leg. I was bad enough on Wednesday but on Thursday it was even worse and I came home useless. Had to bathe my leg as it is raw on the 2 edges. I didn't go anywhere today and stopped in bed 'till noon, too tired and sore and sick of everything to get up.

This afternoon I've been at work packing the bottom of the leg with felt from old hats, cut round and made to fit. Did I tell you I went to the Barracks to see if they could do anything with the leg but they can't and I'm to have a new one as soon as permission comes through to them from the Repatriation Dept. The sooner it comes the better I'll like it. Tomorrow I'm to try the leg I've packed with felt and if it is no good I won't wear it until I get the new one. It is too much agony for me and the people because it makes me too awfully irritable to live with.

After the corking hot days we've had since you went home, it rained last night and solidly all day but I think it is clearing up a little. Now I am to tell you a great secret. Perhaps the Coast application will be in next Wednesdays paper. Perhaps only. So you will get a form from me sooner or later. Now, to make the best impression you can of the Matron. Write as well as you can and get your dad's advice as to what to write.

No wonder your Dad is pleased, don't you think? That white cow brought a record price and I've never heard of the like of that before. Sorry Mr A's horses didn't bring more for him than they did. Who would be a horse dealer at present.

Wonder what sort of a story that Delaney girl is getting up too. Some sticky beak. It beats me how some people won't mind their own business. Glad you had a nice trip up, did you make yourself comfy as I said? You've promised me you would come here when you came down about the examination for the Coast. Get your teeth fixed up *toute suite*.

Every one of the boys seems to have had a good holiday. All talking, not too much work done but plenty to do . One chap had a good experience, he was blown out to sea in a small motor launch from Port Macquarie. He said he thought he'd never be picked up but after drifting for 4 hours he was picked up by a boat and brought in. No damage done to him at all.

Our Babe Tom aged 14, managed to get through his exams and we are helping him with the mechanical side of the question. I've only done 3 hours at my anatomy so far. Visited McGrath Wednesday night. I took him a couple of presents which he deserved. He didn't want to take them as he said it was a pleasure to teach anyone who tried and worked but I prevailed on him. He is a good chap, though he is Irish! I was introduced to some of his relations who had come to see his new house. Listen to the names, Mrs O'Shea, Miss McGillivary and Mrs Dempsey–not an Irish family are they! He isn't a bit priest ridden, he goes to mass when he likes and tells the priests what he thinks of them when they talk Dutch to him about not turning up. I gave McGrath a beautiful pipe an L and Co. the best on the market and 20 cigars so he will be happy for a little while.

Hope you come down Old Girl, there are 2 very fine shows coming here. *Chu Chin Chow* and *Lilac Domino*, I saw them both in London. That fine tree of pears is full of codling moth. We are going to spray it extra well next year. The cow is keeping down the grass on my land very well.

Haven't seen Harold Kershaw lately. I'll remind Didie about the blouse pattern . Are you making any aprons to the pattern of that black one. I liked the beginning and ending of your last letter. You are writing more to the style I like now.

Mr Fisk has had operators listening night and day to the supposed messages from Mars. He says he can hear the G.G.G. very plainly, but that is all the message that comes. Wonder are the Martians trying to communicate. Mr Fisk's engine is going now. [Marconi wireless]

If it doesn't rain by the morning I'm going to bring the bus home but it is no good getting it too wet. Remember the soaking it got going to Artarmon. We know where the house is now next time you want to go. Just when I'm going to sell the bike, I'm so very sorry about parting with it. Best of friends must part mustn't they? That's exactly what I thought when I bade you *adieu* at the train, but it won't be for long will it? Do come down Old Bean.

Ever read any of Robt W Chamber's books? They are nice yet all are the same. You can always depend on a nice ending with him. I bet that carriage we tried to get on wasn't engaged–had we a bit more time I would have asked the station master but you might have had some bother. Perhaps they would have pulled your hair or something. The packet containing those relics, stars, badges and whistles and color came along ok. Mother is guarding them very well. Suppose they have some sentimental value with her. I remember them very acutely.

A baby Triumph would do me if I could only ride solo, but no good taking any risks with my wretched old leg. Blast the Kaiser what would you do with him if you had him? I bet I'd do something quite unladylike if I could cotch him, I've a very good scheme but could not mention it to you. Revenge would be sweet. What would I feel like if I could just wake up and find I've been sleeping all these years and find I've my good old leg back again and that there never had been a war.

We have now found Tom's chain so we surmise that the kiddies, unknown to Arthur broke up the watch.

Do you remember that letter from Capt. Beavis? Well it was to Arthur asking him would he rent the house to him while Thea was in town. Did not notice how cleverly (ahem) I converted he into Thea, meaning Arts wife. Can you also remember who used to make the tails of their Y's like this (curly Y drawn).

Allan Greig is now living at Roseville with his wife. Remember what 2 men in the D.Y. train said about you and your age, funny wasn't it. Look here old bean, You bother to read over your letters, you miss out some words sometimes. Oh that reminds me. The night you went home I received a letter from Miss Vidal, Y.M.C.A. young lady who used to be in Havre. Dad, Mum and I puzzled over it and I can't possibly make out the meaning of fully half of the writing. I'm keeping it to show you. It is funny and silly too when you can't understand. it might just as well be writen in Hebrew or Chinese. From what I make of it, her man was so badly smashed up that she couldn't marry him after all, after being engaged for 7 years. Well she is that sort of girl that legs or arms wouldn't count, so the only thing I can think of is that he must be in an asylum. Awful isn't it. Curse the Kaiser, what say you.

Aunt Eliza [Dunman –Bens great aunt] was buried and the whole funeral was a motor one. Dad said it was quite respectful. The motor hearse went slowly and so did the 6 mourning coaches. Strange idea isn't it.

There is a very big military conference in Melbourne about the defence of Aussie. Wonder what will eventuate? Last night Dad was working with his coat off and he must have caught a chill for mother was up twice to him in the night for cough medicine and rubbing his chest with oil to ease him.

I certainly will go out to see Mr Carroll [William] one of the fine days when I find out Bert is home.

Jean shamed Mother on the station the other day when she was going home. You know the funny little voice and the way she says things. This is it *Gwan I couldn't sleep lars night it was so hot and I woke up once and do you know ow Gwan My Jamrers were simploy sticking to me* Funny little person isn't she.

Aunty Jeannie [married to Rev'd Dykes] has just been up and brought up a kerosene tin half full of blackberries and we have no sugar to make jam.

Now tell me what you want to know about the Coast. We've a friend, Milly Morrison who is out there and who will give you a helping hand. She is a 3rd year nurse.

We are still getting tomatoes and beans, they both repay the labour put on them. I was in bed at 8 last night. How are you feeling old girl O.K.? There is no hope about coming up so please don't tempt me. The principal objection is Dad, I wouldn't like to offend him and he is touchy now he is feeling ill. He has a lot more worries than we think, you know. He supports Grandma as well as this large family and if he thinks I'm spending too much money he tells me.

I'm not going to write any more, I'm still feeling the effects of the leg. Cheeriho

Love Ben

Saturday.

The Austins have to be out of their house by 1.3.20 They have let it to some friends and are buying a house on Long Nose Point right on the water and will buy a motor launch. They have asked me to come and stay over a few weekends with them. Emma Austin is to be married this month sometime.

Well Old Sport, I brought my bike home and she looks and runs *somethink beautiful*. Tom, Kenny and myself have been at work since 2pm and it is now 6pm. We washed it thoroughly, dried it with kerosene and as we had no shinoleum cream, polished it as well as we could. I took out the front well, got in behind all the stays and there is not a speck of dust on it. The man who buys it will have to be fussy if it doesn't please him. Fancy parting with the old dear but she an expensive hobby. Me for carpentering now.

Next week I'm visiting Eric Smith to copy his wardrobe. It's a beauty and I'm just going to stain it with Condi's crystals, no paint, then if I want it another color later on it will be a simple matter to burn it off with oxalic acid.

A most perfect day Bonnie, wish you were here. Don't forget to look in next Wednesdays paper and if you are not selected I'll be heartbroken instead of ordinary (money) broke.

I took Tom into town and we came home together. I forgot to bring my bike licence

---

Monday afternoon

Dear Frank,

Your very disturbing letter to hand. Oh Bonnie I don't know what to say. Of course consider yourself. I can only fall in with your arrangments and I don't think either of us can fail the other and I've your word for it. But remember what it means won't you? I'll have to come and stay in Wallsend during the holidays. Take your mother's advice. You know what style of people are out there and how awkward the train service is. You won't be able to come home often and you'll have to leave mighty early, but as I said before do as you like there no chance of drifting apart. But old sport, you've made me forego the good times I could have given you. No, that wasn't Bruce's father but his uncle. His father is an accountant and is named also Bruce.

Beautiful weather–I was at the Dental Hospital at 8 this morning. Left here by the 7am train came home by 2.30 and have now the bike and all appurtenances all ready for some kind person to come along and buy for 130 pounds.

Bert and family drove over on Sunday. He bought a cow from a chap here and are leaving it in my paddock for a month.

Hope you won't be sorry for your decision which ever way it goes but do let me know at once won't you old girl? I'm just as anxious as you are over the result. Certain news in your letter has made me feel ok again.

Beautful days, I can't settle down to study until I know the results. I thought I'd be able to see you often and do away with the letter writing. I hate letter writing but it's a duty–isn't it? Found 4 of your hankies, post them to you some day.

Very well for you to be gadding about in that motor of Mr Upfold's friend. Did you enjoy yourself muchly? Wait 'till I can afford one. Are the dresses at Wallsend the same as at the Coast. You say you could change later on if necessary but could you without any expenses? Well old sport, I'm a bit unsettled, do let me know how the decision goes.

Fondest love Ben

Remember me to all the family.

FRANK DIARY

8.2.20	Went to church Communion
9.2.	Monday Interviewed Matron gave me ten days to prepare for nursing
10.2.	Helped Mother to do my sewing
11	Wed sewing like billy ho
12.2.	ditto
13.2.	got a nice short note letter form Ben

12.30 Thursday morning

Dear Gug,

So you have at last taken the final step. Well, let us hope it will be for the best advantage for both of us. I was a bit dismal when I read your letter but on telling Mother and her explaining a few things to me, no doubt you will have a splendid opportunity and I'm NOT growling. Besides all this, Mother says it will be so much nicer being nearer to home etc they can do various little things for you which you wouldn't like my Mother to do. So there you are, let it remain, you've decided, But if you find you are not contented there at all, the Coast application will be in next Saturday's paper, but the Nurses application forms are not printed yet.

Do write me an extra long letter in the style I once asked you, just a special letter as the last you can write from home, there's a sport. If you send me the address I guarantee to put a cheerful letter in the post on Thursday night and hope it gets to you on Monday.

Did you see the applicaton I had in the paper for selling the bike? well I've had a number of applications and think I have sold it but the final decision is tonight.

Good Luck, Old Sport in your new venture. Stick at it. I want you to become a Registered Trained Nurse as much as you want to become one. Oh, Old Mrs Smith wanted to know all about you, gave me a big lecture about girls, dear old things she is. I told her you were a country girl and at that she was quite satisfied. Mrs Mackenzie has had a nervous breakdown. The baby has been too much for her so it has been taken away from her and she has been packed off to the country.

Write long letter Bonnie, I'm getting that lonely feeling once again.

Fondest love Ben

It took me 3 hours to get to work this morning and then we had to get out of the train at St Leonards and take the tram down to the Point. A train off the line at the Point. It was extra wretched as I left home in the 3 past 7 train and didnt get to work till 10.15.

Lot of English brides came this morning. Don't know how some chaps got married, must have been drunk when they did the trick. Some had frightful faces and all had that dopey English look

Are you Ok?

Ben

———

Frank

14.2.20 sewing as usual

15.2.20 stayed at home Dr and Mrs Douglas were up

16.2.   Came to Wallsend. to start duty

17.2.   Started work found it pretty hard

18.2.   liked work better hate have to ask questions.

19   Thurs saw Sister dress Lee's leg most awful ever seen

———

15.2.20 Sunday Jura

Dear Frank,

I expect after your bustle, you have begun to settle down at Wallsend Hospital. I expect you will like it tho' things always seem queer for a little while at a new place.

Bert bought a cow on Monday and took it home yesterday–Vera driving the sulky and Bert driving the cow by the side–she was rather frisky and would have pulled the sulky over had Bert tied her on to the back. I expect Ben has told you all about it in his letter There is not any news

Ben and Father have gone to see Felton's this afternoon. Am enclosing the snap Ben took at your place and one of Dee Why and will send the 2 others when printed

No more news

Love from Marjorie

To Frank at Wallsend Hospital

18.2.20 Wednesday night

Dear Bon, Your first letter to hand from hospital. I expect a long one soon telling me all about everything. I've been busy tonight on the skull, so much so, that I've notches, foramen bones and crests all mixed up together so I'm giving it a spell for a few moments. I'll be coming up to Tarro during the week 10th–20th March or somewhere near that so just you make any arrangments you can, please and I'll fall in with them. I've the Coast applicaton forms here, what do you want to do with them? Better leave things as they are now you are settled. Glad you've a friend at least in the Hospital, Winnie Wood I mean. Going to do some crochet. Met a chap today who went through the Dental Hospital 2 years ago and he says he is just making enough money to pay his rent. There is a bright lookout for me. isn't there?

Have had a busy week so far. Everyday in by the 7am train. Got measured and had the plaster cast taken of my stump today for my new leg, this ones give me hell. Getting along quickly now at the Dental Hospital. Also am getting my pension made up to 2 pound by the

Repatriation Dept. Dreadful hot last 2 days, much cooler now though. it is raining. Bought a new saw and plane today, cost me 1 pound for the two. Will finish my bench off on Saturday and order the timber for a wardrobe I'm going to make. Getting ambitions am I not? Were you very tired today? Nurse, my stump is sore, come and massage it. No luck eh? Intermediate results out, Didie sits for her exams on the 2 approaching Saturdays. Ross Smith is making some stunts about. (Kingsford Smith-PF) He deserves all the good times doesn't he? Hope old Poulet reaches Aussie. Mind I must have that nurse photo, no circumventing. Hope you get plenty of tucker Franco, lets know all about everything. Am getting to be an early bird, had Tom out of bed by 6.30am this morning. What a blessing you don't have to shave as you start so early. It is a regular curse shaving. Fondest love, Old Girl look after yourself.–

Do you wear tan shoes?–How many nurses all told are there, is it as big as Newcastle?–How many to one room? are they particular about leaving shoes about etc Have you a good house keeper?–How do you get your letters? Are they put in a rack or do they go to the hospital with patient letters? Have you a separate home as at Newcastle Hospital? Yours Ben

FRANK DIARY

20.2.20 Was given charge of the front verandah

21 Sat Terribly tired didnt come off duty until 10 last night, feet nearly off me, so sore, wanted an evening off and got long afternoon

22 Sun afternoon pass can't got to Church Matron very cranky

28.2.20 Wednesday afternoon

Dear Old Gug,

So you have decided that Wallsend is too callous a place to carry on with your profession. Of course you ask me for my opinion. I can't give it until I've heard everything, but this I know that if your Mother wants you to leave it off for some reasons you've told her, well and good. Nursing is o.k. but if you get into a place where it is made a joke of, and illness and complaints are talked about at the table it is best to get out before you lose all the sympathy and kindness that is in you. Tell me straight what your mother says about it.

The only reason I'm sorry about your leaving is this, that you've built your hopes and ambitions on it and now I don't want you to let them go flop. There are other places remember that, and the Coast is still open to you and I sent you the forms. I quite understand not getting a letter until today because I had reckoned up the days and knew you'd be getting a day off about Monday. The only pity is that you are now back at Wallsend. I'm doubtful as to whether I ought to send this there. Now just you sit down and tell me what the nurses were saying at the dinner time when you had to leave, for on that rests something to me. They ought not to be allowed to even mention nursing there. It is extremely bad form. In the Battalion at mess if anyone mentioned war or anythng like that he would be asked to leave the room, So don't forget tell me.

So Winnie Wood has been a good friend to you has she? Rather strange you saying that you and she are the only ones with natural teeth. Perhaps all the horrible things they say while eating have caused them to decay. So Frank, Old Sport, I've said before and this only proves it once and more to me, that put women over one another and they do get catty. That is not because I'm a mere man. I 've said it, but I 've seen it dozens of times.

I have been awfully busy fighting the Repatriation Dept and now to beat them, my letter has gone on to the Senator Millen and one to Billy Hughes and if that doesn't move them, nothing will.

Come to the Coast Bonnie. Cold bleak day today and very blowey. I broke the support strap of my woody today so Eric Smith and I struggled into the Gentlemans Room at Railway Station and before an admiring audience tied it up with a string and managed to go to dinner with Mr Henderson, Allan and Eric at the Commercial Travellers Club. Some place, had a spanking dinner and feel a bit top heavy still. Plenty to drink too, it was o.k. I had a glimpse of the bill afterward and found it only to be 11/6 each. Glad I didn't have to pay for it.

So sorry about your feet, but so glad you had the grit to get out before it made you ill. Do write and tell me all about everything. Didie got a rise in the Office the other Day. I havent got an almanac here so don't know what date I'll come but somewhere around the 10th I'm not at all well.

This is to be posted straight away in order to catch you at Wallsend.

Love Ben

29.2.20 Sunday afternoon

My dear Bon,

Just had dinner and its one of those beautiful, warm, drowsy, peaceful days, too good to sleep through and yet it makes me want to go down to the river bank and lie in the grass. Mother. Dorothy and Tom are learning their Sunday School lessons and to go to the other extreme, Keith is mending his motor bike out the back.

I expected a letter yesterday telling me for certain that you were leaving the hospital but none came. I promised Dot and Tom a treat for helping me on Friday and Saturday so I turned round and took them to the pictures last night. I was glad I went as there were 2 very nice pictures on.

Had a peculiar day yesterday, very dull and black clouds but no rain came along to help on the weed patches out back. I'm pleased with myself today. That old writing desk came along on Wednesday, so Thursday and Friday I was busy on it. You could not imagine the mess it was in to look at it now. The top had the veneer coming off so that required some patient and skilful letting in of new pieces of gluing. I put 7 coats of Condies fluid on it, then polished it well.

Dot, Tom and Mother helping. We put it in Mother's room yesterday after I had been to town and bought some hinges handles etc. It is quite a nice piece of furniture now and so polished that it makes the chest o'drawers look quite shabby.

You didn't answer all the questions in my last note. Do tell me how you bade farewell to the hospital. It won't be long now until I see your dear old face–hope it is a cheerful one. Will you come into Newcastle to meet me? I may be able to come up a few days earlier now. I received your Mother's note quite safely and as she gave me such a cordial invitation and as I'm not too well I may come on Friday but I'll wire to you the day before I come.

Mr Felton came down to see us before church this morning about a reference for Todd (I don't like them callng him Frank). He starts tomorrow in the Pacific Cable Boards Office–wonder how he will get on. His voice you know is more squeaky then ever it was when you were down.

Just 29 days since you left–what a lot of things have happened to you since then, wonder where are you now 2pm. At the hospital or home? Did you get those Coast applications. I have 2 railway concessions forms given to me by a chap, so I have to go up as Ian Muir and I live at Ultimo. It is not dishonest (not that you would stop me) as I am too busy to go to the University for some more forms.

We had a very fine 8 page letter from Gertrude. She is afraid she and Rupe will have to come down to Sydney to see about his eye as it is very sore and several abscesses have formed there recently.

I bought a new hat the other day and now I find it too small. It is a regular tussle with it when I want to raise it to some damsel or fair fat and forty person.

Bert is doing much better. An award has lately come along whereby he now gets 4 pound and ten shillings.

Those beggars of timber people have not yet delivered my wardrobe timber, the nuisances, and we have been customers there for years.

I am to have some torture tomorrow as am getting Mr Smith to carry on with my teeth. I hate going as I'm so touchy about my front teeth.

Dr Read has most of his bush trees down now. They were undermining his house.

2 cows in my land have made short work of the grass there. Mr Kershaw can't complain now about grass seeds blowing about, in to his fields of roses.

Ray Kershaw is now in England. He had a rather bad time in USA . He became sick with the 'flu and practically ran out of money owing to the large rate of exchange. He only got 1/6 for each pound he cashed, rotten isnt it?

My bike is going well, so the chap who bought it says. He is quite satisfied and so am I. Sesca the man I bought it from sold his car and now has a Bayard car. Saw a beauty in town this other day called a Sizaire–Berwick. It had a nautical appearance, torpedo shaped body with a little venilaters, like on a ship in front to cool the engine.

Captain Beavis and wife are keeping house for Arthur [brother] at Yanco.

Wish you were here. I've to set too and press my grey suit to wear away to your place. Mum is so busy and Edie and Marj don't seem to be able to do anyting in that line. Yesterday afternoon I got some petrol from Keith's bike and ran all over the suit getting out some of the stains from my bike.

The Morley Johnson family are touring Tasmania in their car, then intend to come overland from Melbourne in easy stages. I believe the only way to do Tasmania is by car. You can come from Launceston to Hobart by a beautiful road in a few hours.

Mr Dykes is crook. He is very old you know and so terribly active [Rev'd Dykes, Ben's uncle]. We all went to the Kirk this morning. How is your Uncle Will Carroll? Don't be that it is much use asking questions as I hope to see you at the end of the week. 29 days seems a long time doesnt it. I can't believe only 29 days we came home from Dee Why. Silly letter, I can't write today at all, but as I'll see you soon, please excuse it. Going to put the irons down now to do my suit.

Since writing above I have pressed 2 pair of trousers and 1 coat and have washed a waistcoat, some job. I think they are slighly better than before I touched them. I need a suit but I'm hanged if I'm going to pay the prices they are at present. I'd rather wear a sugar bag instead.

Dad, Keith and Tressie Blackburn have gone out for a walk to the Sanatorium. I can hear Mrs Read romping on the tennis court. Oh Girl, I can't write today, excuse me.

Fondest love Ben

21.3.20 Sunday night

My Dear Bonnie,

Had a very good passage down in the train, not at all crowded so that I had a light sleep. Did you have a good time with the Upfolds? I wish you could have come down with me.

Early on Saturday morning I went along to the ATNA [Australian Trained Nurses Association] and the Secretary told me that a notice had already been sent on to you, so I smiled at her and asked for a duplicate. Took them around to Dad's office and personally saw them attached to your papers, so that in a few weeks you'll hear from them to come down.

Anyhow, I'll be able to pilot you to a show on the night of the day you arrive. Thea [sister in law, wife of Art] has a son. All terribly pleased and he is to be called Clifford Gregory after her brother who was killed in France. [Cliff Gentle] He won't be spoiled will he with 3 sisters older than himself? [I think he was named Roger Lloyd Champion 11.3.20–PF]

Rang up Eric Smith and am meeting him tomorrow and going out to the University together. I aways pity the new comers. I felt awful the 1st day there. There will be some rush to sign on and get lecture tickets tomorrow but a few swings of the woody will soon clear a passage.

Here is something to open your eyes. When I got in to the train yesterday, Clive Inch and Lou Robertson came up to me and said *I believe you gave a ring away the other day* and so I wanted to find out who told them. They said it is all over Hornsby. Now I want to know, did Mrs Niland or Mary tell the Feltons? If they didn't how on earth would Inches know?

Aren't they sticky beaks? Just isn't it wonderful how news flies around? Did you see by Fridays paper that Henderson and Marsland had passed their post examination, so now the old firm will once more be together. I'm not sure yet whether both the girls got through. Great excitement here over the elections when the results come out. Do let me know if Green (on *Kanowna*) got through or not. If he gets in, he is sure to advocate increased pensions.

The clothes went over to Bert today. Father took them over. She is sure to be pleased with them. Mother, of course, said what an awfully wicked woman Mrs Niland must be to waste her time like that but she was very pleased with them. My bags came to Wahroonga by the same train as I did, having missed the connection at Hornsby.

Dot wants to know if the invitation you gave her when you were down still holds good for Easter. If it does she would like to come up, let me know. I've a worseer cold. Been in bed most of the day, no church, did you go?

Tell your father that if he goes to the show to have his dinner at Womens Missionary Association refreshment room, Which is in the Suttor Pavilion under the Grand Stand. Mother expects to be there helping. All proceeds to go towards Foreign Mission, plenty of acco-moderation as the Sgt Major used to say.

Did you get my telegram o.k.? Now Bonnie, don't forget your promise about the Coast when you get there. You have a very good chance as this year Dad says the applications are not as many as usual.

No more news, Old Girl, Fondest love

Yours ever Ben

25.3.20 Thursday night

My dear old FJN,

I've had an awfully tiring week what with signing ??? etc (which I haven't yet done) and trying to settled down to work. It's rotten. I've to learn the whole body by August so you see you won't hear too much of me during the week but I'll never miss a long letter to you over a weekend.

Bert (Carroll) looks well he had a wonderful time up at Brisbane, says his father is not well at all. The whole 1st year dentistry got through. There are 250 doctors starting 1st year this time and if they get through all their years. who is to employ them? Doctors will be dirt cheap.

Haven't forgiven Didie for spreading the news around. Will keep well out of their way and for a long while. You let me wait until Wednesday for a letter and even then didn't say if you were pleased or not that I bustled and spent my time fixing up your papers. Are you pleased or otherwise? I can easily cancel them if you wish.

Look around for some hankies of mine, look in your Dad's old overcoat and in the coat I painted in. Has anyone done anything to the trap? Do shake them up so that I will get the satisfaction of knowing it's on the road after all the work I put on it.

How are you all? I'm losing the nail off my second finger left hand, squeezed it in the vice today at Dental Hospital. Jean loves the clothes your mother made, parading herself around like a manniquin would do at Scotts or Winns.

Just a note to let you know I'm o.k. Don't keep me waiting until Wednesday in future. I'll write a long one on Sunday. Lots of love

Ben

Keith is 21 today.

———

27.3.20

My dear old Pal,

Have you ever felt very pleased with yourself, so much so that you could do anything for anybody. That is how I feel at present, I'll tell you all about it. You know the carpentering job I have on hand, the wardrobe, well the feeling is through that. For some time past I've been planing and sandpapering the timber and by today I had everything cut out and smoothed up. It is a big affair, too big for a stumpy to try to erect on his lonesome, so Alick Macdonald being a large hefty sort of a person came along to give a hand. We started at 8am and worked hard until 4.30 and now I can say the the framework is glued and screwed together all serene. The next job is the making of 2 doors and 3 drawers which are the most ticklish part of the concern and require some fitting.

I went in to see Geoff Johnson and he has promised to order me the mirror at cost price and to supply me with the French Polish. I'm just tired of using varnish. The mirror is to cost between 7/6 and 10/-per square foot but as the job looks well, it is worth it.

Are you in a good mood? At the Alfieries, the kiddies used to look at Mr Alfieries mouth to see if he was in a good *bate* scotch for mood.

So what shape is your mouth tonight? Father and Mother are out at Aunt Florries. Little Florrie (as we call her daughter) is being married, suppose the deed is did now. Mother and Dad gave her a nice silver tea pot. It's some class. Mother said when she got married no one gave her any such expensive presents. Don't know where the people are going for a honeymoon–it is the custom to tell no one these days.

Mother had a very successful Band of Hope concert last night. She spent such a deal of her time over the last week getting the children in order but the Church was simply crowded out. They had 10 little nigger boys song. I had the job of blacking their faces with burnt cork. There were several other musical items and Mother was so pleased it was a success.

Mind now, no more milking. I got a shock when you told me you were milking by hand. It is an awful blow to your Dad. Bert Carroll says the moustache or it is rather a *ziff*, is an improvement. I haven't got rid of it yet. There are too many *gots* in this letter.

Oh, there goes that Marjorie banging away on the piano. No more peace for some time. She went to a concert this afternoon while I was working away. What have you been doing? More crochet or some of that let–in work? When the telegram boy came this afternoon a sigh of relief went up. We've had no news from Gertrude for a month and mother wired her yesterday and also wired a neighbour of hers to find out if Gertrude was sick. So she is O.K. but Ruper had had *quinzy* which is most disagreeable.

Would you mind Bonnie if you only received the weekend letter from me because I've my work cut out these first 2 terms? I'm afraid I've bitten off more than I can chew and it means such a lot to you, as well as to myself that I should pass this anatomy examination.

Bert Carroll says his father is not well but that is all the news I can get out of him so far. I don't like to ask more for fear he might think I'm a sticky beak. Speaking about

Please take an interest in the jobs I've done for my sake. Is the other trap ready for the road yet. Could you tell me if the catches on the buggy house door are still there.

So Miss Houston is engaged but I'm sure she won't have to wait as long as you do. Do you mind? What I minded about Inch saying I was engaged was that he said *Oh I say Ben, you must have paid a good deal for the ring judging from the description.* Don't say a word about it to your folks now. Yes I told Mother and Dad about giving you a ring, they were pleased in a sort of a way, I think that they think that I'm not playing the game binding you when you have to wait so long. Don't say anything about it to your people.

How is Mary and Otto too. Does he still have moods. Bad things are moods. I wrote you a letter on Thursday night. Tell me when you get it so I can get an idea how long it takes to get to Tarro.

The 5th Year Medical students names came out in the papers yesterday and only 49 passed out of 128. That means that 79 failed! The top of the year, the chap who took all the honours, is our lecturer on anatomy. He is only 21 and 3 months. He is such a nice chap and really the best anatomy lecturer I've heard. He is an old Fort St Boy and was in 1st year when I was there. I hope he examines us on anatomy.

We started histology yesterday, examining tissue of the body under the microscope and it is very trying to the eyes. Marsland and Henderson have started to work hard. They have done 3 hours each night this week. I've only done 1 ½ each night.

The Repatriation Dept messed up my University fees so I had to go down to unravel the mystery during the dinner hour yesterday, hence no dinner.

The jammed finger is much better. The broken nail is starting to come off now and as you know from experience it feels much better doesn't it.

How are you? How do you put in the evenings these days when I am not there. Mother made a good job of my coat sleeve—there are no ragged pieces now.

The Show starts this week. Is your Dad coming down? Wonder whether I'll bother to go. I only go to see the horse jumping. I think it good to get away from crowds.

I go down each morning now with a chap named Phil Dixon from Turramurra, nice chap, returned Soldier. His brother is with Ginger Smith in the Sugar Company.

Keith and Tom are playing Bobs on the dining room table. Mum bought a new hat for the wedding but I like her old one the better of the two, although I had tact enough not to say so. Gertrude (last letter) says she made 50 lbs pickles and 20 lbs of jam–good for her isn't it. She is becoming quite domesticated.

I asked Greg Cutler what it felt like to be through his medicine exam. He said as if a ton of bricks had fallen from his head and turned into sovereigns and as if his hat wanted stretching–not a bad sort of a chap but he should have gone to the war, though that doesn't count I know with some people.

Don't you dare ever alter your frizzy hair. I feel as if I'd like to be out with you tonight to some nice musical show in town not to the dopey pictures where wonderful girls shin up drain pipes to top storey windows. All the girls I have ever known have been too scared to do anything like that for fear of I don't know or can't explain the reason.

What sort of a letter is this. I'm puffing away at my pipe and it is sending out sounds quite as musical as Marjories playing. Wonder will the labour Govt turn Verbruggens rise in salary down, hope so. Let him stay at what he is getting, 1, 200 pounds per annum is enough for a foreigner don't you think?

I'm trying to sell all my old last years text books to defray expenses of this years little lot. They come to 4 pound so far. Each book averages 30/–.

When will you be down again–are you on for Dee Why again next year? I've just bitten off the remainder of the jammed nail. Feels better now. Here are Mum and Dad, just in at 8.30pm. I'm off to hear what they say.

.....They say the wedding was nice, not a bit stiff and everything nice and comfy.

Only a week since I saw you, seems ages ago. Bonnie I must have another picture of you soon and not a post card one either–one I can put in a little frame for myself and stand on my dressing table. Are you well? Friend of mine Lieut. Gray out of 19th Battalion married a Miss Tully of Glebe not long ago.

I wonder how Green feels not getting elected. He seemed so confident when I saw him. Waugh rang me up the other night–must meet him in town some day and have lunch. He shouted for the last one so I'll have to square up this time. I'll be able to take an interest in life after this year's exams. Don't have to work so hard in the other years.

Well Old Girl remember and and write. Have this letter in front of you when you write and answer some of my thousand questions. Its seems full of things I want to know. Fondest love

Your Ben.

Remember you have to sleep here when you come down about your Coast application if you dont............(I won't say it)

31.3.20 Wednesday

My dearest Bon,

Enjoyed that phone ring you gave me on Monday night but rings are so unsatisfactory arn't they? You can't really say what you want to and always, after time is up, there are so many questions which I'd like to ask when it is too late.

Now I want you to answer these questions for me. Towards the end of our conversatoin you said *Ben I did today what you told me not to do* I can't remember to what you refer so do tell me about it won't you? The Committee of the Coast have not yet started on the applications and I can't find out about those 2 girls as the papers have left the office.

The kiddies broke up today for a holiday but we have just the bare public holidays. I suppose you are interested in the discussion about the Nurses Home for the Sydney Hospital. The Committee want to put the Home in Woolloomooloo, right in the slums so that the nurses will have 10 minutes walk to and from the Home through the rottenest hole in Sydney. Everyone is naturally protesting. Hope it is fixed up favourably for the nurses.

Didie rang up the other night and in a sarcastic way expressed surprise at the news about you and myself. She was on the boat tonight but I didn't recognised her as I was absolutly too dog tired to say a word to anyone at all. Father is worried. He has appealed to the Arbitration Court re his salary and the appeal comes along on 13.4.20. Some very pointed things were said about the new Chairman of the Public Service Board receiving 2500 pounds per annum in Parliament not long ago. Hope Dad has some satisfaction.

Had rotten luck this afternoon. All my afternoons work went for nothing as I broke (no fault of my own but through cheap plaster they supply us with) a cast which took me 3 hours to do.

Wonder when I'll get a letter.

Geoff Johnson's aunt died in Wahroonga yesterday. Her mother aged 98 is still living though. Don't let your Mother think that because Vera didn't write to her she didn't appreciate the clothes for she didn't exactly know what to do about Jeannie's clothes.

This other business coming on you know and Mother promised she would write for her. I think she did. Anyhow Old Sport they were just the thing and were not just tucked under the arm and said *they'll come in 'andy*.

Are you milking now Albert is gone? Are you well, no colds etc. Well Bonnie,

Cheeriho fondest love Ben.

Don't have any meat tomorrow its 'oly Thursday you know.

1.4.20 Home

My dear Bon,

Many thanks for your long letter which I received yesterday afternoon. I see by the Post mark that if little box is cleared in the afternoon I get the letter the next afternoon.

So you've been having troubles again, never mind they can't last for ever and at the very most it means 4 years. That is if I manage to carry along and have no slips. I'm not at all certain about this anatomy exam, you see we have the whole body and I shirked it last year to make sure of Physics.

Oh I really must tell you about poor Uncle Raphe [Cottam]. He should have come down to the Show but now he is in bed. He was out on a young horse riding around the fences and he had to cross a small creek and his horse slipped and fell on him in the water. His left foot was twisted in the stirrup iron so he talked to his horse so it wouldn't get up and drag him. He is afraid of being dragged ever since he saw a man killed that way. Well then Uncle Raphe lay partly in the water with his horse on his left side until Cousin Arthur came along and freed him. He is awfully disappointed at not being able to come down and he told Dad he doesn't think he will live to the next one.

Good Friday today at the Church of England Church, St Andrews, the bells have been ringing all day. I was glad you told me such a lot of things in your letter and I quite believe them and I'm sure you felt better for having told me. I aways tell you things then they don't seem to worry me anymore. Anyhow what's a chum for but to tell troubles too.

Bert [brother] has been over today to borrow some money from me and to see us all. He has been using a pony for 3 weeks and the man who owns it now wants to sell it for 4 pound so Bert is going to buy it. He is sure it is o.k. as he has used it so much.

You won't forget your promise to me will you. I've had a strenuous 2 days. Yesterday Tom and I went to Turramurra to buy some more timber, brought it home, some load it was and I made one of the drawers for the cabinet. This day I've made the other 2. Now it requires a cornice and I'll do that tomorrow. I was asked out to Newport by Mrs Henderson this weekend but wanted to finish the wardrobe. It looks well old girl and quite good enough for me to keep for good, especially if I can put a good polish on it like I think I can. I bought a beautifully figured piece of wood for the cornice the graining is so beautiful. Old Birdy [General Birdwood] comes in tomorrow. I'm not bothering to go in to see him.

Geoff Johnson is going to build soon. He says he hates flats everyone seems to know each other's business in them.

There is going to be a Doctor of Dentistry Degree at the University, it means going an extra year so I won't, you can't and I [especially] can't wait any longer than is necessary.

I've had a pain in my belt the last few days and have come to the conclusion that it is your old friend indigestion, nice treat isnt it. Dorothy and Marjorie went down to see their little nephew. Dot says he does nothing but try to swallow both his fists at once and that he has Arthur's turned up nose .

We had Tom over April Fools business–had him taking down the mower to Dad (as we said he was in the front garden) but Dad was in bed at the time truly asleep. So Tom tried to catch us all the rest of the morning but he didn't not once. Did you have anybody?

Haven't seen Bruce Rainsford for a long while. Don't see many of my old pals now except when I meet them in the train. The mo is still adorning my face. It must have been scratchy Frank if it wasn't tickly.

So glad you have used the trap as I didn't like the idea of all my work going for nothing you know. Isn't it sickening about the cows and will there be anyone coming in soon? Johnny Hunter gave us such a good anatomy lecture on Wednesday They are keeping him on as a lecturer 12 pounds 12 shillings per week for a chap 21 years old. I told him he ought to get married on it. He smiled. He explained to me very clearly why my leg jumped. It has been doing it a lot lately and I was becoming anxious about it.

Do you like this paper? Mother gave it to me on the 28th. She said *well Ben so you write so much I've got some extra thin sheets*. She doesn't think I or we use both sides. I haven't sent McGrath back his physics text books. I really must but I keep putting it off and off, but he is not as important as you. I don't forget you.

Beautiful weather for the show isn't it. Clear sunny days ever since it started. It must be a record one this year. There goes the church bell again. Terribly fine night Franco, what about a walk. Do you remember a walk to Tarro one Sunday night before I went to the Great War? I do. I really think we ought to preserve that log we sat on while Ruth drove on up the hill.

There is a new motor cycle coming out called the ABC. It is made by the Sopwith Aviation Company. I intend to have a good look at one when they arrive. Our war bonds seem to be looking up don't they? I believe we'll get them in about 2 months time.

Must get out and clean up my Sam Browne belt for the big reunion of The Battalion in Paddington Town Hall–it takes place about the 23 April. Where was I this time 2 years ago down on the Somme? I will have lost my leg 2 years on the 15th of the month. I don't mind the woody so much but those awful back breaking straps. I groan in the mornings when I find out I've to stretch them on to my shoulders.

By the way I'm in pyjamas, as after work this afternoon I had a cold bath and couldn't be bothered getting dressed again. I didn't leave a stump sock up there by any chance did I? I can hardly find a thing here, whether it's because Marjorie does my room out now or not I can't say but the fact remains when I want a thing I have to chase everywhere for it.

Didn't I tell you that the Coogee man who murdered his wife would get off. They didn't have a leg to stand on and they can't hang a man on circumstantial evidence, thank heaven. I know a few inside workings of that case, that is why I took notice of it. John Marsland was acquainted with the people, not intimately you know, but on nodding acquintance so the saying goes.

I am going to get a new suit. I am tired of this grey one so am going to put it away for a while then wear it later on. What colour and sort would you like me to get. I know you like brown and buff colored ones very much. 4 buttons on each pocket and a slit up the back or what, it is your say.

Do you still intend going over to see Mrs Griffin this week? Give her my kind regards please and you needn't wear your left glove all the time like you did at Mrs Douglas' place. They all know about it here, no remarks have been passed by anyone such as Marj. They all expected it and have been putting 2 and 2 together and making 5 out of it.

How are you today? Ok? I'm feeling very good but the constant worry of the pending exam is doing me no good or harm for that matter. Histology is a subject which I think ought to be wrapped in paper and tossed into the sea. It is all the narks of the University rolled into one, it's a cow of a subject. Bert Carroll thinks as I do. I haven' t seen Ray [Carroll] this week. Suppose he is there all right.

Hey what sort of leg pulling did you say to the telephone man. Don't worry about *If Ben could only know* he knows and it will be quite o.k. if you do as you promised me you would and take an interest in things I like to do and remember. Bon I expected just a Birthday wish from you *Just Many Happy Returns* I've never yet forgotten you. Think Frank that's all you have to do. [Bens birthday was 28th March]

Just set to and tell me what Ruth said. Now Bon I want you to burn this page, just this page for me, for I wouldn't like anyone to see what is on it . Here is something, don't be hurt over it for 'tis meant in a kindy way and Bonnie don't forget I love and want you badly. You think too much about yourself and not enough for others. I don't put myself up as an example, I'm far from it and you know my weaknesses, but the whole time, whether I'm with you or not these thoughts are continually running through my mind *what can I do for her,* Anything to make her lot easier, *what would she like* and although I may be frightfully busy and no one can possible know how wretched and tired and sick of myself I am after a days work I think those things above. And when Bon I go to your place and although you maybe busy I can see that you don't think about them because if you did you'd do them. Little things like the bed made etc if I have to do anything for you, I'm actually worried until it is off my mind.

Now old Sport, you aren't hurt are you for even running that risk I must tell you of the things I see. Burn this page please. Tell me what you think of what I have said. I know that if I could only get you to myself I could make you do those things just for sheer love of doing things for you. I've found out that loving a person means waiting on them and giving them everything you've got and shewing them that they are No 1. I never make a person look small if I can help it. I'm not ashamed to let people know that you are THE person.

That night when you and Winnie were in bed and I bent to kiss you as I went out, why did you turn your head so that I couldn't. I saw 'Winnie give a smile. Don't let people think that I am doing all the wanting, you do want me don't you? You are so cold sometimes and it tears my heart out. Have I made you cry old girl.

Now I've put all my lecture on 1 page so that you could burn it. I love you Frank.

Isn't it horrid to be out of matches. We are at present and everytime I want a light I have to go to the gas. Did I tell you that I broke my gas glove mantle trying to do something or other when on crutches, I feel Bon as if I am as helpless as a baby. I really need someone to help me. Just little things that irk me that ordinary people can do on their own. Oh, curse the war and the people who ever started it. Why should I be picked out to lose a leg when so many came back without a scratch . Oh Bon will you help me?

You'll like this wardrobe, gradually I'm going to get things together say for a spare bedroom in case any visitors come.

We are still having plenty of persimmons. Just one little tree supply us with all these. Do you remember the fruit we picked off my land, you in Tom's boots and Ruth's puttees.

Have you seen much of Ruth Upfold? I hope she doesn't love Leonard. She is worth more than him and I hate to see the 2 churches together. It works in rare cases such as yours but not always, does it? [Franks father was RC Irish and her mother C of E Irish]

Such a lot of prominent people are dying lately. Here we have Justice Monday just dead. He, his father and grandfather have all been judges, a good record isn't it? Still more decorations are coming out. There is quite a batch in today's paper. Smiths Weekly had some very clever things on this week. One about the Lords Prayer. It is clever and that is all I can say for it. Well Old Girl, I hope you are sendng me a long letter. Do tell me what you feel like when you read previous page and forgive me if it hurt.

Love Ben (he is not much but trys)

———

15.20 Saturday 5.30pm

Dear Sweetheart,

Good news at last for you. On Monday The Public Service Board will PROBABLY send you a letter asking you to come down and be interviewd by the Matron on Thursday, so be prepared won't you.

Arrangements have been made here for you to sleep and you are to come down at least the day before but 2 days would be nicer for me. Wear your ring down so that Mother can see it will you and I'll promise you nice birthday greetings. Bring also what ever the letter says and your original testimonials. Dad says not to worry, for if you are selected he will see the matron and get you in early. This is the chance of your life time. Don't miss it.

The day before you come, send me a wire Ben Champion Medical School, Sydney University. Do you get that and I'll arrange if possible to meet you at Hornsby, only try to make it Wednesday if at all possible won't you. Even if you sent a telegram on the day you come, to the Uni as long as you send it early in the morning so as I'll get it by 1 oclock.

Who do you think I saw on Newcastle Station when I came down, Bessie Nicolls and her V.C. He is a thin chap, same height as Bessie, looks a nice quiet unassuming sort of cove. He was wearing his VC on his waist coat. We slowed up at Redfern station, the train was 30 minutes late and so he hopped out there instead of coming on to Sydney. I saw you cross the line at Tarro. Sorry I couldn't have the last word with you out of the window owing to the William's girls I made faces at the smaller one all the way to Honeysuckle and she seemed to enjoy it. I met Allan from Cessnock in the train and we came down together.

He shouted tea at Gosford. I'm quite excited at the idea of seeing your old face once again. You've got to stay over the weekend–tell your mother that my mother expects you to stop. Jeannie went home today. Vera is still o.k. Must have been a false alarm on my part.

What about that dream. Did you know that by statistics of Dentists they only live till 50. We've been having fires lately for Dad's sake. Only time you haven't seen me off at Newcastle, but you didn't have the nasty lonesome trip back in the train by yourself did you.

Did Keith say anything to your mother. Oh and how is the sore foot? We had a good shower during the night. I've been putting a flat wash on the wardrobe, brown black when it is polished it goes a mahogany colour and fitting the two doors. I'll order the mirror next week.

Don't disappoint me. I want you to stay over the weekend. How are you feeling Old Girl O.K? I warded off a cold on Thursday night. It is all gone now. When is your Dad leaving for Grafton. Baby Fisk is crying his heart out next door. How did Ruth like milking while you had a sore foot. No news of Claire Bridges. Think she must have tumbled over board.

My hand is shaky this afternoon as it is not used to wielding a plane like I've been doing this afternoon. Went to my coach at the line this morning. Did some more head and neck dissections. It's terribly difficult and hard.

It is a long long while to wait Old Girl but it will be better in the long run. I'll have more money then.

Fancy you 21 on Thursday–some girl. But don't lengthen your dresses, the opposite if any. And you'll look nice in a a cream seater jersey.

No I've not heard any one talk about the reunion at all and I'm not sorry I didn't go. I've been invited to Enid Austin and Arthur Butcher's wedding on Saturday May 22nd–suppose it means a present for them, any suggestions? Oh do come down Bonnie, this is what you've been waiting for a long time isn't it. It seems months since I left Tarro.

Well this simply must get away tonight for if I post this on Sunday it probably won't get to your place until Tuesday Fondest Love.

Bring your approval as the one I put in is only a duplicate and your references too and stay over.

love Ben

Frank had references done for her by:—

J C Douglas L.R.C.S.Ed. (family friend Doctor of Adamstown 18 March 1920); W.A. Howard, Auctioneer and Commission Agent, late Inspector of the State Childrens Dept, of 'Walgahrene' The Hill, Newcastle. Has known since baby hood; Thomas Sydney Champion, Registrar, Public Service Board, Sydney; E.P Evans, Secretary Australian Trained Nurses' Association certificates of Miss Frances J Niland were submitted to The Educational

Committee on the 1st day of April 1919 and were approved. Signed and dated again 20 March 1920 as a true and correct copy of documents by J A Niland J.P.

----

18 March 1920.
Australasian Trained Nurses
Association–approved.

15.5.20

My dear Bonnie,

You are a villianous person. You promised me that I'd get a letter today but none has come although I asked Dad to call there this afternoon. I'm in the throws of a very bad cold. It settled on me during Thursday, a terrific throat and Friday I spent in bed.

Had to go and have my new leg tried on today so I got up and now I feel a little better though I'm coughing as if I've broken all the membranes in my larynx.

I've been very busy this afternoon as I've French Polished and fitted the brass handles and lock on to the wardrobe. I have decided it will be quite good enough for the servants room. I'm sure a State girl like Amy would only be too delighted to hang her dresses in it. If you see any wet spots on the paper you will understand that once again my nose has become unwiped. I ran a bit of a temperature last night. Gee, but I do feel rotten in the top storey.

Geoff Johnson has not been able to get the mirror yet. The whole wardrobe is done with the exception of the mirror so I'm going to move it into Mother's rooms and when the mirror comes I'm going to fit it in there. You see having a Tom in the house, one never knows if he is going to lean his bike or something or other against the wardrobe if I leave it in the trellis verandah.

The new leg is not going too well and I'm really walking so well on this one now. I am practicing short distances without a stick. I walked to the station on Wednesday morning and I didnt sag over on it at all.

Geoff gave me the French Polish, Shellac, and it is mainly shellac in Polish, used to be 1/9 per lb but now it is 12/6 just imagine. He showed me his bed room suite. It is some class. Oak, but it is colored a sort of a white grey, looks so swish. He says he is not going to have a washstand in the whole of his house. He says if he has a friend or so stopping over, they can go to the bathroom as he does. I entirely agree with him. I think washstands in a bed room are a waste too.

I'm terribly pleased about the wardrobe, it is some class and has only cost me 5 pound so far and is worth 16 at least. What a profit these furniture people must make.

Next Saturday I'm to go to Austin–Butcher wedding. I bought her a nice little silver vase. I hope they remember me. If I have a wedding how could my friends go to Tarro, there is no pub for my friends to sleep at. Leave off to look for my 4th hankie today. Shows you how crook my head and cold are when I smoked only 2 cigarettes all day yesterday and only 4 so far today.

Must tell you about the University Commemoration Procession. It took place this morning and I happened to see it as I came from the leg factory. Funny, I can't describe it. If you could only have been there. The idea is to *take off* some thing before the Public's eye. The Federal Police for instance were represented by a dozen or so chaps in police coats on scraggy horses. You never have seen such horses, they all must have been in the last stages of senile decay, scraggy and boney. The policmen all wore short white trousers and on some the coats were so long and the trousers so small that you couldn't see the trousers at all. Then there were dozens of chaps dressed as girls, showing their trousers and legs and things like that. If people like to look on the smutty side of things then of course they could find it but on the whole it was just fun. There were no practical jokes or crackers or anything like that.

The 2nd year dentists took off an advertising dentist's place for injecting. They had a brace and bit, it was so funny. I thought a lady next to me would die laughing too much. Then Medicine 3 had a skit about the Sydney Hospital nurses likely move to the Woolloomoolloo Domain with dossers insulting the nurses. Some of the chaps made excellent nurses too, much prettier than some I've seen in my travels.

I don't mean to say anything against anyone I know in Australia but Franco, some of the nurses in France seemed like washerwomen. Enough about the procession, look it up in the paper.

Oh, Turnbull dressed up as the Matron at the Dental Hospital and Henderson bet him 2/6 he wouldn't kiss a policeman, well he did and I saw him do it. He had rouge on his lips and left a mark on the astonished bobbies face.

This time last Saturday we were on the boat coming from Lane Cove, but I don't know if you got home safely yet. Have you been busy? You didn't give me this cold, I was very hot on Wednesday and I was working down in that horrid old dirty Dental Hospital that did the trick. Things are moving and I believe they will recommence soon to build a new place for us. We need fires–now do you have any at home. Not a week since I left you. Wish you were here now.

How are all getting along at *Oaklands*? Are you boss cocky of the farm and cows?

Oh I have the utmost honour in informing you that you have been accepted by the Coast people. You will get a letter to that effect some day soon. Everyone has not yet been interviewed. Don't be impatient.

I'll see you on the 29th if you can manage to get me an invite and say you want me to come up badly, otherwise I'll work through the vacation at Anatomy. I'm tired and muggy in the head, let's hope you are writing your hardest to cheer me up a bit, for though you work hard too think of what I'm doing.

Earnie Rofe, friend of Keiths died this morning early. He was 21. Suffered with diabetes for years. Hard luck for Mr Rofe, his only son.

What are you doing? did your Dad get away to Grafton safely last Wednesday? Bert and Ray spoke last Monday and told me how sorry they were we couldnt come out but they were all away for the weekend somewhere or other.

Did anyone say anything about the bangle? Must buy some medal ribbons next week to look like a soldier at the Wedding. Saw a chap this morning being fitted for 2 artifical legs and 1 arm. Poor Beggar, but he seemed quite cheerful. Wish I could have had you this morning as I saw Marsland in the distance with a nice girl on his arm.

Why is cream so popular for winter? I'm simply going to do my very damnest to try to get you down to see the Illuminations for the Princes visit. Martin Place the Town Hall, Railway Station etc are simply going to be glorious and it will be a sight which you'll never forget. Will you come if I succeed in the asking. It is cold and my one tootsie is frozen stiff. All the students at Uni are going to a theatre tonight, some mob but they will be orderly I think. They were warned that if they were rowdy there would be no more processions and they wouldn't like that.

I don't feel like work tonight although I haven't done any since Wednesday night. If I don't pass in August there is still a chance for next March that is one consolation and if I don't pass then I'll be a rough bit of a mechanic all my days. I've given up worrying, have found out it does no good at all.

After tea, Do you remember that land that was for sale right next door to the Station, well on the average it fetched 9 pound per foot. Dr Read and Dr Armstong bought the bulk of it. Both of them have too much land as it is but they bought it for a purpose. Word was passed to them that a certain man wanted to buy it to put up a big picture show there, so they put their heads together and said they didn't want a picture show in Wahroonga so they bought it and are going to sell to people who can prove they are going to build houses on it at the same price as they gave for it. I'm so glad, a picture show would have spoilt this dear old place. They paid 1300 pounds for the land and it is not as deep as our place and about 30 foot longer. What a bargain Dad got when he bought this place.

Keith has left the Insurance place and he is going to start at a place called Camelia near Clyde, only a labouring job. Poor chap, where will he end up–he won't study and it really seems as if everything is against him. Lots of people get along without study too. The fates are against him. This is not what you'd call a lovable letter is it? There is too much news in it isn't there,

I received another payment on the bike yesterday, the chap has to pay about 11 pounds more. I had a lot of fun on that bus and some day I'll get another. Then you can learn to ride an Indian as well as an Excelsior. You aren't afraid of much are you? Most girls wouldn't have tackled it. You are awfully afraid of me though? I don't think.

I think I'll go to see a lot of big football matches this year. It is a great sport and I'm sure you'd enjoy them once you understoond the rudiments of the game. Oh what a dopey letter, but I'm dopey myself with this cold. I've tried about everything, even getting mother to rub my chest with a hot brick. Have you ever tried that? But I think you just have to wear them out, drugs etc won't cure them.

Are you O. K.? Hope you haven't been kicked out of the cow bails by a cow yet or had one stand upon your No. 7 sized boots again. How did the poddies behave while you were away? No scours etc You see I'm becoming quite learned in my cow phraseology. When are you going to start the machines going. If you Dad feels like selling out I've still got 6d in the bank. I'd love to be a cocky farmer but come to town to a theatre or something once a fortnight.

Wonder how Gertrude will look when she comes down. Mother helped at the Presbyterian Assembly on Friday. Every year different churches give the ministers luncheon. Mother and the Wahroonga ladies supplied too many good things so Mother had to bring home about 20 lbs of corned meat and tongue. Mother was funny last night. We are not as a rule big meat eaters but last night she piled our plates high with this spare meat, hence castor oil in the middle of the night for Tom and Mother.

There is a very big house just started in Burn's Road, building alone to cost 9000 pounds. Some little cottage Eh What!

Fisks have such a nice gramophone next door. It is just like a miniature band. Marjorie has been to an old Girl's reunion today. Returned home happy and smiling. Oh she has a music pupil, little girl Concanon. [A Concanon KIA Gallipoli] So Marjorie will have a bit more pocket money now. I think she charges 1 ½ guineas per quarter. Hope the little girl is a smart pupil for if she is, more are sure to come.

Well old girl, I've almost come to the end of my tether for news.
I'm feeling dopey on it too and although only 7pm, bed is calling
me. My eyes seem like lead and I want matches to keep them open.
Hoping to see on on the 29 May–Fondest love,

Yours Ben.

Nothing but failures with the photos. These are the only good ones
out of the 1st roll. Have not had the 2nd roll done yet. Had rotten luck, I
either shook the camera or took 2 pictures on the one film.

Love Ben

———

22.5.20 4PM saturday

My Dear Franko,

Many thanks for your 2 big letters this week and Iike the way you
make me curious about things then say *Oh I'll tell you when I see you.*
Of course we both forget these things as we have such a lot of other
things to talk about. Do tell me in the letters this week, 1) why you
say you don't write long letters the reason was to have been told to
me but write it, 2) The second things I've forgotten already but you
mentioned in your last letter. I'm getting consumption (T.B.–PF).
I think my cough is no better indeed I think it is worse. I can get no
relief from anything I take and mother still rubs my chest at night.
That will be your job when or if I come up.

But Old Girl I want letters, you know the sort I haven't had one for
ages and I must have one before I come up. I've been very miserable all
the week with this cold. It is awful and it is not from not wrapping myself
up enough but I think I ought to be wrapping up in cotton wool and left
in a glass case to be out of the way of draughts.

We have an examination on Thursday and the time I've been ill
has been the most important time for the Histology and I can't pick
the work up. No news yet from your Dad? He is most lackadazical? In
writing. I'd be worrying if it were you.

Well I put on my brand new uniform and 3 ribbons, took my
gloves and looking the sweetest Lieut that ever walked ahem! I set out
by the 2 trains for Em Austin's wedding. Bitterly cold too. Arriving

Victor George Austin and family—Ancestry

at St Stephens church in the city, the usual crowd and I didn't know a soul. Later on Jean Austin and family came along. I sat up in the back to be away from the mob but they spied me and hauled me down to the front. Butcher came along looking very red and worried. Why do men look such gawks when they get married. everyone was in uniform so am glad I wore mine.

Tell you now to best of my ability what the bride wore. But being a mere man probably won't be up to your standard Over her hair she had a criss cross of ribbons and seemed to have miles of veil–It floated all over her. The dress was made of Gorgette and the bottom was made of cream satin all crinkled. The bodice was slashed with silver, neck cut moderately low, elbow sleeves the bottoms trimmed with crinkled satin. She had a necklace of pearls and in all she looked as close like an angel as could be without seeing her face. She was late, not her fault though and made an unseemly rush getting up the steps. Anyone looking would think she wanted to be married. Vic gave her away looking very solemn and red as did they all. Miss Essie Milligan sang a sacred song after the service then we adjourned outside and smothered them in confetti down their necks. Then Ann Austin chased me to try to push it down my neck but she didn't succeed. Butcher says it is a much ticklier feeling than after a hair cut with the little bits down your collar.

The wedding breakfast but naturally I didn't go short Trifle, Blancmange, cake etc and cigars afterwards. Drank the brides health in sparkling hock and I got home at 8 feeling tired my leg sore and stuffuped with a cold. I'm getting quite experienced in weddings. I'll know what to do at my own soon. Though how I'm to kneel down I don't know, I havent kneeled since I lost my leg.

There were some bosker dresses at the wedding yesterday. Vic is engaged to such a pretty little girl. She wore a blue voile dress, short sleeves and long white kid gloves, the sleeve ended in a point with a little pompon on the end and she had steel grey colored bead and fancy work, small navy hat and veil.

The trifle was extra nice last night, only the plates were so small I think you ought to have soup plate for trifle.

Jean and Bubs are over here asleep now. Bub cried tonight but Ma kidded her that she was Vera. Didn't speak but just cuddled her off to sleep. Havent seen the Carrolls lately. Well woman I'm to go to Mr Smith next Saturday morning then the leg factory then the Newcastle train if I get an entreating letter this week. Keith has come home for the weekend. He says, all we can get out of him is that it is not too bad. Our little kitten caught a mouse the other day. Imagine an animal that size having the instinct to catch a mouse. Strange the difference between animals and humans. A foal and calf can almost look after themselves after a few days but what of a baby.

I wish you were down here Old Sport. Tom is at the Pictures, Dot has just floated through in her pale blue kimmi and it is time I was in bed too so I'll finish this off tomorrow. Sweet dreams Ben.

Sun is shining bright but I'm still in bed. Jeannie is chatting away to Mother in her room and I'm absolutely stuck for news. I didn't do a stroke of mechanical work at the hospital last week. I made a metal

dies and counter dies to make 2 brass plates on. Did quite a number of
extractions on Thursday afternoon but I couldn't shift one tooth in a
little boys head. I thought if I applied any more force I'd break his jaw
so I let him go and told him not to tell the doc. He was quite pleased. I
think it is horrible for people to eat sardines and onions before they go
to the dentist don't you?

I must tell you about the bother we had with the wardrobe. It is
still reclining in the kitchen. We decided to move it into mother's
room and got it as far as the kitchen door leading into the hall and
we couldn't get it past there because the silly hall walls curve and the
wardrobe won't go past the curve. Anyhow we might do it today as
Keith is home to give me a hand.

Glad the cows are coming up but you are not to milk when I
come up unless your Dad is not at home. Are you hand feeding
much? Look in the papers, there are such a lot of dairies for sale. Am
so sorry your Mother has a cold, give her my sympathy from a fellow
cold person.

Did you get any snaps of the zoo in last week's letter. You didn't
say. I printed and developed the others but they are no good. I'll bring
them up when I come. And what of your sewing cotton? Did you get
that in the bulbs. Don't think of the Coast yet awhile. All the country
girls haven't been interviewed yet. Don't worry you'll get in among the
first lot or so.

My pen is about running out and as Jean can't reach the ink and as
I'm not getting up yet awhile I might have to finish this in pencil.

Bub has such curly hair but she won't be bub for long. We will have
to get used to calling her by her proper name–I forget what it is. Leila is
one of Arthurs kiddies.

I'm out in the sun now, it's snice and Marjorie is just back from doing
the flowers at the church. Had to put a lot there this morning for special
Empire Service.

You would laugh to see us now, Tom, Keith, myself in pyjamas
and overcoats. Dot in her kim, the 2 kiddies and Mother all out on
the logs alongside Keith's bedroom in the sun. We had rhubarb,

peas, silverbeet, the garden is looking well and Edie has carnation plants and Jean is walking around on my crutches with her arms through the cross pieces . We've actually ripe passion fruit too.

Well, fondest love old Dear and if all goes well I'll see you next Saturday evening. You please yourself where you meet me, Newcastle, Tarro or at *Oaklands*, just as you feel fit. I'm catching the 1.5 pm train from Sydney. It gets to Newcastle at 5.3pm now, whether I can catch the 5.5 train from Newcastle I don't know'. The train isn't supposed to call at Hamilton but if it does I'll get out there and catch the Maitland connection. So the best thing you can do is to meet or get some one to meet the 5.39 train at Tarro and if I'm not in that then 20 to 7. So sweet heart, I 'll bid thee farewell, Love and everything else you'd like,

Ben

---

home 24 May 1920

Dear Bonnie,

This is in terrible haste, Dad has just come home and has told me that you are 8th on the list for appointment to the Coast Hospital. They are wanting nurses now, so Dad says as soon as the papers go from their hands to the Dept of Public Health (say in 10 days) time you will be asked how soon you can report. Get Busy. This you can take as official as Dad has seen the papers and knows it to be correct. It's good old Dad to work you in so soon, isn't it? So that supposing it takes you 20 days to get ready, you will get in sooner by getting this note. Order your material or what ever you have to do.

I'll be up on Saturday morning about 12.30. I think I can get that special mail train to stop for me as it did last time. Anyway look out for a wire towards the end of the week. Your mother might like to see this if I haven't made myself clear. Fondest love

Ben

...who said the board wouldn't be taken with your looks (not Bonnie)

Written on small piece of paper

Coast Hospital 13/–per week. There is a waiting list probably 6 months to wait. No wards maids scrubbing to be done. Hours are 6am until 6pm with 1 hour off 4 days per week. 8am to 8pm less 3 hours off 3 days per week. One day a week off. Supply own dresses but if you stand it for 6 months they give you 12 yards of dress materials Compare this with Wallsend

---

5.6.20 Home

Dear Bonnie

Many thanks for the long letter this afternoon. Never mind I didn't expect one so soon. Arrived in plenty of time on Thursday to visit Mr Smith and he hurt awfully. Due to go to him on Wednesday again, after the horrible chamber of torture.

I went to Hordern Bros and asked for that pattern and posted it to you. They said they had posted their reply some days previously so by now I hope the order and cheque are in their hands.

Do tell me about the dresses you are making and hurry up. Have you received any reply fom the Matron re the caps? Gertrude is due in Sydney about the 10th but definate news will come later. I'd give a lot not to have had that discussion which took place last Wednesday night, a mighty lot, as a matter of fact.

It is awfully cold here, colder than at Tarro. It's 49 degree about 3 feet from our fire and although I bought and am wearing a good flannel shirt I'm still cold. Eric Smith, so far has not had a holiday at all.

A chum named Everett who used to be Mr Smith's apprentice before is missing and Eric is helping search for him. It appears that Everett last Tuesday at 3pm left home (Burwood), to go to Stanmore and has not been seen since. I'll let you know if I hear anything more.

How did you get on at Upfolds, have a good day? was Ruth in the best of moods and how about Brook's in the evening? I bet you had a cold time of it coming home. Let me have plenty of letters. I go back to the University on Monday. I've been pottering about on odd jobs trying to get warm. My leg is getting finished now. I ought to have it in 3 weeks time. I was very pleased with it on Friday. Also I went up to the AMP Insurance to be re medically examined so will let you know how I get on when I hear the result.

I'll get that birth certificate for you if you say so. Such a short time since I saw you, I'll now say *adieu* and don't forget to let me know how soon you can come down, and be sure it is not long after the 10th.

Has Cohen replied to you yet?

Yours Ben.

You must see the illuminations and the procession–about 1000 mounted Light Horse , well worth seeing.

———

8.6.20

Dear Bonnie,

Many thanks for your letter yesterday and today. I'm sorry Ruth Foldup [Upfold] is ill. When you see her, tell her that I hope she soon becomes herself once again. Anyhow if one has to be sick this is the best time of the year to spend in bed when it is so cold outside.

Yesterday was a frightful day, I shivered most of the time and in the evening to study by, Mother and I made a fire in my bedroom. We put on a huge log and it caught but just smoulderd away and when I rose this morning there was still a glow there. I'm in the dining room writing this. I don't seem able to study tonight in my room On my right is Marjorie turning over music leaves causing quite a draught and around the bend of the table is Tom turning over leaves in the *Chums*, also a draught.

Lieut. Flora Sandes arrived in Sydney today. She is called the Servian Joan of Arc. She started as a private, fought in the Servia War, wounded several times and rose to the rank of Lieutenant. She had a great hold on the Servian people and they liked her muchly. She is known by Miss Venn-Brown and they are both fundraising.

There is a piece in tonight's paper from some Catholic Soldiers saying that Mannix does not represent all the Catholic Soldiers and for Protestants not to class all Catholics as Sinn Feinners.

Did the Matron say anything in her letter about hurrying up or only just sending the pattern. I'm due at the Dentists tomorrow at 3.

Sergeant Major Flora Sandes

He is sure to hurt me and I hope Bert Solling is kind to you. Dad says he wishes you could come sooner so don't let it be beyond the 20th or so will you.

I'll have your Birth certificate O.K. for you unless you tell me not too. No further news from Gertrude so I suppose she won't be down tomorrow. Wish you'd have my letter in front of you when you reply always, otherwise I don't get my questions answered. Ross [Kingsford] Smith opened up his show today. I didn't see many people going as in his prices are much too high. Can't get anything of a seat under 7/6.

W H Shiers, Sir Keith Smith, Sir Ross Smith and Jim Bennett

Too high a price for people like myself to go. Don't you bother about that basket, get ready is all you have to do. It's much more important. (sermon) It's the stepping out stone for you. Things have been jogging along just the same at Tarro I suppose. Have there been any allusion to the Wednesday night chat, tell me. You won't get anymore letters on Monday if you stop at Tarro, for the last post leaving here Saturday is 3pm, times have been altered but you will only be there 1 more Monday I hope.

More wonderful decorations going up all over Sydney. Thousands on thousands of globes being used. Horderns have right along their front *Advance Australia Fair*. The private buildings look better than the Gov't ones do.

The Feltons have left Hornsby and are living at Gordon. Didie has left the Govt. Service and is now outside somewhere as a typist. Quite a lot of changes eh? I was re insured the other day but have not heard the Doctors verdict yet.

Cheeriho Old Sport,
fondest love Ben

12 .6.20

My Dear Old Girl
(Hand the back page on to your Dad please)
Many thanks for your letters on Monday, Tuesday, Wednesday and this afternoon. But instead of being in my usual good spirits I'm in the opposite. The glands on the right side of my neck are so swollen that today I'v only been able to eat squashy food. I'd like to know the cause of it. I should have gone to Mr Smith this morning to have the inlay he put in last Wednesday afternoon polished but had Mother to ring him up becuase I thought I might give it to him. The throat came last Wednesday but has reached it's climax. I can't swallow my saliva without pain on the right side, so I've been wandering around all day as miserable as a bandicoot, no one to talk too.

Dad is away at bowls and Tom is at Peter Lindsays and so I had nothing to do. I would love to have gone to the football match to see the Englishmen play but what could I do in that crush even if I could have gone. I've no mate to go with, Henderson, Smith, Marsland are playing tennis.

Why aren't you down here with nothing to do. I do so want to go around to matches etc but see how I'm placed I can't. Do you remember me speaking of Malcolm Vicars? Well, he was on his Henderson Bike going along slowly, when a kiddy about 5 rushed across the street, so he ran into a bank of the street to stop himself hitting it and smashed up his leg somehow. So his Dad called here for a loan of a pair of crutches for him. He said he would rather have nearly killed himself than the kiddy. It is a shame to let kiddies roam in the streets on their own isn't it. Thats what I used to notice about London and Edinburgh, NO kiddies on the road in Edinburgh, the good scotch people used to keep them indoors but the Cockneys of London didn't care a hang.

Every morning, but this morning of this week, we've been dissecting the thorax and doing anything we liked in the afternoons. But on Monday we start prompt at 10 on Physiology.

A brand new bed came for you yesterday. Daddy Xmas supplied it and it is up in Majories room ready for you to jump into. Your own special bed. Dad says he'll be disappointed if you don't occupy it when you have the chance. How about coming down on Saturday 19th. Don't be later old bean.

You cannot image what a relief it will be for me to know you are fairly close and can call me by the phone when I can't meet you. The mirror for the wardrobe hasn't come yet and I've ordered the timber for a small book case for Dot's room. I am going to let the centre 2 inches of the shelves come through the side then put a little wooden pin through. Do you get my idea? Then stained mahogany like the wardrobe.

Gertrude and Rupe are not coming down for a little while because the rain has softened the ground so much that Rupe wants to plough. I'm keeping her letter to you for you. What do you propose to do with my letters. If you are not going to burn them or bring them down for me to mind then tie them up well won't you.

We have enjoyed Ross Smith's flights during the dinner hour. He is some flyer. I'm enclosing a slip of paper for your Dad. If you read it do not say any thing about it as it is supposed to be a secret. Keith has just come in. I think he is looking better. Arrangements have been made through the Imperial Service Club to give to the Prince a statement about the Lord Mayor and his disloyal utterances, not a bad scheme eh?

You won't be too late for the Illuminations. I want to show them to you next Saturday night so please catch the early train from Newcastle. And don't bother about luggage. There are tons of Porters at Newcastle. There is someone ringing up Mother for a subscription for something or other. Glad Mother has turned her down.

You are a regular Milko? Did the boy Cameron come back at all? I applied for the birth certificate and expect to get it on Monday at 3pm. Saw Bert on Friday morning at the University. I think I'll go down to Melbourne in September for a week as I've often promised the relations but have never had the manners to go, Cheeriho, Tea is on.

I only could manage a basin of bread and milk for tea, some appetite and sore neck. Jeanie came running in with a china nest egg today saying *Oh Gwan here is a chinamans egg*. Mr Ellis and family from Japan, friends of Dads are in Sydney and the girl had never seen a horse in a vehicle. In Japan, cause men always pull the rickshaws about she said *Oh Mummy look in Sydney they make the poor horses pull the rickshaw and not the men.*

A coke fire tonight–run out of logs. I thought I saw Winnie Wood in the train the other night but thought she was at Wallsend and now you tell me she has left the Hospital. What again? No trace of Everett. No one knows what to think. My own opinion is that for some reason or other he has cleared out because it seem incredible that foul play should come to a man–possibly to a women though.

Have you a supply of hat pins? See one man was sentenced to death during the week for molesitng a girl late at night. I couldn't remember your mother's christian name when I applied for your Birth Certificate so I just put in the initial and the man behind the counter didn't notice the omission. I'm sorry to say that Tabbies cracked tail doesn't provoke me to tears. I would be sorry about the big fellow, Bonnie.

I spent a very intersting afternoon on Thursday at the Sydney Hospital x-ray room. Had it all explained–saw several photos being taken. A cracked malleous fracture and radius and a piece of steel in the arm. They have a cute way of actually knowing the distance from the wound to the piece of steel. They cross pins over the place of entry of the steel so when the negative comes out the x pins are seen and the distance can easily be measured and no extra cuts are made in the skin. I had an X-ray taken of my right upper bicuspid molar teeth.

Marjorie has finished her vieux Rose Jacket and looks o.k. Come early on Saturday I'm glad you are coming

Love Ben.

FROM FRANKS MOTHER

Oaklands Wednesday

My dear old Frank

Just a line or two so you will not be disapointed when you look for a letter. I was so pleased to get Ben's letter and his mother's yesterday. They are good to you—there's no doubt. I hope you'll be able to get these three days off and come up with Ben when he comes.

He told us about that nurse who got bluffing on and was reprimanded for her trouble. Mary also wrote, got her letter last night. She says her hospital is a lovely place. What a pity she did not see you— Am anxious to send this letter before 1pm as it is Wed. and there might be another letter from you—be sure to write to your father about the coat. I hope you like it.

Such a terrible thing happend this morning at the Garners. When they all went back home after milking they found Mrs Garner dead. She had cut her throat with a razor. Poor old thing! I do feel sorry about it. I've just heard they had thought for sometime she was a bit strange–so she couldn't have been in her right mind when she did it. Alma was at Mrs Fred's last night at the dance too. All these things do make one feel depressed and I think we should take them as warnings of how surely Death steps in and try to live better lives than we do.

I went to Maitland yesterday Frank–first to the gardens and I could not walk any further. My foot was too painful. It was the first outing since I did it. It does seem a long time since you left Frank and we do miss you. I was telling Ben, I believe old Bonnie the cat often thinks of you, for he does look mournful with us and we try to pet him up so I must take him in hand and look after him. He seems to be getting very old and old Bluey too. He will be glad to see you when you come.

Probably Mary and Aunt Emm, [Rumery] are having lunch with Aunt Carrie [Carroll] today. They were invited. Oh Frank, I'll get Ruth to make a cake for you as soon as I can. I was thinking the other day you might like one.

Now I must send, as I want to send a few lines to Mary as well and it is getting time for Ruth to go for the mail and post this. Claire is at home today, bad cold and headache so I put her feet in hot water and fixed her up comfortably.

Aunt Carrie's address is *St Ives* Redmyre Rd, Strathfield–easy to find–it is 4th house. You could spend a day off with them sometime. I'll say goodbye now

with love from Mother

———

From Frank–at The Coast–
I'm off duty 2 p.m.

My dear Bennie

Suppose you got my note o.k.–left in front of the looking glass. This is a great place but I wish you could come out and see me. I'm awfully you know (love sick) Went on duty at 6 last night and came off at 8 pm this afternoon. I'm coming into town some afternoon you are at the hospital. I'll just have time to have an hour and half with you.

Matron Medcalf, at least she is only acting matron, we call her sister. She is so nice. She took me into her office for particulars and kept me there for about an hour talking to me and showing me how to fix my caps etc and she actually told me my hair was beautiful.

Ben, I have something to tell you about Geo Flower. He is still here and I don't think he will ever be anywhere else. There are incurables here aren't there? At least he is. Must go now, my dear old Boy.

Love from Yours Frank

write me soon won't you

From Mary

Oaklands Tarro

29.6.20

My dear Frank

Am actually enjoying my holidays at last, came home last night, came off night duty and yesterday morning went to bed 8.30 called 12.30 and had to go on duty (day from 2pm til 6pm) So I will go back on day duty, so you can guess I was very tired last night when I came home. I didn't know 'till Sunday night that I was to begin holidays so soon.

Our exam has been postponed till end of July, hence we holidays early. I'm not sure when I will be going to Sydney but will let you know and go out to see you.

Am glad you are contented and like being there. Is there a Nurse Mann there? She started the same day as you. I think she has a sister in 3rd year at Newcastle. Yesterday was the last time for me to wear my poor old lilac uniform.

I have had a very sore eye–had to go and let Dr Roberts see it—was one night. Had to have it bathed two hourly ad tied up. Dr Brown came every night to see how it was and told Norman one night if I needed holding down while she bathed it for me he'd hold me down and wanted to wheel me about in an invalids chair. It is much better now, thanks goodness.

I have a cold still and my throat gets terribly sore too. Thought I was getting Diphtheria the other morning. Had some white patches at the back of my throat. Did you see the Prince. We did, the night staff were allowed to get up for half an hour to see him and then back to bed. I didn't see why we should get fully dressed for half an hour, so put my uniform on over my nightie. I looked simply lovely.

Everyone in Newcastle came out to see him I think. The wards were all decorated in his honor. We are going to have a surprise party here next Friday. Mum and Father are not supposed to know anything about it but of course they do. I'm going to invite William Neilsen up for the occasion.

Dr Roberts leaves on Wednesday and Howell has gone. Mrs Felton spent the night here last Friday. She, Mr Felton and Noel motored to Kempsey with Mrs Saul. Ruth and I are going over to the ?

So Goodbye, love from Mary

September 1920 Wednesday
Newport

Dear Frank,

I'm having a splendid time down here, just Alan Henderson, Eric Smith and myself. We, of course, cook for ourselves, generally sausages and salad. Henderson makes fine salads. We were very lucky coming down here. Only took us 40 minutes as we came in a Buick car. Friends of Smiths happened to know we were coming down, so of their own accord came to meet us at Manly and brought us down. Eric drove the car. It was O.K.

Did you go to see your Aunt? I wish you would go. But next term being a slack one I'll be able to see more of you then. Marjorie carried my bag to Manly wharf as I did not like the idea of getting a sore leg again.

How are you? I've got out of the habit of writing letters, aren't you? Have not taken any pictures yet but I expect to do so today. Have not yet put on my leg so far as I am giving my stump a chance. Hope your tootsies are o.k. again. No more news–will see you next week.

Fondest love Ben

Maybe

A soldier stands, proud and stiff,
in the centre of our town,
With a rifle, never to fire again,
with its barrel pointing to the ground.

Through, rain, hail, shine and wind,
he reminds us as time passes by,
That life doesn't always go your way,
it's just a beautiful lie.

The plaque that has those 'respectful' words,
moulded in the brass,
Really, doesn't mean anything,
for everyone is the same as the last.

But, for our tall, strong soldier,
and each one of his mates,
Each experience was different,
each with different fates.

Now, we know nothing of this soldier and nothing of his life,
We can only assume, his memories, his fears,
if he had children or a wife.

Maybe, he was just 16,
and needed life's thrill,
Maybe, living on rations was easy for him,
or maybe he couldn't kill.

Maybe, he was 18, his life just finding its place,
Maybe, he was lost in the mud, unable to be retraced.

Maybe, he was 21, with a sweetheart waiting at home,
Maybe, he had her portrait, resting in his pocket,
along with his watch and comb.

Maybe, he was a young man,
believing a job had to be done,
Maybe, he thought this wouldn't kill me,
this is gonna be fun.

Stone, flesh, soul and pride.
Is the legacy of this man,
He's very special, to each of us,
cause he helped save our land.

So maybe this soldier is made of rock,
but his life is special and old,
Maybe, this town keeps our eye out for him,
for we know his memories are gold.

– Chloe Smith

Ben's Mates

Chloe Estella Smith was aged 13 years when she submitted her poem to ANZAC LIVE. She has kindly given permission for me to reproduce this in Ben and his Mates. Chloe has written other poems and short stories and is passionate about remembering The Anzacs.

She remembers her family soldier who Died of Wounds in France.

> Noel James Black, Private, 3348 Enlisted 26.7.15, 7th reinforcements, 24 Battalion, aged 20 years, labourer, born Winchelsea Geelong VIC. NOK father James J Black of 28 Bourke Cresc., Geelong. He was 5'7 'with dark complexion black hair and brown eyes. Trasnferred to join 8th Bn 24.2.16 at Zeitoun. Hospital with mumps and rejoined Bn at Serepeum. Disembarked with British Expeditionary Force at Marseille with 8 Bn 31.3.16. Tonsillitis 25.10.16. Wounded 22 April 1917 and Died of Wounds 26.4.17. GSW to head, face and leg at 3rd Casuality Clearing Station. Buried Grevillers British Cemetery 27.4.17 3 kms from Bapaume. His pension went to his mother Catherine and medals to father James Black.

Red Cross Report says he was with D Coy 14 Platoon 8 Bn, a Lewis Machine Gunner in No 1 position on the gun. They were positioned on right of Lagnicourt. Battalion records are online at Australian War Memorial.

Abbreviations

I have marked those who died as a consequence of the war with*

Private	Pte,
Lance Corporal	L/Corp
Corporal	Corp
Sergeant	Sgt
Sergeant Major-Regimental	RSM
Sergeant Major-Company	CSM
Warrant Officer	WO
Second Lieutenant	2/Lt
Lieutenant	Lt
Captain	Capt
Major	Maj
Colonel	Col
Tommies	English soldiers
MM	Military Medal
MC	Military Cross
DSO	Distinguished Service Order,
RTA	Returned to Australia
KIA	Killed in Action and
DOW	Died of Wounds.

VOLUNTEERS ALL
LEST WE FORGET

In recognition of the men who volunteered to serve their Country and were part of Ben's life from 1915 until 1920.

Significantly their records show how often men were wounded or sick, how they were patched up in comfort and then sent back to the horrors they knew awaited them. For those who survived and returned to Australia, many continued to suffer throughout their lives and others died prematurely. The consequences of this war effected all soldiers and their families and they were never the same again.

Wounds were not the only cause of pain and discomfort for many soldiers contracted Influenza, malaria, measles, mumps, rheumatism, trench feet and trench fever, appendicitis, tonsillitis. Many also were infected with venereal disease and it is important to remember that antibiotics as we know them were not available and some medical treatments we would now consider inadequate or even primitive.

Any cases of courts martial, charges or venereal disease have not been included. We pay tribute to their service to our Country and acknowledge they were all volunteers.

All effort has been made to identify the records of the surnames of the men who are identified in this book. Searches have been made against the records which are available online at the National Australian Archives, The AIF Project, The Australian War Memorial records and also from the nominal roll found in the book First Battalion A.I.F. 1914-1919. In some instances Trove has also been checked.

The compilation per entry is not complete and some names have more information than others so please check first with record search/name search at Australian National Archives.

If there are any corrections to be made please contact the publisher

Soldiers are listed first and then acquaintances of Ben and Frank are indexed after the soldiers.

An incomplete list of nurses who returned sick from Duty at Salonika on *Kanowna* are then listed.

List of Honour Roll at Wahroonga War Memorial

A

A'BECKETT Hastings Elwin, Lt., MC. for action at Gueudecourt. Station manager of *Whitwell* Wellington NSW. Enlist 6th L.H. to 1ˢᵗ Bn, Wounded x 3. GSW to jaw, RTA *Argyllshire* 8.12.18.	293-4, 299, 301, 303, 332, 408-9, 411, 419, 436, 446
ADAMS Alan Moysey, *Moisie*, Lt., Gentleman, aged 25, born Kingsbridge South Devon. 7th Rfts 1ˢᵗ Bn to 53rd Bn. Double Broncho- pneumonia Adjutant to Overseas Training Bgde, to 4 Bn., RTA 24.01.1920 per *Osterley*. Grandson says he went to Australia with no money to become a adventurer swagman and walked all over eastern Australia- some 4000 miles in all - getting odd jobs where he could. During this period, he met my Grandmother Florence, who was teaching in, I think, Toowoomba ' She went to England to marry. Even as a swagman people recognised Moysey as a gentleman. Ben thought he was a remittance man but it seems he was quite broke. After the war Moysey continued his adventuring and lived on Dolores Estate, Punta Gorda, Belize Honduras with wife and two children. They did return to England to live.	76, 93
*AGNEW Harry Rowan, Gunner, clerk born SCOT.7th Bn. to 11 Aus. Field Artillery Brig., KIA 15.4.17 HAC Cemetery Ecouste St Mein Arras Nord Pas de Calais near Bapaume. Ben wrote wounded in back, Is there another AGNEW who was at Instructors School with Ben of 4th Bn (McMahon Symington)	313, 334
ALLAN Herbert *Bert* or *Slab* Washington Tinning, Lt., MM., *French Medaille Militaire* at Pozieres. Enlist 11.8.15 aged 18 Bathurst school student. 13 Bn to 4th Machine Gun Bn., 1ˢᵗ Bn 1.5.16 1) GSW 1.5.18 2) GSW R arm neck and chest/back severe 8.8.18 Villers-Bretonneux RTA per H.T. *Leicestershire* 9.12.18. Dentistry with Ben but left after one year. Died 1951. His brother Stanley Tinning Allan was taken POW at the same battle of Bullecourt.	632, 633, 634, 643, 644, 647
ALLAN Douglas Fraser, Sgt. MM. Lone Pine and Bar Gueudecourt. Born Aberdeen SCT, mother of *Kinnallan*. Enlist 23.11.14 –Lived at Lane Cove. 6ᵗʰ Aust. Infantry Brigade 1915 1st Bn 18.9.15., On *Ivernia* to Marseille, Bombing School 11.5.16 Sgt. vice Sgt. Brainwood trans to 53 Bn. Wounded Gueudecourt 5.11.16 to 3 London General Hospital GSW thigh, RTA 16.12.17, H. T. *Port Lyttleton* Discharged 26.2.18	294
ANDERSON C 81 Beach St, Coogee	

ANDREWS Oswald *Os* Alfred Stanley Waldon, of *Taree* Grosvenor St, Wahroonga NSW. Tried to enlist 9.10.17, born Marrickville, aged 23 years, commercial traveller. not accepted, has mitral incompetence. No further Information ANA. Only 3 pages	556, 560, 571, 778, 781
ARNOLD James Edwin, Lt., Enlist 9.8.15 aged 24, grip man, 6th Bn., Wounded multiple GSW abdomen wall, r leg, l arm, shoulder severe. RTA *Kanowna* with Ben, to Melbourne.	
ATKINSON, Lt., Ben says KIA Pozieres. - none in 1st Bn Nominal Roll. Thomas Henry Atkinson 7th Rfts 1st Bn was a deserter from *Orsova*. To match date of death I have changed to Atkins. PF	
*ATKINS Harold Augustus Randolph, 2/ Lt., Enlist 11.8.14 F Company. Discharged. Re enlist 28.7.15 16 Rfts 1st Bn. Born Bathurst aged 26 Customs Officer. KIA 23 July Pozieres. Memorial Villers-Bretonneux	
AUSTIN Victor George, Pt., Enlist 17.6.18, clerk, age 21, NOK sister Miss Jean Austin *Sunnybrae* Wahroonga. 2nd Bn Aus. Inf. Base Depot H.Q.–RTA 8.9.19 *Chemnitz*. Austin Family WW11 Austin, Victor George–*Kokoda and Beyond*, the Story of the 39th Bn. This unit existed for only 24 months of WWII but it is one of the most unusual and proudest in the annals of Australian Military History. Melbourne University Press.	xiii, 290, 480, 485, 510, 582, 598, 603, 613, 647, 651, 654, 656, 662, 686, 688, 692, 693, 694, 721, 777

B

BACKHOUSE Alan Norman, Lt., enlist 5 Rfts 3 Bn to 1st Bn. Aged 19 Draughtsman, born Katoomba, father of Strathfield. Wounded x 3	379
BARBER Albert Edward, CSM / W.O., Enlist 17.8.14, 31 years, bookseller, married of Lidcombe. 1st Bn. A Coy., Jaundice Dysentery Gallipoli, trench fever, GSW l Arm RTA *Orontes* 13.5.18 Discharged 10.10.18 medically unfit. Died 1942 war related.	104, 247
BARBOUR Henry Arnold, Lt., Enlist 25.1.16 Born Vic, aged 30 years, bank manager, father of Hampton VIC. 37 Bn. Wounded 23.4.17. Central Training School Havre. 3.6.17 Wounded 23.4.18 to Eng. GSW # Fibula RTA *Rio Padre* 27.5.19 Disembark Adelaide to Vic 17.7.19 Discharge 4.9.19. Did Trench Art with Ben at Havre	

BELLAMY Thomas, Lt., born ENG Enlisted 8.1.14. West Maitland, aged 23, miner, 43 Bn. Many Courses of Instruction16.3.18 to be Lieut., 9.4.18 Wounded GSW hand and jaw severe To England 3rd London General Hospital Wandsworth (with Ben) RTA *Medic* 13.10.18. Discharge Medical Unfit 29.10.19. Family of Dallas Bellamy who was a child patient of Bens at Newcastle	818
BAYNE William Alexander, Pte, Enlist 19.8.14 born SCOT aged 26, Mining. H Coy 1st Bn., Wounded 1) Gallipoli 6.9.15 B W R arm. to 53 Bn Tel el Kebir, special 1st Camel Corps. Wounded 2) shrapnel to forehead France 19.7.16 to 1st Bn. Wounded 3) Demicourt 9.4.17 GSW both legs. 1.11.17 RTA *Anchises* 4.1.18 Discharge 11.2.18. GSW R Leg Ben has L/Corp. Archie Barwick's friend. Applied for Anzac medal in 1967	332
THE BARWICK Brothers	
BARWICK Leonard George, Sgt., Enlist 26.10.14. Born Tasmania, aged 20 years, farmer, father of Tasmania. 22.3.16 *Ivernia* with Ben. L/ Corp 12.3.16. School of Sniping. Corp. vice T/Sgt Mackie 4.10.16, Marched in as replacement to 1st Bn. 4.11.17. l/ Sgt 1.1.18 Overseas Tng. Bgde. RTA from Taranto Italy on transport duty on *Port Sydney* 1.12.18, Discharge 31.1.19. His brother	386
BARWICK Archie Albert, Sgt., *Croix de Geurre*, also in 1st Bn. Archie's diary is at Mitchell Library and online In it Ben is mentioned a few times as are other soldiers mentioned in *Ben and his Mates*	714, 726, 746, 787-8, 820
*BARWICK brother Norman Stan enlist 8.7.16 farmer of Campania Tas aged 25 years 12 Bn. KIA 8.10.17 Menin Gate Memorial	384, 728, 786
*BAYLISS Walter Norman, Pt. Enlist aged 22, accountant from Petersham. 1st Bn. A Coy, GSW Abdomen. DOW 25.7.1916, Pozieres, Cemetery Warloy-Baillon Communal Cemetery Extension near Albert His brother	
* BAYLISS A.J. Gunner 5th Field Artillery KIA 3.5.1917	243, 280
BEDFORD Frank 2/Lt., Enlist 23.2.15 QLD., born ENG. aged 28 years, carpenter, NOK wife in England. 25 Bn., GSW left shoulder, 2) 4.10.17 SW foot. Amp. 3rd London General Hospital. RTA *Kanowna* . Living in England 1920	452
BEALE William Frederick, Sgt., Medaille Militaire. Enlist aged 21, clerk, born London. 5th Rfts 31 Bn to 5th Pioneer Bn, special leave granted for Aeroplane construction, attending aircraft. Demob. ENG 19.8.19. 1925 To join 22nd London Armoured Car Coy, Royal Tank Corps.	393

BEAVIS Horace Weston, Capt., 1st Bn. school teacher, family from Bathurst. Took responsibility writing to families after Pozieres. Invalided to Aus. with neurasthenia *Kanowna* 14.9.17, married Miss McLeod 29 Oct 1919 St Stephens Sydney with Ben as Best Man. Ben would not know that Beavis father died in 1917. Died 1965	152, 156, 158, 163, 198, 219, 241, 243, 244-5, 261, 274, 298, 339, 412, 610, 622-4, 641, 647, 652, 661, 671, 715, 750, 752, 780
*BEAVIS Edward Bathurst KIA Gallipoli 1915. Brother to above.	
*BENNETT James *Norman*, Lt. born on a fairly large Herefordshire farm called *Ingestone*, in Foy. He came from a line of Bennetts that had farmed in this area of Herefordshire for at least 400 years. The family had something of a global outlook and traded polo horses and Herefordshire cattle in particular. It is not known why 'Norman 'as he was known, was in Australia but the family members did a lot of travelling and investing '. Info from Nigel Edwards his great nephew. Enlisted 21 years, station overseer, 1st Bn ex 6th Aus. Light Horse, wound 13.4.17 GSW face severe. KIA Broodseinde Ridge Belgium 3.10.17 Buried in field 1000 yds. S. E. of Zonnebeke, exhumed to Tyne Cot British Cemetery. Passchendaele near Ypres. His brother Philip John Bennett 'Jack' served in English Machine Gun Corps and survived the war.	334, 379
BERGELIN Rupert *Rupe* Wilhelm, Trooper, Enlist aged almost 30, clerk of Sydney, 2nd Light Horse Brig., 6th Light Horse Regiment. Lost eye shrapnel Gallipoli RTA 8.10.1915 H.M.T. *Suevic*, Discharged 13.3.1916, married Gertrude Champion 1919	xiii, 470, 479, 516, 546, 548, 550, 558, 571, 591, 594, 609.612, 616, 625, 646, 647, 670, 675, 778, 806, 806

BEYNON Frank, Sgt., Enlist 31.8.14 aged 26, Balmain, store man. Ben says ex Petty Officer. 1st Bn, Gallipoli, France, Mentioned dispatches. Reported Missing 20.1.18., German prisoner of war Limburg 19.1.18 Ypres., Repatriated to England 17.12.18., RTA *Derbyshire* arrived 17.4.19	403
*BINGLEY Frederick Joseph, Sgt., Enlist 15.8.15, aged 18, junior clerk from Darlington Sydney. 12 Rfts 4 Bn to 1st Bn., KIA. 18.9.18 attack on Hargicourt near Brusle with no known grave. Villers--Bretonneux Memorial. Photo AWM	
*BINGLEY Claude William KIA 1917	733
BINGLEY George Edward Sgt., RTA	247, 268
BITMEAD George, Lt., Enlist age 27, Sydney, railway guard, 2nd Bn to 1st Bn., Wounded x 4 including Gallipoli and Pozieres. RTA *Wahene* OC Troops to Sydney.1.7.19. Married overseas. Note 1st Bn. Meteren officers photograph	375, 384, 386, 410, 419
BLACK Noel James, see Chloe Estella Smith Poem	711
*BLACK Archibald John, Sgt., Enlist. 14.5.15 Public school teacher from Stanmore, aged 30, 7th Rfts. 1st Bn., to 53rd Bn, KIA 19.07.1916, Battle of Fromelles, Fleurbaix France. Fromelles cemetery, Bulls Rd, V.C. corner Australian Cemetery France. Fair complexion, grey eyes and dark brown hair, 5'10 '	93, 152, 152, 248
*BLACK Leslie Malcolm, Sgt., Enlist 18.5.15. age 26, born Junee, Fireman railway, Mother of VIC., 5th Rfts 1st Bn, Shell wound Gallipoli. Corp. Tel el Kebir. *Ivernia.* Sgt. vice Sgt. Steele. Commissioned KIA 5.11.1916. Sgt Black KIA .1.1.17 Cemetery Bulls Rd, Flers, France near Combles. Sergeants photo 5 foot 9 inches, Dark complexion, eyes and hair. Brother	
BLACK A.E. Pt. 1st Field Ambulance	269, 248
* BLACKMORE Lewis Gordon, 2/Lt., Enlist. aged 19 farmer/ grazier of Mattamondara NSW, 6th L.H. to 1st Bn., wounded Gallipoli. KIA 23.7.16 Pozieres, buried to R of Communication Trench leading to old German No 1 trench, buried in heat of action, no minister, no grave. Villers -Bretonneau Memorial.	244
BLAKE Wesley Mervyn, Lt., also ADJ. MC., Enlist 11.8.15 age 21 real estate agent of *Ontario* Gerald Ave Roseville. 9th Rfts 1st Bn., 1.9.18 near Chignelles 2 x GSW and buried by shell. RTA OC Troops HT *Wahene* 1.7.19 Sydney with wife Violet. Married 30.4.19 Kensington Parish Church ENG. Died 1937 aged 42 years.	329, 375, 379, 398, 565
BLEWITT Percy Charles	

BOARDMAN Herbert, Lt., Enlist 1.9.15 aged 23 years, warehouseman from Woollahra, father of Vaucluse. 1st Field ambulance Reg. to 1st Bn., Adj. vice Lt. F.L. Flannery 11.12.17. RTA special 1914 furlough, transport Duty 13.10.18 – 24.12.18. H.M.A. T. *Durham*. Discharge 22.2.19 Also served Capt. WW11 1940-1947., died 17.3.1981	299, 302, 364, 401, 409, 419
BOWES 2nd Bn hurt in mouth Feb 1918 playing football	
BOILEAU Angus Herbert, Lt., and Flying Officer., MM. 3 Bn to Australian Flying Corps. Attended 1st Div. Training school, June and Sept. and then instructor 1.12.17, on Bens menu as Adj. RTA *Kaiser Hind* with his brother BOILEAU Charles Lestock 19.6.19 (3 brothers at war)	
BOILEAU - Cecil McIntosh AIF terminated 14.1.18 and joined India Army with Commission	313, 314
BOOTH C Coy 1st Bn Feb 1918. Probably BOOTH Charles Lt., prev. record over 4 yrs. 14th Kings Hussars, Aug 1914-15 European Armed Constab. in Papua, Aug 1915 to March 1916 Commission 17.1.1916. Enlist 29.8.15 aged 26 Plantar and native recruiter Papua to Base Light Horse, 16 Rfts, - 2nd L.H. -1st LH Training Reg – 2 LH Sqdn. Adj., 1st LHTR, 61 Bn., Gen Inf. Rfts., posted to 1st Bn 16.10.17, Aust. Corp School 23.2.18 re-joined 1st Bn, Wounded 21.9.18 GSW Elbow thigh and leg RTA *Kanowna* 7.3.19 Term., 14.6.19	391, 411
BOOTH Edgar Harold, Capt., MC. 30.10.17. Enlist 19.8.15 aged 22 years 6 months Lecturer in Physics, Uni of Sydney and Engineer. Father of Chatswood. 1 Rfts Med Trench Mortar Battery to Heavy Trench Mortar Batteries. RTA *Kashmir* 14.3.19	
BOOTH Clarence Enlist 7th Reinforcements 1st Bn with Ben, aged 24 years teacher, married. KIA 30.9.15 Gallipoli. Lone Pine Memorial	
BOOTLE John Carlisle, Capt., Adj. MC., Enlist 22.1.15 aged 20 years 6 months born Moree, draftsman 5th Rfts to 4 Bn to 1st Bn., Gallipoli # humorous RTA. 22.5.19 Adj.- Capt., OC Troops, H.T. *City of Poonah* to Melbourne trans Newcastle. Discharged 25.7.19 Also served WW11. Lt. Col J.C. Bootle., MCED. Brother	
BOOTLE Norman Austin Charles. RTA Dec. 1919. Discharged Western Australia. In March 1926 he disappeared and was not found.	

*BOOTLE Francis William Courtney Died of Disease February 1917 England	163, 165, 231, 239, 252, 253, 254, 256, 383, 419 536, 562, 730,
BOWLING Peter Pte, MM., Enlist 20.4.16. 19 years, labourer, mother of Swansea, Wounded 10.2.14, Sick, Sick, Trench Fever RTA *Orsova* 2.3.19 Discharge 10.4.19	331
BOYER Richard James Fildes, Lt., Enlist b Taree, age 24, student, father Rev Boyer, 24.5.15 24 Rfts 1st Bn. Div. team postal service. Enteric to Malta RTA for 3 months home duty per *Commonwealth*. Re-joined 2.9.15 A Coy 26 Bn to 3rd Bn. Duntroon School 20.6.16 to 1st Tng Bn and Officers and NCS School 20.6.16 – Commission. 24.10.16. 1st Bn wounded Duchess of Westminster La Touquet with gas poisoning severe to Eng. then more schools. RTA HT *Malta* with Broncho pneumonia discharge 13.8.18 Clergyman. Parents died while at War. Made Knight 1956. Died Wahroonga 1961. *Who's Who Australia*, R Boyer, c/- H Small Esq., Collingwood St, Drummoyne	364, 371, 379, 419
BRAINWOOD Harold Charles, R.S.M. Croix de Geurre and Meritorious Service Medal. Enlist age 25, boiler maker, North Sydney. 6th Rfts 1st Bn; wounded x 2 RTA *Leicestershire* 22.6.19	178, 231, 713
BRAMMELL 2/Lt CTS Havre	
*BRAY Charles Wynwood, Maj. Medical Officer ANMEF. Rabaul, Madang, Enlist 25.11.15 aged 23, Medical officer, Mother living in California previously lived Raglan St Mosman. Discharge Sydney 5.5.19. Died 3.8.19 influenza	622, 627
BRAY *Bob*. NAVY	500
* BREWER Harold, CSM, W.O., Enlist 14.5.15 aged 31 years, 7th Rfts 1st Bn., Public school teacher, from Lismore NSW, to 53rd Battalion, Wounded Gallipoli, at Malta with Ben. KIA 26.9.17 Polygon Wood. no known grave, near The Butte, Cemetery Menin Gate Ypres, panel 156.,	4, 93, 109, 111, 126, 136, 149, 152, 219
*BROTHERTON Herbert James, Pt., Enlist 9.1.16 aged 20, labourer, *Dundundera* Bombala, NSW. Cyclist Training Bn to 1st Bn. KIA 29.10.16. Buried in field in vicinity of Delville Wood near Longueval. Reinterred Bulls Rd British Cemetery Bapaume.	288

*BROUGH Joseph Potts, Pt., Enlist. 14.8.15, born Eng, age 27, labourer. (pic at Tel el Kebir with camels) 12th Rfts 1st Bn. A Coy., *Ivernia* with Ben to Marseilles., KIA Belgium 4 10. 1916. Bedford House Cemetery 1 mile S of Ypres.	160, 280
BROWN 'Tom' Thomas, Corp., Enlist 28.6.15. Born Essex, aged 26, carpenter, Mother of Hertford, wife of Ackworth near Pontefract Yorkshire. 9th Rfts Tel el Kebir. 6.1.16. *Ivernia*. Mumps 12.4.16 Wounded 10.6.16 GSW neck to England North Evington Nottingham. Re-joined Bn 24.9.16 Corporal vice Champion 26.10.16 GSW head 8.11.16 RTA *Miltiades*. Discharge 4.8.17.	
BROWN Tom, 5 Theaton St., Moor Top, Ackworth Yorkshire; 87 Jersey Rd Woollahra, 124 Bland St Ashfield. Wife and child arrived June 1919	198, 206, 210, 211, 212, 214, 223, 225, 239, 248, 251, 286, 317, 555, 556, 601, 652, 657
ASHLEY-BROWN William, Revd., Captain Chaplain, Rector C of E Coffs Harbour, married aged 28 years. Posted 1st Aus. Div. 1.9.15 to 9th Bn, 3rd Inf Bgde 28.1.16 to 1st Inf Bgde, Aus. Div. Hdgtrs. Mumps orchitis. Discharge by own request AIF 25.10.17 in England. Accepted position with Indian Army.	
BROWNLEE James, Sgt., Enlist 19.4.15., age 24. born Lanarkshire, miner. 1st Bn – 1st Machine Gun Coy – 1 Bn B Coy., one of covering party at Gallipoli in Torpedo boat *The Partridge*. Wound face and leg at Hill 60 Belgium 11.9.16. RTA H.T. *Somali* 10.12.18. Discharged 12.4.19 medical unfit. Died Newcastle 1973	267
*BROWNLIE Albert Thomas 'Tom', Lt., 9th Rfts 1st Bn, RTA 20.4.19 *Boonah*, died Alfred Hospital Melbourne 31.10.19 aged 28 years buried Brighton Cemetery. His mother Mrs. Brownlie, 5 Longmore St Kilda, MELBOURNE	220, 263, 391, 393, 410, 416, 419, 561, 565, 567, 600, 601, 602, 603, 625, 629

*BRUTON Fernleigh John, Lt., MC., joined with previous military experience. Enlist 27.8.14 1st Bn, born Yorkshire, aged 24, chef, father of London. Married Carlotta Pierina of Turin Italy by British Consul in Egypt. Gallipoli debility Paymaster at Tel el Kebir. To 5th Aust. Div. Depot as Adj., to 1st Bn 9.12.16. Lt. 18.2.17., MC. 2.7.17 stunt. Sick, 20.9.17 Ypres GSW chest ankle leg to ENG. RTA 16.2.18 HMAT *Kanowna* GSW chest, haemothorax, R arm, Discharged 15.8.18. Died 26.11.18 after discharge of peritonitis, intestinal obstruction at Garrison Hospital Sydney	308, 371, 379
BUBEAR George Thomas, CQMS, Enlist 29.8.14 born ENG age 23 labourer. 14 Bn to 1st Inf. Brig. 1st Battalion A Coy, RTA *Port Sydney* from Suez to Melbourne for Sydney 2.12.18. Discharged 3.2.19. JOINED Naval and Military Expeditionary Force 29.7.19 is Taken on Strength Rabaul Forces at Garrison. Seconded to duty Dept. of Post and telephones 2.9.19., 30.9.20 Hon. Corporal to Officers Mess. Returned to Aust. furlough 16.2.21 per S.S. *Melusia*, Discharge medically unfit from N & MEF at Sydney, disability malaria 15.4.21 (PF – pic of SGT., 16.09.1916)	269
BUCKLEY William James, Enlist born Merriwa, aged 18, labourer, father of Gulgong. 6 foot 6 inches on *Borda* 18.10.15. 8 Rfts 1st Bn *Runic*. to France *Ivernia*.27.3.17 to Division Traffic Control Aust. Div. HQ.23.3.17 return to 1st Bn. 14.10.17 back to Traffic Control Detachment, 9.11.17 to hospital sick enteritis and peritonsillar abscess, RTA *Suffolk* to Armagh 5.4.19	329, 788
*BULL Lewis Marsden, Lt., only child, Sydney Grammar School. Enlist 13.9.15 aged 19, engineering student from Strathfield. 15th Rfts 3 Bn - 55 Bn - 1st Bn A Coy; Severe frost bite and neuritis Ypres Feb 1918; KIA 18.9.18 Hesbecourt France by shell fire. Buried Hesbecourt Cemetery exhumed to Roisel Communal Cemetery Extension.	364, 366, 371, 398, 403
*BULMER, Walter Edgar, Pt., Enlist age 18, Farm hand, 23.8.15. 12 Rfts 1st Bn., *Ivernia* to Marseilles with Ben. KIA 25.8.16 Buried in vicinity of Pozieres. – Villers -Bretonneux Memorial. Pic AWM	260
*BULMER Robert Henry, Sgt., Enlist 24.8.14. age 24, pattern maker of Carlton Sydney. Brother to above. 1 Field Amb. 3rd Bn, KIA 16.7.15 Anzac., Shrapnel Valley Cemetery.	260

*BURRIN David James, Lt., Enlist 1st Rfts 1st Bn 15.10.14. born ENG. aged 24 years, clerk and orchardist. Previous military experience. Gallipoli GSW Wound R hand and left leg to ENG. Re-joined Bn 15.5.16. Wounded Pozieres 22.25.7.16 GSW r leg severe to ENG. To 1st Bn. 18.12.16 Officers School Cambridge. Mustard Gas Shell at Messines 19.3.18 to ENG. Made Lt. 15.5.18. KIA 23.8.18. Heath Cemetery Harbonnieres	389, 419
BUTCHARD W.J. Sgt., MM. Enlist 12.1.15. 5 Rfts 1st Bn. Aged 23, labourer, born Darlinghurst mother of same. Wounded Gallipoli BW leg and arm. L/Corp 12.3.16. Pozieres wounded 21.6.16 wounded GSW neck mastoid serious to Eng. Re-joined Bn 16.1.17 Bronchitis. made Sgt 19.7.17. RTA *Delta* 3.2.19 MM dated Hargicourt 18-21.9.18	220
*BURSTALL Richard Stewart, 2/Lt., Enlist 5.6.15 age 23, Stock and Station agent. Father address Inspector in charge Bank of NSW, Townsville, then Brisbane then Sydney. 15 Rfts 1st Bn., KIA 25.7.16 Poziers, France. Unknown grave. Villers-Bretonneaux Memorial	218, 241, 244
BUTCHER Arthur Albert, Lt., MM 1.11.17, Enlist 1.7.1915 aged 23, Motor mechanic of *Brundah* Buller Rd Artarmon, 10 Rfts 8th Army Service Corps, 301st Coy Mechanic Transport Army Services Corp, Motor Transport Driver ex mechanic. RTA 7.7.19 *Chemnitz* Discharge Nov 1919. Married 22.5.20. Emilie Kathleen Austin died 1957. Also served WW11. Enlist 6.1.42 to 18.10.43 as Lt. Died Newcastle 1975. His brother	510, 686, 688, 693, 694
BUTCHER Sydney Alfred. He also served	
BUXTON Jack Oscar, Corp., Enlist 17.8.14 age almost 21, Engineer with Clyde Engineers Coy. 3rd Bn 1st AIF, Wounded Gallipoli ear/deafness and wound back and knee. Admitted Malta 24.5.15 RTA *Suevic* 8.10.15 Discharge 21.5.16 Became recruiting sergeant. Lived at 73 Lindsay St Hamilton Newcastle, Died 1961 Hamilton	537, 563, 630
BYERS James L/Corp., MM. Enlist 26.5.15 aged 29 years, labourer, born and father of Nth Sydney. Previous British Territorials, left to go to sea. 7th Rfts 1st Bn., On *Orsova* with Ben. Wounded Gallipoli. L/Corp 26.10.16 Pigeon School of Instruction. MM 20.7.17 Wounded 5-8.5.17 Demicourt both legs. R thigh amputated. RTA *Anchises* 1.11.17 Discharge 3.7.18 Died 1941	
BYRNE Jack Edington, Gunner, Enlist 9.2.17 aged 18 Agri. Student, *Aloha* Grosvenor Rd, Wahroonga. 28 Rfts 1st Field Artil. Bgde to 10th Field Artillery Bn. Wounded mustard gas 1.6.18. RTA disembark 20.8.19 *Frankfurt* Discharge 13.9.19. Married Gladys Phillips 1923. Sister Jess Byrne. Also served WW11 Citizen Militia	477, 603, 604, 619, 649

C

CALLAWAY Edward, Driver, enlist 1.9.14, born Mudgee, cook, aged 34 years Sister Mrs W Price, Ashfield. RTA 23.10.18 *Durham* Discharge 22.2.19	
CARROLL *Bert* Herbert Buckworth, Lt., Enlist 28.9.15 age 22, Uni student engineering, father address Marrickville. 4th Rfts D.A.C. to 25 Battery 7th Field Artil. Brigade. 3.6.17 Evac wounded GSW thigh, severe, damage to Sciatic nerve. RTA 13.12.17 H.M.A.T. *Beltana*, struck off 11.6.18 medically unfit. Bert transferred to Medical school as Engineering difficult with his damaged leg and eventually became an E.N.T. specialist, 193 Macquarie Street Sydney. Married and had two boys. See other Carroll family under Franks connections.	359, 427, 480, 508, 518, 540, 545, 563, 574, 616, 673, 675, 682
CARSTAIRS George James, Pt., 24 Rfts 1st Bn., Enlist 24.1.17, aged 18, Porter, mother lived Leichhardt NSW. 1st Division football team. Injured whilst playing football. Played Australia 1921-22 against England. RTA *Boorara* 6.7.19. Died war causes 1966	408
*CARTER David William, Sgt., Enlist 3.9.16 age 22, shunter railways from Goondiwindi QLD. 1st Bn, GSW Gallipoli. *Ivernia* to Marseille with Ben, KIA 22- 25.7.1916 in the field Pozieres. Pozieres British Cemetery, France.	239
CASSIDY John, Lt., 3rd Pioneer to 41st Bn. RTA *Wandilla - Kanowna* to travel as cot case. Wounded 27.4.18, perforating GSW entry over left supra scapular, exit lumbar region, thorax injured, heart displaced, # scalp. Struck of strength 25.6.18 Declared medically unfit 1.11.18. Died 1956	448, 452
*CASSIDY Robert Alfred *DIck*, 2/Lt., Enlist 29.9.14 age 22, labourer of Redfern. A Coy 1st Battalion, 6.8.15 Wounded Lone Pine BW knee. Wounded 22.25.7.16 Pozieres + shell shock. KIA 9.4.17 Dernicourt France. Buried Dernancourt, 6 miles NNW Gouzeancourt. Exhumed / interred Hermies Hill British Cemetery.	156, 178, 309, 323, 332, 337, 420
CHAMPION Ben William, Lt., Enlist 22.5.15 aged 18, dental apprentice to Donald Smith, Father T.S. of *Jura* Stuart St Wahroonga. 5'9 'fair complex, eyes grey, hair brown. 7th Rfts 1 Bn., 1) Gallipoli 29.11.15 Wounded SW and malaria to St Elmo Military Hospital Valetta Malta, 15.4.16 School of Instruction, Outersteers. 29.12.16 School of Instruction France 23.5.17 Command 1 ADBD as instructor. 24.5.17 No 1 Training School to Central Training School at Havre. 7.7.17 Depot Class TB Havre 5.7.17 returned to Base Dept as Instructor Havre 19.7.17 Michelham Convalescent Hospital Dieppe (see over)	

CHAMPION Ben William (cont) 2) 17.9.17 SW France to Duchess of Westminster Hospital La Touquet. 14.12.17 Commandant Mt Kemmel, 22.3.18 2nd Arm musketry School and 3)15.4.18 SW leg compound # France severe, leg amp to 3rd London Hospital Wandsworth then to Moreton Gardens 30.5.18 England. RTA 25.6.18, HT *Wandilla to* Suez then trans-shipped H.T. *Kanowna,* 16.7.18, Medically unfit 5.4.19. Married Frank in 1923. Two girls	419
CHAMPION Herbert, Sapper. Enlist 2) 19.11.17 (musician) electrician, aged 24 years, married 1 child, N.O.K. wife Vera, Father T.S. Champion of Stuart St, Wahroonga. Joined first as Trumpeter Light Horse Band then second enlistment to Engineer Rfts, trained through EOTS (Engineers Officer's Training School) 1st Field Sqdn Engineers. RTA 3.8.18, H.T. *Wandilla.* Discharge medical unfit 4.7.19. Was Band Master at Hornsby aged 17 years. Band master 45 Battalion post war and Tuggerah Lakes District Band. Married Vera Barlow. His son-	
CHAMPION Roy Edwin WW11.Source his children Gary and Kaye. Dad was in New Guinea on the Kokoda Track. Then in Hiroshima as part of the occupation forces. Lived on a small boat apparently with a dog. Was there as a driver to an American General I believe. Then went briefly to Korea when the war began there. Was 15 when he enlisted. I am trying to track down a pic of Dad with a mate during the war on the Golden Stairway section of the track. I believe this pic was used as a window display in Myer Melbourne to encourage people to buy war bonds.	xiii, 806
CHAMPION Keith Henry, Pt., Enlist 15.5.18 aged 19, clerk of Stuart St, Wahroonga. Rfts 3 Bn, Appendicitis bronchitis nephritis. RTA *Euripides* Sydney 20.4.19. Discharge 26.6.19. Married 1925 Canberra, Edna Alexandra Horsburgh 1903-1969. Two children. Died 1973	
*CHAPMAN Alfred George Pt., Enlist. 22.8.14 aged 28, salesman, Redfern, Sydney. D Coy 1st Bn., wounded x 2 then KIA head blown off when with Ben when he was wounded 29.11.15 Gallipoli. Shell Green Cemetery Gallipoli Peninsula	119
CHAPMAN William Simeon Bailey, Lt., Enlist 30.9.15 born Camperdown Sydney 19 years bank clerk, 25th Div. Cyclist Corps to 2nd Anzac Cyclist Bn to 17 Bn. 24.5.18 GSW # arm amputated RTA *Kanowna* with Ben	446, 462

CHEDGEY Hubert Victor, Lt., Enlist 26.4.16 aged 23, solicitor, father at Arncliffe. 3rd Div. cyclists Bn to 1st Bn., 26.4.16 wounded penetrating GSW (bomb) to chest, abdo. and l arm severe., RTA *Argyllshire* to Sydney 22.9.19., Discharge fit 24.9.19. C/- R N Henderson 88 Pitt St Sydney	398, 403, 407
CHESLYN Harry George, Corp., MM., Enlist 29.8.14 aged 24 fireman born London. To Head Quarters Signallers. Enteric Gallipoli. L/Corp 27.4.15. Trench fever. 30.11.16. GSW upper arm France 22.4.18. MM 13.9.18. Transport Duty *Kaiser Hind* RTA *Devon* Discharge 23.1.19. Died 1940	251
*CHISHOLM Forester Joseph Joe Milthorpe, Pte, Enlist 21.5.15. born Sydney, aged 25, book keeper accountant, mother of Marrickville. To Peninsula 7th Rfts 1st Bn. Influenza pneumonia with cardiac complications to Alexandria to Cairo. RTA *Runic* 18.4.16 Discharge 24.9.16 medical unfit Died 25.7.1927 Prince of Wales Repat. Hospital due to war Service Both parents deceased at death and one brother Lt. AIF.	
CLARKE Claude Augustus, Lt., Enlist 3.5.16. Born Dubbo. aged 26. Clerk. father of Bathurst. Officer Training School Duntroon 30.8.16. 25 Rfts 1st Bn., Lt., 24.11.17 Flu, 3.6.18, Wounded GSW face mild 23.9.18. Shell wound to knee mild 19.7.18. GSW back 19.9.18 to Eng. To 1st Bn 24.12.18. 1st Bgde HQ as town mayor Gougnies 8.3.19. RTA *Wiltshire* 4.7.19. Discharge 19.9.19. Meteren Photo	391, 419
CLARKE, Gallipoli *swaggy*. Could be CLARKE John, Sgt., Enlist 27.1.15 aged 44, carpenter, born Mudgee, wife of Enmore Sydney. Embarked 25.6.18. 5 Rfts 1st Bn. Wounded 7.8.15 BW hip to Heliopolis, 3.9.15 SW head, Hospital jaundice 23.11.15 Changed to 53 Bn Tel- l- Kebir. GSW back/chest to Boulogne to Eng., Influenza. 11.4.17 RTA *Nestor* 22.10. 1917 senility. Discharge 22 10.17 Died 30.7.51	109
*CLELAND Albert Victor Vic., Gunner, enlist 20.10.15 Born Sydney, aged 27, sales- man, father of Stanmore. 13 Rfts 1st Field Artillery to 14 Field Artillery DAC Cairo. 24.1.16. Gassed 29.10.17 Died Gas poisoning 6.11.17 Bur Boulogne Eastern Cemetery.	386
CLEPHANE James, Pt., driver, Enlist Sydney 3.3.16 born SCOT, aged 24 Milk carter, Cootamundra. Previous Territorial 7thBn Royal Scots to 20 Rfts A Coy to C 1st Bn, wounded France GSW arm and shoulder. Followed Ben at Mt Kemmel Command, Married girl from Leith 23.4.19. RTA *Aeneas* Sydney 12.7.19.	397
*CLOUSON Bert, Pte, 6th Bn late 2nd Pioneers, aged 24 years, labourer, born VIC. Influenza 1.5.16 KIA Villers- Bretonneaux	552

CLOW Henry Alfred, Lt., Enlist 17.9.14 Born London, aged 30 years, chauffeur, Sister of Eng. Previous military experience. 6th Aust. Light Horse, trooper. S/Quarter Master Sergeant 28.9.15. Hospital, to 1st Bn 6.9.16 to 4th Bn to 1st Bn. Cadet School of instruction 3.4.17 Wounded 21.9.17 GSW # arm. made Lt 24.11.17. Wounded. 30.1.18 GSW R arm # compound RTA *Euripides* 22.3.18 Discharge 26.8.18	370, 371, 379
COLLINS Archibald John, Major, MC., DSO., Enlist 4.10.15. Medical practitioner, age 25 years, born Lismore, mother of Randwick. AAMC Capt 1.10.15 RTA *Wiltshire* 26.8.19 Discharge 27.10.19	267
* COOK Reginald Reg Hastings, Pt., Enlist 26.5.15 aged 21, warehouse man of Sydney City. 7th Rfts 1st Bn., KIA Larges Post, Gallipoli by sniper 25.11.1915. Shell Green cemetery, Gallipoli	115, 126
*CONCANON George Lewis Blake enlist 27.8.1914, ex Sherwood Foresters, he was already serving with 19th Inf. AMF in command of Hornsby Coy. (19b with Ben). c/o National Bank of Australia and *Moylagh* 21 Cleveland St Wahroonga (Now St Lucy's School) 2 Bn KIA 27.4. 1914 Gallipoli. Married with a daughter Patricia. Buried where he fell. Lone Pine Cemetery Memorial-see photo group 19b	2, 3, 691
*CORMACK James Alexander Alex McDonald. Gunner was in 19B with Ben. Enlist 16.12.15 aged 18 years postal assist. Only child. Parents Kintore St., Wahroonga. 1st Rfts. 7th Field Artill. Brig., KIA 23.7.17 Messines Ridge. Buried Kandahar Farm Military Cem. Belgium.	3
COX Horace, Pte, Enlist 16.7.15. Born ENG, lorry driver-labourer. aged 23 years. Wife of Nth Sydney. 11 Rfts 1st Bn, on *Ivernia*. 21.7.16 shell shock buried Pozieres Abrasion to knee to ENG. Absent. To 63 Bn 28.4.17 – 18.9.17 to 1st Bn 19.9.17 RTA *Persic* 14.2.18 medical unfit, chronic bronchitis, tachycardia Discharge 2.5.18	383
CRAIG Robert Gordon, Lt. Col., Enlist 10.5.15 age 45 years Civil Surgeon of 185 Macquarie St Sydney. Medical Officer ships. 17.6.15 Australian Medical Corp. Re-signed commission to Surgical Specialist at No 4 AGH Randwick, NSW	467, 471, 473, 486, 492, 546
CRUISE Albert John Lt., M.B.E. Enlist aged 29, accountant, wife living at Chatswood. Enlisted 19th Rfts 1st Bn to Gallipoli RTA 20.1.16 *Karoora* from Suez with enteric and pneumonia via Malta. Returned to Action *Wiltshire* 22.8.16., 1st Bn to 1st Div. Salvage Coy. RTA HT *Takada* 1919. Discharged 7.11.19	405

*CUDDEFORD Ralph Sydney, Pt., Enlist 4.7.15 at Holdsworthy, aged 22 bank clerk. 12 Rfts 1st Bn, B Coy, KIA 23 July 1916 vicinity of Poziers, body not recovered, Villers-Bretonneau Memorial. Ben has Sgt. Photo AWM	239
CUNNEEN William John, Pt., Enlist aged 22 years, bootmaker from Dubbo. 7th Rfts 1st Bn to 45 Bn. Sick+ deserter, RTA *Delta* to Sydney 22.3.19. Discharged 8.4.19. medically unfit 17.5.19.	161
CUNNINGHAM Stanmore school	225

D

DAVIDSON James Sydney, Corp., Enlist 21.5.15 aged 23, clerk Dulwich Hill. 7th Rfts 1st Bn., wounded 1) 15.4.17 2) 10.9.17 GSW head severe RTA *Persic* from Eng. 14.2.18, transhipped RMT *Ormonde* for Sydney. Discharged medically unfit 26.6.18	93, 126
*DAVIDSON William, Major, born 1866 Scotland. Wife Annie living in Oatley NSW. Capt. made Major 26.4.15 Gallipoli transferred from Head Quarters to A Coy 1st Bn 30.5.15. Died of wounds 16.8.15 GSW R Side died at sea buried *Guildford Castle*. Memorial Lone Pine Gallipoli	111, 119 787
*DAVIDSON John Charles, 2/Lt, enlist 24.9.15 13 Rfts 1st Bn. Aged 21 years, carpenter, father James of Bellingen. A Coy. Accidentally killed, Shot to abdomen at Moubecau Rifle Range 3.6.16. Buried Hazebrouck Cemetery. 1st Bn., AWM photo. Sgt Archie Barwick in his diaries also of 1st Bn said that Lt Davidson was the son of Major Davidson but records show he was the son of James Davidson of Bellingen.	787
DAVIS William James, Corp., Enlist 17.5.15. Born QLD, aged 23, tinsmith, father of Adamstown Newcastle. on *Borda*. Corp to L Sergeant 8.5.16 Wounded hand 22.7.16 Gallipoli to Alexandria RTA *Beltana* 17.3.17 Amputated left forearm. Discharge 20.10.17	
DAVIS Harold Hand, Lt., MC., Enlist 23.8.14 born Eng., aged 27, railway shunter. 2nd Bn. Influenza Cairo, 5.10.16 Officer Cadet School Oxford. to 1st Bn 22.2.17 made Lt., Wounded GSW R thigh 7.10.17, Signalling officer vice Lt., Bruton. Measles Returned 1st Bn 15.11.17 RTA *Khyber* ships subaltern 31.3.19 Discharge 21.5.19 Meteren photo	391, 401, 411, 419, 793
*DEVLIN John, Pt., real name John SHARKEY., Enlist as Devlin 5.5.15 aged 27 years, barber from Belfast Ireland. 7th Rfts 1 Bn., KIA between 5-8 May 1917 Buried vicinity of Bullecourt. Villers-Bretonneau Memorial. John Sharkey died aged 32.	5

DEWAR James Sgt., Enlist 17.8.14. born Glasgow. aged 23 years. labourer, G Coy 1st Bn. Signaller Sgt 6.8.16. Aeroplane Signal School and other Schools of Instruction Granted 75 days leave with pay in Eng. to attend Steel Co - Ltd in Glasgow. Married Elizabeth Lydia Swinney St Mary Cathedral Glasgow 15.4.18. RTA *Megantic* 9.1.20 Discharge 12.3.20	225
DIMOCK Victor Thomas, Sgt., H Coy 1st Bn. Enlist 19.8.14 born New Zealand. 23 years. Wounded Gallipoli bomb to feet and side, many visits to hospital for other reasons. RTA *Somerset* 4.12.18 Discharge 17.3.19. In photo with Yates	794
*DINGLE Henry, 2/Lt., MM., Enlist 8.4.15 aged 21, Commission agent, from Stanmore. 6th Rfts 1st Field Ambulance to 1st Bn., 19.2.17 accidently wounded bomb blast, died 20 Feb 1917 France. Cemetery Dernancourt Communal Cemetery Extension, Bresle near Albert	321, 364
DIXON Phillip Vernon, L/ Corp) Enlist 17.6.15 age 18, Uni student from *Brenty* Warrange St, Turramurra. Also in 19b. 10 Rfts 17th Bn., to 64 Bn Windmill Hill. 28.4.17 to 17 Bn. trench feet 16.11.16 Mumps and 5.10.18 gassed. RTA 2.1.19 *Aeneas* discharge 31.3.19 medic unfit. Uni of Sydney as Bachelor of Medicine 1924 and then General Practice	677
DOBSON Squire Walter, 12 Bn. Enlist 28.8.14 aged 23 years, born SCOT., gardener, enlist Tasmania. Made Lt., 5.11.16. Served Gallipoli wounded, Pozieres, Mouquet Farm, Le Barque wounded, Polygon Wood, Zonnebeke. RTA 20.7.18 Trench art with Ben at Havre	
*DONNELLY Arthur James, L/Corp. Enlist 18.4.15 born Nth Sydney, aged 23 years, carpenter. 6.8.15 sick Gallipoli, re-joined Bn, on *Ivernia*. Wounded 22.26-7.16 Pozieres GSW R Arm. Re-joined 1st Bn. Sick, Sick, Trench Fever Re-joined 10.10.17. Re-joined 30.1.18. Made L/ Corp 11.2.18. Sick re-joined 11.3.18. KIA 15.4.18 Buried Pradelles near Hazebrouck/ Borre. Exhumed to The Grand Hazzard Military Cemetery, He left an illegitimate son	241
DOWNES *Drummy* Charles Edward, Gunner Sgt., Enlist 17.8.14 Ex 2nd Bn Devonshire Regt. England, Africa, India, born India, age 34, musician. 1st Bn, 1st AIF. RTA on submarine guard duty per *Medic* 9.10.18 Discharge 12.12.18. Was on *Ivernia* with Ben from Alexandria to Marseilles 22.3.16 Attached to H.Q. 1st Bn. Ben says an old soldier with curly golden moustaches who liked his rum issue	167

DOWNTON John Hartnell, Lt., Enlist 21.8.14 born Narrabri, aged 20 years, bank clerk, father of Eden. 1st Field Coy. HQ 16.6.15 Gallipoli enteric to Malta. Transferred to 3rd Echelon Base records Did many instruction courses and officer cadet school. 1st Bn 21.8.17. Hospital # lower fibula accidentally to Eng. Made Lt 2.2.18. Re-join 1st Bn 24.2.18. to Hospital cellulitis arm. Wounded SW back 10.8.18 to Eng. 21.9.18 re-joined Bn RTA *Somali* 10.12.18 Discharge 15.4.19	398, 408
*DRUMMOND John Albert *Uncle*, Pte., Enlist 26.5.15 aged 44, railway plate layer, Sister address of Surrey Hills. 7th Rfts 1st Bn., KIA bullet to head, 20.11.15 Gallipoli., Shell Green Cemetery Gallipoli	113, 126
*DWYER William. See Charles Oscar HOPE	321

E

EADE Albert, Sgt., Enlist 14.8.15. born Wallsend, Aged 21, labourer, father of Wingham. Brother in law to JP Brough. 12 Rfts 1st Bn. On *Ivernia*. GSW shoulder 7.5.16. SW L thigh 3.10.17. RTA 31.7.18 HMAT *Osterley* Discharge 21.7.18	280
*EATHER Frank, Sgt., Enlist 3.11.14 aged 30, operator of Windsor, 2 Rfts 1st Bn. Dysentery, Gallipoli. KIA 5-8 May 1917 body not recovered, blown to pieces vicinity of Bullecourt. Court of Enquiry. Villers-Bretonneau Memorial	333
*EDGAR Alexander Joseph, Pt., Enlist 5.8.16, share farmer, mother of Bondi, aged 21, 22 Rfts 1st Bn O Coy. KIA 27.10.17 Ypres. Belgium Battery Corner Cemetery, Ypres Belgium.	384
EDGLEY Louis Norman, Capt., Croix de Guerre Belgium. Enlist 8.5.15 aged 28 merchant of Bathurst. 9th Rfts 4th Bn to 1st Bn., Mumps Tel el Kebir 1.5.16 Wounded abdomen and liver RTA thrombosis femoral vein H.T. *Ruahine* 5.7.18 Discharge 30.11.18, Also on *Ivernia* with Ben. Died 1956.	294, 408
ELLIS Arthur John, Pte, Enlist 6.3.16. Conductor, 18.4.16. 19 Rfts 1st Bn A Coy. Absent. Re-joined Bn 4.7.18 to 2nd Bn. Wounded GSW 16.8.18. RTA *Port Darwin* 28.7.19. Discharge 11.9.19	
ELLIS Horace, Pt., Enlist 16.7.15 born ENG, aged 23 years, labourer lorry driver, wife of Willoughby, .11 Rfts 1st Bn to 63 Bn 28.4.17 -18.9.17 to 1st Bn. RTA *Persic* 14.2.18 medical unfit chronic bronchitis tachycardia. Discharged 2.5.18	
EVANS Arthur. Lance Sergeant. Enlist 20.1.15 born Geelong, aged 36 years, accountant, 7th Rfts 1st Bn., to 53 Tel el Kebir. Wounded GSW abdomen 19.7.16 to Pay Corps 14.12.18 as Lance Sgt. RTA *Konig F August* with wife 6.8.19 Discharge 6.10.19. In 1923 Bull St, Mayfield Newcastle.	49

EVE Richard Dick William, Corp., Enlist 16.5.15 aged 22 draughtsman. Father William Henry of Annandale. B Coy 18 Bn., 5th Inf. Brig., to Anzac Provost Corps. Wounded GSW thigh 4.8.16 2) GSW thigh 23.4.18., RTA *Bahia Castillo* 21.6.20 Discharged 20.9.20. Ben's cousin	365-6
*EVERITT Frank Edward, 2/Lt., Age 22 scholarship to Moore Theological College from England, 14th Rfts 1st Bn D.O.W. 103 Field Ambulance. GSW humorous and gas 20.7.1916, Cemetery Albert Communal Extension France.	241
EVERETT George Lt., Enlist 22.2.16. Born Ultimo, aged 27, dental surgeon. Mother of Woolwich Sydney. Dental apprentice to Mr D Smith Macquarie St. Over 6 foot. (*Pull Through*) Sapper 2nd Engineer Rfts, to 1 Sig Wireless to 16 Dental Unit attached to 12 Light Horse then to 6th LH. Wounded severe Moascar Belah, bomb wound knee and ankle to Abbassia RTA *Neuralia* to Durban then HT *Oxfordshire* then HS *Karoola* to Aust. 28.7.17 Discharge 21.5.18	212, 697, 702
EVERETT Sydney Bedford, Sapper, 30.6.17 born Nth Sydney aged 24 poultry farmer, father of Lucinda Ave Wahroonga Engineer Rfts 4.7.17 RTA *Karmala* 1.7.19 Discharge 10.9.19	

F

*FARLOW John, Pt., Enlist 22.5.15 age 28, drover from Homebush. 7th Rfts.1st Bn., At Gallipoli. On *Ivernia* KIA France between 22-25.7.16 in vicinity of Poziers. – no known burial, Villers- Bretonneaux Memorial; brother FARLOW Henry in 1st Pioneers. His will left all possessions to Oswald Martinere. Witnesses from 1st Bn are G Howell, Pt. A Selkeld, D Thomas Esq, Pt. M Meigenh.	222
FARMER Eric Maynard, Lt., 15 Rfts 3 Bn to 55 Bn., enlist 5.7.15 aged 27, married, Draughtsman Lands Depart. NSW of Dulwich Hill NSW, 2.10.16 Trench Mortar School, 19.8.18 School of Instruction. Displaced cartilage Knee, Wounded GSW buttocks. RTA *Ascanius* 23.9.1919 Discharge 30.9.19	
*FELTON Arthur Art Alfred, Lt., Enlisted with Ben, one I.D. number different, aged 18, analytical chemist, from Junction Rd Hornsby NSW. 7th Rfts 1st Bn to 53 Bn to 4th Bn., KIA 17.4.1918 sniper bullet to head. Buried with two others but later no evidence of bodies, obliterated by shells. Battle of Lys, Strazeele, France, Villers-Bretonneau Memorial wall panel 40, The family home was renamed *Arthursleith* in William St Gordon in 1921.	2, 33, 73, 74, 109, 126.142, 148, 228, 243, 262, 279, 292, 391.397, 415, 439, 777, 794, 821

*FARRY Charles, 2/Lt., 9 Rfts 1 Bn., Enlist 13.6.15 aged 29 years, Grocer, of Ashfield. Parents deceased. On *Ivernia*. Wounded GSW Pozieres. Missing then KIA Broodseinde Ridge 4.10.1917 Menin Gate Memorial, Ypres, Flanders Belgium. NOK Henry FARRY on active service. RTA Discharge 23.3.19. Medals to eldest brother Michael Joseph Farry.	362, 366, 377, 379,
*FINLAYSON Ronald Berry, Lt., 16 Rfts 1st Bn. Enlist 4.1.16 aged 25 years, former bank officer from Wollongong. Sydney Grammar School. Applied for commission. Missing in Action/KIA 5.11.1916 Flers/Gueudecourt. Exhumed to Bancourt British Cemetery Picardie France, East of Bapaume.	294, 323, 324, 364
Brother Captain M.R. FINLAYSON, AAMC. Pic AWM	
FLANNERY Francis Leonard, Lt., vice Bootle, Enlist age 24 years, student BA and final year Faculty of Law of Dulwich Hill Sydney. 6th Rfts 1 Bn, Adj. 1st Aus. Div. Hdqts, Typhoid Gallipoli, 5.10.16 bomb wound to back, sick+++, Granted leave to attend Council of Legal Education Lincoln Inn London RTA *Mahene* 25.9.1919	293, 366, 394, 396, 403, 717
*FLETCHER Alfred Edward, born Francis Edward FLITCROFT, Pt., 4 Rfts 1st Bn., Enlist 8.1.15 aged 24, labourer, fireman, mother of Glebe, Gallipoli (Cook) KIA 22.6.1916 A coy 1st Bn. BW head and breast Wye Farm Cemetery south of Armentieres	222
FLOWER George Victor, Sgt., Enlist 2.12.14 born IRE, aged 27 years, engineer, mother of Islington Newcastle. 2nd Rfts 2 Bn., Wounded Gallipoli 8.5.15 GSW L leg thigh. Wounded Gallipoli 6.6.15 GSW Wounded Gallipoli x 3. 16.8.15 Shrapnel shoulder and chest to Valetta Malta to ENG. Invalided to Aust. per *Kanowna* 11.5.16. Discharge 7.9.16.	705
FOOTT John Lance, Lt., Enlist 19.8.14 aged 25 farmer from Victoria, 8th Bn., wounded head Gallipoli, GSW France, Mustard gas France, 17.7.18 France SW leg amp. R leg severe RTA *Kanowna* Disembark. Melbourne. Discharge 25.10.18	
FORD Bernard Francis, Sgt MM., Enlist 17.9.14 born Armidale, aged 28, Railway Employee, Previous 5th ALH 8 years. AAMC to 1st Bn AMC. Lance Sgt vice Sgt Bingley KIA 29.3.17. Slightly wounded 5.11.16, influenza, MM 15.12.17 and Meritorious Service Medal. RTA *Norman* 20.8.19 for nursing staff. Discharge med unfit 9.4.20	104, 119

FORREST Richard John, Staff Sergeant. Hon Captain. (Quarter Master) MC., Enlist 23.7.15 aged 27 years, born Melbourne, paymaster clerk, father of Geelong. Aust. Pay Corps, Field Cashier 1st Aust. Div. Cairo. Pay Office Boulogne. Pay Office London 10.5.17. QM and Hon Lt.13.7.18, 29.7.17 1st Bn in Field from Pay Corps, Influenza, Military Cross 4.6.18, Re-joined Bn 24.9.18 on Command American Division. RTA *City of Poona* permanent ship staff to Melbourne Discharge 27.7.19 Living Killara 1953. Died 28.4.1960	366, 407, 419
FORREST H F., Lt., MC. Not listed on Nominal roll of 1st Battalion but in Meteren Officers Photo	401, 415, 431, 419
*FOSTER Francis *Frank* Joseph, Pt., Enlist 26 years, married, 2 children from Sydney NSW. 12 Rfts. 1st Bn. D.O.W. 16.6.1916 2nd Aus. Field Ambulance France. Military Cemetery Rue-David near Armentieres east of Levante Fleurbaix Bethune, Nord Pas de Calais France	215
FOSTER Reginald Francis, Lt., Enlist 28.5.15 born Colac VIC, aged 26, clerk, mother of Ballarat. 7th Rfts 14 Bn to 46 Bn Corp, Officer Training Camp Oxford. Wounded GSW severe both legs To Duchess of Westminster Le Touquet then to 3rd London Westminster 13.4.18. RTA 25.6.18 *Kanowna* GSW both legs with Amp right thigh. Discharge 3 MD 1.9.19 Photo ID 5.5. Dark Complex Blue eyes dark brown hair. Ben photos *Kanowna*	449
FOWLER Wallace *Vic* Victor, Lt., *Petit Noir Sergeant* Enlist age 24 years accountant 1st Bn. B Coy., GSW severe R. foot. RTA 10.12.1918 on furlough 1914 leave to Australia *Somali* Terminated 9.4.19 medically unfit. (lived to 93 years +)	181, 206, 207, 226, 230, 231, 269, 392, 403, 410, 420, 540, 551, 561, 602, 649
FUNNELL Eric Winton, Corp. Enlist 10.5.15. Born Cobbity, aged 18, clerk, father of *Arthgarrett*, Bridge Rd, Hornsby. of 19b to 7th Rfts 1st Bn. To 1st Field Coy engineers 12.12.15 to 14th Engineers. Requested discharge in Eng. 22.5.19 to do course in constructional drafting Railway Electric Mounds and then to USA for experience and to return to NSW Railways. Married 25.1.19 in England.	126
FUSSELL John *Jack* Rich, L/Corp., Enlist 15.9.14 born Eng. Seaman, B Coy 4th Bn, 28.5.15 wounded Gallipoli, Amp right thigh RTA 30.4.16 Discharge medic unfit 15.6.16.	499

G

GASCOIGNE-*Roy* Rupert Hugh Lt., Enlist born Narrandera, aged 19, clerk, mother of Nth Sydney. Made Sgt 29.3.15 18 Bn., GSW 28.8.15. Made Lt., 18.1.18. Wounded 2) 15.4.18 GSW R Leg amputated below knee to 3rd General Hospital. RTA *Wandilla* to *Kanowna* Says *Karoola*. MD 2 Discharge 10.4.19 18 Bn.	
GELDARD Herbert Stanley, Lt., MC., Enlist born Armidale, age 23, bank clerk, 7th Rfts., 1st Bn. to 53 Bn at Tel el Kebir, School of Instruction 16.3.16. Corps School. 18.5.17 Wounded GSW hand and thigh to ENG, Wounded gas shell 17.4.18 RTA *Kildonian Castle* 21.3.19 on Duty, Discharge 14.7.19. WWII	152
*GENTLE Clifford Gladstone, Gunner. Enlist 6.11.15, almost 24, clerk, born Armidale NSW. mother of Artarmon, father deceased. KIA 5.6.17. 7th Australian Field Artillery Brig. Belgium, Cemetery Strand Military Cemetery Ploegsteert Wallonie Belgium. Brother of Ben's Sister -in -law Althea nee Gentle, wife of Arthur Champion	228, 359, 407, 414, 672
GOLDER John George, L/Corp., Enlist 21.8.14 aged 27, postal worker from North Sydney. 1st Bn., Gallipoli, flu pneumonia diarrhoea. Egypt. Wounded bomb wound both feet and R thigh, l forearm Re-join Bn 3.11.16 Wounded 5-8.5.18 GSW R thigh. Wounded 14.4.18 GSW R thigh # femur RTA *Suevic* 6.1.19. Discharge medic unfit 4.5.19.	220
*GOODE William *Billy* John, Pt., Enlist teacher, aged 24 years, father near Parkes NSW, 7th Rfts. 1st Bn. DOW 15.12.15 Gallipoli. Cemetery, Chatby War Memorial Cemetery Egypt. Brother	
*GOODE Norman George KIA 3.5.1917	4, 93, 108, 116, 219
*GORRIE, Campbell Robertson, Staff Sgt., Enlist 15.2.17 aged 22, father in Ermington Sydney. Also of *Coorparoo* Grosvenor Rd, Lindfield. 6 LH attach 2nd Bgde Hdqts, Time in Ismailia and malaria x 3. RTA *Madras* 3.8.19. Died Bougainville 1923 of Malaria aged 24 years	147
GRAHAM Frederick Archibald, *Grum* First Enlist 11.8.14 N &MEF. Born Sydney aged 21 carpenter Father of The Spit Mosman. Discharged 4.3.15. Re enlist occupation business proprietor 6.1.16 Tel el Kebir as 2 / Lt 11 Rfts 1st Bn. On *Ivernia* to France.28.4.16 made Lt., 21.7.16 Pozieres, Gas and shell shock severe to ENG. Many schools of instruction. Sickness, knee synovitis, tonsillitis, bronchitis. To 6th Aust. Div. and back to 1st Bn. Ceased to hold rank of Capt. on relinquishing command of A Coy 29.3.18. RTA *Boonah* 20.4.18	234, 241, 299, 394, 409, 410, 419, 425,

*GRANGE, Sgt., 31.10.17. M.M., Enlist 25.2.1915 born Newtown aged 20 years clerk of Wollstonecraft, C Coy 17 Bn., 9.10.17 Missing then KIA Passchendaele. Buried in Vicinity of Broodseinde Belgium.	95
GRANT Robert *Bob* Anthony, Pt., Enlist born Gympie, aged 26 years, student, married, father of Gympie. Gallipoli wounded 6/9-8.15 Compound fracture R femur – to Valetta Malta to Eng. to Egypt Heliopolis. Amputation R leg severe. on return tranship *Kanowna* 28.1.16. Discharge 2.11.16	624, 625, 641, 780
GRAY John Lt., MC. Enlist 13.3.16 born QLD, aged 31 years, station hand. NOK England. 19 Bn., Enteritis, Wounded 1917 GSW hand and arm, April 1918 GSW R leg and Abdo contusion 3rd London Hosp to 6th Aust. Aux Hospital (Moreton Gardens) RTA stretcher case *Kanowna* with Ben. Discharge 6.4.19. Lived in Mosman, NSW	441, 449, 452 462, 678
GREEN Roland Frederick Herbert, Lt., Enlist 19.12.14 aged 28 years, married. 6th LH to 6th Bn. GSW at Menin Road Belgium Sept.1917, Amputated mid-thigh. Has RTA *Karoola* but we know RTA 22.7.18 per *Wandilla* tran- shipped H.T. *Kanowna* from Suez with Ben 4.9.18. MD 2. 1922-1937 MLA Country party for Richmond, House of Representatives. Married 1924. Died 1947 Photo	448, 449, 450, 452, 479, 486, 569, 573, 672, 678
GREEN Edward Prior, Lt., Enlist 29.8.14 born ENG, aged 25, joiner. 4th Bn., Severely wounded 1916 then GSW thigh 1918. RTA 22.7.18 per *Wandilla* trans-shipped H.T. *Kanowna* from Suez. MD 2 With Ben. Died 1950	452, 462
GREIG Allan, Pt., enlist 22.10.18, 21 years, chemist, of *Glen Ayr*, Burns Rd Wahroonga. Dux of Eltham College Wahroonga 1910. Prize given by Dr Reid, neighbour of Ben.	78, 521, 547, 566, 661
*GRIFFIN, Keith Eric, L/Corp., 13 Rfts 1 Bn., Enlist 30.8.15 Newcastle, born West Maitland, Mother Jeanne of Hinton Morpeth, aged 21 years, public servant –Customs. GSW head DOW 29.7.1916 No 26 General Hosp Etaples France. Etaples Military Cemetery (for photo comparison 5.8, fair complex, fair hair with blue eyes. pic AWM Ben had a copy and marked it. Mrs Griffin now Mrs Loddon, Kenilworth Hinton	498.248 511, 536, 546, 561, 598, 682
GRIFFITHS Francis Lt., Enlist 13.10.14, aged 21, Grazier Coonabarabran, NSW then Stock and Station agent in Sydney, NOK brother Dr F Guy Griffiths of Killara and Macquarie St (4 brothers at war) 6 LH, wounded Gallipoli amp finger damaged hand RTA AUS 17.5.16. Re embark and return to duty. 30.10.16 1st Bn. Many schools of instruction. Made Lt. Demicourt 11.4.17 Influenza, trench fever, Wounded Hazebrouck R leg and abdomen. Divorced. Suicide in 39th year. RTA 28.2.19 *Anchises* Other brothers	362, 365, 419

Dr GRIFFITHS Frederick Guy,	
* Dr GRIFFITHS John Neville KIA Bapaume,	
* GRIFFITHS Hugh KIA Gallipoli Lone Pine	
HAILE John Lindsay, Pt., Enlist 10.10.16. aged 21, farmer born Woodberry Tarro, father address c/- Tarro Railway Station. 53 Bn, shell shock and trench fever, GSW arm & leg. RTA 3.2.19 *Orontes*, Medical unfit 5.3.19	
HAILE William Henry, Pt., Enlist 24.10.16 aged 22, printer, Father Thomas of Woodberry Tarro. 53 Bn., Shell gas severe. RTA *Kildonian Castle* 21.3.19. Discharged 17.6.19	54, 492, 533, 538, 576, 593, 648
GRIFFITHS C.H. Lt., 57 Bn., aged 34. Doctor of Dentistry, born Inglewood. *Kanowna* 3 MD	

H

*HAMBLING Charles, Pt. Enlist 5.7.15. Tile maker b Liverpool aged 21 years, B Coy 10 Rfts 1st Bn Wounded 22-25.7.16 GSW r hand to hospital Rouen re-joined 1st Bn 26.8.16. Wounded 27.9.16 GSW head to hosp. Rt Bn D Coy., 3.11.16. KIA 5.11.1916 at Flers. Villers- Bretonneaux Memorial	
HAMILTON Latham, Lt., Enlist aged 22 years, chemist, born New Zealand father of same. G Coy 3rd Bn 17.8.14. Gallipoli Pleurisy diarrhoea to Div. Salvage Corps to 1st Bn Div. Salvage Corps. 22.1.17 to 3rd Bn. made Lt., 1st Bn 24.11.17. Synovitis knee, sick ++ Wounded 11.5.18 GSW multiple leg at Ypres to Eng. RTA *Borda* Discharge 20.2.19	391, 438, 441
*HAMPTON Sydney Victor Syd, l/Corp., 7th Rfts 1 Bn., Enlist 21.5.15 aged 22 years, clerk of Marrickville. 1.8.16 1st Charge at Pozieres. Brother carried him to 2/1 South Midland Casualty Clearing Station Warloy, transferred to Warloy Hosp D.O.W. G.S.W. abdomen. Buried Warloy Baillon Community Cemetery Extension, Warloy	126, 263-4
HAMPTON C.W. Pt, 1ˢᵗ Battalion	
HANSEN Carl James, Sgt., Farmer aged 33 years. 7th Rfts 1st Bn., to 5th Machine Gun Bn, Wounded GSW face. (total x 3 times wounded) RTA 25.5.19 *Trans Montes* discharged Sydney, medically unfit.	
HARCOURT Cecil Andrew, Sapper., Enlist 4.12.16 age 26, store keeper with wife born Sydney, 2 Signallers Sqd. Engineers, Wireless operator., RTA *City of Exeter*, debility 2.3.19. Franks cousin	492
HARRIS, (Sister), Valetta Hospital Malta, then Cammerata Valetta Malta. Have checked online resources but no luck	128, 136, 141, 166

HART William Eric Ewart, Lt., Enlist age 30, born Parramatta, Dental Surgeon to Australian Flying Corps as 1st Lt – Perm unfit due to Epilepsy was Pioneer of Aviation in Australia and was in contact with Dept of Defence 1912. Hyde Park Camp City. Interesting history	
HASLAM Hector Albert, Lt., Enlist7.9.14. Born Vic, bank clerk, aged 20 years. 11 Bn to 51st Bn. Wounded Gallipoli. Wounded 15.8.16 Pozieres, GSW# fibula to ENG. Made Lt. 1.12.16. Cellulitis of hand. ADAD Havre. 1.6.17. To Duchess of Westminster Hospital Le Touquet 14.10.17. 26.4.18 SW l foot to ENG 3rd London Gen Hospital. RTA *Dimboola* 29.12.18 Discharge 11.3.19 to Western Australia. Died 1965. Trench Art at Havre with Ben	
HAWKINS Alfred Roy, Lt., Enlist 1.9.14, born Narrabri, aged 23 years, horse trainer. Gallipoli wounded x 2, 6-9/5/15 BW thigh Re-join Bn 19.8.15. *Ivernia* with 1st Bn to France 8.6.16. Pozieres shell shock then to 54 Bn to 55 Bn. made Lt. 27.6.17. Bombing officer to 14 Tng. Bn to 2nd AUS Div. Admin HGTRS London to 1st Tng. Bn. RTA *Nevasa* Discharge 10.5.19 Died 1942	285
HAWKINS Maurice Hunter, Pt., Enlist born Sydney, aged 21, Commercial traveller, father of Lindfield. At 19b with Ben. 16 Rfts 3rd Bn., Wounded GSW head slight. 3.5.17 then eye troubles Pleurisy, RTA HMAT *Suevic* 20.11.17 Discharge 21.12.17	3, 514
HEANE James, (Brig-Gen), CB, CMG, DSO, VD, Croix de Guerre. Enlist 3.9.14 aged 40 years, Accountant/Orchardist, Beecroft Pennant Hills, Mother of Dubbo. Illustrious career-see in full, National Archives of Australia, Capt. Heane applied for commission from 4 Bn to LH Reg to 2nd Inf. Bd-1st Inf. Bd. to 1st Bn. Wounded Lone Pine and Gueudecourt. Assumed Command of 1st Bn 15.1.16, - replace Colonel Smythe as Command 1st Inf. Brigade to 2nd Inf. Bgde. RTA *Euripides* 6.9.19. Appt terminated. 7.1.20. Died 20.8.1954.	148, 149, 161, 167, 175, 186, 193, 205, 230, 231, 242, 258, 259, 261, 280, 294, 298, 300, 301, 307, 400
HEDLEY Ernest Barnes (Barnes- Hedley). CSM and WO11 and Lt. Enlist 22.8.14. Born London, aged 28 years, engineer, mother of ENG. B Coy 1st Bn 17.8.14 –1.9.14 Machine Gun Section 1.9.14, Made Sgt 4.3.15 to 1st Bgde Machine Gun Coy. CSM and WO11 10.4.16 of 1st Bgde Machine Gun Coy. Discharged AIF 4.4.17 Joined Royal Flying School 30.10.16 Became Lt., Barnes- Hedley living in Killara 1946.	382

HENDERSON Alan Stuart, Gunner. Enlist 23.4.17 aged 18, student, father of 271 Edgecliff Rd Woollahra., 31 Rfts – 7th Field Artillery. RTA 25.3.19 Discharge 5.6.19 Fort Denison. After war Gordon Road Lindfield. Graduated Dentistry 1923 with Ben. L.C. Henderson 4 Castlereagh St City	617, 626, 632, 633, 642, 644, 645, 658, 668, 672, 676, 680, 689, 706, 779
* HESKETH Leonard Wykham, Pt., Enlist 23 years, railway signalman of *Kanevalla* Station St, Pymble. Mrs. Hesketh. 9th Rfts., 1st Bn A Coy., KIA 20.8.16. sniped near Courcelette in the hollow and Mouquet Farm. Villers-Bretonneaux Memorial, Picardie France.	206, 259, 260, 304, 479, 600, 603, 625
HESLOP Joseph Bagshaw, Lt., MC., Enlist. 23.8.15 Melbourne aged 21, manager boot factory, 2nd Field Artillery, GSW knee 6.5.17 Amputation. RTA *Kanowna* with Ben. Disembark 1.9.18 Melbourne. MD 3 Struck off 22.7.18. *Fairholm* 46 Riversdale Rd, Hawthorn Melbourne.	448, 449, 450
*HIGGINSON Ernest Everard Chester, *Chas*, Sgt., C Coy 2 Bn., Enlist 17.8.1914 aged 21, Porter in Charge of Trans shipment yards, Mother of West Maitland, only child. KIA 20.5.16 Gallipoli. Buried Browns Dip Cemetery. exhumed to Lone Pine Cemetery.	22, 28, 113, 117
HODGE Russell Frederick, *Fred*, 2/ Lt has Lt on record too., Enlist 21.8.14, born Hill End, aged 20 years, teacher, father of Hill End. 1st Bn to 1st Pioneers. Gallipoli dysentery and rheumatism. L/ Corp 22.4.15, 1st Pioneer Bn 10.3.16. Sgt 15.3.16 Schools of instruction. Warrant Officer 1.3.18, 2/ Lt 2.1.19. Was at Coffs Harbour High School in 1935. RTA *Ascanus* 9.2.19 as ship subaltern. Discharge 9.2.19 WW11 died before Gallipoli medal	226
HOLCOMBE Tristram Essex Young, Lt., Enlist 17.8.14 aged 20 years, clerk, Mother Magistrate of Forbes also of Hunters Hill. 4th Bn GSW knee Gallipoli, St Elmo Hospital Malta. RTA *Kanowna* 29.1.16 Discharged. Re-joined 7.11.18. Friend of Teitzel in Malta 4 Bn. Photo ID in Malta	133

HOLDEN Leslie Hubert, Capt. and Squadron Commander. Aus. Flying Cross and MC. Enlist 26.5.15 aged 26 years, salesman, of Turramurra, NSW. Was in 19b Ku ring gai E Coy, 4th Light Horse Brigade HQ aged 20 of *Lynwood* Winton St Turramurra, father gave consent. 2nd Aust. Bn., 5.12.1916 To Royal Flying School military aeronautics to No 2 Sqdn AFC to 6 Training School Squadron 28.4.18 RTA *Kaiser Hind* 18.8.19 Discharge. Married 1924. On return did aerial tour of NSW in support of the Commonwealth Government's Peace Loan. Found the missing Southern Cross and her pilots Charles Kingsford Smith and Charles Ulm. As a passenger he was killed in air disaster 1932	3, 597, 598, 608
*HOLLINGWORTH Roland Edwin, Pt., Enlist 16.11.1915. 1st Vet section to mobile vet section to D coy 1st Bn., age 19, agriculture student, born Sydney, father Albert Charles Hollingworth of 2 Grosvenor Gardens, Muswell Hill London, Also AMP Society 37 Threadneedle St London. Lewis Gun School of Instruction, 5.11.1916 Missing then KIA Flers north of Gueudecourt, exhumed to Grevillers British Cemetery, Picardie France- *attacking waves of troops were sucked down by cloying mud and they were unable to keep up with the creeping artillery -became easy targets for German machine gunners and riflemen*	278, 324, 339, 396
*HOPE Charles Oscar, Pt., Enlisted see William DWYER. Born Cowra, aged 21 years, labourer. Enlist Bathurst. 6 Rfts 33 Bn to 9th training Bn to 1st Bn 10.6.17 Havre. Sworn declaration that his correct name is Charles Oscar Hope, father James Hope and his mother states his age as 18 years and 5 months. Former employee of ES Twiggs, Mayfield Estate. Given watch by Rev. James Barr on behalf of Mayfield and Mulyar friends on rail departure. KIA 3.10.17 Belgium. 3rd Battle of Ypres -Passchendaele. Effects not returned to family. Menin Gate Memorial Ypres.	321
* HOLT., Gordon Cyril, 2/Lt., 2nd Bn – 1st Bn from Enlist 24.8.14, Mother lives Newcastle, born Wilcannia. Wounded 1)1.11.16, 2)23.7.16, 3)5.5.17 and DOW SW head # skull 4) 9.10.17 Bur Lijssenthoek Military Cem. Near Poperinghe Belgium.	
HORNIMAN Robert Geoffrey, Capt., MC for Hargicourt15.2.19., Enlist 6.4.14 born Hinton, age 24, clerk, from C Coy 17th Bn to Depot Training Bn to 8th Rfts 3rd Bn, 45 Howitzer Bn., 4 Bn 19.3.16. Bomb wound left thigh Fleurbaix 1.7.17. Convalescence at No.6.London Moreton Gardens. School of Instruction 29.11.16, Duty at ADBD 26.8.17, Central Army Training School Havre 28.7.17 and 24.10.17 to 1st Aust. Div. at Havre. 5th Army Musketry School, Training Bn England, Lewis Gun School Tidworth. CO officer 1st Training Bn England back to 4th Bn, 1st NSW Training Bn, Training Corp. Wing France 11.1.19, RTA *Boorawa* 6.7.19. Discharge 12.12.19	227

HOWELL George Julian *Snowy*, Sgt., V.C. Bullecourt and MM Demicourt., 7th Reinforcements 1st Bn joined with Ben, On *Ivernia*. Find full record www of illustrious career during WW1 and afterwards WW11 or on National Archives. Married 1.3.19 St Stephens Presbyterian Church Sydney, nurse Sarah *Sadie* Lillian Yates. Also served WW11 Wedding photo Daily Mail.	308, 335, 505
HOWELL- PRICE brothers are listed under Price	
HUGO Fred, Lt., Enlist 8.2.16 aged 24 electrician from Victoria, 28th Bn late 44th Bn., 28.3.17 SW R leg amputated thigh. RTA *Kanowna* MD6 Struck of Strength 15.7.18	448, 449, 450, 451, 452
*HUMPHREYS Robert *Bob*, Lt., MM., Enlist 22.8.14. born Wollongong. aged 25. Carpenter. father of Eastwood and South Africa. 1st Battalion. On *Ivernia* Many Schools of Instruction. KIA 16.4.18 bur Nth of Strazeele in field, exhumed to Le Grand Military Cemetery near Hazebrouck	
* HUMPHREYS Harry Bolton Pt, KIA Pozieres 22.7.16. 1st Battalion	401, 402, 419
HUNT John *Billy* William, Lt., Enlist 26.5.15. 22 years, comm. Traveller 73 Spofforth St, Mosman. 7th Rfts., 1st Bn., On *Ivernia* 12.4.16 shrapnel wounds, 23.6.16 multiple GSW, 18.4.18 GSW arm severe, 3rd London Gen. Hospital, RTA 22.7.18 *Kanowna* from Suez with Ben. Randwick Hospital treatment to April 1919. See photos on *Kanowna*. Kept records of all enlistments up until 10 Rfts for 1st Bn, at AWM that Penny used. 14 Glen St Bondi	ii, ix, 4, 49, 73, 74, 80, 81, 126, 142, 148, 152, 154, 166, 169, 196, 204, 206, 219, 225-6, 272, 388, 389, 402, 444, 446, 447, 448, 450, 451, 452, 462, 479, 486, 488, 491, 498, 569, 573, 788-9, 820

HUTCHISON Edward James, Sgt., Enlist 19.9.14. born Balmain, aged 20 years, painter, mother of Nth Sydney. 1st Bn. On *Ivernia* L/Corp 12.3.16 Pozieres shell shock 22-25 /7/16 to 62 Bn Windmill Hill. Made Corp 7.5.17, Sgt 8.5.17 Trans to 1st Bn as Sgt 23.2.18. wounded 17.4.18 GSW abdomen, 7.8.17. Ypres SW leg to ENG. to Aust. Inf Base Depot 26.7.18 RTA 13.12.18 HT *Balmoral Castle* 1.2.18. Died 1944	202, 211, 212

I

INCH Clive Stephen, A/Clerk. Enlist 10.2.16, aged 18 years, bank clerk on enlistment, of Junction Rd Hornsby. 4th Bn to 2nd Sqdn to 68 Squadron. Wounded x 2, RTA Acting Flight Sergeant 2nd Sqdn Australian Flying Corps., RTA *Kaiser L Hind* 19.7.19. – Married 1923 Murwillumbah. Town clerk Mullumbimby 1930 Town Clerk Goulburn 1958.	577, 597, 672

J

JACKS Capt., MC. Ox and Bucks Regt. Bull ring Officer	
JACK see 1918 officer not 1st Bn	
JACKSON Albert Edward, Capt., MC. Enlist 22.8.14. born Sydney. 20 years. joiner. Colour Sgt and Coy QMS 22.5.15. Wounded Gallipoli GSW R thigh then double pneumonia to Malta re-joined Bn at Gallipoli. To Tel el Kebir, 53 Bn. 2nd Lt., at Petillon. All his men killed July 1916. Bn Bombing Officer. School of Instruction 3.7.16, 5th Army School 7.7.17. Wounded 20.7.16 GSW wrist and back, to Eng. Wounded 10.4.18 to 3rd London Gen Hospital. Back to unit 12.8.18 for duty with 14 Training Bn. Married Edith Shepherd 11.11.16 at Gillingham ENG. Captain of C Coy 1st Bn with Ben as 2/Lt. RTA 28.3.19 *City of Poona* Discharge 31.5.19. Died 1955	294, 791, 299
JACOBS Harold, Maj., Enlist 21.9.14, aged 25 years, born Hornsby. Officer in 19b., 1st Rfts 4 Bn., Capt. 1st Bn 1.5.15 enteric Nov 1915. To 61st Bn. Made Major 10.12.16 1st Bn. To 1st Bn 15.9.17. To 55 Bn.12.3.16 to 1st Bn., 31.7.16 sick influenza 3.2.18. Wounded 15.4.18 GSW cheek and R thigh. RTA *Derbyshire* OC Troops 2.3.19. Discharge 30.10.19. C/- Commercial Banking Coy of Sydney; 18 Binchin Lane, Lombard St, London; *Orani* Buller Road Artarmon Sydney in 1921	2, 3 , 206, 294, 299, 327, 391, 425, 433, 446, 631
JARVIS Frederick John, Lt., Enlist, school teacher, born Eng., aged 30 years. G Coy 3rd Bn., Enteritis Gallipoli. On leave to Paris 30.11.17. RTA *Aeneas* 22.11.19. Discharge 12.3.20	392

JENSEN Rennie Hendri Vivian, Lt., Enlist bank clerk aged 19 of Ipswich QLD. 5 Aus. Light Horse to 1st Battalion. RTA 20.10.18 *Borda* Discharge 21.9.19. WW11 Capt., age 44, grazier, QLD 15.7.1940 discharge Aus. Intel Corps 10.12.43 Meteren photo and Pioneers.	366, 370, 391, 392, 393, 394, 405, 419
*JOHNS Frederick Charles, Pt. Enlist 26.5.15. 7th Rfts 1st Bn., born London, labourer, aged 23 years, mother England. At Gallipoli parcel from Miss Smith. *Ivernia* with Ben KIA 22-25 7.16 Pozieres.	105,
JOHNSON Geoffrey Allan, Lt., MM as signaller with 107th Howitzer Battery. Enlist 21.12.15 aged 20 of Turramurra. Father William Morley Johnson of *Gainsborough* Turramurra. Bombardier 7th Field Artillery to 3rd Div. Ammunition. RTA *Karmala* 1.7.19. Married 1919 Mary Bella Murdoch dau. of Commissioner Lt- Col Murdoch, later knighted, of *Midhope* Burns Road Wahroonga 1930 elect roll, house furnisher. Established Geoffrey Johnson Wing of Burnside Homes for Babies and Toddlers 1970. Awarded MBE 1966. Sister Miss Nancy Annie Elizabeth Johnson married Capt., John William Wright, DFC., at Wahroonga Presb. Church 24.9.19	282, 402, 483, 547, 548, 564, 569, 586, 596, 608, 616, 624, 626, 631, 638, 639, 640, 643, 649, 671, 674, 679, 680, 687,
JOHNSTON (No E) William John, Lt., Enlist 29.9.15. 20 Rfts 1st Bn., born Glebe, aged 29 years, property salesman, father of Annandale. Made Lt., 5.6.17 Ypres. Wounded SW R leg, groin and R upper arm, Gassed 21.5.18. RTA *Ascanius* 23.1.19	99, 362, 379
JONES *Harry* Henry Smith *Edwin*. Driver. Enlist 6.3.1916 aged 22 years, student, his father of *The Grange* Grosvenor Rd Wahroonga. His father Mr. Harry S. Edwin Jones has presented to the Army Medical Corps a 25 h.p. motor ambulance fully equipped. Mr. Edwin Jones has enlisted in the AMC and will proceed to the front ' where he will drive the car himself. Then assigned to Army Motor Transport Service with the rank of Driver then to England where he served primarily at Parkhouse and Bhurtpore Barracks near Tidworth Camp Wiltshire. 1917 and 1918. ill health and influenza. RTA 22 Sept 1919 *Argyllshire* and was discharged 15 November 1919 Sister Enid Jones. His father Edwin Jones served as Sunday School Superintendent for 32 years at Wahroonga Presbyterian Church later St Johns Presbyterian	515, 524, 528, 604, 605, 649

JONES Frederick Harold, *Shiny Buttons*, Sgt., Enlist 21.6.16. with Ben, born Chester ENG. Father of Birkenhead ENG aged 22 steward and writer. 5.9 inches. 7th Rfts., 1st Bn to 5th Pioneers. Influenza and Pleurisy. Wounded Pozieres RTA *Wahehe* Discharge 30.5.19. Married 1923 aged 28 years to Isabel Jolly. On his death certificate it said he was born Pontypridd Wales and had been in NSW 11 years. He died aged 31years, 6 October 1925 at Prince of Wales Hospital, Randwick, soldier and seaman, of Pulmonary and Laryngeal Tuberculosis with toxaemia. At his death he lived in Balmain and had one son Ronald, aged 1 year. Buried Field of Mars Presbyterian. Note TB in those days and even into the 1960s was a dreadful disease with little treatment and Shiny was probably kept in isolation-PF	105, 192, 194, 195, 213, 217, 221, 222, 490, 491, 495, 498
JUDD Clifford Charles, Lt., MM., Enlist 22.8.14, born Melbourne, aged 22, operating porter. 1st Bn., Wounded scalp Gallipoli. Made 1/ Corp 24.7.15 Pneumonia gastritis 30.12.15. Trans to Audit Section. 2) GSW hand severe 4.10.17 to Duchess of Westminster to 3rd London Gen Hospital. 18.9.18. 3rd occasion, GSW Chest wall, fractured scapula RTA *Nestor* 12.12.18 Discharge 30.6.19	

K

KEEP John Leonard, Lt., Enlist 3.11.15 aged 21, C/- John Keep and Sons Ltd Clarence St, Sydney. Rfts to 3rd Div. Artillery then to 7th Field Artillery Bombardier. To Royal Artillery Cadet School. RTA Orvieto 15.12.19 Discharge 6.2.20 Married 1920 Died 1966	
KEIGHTLEY John Broughton, Sapper, 1st Div. Signal Corps, Engineer Rfts 2 MD Tunnelling Corps. Enlist 19.6.17, aged 35 years, mining Engineer, born Newcastle, Wife The Hill Newcastle. Old injury prior to war aggravated. Amp toe. Was at Moreton Gardens with Ben. Discharged medically unfit in ENG 14.3.19 went to USA	441
KELLAWAY Charles, Capt., Enlist embark 25.9.15 born Lismore, aged 29 years, accountant, mother of Glebe. 11 Rfts. 1st Bn. To 2nd Bn to 1st Bn 16.2.16. on *Ivernia*. Wounded GSW R Buttock 2.7.16, severe to ENG to 6th Aux Hospital Sth Kensington Moreton Gardens 30.7.16. To Michelham Home 24.2.18. 9.8.16 GSW arm Made Captain 21.10.18. Influenza, to Sports Control Board for Duty 2.5.19. RTA *Orsova*. 18.7.19. Discharge 12.12.19	141, 227, 394, 491, 787
KENYON William Duncan. Capt., MC., Enlist 20.7.15 born Toowoomba QLD., aged 33 contractor builder 15 Rfts 15 Bn., Made Captain 5.10.17. Wounded Bullecourt 11.4.17. GSW fractured bones R leg, Amputation below knee. No 3 London Hospital to Moreton Gardens. RTA *Kanowna* with Ben.	

KERSHAW Harold George Augustus, L/Sgt., MM., at Broodseinde 22 Oct 1917. Enlist 12.1.15 aged 19, nurseryman of Billyard Ave Wahroonga. 4th Rfts 13 Bn to 13 Bn Machine Gun section to 4th MG Coy. June 1918 neurasthenia before completing officers training course RTA *Borda* 29.8.19. Married Miss Frances Mary King of Somerset ENG 1920. She came out to marry. The nursery was also in Billyard Ave. Wahroonga. Harold Kershaw planted a rose garden in Wahroonga Park in memory of his father George Wilkinson Kershaw who was a rose specialist who died 1924. Harold also served as a WW1 veteran for home duties in WW11. Had seed distribution business. Died 1968.	2, 65, 89, 153, 196, 243, 297, 347, 480, 493, 519, 565, 599, 608, 609, 613, 614, 622, 633, 634, 641, 648, 660, 670
KERSHAW Raymond Newton, Lt., MC., At Villers-Bretonneau 4.7.18. 22 Machine Gun Coy at Villers- Bretonneau. Enlist 20.3.1916 aged 18 years, uni student. 1916 pneumonia 2nd machine gun Bn., disabled left arm ulnar nerve damage. RTA *Nestor* 12.12.19, Back to Sydney Uni, Rhodes Scholar 1918 to Oxford Went via USA –sick. To Switzerland as Member of League of Nations Secretariat, Married 1925 in Hampstead ENG. Illustrious career as banker and economist 1947 Companion of the Order of St Michael and St George (CMG)	480, 487, 491, 500, 508, 515, 516, 585, 670
*KING Charles Wesley, Driver. Enlist 22.3.15, aged 24 years, born Sydney, motor mechanic, parents Charles and Esther King of Neringah Ave Wahroonga then George St Hornsby. A Coy 17 Bn. Missing KIA 27.8.15 Gallipoli. Lone Pine Memorial. Of St Johns Presbyterian Wahroonga.	
*KIRKLAND Hugh Edward, Capt., MC., Enlist 10.1.15. AAMC born Bathurst aged 23 Medical Practitioner, mother of Lithgow. KIA 3.10.18 buried Roisel Communal Cemetery near Peronne 2nd Aust. Field Artill and also Transport Duty. Brothers. Both had each other as NOK and mother died as well during service so estates to cousin.	
*KIRKLAND William Duncan, Major., MC., Enlist 19.5.16. AAMC, aged 25 years Medical Practitioner mother of Lithgow. 2nd Field Ambulance to 1st Division Artillery. 1.2.17 KIA 22.7.17 at or near Ypres. Reningheist Military Cemetery Poperinghe Belgium	

KIRKPATRICK James Hunter, Driver. Enlist 2.6.15 aged 24 years, lead light worker, mother of Manly.7th Rfts 1st Bn, B Coy to Transport Section. In Corps boxing France. Probably Ben's Champion boxer. RTA *Kildonian Castle* 26.3.19. photo recognition 5'10", fair complex, grey eyes and light brown hair. Brother to below. Both 7th Rfts 1st Bn. 1st Bn Transport	
KIRKPATRICK Richard Sydney, Driver-L/Corp., Enlist 31.5.15, aged 21 years, motor mechanic, mother at Narrabeen. 7th Rfts 1st Bn, Pack Animal driver at Tel el Kebir. RTA *Kildonian Castle* 26.3.19 (Description to identify photos, height 5'8 'fair complex, grey eyes and light brown hair). possibly in photos at Tel el Kebir and with camels in desert.	248,
KIRKPATRICK Frances Clunes Sapper 27.6.18 – 20.11.18 Wireless Training School, age 22 law student apprentice of MacIntosh St Gordon	
KIRKWOOD Noel Edmund, Major, MC., Enlist 27.5.1915 Medical Practitioner Sydney Uni to 1st Aust. General Hospital. To 1st Bn as Medical Officer 12.6.15. RTA 7.3.18 HT *Corinthic* 18.1.18 Discharged 10.7.18	289, 293, 327, 365
KNIGHTLEY Alfred Rainald, Major, MC. Enlisted 25.6.14 aged 29 years to 9 Bn. Officer School. Wounded GSW – Amp R. leg, buttock/ hip, hand, R and L arm to 3rd London General Hospital to No 6 Moreton Gardens. RTA *Wandilla / Kanowna* with Ben 1918	452

L

LACEY James Jimmy at Oaklands. Enlist 5.4.16 born Crows Nest, Labourer, aged 22 years, father of Paddington. 3rd Rfts 33 Bn., Missed embarkation. Deserter Rutherford. Field Service tunic britches and puttees not returned.	552, 532, 576, 590,
LAMBERT Clarence *Clarrie* Charles, Lt., commercial traveller of *Iandra* Clanville Rd, Roseville NSW 7th Rfts., 1st Bn, attached to 1st Light Trench Mortar Battery. RTA *Boonah* 20.4.19.	301, 403
LANDON Sydney Clark, Pt., born Dubbo, aged 21, carpenter, mother of Cronulla Enlist 19 Rfts 1st Bn. Wounded x 3. RTA *Ormond* 4.8.19	330, 331
LANE William Henry, Pioneer Sgt., but comes up as William George on NAA site SERN 2604. Enlist 13.6.1915 born London, aged 44, plasterer, wife Georgina Hannah of 2nd Street, Wentworthville. 8th Rfts 1st Bn., 18.10.15 on *Borda* C Coy. 1st Bn to Bn HG to Sgt Pioneers, influenza, RTA Home Service. Arterio- sclerosis *Demosthenes* 29.9.17 Discharge 15.12.17. Died 26.10.1934. Ben was on *Borda* with father William Henry LANE and youngest son Sidney George Lane met up with other two sons at Alexandria	

LANE Sidney George, Sapper. Enlist aged 21, plasterer, father W.H. Lane of Second St, Wentworthville. 8 Rfts 1st Bn, Field Coy 1st Bn to 14 Field Coy Engineers. Wounded GSW nose, # r eye socket, chest and shoulder. RTA *Port Melbourne* 5.7.19 Discharge 11.6.1920	
LANE Frank Herbert, Corp, Enlist 28.12.14 aged 21 plumber. 14 Rfts 2nd LH Bgde Training end up 4th Inf Bn. RTA *Tranos Montes* 7.4.19 Discharge 25.7.19	
LANE Gordon Lewis aged 22, fireman 4.7.15. Early return to AUS with muscular dystrophy HT *Beltana* 17.3.17	100
* LANSER Henry Miller, 2/Lt., Enlist 2.9.14 motor mechanic, father of Chatswood Sydney, 1st Bn., 6.8.15 Gallipoli GSW l Knee, 28.8.15 GSW Chest arm Gallipoli, School of instruction 5.5.16, Stokes gun and Lewis Gun Schools. KIA 5.11.1916 Flers/Gueudecourt Bayonet Trench, France SSW of Bapaume. Exhumed to Grevillers British Cemetery France. Has own memorial Face Book page set up by his family	251, 294, 296, 364
LAZARUS Julius Samuel, Major, Enlist 23.4.15. 6 Rfts 14 Bn., to 5th Bn. Born 1861 at Frankston. Civil and Hydraulic Engineer. Relieved of Duty Dardanelles 4.12.15 RTA *Runic* 11.4.16 Discharge 28.5.16 med unfit. Died 1951.	84
LEE Robert Arthur, Lt., Enlist 15.1.16. aged 23, born Petersham. Architect. 9 Rfts 53 Bn. Many training courses. Demob. ENG for course in Architecture. RTA *Euripides* 26.10.19,	384, 403, 429, 561, 665
LEE Charles Hubert, Lt., Enlist 25.6.15 born Canada age 35 merchant with varicose veins 8 Rfts 1st Bn, Embark *Runic*, wounded GSW bomb face and back Made Lt. 2.7.16 Suffered debility insomnia and exhaustion RTA *Boonah* 3.6.19 Discharge 10.19	
LEIFERMANN Augustus Frederick, L/Corp., Enlist 1915. aged 27, store manager, born and NOK Condobolin. 11 Rfts 1st Bn. Wounded 8.9.16 GSW Compound metacarpal's. RTA *Benalla* 11.5.17	267
LEWIS 2/Lt, 9 Bn. Royal Irish Rifles at Havre with Ben, trench art.	
*LINDEMAN Frank William, Maj., Enlist 29.3.15. Sydney Grammar School previous military service. Applied for Commission in 19 Infantry Bn. Made Capt. and Adj., July 1915. Age 23, married wife of Mosman, stock and station agent Dalgety. To 1st Bn 5.5.16 D.O.W. 28.7.16 Pozieres, Becourt Military Cemetery near Albert. Son Frederick Sampson Lindeman born 8.12.15	202, 210, 235, 241, 244, 773-4

*LIPSCOMB Neville Henry, Gunner. Enlist 22.8.14, aged 19, student Father W.J. of Normanhurst. 1st Light Horse Field Amb. to 10th Field Artillery. KIA 23.4.17 Ecoust near Bullecourt. France. Buried Ecoust Embankment Military Cemetery near Bapaume.	
* LIPSCOMB Eric John, Pt., Enlist 1.8.16 aged 21 Farmer, Father William John of *Nevilleton* Pennant Hills Rd Normanhurst. Father butcher at Wahroonga.4 Rfts 34 Bn, KIA 16.5.17. Le Touquet near Armentieres. Buried Tancrez Farm Military Cemetery, Plogsteert, Belgium	
LIPSCOMBE Frederick Wounded RTA	
LITTLE George Campbell, Lt., MC., Enlist aged 33, soldier, of Bondi. Aus. Perm Military Forces instructional staff, ex Duntroon, ex Scots Guards, N.Z. Instruction staff to 1st Bn. RTA *Ypiranga* 15.11.19. Discharge Jan 1920.	206, 223
*LUBLIN Norman, (Lubbin) Pte, enlist 7.1.16, born Sydney, mother of Strathfield, aged 33 years, tailors presser. 18 Rfts 1st Bn. Wounded accidentally, premature explosion of bomb. Died of Wounds 3rd Field Ambulance Rest Station 19.2.17. buried Heilly Cemetery.	321
LUCK Douglas Seymour, L/Corp., Enlist 17.6.15 born Tas, 20 years, labourer, father of Mt Seymour Tas. Gallipoli Shrapnel to shoulder chest abdo to St Elmo Hospital Malta then All Saints Convalescent Hosp. Malta. *Bornu* to Egypt with Ben 26.2.16. 26 Bn. Flu 6.1.17 RTA *Tasos Montes* 3.4.19 Discharge 11.8.19	140, 139
LUFFT Stanley Ernest, Sgt., Gunner. Enlist 1.11.16 aged 26 engineer from Wahroonga. 5th Bn. AIF HQ., RTA *Kanowna* 26.10.19. Died 1949. Ben says another Lufft boy KIA	626
LYNCH Arthur Wilfred, Pte, Enlist 20.5.15 Born Forbes aged 24 Carpenter Mother of Sydney. Deserted *Orsova* Fremantle. *Demosthenes* stowaway to Egypt. more record	165

M

McDONALD /MACDONALD *Alick* William, also known as Alexander, Corp., Enlist 14.4.16 Of *Elderslie*, Coila St, Wahroonga, draughtsman and carpenter 35 Bn., G.S.W. to hand severe. RTA invalided *Suevic* 5.1.19., In No 6 A.A. Hospital, 1 Moreton Gardens, South Kensington London like Ben. Discharge 30.5.19 medically unfit. Living 8 Bar Beach Newcastle in 1951	153, 362, 382, 485, 674
McINTYRE Andrew Kirkland Sapper Born Wallsend aged 21, wheeler father AK McIntyre Mother Elle of Carrington St Wet Wallsend. Enlist 4.3.15 20 Bn Gallipoli enteric and septic leg to Mudros to 4th Field Coy Engineers, KIA 5.7.18 Buried La Neuville British Cemetery near Corbie	

* MACKENZIE Arthur Cobcroft, Capt., Enlist 24.6.15 aged 24, Master Baker of Drummoyne. 8th Rfts. 1st Bn., KIA 23.7.16 Pozieres, France. Pozieres British Cemetery Ovillers - La Boisselle Pozieres Picardie France,	152, 156, 163, 186, 190, 193, 211, 219, 221, 231, 239, 244, 749
MACKENZIE Alexander Kenneth, Lt.-Col., DSO Hargicourt, MC., Bullecourt. Enlist 27.8.14 aged 26 clerk, of *Caerlock* Bondi. As 2/Lt 1st Bn. to Gallipoli, On *Ivernia* to France. Temporary CO Major vice Woodforde, DOW 2nd Bullecourt. (DSO) 1st Bn then CO of 4th Bn then to 3rd Bn vice Sasse. To 1st Bn vice Lt.- Col. Stacy RTA *Leicestershire* OC of Troops 9.5.19. Died 20.11.1925 aged 37 years. Ben says died of appendicitis	219, 330, 333, 334, 341, 366, 413, 429, 791, 793, 794
*MACKIE John *Jock*, Sgt., Enlist 31.8.14 aged 29 labourer from Aberdeenshire SCOT. C Coy, 1st Bn., G.S.W. to arm severe 20.4.18 DOW 15 Cas. Clearing Station France, Buried Ebblingham British Cemetery near Hazebrouck. Made Sgt., vice Lanser H.M., KIA. Archie Barwick's friend. see his diary online Mitchell Library	299, 343, 793, 794
MACKINNON Oct 17 wounded	
*MACKLEY Tom. Pt., MM., Enlist 7th Rfts A Coy 1st Bn. Aged 24, train conductor, born Surrey Hills. Mother of Leichardt NSW. Sick Egypt re-joined Bn 23.5.16. Wounded Pozieres shellshock. sick other teeth. KIA 5-8 /5/17 Bullecourt. Memorial Villers Bretonneaux. Ben said Mackley was a wag in his platoon. He keeps us amused with his cheerfulness and pronunciation of French	152, 218
MACVEAN Mafra William, Capt., MC., Enlist 21.8.14 Randwick, born Melbourne, stock and station agent, father in London. BW Thigh at Landing Gallipoli, 1st Bn., 2nd in Command of 1st Div. rear-guard at evacuation of Gallipoli. Hospital Influenza, 28.7.16. Pozieres GSW 1 Humorous with paralysis RTA 15.5.17 H.M.A.T. *Beltana*	241
*MADSEN Olaf, (Oscar Madison) Corp., Enlist 29.8.14 born Denmark, father of Denmark, aged 23, labourer.5'11 'fair hair complexion and blue eyes 1st Bn, GSW Gallipoli, Re-join Bn 7.6.16 ingrown toenail, 9.7.16 Re-join Bn July 17. Missing, KIA attached to 1st Field Coy engineers Belgium 21.9.17. Memorial Menin Gate Ypres.	206

MAITLAND George Duncan Lt, Enlist 1.2.16. born Sydney., aged 19, clerk, mother of Ryde. was in 19th Bn militia. To 34th Reg Transport, to Officers Cadet school. Wounded 1.10.17 to 3rd London GH., Compound fracture R Femur severe. RTA *Wandilla* to Suez *Kanowna* (NAA says Karoola) MD 2 Discharge 4.4.19 *Kanowna*	3, 447
MANN John Spencer, Lt., Enlist 5.11.15 Hawthorn Vic, aged 21, geologist. Signal School. Sgt 27.8.15 59 Bn to 39 Bn. Made Lt. 4.10.16. Many Schools of Instruction. Wounded 16.9.17 SW R Leg, R Ankle and L Leg To Le Touquet Duchess of West- minster Hospital to 3rd London. RTA 30.6.18 D 14 *Wandilla* with Ben and *Kanowna*. Discharge 6.11.18 to Victoria 3 MD. J.S. Mann, *Cestria* Myrtle Rd Canterbury VIC. Pic on *Kanowna*	452, 450
MANN James, Corp., Enlist 31.8.14. born SCOT, married wife of SCOT, age 19 years, farmer. To 1st Bn E Coy., Sun fever 11.7.15 Pneumonia 18.7.15 to Malta to ENG Re-join 20.1.17 then on 15.5.17 Married Twice Mary Beaucourt 12.3.15 in Cairo and Marion Deas Doughty at Sutton Veny in The Parish Church 21.12.17. Corp. vice Corp. O. Madson KIA. Made Assistant Instructor gas. To 1st Training Bn 19.12.17 Admit Sutton Veny gas poisoning. Court of Enquiry accidental poisoning drift from faulty chamber. RTA *Trasos Montes* 8.4.19 Discharge 26.6.19. Died 1974	
MANSELL Charles William *Bluey*, Pt. Enlist 22.5.16 aged 18, shop assistant, born Redfern, Father of Annandale, hair auburn. B Coy 1st Bn to 1st MG Coy. Missing Prisoner of war 19.1.18 Ypres Wytschaete. To Carolus Magna Mine. RTA Aeneas 3.6.19 Discharge 20.4.19, Reveille 1933 Died 3Sept 1950 Collaroy War Veterans Home	403, 783-4
MANT John Francis, Lt., Enlist 4.3.16. born Sydney, aged 19, station hand and clerk, mother of Woollahra. Father The Hon R.A. Mant of India. 3rd Div. Cycling Training Bn to 1st Bn – 3rd Bn to 1st Bn. Many courses including officer cadet course at Oxford. RTA via India extended special leave. Discharge Aus. 23.7.1920. WW11 Lt-Colonel MANT W H, (Mrs.) 'Splinter ', 2 Albert St Woollahra Sydney	384, 398
MANTON Willoughby, Lt., MC. Enlist 1.9.15. aged 43, mining engineer, wife of Paddington to No.1 Mining Corps then final to 1st Tunnelling Corps. Was in Michelham Convalescence Home 13.1.17 – was for return but held on duty with war records until 26.5.19 then attended course in London on Steel. RTA *Ypindirqa* 15.11.19	

MARKS George Moss, Sgt., Enlist 19.5.15. 7th Rfts 1st Bn, born London, aged 23, bread carter. Wounded GSW shoulder 12.5.17 and influenza, vice Brownlie, to 1st Training Bn in ENG, Lyndhurst bombing school RTA *Klyber* Sydney 16.5.19 (Pic of Sgts 16.9.16 of A Coy)	269
MARSDEN, Dick cleft palate. John Patrick Pt, only Marsden/Marsdon on 1ˢᵗ Bn Nominal Roll. 12 Rfts 1ˢᵗ Bn, aged 18, mill hand, Enlist 11.9.15, foster mother. Wounded France GSW l arm at Pozieres, then sick bronchitis, Sniping School Wounded 19.4.17 r arm and back, RTA *Orca* 19.3.19 Discharge 25.5.19 Married Annie Johnstone of Glasgow 19.6.18 R.C. Govan. Living at Dungog in 1957	269
MARR Ernest, *Barney* Pt. Enlist 13.9.15 born London, aged 23 years, labourer, mother of London. 15 Rfts 1st Bn., B Coy., to 53 Bn 21.4.16. Shell Shock 19.5.16. Wounded France 19.7.16 derangement of Knee. RTA Chronic Synovitis of Knee HT *Malta*.30.9.18 Discharge 16.2.19. Marriage St George Hanover Square Reg. Office 15.9.17 to Edith Eva Dennis. Photo ID 5'7 'blue eyes, dark hair and complexion. Photo at Tel el Kebir.	256
MARSLAND John Woodward, Gunner. Enlist 11.1.16 aged 18 years, born Sydney, student mother of QLD. 4th Dept. of Supply, 10 FAB, 1st Anzac Cycle RTA invalided shell shock 13 April 1917 Ecouste, *Balmoral Castle* 18.12.18. Graduated dentistry 1923 with Ben. Harriet St., Neutral Bay, Valetta Lower Wycombe St Neutral Bay	527, 539, 626, 637, 672, 676, 682, 690, 701
MATTHEWS of 4th BN	
MAUGHAM Collingwood William Ryott, Lt., Enlist. 2.3.16, aged 24, clerk from Melbourne. 1st Field Artillery Rfts, 5th Div. Artillery. Wounded 16.5.18 GSW both legs. RTA *Kanowna* with Ben. MD 2	452
McAULIFFE Edmund, Capt., Chaplain R.C., O.B.E., Enlist 11.9.14 from St Mary's Cathedral Sydney. Served Egypt., Gallipoli France. RTA *Kanowna*. Appointment terminated 18.9.18 to St Mary's Presbytery Newcastle.	452
McCONNEL Kenneth Hamlyn, Lt., Enlist born Brisbane aged 19, grazier, mother of London to 5th LH Reg. 2.3.16 1st Bn., On *Ivernia*. Lt. 12.8.16. Wounded Pozieres GSW leg to Wandsworth ENG.1st Brigade Gas Officer and Transport Officer last 6 months RTA *Kaiser Hind* 6.5.19 Discharge 19.8.19. Captain Enlist 1941 WW11.	
McCONNEL Cressbrook P., 35 Kensington Park Gardens London	402, 391, 384

McDOWELL John Ambrose, Maj., C.O. 36th Bn., enlist 14.8.14, aged 26, civil servant from Coogee, 1st N and M E F at Rabaul, To Gallipoli and evac home with shell concussion. Re enlisted 29.4.16 as Capt., 34 Bn- 25 Bn to 36 Bn as Major C O. Wounded 30.6.18 GSW scalp L forearm and both legs. RTA *Kanowna*. National Archives has *Karoola* but definitely *Kanowna* with Ben	452
McGREGOR /MacGREGOR Roderick Ian Clarence, Capt., MC. Enlist 22.8.14 aged 22 years, born and mother India, farmer, 1st Bn. Gallipoli wounded GSW back. 25.4.15. Lt., synovitis 22.7.15. on *Ivernia* Wounded France accident bomb burns face and hands, Made Captain vice Capt. AC MacKenzie KIA. GSW arm # end of radius 5.11.16 Flers. to ENG. 3rd wound, 1.12.18 laryngitis due to gas at Messines. RTA 12.7.19 H.T. *Aeneas* Discharge 10.2.20	242, 294, 303, 306, 401, 791
* MCKELL Victor Cleveland, Lt., Enlist 21.8.14 aged 26, Bank clerk, mother in Mosman. 20 Rfts 1st Bn. To 53 Bn., KIA 4 Oct 1917 3rd Battle Ypres Belgium. C Menin Gate Memorial Ypres Flanders Belgium	379
* MCKENNA Hugh Patrick, Pt., Enlist 28.5.15 born Scot. Aged 28 years, steward. 7th Rfts 1st Bn; B Coy., DOW perforating chest wound 26.11.15 Gallipoli; Shell Green Cemetery Gallipoli. Photo ID. Med complex, grey eyes, light brown hair, 5'8 'see pic with Ben	4, 115, 117, 118
MCKENZIE William, FIGHTING MAC Major, MC, Chaplain (Salvation Army) Enlist 1914 aged 44 from Bendigo, late Brigadier Salvation Army, married with children. 1st AIF. 4 Bn. RTA 10.1.18 to Melbourne Terminated 17.3.18. Became Commissioner Salvation Army. Mentioned in *Reveille* 1932	108, 271, 252, 254-5, 272, 468, 583, 791, 794
*MCKENZIE George Roith, Pt., Enlist 17.1.16, 16 Rfts 1st Bn., born SCOT aged 38 years, engineers labourer, from Sydney, married. Missing KIA 5.11.16 bur 450 yds NNW of Gueudecourt re bur. Grevillers British Military Cemetery Picardie France.	324
McKENZIE/MACKENZIE Robert John, Sgt., Enlist 21.8.14, born Rockhampton, aged 23 years, carter, wife of Manly. A Coy 1st Bn. To France *Ivernia* with Ben. Made Corp 2.5.16. Wounded 22.8.16 GSW R arm. To 53 Bn to 1st Bn. Made Sgt. 6.2.17. Wounded SW R thigh 19.5.17, Neurasthenia, SW head and thigh to ENG. 18.4.17 Wounded 4) gassed 9.3.18. RTA 17.6.18 gassed and heart H.T. *Matatua*. Discharge 8.10.18. Died in Callam Park Psych Hospital 1967. This is probably Ponto MacKenzie on leave 23.6.16	206, 210, 211, 220, 254

*McLEOD David Ferguson, L/Corp., Enlisted 22.8.14 born Edinburgh SCOT, aged 24 years, clerk, 1st Bn., Wounded GSW face and upper arm April 15. Wounded 2. GSW neck bomb wound 9.8.15 then DOW 10.8.15. aboard H.T. *Davanha* buried at sea 10.8.15., Lone Pine Memorial, Peninsula Turkey. Brother of Miss Isabella Gibson McLeod who married Beavis	371,
Mc LEOD Bruce Burton, Lt., Enlist born Sth. Aust., age 29 years, clerk, 24 Rfts 1st Bn., Ex Hussars, Ex Hampshire Yeomanry Ex Duntroon. GSW back, humorous severe 16.9.17 to England RTA *Wandilla* to Suez 16.3.18 *Kanowna* 25.5.18 Discharge 24.11.18 Wife of Mosman Sydney, Later of Bondi 1919	
*MCMAHON Randolph George Finlay, Lt. MC., Enlist 8.9.14 4th Bn, born Edinburgh, 24 yrs., clerk, mother in Mosman, farmer, previously of Leeton via Yanko. Wounded x 3. 23.2.1919 Died Belgium of 'flu, Halle Communal Cemetery	311, 313, 315, 411
*McSHANE Noel Edmund, Lt., 1st Bn. Enlist 21.8.14. Aged 21 years, clerk, father of Woollahra. 2/Lt., 7.10.15 Transport Section, Lt 12.3.16. 1st Brig., KIA 25.7.1916 Pozieres in A Coy, Villers-Bretonneaux Memorial, Photo AWM	244
McTACKETT (Ben had McTaggart)Thomas William, Corp., MM. Enlist 4.9.14 aged 19 yrs., labourer of Willoughby, 1st Bn. wounded Gallipoli, Pozieres shellshock went dumb but carried on 22-25.7.16 Bayonet wound to leg RTA 20.12.17 H.T. *Runic* Discharge 12.8.18	109, 228, 240
MIFSUD Alfred Eugene, MD FRCS (Ed.) Surgeon- Major, Valetta Hospital Malta. Royal Malta Artillery. Medical Officer 1st Royal Malta Regiment of Militia from 1887 Retired June 1919. Mrs Mifsud- Lady Superintendent of St John Ambulance Brigade Valletta. All applicants to join Military Hospitals as nurses were to be made through her.	126, 134
*MILLER Charles., Pte, Enlist 23.9.15. born Orange, aged 24, painter, Sister of Wahroonga. On *Ivernia*. 14 Rfts 1st Bn, Mouquet Farm KIA 18.8.16. Ben says leg blown off	
*Robert Donald Miller. Pt, Enlist. 15.12.15 16 Rfts 1st Bn. blacksmith aged 23, mother of Glebe. KIA E Coy 1st Bn Flers 5.11.16. Buried 250 yds from Gueudecourt. Villers Bretonneaux Memorial	
MILLINGTON *Australia* Petty Officer	478

MOAG Roger Henry Patrick Farnham, Lt., Enlisted 7th Rfts 1st Bn with Ben. Medals on enlistment. Australian Army for Boer War Aug 1911 to 1902;1806 Zululand;1910 China1910-1912 China Rebellion. ;1914 European war China; King Edward 11 Coronation, Queen Victoria Boer war, King Edward Boer War; Zulu land. China. Royal Humane Society 1911.	4, 5, 31, 33, 38, 39, 40, 42, 57, 73, 79, 82, 94, 99, 216,
Returned to Australia 3 March 1916 for disciplinary reasons and dismissed. Fascinating War Record and amazing man. Read his full war record on National Archives of Australia and Info on Ancestry and Trove and Us World War Draft Registration Card. MOAG Roger with alias. After returning to Australia in 1916. Joined Canada Mounted Rifles in November 1916 as Roger Henry Moag Levy and was chosen for service in Royal Flying Corps in England. Second Court Martial at Westminster for wearing a officers uniform and decorations without authority. See *The Argus* (Melbourne – Saturday 9 June 1917 page 6. Wore DSO, Zulu, Egypt and other decorations. Passed in West End London as Capt. Maxwell Farnham. Escaped Flying Corps. (continued oveleaf) MOAG Roger (c0nt)Then he enlisted in Machine Gun Section of the New Zealand Forces in the name of Moag.3rd Mate Roger Moag SS *Halifax* presumed drowned 12 December 1917 age 38 Son of Francis and Ann Moag, husband of Mary Moag nee Miley of 449 West 206th St New York. Born in Dunedin. Commonwealth War Graves. Did his wife know he was deceased when she petitioned for a divorce 23 December 1920. 9 Jan 1929 NSW Police Gazette charged with disobeying a magisterial order for the support of wife and children He is about 40 years of age 5'11, ' thin build, ruddy complexion, auburn hair, brown eyes, clean shaven. Tattoos on chest and forearm, native of New Zealand, master mariner. More to this story elsewhere.	

MOFFAT/MOFFATT (Nom Roll TT) Haywood Hugh Guthrie, Capt., MC. Enlist 1.10.14, born Albury, aged 28 years, pastoralist of Longreach QLD. 6th L. H. Regt to 1st Bn. 24.2.16. Wounded Gallipoli forehead detach retina. Took Beavis place as Capt., DOW 21.9.18. Bur. La Chapelette near Perrone. Diary of First Battalion A.I.F. 1914-1919 ' The death of Capt. Moffatt was a very real loss to us all. His personality was one that would have made him stand out in any company for his almost remarkable qualities of courage, cheerfulness and entire lack of anything approaching pettiness or spite endeared him to every officer and to every man. His last day was typical of his great-hearted courage and unselfish regard for others. His wound was severe and painful but he resolutely refused to be assisted on his way to the dressing station. Struggling on he reached the station at last and they saw that he must be sent to the main dressing station without delay. This he refused to do until someone had been summoned from the Brigade. so that he could inform. at once the position in the front line. So, passed one of the most gallant of the many gallant soldiers whose lives and deaths were bound up in the fortunes of the 1st Battalion.	372, 794, 206, 230, 293, 331, 332, 365, 366, 383, 400
MOORE, W.S.T. Major sniped in left shoulder Battle of Moquet Farm. Became Brigadier.	258
Lt Moore re-joined Co after Pozieres	242, 243, 264, 266
*MOORE Charles James, Corp. Enlist 20.6.15 born Leichhardt, aged 21 years, father of Artarmon. 7th Rfts 1st Bn to 53 Bn to 14 Machine Gun Coy 26.3.16. Wounded Gallipoli 10.12.15 then KIA 20.7.16 Villers- Bretonneaux (has Pte) made Corp 11.7.16	93, 126,
* MORGAN John *Jack* Philip, Gunner, Enlist 4.9.15 aged 28 years, caretaker, wife Dorothea Realph Morgan. Will in care of W H Champion Esq., *Strathalbyn* Kingston Rd, Camperdown. Sydney. Ben's uncle. 36th Australian Heavy Artillery Group. DOW 5 Oct 1917. Cemetery Ypres Reservoir North Cemetery Ypres Belgium. Jack Ben's first cousin	354
*MORGAN Reginald Roy, Lt., Enlist 10.7.15 aged 23, Bank officer, father B Morgan Esq., *Ivanhoe*, Boorawa NSW 10 Rfts 3rd Bn., On command 1st Aust. Divisional School of Instruction. 25.9.16 and 2nd time 28.12.16. Made 2 Lt., 7.11.16, Made Lt., 15.3.17. DOW GSW R thigh and head 5.5.17 Buried Grevillers British Cemetery near Bapaume. Morgan of 3rd Bn at School of Instruction with Ben	313, 314

MORLEY Claude Ronald, Lt., MC. Dated 15.10.18. Enlist 25.5.15, aged 25, analytical chemist C.S.I.R.O., father lives Lindfield. 7 Rfts 4 Bn., to 1st Inf. Bgde Machine Gun Coy., Schools of Instruction. RTA as OC Troops *Boonah* 20.4.19. Discharge 10.8.19.	408, 420, 428, 419
*MORRIS Francis Robert, Pt., Enlist 9.6.15 aged 34, fisherman, father lives Botany. 7 Rfts 1st Bn., KIA Gallipoli 9.11.15. Shot between eyes. Shell Green Cemetery Gallipoli.	109
MORTLOCK Kenneth Charles, Lt., MC., Enlist 13.3.16 age 23, clerk, father of City. 21 Rfts 1st Bn, RTA *Leicestershire* 3.5.19 Terminated 2.8.19.	384, 391, 409, 410, 419
MURDOCH Sir James Anderson Lt Col, DSO. 1867-1939. Edinburgh born retailer who established Murdoch men's mercery in Park Street City. Served in WW1 as a Commissioner of Red Cross. Lt Col Murdoch volunteered for service (at his own expense) with the Australian branch of the British Red Cross Society in October 1915. He worked in Egypt and France before being appointed honorary Lt Col and chief commissioner in England in 1917. He was appointed CMG in 1918 and returned to Sydney in December 1918. Prominent in Scottish and Presbyterian causes being chairman of Burnside Homes 1923-1927. MLC 10223-1934. Member of St John's Presbyterian Church Wahroonga. Father of Mary Bella who married Geoff Johnson. Ben met the Colonel in London and knew the family.	441, 472, 626
MURDOCH Mary Bella	470, 626, 639, 740
MUSGRAVE Vic, Ex Fort Street High School, tried to enlist 3 years in a row. *Norwood* Campbell St North Sydney	488
*MURRAY, Robert Cooper James, acting L/Corp Enlist 6.2.16. Said by his mother to be 16 ½ years at death. Born Parramatta, accountants' clerk. Uncle also 1st Bn, KIA Gallipoli. Enlist aged 18 years clerk. He put next of kin his aunt who 'signed ' permission as father overseas and mother deceased. His father was Pt. R.E. Murray overseas and his mother was alive in Sydney. Age not determined with birth registration. 18 Rfts 1st Bn, B Coy DOW, 4.10.16 GSW shattered both ankles and feet. Lijssenthoek Military Cemetery near Poperinghe	280

N

NANKING of 5th with Ben at Training school	
* NEILL Reuben *Rupe*, Sgt., Enlist 28.5.15 Sydney, Salesman, aged 19, father dead, mother of North Sydney.7th Rfts 1st Bn, to 53rd Bn. Gallipoli, Ismailia 3.5.16 Missing in action and KIA 19.7.1915 Fromelles Cemetery VC Corner Australian Cemetery. For photo description 5 4 ̓ Dark complex, blue eyes, dark hair. Sister Irene Neil not married. medal 1967	4, 73, 74, 78, 80, 81, 126, 148, 149.152, 154, 219, 273, 285
NIELSEN Hans Martin, L/Corp., Enlist 13.7.15 Sydney Born o/s, age nearly 43, gas stoker married. 12 Rfts 1st Bn, Wounded GSW head. Discharged Rheumatism RTA *Essex* 10.9.18.	198
NEWING Harry Henry Joseph, S / Sgt., 1) 16.8.14 Naval & Military Exped Force German Papua. 2) 7th Rfts 1st Bn, Enlisted 18.1.15 aged 28, farmer, mother at Albion St Harris Park. Sgt., 8.3.16. Description for photos 5.10 ̓ dark complexion, dark eyes and hair (check photos) to Australian Army Ordnance Corps, HDQTS. Discharge England 14.9.20 permission to go to USA to study intensive farming, pigs, irrigation and return to his 300 acres at Dorrigo	73, 74, 77, 78, 80, 81, 154
NORRIS Raymond Gladstone Lt., MC., Enlist 5.5.15 aged 30 years, Station Manager, father of Sydney. 2nd Bn late 5 Rfts 7th Light Horse. Many Schools of Instruction including Oct 17 and Dec 17. RTA HT *Boonah* 20.4.19. WW11 Major 11 Garrison Bn 1939 at POW Camp Cowra. In 1943 of Jersey Rd Artarmon NSW.	313
NORTHCOTT Arthur Norman, Lt., Enlist 14.12.15. born Victoria, aged 28, commercial teacher, mother of Dulwich Hill. Father Dr Northcott of Leichhardt. 19 Rfts 1st Bn A Coy 17.5.16. Joined Officers Cadet Bn Oxford. Originally joined Expeditionary Force and discharged medical unfit due to malaria 23.7.15 Joined 1st Bn Havre 20.7.17, cellulitis leg. Wounded 30.4.18 GSW multiple head and concussion Made Lt 15.5.18. Night blindness. Wounded gassed 10.8.18 RTA *Orsova* Feb 1919 Discharge 21.7.19 Died 1941	

O

O'BYRNE Gerald, Lt., Enlist 13.9.15 aged 21, clerk, from Wellington. 34 Bn 9 Inf. Bgde. Wound GSW Buttock then 17.7.17 GSW arm and thigh # femur and l forearm. RTA *Kanowna*. MD 2 Died 1955	452
ORAM Reginald John, Lt, Enlist 11.5.15. 9 Rfts 1st Bn at Tel el Kebir. born Sydney, Clerk, father of Petersham. On *Ivernia* Pozieres buried and shellshock. Sick+. RTA *Karagola* 30.4.19 Discharge 6.8.19	241

ORAMES Benjamin, Capt., and Chaplain (Salvation Army). Enlist Melbourne. 5th Division troops, Enlist 1.3.16 *Kanowna*. Disembark. Melbourne 1.9.18 Discharge 15.9.18	449
OSBORN old 19b which one	
*OSHEA Eugene Pt. Enlist 23.10.16 Aged 41, born Kerry IRE Blacksmith Striker, B Coy 23rd RFTS 1st Bn. 4.10.17 SW Head, Influenza 26.6.18 KIA 18.9.18 Bellicourt British Cemetery.	5
O'SHEA Patrick Joseph Francis, Capt., MC with Bar, DSO, AAMC. Enlist 6.9.16 aged 24, born Sydney, Medical Practitioner, father of Granville. Gas poisoning 17.3.18 Ypres. Attached to 1st Bn 30.12.17. RTA *Shropshire* 1.4.19 Discharge 29.7.19 not in 1st Bn Nominal Roll	409, 419

P

PAGE Harry Frederick, Lt., Enlist 8.3.15. Born MDX ENG., Bank teller, married, 27 years, 7th Rfts 1st Bn, 31.12.15 Concussion Gallipoli, to 61st Bn. 2 /Lt Qual for Commission from Cadet Bn 28.10.16. 11.5.17 to 1st Bn., 15.9.17 Made Lt. 24.11.17. 18.9.18 Wounded SW chest to Eng. 3rd London 24.9.18 (Pic) in reed hamper 30.4.18 RTA, G.S.W. to chest penetrating wound. RTA HT *Ulysses* 4.3.19. Discharge 2.11.19 *Carlotta* Hampden Rd Artarmon NSW 1920.	57, 303, 304, 308, 441, 442, 438, 788-90, 792, 793, 794
PARISH Stanley Josiah, Corp., MM. for 10.5.17. Enlist 13.2.15 born Orange, aged 20 years, bookbinder / labourer. 6th Rfts. 1st Bn. Wounded Gallipoli SW nose and R knee & buttock to Malta St Elmo. RTA *City of Poona* 17.5.19.	
PARISH Eric Charles Pte, Enlist 11.7.15. Born Orange, aged 18 years, labourer, 11 Rfts 1st Bn., *Ivernia* with Ben, GSW R leg 22.6.16 Pozieres. Aust. Div. School of Instruction 3.3.17. Discovered to be underage, to working parties and to Custody Compound Gaol time. RTA *Soudon* 12.5.19 Discharge 6.1.20	222
PARKINSON Walter George Lt., MM. Enlist. 18.11.14 aged 22. Blacksmith, from Victoria. 1st Div. Trench Mortars. Rheumatism Gallipoli, 3rd FAB, Trench Mortar Bn, RA Cadet School. RTA Suffolk Disembark. Melbourne 5.6.19 Meteren Photo is W.H. Parkinson	401, 402, 410, 411, 419
PARKES Lifton Villiers, Lt., Enlist born South Australia father of same, aged 19 years, orchardist Made Lt., 27 Bn, 19.3.17, Accident shot GSW L hand foot and back.2.4.17 to ENG. Influenza Wounded 3) GSW Back shoulders and scrotum severe to ENG RTA *Wandilla* to *Kanowna* to 4 MD 1.9.18 Discharge. Died before 1967, Son Gallipoli medal.	452

PEACOCK Charles, Pt., Enlist 3.2.17. Born Raymond Terrace, 19 years, miner, father of East Maitland. 9th Trng Bn to 7 Rfts 36 Bn to 33 Bn. Wounded SW jaw severe. RTA HT *Takada* 16.2.19 Discharge 23.9.19	84
*PEARCE Eddie, Pte, Enlist 11.10.15. born Richmond, aged 24, farmer, father Edward of Richmond, 12 Rfts 4 Bn to 1st Bn. *Ivernia* KIA 19.8.16 before Mouquet Farm, Sunken Road. British Cemetery Albert. stretcher bearer 19.8.16. Ben called him Bill, maybe because his father was Edward too.	254
PEARCE Frank, Pt. 17 Bn his brother	
PEGG John, R.S.M. and WO. Enlist 17.8.14. born ENG, aged 32, shopkeeper, wife of Annandale. G Coy 1st Bn., Tel el Kebir Regimental Sgt Major and WO 10.12.16 on *Ivernia*. Sick, ++ wounded gas 14.8.18. Transport Duty *Kaisir A Hind* -Taranto Italy. RTA trans- shipped *Devon* 24.11.18 disability dyspnea and weakness 12.7.19	156
*PHILLIPS Frederick Stobo, 2/Lt., MM. Enlist 9.11.14 born Surrey Hills, 30 years, farmer. NOK Sister Mrs Read, *The Wurley*, Cleveland St, Wahroonga. AAMC No 2 Aust. Gen. Hospital to 1st Bn. Made 2/ Lt 5.8.16. KIA 5.11.16 Gueudecourt. Bulls Rd Cemetery Flers France.	251, 294, 364
*POCKLEY Brien Colden Antill, Capt., Medical Practitioner, ex Sydney Hospital. Enlist 14.8.14, aged 24 years, Naval and Military Expeditionary Force. KIA 11.9.14 at Kabakaul in taking of German New Guinea: exhumed to H.M.A.S. *Una* and remains to Rabaul Cemetery with full military honours 11.7.19. Father Dr F. Antill Pockley of Macquarie St and *Grayslanes* Wahroonga. Brien Pockley diary online at Mitchell Library WW1 diaries.	
*POCKLEY John Graham Antill, Lt., Enlist 27.3.15, aged 25 years of *Rockby* Wahroonga and his widow c/- Sargood of Rippon Grange Wahroonga. 33 Bn KIA 30.3.18 Morgemont Wood France, body not recovered after Germans retook position. Crucifix Cemetery. Father Dr Pockley gave an address at the opening of Wahroonga Returned Soldiers Memorial in 1918	478
PONT Reginal John., Corp. Enlist born Maitland, aged 27 years, iron moulder, father of Morpeth. 20 Bn to 1st Bn 10.11.16. Myalgia, rheumatism, trench fever, dermatitis, flu. Wounded 23.8.18 GSW Shoulder wrist. RTA *Aeneas* 31.5.19 Discharge 28.8.19	386
*POTTER, Daniel, Pt., Enlist 24.6.15, 23 years, labourer, mother of Nananga QLD. 49 Bn to 9 Bn KIA 20.9.17 Belgium. Menin Gate	370

POTTER Walter Leslie, Enlist 2.8.15. Born Sydney, aged 21, Stove fitter, 11 Rfts 1 Bn., On *Ivernia*. Wounded Pozieres shell shock to ENG. Wounded 9.4.17 Shell shock confusion debilitation. RTA *Chemnitz* 7.7.19 Cape Town 1.8.19 Re embarked Dun- bar 5.8.19 Discharged 8.10.19.	
PRESNELL Frederick Arthur, Lt., Enlist Born Victoria, aged 21 years, bank officer. 14 Rfts 6 Bn to 1st Bn. Many courses. Defensive measures, sniping school, Aust. Div. Intel. School, 1st Training Bn. RTA *Frankfurt* 1.7.19	366, 370, 382, 384, 391, 398, 409, 411, 419, 498
PRESTON Raymond, Lt., 22.10.17. Enlist b Scarsdale Vic, age 22, clerk, father of Subiaco. 12 Rfts 11 Bn to 10 Rfts 28 Bn. Wounded 28.4.17 BW hands face thigh. Wounded 9.4.18 # r leg severe, 3rd London GH, Moreton Gardens RTA *Kanowna* with Ben. MD 5 WW11 Captain 1939-1944 CMF and Garrison	448, 452
* HOWELL - PRICE Owen Glendower, Lt., Col., DSO., and despatches. MC for attack at Lone Pine. Enlist: born Kiama, agriculturalist from Richmond NSW. Major at Gallipoli in hand to hand combat. Led 3rd Bn at Pozieres and Mouquet Farm and at Flers when hit by rifle fire 2.11.17 and DOW 4.Nov 1917, aged 26 years. GSW cheek penetrating head near Flers. Heilly Station Cemetery Mericourt near Corbie. Memorial Menin Gate Made Lt Col., and CO of 3rd Bn 13.2.16. Note: There is an additional index item 798-9	253
* HOWELL-PRICE Philip Llewellyn, Maj. DSO, MM. Enlist: 17.8.14, born Mt Wilson, aged 20 years, bank clerk, father of Balmain East. To Gallipoli 30.6.15. Wounded bomb to back. Re-joined 1st Bn 7.12.15. Made Capt. Tel El Kebir 28.1.16. on *Ivernia*. Wounded 1.3.17 remained on duty SW R. thigh and shoulder. Awarded Military Cross 3.6.17. Made Major vice Sasse 7.6.17. Missing in Action- KIA 4.10.17 Broodseinde Belgium. Cemetery Menin Gate Memorial Ypres Flanders Belgium, Note: There is an additional index item 798-9	225, 241, 293, 294, 309, 372, 377, 362, 364, 366, 369, 372, 376, 377, 379, 384, 740
* HOWELL- PRICE. Richmond Dick Gordon, 2/Lt., MC. Enlist 14.12.15, aged 19, farmer, born Victoria. 16 Rfts 6 Light Horse to 1st Bn 6.12.16. 2/Lt., 13.12.16. Div. School of Instruction with Ben 5.1.17 then Lewis Gun school. DOW 4.5.17 Bullecourt- Vraucourt Copse British Cemetery. Note: There is an additional index item 798-9	311, 314, 309, 329, 331, 335, 353

HOWELL-PRICE Frederick Phillimore, Major, DSO and DMC enlist 17.9.14 age 26. To Army Service Corps to 7th LH Reg. to Requisitioning Officer Div. Hdgtrs Australian Army Service Corps. RTA *Devanha* from Port Said. Discharge 25.8.19. living in Sumatra in 1931 and Vaucluse 1967. Not mentioned in book Note: There is an additional index item 798-9	740
HOWELL-PRICE John, Lt., DSC., DSO., 1886-1937. Ran away to sea aged 14. 1915 made Lt., armed merchant cruiser *Alcantura*. Met German raider *Greif* both ships sunk. DSC of the Navy. Then to Submarines. Discharge 1921 then returned to Merchant Navy. Not mentioned in book Note: There is an additional index item 798-9	740
* PRIESTLY George Henry, Lance/ Corp., Enlist 20.4.15 age 21 years, farmer, father of Gostwyck Martins Creek via Paterson NSW. 6th Rfts 1st Bn A Coy. Wounded Gallipoli bomb wound to r leg to Malta, Influenza, KIA 11.2.17 France, Warlencourt British Cemetery SW of Bapaume France, sniped 10.2.17 George, from Raymond Terrace -Ben	320
PRIOR E. William Henry, Capt., MBE. Enlist 11.8.15 Bank officer, aged 26, father of Artarmon. 9 Rfts 3 Bn to 1st Bn Tel el Kebir. Wounded 28.6.16 Pozieres. Disch. to Captain Sherrington HQ London. Officer in Charge of Civilian Personnel AIF. Discharge 28.11.20 *Nartundo* Duty OC troops 9.7.20 Died 1937	206, 163, 223, 441, 445
* PUNCH William Joseph, Pt. Enlisted Goulburn from Queensland. 17th Rfts 1st Bn. (aboriginal) aged 31 years. To 53 Bn 20.5.16. Trench Feet 7.9.16, 1st Bn, Wounded, 20.9.16, Wounded 5.4.17 and 18.4.17. Died 29.8.17 Pneumonia and endocarditis Mont Dora Military Hospital. England. Full Military Honours East Cemetery Bournemouth England. Michael Kelly The Australia Jan 2015: William Punch was believed to have been born in the Bland River region of NSW about 1880 to an indigenous family. Following the murder of his family soon after his birth he was taken in by the Siggs family of Goulburn. He attended the local school and was a good student. He enjoyed music and became an accomplished violin player. He went to music lessons with the Siggs children in Crookwell. He was a popular member of his community and along with some of his friends provided musical entertainment at community functions. Information from Geoff Speer in *Simply Hell Let Loose* Stories of Australians at War. Dep of Veterans Affairs. Article written by Albert Speer MBE in Goulburn and District Historical Society newsletter	267, 277, 278

PURCELL, Montague Horatio Charles, L/Corp. Born Sydney, aged 18 years, Smiths striker, mother of Ryde. 26.7.15 Tel el Kebir to 11 Rfts 1st Bn, *Ivernia* to France. Wounded 28.7.16 GSW neck, re-join 1st Bn 27.11.16. Septic foot 19.1.17 Re-join1st Bn, C Coy 15.2.17. KIA 7.4.17 Villers-Bretonneux Memorial	243
PURCELL James Dudley, Pt., Enlist 12 Rfts 1st Bn., A Coy., aged 24 of Marrickville. Flu, Wounded 22.7.16. DOW 25.7.16. Becourt Military Cemetery Albert.	

Q

* QUINLAN William, Pt., Enlist 1.9.15 born Glebe aged 36 years, shop assistant 12 Rfts 1st Bn., 4.5.16 SW back leg and arm Weathercock House, DOW 25. 5. 16. Merville Cemetery, France	207

R

RAINSFORD Walter Bruce. Staff Sgt. Enlist 14.10.15 born Wahroonga, age 18 years, clerk, AAMC to No 2 Field Amb. to 3rd Canadian Clearing St, France. 14 Field Amb. RTA *Port Lyttleton* 25.12.18 Chartered accountant 350 George St Sydney NSW. Dr Bruce Rainsford 31 Post Office Chambers 114a Pitt St Sydney. His WW1war diary online at Mitchell Library. He mentions Ben and Art, *Ancestry* Peter Crocker USA: Walter Bruce Rainsford left Southampton, UK for New York, USA on 29/11/1936 and lived in California for some years before returning to the UK. He returned to Melbourne, Australia from Liverpool, UK in September 1947.	2, 65, 69, 74, 153, 220, 381, 470, 478, 482, 500, 516, 533, 615
RAINSFORD Bruce's sister. nurse at Royal Prince Alfred Hospital Sydney	
RATCLIFF Sidney Castle S/Sgt., Enlist 12.7.15 born Eng. Aged 41 years, Sydney Uni Dental Student, married of Fivedock Sydney. Dental Corp 2nd Aust. General Hospital. Epistaxis Cairo. On strength 13.8.15 On *Orsova* with Ben. RTA *Borda* on nursing duties Discharge 21.1.16 Transfer to Dental Hospital. Re enlist 29.9.18 Discharge 31.12.18 Now dentist with Uni of Sydney Company aged 44, Dentist, wife of Vaucluse. Aust. General Hospital, Ben's address book has D.G. Radcliffe 433 Bourke St Darlinghurst	40, 46
RADCLIFFE Frederick, L/ Corp., enlist 27.1.15, born ENG, father of Manchester, aged 23, Engineers draftsman. 5th Rfts 1st Bn. Gallipoli 6/11.8.15 Missing then KIA Buried Browns Dip North, Exhumed to Lone Pine. Red Cross report from Pt Byers, wounded, in Malta, A Coy 1 AIF	

REDMOND Johnston. Capt., C of E Chaplain. Enlist 18.9.16, aged 34 years, married, born Ireland, lives Victoria, 1st Bn. RTA with Ben *Wandilla* to *Kanowna* on transport Duty, Melbourne 12.5.18. No ship Picture but Meteren Officers Pic	419
RICHARDS Thomas *Tom* James, Lt., MM., Enlist 26.8.14 aged 31, traveller, born Armidale, mother of Brisbane. 1st Field Ambulance and stretcher bearer to 1st Bn. 2/Lt 1.12.16. Malaria, debility lumbago. Wounded accidentally 19.5.17 whilst at 1st Anzac Corps School by bomb explosion to back and shoulders, to ENG. 17.9.17 GSW R Arm to ENG. Also sick to hospital with osteo-arthritis of spine. RTA 31.7.18 with a stop-over in South Africa. Terminated 2.3.19 MD 2. Tom RICHARDS, Beach Court Manly. Also in Meteren photo Before the war 'Rusty' Richards had a successful career in rugby union. As an international player, Richards travelled to South Africa and England, representing both Australia and Britain, and won a rugby Olympic gold medal for Australia at the London Olympics in 1908. He retired from football in 1913. Source AWM Anzac Live. Rusty died at Rosemount Repat. Hospital Brisbane of advanced TB in 1935	301, 364, 366, 369, 371, 379, 409, 438, 441, 419
ROBERTS George Arthur, Maj., Embark 9.11.16. 2nd Rfts 1st Bn. Born Linton VIC. Age 40. Architect. wife of Milsons Pt then Roseville. Soldier at Boer War and many local infantry regiments with training prior to 1914. Wounded Gallipoli. 29.5.15 to 1st Bn Tel el Kebir. 25.2.16 to 1st Training Bn. RTA *Seang Bee* 29.4.16 then on Transport Duty. RTA *Balmoral Castle* OC Troops medically unfit, neurasthenia.	158, 162, 163
ROBERTS Kenneth Walter. Pt., Enlist 19.9.16 aged 23, engine driver / engineer of Tarro, NSW. 36th Bn. Invalided to Australia with mitral heart defect considered pre-exist condition HT Port Lyttleton 19.10.17 Melbourne thence overland to Sydney. Discharge 23.1.18	581
ROBERTSON Louis Leighton, Gunner, MM. draughtsman, apprenticed to architect father, for 5/- per week. Family home *Birklands* Dural Rd Hornsby. 1st Siege Battery 36th Bgde., RTA 17.4.19., H.T. *Derbyshire*.	
ROBERTSON Norman Howard, Gunner, enlist 8.10.16. clerk. 6th Army Brig. A.F.A. 17th Battery, brother to Louis, Gassed RTA *Halia* 20.7.19	567, 672

ROBERTSON Thomas Abraham, Lt., Enlist 22.6.15. Born Sydney, aged 22 years, analytical chemist, mother of Petersham. 21st Rfts 1st Bn., C Coy 13.3.16. 1st. ADBD Etaples 27.4.17-40.4.17 to 39 General Hospital Havre 14.5.17. Returned 1st Bn 30.6.17. Wounded 7.1.17, SW left knee R leg to Eng. Influenza 18.6.18 RTA *City of Poona* 14.1.19 as Quarter Master on Duty. Discharge 21.7.19. Did trench art at Havre	360
ROBINSON Leonard *Len* Gladwin, Pt. Enlist 14.1.17 aged 19, born Bundaberg, motor engineer. 8 Rfts 34 Bn. To Aust. Field Artil. 18.5.18 Gas poisoning. Marriage to Kate Edith Powell at Christ Church Warminster 7.8.19 bought out wife and mother in law. RTA *Runic* 20.12.19 Discharge 19.3.20	383, 521
*ROWLANDS Dad Verner Stanley, Maj., Enlist 7.10.14 Ex 33rd Inf Reg., aged 26 years, auctioneer. Embarked for Gallipoli 5.4.15 made Capt. 7.8.15. KIA 30.9.16, Bed-ford House New Cemetery, 1mile S of Ypres.	276
ROWLAND William Joseph, Maj., Enlist 18.6.15, Born Bundarra, aged 31 years, mother of Mosman. 4 Rfts 1st Bn C Coy. Wounded Gallipoli, CO of 1st Bn 3.9.15. to 53 Bn Tel el Kebir. To 45 Bn to 12 Training Bn ENG. 25.8.16 RTA 3.10.18 *Olympic* via USA then *Sonoma* to Sydney Discharge 1.12.18	152, 158
RYAN Cyril Housden, Captain, MC., Member Victorian Order. Enlist 20.10.15 aged 24 years. Born Rockhampton, commercial traveller, father of *Allowah* Nundah QLD. 15th Rfts 9th Bn. Many training courses, No 1 training Bn, 25.8.17 Corps School, 2nd Army Central School, Lewis Gun School. To Kings Guard, back to 9th Bn. Overseas Training Bgde. RTA *Borda* 27.9.18 Term. 13.8.19	365, 372

S

SADDINGTON Douglas Vernon, L/Corp., Enlist born Sydney, age 20, audit clerk, father of *Bellbourie* Water St Wahroonga 29.5.15. 23 AAMC 15th Field Ambulance RTA *City of Poona* 28.3.19 as nursing staff on duty Discharge 9.7.19 Doug Saddington Expropriation Board Rabaul	
SADDINGTON Roy Menzies Enlist 24.10.18, 26 years, pay clerk, brother to Doug	533, 617, 619
SAMPSON Reginald William, Lt., MC. and Bar. Enlist 13.9.15. Aged 29 years, accountant of Leichardt. RTA Melbourne *Aeneas* then by rail to Sydney. Appoint terminated 28.8.19; c/- Dangar Gedye and Co, Young St, City. Meteren Photo	331, 332, 335, 391, 398, 417, 419, 437

*SAMUELS Robert Oswald, Lt., Enlist 27.7.15 aged 27 years, motor mechanic, father of Narromine NSW. 13 Rfts 1st Bn to 54 Bn at Tel el Kebir -5th Div. Hdgtrs – Anzac Provost – 5th Div. Hdgtrs-1st Bn-Officer Cadet Bn-1st Training Bn Eng., KIA France 9.8.18 France Adelaide Military Cemetery France-Villers-Bretonneux	
SANDERS Charles, Bombardier, Corp. MM., 28.10.17. Enlist 9.12.14, aged 21, farmer, father living Billiard Ave Wahroonga. Married in England. 6 Light Horse then 15th Field Artillery to 58 Bn. Wounded gas 5.6.18 Rheumatism and reaction paralysis 7.11.15. Wounded deafness gunfire 3rd Artil Bn . RTA *Berrima* 2.1.19 to Melbourne then ship to Sydney Discharged 23.4.19. Died 1957. Brother Bert and Sister Mary Sanders, Nurse at The Coast Hospital	490, 494, 495, 514, 576
SANDES Flora, Capt., Known as Servian Joan of Arc. Helped Rose Venn-Smith with fundraising. photo from Archives see Google	698, 699
SCALES Frederick Hudson, Lt., Enlist 9.7.15 Born ENG aged 31, clerk. 12 Rfts 1st Bn., GSW chest, leg serious, prem. explosion of bomb, accidentally wounded. RTA *Anchises* with wife and child Struck off 22.8.19.	321
SCOTT Edward Irvine Charles, Maj. Born 1873. Kempsey. Agent from Sydney. Previous Boer War and 6 months Pacific Islands. Lt., 7th Rfts 1st Bn.to 53 Bn to CO 5th Pioneer Bn. RTA 31.7.18. Died Mosman 1941. For photo ID He is described as a big lump of a well- dressed fellow. source Trove. AIF ID 6', 12 stone, chest 38-41, fair complexion, grey eyes, and brown hair. Wore Queen Victoria Boer war with 5 clasps and ANMEF Pacific Islands	4, 5, 38, 82, 83, 149, 347, 439
SALKELD Alexander, Corp., Enlist 1.2.15. 5 Rfts A Coy 1st Bn., born Eng., aged 23, seaman. Wounded Gallipoli Anzac to Valetta Hosp. Malta to Eng., Tel-el Kebir 15.1.16 *Ivernia* Many Schools of Instruction. L/Corp 26.10.16 RTA *Burmah* 30.12.18 Discharge 24.3.19. Married Eng., Agnes Maud Patterson, South Shields Durham 22.8.17. Died before Gallipoli Medallion 1967.	220
SCOTTON William Henry L/Corp Enlist 31.5.16 born Newtown age 30 wife of Waterloo B Coy 1st Bn, B Coy 3rd Bn – 20 Bn RTA *Delta* 7.3.19. W. Scotton Mann St Armidale in Bens address book	
SCHULZ John, Lt., MC. Enlist 20.7.15. aged 21 years, born Rockhampton, station hand, 2nd Rfts 31 Bn., to 47 Bn., for photo ID 5 11 ' fair grey fair. Wounded SW l knee 7.8.16. Wounded 5.9.18 GSW R leg fractured tibia. Wounded 25.3.18 GSW face and fractured mandible Messines 7.6.17 RTA *Kanowna* 5.9.18	452

SHANNON Frederick Patrick Lt., Enlist 29.12.14. Born Eng, aged 18, farm hand. Gallipoli Enteric Dysentery to Malta. Many Schools of Instruction and cadet School at Trinity College Cambridge to 1st Bn 18.1.17 Crushed foot 14.7.17 Wounded 1.3.18 SW fracture left femur to 3rd London and Moreton Gardens *Kanowna* 7.3.19 Discharge 30.8.19. His new bride 7.9.18 in England lost contact with him. In Brisbane 1928. C/- A J Biggs Esq., 25 Caldervale Rd Clapham Park London. Meteren Photo	409, 416, 419.438, 441
SHAW Abraham Nevison *Joe*. Sgt., Enlist 20.4.15. born ENG. aged 35, Compositor, wife of Waverley. Previous service. Made Sgt., Tel el Kebir 2.2.16. On *Ivernia*. Rheumatism to hospital 29.6.16 Sgt Shaw has re-joined No 2 Platoon. 28.1.17 Trench fever, Bronchitis to ENG Re-join 1 Bn 2.4.17 Sgt vice Sgt Marks 29.6.18 RTA *Burmah* 30.12.18 Discharge 24.3.19. Joe Shaw, 21 Little West St Darlinghurst; Mrs. J Shaw 6 Queen St Woollahara. P H Shaw manager Comm Ass Co., 65 Scott St Newcastle Bens address book	256, 258, 269, 343, 791, 794
SHEPHERD Charles Lt., *Medaille Militaire*. Enlist 1.9.14 born Ballarat, aged 24, plumber, father of VIC. 2 Field Coy Engineers. Gallipoli bullet to sole of foot, Dysenteric to Malta Made Lt. 5.4.18 4th Pioneers GSW Thigh amputated l thigh to 3rd London Hospital RTA *Wandilla* to *Kanowna* Discharge 3 MD 1.9.18 Died 1964	
* SHERIDAN John Joseph *Johnnie*, Pt., Enlist 13.5.15. aged 20 years, cable clerk from Five Dock 6th Rfts. 4th Bn., DOW 17 Gen. Hospital Alexandria from GSW head side back and leg 7.8.15 received on Gallipoli. Buried Chatby Military War Memorial Cemetery, Alexandria Egypt	161
SHOEBRIDGE Alfred Arthur. E.R. WO 1. Enlist 24.8.14. born Hornsby, aged 20, civil servant, father of Peats Ridge Rd Hornsby. Senior cadets 19b Corps. Brigade Ammun. Column. Dysentery Gallipoli. Tonsillitis seriously ill April 1917 Duty with Kit Stores RTA *Ceramic* 12.3.20 Discharge 5.6.20	
SIMPSON Lt., J.W.S. 1/8 Middlesex Regt – trench art at Havre	
SMITH Albert Ernest Jeffrey, Sapper, Enlist 8.2.16 age 27, school teacher, father of *Arcadia* O'Brien St, Bondi, 1st Div., 2nd Div. Signallers Coy, Engineers NSW Signals Corps, Signal Rfts. Wounded SW R thigh 29.4.18 France. RTA *Bakara* 19.2.19 Discharge 10.4.19 med unfit - Ben's brother in law who married sister Dot Champion. Widowed when she was 50 years. Excerpts from his diary 1918 included which were in possession of T S Champion., Ben said in cardex that he never fully recovered from his war wounds and that he came to see Ben when he was hit at Pradelles	xiii, 375, 377, 416, 805

*ASHER-SMITH Charles Donaldson, Pte, enlist 20.9.17 of *Alvah* Burns Road, Wahroonga. St Johns Presbyterian. 20 Bn., KIA 9.10.17 Passchendaele, body not retrieved. Memorial Menin Gate. Charlie Smith of St Johns Presbyterian Church Wahroonga Honour Roll	407
ASHER-SMITH George aged 19, Enlist 12.7.18 born Sydney, law student, father Alexander Asher -Smith of Burns Road Wahroonga. St Johns Presbyterian	
SMITH Donald, Major.	787
SMITH Donald Ian Robertson, Capt., born Nth Sydney, aged 24 years, Doctor, senior resident Sydney Hospital, NOK Donald father 159 Macquarie Street Sydney. AMC Rfts 1.3.16 Enteric Fever 13.6.17. Typhoid 2.7.17 RTA *Katoomba* on duty 8.8.19 Discharge 14.11.19	500, 808
SMITH Eric Alfred Fell, Lt., Enlist 9.5.16 aged 18, dental student, North Sydney. Father Mr Donald Smith, dentist, Macquarie St Sydney. Army Dental Corps to 4th Div. Artillery, 11 Field Artill Bn. Awarded best all-round cadet at St John's Wood with papers marked excellent all round with mark of 95%. Dec. 1917.Wounded SW R Arm France RTA *Anchises* Wounded R. knee at sea accidentally 3.3.19 Arrived Melbourne 13.4.19 then to Sydney. Terminated 9.6.19. graduated Dentistry 1923 with Ben. Best man Bens wedding 1923. WW11 Citizen Militia Forces. Married twice. Died 1965 Victoria.	500, 513, 521, 526, 543, 547, 561, 585, 592, 616, 628, 631, 634, 658, 663, 668, 672, 697, 706, 809, 815
SMITH Noel Ginger Watson Munroe, Lt., Enlist 8.6.15. aged 19. analytical chemist. born North Sydney Father Major Donald Smith, dentist Macquarie St Sydney. 10 Rfts 1st Field Artillery. Influenza. Returned to Aust. by permission to finish Dental Course. RTA as quarter master ships staff H.T. *Gaika* 29.12.18 Sydney. Discharge.4.2.19	15, 24, 149, 212, 213, 486, 499, 500 503, 508, 509, 561, 585, 677, 500, 201, 251

SMITH Ross Macpherson. Sir Enlist 19.8.14 Born Adelaide Mother of Gilberton South Australia aged 21 years warehouseman for Harris Skarfe. B Sgdn 3rd Light Horse Regiment. See complete record ANA record search and ANZAC LIVE for more complete history. Trained as pilot in July 1917 with Australian Flying Corps. Flew supplies to Laurence of Arabia in Azrak. After Armistice Prime Minister Billy Hughes offered 10, 000 pounds to the first Australians who could fly England to Darwin. Vickers Vemy 4 engine bomber with his brother Lt Keith Smith with Jim Bennett and Sgt. Wally Shiers as mechanics. The brothers were knighted and the money split 4 ways. The Smith brothers then planned a round- the-world flight in a single engine Vickers Viking starting on Anzac Day 1922. 9 days earlier Ross and mechanic Jim were trying out the aeroplane and as Keith was late took off without him. Both men died. Ross, aged 29 years.	667, 699, 702
MARTIN-SMITH Harry, Lt. Enlist 2.3.15 aged 21, farmer of Wahroonga.19 Bn to 5th Aus. Machine Gun Corp to 2nd Machine Gun Bn. GSW and gassed x 2. RTA 9.1.19 *Margha*. Also served WW11	3
SMITH Harold Charles, Driver, enlist 29.5.15 born Sydney, aged 19, in 19b Hornsby. 7 Rfts 1st Bn., White Camp on Anzac to 53 Bn at Tel el Kebir, mumps bronchitis to 62 Bn. 19.4.18 GSW face RTA *Konig Frederick August* 20.6.19 Discharge 10.10.19	
SOLMON A., 10th London Regiment CTS Havre - did trench art in Ben's diary	
SOMERSET Charles William Henry Rollo, Capt., Enlist 3.10.14 from Esk QLD, 19 years, station hand. 5th Light Horse Bgde – 1st Bn. 5.6.16 Lewis Gun MG School 31.5.17 5th Army School 1st Bgde School to 1st Bn. 17.7.18 Accidental # ribs to Eng- land 28.9.18 To 1st Bn. RTA Leicestershire 9.12.18 Died 20.2.1936	293, 294, 301, 303, 335, 362, 364, 366, 396, 398, 408, 411
*SPARKE Edward Rashleigh, MC. Lt., 25.8.14 born Newcastle, aged 19, law student, parents Newcastle. 1st Field Ambulance to 1st Bn. France. Sniping, Light Mortar Schools., M.C. 6.12.16 Wound bomb Rt shoulder and # humorous to ENG. RTA Euripides, discharge 18.2.18. Joined Censor team at 4 Aust. General Hospital and died of Pneumonia influenza, bronchitis and cardiac failure 22.6.19 aged 24. Unfortunately, death not considered war related. His diary online at Mitchell Library WW1 diaries	253, 267, 294, 299, 301, 302, 445, 499, 625

*SPINKS Leslie Gilbert, L/Corp, MM. dated 12.7.16, Enlist 28.6.15 Born Vic, carpenter, aged 23 years, wife of Paddington. 9 Rfts 1st Bn A Coy. Made L/ Corp. 12.3.16. Wounded Pozieres 22-25 /7/16 BSW lower extremities R leg and knee also buried, RTA HT *Barambah* 10.6.17 Discharge 15.8.19 Died 1921 at Auburn VIC. Also was able seaman in RAN on HMAS *Encounter* and saw service. Deserted. 1.7.15 and immediately re-joined the AIF. Died after discharge but War related so I have included him in died due to war	230, 232
STACEY Bertie Vandeleur, Lt-Col., CMG, DSO and Bar. Enlist 17.8.14 as Pte in 4th Bn commissioned 14 Sept 1914. Wounded Gallipoli. To France as Major. OC Coy serving at Pozieres and throughout 1916. 4th Bn. Lt. Col., 17 .3.17 CO 1st Bn after Bullecourt. Battles of Messines, Broodseinde where wounded and Passchendaele 1917. Wounded 6.10.17 rejoin1st Bn 19.10.17. Led Bn from March to August 1918 and Armistice. Granted leave to continue legal studies RTA 6.7.19. Appointed Judge 1939. Denman Chambers Phillip St Sydney. Died 1971 Sydney.	327, 332, 335, 364, 366, 379, 386, 392, 407, 410, 411, 419, 423, 439, 440, 446, 630
STARKEY James Alexander, Sgt., Enlist 18, 8, 14, born Sydney aged 22 years labourer father of Manly. 5'11 'to H Coy 1st Bn., Made Sgt 19.3.17 France. 49th Army Course Musketry School O seas Tng Bgde, 49 Army Course Aldershot RTA 20.11.18 submarine guard duty *Suevic* Discharge 7.3.19. Post war, Orchard Rd Brookvale Manly	303
STEDMAN Ernest Lloyd, Pte, 1st Bn. Enlist 19.4.15. born Kent. wife in Eng. 31 years stoker. Wounded Gallipoli SW left leg. Wounded 23.5.16 Pozieres bomb GSW both legs R leg amp mid-thigh to 3rd London Gen. Hospital. Discharged in England 6.1.17 unfit for home or abroad. Lived in USA	222, 227
STEEN George Lt., then Captain. 1.with 1st Bn, enlist born Victoria, mother of Annandale NSW aged 29, Civil Servant. Gallipoli, wounded x 3, wounded debility and GSW foot 25/29.4.15. RTA 11.4.16 neurasthenia and enteric fever for 3 months recovery per *Kanowna* 2. Re-joined 24 Rfts 3 Bn to 1st Bn as Lt. 15.7.17 10 Corps School, Lewis Gun and Trench Mortar School, 23.8.18 Lacerate hand and sprained thigh. Commission, Captain and Adj. 21.8.18 vice Boardman. Held on Base Records Duty to 26.5.19 RTA *Kanowna* 25.9.19	403
SOUTER C.S. Nurse on HMHS *Karapara*. 'Bracklinn" Arbroath Scotland	
*STEEL Arthur Valentine 2/Lt., Enlist 17.8.14. born *Ballanglen* Wangaretta Vic. 19 years, postal assistant. E Coy 1st Bn to HQ Signallers, medical unfit, re-joined 1st Bn. Lewis Gun School 22.9.16. KIA Flers- Gueudecourt 5.11. 1916 ½ mile NNW of Flers exhumed to Grevillers British Cemetery	251, 294, 296, 364

STEVENS *Sticky* Arthur Borlase, Lt-Col., CMG, DSO., Enlist 27.8.14, born Sydney, aged 34, employee of NSW Railways. Previous war history Boer War, 2nd Lt., NSW Lancers 1910. Capt. Adjutant 2nd Bn. Lt Col., CO of 2nd Bn 12.3.16. Pozieres and Mouquet Farm. Nov 1916 appointed OC Base Depot. Resumed command Bn 19 Dec 17. Led Bn 1918 Battles. RTA 24.9.1918. Served WW11 Died 1965 Sydney.	310, 360, 410
STREET Geoffrey Austin, Major. MC., Enlist 10.9.14 born Double Bay, age 20 years, university student, father JW Street of Inniskillen Elizabeth Bay. 1st Bn. 30.4.15 GSW wound slight head, On *Ivernia* with Ben. 14.11.18 GSW wrist RTA *Wyremia* 13.4.19 Discharge 15.3.19	211, 231
STRINGER Kenneth Kelly, Pt., Enlist Childers QLD, aged 20 years, dental student. 18 Rfts 36 Bn Heavy Artillery, RTA *Kildonian Castle* Discharge 30.5.19 Dental school with Ben	809
STOBO Alexander Jarvie Hood, Lt., Enlist 18 years, medical student, father of Brisbane, born Harwood Island Clarence River. 12 Rfts 4 Bn to 1st Bn at Serapeum, wounded 21.7.15 SW scalp forehead. Div. school of Instruction 25.9.16 On Command Officers School of Instruction. Wounded 28.6.16 re-joined unit 6.7.16 to No 6 Officers Cadet Bn Oxford, Wounded Pozieres France, gas shell poisoning severe, Hernia operation 4.8.16 Div. School of Instruction. Wounded GSW chest 8.5.17 Command sniping School 10.6.17. Intelligence duties command to 1st Bgde, GHQ small arms School Musketry Instruction School. To Corps Intel. School 28.6.18, Bgde 22.7.18 1st Aus. Inf Bgde 8.9.18 30 Div. Armies 24.9.18 Intel Officer 21.9.18 – 1st Training Bgde 15.2.19. RTA 16.3.19 *Czaritzn* Transhipped *Dunluce Castle* and *City of Poona* 18.5.19 to Brisbane. With Ben when wounded. Wesley College.	230, 231, 410, 419, 420, 436, 438, 444, 567, 625, 636
STUDDY William Gordon Bradridge, Gunner. Enlist 1.2.18 student, born Riverstone NSW, father Dr Studdy of Berry St North Sydney. 34 FAB to 1st FAB. Synovitis Knee 1918. RTA *Balmoral Castle* 25.2.19 Discharge 15.4.19. Post war Glencoe Boggabri	
SUTHERLAND John Miller Lt., Enlist 11.3.15. Born Melbourne, aged 23, accountant, to Army Pay Corps, 22 Bn. to Officers School Oxford. Wounded 22.4.18 GSW R Leg, Cheek and Abdomen. To Le Touquet to No 3 Hospital London. Made L. 18.5.18 RTA *Kanowna* with Ben	452
SYMONS Albert Edward Lt., Enlist 18.9.16. aged 24 years, assistant secretary to Ltd Co, married, 9th Rfts 22nd BH – 22 FAB – 1st FAB to RA Cadet School ENG 13 F. Artil Bgde., RTA *Friedrichruch*, 3.7.19 as Education Officer on board. In Meteren Officers.	419,

SYMONDS Hyman, Capt. Enlist 25.4.17 aged 25 years, medical practitioner at Sydney Hospital, father of Paddington. AMC to 1st Aust. Field Amb to 1st Aust. General Hospital 4 Base to 15 Field Amb to 5th Pioneers Bn as MO. 1st Bn 11.3.18. Gas School and School of Instruction for MO. Wounded when patching up Ben on 15.4.18. GSW foot to Eng. To 1st Aust. General Hospital 7.7.18, 10.9.19 to ADMS Depots. In AIF UK. Relinquishing MO duties 3.10.19. RTA *Orantes* on duty, with wife. Discharge 15.1.20. Married Dora Israelson at Hamstead Synagogue 10.9.19. Capt., H Symonds 144 Fordwych Rd, Cricklewood London	364, 386, 394, 398, 436, 446
SYMINGTON Jack Evill, Lt., DCM. 20.11.17. Enlist 31.7.15 age 21, Stockman, b Maitland, father of Mosman. 8 Rfts 4 Bn. Wounded limbs and face, broncho pneumonia x 4 include accident shot in leg, 23.2.17 Div. Signal School. Inf Cadet Course.13.1.18. RTA *Aeneas* 31.5.19 Discharge 19.9.19. 1950 of North Manly. Enlist WW11 and served in New Guinea	313

T

TAIT Robert *Bob* Frederick, dentist of Wahroonga, born 1899 Townsville, also of Stanton Hill Townsville. Married Sydney 1927. Of *SunnyBraie* Neringale Ave Wahroonga. Died 1980 Wahroonga. Dentist. Served WW11.	
TEAZE Alexander, Pt., born ENG aged 24, farmer from Liverpool NSW. 1st Bn, RTA gunshot / bomb wound to foot and leg. HT *Barambah* 10.6.17.	222
TEASDALE W.J. Lt., Enlist 22.2.16. Born Cork IRE., aged 31 years, Police Constable, wife of Auburn. To 55 Bn 31.6.16. 1st Training School as Instructor Etaples 4.7.16. To Duchess of Westminster at Le Touquet 3.2.17 Bronchitis. To 1st Tng Camp Etaples 25.2.17 to Central Training School Havre as Instructor 30.5.17. Also other Schools of Instruction. Wounded 20.8.18 face, eye and tibia to Eng. RTA *Berrima* 17.4.19 Discharge 23.4.20. Died 1947 Did Trench Art with Ben. The trench art was squiggles on a piece of paper, Ben's diary, then using those lines an image was drawn.	
*TEITZEL Louis Walter, Lt., Enlist 15.2.15 age 28, Telegraphist Post master., father HAC Teitzel from Warwick Queensland. 25th Bn, For photo ID. 5'10 'fair complex blue eyes and brown hair Presbyterian. Wounded bomb wound to foot and frost bite 27.11.15 Gallipoli per *Karapora* to St Elmo Hospital Malta. Friend of Ben. Missing then KIA 12.30 am 'said I am blind Find Sgt and tell him to carry on. Body lost '. Pozieres Mouquet Farm area 29.7.16. ID disc recovered 1927. Cemetery AIF Burial Ground, Grass Lane Flers France. Brother Arthur also served	123, 124, 125, 129, 131, 132, 133, 134, 135, 136, 140, 360

TEMPLE William Arnold, Lt., Enlist 22.8.15 aged 21 clerk of Lakemba. 18th Bn. Wounded x 3. 20.5.18 GSW Foot. RTA *Kanowna*. Term. 22.3.19	452, 462
THOMPSON Clive Wentworth, Lt. Col., DSO., MC., VD., Bsc. MB. Enlisted 3.9.14 to Gallipoli as Regimental Medical Officer. 1st Bn. with AMC. Was with General Bridges when mortally wounded. Wounded GSW back multiples 26.9.17 to ENG. RTA *Durham* 23.12.18 Discharge 22.2.19	105
THOMPSON C. killed 22.6.16 Pt., CW	
THOMPSON Fred William, BQMS, Enlist 24.8.14 aged 24, book keeper, of *Bungey* Coonanbarra St, Wahroonga. 1st Bn to 2nd Battery 1st Field Artillery. (FAB). Re-joined 1st Bn 9.12.17 ex instruction Hurdcutt. Wounded x 2 + trench feet and gassed, RTA special 1914 leave *Durham* Sydney 24.12.18. A brother drowned whilst he was away and his father died. Also served WW11 as Capt.	149, 480, 582
THOMPSON Walter Raleigh- Artificer, Enlist 11.12.15 born Eng, Attestation front page missing. Brother to Fred. 1st Bn to A.M.A.T. Mechanical Trans section 1st Bn., M/O to Bhutpore Barracks Tidworth. Much illness including Influenza RTA *Koroa* 20.5.19 Disch 20.1.20 Was with Ben in 1917 check again	149, 296, 480, 394, 569, 581, 781
TIBBETT John George, Sapper, Enlist 24.10.17 aged 18, clerk, of Peats Ferry Rd Wahroonga. Wireless Sqdn Rfts, Service in Kurdistan. RTA Medic Discharged 13.1.20.	362
TINDALE Allen Reginald, Lt., Enlist 1.9.14 aged 19 years, clerk, father of Mosman 1st Bn, wounded Steeles Post Gallipoli 2) France then 3) GSW leg serious also neurosis RTA *Athenic* to Cape Town trans shipped Sydney 15.10.17. Struck of Strength 9.10.17.	162, 193, 375
TRAILL *Bob* Sydney Robert, Lt., *Croix de Guerre* Belgium. Enlist 28.8.14 aged 19, clerk, father of Burwood 1st Bn., Wounded GSW x 3 times RTA *Wahene* Sydney 1.7.19.	635
TUDEHOPE Archibald Edward, Lt., Enlist 30.8.15. born Paddington, aged 27, motor salesman, father of Paddington. Depot Bn Casula CSM. To 1st Bn 20 Rfts. Made 2/ Lt 1.3.16 Made Lt., 5.6.17 Sick cellulitis neck. Wounded 3.10.17 GSW l Arm to La Touquet to Eng, fractured humorous. RTA *Orontes* 13.5.18 left Capetown 19.4.18 Also has *Durham Castle*. Discharge 12.11.18. 1952 address Crowncliff Berowra. in 1952 Bens address book has Glen Tudehope and Co Wentworth Ave	

TURNBULL Sydney Moffatt, Pt, Enlist aged 20 years, student, father of Bondi 5.11.18 Discharge. consequence of expiration of period of enlistment. Post war of Birrell St Bondi.	
TURNER E. Nelson 25 Bn. Havre trench art	
TURNER Frederick George Freddie, Meritorious Service medal for duties as RQMS. Reg Sgt Major also was WO 11 and RQMS between wounds. Enlist 22.8.14 aged 27, soldier also says clerk, father of ENG. Joined B Coy 1st Bn. Lone Pine wounded arm, Wounded Poziers and Hill 60. In C Coy 1st Bn., RTA *Delta* 7.3.19 Discharge 13.6.19. In 1933 wrote to Dept saying he had not given accurate info on attestation. Was living in Leichhardt in 1967 for Gallipoli medal	
*TYSON James Gordon, Capt., MC., Enlist aged 20, pastoralist of Chatswood. 1st Bn to 3rd Bn, embarked *Orsova* 2/Lt., with Ben, Wounded, trench fever and brain fatigue and inability to collect thoughts post Ypres. KIA 3.5.17 Buried Vaulx A.D.S. British Cemetery exhumed to Vraucourt Copse Cemetery near Bapaume.	
* His brother Pt. H.H. Tyson, 19th Bn. also KIA buried Queant Rd Cemetery	40

V

VICARS James Malcolm Kither, Pt., Enlist age 18, woollen manufacturer, born Adelaide SA. Father of *Narrango* Burns Rd, Wahroonga. Father gave permission.to enlist in Hospital Service as previously refused due to heart troubles. A.MC. 2 Casualty Clearing Station. RTA 18.4.16 invalided H.S. *Runic* cardiac debility, pneumonia, anaemia.	701

W

WALKER Westby *DAD* Lionel, Capt., Enlist 20.3.15. Born Toowoomba, aged 40, Banker. Mother of 26 Mona Road Darlingpoint. 6 Rfts LH to 1st Bn 2 / Lt., 28.11.15. Made Lt., 28.5.16 GSW Wound x 2 thigh mild, May16 to Eng. RTA *Czar* 23.3.19 tranship *Dongola* 19.5.19. Discharge 8.7.19. Meteren photo	419, 391, 206
WALLEN Thomas, 2/Corp., Enlist. 7.10.14 aged 36, New Zealand, Telegraphist and poultry farmer of Neutral Bay. 1st Rfts 1st Bn, to 53 Bn-1st Anzac wireless section- 5th Pioneers, 1st Anzac wireless school-4th army. l/corp 1st Anzac wireless 28, 6.17 RTA *Kenilworth Castle* as staff. To ENG RTA *Field Marshall* 23.5.18 Medically unfit. Heart problems aggravated by war. Died 1936. pic of Sergeants 16.9.16 says l/ corp.	269,
WARD Samuel Edward Syd, Pt. Enlist 20.6.18 aged 18 years, student, Mother of *Myrtleville* Billyard Ave Wahroonga. 18 Rfts 3rd Bn., GSW R thigh, amputation., RTA *Euripides* Discharge 2.11.19. Married Maude Kershaw 1920	510, 511, 619, 780

WARNE Frank Edward, Pt. Enlist 14.8.15 aged 43 labourer/ fitter, married of Dulwich Hill. 12 Rfts 1st Bn., RTA *Nestor* medically unfit, pleurisy and pneumonia, overage. Discharged 25.10.17 on part pension	210, 211,
WAUGH Frederick Murchison, Lt. MC, enlist 3.4.16, aged 21, public servant from Ashfield. 11 Rfts 20 Bn, to 34 Bn., 5.6.17 GSW R leg, gas gangrene, amp. leg., RTA *Wandilla* transhipped *Kanowna* 22.7.18 with Ben. *Kelvyn Side* King St Ashfield. Living Coolangatta 1957	448, 450, 452, 462, 479, 480, 482, 483, 486, 491, 493, 501, 523, 531, 533, 536, 552, 557, 612, 629, 678
WAUGH *Carl* Carlton John, enlisted as John Carlton. Lt., Enlist aged 20 yrs., horse- breaker, father Mt Druitt., for photo I.D. fair all, complex, eyes and hair. 5'11 '-17.8.14 1st Bn, Transport section Maadi, appendicitis, many training courses. RTA *Caledonian Castle* 21.3.19; Cobcroft and Waugh 80 Pitt St Sydney post war.	154, 284, 302, 316, 329, 332, 401, 409, 419, 410
* WEBB Ernest Charles, Lt. and Q.M. Enlist 26.7.15 aged 26 of Illo Dural Rd Hornsby and The Junction Pharmacy Hornsby, Enrolled 2 Bn then 1st Bn. A Coy, KIA 5.5.17 Bullecourt, shell fire to head and body – burial not certain. Cemetery Villers - Bretonneux Memorial France late chemist from Hornsby Ben's postcard portrait. Sister Theodora Flora A Webb	299, 301, 305, 789
WELLS Frederick William, Lt., Enlist 7.10.16 aged 22 years, farmer/grazier, father of East Gresford. 21st Rfts 1st Bn., RTA *Ascanius* Struck of Strength 30.9.19. Meteren Photo	419, 410
WELLS Henry, Hon Capt., 1st Bn Quarter Master. Enlist 24.8.14, aged 37, born Eng, Tramway Inspector. Previous history Boer War. Colour Sgt. D Coy 1st Bn. 18.10.14 Wounded Gallipoli, sick, sick, Sick to hospital 24.12.16 arteriosclerosis. To 1st Training Bn as QM. RTA *Durham Castle* debility. Discharge 23.7.18	304
* WELLS also COSGROVE George Edward, Sgt. MM., Enlist aged 25 years, labourer, born NZ, 11 Rfts 1st Bn Tel el Kebir, Made Sgt 12.7.16 Missing then KIA 5.11.16. Bayonet Trench Cemetery Gueudecourt near Bapaume. Exhumed to Grevillers British Cemetery	294, 324

*WEST Claude Bertie 2/Lt., Enlist 24.8.14 Born Bourke, aged 23 years, clerk, father of Cooks Hill and Orange, Corp 5.8.16 to 4th Bn to 1st Field Ambulance as Driver at Alexandria, Mastitis of ear and enteritis RTA for 3 months Returned to Service. Wagon orderly 1st Field Ambulance to 4th Bn 29.9.16 Officers school of Instruction, 2/Lt 25.1.17 to 1st Bn 22.2.17 Wounded 5-8 /5.17 GSW # thigh and chest severe DOW 16.5.17 Bullecourt. Etaples Military Cemetery.	364
WHATMAN William John. Driver. MM., Enlist 2.2.16 Born Mossvale, aged 20 years, labourer. 12.11.16 Mumps.10.7.16 33rd Bn to 1st Bn. MM dated 10.5.17 Demicourt. RTA *Boonah* 11.6.19. Died 1946	332
WHETTON Frank Pt., 1st Pioneers to 4th Bn. Enlist 7.1.16 born Granville, Sydney, age 28, carpenter, wharf labourer, photo id., tattoos neck and shoulders and arms 5'5 '. GSW legs and head, 4.10.17 Demicourt. l leg amp above knee and R femur not united. RTA *Kanowna* 22.7.18 Discharge 30.3.19. Died 1941	
WETTON Ernest Albert, Pt, Enlist Embark. 14.4.16 born Homebush, aged 22, butcher, 2 Rfts 53 Bn Wounded 13.3.17 GSW head, sick etc 30.7.18 Amp Right Thigh RTA *Kanowna* 5.1.19	
WHITFIELD Norman Harold, Capt., MC. + Bar, Enlist 11.5.15. ANMEF. ex Rabaul duty aged 20, electrician, to 7th Rfts 1st Bn on *Orsova*. Height 5.11 '. to 53 Bn to 5th Pioneer Bn. Court Martial Duty in England 12.10.18. Tonsillitis, Wounded slight, Influenza RTA Transport Duty *Berrima* Sydney.2.1.19	4, 39, 529, 531, 545
WILKINS James Earle, Lt., Enlist. Aged 29 customs officer married. 20th Bn, 27.9.17 GSW Leg and knee. R leg amputated 5.10.17. HT *Kanowna* embark. 3.9.18. Terminated 22.3.19.	448, 452, 462, 486, 523
WILKINSON Thomas Russell Bowman, Lt., MM., 14 Rfts 1st Bn. Enlist 4.8.15. Aged 24, bank clerk, father of Chatswood.1st. Bn 20.2.16 Tel el Kebir, on *Ivernia*, L/Corp 13.5.16, MM 12.7.16. 2/Lt 5.8.16. Bronchitis- sprained ankle, Wounded 24.8.18 GSW # humorous. RTA *Ascanius* 23.9.19 Discharge 25.5.20	230, 232, 371
WILSON L.G. *Mafney* Southport, Rosewood. South Queensland, Ben's address book	
WILSON Sid 17.6.16 -19.6.16 missing for a while	218
WITHY Charles Burton, Capt. Landing at Gallipoli 1st AIF. Diphtheria 8.11.15. School of Instruction Ismailia. Return to Egypt with horses. 18.8.16 shell wound thigh severe, 21.8.16 Duchess of Westminster Hosp., Le Touquet to 4th London Gen Hosp. Influenza. RTA *Leicestershire* 3.5.19 as Duty Adjutant. Discharge 24.8.19. Meteren photo	419

WITHY (continued) WW11 Lt-Col., DSO, MC, Ed., Enlist age 47 years, Company Manager, married. Previously 1st Bn Gallipoli and France. CO 2/25 Bn., middle East and New Guinea. WW11 Lt-Col., DSO, MC, Ed., Enlist age 47 years, Company Manager, married. Previously 1st Bn Gallipoli and France.	419
WHITE Lt KIA Pozieres	
WHITE Bevis Gerald, Capt. Enlist born Trinidad, 30 years, farmer father of Jersey Channel Islands. 25.8.14 2nd Light Horse, transferred to 1st Bn 26.9.15, made 2 Lt. 19.11.15 Gastritis Gallipoli to Malta. Made Captain vice Withy. Gas poisoning 10.8.16 to Eng. RTA *Kaiser J Hind* 6.5.19 Discharge 9 .7.19 -living at Monabool, Yimbun. QLD.	235, 241,
WOODS Sgt on *Orsova* exhibitions and theatre performer	
WOOD Andrew Thomas, Driver, Enlist 18.10.16. Rfts 1st Supply Column Motor Transport. Aged 27 years, Motor Car proprietor, Married since enlistment, of Billyard Ave Wahroonga. Father Roderick Wood. For photo id. 5 11 'dark complexion, grey eyes and dark brown hair. weight 162 lbs. Shoemakers chest. 4 Motor Transport, Supply Column, also in 1st Pioneer Bn. RTA 31.12.18 Sardinia Discharge 19.3.19 suspected TB but Scoliosis	656
WOOD George Sgt, MM + Bar. 5256. Enlist 14.9.15. born Sydney, aged 21, clerk, Made l/ Corp 31.7.16 Wounded 5.11.15 GSW thigh. 9.4.17 GSW R Hand. RTA *Konig Friedrich August* 20.6.19 Disembark Capetown for duty as pay and record Sgt in South Africa. Disembark Sydney 10.8.19 MM at Boursies 10.5.17 and Bar 5.7.18 (also known as Wilson George Wood	
*WOODFORDE Phillip Sidney Soane, Maj., Enlist 3.9.14. 1st Bn., aged 20, wool buyer, mother of Mosman. Applied for commission, Wounded GSW leg to Hosp back to Gallipoli, debility. *Ivernia* to Marseille. Wounded Weathercock House. Led Bn at Bullecourt April-May 1917 back to Eng – 1st Bn. 24.7.16 Major vice FWW Lindeman DOW 24.6.15. Wounded GSW upper and lower extremities and abdo. DOW 6.5.17. Buried Grevillers Military Cem. Picardie France. Brother also served, became architect.	193, 202, 207, 260, 283, 335, 336
WOOTTEN George Frederick, Major, DSO. Enlist 1st Bn 10.10.14 Diphtheria GSW Wound thigh to Duchess of Westminster Le Touquet 3.10.17.	
WRAY Mick, Ypres 11.9.16	
WRIGHT John William Jack ; DFC., CAPTE., and Flight Commander, enlist Light Horse 1915 to 4th Sqdn, Aus. Flying Corps., RTA *Kaiser Hind* 19.6.19. Married Nancy Johnson 24.9.19 enlist	564, 569, 605

Y	
YATES Harold Francis, Lt., MM., Enlist. 5.11.15, age 23, surveyor, of Newtown Sydney. Tfd School of Instruction Hayling Island to 16 Rfts 1st Bn 13.2.17.Acting Reg. Ships Sgt. Major 1.4.16. *Ivernia* L/ Corp to Officers Cadet Bn 7.6.18. 2/ Lt., 31.6.19. Lt. RTA 25.9.19 Katoomba, disembark Sydney with wife Marie Josephy formerly from Belgium. Married by License in Eng. Photo ID 5'9 'fresh complex blue eyes and brown hair.	445
YATES Walter Reginald. Lt. MC., Enlist 27.8.14. 1st Bn .Born Parramatta aged 21, mechanic, mother of Summer Hill. 5 Foot 11 inches. Influenza Gallipoli Made Sgt. 14.12.15 on *Ivernia* with Ben. Sniping School. School of Instruction and Cadet Officer School. Made Lt, wounded GSW Head frontal lobe 8.7.15. RTA *Kanowna* 14.12.17 Discharge 14.12.17 Major in Militia 1930. In West Aust in 1967 for Gallipoli medal.	168,
*YEOMANS Geoffrey Heron. Lt. Enlist 5.10.14 Grazier of Gilgoin Brewarrina NSW. Father of same. Mother of Woollahra. Trooper 6th LHR to 1st Bn. Shrapnel arm to Malta Lt. 12.3.16. KIA. night of 22 July 1916 prior to attack on Pozieres, with Major Lindeman, somewhere near Chalk Pit Contalmaison. - Exhumed to Pozieres British Military Cemetery.	235, 241, 244, 284
*YOUMAN James, Pt. Enlist 14.5.15, aged 37, teacher from Robertson Black Mountain NSW. 7th Rfts 1st Bn. to 53 Bn., KIA 30.9.18., Bullecourt, Tincourt New British Cemetery France,	93, 219
YOUNG David Kinlock, Sgt., aged 22 years, clerk, 7th Rfts 1 Bn., -1st Field Engineers – Army Pay Corps 53 Bn. Wounded 16.9.17 GSW R thigh. RTA *City of Poonah* Disembark Sydney 16.5.19	49, 74, 80, 126
YOUNG Eric Maclean, Capt. 59 Bn	
YOUNG Leonard Grace Gifford, Lt., Enlist 1.2.15 aged 23 music teacher, family of Adelong. 7th Rfts 1st Bn, Gallipoli with Ben. Imperial Camel Corps – 3rd Anzac Bn Imperial Camel corps. Wounded GSW both arms and knee Sinai Peninsula. RTA Suez *Neuralia* to Cape Town. HMT *Nestor* to Australia 21.5.17 Arrived Sydney. 28.11.17. suicide 1939	126,

Non-military connections to Frank

ADAMSON Heather, Miss, 3 year Arts, 63 Middle Street Stanmore NSW (friend of Frank). Heather Stuart Adamson daughter of Thomas G Adamson and Margaret C. 30.1.22 Junior staff Broken Hill High School. Married 1925	117, 525, 546, 562, 583, 591, 612, 652
CARROLL Peter, patriarch of Windsor NSW and grandfather to Frank. He became a successful business man. The son of an Irish convict, married to Caroline Morgan also the daughter of a convict. She was raised and schooled on the Hassall property Denbigh at Cobbitty NSW	153, 203
CARROLL William Raymond Ray, Public Works Depart. as engineer assistant in 1922 and was supervising engineer of the city underground railway and the Sydney Harbour Bridge (opened 1932) in association with Dr. J.J. Bradfield. He eventually became Director of Public Works. He was also largely responsible for supervising construction of Adaminaby Dam and the Inner Harbour of Port Kembla. He married and had three children. Photo from *Pickett Lines* courtesy of Lorraine Nelson	152, 510, 535, 585, 566, 575
CARROLL William Henry, school teacher (Uncle of Frank), his father Peter Carroll, patriarch of Windsor. His sons Bert, Ray and Philip. Died April 1920	xxii, 152, 557, 635, 662, 671
HARDING Mrs Horace (nee Lucina Carroll, Mrs Niland's sister) Genoa Flats. Musgrave. St Mosman	509, 510, 607, 656
NILAND Agnes Claire, Franks sister, married Helge Jack Molvig and lived at Belmont NSW. They had no children together	
NILAND, Cecilia Kitty, Franks sister, became dental assistant to Ben and it was he who diagnosed her with fatal leukaemia. She died in 1951. She married Peter Wilson. No children	
NILAND Frances Julia 'Frank' initially helped Ben in his Dental Practice after they married in 1923. They lived near the Newcastle Railway Station (coal trains and dust) and they had limited money so their first daughter spent much of her early years with the Niland grandparents and the doting aunts at *Tarro* on the farm. They built 83 Janet Street Merewether and then about 1937 *Jura* 214 Croudace St New Lambton Heights. Frank and Ben had two daughters.	

NILAND Mary started nursing in 1918 and graduated Dec 1921 at Newcastle Hospital and did her midwifery at Crown Street Hospital for Mothers and Babies. She owned a small private hospital at Bolworra. Her first husband died and she married her childhood sweetheart Billy Nielsen who was also widowed. (see 1918 photo) No children	
NILAND Ruth Caroline 1900-1952. Finished her nursing. Married Angus Roy Humphries. They had two daughters, one adopted	
RUMERY, Emma nee Carroll, sister of Mrs Niland. (Mrs.), *Denbigh* Riverstone NSW, children Fred and Marjorie . Fred left 1000 pounds to Frank in his will. Don't know if the sisters also received some money.	13, 301, 555, 589, 606 pic, 607, 704, 782,
Ruth UPFOLD bridesmaid to Frank in 1923 She had a sister Lena	562, 602, 614, 616, 618, 629, 653, 654, 664, 672, 684, 697, 698, 782, 815

Non-military connections to Ben

A ALLEN A. A. Lorne Avenue Killara NSW J3126	
ALFIERI Family, Mrs. F E and Miss Clare, *Horn Lodge*, Battle Sussex, ENGLAND	382, 394, 402, 408, 412, 413, 415, 439, 445, 446, 544, 581, 584, 629, 635, 651, 674
ANDERSON Charles Wyndham, graduated dentistry 1923, Coogee NSW	542
AUSTIN family. Enid, Mary, Jean etc .mostly pages under Vic Austin	
BRIDGES Miss Claire, Dovedale 29 Woodfield Rd Kings Heath, Birmingham thought to be Art Felton's English fiancé. His belongings were sent to her first and then to the Fentons.	397, 439, 468, 686, 782
VENN-BROWN Miss Rose. Y.MC.A. worker at Havre from Lane Cove Rd Wahroonga. See Trove. *A Sydney Girl in Havre* Sept 1916. RTA *Wahene*.1920 Instrumental in organizing Australian Peace Loan and asked to be one of speakers for the campaign, 1921 *A Business Girl in Shanghai China*	343, 698
CHAMPION Arthur Leslie, Bens eldest brother, 1887-1972 of Victoria St Roseville NSW. Irrigation officer, Leeton, Draftsman in Armidale in 1909 married in Armidale 1913 Althea Gentle 1885-1957. Head injury prior to the war and in Ben notes, had a plate in his head. Had 5 children	
CHAMPION William Henry, Esq., Strathalbyn Kingston Rd Camperdown Uncle Will. Compositor with Government Printing Office. His mother Louisa lived with him and he died before her in 1921. He helped Thomas Sydney Champion buy *Jura* Stuart St Wahroonga from the Hordern family and in his will forgave any debt. He was said to look like the Champion side of the family whereas Thomas took after his mother's side of the family.	

CHAMPION Gertrude Elsie 1891-1935, Worked Mines Department Lands Office, Bent St Sydney. Probably met there and married 1919 Rupert Bergelin. (See list of those who served) Gertrude died 1935 leaving Rupe and 4 young children. Eldest son Flight Sgt., Rupert Bergelin KIA 1944, Second son Tom Frank 1926-1953 Served WW11. Two daughters with families.	
CHAMPION Dorothy 1903-1993 Married 1930 Albert Ernest Jeffrey Smith (see list of those who served). She was a pitman stenographer before her marriage. They had one daughter. The Miss Smith who wrote to a soldier and was Gertrude's friend was Mabel Smith, Albert's sister who married Andrews.	
CHAMPION Tom 1907-1974 Married 1930 Grace Annie Louise Bradley. WW11 1940-45 A.C.I. Electrical fitter in RAAF. Ben's notes 'Pacific areas especially Rabaul area flying in crocks without doors' No children.	
CHAMPION Thomas Sydney. See family introduction. Secretary to Public Service Board 1920. 30 Hunter St Sydney. Died after Jessie in 1949 late of 1 Kissing Point Road Turramurra.	
CHAMPION Edie-was the stay at home daughter and after TS Champion died she married but became widowed fairly soon after and returned to Sydney.	
CHAMPION Eva *Marjorie* led a very active life with music teaching in High Schools and life in the church and she was a choir mistress. She was a constant in the family, writing and checking on other members. She loved her music and also wrote poetry particularly in later life. She died 1983 at Sydney Adventist Hospital.	
CHAMPION Boys Arthur Bert, Ben, Keith Tom throughout the book	
DEAN Harold Edward, aged 15 of Wahroonga. Shot in the back, killed, accidently by his friend when shooting cans.	147
DENTAL DRILL. Ben had a similar foot pedal dentist drill see pic 5.6.20 which he converted to make a foot pedal pottery wheel which I still have–PF. I think it is possible that Ben may have had some injury to his teeth when he was hit at Gallipoli as his teeth were fixed before he went away. He needed a lot of work when he returned. Ben was an early advocate and was instrumental in having fluoride put into the town water in Newcastle.	

Fiston DAVERNES 7 Rue Le Vasseur, Pollet Dieppe	
FISHER, Mr W Esq., AMP society 37 Threadneedle St London E.C.	403, 411, 438, 444, 784
FISK Ernest., Marconi wireless engineer. In 1918, a suburban house Lucania on the corner of Cleveland and Stuart Streets, Wahroonga was the unlikely setting for a world first in the history of communication. With Government permission Ernest Fisk set up a radio receiver in his home. The first wireless radio message on 22 Sept 1918 sent from the UK by Prime Minister Billy Hughes to Australia was received here, making it the longest distance wireless message ever sent, beating all previous distance records for a radio message. May Day calls from Titanic 1912 were sent via Marconi wireless. The Fisk Memorial – was unveiled outside the Wahroonga house in 1935. This was next door to Jura which is no longer there. He was knighted in 1937	, 544, 660, 686, 691, 784
FELL David, Weybridge Surrey, brother to Mrs. Donald Smith	
FELTON Didie. Married a returned soldier Frederick Rout in 1927 and lived at Forbes. She had one son and he had children.	28, 93, 151, 159, 164, 232, 290, 402, 473, 477, 480, 481, 501, 514, 518, 526, 535, 552, 554, 555, 556, 566, 577, 587, 591, 597, 631, 636, 643, 653, 658, 660, 667, 669, 673, 679, 700, 784,
HENDERSON L C, Esq., father of Alan, 4 Castlereagh St Sydney	

HIRST H, (Mrs.) and family, *Horncote* 124 Wright St, Middle Park Melbourne VIC. Ben's aunt Eliza nee Champion and her family including dentist family members	289, 564, 604, 801
KERSHAW Miss Maude Powell married Samuel 'Syd' Edward Ward 1920. See KERSHAW Bros and Sam Ward	
Peter LINDSAY. Tom Champion's young friend, lived in Burns Road. His father artist Sir Lionel Lindsay and mother Lady Lindsay known as Bingo. His uncle was artist Norman Lindsay	601, 608, 611, 620, 637, 653, 700
McGRATH M. J. Bsc., Kelvin Grove, Market St, Narremburn previous Lane Cove Road, Greenwich	516, 533, 567, 572, 573, 583, 592, 596, 612, 613, 617, 625, 635, 646, 648, 649, 651-3, 658, 659, 660.682, 784
MCLEOD, (Mrs.), 29 Polwarth Gardens Edinburgh; Miss Isabel Gibson McLeod of Edinburgh SCOT, married Capt., Beavis 29.10.19 St Stephens Sydney, notice SMH	
1.11.19 Ben was Best man and she was given away by Bob Grant the friend of her brother David McCleod, 1st Bn, KIA Gallipoli	629, 412, 785
NIELSEN William *Billy* Mitthius - Husband to Mary Niland (Kirkwood) and vet to Phar Lap when he died in USA.	649, 469, 782,
READ Dr William Henry and his wife Irene Victoria nee Phillips OBE.	
The Wurley, Cleveland St. Wahroonga. (back fence to Ben) She was sister to Frederick Stobo Phillips KIA Gueudecourt 5.11.16	294, 471, 555, 653, 654, 670, 690, 785

REID Andrew, near neighbours in Neriga Ave, Wahroonga Andrew Thyne Reid (1901-1964), engineer, businessman and benefactor, was born on 20 December 1901 at Randwick, Sydney, eldest of three sons of Scottish-born parents Andrew Reid, general importer, and his wife Margaret, née Thyne. Made a partner in James Hardie & Co. in 1896, Andrew senior became sole proprietor in 1912 and built the firm into a large industrial enterprise. In 1920 it was registered as a public company. Among other building products, the firm manufactured Fibrolite cement sheets. Andrew Reid senior was a benefactor of many causes including the Fairbridge Farm Schools and Burnside Homes. N.B. Ben had an introduction to Mrs. Reid's brother, Dr. Thyne 101 Earlsfield Rd Wandsworth, UK.	578, 439.
ROFE Ernest Fulton Gladstone 1899- 15.5.1920 at Wahroonga (aged 21 years). His sister Minnie Edith Rofe married Oswald *Os* Alfred Waldon Andrews in Nov 1920. Walter Thompson was best man. She died two years later. Their father Thomas Ernest Rofe, *Neringia* Wahroonga was a philanthropist amongst many things and Rofe Park at Hornsby is named after him. (source from Ancestry)	582, 689
ST ELMO Military Hospital Valletta Malta. Malta was known as *The Nurse of The Mediterranean* as there were so many hospitals on the island. In July 1915, two civil Government Schools, St John's and St Elmo, which occupied the site where now stands the Evans building in Merchant Street Valletta, were refurbished and converted into a hospital. St Elmo school was destroyed by bombing in the Second World War which also demolished the nearby historic Nibbia Chapel. The basements were used for stores. School children were moved to the old barrack rooms at Fort Lower St Elmo. St Elmo Hospital became operational on 12 August 1915. It had 218 beds with the verandah running along the class rooms accommodating an extra 100 beds. The hospital admitted mainly surgical casualties. It remained a surgical hospital even when the rush of enteric cases had transformed most of the other surgical units into medical ones. Miss Stones was Matron of St Elmo Hospital. The hospital closed in 1918.	122, 125, 130, 138, 205, 722, 736, 745, 755, 768,

16   REVEILLE   *January 1, 1933*

1st Bn. Patrol : No Man's Land Clash

(By Sgt. Norman Langford, 1st Bn., A.I.F.)

THIS story describes the circumstances in which Pte. Chas. Mansell, "D" Coy., 1st Bn., keen and fearless, who enlisted at the age of 17, was taken prisoner; and the subsequent experiences of himself and fellow-captive at the hands of the Germans.

A member of a patrol led by Lieut. L. M. Bull, shortly after the 1st Bn. took over the trenches in the Messines-Wytschaete Sector, Mansell, together with a companion, Sgt. Beynon, was taken prisoner in January, 1918.

The line held by the 1st Bn. at this time was bounded by the Roozebeek on the right and the Hollebeke on the left, with advanced headquarters in the Ravine. From the Ravine steps led up to the communication trench, which led to outposts—a series of shell-holes, practically bare of cover.

The practice was to withdraw the outposts before daylight, the men then sheltering in adjacent pill boxes or in a sap of the main communication trench. Being mid-winter, the ground was frozen hard except in places where it had been churned into a sea of mud.

The posts were separated from each other by about 50 or 60 yards, and every hour an N.C.O. and man would leave their posts on patrol, crawling through the slush to the next post, and daring all the dangers to which these outposts had gained in reputation. But this system ensured an hourly patrol of the gaps between the posts.

Sometimes the garrisons would be alarmed by a stealthy creeping or hushed voices—sometimes a muttered curse—but invariably the wanderers turned out to be our own ration carriers, slipping or falling in the treacherous mud, or ducking down to escape a burst of enemy machine-gun fire.

To our front lay pools of water, which were caught in the reflection of the flares, and gleamed up still and forbidding. In the outposts, sometimes full of water, the men lay cramped with their feet almost frozen.

Of one of the posts, a pill box on the left, I cannot now recall who was in charge, but next to it was one under Sgt. J. Coppin, M.M. (later killed at Proyart), then came my own, followed by Lieut. Stobo's and Sgt. Wilcsmith's on the extreme right.

In our front were several huge pill boxes, called the Giants, Twins, 400 yards or more out, and as these were suspected of concealing parties of enemy machine-gunners, our trench mortars had been, the day previously, ordered to demolish the pill boxes. The following night a patrol of six, consisting of Lieut. Bull, Sgt. Beynon, Sgt. D. Scott, D.C.M., M.S.M., and Ptes. C. Mansell, Vasserotti, and Fish, were ordered to investigate the result of the trench mortars' shooting.

Leaving the Elephant Castle pill box on the left at 6 p.m., Lieut. Bull's patrol set out, not having had anything to eat, as an early return was anticipated. Moving down to the right to pass through Sgt. Coppins' post, and dressed in brown patrol suits and gum-boots, Bull and his party moved out into "No Mans Land" and made direct for the German pill box behind the enemy barbed wire.

Just as they were near the wire they heard a noise, as if a plank had fallen in the mud, but decided to move on, explore the pill boxes first, then return and investigate the cause of the noise. Bull halted the patrol and alone courageously crawled through the wire, instructing the others that if he did not return they were to go back and report. He scrambled through into the pill boxes, found them smashed up, and full of water, with no sign of the enemy. Rejoining his anxious patrol, he retraced his steps, in the direction whence previously a noise had been heard.

The party had not gone far when suddenly a flare shot up, not 20 yards away. The patrol at once sought cover in shell-holes. The enemy opened out with rifle and machine-gun, and also threw bombs. While a flare was still burning, Lieut. Bull knelt down, and by the aid of its light fired six shots from his revolver, hitting two of the enemy. One of the Aussies was wounded by a grenade. Seeing this, Mansell crawled to where he had last seen his officer to report, but in the darkness could not find him. He rejoined Sgt. Beynon, and together they got the wounded man back to the others. The rifles of the party were clogged with mud and out of action, and they decided to return to their lines as quickly as possible.

The enemy was in the meantime using his machine-gun, searching for the patrol. The wounded man, who was helpless, had to be carried, and the party made for the road, as offering easier going than crossing shell-holes and dodging stumps.

Treading gingerly and ducking down at each burst of machine-gun fire, the party came to a fork in the road. Having the choice of two posts to return by, the patrol took the nearest—the one on the left—but this post mistook the identity of the patrol, and sent up a flare, and then opened fire. The patrol, failing to get its password heard, ducked back into "No Man's Land" and took shelter near a big tree stump. After a further council of war, Sgt Beynon and Pte. Mansell left Sgt. Scott with the others, including the wounded man, while they tried to locate another way into our lines.

They had been gone about an hour when they were suddenly challenged from a post. They answered with the password. Having some misgivings as to the bona fides of this post, they crawled back to where they had left the others, but found their mates had gone. Strange to relate, the Germans had a habit of using our passwords in this area, and so the password was changed every night. The pair, now wet, hungry, and exhausted—it was now hours since the patrol had set out—agreed that it would be safer to seek cover and await daybreak, pick up their bearings, and return the next night. So they made their way to an old trench and took shelter. However, they were again challenged from a post, a little to the left of the previous one. They gave

(Continued on page 28)

Chas. Mansell.

REVEILLE   *January 1, 1933*

1st Bn. Patrol —*(From page 16)*

(From page 16)

the password, but realised their mistake too late; a sentry calling out "*Rous, Rous,*" and Germans immediately rushed up and covered them. The position was hopeless; their rifles were useless and fight was out of the question.

They were at once grabbed and searched and then conducted to company Hqrs. The company commander asked them several questions, particularly as to the position of our trench mortars, which had destroyed the pill-boxes the day previously. The Germans seemed very annoyed about it all, but the prisoners, faithful to their duty, knew nothing. They were then escorted to Bn. Hqrs., arriving at daylight, and were given hot coffee and food, and their clothing taken away and dried. This act of mercy by the enemy was appreciated. The captives inquired about Lt. Bull, but he had not been captured, as far as those Germans, hereabouts, knew, so the prisoners concluded that he must have been hit during the scrap and died on the way to our lines.

JOKE ON GUARD.

Utterly exhausted, the pair fell asleep, and later in the morning were taken to Courtrai, and after lunch, were sent to Alost, under the keen eye of a mounted Uhlan. At Alost they remained three or four days, pending the arrival of a batch of English prisoners to accompany them to Germany. During the journey through Belgium, the people showed kindness towards the prisoners, endeavouring to give them food. Sometimes the Belgians would be allowed to hand over their gifts; at other times the German escort hunted them away. The trip occupied three days, and there was an amusing incident during the train journey, when one of the prisoners with a sense of humour, sneaked up to one of the guards, quietly unloaded the rifle magazine and threw the cartridge out of the carriage window, returning the rifle as he found it.

When the prisoners arrived at Dulmen camp, in Westphalia, Germany, they were lined up for inspection, and the order was given to the escort to unload rifles. The look of bewilderment on the face of the escort who had been "souvenired" was worth going miles to see. Whether he woke up to the joke played upon him, the prisoners never found out. Perhaps it was just as well for them that he was not suspicious. The prisoners were drafted to a compound and were not inside ten minutes before an inquiry was made for any Australians to gather at the fence dividing the new arrivals from the next compound. The only other Australians in the party besides Sgt. Beynon and Pte. Mansell, was Cpl. Frost —a private of Capt. Jacka's Bn. The three Australians went over to the fence and were pleased to meet a couple of other Australians, one of them, a 4th Bn. Digger, hailing from Botany. (N.S.W.). Naturally, the older hands were glad to see the new arrivals from whom they got the latest news.

RED CROSS PARCELS.

The food supplied to the prisoners was not up to expectations by a long way. It consisted of soup, twice daily, a little bread—nothing else. Prisoners, in other compounds, who were receiving Red Cross parcels from England, sent their prison rations across to the new arrivals, who presented a pitiful sight, lining up for spare food. More fortunate were the Australians, in the new batch, in receiving from their compatriots smokes, bread, tea, milk, and other things.

The second day in camp Mansell and Sgt. Beynon parted company. Mansell was drafted to a party of 16, including another Australian, a Gordon Highlander, and a Canadian, and was sent to Carolus Magnus I coal mine at Berger-borbeck near Essen. The prison here was a three-storyed building, about 1½ miles from the mine, and among its confines were 70 Russians and 50 Frenchmen. Mansell named a Russian named Luscius, who was an adept in escaping. He and Mansell chummed up, but not long after the Russian "caught" Mansell for his boots. The Russian and a Frenchman had planned to escape to Holland. The Russian, who had made 11 or 12 previous bids for liberty, had no boots, so Mansell lent him his on the understanding that if he was caught, he was to return the footwear, and take Mansell with him the next time he made an escape attempt. After two or three weeks the Russian returned under guard, and for punishment was given solitary cell confinement. with bread and water diet. Work in the mines was very severe and the hours were long. Mansell's Australian mate became ill and was sent to Switzerland.

About a month before the Armistice the Russian Luscius, false to his

War Decorations: General's Strictures

Lt.-Col. H. C. Metcalf, Chief Constable of Somerset, who commanded a battalion in the Brigade led by Brig.-Gen. Crozier (author of "A Brass Hat in No Man's Land"), was only three months in action, and was awarded the D.S.O. and Bar—both decorations being gazetted on the same day.

Another one of Crozier's officers, J. F. Plunkett, started as a sgt.-mjr, at Mons, and within three years was a Colonel, D.S.O. (2 Bars), M.C., D.C.M. Crozier relates in his book that he tried hard to get Plunkett a V.C. for "30 hours continuous and sustained valor" at Bourlon Wood.

"He does not get the V.C., but a D.S.O. Indeed, as I have already put him in for the half yearly D.S.O., he gets two. The blue pencil is mightier than the sword once the battle is over. It is easier to hold the line against repeated counter attacks than to persuade an officer 50 miles away at G.H.Q. that '30 hours valor' is better than a flash in the pan action, however brave the latter may be. 'But he was only doing his duty,' I am told by the red-banded clerk-officer, who had never seen a shot fired.

"The truth is the war has made people dishonest. Men are scrambling for honors and rewards, and people are recommended for rewards on account of friendship, favouritism, and the like, on a larger scale than ever in our time before. . . . The lists are choc-a-block with names put in by favor, and when occasionally a hard-fighting man without interest gets recommended, he is left out, as there is no one to push him. It's a scandal and a slur.

" 'But look generally at the thousands of awards made,' says the officer-clerk. 'Quite so,' I say, 'I can tell you off-hand of 20 unmerited D.S.O.'s awarded in this war. . . .' I recommended, when asked, that all honors should be abolished for the duration. There's no good of having decorations unless they are given the right way. . . .' "

promise to Mansell, skedaddled with another Russian and a Scotchie who had been a prisoner since Mons, 1914. The trio collected decent abes, biscuits and tinned stuff (also civilian clothes, a map and compass), and, descending from the roof by a rope made of light chains, smuggled up from the mines, reached the ground safely, all with the exception of Sandy, under whose weight the rope broke. Sandy, being an old soldier and a hero, lay where he fell for four hours to give his companions a good start and then crawled to the sentry box for assistance, as he had been severely hurt in his fall. The two Russians reached the Dutch border after untold hardships, only to be attacked by savage dogs. While Luscius battled with the dogs, his companion crawled through the high voltage wire. Luscius was recaptured and returned to camp, and orders were given to the guards to shoot him if he broke prison again.

About this time the camp was ravaged by Spanish 'flu, but Mansell escaped the scourge. After the Armistice, a batch of British prisoners, including Mansell, was sent to Holland to await a train for Amsterdam, and thence aboard a boat for England.

Charles Mansell is once more in Australia among his own people. While we of the old Bn. were still fighting and suffering hardships, our prisoners of war in enemy hands were suffering perhaps even more than we. In fairness to the Germans, who were on our front at the time Beynon and Mansell were captured, let it be said that they treated their captives decently. Lieut. Bull escaped capture after being lost behind the German lines for two days and three nights. He suffered severely with trench feet as a result of exposure, and the only food he had during that time was a turnip picked up in No Man's Land. Lieut. Bull rejoined the Bn. just before Armistice, and the next time he went into the line he fell, gallantly, struck by a piece of shell which landed among officers of "A" Coy., with whom he was standing.

The Scottish Australasian April 1918
Major DONALD SMITH 'The Scot We Know'

Few people know how many offices he holds in the community, although everyone knows him for a busy man, a tiger for work, a tactful, able representative of an honourable profession and withal a good citizen.

Born Christmas Day 1864 Port Glasgow. His mother was Miss Janet Robertson and her brother and sister were well known in Sydney as Captain William Robertson of Messrs Flood and Co and Mrs Frederick MacKellar, mother of Sir Charles MacKellar, KCMG. He was educated at Kilblain Academy Glasgow and later at the Royal College Mauritius to which place the family removed and resided for about ten years. This island was noted for its sugar production and it was in this industry our Scots father was engaged as was his son for a time. 3 of Major Smiths brothers are in the sugar industry. Mr J. R. Smith is a manager. Mr John Smith is an inspector and Mr George Smith an accountant. Further a sister became the wife of another inspector in the CSR Company's service, Mr Buchanon. Others sisters are Miss Smith and Mrs English. From Mauritius the family came to Sydney.

He took up the study of Dentistry gaining a good insight into it. He joined Dr D. Magnus. Major Smith has been lecturer in clinical dentistry at the University of Sydney since 1907. He was President of the Dental Board, a post he has filled since 1910. He is also a member of the Control and honorary secretary of the United Dental Hospital being elected in 1903 and continuing in the office ever since. He was a founder of the Odonatological Society and is a visiting dental surgeon for the Department for the Insane beside being honorary dental surgeon for the Women's Hospital, the Benevolent Society and several other kindred institutions. He is a Councillor for the Highland Society of New South Wales and President of the Burns Club and Entertainment Committee. Major Smith is as all his friends know, very musical and finds himself interested in many musical institutions. He is councillor of Madrigal Society, holds the teacher's Diploma of Licentiate of Trinity College London and for over twenty years has been member and conductor of the choir at St Peters Presbyterian Church North Sydney in which church he is a senior elder.

Major DONALD SMITH (cont)	
Of the Major's 5 sons, 3 are on active service, viz, Capt. Donald Ian Smith who has served two years with the Army Medical Corps, Lieut. Noel Watson Smith who at 22 years has credit for three years and six month's service with the Field Artillery and Lieut. Eric Alfred Smith who is only 20 but has been with the Field Artillery for 18 months These lads are all with our Australian forces abroad. Capt. Smith has been x-ray specialist at the great Wimmereaux Hospitals in France for 18 months The two lieutenants left Australia as gunners but both were promoted in the field to commissioned rank a fact which speaks for itself. Upon the outbreak of war in 1914, Donald Smith assisted in organising and man- aged the Voluntary Dental Service at the United Dental Hospital and when the Defence Department decided to form a Dental Corps as part of the Army Medical Corps he was chosen to be the first dentist to hold a commissioned rank in Australia becoming Senior Dental Officer, Commanding in NSW in Feb 1915. This branch of national service with small beginnings has grown tremendously and Major Smith has been in command all through. The corps makes fully ten thousand men per annum fit for service in our national armies who would otherwise be registered as unfit in this state alone. So satisfactory has been the results of this corps that to it has been entrusted the dental work of the Navy , the returned soldiers and the prisoners of war. This necessitates widespread organisation and there has to be a network of agencies all over the State.	
STRANG Mrs. Evelyn. President of the Women's Christian Temperance Union died aged 87 in her sleep in Burns Rd Wahroonga in 1954. She was a member of WCTU for 70 years, travelled overseas as representative and was also vice President and former local union president. Funeral at St Johns Presbyterian Wahroonga. Wife of Walter Symington Strang died 1914. Mother of Lilias who married George Edward Bryant and died 1950 mother of two girls. Her sister Mrs Marion Scott	539, 548, 563

THE BAND OF HOPE was formed in 1906. In it the principles of Temperance were inculcated and the juniors encourages in singing and reciting. The meetings were mainly held in the summer and many lectures on various subjects were delivered. Lantern evenings were always well attended. Written by TS Champion	xviii, 572
THE POINT referred to was Milsons Point, the end of the train ride on the North- ern line from Hornsby. The rail terminated closer to the water before the Harbour Bridge was built. Ferries then went to the Quay.	
TRAPENARDE, Alexis 66 Bis Rue de St Didier Paris	
VIDAL Miss Dorothy Vidal, 3 Butter Market Ipswich ENG or c/- London County and Westminster Bank Oxford. Miss Lois Vidal, YMCA, 30 Rue de Rivage Etaples	
WAHROONGA Grammar School in Burns Road where Ben was taught first. Mas- ter W Stewart Page, M.A., a member of congregation of Wahroonga Presbyterian Church.	
WAHROONGA Presbyterian Church. The old church, Ben describes in his diaries and letters which he and his family attended was demolished in 1926. Services were then held in the new lecture hall and kindergarten until the new St Johns Presbyte- rian Church was opened on 26 April 1930. Until Knox Grammar School built their own chapel this was the School Church. It is now St John's Uniting Church, on the corner of Stuart St Wahroonga. As part of the Commmemoration Cememony TS Champion as elder, was given the honour of sliding back one of the doors to the new church to allow the official party and congregation to enter.	

Kanowna Nursing staff both patients and on duty

Nurses on Duty on *Kanowna* (this was not clearly defined as On duty). Some names were not listed on MD but were listed on Ships Indent at AWM

DOUBLEDAY Rita Mabel, S/N born Ashfield, Sydney aged 26
NEILSEN L.F. Pt, Aust Mtd, Inv HQ
COCKING Sister Alice Elizabeth 14 AGH. AMC. Born Clunes Vic aged 36
SHEIL Emil Jane, RTA on nursing duties 4.9.18 on *Kanowna*
MURPHY Matron J

Nurses embarked at Suez from Salonika

1 Military District
CAVE Annie Freda, S/N, ANB born Barcaldine aged 29
PARTRIDGE Cyril William Robert, Pt, male nurse 14 AGH born Brisbane, aged 19
   2 Military District
MURPHY Matron J
BROWLOW Olive, S/N AANS, born Rockley NSW, aged 29
HUTTON Mary Ann Sister AMC, AANS. Born Glenn Innes aged 45
MURRELL Elizabeth Ellen "Beth" S/N. AMC. Born Sydney, aged 36
SCAHIL Alice Cecilia, S/N, AMC. Born Canterbury, aged 24
McKENZIE Mary Elizabeth, Sister. AANS. Born Newport, aged 27
   3 Military District
CAMPBELL Olive Catherine Emma S/N. AANS. born Nhill Vic. aged 31
HARTRIDGE Alice S/N. AANS. Born ENG, aged 28
McLENNAN Thora S/N AAMC. Born Dimboola Vic, aged 32
McPHAIL Irene, S/N, AAMC. Born Echua. Aged 24
POWER Florence Louise, S/N, AAMC> Born Melbourne aged 36
RODGER Elonie, S/N born Ballarat, aged 25
SHELDON Caroline Hannah, S/N/ Born Bendigo, aged 41
KIRK Myrtle Hannah S/N AAMC. Born Camperdown Vic. Aged 26
WATT Ruby Mary, S/N/ AAMC born Fairfield NSW. Aged 26
COATE Agnes S/N. AMC. Born Woodend Vic. Aged 32
   Male Nurses
BURNETT Ernest Arnold, Corporal, 14 AGH born Illabreck VIC aged 26, farmer
MILNES Arnold William Claud, Sergt., 14 AGH. Born ENG. Aged 26, farmer
TATTERSON James, Pt, 3 LHFA. Born Essenden VIC, aged 19, clerk

4 Military District

McNALLY Mary Theresa, S/N, AANS, born Keswick S.A. aged 30

5th Military District

WINTON Leslie Clifton Pt., Male Nurse 2nd ASH, born Port Pirie, aged 19

6 Military District

BAILEY Hilda Jane, S/N, AANS, Born Launceston TAS, aged 25

BERESFORD Ruby Evelyn S/N, AANS, burn Burnie Tas, aged 28

Nurses

CHERRY Enid Sister RTA. end of 1918

Nurses in Salonika

MOULE Eva Gladys S/N

BIGGS Ethel Maud. Sister pic

GIDDINGS Ethel. Sister

GILLINGHAM Ethel Mary, Sister

MALCOLM Edith Eileen, S/N pic

McINTYRE Daisy Florence, S/N

PETERSEN Olive Winifred, S/N

APPLETON Laura Mary, S/N

BEGLEY Laura Beatrice, Sister

ALLEN Anne, Sister

60th General Hospital Hortiach Staff not necessarily on *Kanowna*

GREENTREE Vida Mitylene, 3 different photographs of 60th Hospital online

CAMPBELL Matron Beryl, Salonica in 1917

KELLETT Matron Adelaide, in 1919 at Hortiach on *Kanowna*

SORENSON Matron Christine, AIF. 60 th General Hospital 1919

McDONALD Baxter Jessie.

SOLLING Nurse, not on *Kanowna*

MUNRO Gertrude Evelyn Munro Sister and

CHRISTIE Amy, Sister. photo of last two online

McLENNAN Jane, Nurse. With 300 nurses per *Mooltan* arrived to Suez, to Cairo, to Alexandria to Salonika Greece. 9.6.17 RTA March 1918 with heart disease. Her Diaries and photographs are now online The John Oxley Library, Queensland State Library. 60th General Tent Hospital had capacity of 2000 patients.

Theses nurses are not a complete list but those I have come across.

There are more photographs of the sisters on board that are not in the book and these could be used to identify, perhaps those on *Kanowna*–Editor Penny Ferguson

Sergeant Archie Barwick diaries

Diaries online and at State Library of NSW itchellLibrary

Snippets with reference to Ben Champion and other mutual acquaintances

(Not necessarily in chronological correct order)

FL530164 15 Jan – March 1917

In the afternoon the whole Coy marched out and went bomb throwing, one of our new chaps nearly settled Mr Champion. He was evidently frightened and didn't let go at top of throw.

There is some talk of Mr Beckett leaving us tomorrow and I hope he doesn't for he is a very fine officer and admired by all throughout the whole Battalion

The food today was very crook and I called our officer Mr Champion down to have a look at it, he is going to kick up a row over it.

Sgt Major Shaw

Archie was in C Company

Arranged boxing match between Mellish of Transports and Norton A Coy.

Page 198 end of March

Major Davidson was a bonzer chap he was killed at Lone Pine on 18 August last year. We were all sorry he went under. I hear that Lt Davidson was shot dead accidently yesterday by some of our chaps at the musketry school. I feel sorry for his mother for she has lost both her husband her son. (According to National Archives they were not father and son unless there is another Lt JC Davidson)

Archive/ 110226347 Diary 10 May 23-July 1916

This evening page 42 we had a fine bit of fun we had a lot of officers up on our pitch having a strike, Kellaway, Withy, Jackson, MacKenzie, Graham, Laurence, MacGregor and a few more the fun was fast and furious for a time. (Kellaway was a renowned cricketer)

Lots of rivalry between A and C Companies over the platoon drilling so this morning each platoon selected their 6 best men. They were put in a special squad and they shaped up real well. There is a thought of a competition coming up.Bapaume

Archie thought Old Mac was the finest man in the Division. Salvation Army Mackenzie. Loved by all the men.

Had the best news today that we have had for a long time. Mr Champion hurried around with a map in his hand and showed us where the 5th Division had advanced during the night and captured Bapuame Bivalios and Le Transloy. What a splendid victory for the Australians.

19 March. Jack Starkey was made a Sgt tonight

3.6.17

One of A Coy Sergeants was killed and they buried him and now have to dig him up again and take him down to Brigade Headquarters to a small cemetery there.

We have a character of an officer at present, Page is his name. How he came to get a commission is beyond me for he is perfectly useless The other morning just as we were leaving the trenches his batman wanted to get up and get a pair of dry gumboots for his own were all wet. Page yells out Sgt Barwick you get Hunt (his batman)....Mr Broughton a fine little officer then chipped in, Hunt he said you go out and get yourself your own boots.

Archie Barwick. I am not feeling well-Jack Price (brother of Capt Philip Price) brought me up a nice plate of porridge and I felt much better.

Refers to big bill Buckley and he is 6'7" I think he must be Ben's Lofty Buckley

31.1.17

Mr Champion and I to get some barbed wire and block up an old sap in front. The wire rotten stuff to handle too

Sunday 15 August

Met Ben Champion at 6pm and we had a walk around town.

There was a knock on the door and in rushed Capt Mackenzie, Mr Beckett, Mr Champion and a few more. They were very excited, all sorts of things were happening and they had a lot of orders. Freddie Turner had to get up and go with transport and go to Bazentin and draw bombs, ammunition, sand bags etc This made Freddie swear as he was pretty crook but up he got and went after them The Captain had a big map of the sector.

April–May 1917 7th

Put the day in, cramped up in an old dugout. Mr Champion, Starkey and myself. Never got a wink of sleep the whole day for Fritz shelled heavily, some of them lobbing uncomfortably close to us. Towards evening rain and hail set in and we were faced with a bonza night

18 March 1917 Page 181

This evening all C Coy Sergts were invited over to the Officers Mess for an evening of fun. So over we went The evening started off the usual toasts and then followed the dinner which was very good. After dinner more toasts and so they went round. At first some of them were cunning and only sipped their whisky but soon all was changed and they were tipping it down wholesale. I think the Captain set himself out to get the Reg. Sergeant Major (George Gould) drunk and he succeeded admirably for George was speechless about 10.30 and old Bell (Bellchambers) and Mr Beckett were keeping him company. They tried to get me to drink the whisky but nothing doing. It would take a good man to make me drink against my will. After dinner we had a card party and finished up about 11.45. We all had a most enjoyable evening and had some fun. The Sergeants who were present were RSM Gould, RQMS Turner, CQMS Hayes, CSM Bellchambers and Sergts Mackie, Price, Graham, Hunt and myself. The officers, Captain Mackenzie, Lieuts Page and Champion, Davis, Gallagher, A'Beckett and Webb. There is not many officers would do this but our officers are sports.

Jan-March 1917 Page 196.

In the evening we had a spread, for the sergeants of C Coy entertained the officers. The French let us have their front room and lent us tables, chairs, plates, glasses and everything that would be of any use to us. We started off at 6.30pm and had a good tea after that the grog came on and the fun commenced toast after toast went on and on and soon some of them did not know whether they were standing on their head or feet. Sgt Starkey was the first to go They made the pace too hot for him when everything was going merrily, Mr Page suddenly leaps off his seat and grabs hold of his thigh. I thought he must have sat on a pin or something. When the laughing had died down a little he explained that he had a cramp in his leg. More laughing and plenty offers of assistance to rub him down etc..but we fired him after a while and the game proceeded. This followed by some recitations and pretty hot ones too and afterward songs and stories. Altogether we had a most pleasant evening and I think it will be remembered by all of us for many many a day to come. Of course, according to Kings Rules and Regulations this sort of thing is altogether wrong

Later page 198 …..such as Sergeants entertaining and meeting their officers on almost level terms and vice versa and I dare say unheard of in the English Army but it is a jolly good idea for it brings the officers and NCO's together and they understand one another all the more and instead of being bad for discipline I think it is the reverse.

13th

Had charge of Platoon this morning as Mr Champion has gone away to Gas school. Our platoon got new Lewis Gun this morning

Archies main friends mentioned are Jock Mackie, Bayne. Joe Shaw. Dimock. His brother Len was also in 1st Bn but was in other units and at Headquarters. He was a very good sniper. As did Ben he had a very high regard for Howard Moffatt and Old Mac, Salvation Army MacKenzie. He disliked Lt Page and for a while Captain MacKenzie and Archie did not get on but then they developed a mutual regard for each other. Archie thought someone was putting bad reports in behind his back to the Captain. He and Captain Price it seems did not get along either.

He mentions going over to see his brother Stan who he was very close too and was told he had been KIA

Bruce Rainsford Diary also at Mitchell Library.

Had a long association with the Scout movement and continued his interest in Egypt. He thought it also kept him on straight and narrow away from temptation as he concentrated on learning French and Arabic and attending the different Scout meetings held frequently each week.

He mentions his excursions with Ben and Art

Wahroonga War Memorial

– for further details check books Vol.1-4 of Ku- ring- gai Historical
Society who have done extensive research into these and many other
soldiers from the region.

ARFORD Abel Henry aka Abel Hebel PHOO

Born Nundle NSW, aged 23 years, carter, Enlist 2.10.15, 9 Rfts 20 Bn,
NOK sister C/- Mrs Smith Coonanbarra Rd Wahroonga. Was sent to Boys
home as child and given name change. Influenza serious 14.4.16. Wounded
10.11.16, KIA 25.2.17. Buried Warlencourt British Cemetery SW of
Bapaume.

BRUCE John Kemp, Captain, Presbyterian Chaplain,

The Manse Wahroonga, aged 63. Enlisted for voyage and died influenza
and cardiac complications on return on HMHS *Karoola and* buried at sea.
9.2.18

CARDEW Thuiller Lake Pt

Born Woollahra, aged 24 years, farmer, father J Haydon Cardew of Pitt
St and *St Enne* Ingram St, Wahroonga. Enlist 22.6.15 joined 2 Bn, at Tel
el Kebir to 54 Bn. KIA 19.7.16 Fleurbaix/Fromelles, buried VC Corner
Cemetery

CORMACK James Alexander, Gunner.

1Rfts 7th Brigade 16.12.15, born Sydney, aged 18 years postal assistant,
mother Elizabeth and father William of Kintore St Wahroonga.
Presbyterian. Was in 19 b militia. KIA 23.7.17 Messines. 7th Field Artillery
Brigade. Buried Kandahar Farm Military Cemetery

CARTER Edward Moore, Sapper

Born Sydney, aged 29 years, engineer Enlist 19.2.15 of *Carrawilla* Kintore
St, Wahroonga. Australian Engineers to 1st Field. Evacuated from Gallipoli.
DOW GSW leg and tetanus, Malta 21.7.15. Buried Pieta Cemetery, Malta

CHAMBERLAIN Frank, Pt.

Born Wahroonga, aged 19, butcher, mother Florence of Kintore St, Wahroonga. Enlisted 4.1.16 to 16 Rfts 4 Bn. Was in militia? 19b. Died of Illness 3.7.16 Tidworth ENG of cerebro-spinal meningitis. Buried Tidworth Military Cemetery. 'Father died 14 months prior and now no breadwinner to maintain a large family of small children'.

CLARKE Gother Robert Carlisle, Major, Medical Officer

Enlist 29.4.15, 34 Bn to 56 Bn, KIA Passchendaele 12.10.17. Buttes New British Cemetery Polygon Wood Belgium. His father died in 1917

COOK Reg

It may have been Ben who wrote to his parents with details of his death if not Ben then Arthur Felton see Bens mates index

COOKE W (McNab)

Enlist Dec 1916, born SCOT, sister of *Craigielea* Coonanbarra Rd Wahroonga. engineer fitter. 14 FCC in Longueval Gueudecourt area KIA 27.10.17. Menin Road Sth Military Cemetery Belgium

DAVIDSON Charles Bernard, Pt,

Enlist 1.12.14, 2 Rfts 12 Bn, Aged 23 years, civil servant, father George of *Woodlands* Wahroonga Ave, Wahroonga. Father died in 1917, NOK Mother, Grace of Kintore Rd, Wahroonga. KIA 20.7.15 Gallipoli, buried Browns Dip and exhumed to Lone Pine Cemetery. Also his brother

DONALDSON John Ebenezer, Capt.

Aged 27 years of Kintore Rd Wahroonga, married, resident pathologist at Sydney Hospital, attached to 19 Bn. DOW 11.8.16 Le Touquet Hospital of pneumonia following GSW back paraplegia. Buried Etaples Military Cemetery. Another son also served but survived He was wounded 5 times Gallipoli medal to sister as no relations left. Mother lost 3 of her men in 3 years

FERGUSSON Maurice Cameron, Corp

Enlist 14.9.14 aged 20, draughtsman, of Water St, Wahroonga, Father Ian Fergusson, Presbyterian, 13 Bn, KIA Gallipoli 4.5.15. Buried Lone Pine Cemetery 11.5.15

FITZGERALD Leslie Thomas Manning, Sergeant

Enlist 11.3.15, 6th Rfts 9 Bn, Wounded 30.10.15, DOW 21.9.16 Mouquet Farm, Warloy Baillon Communal Cemetery extension near Amiens

HESKETH Leonard

Also at Fort St School. See Ben Index.

Villers Bretonneaux. Cairns Post Wednesday 1.11.16 A Corporals unvarnished account A Terrible Week see *Rallying the Troops* p 218 9^{Rfts} 1st Bn 13.6.15 aged 23 years

HUGHES Starby David

Enlist 29.8.14, aged 21 years, blacksmith, Mother of Hinemoa Ave, Wahroonga, killed accidently when fishing in Somme with stokes mortar bomb fuse when exploded 4.9.18. 1st Field Artillery. Memorial Villers-Bretonneaux

KING Charles Wesley.

Enlist 22.3.15, aged 24, motor mechanic, mother Esther of Neringah Ave, Wahroonga. 17 Bn. KIA 27.8.15 Gallipoli, Lone Pine Cemetery.

Also lived at Coonanbarra Rd. His father Charles died 1921 was a well known Wahroonga cab proprietor operating livery stables near Wahroonga Park. Brothers William and Henry

Source: *Rallying the Troops*

LIPSCOMBE Brothers. See Ben Index

Eric John Lipscombe KIA 23 days after brother Neville

William Henry Lipscombe KIA was in 19b militia

McCULLOCH Colin Vernon, Lt,

Enlist 18.1.16 aged 24, Uni grad law, father of *Entally* Lane Cove Rd, Warrawee. 2nd Bn. pneumonia 7.2.17, Wounded 15.9.17, KIA 11.4.18. Bur St Pierre Military Cemetery, Amiens

O'DONNELL James Francis

Enlist 20.3.16. 20 years, labourer, father of Bundarra Rd, Wahroonga, belonged to citizen militia? 19b. 4 Rfts 56 Bn. Wounded 6.4.17, 23.6.17 Trench feet, 54 Bn KIA 1.9.18 Bur. Hem Farm British Military Cemetery near Peronne

OWEN George Burgoyne, Capt.,

Enlist 1.4.16 architect. 30 years, father dead, mother Mrs Culver of Stuart St Wahroonga. Died Influenza pneumonia 5.11.18. 3rd Division Field Artillery. Bur Busigny Communal Cemetery

RAMSEY William Bernard

Enlist 15.3.16, 30 Rfts 4 Bn, Carter, of Blytheswood Ave, Warrawee. KIA 15.4.17 Demicourt. 11 April relieved 1st Bn at Demicourt. Memorial Villers- Bretonneux

ROE Arthur Charles, Lance Corp

Mother of *The Laurels* Cleveland St, Wahroonga Enlist 6.8.15, aged 28 years, A Coy 1st Bn., KIA Battle of Lone Pine Gallipoli, Lone Pine Cemetery

ROWLEY Thomas Mountford, Pt, Lewis Gunner

Enlist 3.12.15, of *Lowallan* Lochville St, Wahroonga. Boundary rider and station hand, 2Rfts 55 Bn. Pneumonia to 57 Bn. DOW Beaulencourt. 16.3.17 Bernafroy Wood British Cemetery

SCOTT Alan Humphrey, Lt-Col., DSO.

Enlist 5.9.14 with previous military history. Clerk, Dalgety and Co., father of *Edgemend*, Lane Cove Rd, Wahroonga. B Coy 4th Bn to finally 56 Bn. Sniped KIA 1.10.17 buried near Zonnebeke, exhumed to Buttes New British Cemetery Polygon Wood

SCRUTTON Arthur Edward, Pt.

Born Petersham, enlist Dubbo, aged 33, chemist, wife of *Koorawatha* Cleveland St, Wahroonga. Enlist 10.4.16 KIA 54 Bn 29.3.17 Vaulx Vraucourt British Cemetery near Bapaume.

SWAN Frederick

electrical engineer, Signaller, 20 Bn. KIA 5.8.16

SLADE Elliott Darcy, Lt.,

Enlist 25.3.15 aged 20 years articled clerk Uni, of *Ellerken* Cleveland St Wahroonga 7th Rfts 33 Bn -63 bn-33Bn. KIA 30.3.18

ASHER-SMITH Charles Donaldson (Charlie Smith)

Enlist 11.12.16 aged 19, also at Fort St High School, of *Alvah* Burns Rd, Wahroonga, served militia? 19b. 19 Rfts 20 Bn, KIA 9.10.17 Memorial Menin Gate Belgium

UNDERWOOD Albert Charles

Enlist 28.7.15, aged 21, grocer, NOK brother in law Fred Wooding, Westbrooke Ave, Wahroonga, father of England. 6 Rfts 20 Bn -56 Bn-Infant Bde – 60 Bn. Missing KIA 19.7.16

WALKER E

WINTER W

WOODERSON James

Enlist 6.1.16. aged 25 years. Gardener. wife Alice and child of *Te Kinli* and *Haarlem* Isis St, Wahroonga. Widow of Raymond Ave Turramurra. 36 Bn-53 Bn – 14 Light Trench Mortars KIA 15.5.17

Additional index items

Pill Boxes

A key feature of the battlefield between Ypres and Passchendaele in 1917 was the pillbox. Along with the dreadful conditions and intense artillery bombardments, pillboxes forced a particularly grim situation upon the combatants that led to very bitter and costly fighting. The Germans had begun a program of building concrete field fortifications in the latter stages of 1916 and early 1917, particularly in their new defensive position along the Hindenburg Line.

Their primary role was to protect German troops from artillery bombardments. Low and squat, they were built in many different sizes, some designed to house only half a dozen men, while others, the size of a single-car garage, might house 10-20 men. Still others were even bigger (with some having two storeys) and might house up to 40.

The terrain conditions in the Ypres salient, more than any other place, meant that pillboxes would play an important role there. With a high-water table and high rainfall, trenches proved largely impractical.

In the Ypres sector, many of the pillboxes were individually marked on detailed battle maps. Like any features on the battlefield they were given names to identify them. Pillboxes in the area had a variety of names such as Israel, Potsdam, Judah, Thames, Seine, Waterfields, Anzac, Helles, Kit, Kat, Hamburg and so on. The shelters and pillboxes were often used as first aid stations and as command and communication posts, the latter making them important tactical objectives. this inevitably meant these places became the scenes of numerous bitter struggles.

Anzac Commemorative Medallion

The Anzac Commemorative Medallion was instituted 1967. It was awarded to surviving members of the Australian forces who served on the Gallipoli Peninsula, or in direct support of the operations from close off shore, at any time during the period from the first Anzac Day in April 1915 to the date of final evacuation in January 1916.

Next of kin, or other entitled persons, are entitled to receive the medallion on behalf of their relatives if the medallion has not been issued.

The soldier's name is engraved on the reverse side. (My local Military shop had not seen one before-editor)

Trench Art

To help reduce boredom in the trenches and hospitals, soldiers would do what is called trench art which took many forms of creativity. Ben's version in his diary done at Havre was a squiggle was put on one page and on the other the soldier did a drawing using the squiggles from the other page. About ten soldiers participated, some English soldiers, and two examples are put in this book. The picture of Ben done by Vaux was done in this way and also the picture done by Teasdale of 55 Bn. of the North Shore Line. Others included drawings of trenches with names such as Byron Bay etc and stick pictures of life in the trenches.

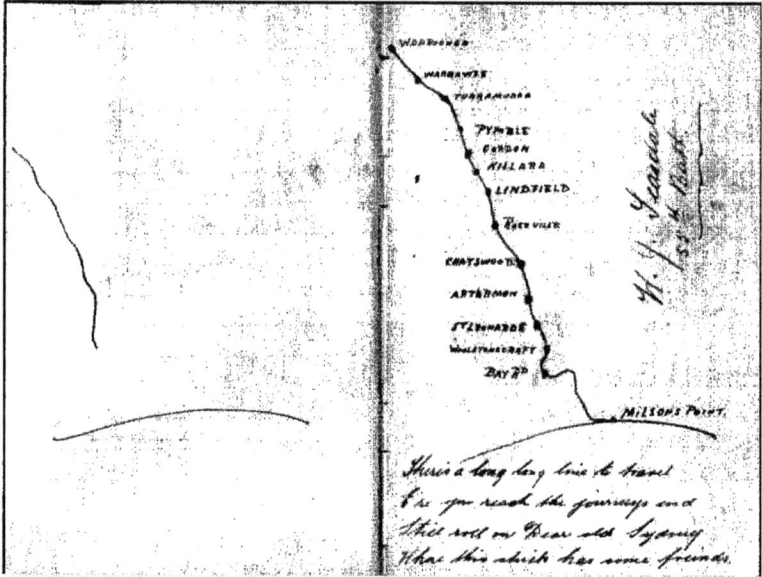

Example of Trench Art, done by Teasdale.

HOWELL-PRICE Brothers on AWM website

The story of the Howell-Price brothers is one of the most remarkable examples of a family at war. Six Howell-Price brothers served during the First World War. They were sons of a Welsh clergyman, Rev. John Howell-Price, who for many years was the vicar of St Silas's Anglican Church in Waterloo, Sydney.

When war broke out in 1914, the brothers ranged in age from David, 33, to down to Richmond, 18. All the brothers except David served overseas with distinction and were highly decorated. Sadly, the three youngest brothers were all killed in action on the Western Front. (See more information on Trove)

David Clayton Winchcombe Howell-Price

The eldest of the family, (b.1881), David served in the South African War, and in Australia on the Army's Administrative and Instructional Staff and as the adjutant of a light horse (militia) regiment.

John Howell-Price DSO, DSC, Sub-Lieutenant (later Lieutenant Commander) (1886-1937)

John Howell-Price served with the Royal Naval Reserve from 1915 to 1918 and in the Royal Australian Navy from 1918 to 1921. He survived the sinking of the HMS *Alcantara* in February 1916. For his part in the engagement John was awarded the Distinguished Service Cross. He later transferred to submarine service and was promoted temporary lieutenant, R.N.R., on 24 July 1917. He was second-in-command and navigator of the old British submarine *C3* which, filled with explosives, was blown up at Zeebrugge, Belgium, on the night of 22-23 April 1918. The commander of the submarine was awarded the Victoria Cross and John Howell-Price the Distinguished Service Order. After the war he transferred to the Royal Australian Navy in the same rank and returned to Australia in command of the submarine *J3*; he served with the R.A.N. until 1921 when he rejoined the merchant navy as a master.

Major Frederick Phillimore Howell-Price DSO (1888-1978)

Frederick Howell-Price enlisted as a Driver in 6 Company, Australian Army Service Corps, attached to the 2nd Light Horse Brigade. He served at Gallipoli from September to December 1915 and also during the Romani, Beersheba, Jericho Valley and Syrian Operations in 1916 and 1917. During this time he was awarded the Distinguished Service Order and twice mentioned in despatches. He returned to Australia in May 1919.

Owen Glendower Howell-Price

Owen served for a period in the citizen forces and on 27 August 1914 was commissioned second lieutenant in the 3rd Battalion, A.I.F. The battalion left Sydney in October and arrived in Egypt in December. During this time he was appointed assistant adjutant and when the adjutant was killed on the first day of the Gallipoli landing he succeeded him. He was promoted captain on 4 August 1915. During the fighting at Lone Pine he won the Military Cross and was also mentioned in dispatches. Casualties were heavy and on 5 September he was promoted temporary major and assumed temporary command of the battalion. He was wounded on 9 September but remained on duty. Having revealed his ability as a fine trainer and organizer, Owen was confirmed in rank on 1 December. For a short period in egypt after the evacuation he was temporarily superseded in command. He died of wounds on 4 november 1916 near flers, France. His final words were 'give my love to the battalion'.

Philip Llewellyn Howell-Price

Philip was commissioned as a Second Lieutenant in the 1st Battalion AIF and subsequently served at Gallipoli. It was here he was mentioned in despatches for work in the Lone Pine Battles. He also fought at Armentieres, France, June 1916 for which he received the Distinguished Service Order, the Somme in July, Flers in November and at Bullecourt in March 1917. He was awarded the Military Cross and was later to die at Broodseinde, Belgium on 4 October 1917.Lieutenant (later) Major Philip Llewellyn Howell-Price DSO, MC (1894-1917). C41640

Lieutenant Richmond Gordon Howell-Price MC (1896-1917)

Richmond Gordon Howell-Price enlisted in December 1915 and served as a Trooper and Corporal in Light Horse units in the Middle East and was commissioned as a 2nd Lieutenant in the 1st Battalion AIF in December 1916. He was killed in action at Bullecourt, France 4 May 1917 and was posthumously awarded the Military Cross.

Post 1920 Family Photographs

Gertrude, Althea (seated) with Helen Victoria and Olive Ruth, and Arthur (standing) holding Leila Francis, at Leeton. Photo Helen–Watling.

Arthur's children: Helen Victoria 1914, Olive Ruth 1916, Leila F 1918, Roger Lloyd 1920 and Ian Russell 1921

Thomas Sydney Champion (centre), Arthur's daughter Olive Lord (left), with her children, Helen and Graham and Marjore Champion.

Marjorie Champion (left), Dorothy Champion (right)

1930 Wedding portrait of Albert Smith and Dorothy Champion.
Photo–Margaret McAlpine

Lyndsay Warwick Champion as a cadet. Photo–
Duncan Warwick Champion

Tom Wilfred Champion WWII.

*Roy Edwin Champion, WW11 Taken on Golden
Stairway Kokoda. He then went to Hiroshima, then to
Korea, son of Bert Champion*

Other family members who served in the Australian forces in WWII:Rupert Bergelin (KIA)
and Tom Bergelin, sons of Gertrude; Lyndsay Warwick Championm son of Keith; Kevin
Gurney, son-in-law of Keith; Bruce Dolman, son-in-law of Ben; Roger Lloyd Champion, son
of Charles Lloyd and Frank Fox Lord, sons-in-law of Arthur.

Hirst Family group–golden wedding anniversary of Harris and Eliza Hurst, taken at Ennis Vale,
Albert Park, Melbourne, 1923.
Standing (L-R): Jean Sara Hirst, Harris Dunman (Hary) Hirst, William Harris Hirst, Arthur R
Lamborn, Elsie Champion Lamborn, Alan Hirst, Arthur William Hirst,
Ethel (Brenda) Hirst, Eva Lorna (Lorna) Sundstrom, Colin Arthur,
Elsie Mavis (Mavis) Sundstrom
Seated (L-R): Sara Hirst (née Thompson), Elisa Emma Hirst (née Champion),
Harris Hirst, Eva Lockwood Sundstrom.
Seated on ground (L-R) Emily (Nin) Hirst (with dog), Noel Coulton Hirst, Leigh Hirst, Ian
Roland Lamborn.

Esme Warwick Champion, daughter of Keith, married Kevin Gurney–Vietnam War..

Ben's certificate to practice as a Dentist. Note that it is signed by Donald Smith.

University graduation portrait of Ben, 1923.

University graduation group photograph 1923. Ben seated front row 4th from the left between Ken Stringer and Eric Smith (in light suit).

Standing (L-R): Tom Bergelin, Rupert Jr, known as Boyd and Mother Gertrude Bergelin.
Front (L-R): Marjorie, Elsie amd Jean Bergelin with Edie Champion.
The photo was taken not long before Gertrude's death.

Jean Bergelin with Ruth Champion and Lindsay Warwick Champion taken at
Jura Wahroonga. Photo–Newcastle Region Library

Ben's eldest grandchildren; John, Penny, Adrian Dolman.

Patron of the Newcastle Pipe Band, Ben on his 60th Birthday with (neigbour) Mona Flower (R)
then his younger grandchildren, Sarah Helen Wheeler,
Claudia Ruth Dolman and Samuel P Wheeler.

Back (L-R): Tom Bergelin, Ruth Champion and Rupert Jnr known as Boyde Bergelin.
Front (L-R)Jean and Elsie Bergelin and Mary Wheeler.

Keith, Dorothy, Marjorie and Tom Champion.

Dorothys grandchildren, Ian McAlpine aged 6 and-Jeannette McAlpine aged 8

Ray Carroll atop the Sydney Harbour Bridge. He was in charge of construction from the North side.

Newcastle Morning Herald: Tuesday, Nov 21, 1978

Historian dies, aged 81

Dr Champion

Newcastle dental surgeon and historian, Dr Benjamin William Champion, who died on November 14, aged 81, finished the last volume of his work, Hunter Valley Register, only weeks before his death.

The register, which lists births, deaths and marriages recorded in the region between 843 and 1905, is held in Australian parliamentary libraries, most Australian universities and Utah University in the United States.

Dr Champion published the first volume of the register in 1973.

A funeral service and private cremation were held for Dr Champion on Saturday.

Dr Champion was born in 1897, son of a secretary of the NSW Public Service Board. He was educated at Wahroonga Boys College (later Knox Grammar School) and the Fort Street School before joining the Army in World War I.

He rose through the ranks from private to lieutenant, serving at Gallipoli and in France. After losing a leg, Dr Champion returned to Australia in 1918 and studied dentistry at Sydney University.

He gained a doctorate of dental science from Sydney University in 1933, was elected a Fellow of the International College of Dentists in 1958 and became a Fellow of the Royal Australiasian College of Dental Surgeons in 1963.

Dr Champion helped establish the dental unit at Royal Newcastle Hospital.

Dr Champion is survived by his daughters, Mrs Ruth Dolman and Mrs Mary Wheeler, and grandchildren.

Ben's obituary from the Newcastle Morning Herald, Nov 21 1978.

Bens Life.

Benjamin William Champion. D.D.Sc., F.I.C.D., F.R.A.C.D.S.
1897-1978

In reading Bens war diaries, it seems he was used as a forward soldier to obtain billets for the Battalion as they moved around the battlefields and then to lead the Battalion in by the best route.

No doubt, the fact he could speak some rudimentary French made him a good candidate for this in talking to the local population. It seems he was also used as a scout and messenger.

Before Ben went to war he was an able sprinter and had medallions to demonstrate this, so he was quick on his feet and when he says he played rugby It would seem he played on the wing as he was still slight of build and fast. He was younger than many of the other more mature rugby players.

Ben and Frank married in 1923 at St Philip's Church of England, Church Hill, City of Sydney. Eric Smith was best man and Ruth Upfold was bridesmaid

After Ben moved to Newcastle in 1923 he became involved in worthy movements which attracted and maintained his support such as Legacy, Freemasonry, The Crippled Children's Association and Rotary, not to mention the Australian Dental Association. He continued to use his manual dexterity in the hobbies of woodwork, pottery, photography, ceramics and weaving. Above his garage he had a kiln and everything he needed for his hobbies. He converted his old foot drill into a potter's wheel. He loved his cars. His last was a 3.8. Jaguar with his number plate. W.C. but he had a Morris Major to go to work which he had for all of my memories from a little girl. (PF editor)

Newcastle Morning Herald 4 May 1933

Dental Degree

At the last meeting of the Senate of the University of Sydney it was resolved to admit Mr Ben W Champion B.DS., of Newcastle to the degree of Doctor of Dental Science one rarely conferred in Australian Universities for his thesis on mouths of mental deficients. In 1932 He took First Class Honours in Dental Surgery at Sydney University. Dr Champion is the honorary dental surgeon in the Truby King Mothercraft Centre (became Karitane) and the RSL and he has for the past 10 years fulfilled a similar position at the mental hospitals at Newcastle and Stockton.

In 1958 he was elected a Fellow of the International College of Dentist and Fellow of the Royal Australasian College of Dental Surgeons in 1963. He helped establish the dental unit at Royal Newcastle Hospital.

His interest and work in historical matters particularly of the local district are well known. He was determined not to die until he had finished his self-published volumes of The Hunter Valley Registers. All information of Births Deaths and Marriages from the regional newspapers, with other notes of individuals of selected professions taken and then put onto his cardex system and then typed out. This today is still an important resource even with internet research as Ben was able to annotate his records and add information of, e.g. family relationships and gossip, because of his vast knowledge of the families in the region.

Ben suffered from emphysema due to being gassed in WW1. To improve his lung capacity, he took up the bag pipes to improve them, much to the terror of the dogs in the neighbourhood who could be heard for miles. He also became a complete scotophile with tartan ties, berets, waistcoat, rugs etc and kilts for the girls. In 1964 on his birthday, to honour their Patron, the full Newcastle Pipe Band marched down the street and onto the lawn at 'Jura' and played for some time to the family and neighbours.

Ben was well known in Newcastle and he was no shrinking violet. He was always whistling mostly Scottish tunes and with his walking stick managed to 'shoot' many little boys. Not so PC today. He always talked to people on the street and only once was he very annoyed with me because I did not offer my hand to a gentleman. I must have been about 12. Ben was known as Fa Fa and he and Gran were very good grandparents to visit me regularly at school in Armidale where they got to know some of my friends and took us out on long weekends. Things I remember about them both is Fa Fa's jumpy stump, affected by weather changes, with the leg and braces over the chair in the bedroom and Gran's pink satin whalebone corset over her chair. His whistling drove Gran mad. He always had some Irish, Scottish, church or classical music playing.

Gran was not such an obvious person but she was very much in charge. She loved her cooking and was a wonderful home maker. She loved beautiful things but does not seem to have kept up her painting. She did a lot of sewing in her sewing room with Mrs Gallymore. My little girl dresses were the envy of my local neighbourhood. In those days everything was home / hand made. Gran developed a 'heart' when quite young which kept her from doing many things she would have enjoyed doing. She loved her dachshunds. She was famous for her hydrangeas which were massed in every hue but poor old Fa Fa had to pay enormous water rates and was often penalised. Her best friends were her sisters. When she died in 1972, Ben sold up *Jura* at New Lambton Heights (now across from John Hunter Hospital) and adjacent developed land and the household contents were auctioned. Ben then moved to a new unit block, Union Towers in Union Street which he hated. He enjoyed visiting Mrs von Bertough's Gallery and acquired many pieces.

In 1975 Ben was awarded *Croix des Vétérans du Roi Albert 1er* by Comité Fédéral decerne a 84551. This was a gold leaf to put on his medals and also a lapel pin with the Belgium colours which came with the certificate. A friend of his had taken one of his diaries to Belgium and apparently it was well thought of and copied and so Ben got this award.

He died in Royal Newcastle Hospital in 1978

Letter from Dallas Bellamy.2018

I first met Ben Champion as a boy of 2 years old and that would be around 1953 and Ben would have been 56 years old. He was a dentist in the AMP Building in Hunter Street, Newcastle.

I remember clearly his dental surgery, the lovely terrazzo floors, wrought iron balustrading and ornate wash basins and tap wear in the toilets. His fellow dentist Dr.Solomon had the rooms down the corridor. I'm not sure how my parents got to know Ben, probably via the Royal Newcastle Dental Hospital.

I was born with a bi-lateral cleft palate and needed specialist dentistry from an early age, especially a prosthetic upper denture.

My father was a professional fisherman in Lake Macquarie and often brought fresh fish to Ben at his house in New Lambton Heights.

"Do you know that was the only payment he wanted for his professional services". He asked one day for some shell grit for his birds and I remember dad & I going to the beach to get it.

I was very young at the time and did not quite understand the significance of our trip to the beach but I sensed that my father thought it was very important.

From my memory he was a very compassionate disarming man and that worked perfectly for working with frightened apprehensive children.

He would say, 'Hop up here my boy' when getting into the chair. I remember his moustache and his 'hoppy' leg. He was always on about wanting my mum to have more children, but she never did, maybe he could see their folly of not wanting to.

Prior to one visit I had to have a skin cancer removed from the top of my right ear lobe and after having climbed up into the dentist's chair, I quickly relayed my concern to him about the big chunk out of my ear.

He quickly replied 'Don't worry about that, don't you know that all good bulls are marked '

I will never forget that.

Notes on Bibliography

Although I have extensively read books on WW1 and noted other's references to Ben's diaries I have not mentioned these as sources. When there is an outside source used this is usually credited as the reference on the same page.

All the wording in *Ben and his Mates* is from Ben.

The National Australian Archives,search-Service Records, Record Search, name search,WWI

The Australian War Memorial web site.

The AIF Project. The nominal roll of 7th Rfts 1st Battalion.

Ben's annotated copy of the book *The First Battalion AIF 1914-1919*. History Committee BV Stacey,Lt-Col FJ Kindon, Lt Col HV Chedgey.The nominal roll of the 1st Battalion was especially helpful in identifying soldiers with names not identifiable because of many similar names on National Archives soldier search site. Some text and photographs have been taken for this book.

Trove – a good source

Extract Bill Gammage *The Broken Years* Sydney 1990

Some reference books

Combat Colonels of the AIF in the Great War David Clare Holloway 1914

Beneath Hill 60, Will Davies 2010

Passchendaele Requiem for Doomed Youth, Paul Ham 2016

Fromelles and Pozieres, Peter Fitzsimons

Liams Story, Ann Victoria Roberts 1991

Poziers, Peter Charlton 1986

Lost Anzacs, The Story of two brothers, Greg Kerr

The Hunter Region in The Great War, Greg and Sylvia Ray

Ben's copy of *Shrapnel and Smiles* for original photographs

John William *Bill* Hunt's record at AWM of those who enlisted 1-10 Rfts 1st Battalion.

The Ku-ring gai Historical Society has published *Rallying the Troops*, an alphabetical index of all WW1 soldiers from the region with histories of their family and war service. I have rarely needed to use information from this award winning resource but I would recommend these wonderfully presented and researched beautiful editions to anyone who has soldiers and perhaps family from this region.

I have used extensively the original military records at the NAA of the men mentioned by Ben and I have spoken with family members. This book has an emphasis about individual soldiers from the 1st Battalion and only some from Ben's home area of Wahroonga.

St John's Wahroonga. The first 100 Years 1898-1998. Hon Editor David R.V. Wood, which included a booklet written by Thomas Sydney Champion on Wahroonga Presbyterian Church. I learnt facts about the family that I would otherwise have been unaware. I was surprised when visiting the church to find a portrait of Thomas Sydney Champion still on the wall in the office. Dr John Dykes is also there and has a stained glass window.

Extracts from the WW1 Diary of Archie Barwick which mention Ben and other Mates which is online at WW1 Diaries at The Mitchell Library,

State library of NSW. Bruce Rainsford also mentions Ben and Art Felton in Egypt in his online diary at The Mitchell Library

A · SECTION · OF · NORTHERN · FRANCE · AND · BELGIUM

SHOWING · THE · MOVEMENTS · OF · THE · FIRST · AUSTRALIAN · INFANTRY · BATTALION

FROM · MARCH · 1916 · TO · THE · END · OF · 1918

LEGEND.

1916	SHOWN THUS	....
1917	" "	— — — —
1918	" "	— · — · — ·

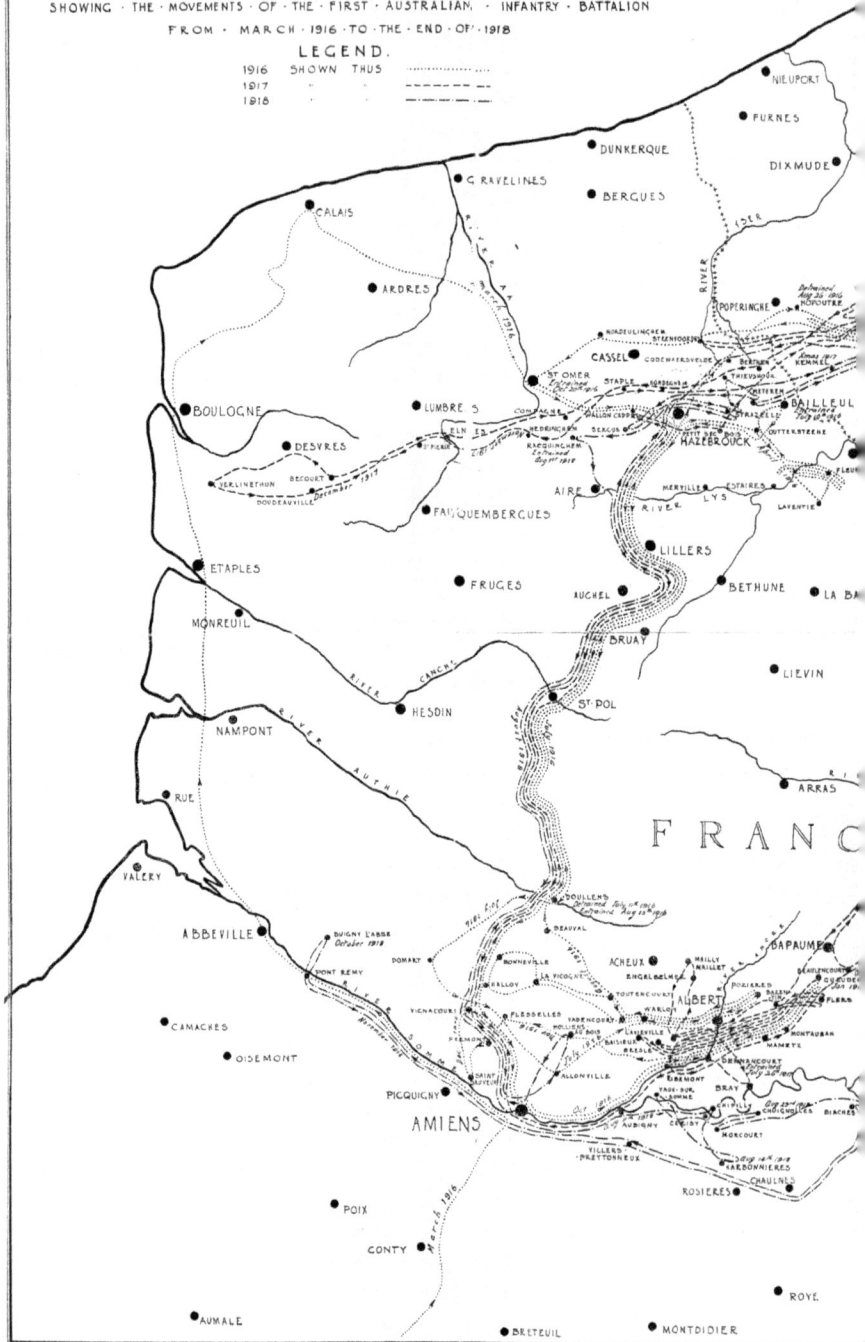

NIEUPORT
FURNES
DUNKERQUE
DIXMUDE
GRAVELINES
BERGUES
CALAIS
POPERINGHE
Defended Aug 26 1916 POPERINGHE
ARDRES
HAZEULINCKEM STEENVOORDE
CASSEL CODEWAERSVELDE
ST OMER Amos 16-17 KEMMEL
STAPLE WYTSCHAETE
BOULOGNE LUMBRE S BAILLEUL Rally of the
HERRINGHEM SERCUS WEST BAC BOIS
HALLOY CADE
DESVRES KARQUINGHEM HAZEBROUCK
ELN 15 OUTTERSTEENE
BECOURT PIERRE Defended FLEUR
VERLINETHUN December 1917 Aug 1st 1918
DOUDEAUVILLE AIRE MERVILLE ESTAIRES
FAUQUEMBERGUES RIVER LYS LAVENTIE
ETAPLES LILLERS
FRUGES AUCHEL BETHUNE LA BA
MONREUIL BRUAY
RIVER CANCHE LIEVIN
HESDIN ST POL
NAMPONT RIVER AUTHIE ARRAS
RUE

F R A N C

VALERY
DOULLENS Defended July 1st 1918 Defended Aug 15 1918
ABBEVILLE QUIGNY L'ABBE October 1918 BEAUVAL
DOMART BAPAUME
PONT REMY BONNEVILLE ACHEUX MAILLY MAILLET
HALLOY LA PICQUET ENGELBELMER BEAUCOURT
VIGNACOURT TOUTENCOURT ALBERT
CAMACHES FLESSELLES VADENCOURT WARLOY
OISEMONT MOLLIENS BAIZIEUX
PIEMONT LAVIEVILLE BECORDEL
SAINT ALLONVILLE BRAY
PICQUIGNY AUBIGNY CERISY
AMIENS VILLERS
BRETTONNEUX CHAULNES
POIX ROSIERES
CONTY ROYE
AUMALE BRETEUIL MONTDIDIER

BRUCES

EECLOO

ANTWERP

THOUROUT

THIELT

GHENT

MALINES

WETTEREN

ROULERS

ISEYHEM

ALOST

KENDE-RIDGE
1917

RIVER SCHELDE

MENIN

COURTRAI

AUDENARDE

BRUSSELS

FRANCO

TOURCOING

RENAIX

GRAMMONT

RUBAIX

BELGIUM

LLE

ATH

BELCIAN

TOURNAI

SOIGNIES

ORCHIES

NIVELLE

RIVER SAMBRE

BORDER

MONS

CHARLEROI

St AMAND

GOUGNIES

OUAI

VALENCIENNES

DENAIN

GOUDINNES

MAUBEUGE

BEAUMONT

COUSOLRE

SOLRE-ST-GERY

AULNOYE

SOLRE-LE-CHATEAU

PHILIPPEVILLE

CAMBRAI

AVESHES

LE-CATEAU
BAZUEL
Nov 4 th 1918

AVESNELLES

PRISCHES

Nov 1918

St SOUPLET

LE-HOUYION

CHIMAY

Sept 29 th 1918
BELLICOURT
BARGICOURT

BOHAIN

ROCROI

GUISE

RIVER OISE

MIRSON

St QUENTIN

VERVINS

LIART

MARLE

MONTCORNET

LA FERE